THEORIES OF
ABSTRACT AUTOMATA

Prentice-Hall
Series in Automatic Computation

George Forsythe, editor

THEORIES OF
ABSTRACT AUTOMATA

MICHAEL A. ARBIB

Stanford Electronics Laboratories
Stanford University

PRENTICE-HALL, INC.

Englewood Cliffs, N. J.

13-913368-2
Library of Congress Catalogue Card No.: 72-82901

Printed in the United States of America
Current printing (last digit):
10 9 8 7 6 5 4 3 2 1

PRENTICE-HALL INTERNATIONAL, INC., *London*
PRENTICE-HALL OF AUSTRALIA, PTY. LTD., *Sydney*
PRENTICE-HALL OF CANADA, LTD., *Toronto*
PRENTICE-HALL OF INDIA PRIVATE LTD., *New Delhi*
PRENTICE-HALL OF JAPAN, INC., *Tokyo*

For my friends in Czechoslovakia

PREFACE

Abstract automata theory may be defined, approximately, as the mathematical investigation of the *general* questions raised by the study of information-processing systems, be they men or machines. In particular, it focuses on the algebraic and combinatorial problems so raised.

Automata theorists have attacked a wide range of problems. No book could—or should—attempt to summarize all their studies. What this book does do is present an overview of the classical results of automata theory, as well as sample some of the most exciting areas of current research.

This book is perhaps the first advanced textbook in automata theory—its scope is broader than that of any other book on automata theory, and it treats many topics in greater depth than can be found outside specialized research monographs. Yet the book is not exceptionally long, and it is self-contained. A special feature that aids this compactness is that if the idea of a proof can be made clear in a few lines, then the proof will be presented heuristically to aid first-reading comprehension—details can then be supplied by the serious student on a second reading, as he works the clearly marked exercises which are distributed in appropriate places throughout the text.

The reader should have sufficient background in abstract algebra to be able to assimilate a concise treatment of the basic notions of automata theory, or know enough automata theory to be able to use Chapter 2 to acclimate himself to the abstract mathematical approach.

An algebraic background might include the elements of set theory together with a course in group theory, up to and including the Jordan-Hölder Theorem. A reader who is completely at home with such material should have no undue trouble with this book—and need have no previous study of automata theory. This book should be well suited for a first course in automata theory for mathematicians.

A background in automata theory may be provided by any one of the excellent new introductory texts available, such as BOOTH [1967], HENNIE [1968], or MINSKY [1967]. I have been asked whether there is need for a text in automata theory intermediate in level between such texts and the present volume. My answere is *no*—but there may be need of intermediate study of abstract algebra. Thus the instructor using this book as text for a second course in automata theory for computer scientists or engineers may need to devote a few lectures to giving exercises and motivation to supplement the summary of mathematical background given in Chapter 2 of this book.

Let us summarize the three parts of this book.

The first part is background. In Chapter 1, we present a mildly mathematical survey of automata theory—an overview of the structures of automata theory and the main questions which we ask about them. This provides a framework wherein we may locate the many topics of Parts II and III. In Chapter 2, we summarize the mathematical concepts needed in abstract automata theory—distinguishing the tools that must be used throughout from those that are needed in one or two special investigations.

The second part might be subtitled "What every literate automata theorist ought to know." It contains my choice of the topics without which one cannot hope to follow the research literature. Chapter 3 treats finite automata, their minimization, circuits which realize them (and the complexity thereof), the languages they characterize, and their relation to semigroups. Chapter 4 treats Turing machines, even polycephalic ones, looks at the functions they compute, studies the sets they define, and introduces the reader to unsolvable decision problems (and proves Gödel's incompleteness theorem as an application). Chapter 5 examines Post's canonical systems, and then concentrates on the context-sensitive and context-free grammars, relating them to push-down automata and linear bounded automata, and proves the basic results on ambiguity and undecidability of context-free languages. By and large, then, Part II contains the material that most automata theorists would want to see included in any thoroughgoing text.

The third part, after a preliminary study of partial recursive functions, is devoted to the presentation of four of the many topics now at the forefront of research in automata theory. They are: complexity of computation, algebraic decomposition theory, stochastic automata, and machines which compute and construct. Here my choice is purely personal—I suspect that the three main omissions which might be lamented are advanced topics in language theory, the theory of algebra automata, and the relation between mathematical logic and automata. But here we begin to leave the domain of the general textbook and start to debate which monographs should best be written to complement the basis which this book seeks to provide.

This book grew from lextures given at Imperial College, in London, in 1964, and at the University of New South Wales, in Sydney, in 1965. It has improved greatly from the comments of my friends and students there, and in the last three years at Stanford. My main debt is to my fellow automata theorists whose papers, correspondence, and discussion at meetings, have provided much material and stimulation. I have tried to guide the reader to their writings to shed more light on the material I have presented, but have made no attempt to establish priority, or to find references for material which is by now classical (which means, I suppose, that the material had appeared in a textbook by 1963). The book has benefited much from my discussion with Manuel Blum, P. C. Fischer, Shafee Give'on, J. Hartmanis, R. E. Kalman, Bill Kilmer, W. Ogden, J. Rhodes, Fred Roberts, Bill Rounds, P. M. Spira, Don Stanat and Paul Zeiger. To those others whose valued comments are not explicitly acknowledged, my thanks and apologies, and a sincere hope that they will read the book and find that their comments did not fall on deaf ears. Finally, my thanks to Mrs. Rowena Swanson, who monitored the support given by the Air Force Office of Scientific Research, Information Science Directorate, for much of my research reported herein. May this research prove of interest to men of all nations, so that defense yields to the making of friends.

MICHAEL A. ARBIB

Stanford, California

A NOTE
TO THE READER

All items, except figures, are numbered consecutively within each section. A reference to item **a** means item **a** of the present section; to item **b.a** means item **a** of section **b** of the present chapter; and to item **c.b.a** means item **a** of section **b** of chapter **c** of the present volume.

I have not presumed to tell the reader which sections to omit on a first reading, but I have used a smaller typeface for material which the reader may safely omit on a first reading of the section in which it occurs. Note that this means that if an exercise is set in full-size type, then it is an integral part of the text, and should be read and understood by the reader even if he is in no mood actually to solve the stated problem.

The symbol □ indicates that no more proof will be given of the last numbered proposition that precedes it.

One more comment. This book will be published at least a year after completion of the manuscript. Looking back, I think this book has stood the test of time in that all the material in parts I and II and most of part III, is still essential for the repertoire of the automata theorist. However, the subject is continually growing in breadth and depth, and the reader should augment his study of this (or any other) textbook by a determined assault on the symposium volumes of the *IEEE Symposia on Switching and Automata Theory,* and of the *ACM Symposia on Theory of Computing,* and on journals such as the *Journal of the Association for Computing Machinery, Information and Control,* and the *IEEE Transactions on Computers,* which are cited again and again in the bibliography.

CONTENTS

THEORIES OF
ABSTRACT AUTOMATA

BACKGROUND

1 AN OVERVIEW
OF AUTOMATA THEORY

This is the sort of introduction that should be read quickly before the rest of the book, and slowly afterward. I do not attempt to give a detailed tour of the subject matter of this book, nor a survey of those important theorems which this book omits. Rather I try to provide a conceptual framework in which the diverse topics of automata theory may be fitted. So many different descriptions, so many different devices, engage our attention that at times we wonder whether we are getting entangled unnecessarily in idiosyncratic formalizations. While expecting that future research will polish many of the results treated in this book, and reveal some of them as aspects of deeper truths, nonetheless I hope to show that much of the diversity we encounter is desirable, stemming from our need to ask different types of questions about a basically coherent subject matter.

1.1 THE AIMS OF ABSTRACT AUTOMATA THEORY

The *Oxford English Dictionary* defines an *automaton* (plural, *automata*) as "Something which has the power of spontaneous movement or self-motion; a piece of mechanism having its motive power so concealed that it appears to move spontaneously; now usually applied to figures which simulate the

3

actions of living beings, as clockwork mice, etc." Today the computer has replaced the clockwork mouse as the archetype of the automaton; and with it, our emphasis shifts from simulation of motion to simulation of information processing. Automata theory, in its widest sense, might now embrace such diverse activities as the building of a space station's control system or the programming of a computer to play chess. In the theory of *abstract* automata, we are less concerned with the design of automata to do specific tasks, and more concerned with understanding the capabilities and limitations of whole *classes* of automata. One might say, then, that "Automata theory (the qualification abstract is henceforth implied) is the pure mathematics of computer science." Of the several possible interpretations, the one I intend is that, just as much of today's pure mathematics can be seen to have evolved from formalisms suggested by the problems of physics, so automata theory is a branch of mathematics which draws inspiration and intuition from asking questions about biological and electronic computers. The mathematics is pure in that many of the questions are pursued for their intrinsic interest, rather than in the hope of applications. And as answers to these questions accumulate, one is led to look for mathematical generalizations which lay bare the essential logic of the situation, stripped of the details unessential to gaining a general understanding of the processes involved. That we persevere even though some of these details were essential to the "real-world" problem of getting an answer out of a computer by next Tuesday is what makes us—at least on this occasion—automata theorists, rather than programmers or designers of actual circuitry. I like to dream that automata theorists will one day do for computer science what group theorists did for physics. Be that as it may, it must be emphasized that automata theory is *not* to be thought of as the study of a limited number of presently formalized objects. Rather, it is a growing subject which gains richness and power from the intuition one obtains by thinking about information-processing, and the consequent interplay between rigorous mathematics and the search for appropriate formalizations for this intuition.

If automata theory does not yet provide a magical key to the solution of problems of everyday information-processing, it does have the following virtues: (a) it is a fascinating branch of mathematics; (b) it provides a form of mental discipline which will benefit system theorists, computer scientists, and logical designers by giving them a powerful set of languages for setting out their problems, even though it may not provide methods that can be "plugged in"; and (c) certain techniques of automata theory are already directly useful (though, in this book, I shall generally leave this implicit) and, what is more important, automata theory is slowly building up for us a feel for information-processing that will eventually help us do things for which no amount of program-writing could provide the basis. We may note that automata theory has already provided the following:

(1) A characterization of *all* computable functions (e.g., as those computable by Turing machines)—it being now a highly active area of research to find which of the concomitant computations are *practicable*—together with the demonstration that no computer can compute, of an arbitrary computer, whether or not that second computer will ever halt.

(2) The demonstration of *universality*—that there is a computer which can do the job of any other computer provided that it is suitably programmed.

(3) Parsing systems for formal languages, and concomitant automata, which form the basis for a rigorous treatment of compilers for computer languages.

We may expect further progress in automata theory to provide an ever richer *framework* for the solution of practical problems—as the theorist proves theorems of the kind "Every X in the relation R to Y must have property Z," so will the circuit designer learn to check the Z factor each time he builds an R device.

1.2   THE MANIPULATION OF STRINGS OF SYMBOLS

Consider the item displayed on the next line:

$$1 \quad 0 \quad 0 \quad 1 \quad 1$$

Is it "ten thousand and eleven" or "nineteen in binary notation"? Clearly, it is in fact a string (we use "string" as a synonym for "sequence") of five symbols, of which the first, fourth, and fifth are 1's, while the second and third are 0's. Whether we choose to interpret this string of symbols as a decimal number or binary number, or as something else, depends on our "mental set," on the context. To a binary computer 1 0 0 1 1 is "nineteen"; to a decimal computer it is "ten thousand and eleven." Similarly, the function which places 0 at the end of a string of 0's and 1's is, to a binary computer, "multiplication by two," whereas to a decimal computer, it is "multiplication by ten."

The point I am trying to make, then, is the familiar one that computers are symbol-manipulation devices. What needs further emphasis is that they are thus numerical processors, but *the numerical processing that they undertake is only specified when we state how numbers are to be **encoded** as strings of symbols which may be fed into the computer, and how the strings of symbols printed out by the computer are to be **decoded** to yield the numerical result of the computation.*

Our emphasis in what follows, then, is on the ways in which information-processing structures (henceforth called automata) transform strings of symbols into other strings of symbols. Sometimes it will be convenient to emphasize the interpretation of these strings as encodings of numbers, but in many cases we shall deem it better not to do so.

Let us, then, introduce some basic terminology. We shall usually use X to denote the *input alphabet*, the set of symbols from which we may build up strings suitable for feeding into our automaton. The symbol Y will usually denote the *output alphabet*, our automaton emitting strings of symbols from Y.

Given any set A, we shall denote by A^* the set of all finite sequences of elements from A, and shall call the number of symbols, $l(\alpha)$, in a sequence α the *length* of α. For mathematical convenience, we shall include in A^* the *empty sequence* Λ of length 0. We need Λ for the same reason that we had to invent the number 0. Just as it became distinctly unhelpful to write "x with nothing added to it" instead of "$x + 0$," so we prefer to say "input Λ" rather than "no input was supplied." It allows us to state many theorems in general form, without having to treat "no input" as a special case. Given two sequences $\alpha = a_1 \ldots a_n$ and $\beta = b_1 \ldots b_m$ we may *concatenate* them to obtain $\alpha \cdot \beta = a_1 \ldots a_n b_1 \ldots b_m$, and for all α we set $\alpha \cdot \Lambda = \Lambda \cdot \alpha = \alpha$.

Thus X^* will usually denote the set of all input strings to our automaton, and Y^* will indicate a set which includes all possible output strings of our automaton.

Our general notion of an automaton, then, is a device to which we may present a string of symbols from X^*. If and when the machine finishes computing on this string, the result will be an element of Y^*. We say "if" because certain input strings may drive the computer into a "runaway" condition—e.g., endless cycling through a loop—from which a halt is impossible without external intervention (which amounts to changing the input string). This case might correspond to associating with the machine a device which produces an infinite string of elements of Y for each string in X^*—but, in fact, this viewpoint will only be taken in Section 7.2, and so we shall not treat it further in this chapter.

Thus, in a very general form, we may say that automata theory is the study of *partial* functions $F: X^* \to Y^*$—that is, ways whereby *some* of the strings in X^* have assigned to them output strings from Y^*, it being understood that for other input strings x, the function $F(x)$ may not be defined at all. However, such a function becomes truly a part of "classical" automata theory only if we can relate it to a *finitely specifiable substrate*—or if we are eager to prove that no such substrate exists for it. Of course, once one has developed a body of theorems, one sees how they can be generalized if the finiteness condition is removed, so this criterion does not cover all of present-day automata theory.

1.3   ON-LINE AND OFF-LINE MACHINES

We have said that automata theory deals with the realization of *partial* functions $F: X^* \to Y^*$ by some finitely specifiable substrate. Before we specify in more detail the forms (of which the Turing machine is one) of substrate which have figured most prominently in automata theory, it is useful to distinguish *on-line* machines from *off-line* machines. An on-line machine is one that may be thought of as processing data in an interactive situation—in processing a string it must yield a continual flow of outputs, processing each symbol completely (albeit in a way dependent on prior inputs) before it reads in the next symbol. This means that the corresponding function $F: X^* \to Y^*$ must have the following special property:

1   For each nonempty string u of X^* there exists a function $F_u: X^* \to Y^*$ such that for every nonempty v in X^*

$$F(uv) = F(u) \cdot F_u(v)$$

that is, the input string u causes the machine to put out the string $F(u)$ and to "change state" in such a way that it henceforth processes inputs according to a function F_u determined solely by F and u. We call a function *sequential* if it satisfies property **1**. If we define $f(\Lambda) = F(\Lambda)$, whereas, for $x \neq \Lambda$, the function $f(x)$ is the substring of $F(x)$ produced in response to the last symbol of x, we see that $f: X^* \to Y^*$ allows us to reconstruct F by the formula

$$F(x_1 x_2 \ldots x_n) = f(\Lambda) f(x_1) f(x_1 x_2) \ldots f(x_1 x_2 \ldots x_n)$$

if each $x_1, \ldots, x_n$ is in X. Conversely,

$$f(x_1 x_2 \ldots x_n) = F_{x_1 x_2 \ldots x_{n-1}}(x_n)$$

Let us define, for any u in X^* the function $L: X^* \to X^*$ which simply places u to the left of any string: $L_u(x) = ux$. Then we see that f_u, the function corresponding to F_u, has the simple form

2 $$f_u(x) = f L_u(x)$$

and for a string uv we find, by changing f to f_u, and u to v in **2**, that

$$f_{uv}(x) = f_u L_v(x) = f L_u L_v(x)$$

It thus makes sense to speak of each function f_u for u in X^* (so that $f = f_\Lambda$) as a *state* of the sequential function F—with the input v serving to change state f_u to state f_{uv}, while the output corresponding to state f_u is $f_u(\Lambda) - fL_u(\Lambda) = f(u)$. Thus the evaluation of F may be captured by the input-state-output sequence shown in Table 1.1.

Table 1.1

Input string: Sequence of symbols from X	x_1	x_2	$\ldots$	x_n
State string: Sequence of functions f_u	f f_{x_1}	$f_{x_1 x_2}$	$\ldots$	$f_{x_1 x_2 \cdots x_n}$
Output string: Sequence of strings on Y^*	$f(\Lambda)$ $f(x_1)$ $f(x_1 x_2)$		$\ldots$	$f(x_1 x_2 \ldots x_n)$

$$F(x_1 x_2 \ldots x_n)$$

Three portraits of a sequential machine are shown in Fig. 1.1. Since we are in the habit of considering the first letter of a string to be the leftmost letter (translators of this text into Hebrew, please take care!), it seems appropriate (although perhaps a majority of authors use the opposite convention) to have the input line drawn to the right of the box—so that the first input symbol is the first to reach the box—and the output line drawn to the left of the box—so that the last output symbol is the last to leave the box.

A sequential machine M is specified by three sets, the set X of inputs, the set Y of outputs and the set Q of states together with a next-state function $\delta: Q \times X \to Q$ and an output function $\beta: Q \to Y$. If we have $\beta: Q \to Y^*$, we usually call M a *generalized* sequential machine.

We say that a sequential function F is *finite-state* if there are only finitely many distinct functions of the form fL_u.

Suppose that F has n states, and consider the effect of an input string of n identical inputs, each, say, 0. Then we have a sequence of $n + 1$ states

$$f_\Lambda, f_0, f_{00}, \ldots, f_{0^n}$$

(where 0^n stands for a string of n 0's—i.e., the nth power of 0 with respect to *concatenation*. We may write 0^0 for Λ). Since F has only n states, at least two of the above, say f_{0^i} and f_{0^j} with $i < j$, must be equal, and thus f_{0^n} equals $f_{0^i} L_{0^{n-i}} = f_{0^i} L_{0^{n-i}} = f_{0^{n-(j-i)}}$. Thus

3   If F has only n states, we cannot enter a state of F for the first time after applying n identical inputs.

4   It is clear that if F is finite-state with n states, then every F_u, for u in X^*, is finite-state with $\leq n$ states.

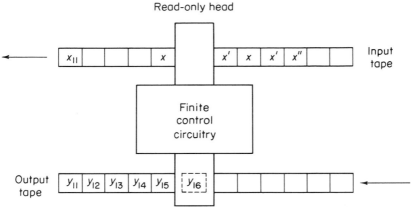

(a)

(b)

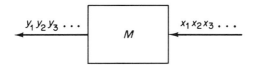

(c)

Fig. 1.1

5   EXAMPLE

(i) Let $F: \{0, 1\}^* \to \{0, 1\}^*$ be the function, with state $f: \{0, 1\}^* \to \{0, 1\}$,

$$f(x_1x_2 \ldots x_n) = \begin{cases} 1 & \text{if an even number of } x_j\text{'s are 1} \\ 0 & \text{if not} \end{cases}$$

Then F is sequential, and is finite-state with only two states $f_0 = f$ and f_1, with the relations

$$f_1 = f_1L_0 = f_0L_1$$
$$f_0 = f_1L_1 = f_0L_0$$

that is, we only change state (parity) if the input is one.

(ii) Let $G: \begin{pmatrix} 0 & 0 & 1 & 1 \\ 0, & 1, & 0, & 1 \end{pmatrix}^* \to \{0, 1\}^*$ be the function

$$G \begin{pmatrix} u_1 & u_2 & u_3 & & u_n \\ v_1, & v_2, & v_3, & \ldots, & v_n \end{pmatrix} =$$ the n lowest-order digits, with lowest-order digit first, of the binary expansion of the product of the binary numbers $u_1 u_2 \ldots u_n$ and $v_1 v_2 \ldots v_n$.

Then G is clearly sequential. However, G is *not* finite-state—we shall derive a contradiction from the assumption that G has a finite number n of internal states.

Suppose G had to multiply 2^n by itself fed to the machine as the string $\begin{pmatrix} 0 \\ 0 \end{pmatrix}^n 1 \begin{pmatrix} 0 \\ 0 \end{pmatrix}^n$ to yield 2^{2n}, that is, the string $0^{2n}1$. This would mean that after it had received its last nonzero input, G would have to print n more symbols, all zeros save for the last. But this would require that, setting $\hat{g} = fL_{\begin{pmatrix} 0 \\ 0 \end{pmatrix}^{n_1}}$, the state $\hat{g}_{\begin{pmatrix} 0 \\ 0 \end{pmatrix}^n}$ is different from each state $\hat{g}_{\begin{pmatrix} 0 \\ 0 \end{pmatrix}^j}$, for $0 \leq j < n$, contradicting **3** and **4**.

(iii) The function $H: \{0, 1\}^* \to \{0, 1\}^*$ with

$$H(x_1 x_2 \ldots x_n) = x_n \ldots x_2 x_1$$

is *not* sequential—for instance, $H(01)$ does not begin with the string $H(0)$.

Thus by restricting a machine to process a string one symbol at a time, or to preserve information about prior symbols by the present state from a *finite* set of possible states, we severely limit which functions from X^* to Y^* may be realized.

We are thus led to consider *off-line* machines, which may be simply defined as those functions which need not be sequential. We imagine that the whole string may be presented to the machine before any computation need take place. It is perhaps useful to think of the input string as read into a data structure which the machine may operate upon over a period of time, it usually being assumed that time is quantized, and that only a *finite* portion of the data structure is affected during each unit of time. (This condition will only be relaxed when we consider tesselations in Chapter 10.)

There is a sense, then, in which we may view an on-line computation as treating an input string as distributed in time, whereas an off-line computation treats the string as distributed in space.

A major question, then, is this: Can we formally define a class of machines which can compute all partial functions $F: X^* \to Y^*$ which may be obtained by a well-defined machine when we place a finiteness condition not upon its memory but only upon its access to that memory? Since the notion of machine is informal in the last sentence, this amounts to finding a precise mathematical definition to replace our intuitive notion of an *effective procedure* for going (not always successfully, since the function may be partial) from a string of X^* to a string of Y^*.

The first candidate for the notion of *effectively computable function* will be that of a *function computable by a Turing machine*. As we develop other theories of computation in this book, we shall see again and again that each computable function we specify can also be computed by a Turing machine. This will bolster our conviction that the notion of *Turing-computable* (and its equivalents) is indeed an adequate formalization of our intuitive notion of effectively computable. However, Turing machines often carry out their computations most inefficiently, and an important task of the automata theorist is to find more efficient automata to compute various classes of functions.

Let us emphasize that we are now considering what effective computations are possible, without placing any bounds on the time or the storage space required to complete the computation. In Chapter 7 we shall turn to the more intricate questions of difficulty or complexity of computation: "Among all the *possible* effective computations, which ones are practicable when we impose certain restrictions on computation time or computer growth?"

At this stage, we had better crystallize the idea of an *effective procedure*. There are certain computations for which there exist mechanical rules, or *algorithms*, e.g., the euclidean algorithm for finding the greatest common divisor of two integers. Certainly, any computation which can be carried out by a digital computer is governed by purely mechanical rules. We say, then, that there exists an effective procedure for carrying out these computations. There are many cases in which we do not really know how to write a program which would cause a given computer to carry out the desired computation, but we do have a strong intuitive feeling that a suitable effective procedure exists.

Abstract automata theory may be said to start with the simultaneous publications of TURING [1936] and POST [1936], who gave independent—and equivalent—formulations of machines which could carry out any effective procedure provided that they were adequately programmed. (Of course, such a statement is informal—we cannot prove that the formally defined class of procedures implementable by Post or Turing machines will be the same as our intuitive hazy notions of effective procedure. Suffice to say that this class has been proved equivalent to many other formal classes, and that no one has produced a procedure which is intuitively effective but cannot be translated into a program for one of their machines.)

The basic idea of the Post and Turing formalisms is as follows (see Fig.

1.2). The machine consists of (i) a control box in which may be placed a *finite* program ⌊i.e., which may be in one of a finite number of states⌋; (ii) a potentially infinite tape, divided lengthwise into squares (i.e., depending on our choice of mathematical fiction, we may consider the tape as comprising

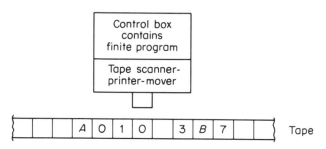

Fig. 1.2. A Turing Machine

an infinite string of squares of which all but finitely many are blank, or as a finite tape to the ends of which arbitrarily many new squares may be added as required); and (iii) a device for scanning, or printing on, one square of the tape at a time, and for moving along the tape, all under the command of the control box.

We start the machine with a finite string from X^* on the tape, and with a program in the control box. The symbol scanned and the instruction presently being executed (that is, current state of the control box) uniquely determine what new symbol shall be printed on the square, how the head shall be moved, and what instruction is to be executed next (that is, what shall be the next state of the control box). Thus the control box of a Turing machine may be thought of as a finite-state sequential machine whose output can be either a halt instruction, or a print-and-move instruction. *If* and when the machine stops, the result of our computation, a new string from X^*, may be read off the tape.

We shall see that computation more efficient than that of ordinary Turing machines can be obtained simply by allowing the Turing machine to have several tapes—and these not necessarily one-dimensional—each acted on by one or more heads which report back to a single control box which coordinates their printing and moving on their respective tapes. We shall see in Section 4.3 that any job that can be done by such a "polycephalic" Turing machine can be simulated by an ordinary Turing machine—thus reassuring ourselves of the breadth of the notion of a Turing-machine-computable (henceforth: TM-computable) function (which, incidentally, we shall prove in Chapter 6 to be coextensive with the notion of partial recursive function introduced by the logicians in the 1930s as an alternative formalization of the effectively computable functions). Further, we shall show in

Chapter 7 that these polycephalic machines do indeed give us the expected gain in efficiency. We shall also see that they not only have the great virtue of being more efficient in that they take less time to complete a computation, but also are easier to write programs for. With these "polycephalic" machines we shall, in fact, have a realistic model of computers—a virtue we do not claim for the ordinary Turing machine, useful though it is in allowing us to construct a theory of the computable. With these machines we are also made aware that there is no reason to restrict automata theory to functions of the form $F: X^* \rightarrow Y^*$. With multidimensional tapes, our automata may as well process planar or higher-dimensional configurations as the linear strings of X^*. However, we shall not pursue this line of study in this book, save for a brief look at pattern recognition in Section 3.2, and in our study of tessellations in Chapter 10.

McCulloch and Pitts [1943] introduced nets of formalized neurons, and showed that such nets could carry out the control operations of a Turing machine—providing, if you will, a formal "brain" for the formal machine which could carry out any effective procedure (cf. Chapter 1 of Arbib [1964]). These nets comprised synchronized elements, each capable of some boolean function, such as "and," "or," and "not." It was his knowledge of these networks that inspired von Neumann in establishing his logical design for digital computers with stored programs, which is of basic importance to the present day. (In 1948, von Neumann [1951] added to the computational and logical questions of automata theory, the new questions of construction and self-reproduction which we shall take up in Chapter 10.)

In 1956 the collection "Automata Studies" (Shannon and McCarthy [1956]) was published, and automata theory emerged as a relatively autonomous discipline. Besides the "infinite-state" Turing-Post machines, much interest centered on finite-state sequential machines, which first arose not in the abstract form of our above discussion, but in connection with the input-output behavior of a McCulloch-Pitts net or an "isolated" Turing machine control box.

Turing's paper [1936] contains a charming "pseudopsychological" account of why we might expect any algorithm to be implementable by a suitable A-machine (his name for Turing machines). We reproduce excerpts from this below. Bear in mind that when Turing wrote this, "computer" meant a human who carried out computations!

> All arguments which can be given are bound to be, fundamentally, appeals to intuition [since the notion of effective procedure is intuitive] and for this reason, rather unsatisfactory mathematically . . . . Computing is normally done by writing certain symbols on paper. We may suppose this paper is divided into squares like a child's arithmetic book. In elementary arithmetic, the 2-dimensional character of the paper is sometimes used. But such a use is

always avoidable, and I think that it will be agreed that the 2-dimensional character of paper is no essential of computation. I assume then that the computation is carried out on one-dimensional paper, i.e., on a tape divided into squares. I shall also suppose that the number of symbols which may be printed is finite. If we were to allow an infinity of symbols, then there would be symbols differing to an arbitrarily small extent. . . . It is always possible to use sequences of symbols in the place of single symbols. . . . The difference from our point of view between the single and compound symbols is that the compound symbols, if they are too lengthy, cannot be observed at one glance. . . . We cannot tell at one glance whether 9999999999 and 99999999999 are the same.

The behavior of the computer at any moment is determined by the symbols which he is observing, and his "state of mind" at that moment. We may suppose that there is a bound B to the number of symbols on squares which the computer can observe at any moment. If he wishes to use more, he must use successive observations. We will also suppose that the number of states of mind which need to be taken into account is finite. The reasons for this are of the same character as those which restrict the number of symbols . . . . Let us imagine that the operations performed by the computer are split up into "simple operations," which are so elementary that it is not easy to imagine them further divided. Every such operation consists of some change of the physical system consisting of the computer and his tape. We know the state of the system if we know the sequence of symbols on the tape, which of those are observed by the computer (possibly with a special order), and the state of mind of the computer. We may suppose that in a simple operation not more than one symbol is altered, [and] . . . without loss of generality assume that the squares whose symbols are changed are always "observed" squares.

Besides these changes of symbols, the simple operations must include changes of distribution of observed squares. The new observed squares must be immediately recognizable by the computer . . . . Let us say that each of the new observed squares is within L squares of an immediately previously observed square.

The simple operations must therefore include:
(a) Changes of the symbol on one of the observed squares.
(b) Changes of one of the squares observed to another square within L squares of one of the previously observed squares.

It may be that some of these changes necessarily involve a change of state of mind . . . . The operation actually performed is determined . . . by the state of mind of the computer and the observed symbols. In particular they determine the state of mind of the computer after the operation is carried out.

We may now construct a machine to do the work of this computer. To each state of mind of the computer corresponds an [internal state] of the machine. The machine scans B squares corresponding to the B squares observed by the computer. In any move the machine can change a symbol on a scanned square, or can change any one of the scanned squares to another square distant not more than L squares from one of the other scanned squares.

The move which is done, and the succeeding [internal state] are determined by the scanned symbol and the internal state. The machines just described do not differ very essentially from [Turing machines] . . . [and so, a Turing machine] can be constructed to compute . . . the sequence computed by the computer.

We associate with a Turing machine Z a function $F_Z: X^* \rightarrow X^*$ by defining $F_Z(u)$ to be the expression printed on the tape when Z stops, if started in a specified initial state, say q_0, scanning the leftmost letter of the string u—if Z never stops after being so started, $F_Z(u)$ is to be left undefined.

Note that F_Z may be always defined, sometimes defined, or never defined. Trivial examples of the three cases are, respectively, a machine which halts under all circumstances; a machine which halts if it scans a 1, but moves right if it scans any other symbol; and the machine which, no matter what state it is in and no matter what it sees, always moves right.‡

If we think of Turing machines as actual physical devices, it is clear that the input symbols could be configurations of holes on punched tape, patterns of magnetization or handwritten characters, or the like, whereas the states could be that of a clockwork, of a piece of electronic apparatus, or of an ingenious hydraulic device. Such details are irrelevant to our study, and so if there are m inputs in X, we shall feel free to refer to them as $x_0, x_1, \ldots, x_{m-1}$ without feeling impelled to provide further specification; and if there are n states, we shall similarly find it useful to lable them $q_0, q_1, \ldots, q_{n-1}$. I mention this because I want it to be clear that automata theory deals with abstract descriptions of machines, not their implementations. For each such abstract description there are many implementations—depending, e.g., on whether we interpret x_3 as a 0 or a 1, as a pattern of magnetization or a configuration of holes in a punched tape—but it should be clear that, from the information-processing point of view, there is a very real sense in which all these machines may be considered the *same* machine.

Since each Turing machine is described by a finite list of instructions, it is easy to show that we may *effectively* enumerate the Turing machines

$$Z_1, Z_2, Z_3, \ldots$$

so that, given n we may effectively find Z_n, and given the list of instructions for Z, we may effectively find the n for which $Z = Z_n$.

This implies that we can effectively enumerate all TM-computable (that is, Turing machine computable) functions as

$$f_1, f_2, f_3, \ldots$$

simply by setting $f_n = F_{Z_n}$. Such effective enumeration lies at the heart of

---

‡ This is the John Birch machine. Teachers at more conservative campuses may replace this example with a suitably insidious device which always moves left.

much of our study of the computable in Chapter 4. For example, if we say that f_n is *total* if $f_n(u)$ is defined for all u, we might ask: Is there an effective procedure for telling whether or not f_n is total; e.g., does there exist a total TM-computable function h such that f_n is total if and only if $n = h(m)$ for some m (identifying a string with a suitable number that encodes it)? The answer is "NO," for if such an h existed, we could define f by

$$f(n) = f_{h(n)}(n) + 1$$

Then f would be total recursive, and so $f = f_{h(m)}$ for some m.

Then $f_{h(m)}(m) = f_{h(m)}(m) + 1$, a contradiction!

This is just one example of the many things we can prove to be undecidable by any effective procedure. To say that we cannot effectively tell that f_n is *total* is just the same as saying that we cannot tell effectively whether Z_n will stop computing no matter what tape it is started on. We may thus say that "the halting problem for Turing machines is unsolvable."

A most interesting result of Turing's paper is that there is a *universal* Turing machine, i.e., one which, when given a coded description of Z_n on its tape, as well as the data x, will then proceed to compute $f_n(x)$, if it is defined. This is obvious if we accept that every effective computation may be executed by a Turing machine: For given n and x we find Z_n effectively, and then use it to compute $f_n(x)$, and so there should exist a Turing machine to implement the effective procedure of going from the *pair* (n, x) to the value $f_n(x)$. A proper proof (Section 4.5) takes somewhat longer! The universal Turing machine is the intellectual forebear of today's stored-program digital computer.

1.4 FORMAL LANGUAGES

We have spoken of automata as finitely specifiable substrates for partial functions $F: X^* \rightarrow Y^*$. Let us now see ways in which functions may define sets, thus learning to associate classes of sets with classes of automata. We follow the terminology of SCOTT [1967].

We shall say that a subset S of X^* is *decidable* by $F: X^* \rightarrow Y^*$ if there exist two distinct elements a and b of Y^* such that $F(u) = a$ if u is in S, whereas $F(u) = b$ if u is not in S. In other words, if we can compute the function F, we have a straightforward method for *deciding* whether or not u belongs to S.

We shall say that a subset S of X^* is *acceptable* by $F: X^* \rightarrow Y^*$ if there exists an element a of Y^* such that $F(u) = a$ if u is in S. Note that if F is a *total* function (i.e., defined for all u in X^*), then we may use F to decide whether or not any u belongs to S. Suppose, however, F is only partially defined, and we set some automaton going to decide u. Then if after a period of time the automaton has not halted, we may not be sure whether it will never halt, so that u is not in S, or whether it will eventually halt, at which time we would know that u belonged to S iff‡ the output of the automaton were a. We have already mentioned that there is no effective procedure to tell of a Turing machine whether or not it will halt.

We shall say that a subset S of Y^* is *generable* by F: $X^* \to Y^*$ just in case S is the *range* of F, that is, $S = F(X^*) = \{F(u) | u \text{ is in } X^*\}$.

We shall usually speak of subsets of X^* or Y^* as *languages*. Thinking of X, say, as the vocabulary, we think of the strings of X^* as the possible utterances in the vocabulary, with the strings of the given subset as being, in some sense, grammatical or well-formed. We shall associate different *classes* of languages with different *classes* of automata and explore the formal properties of these associations, leaving it for texts on linguistics to assess what relevance such studies have to the structure of the real languages of human discourse.

We may note that if we consider functions f: $X^* \to Y$ corresponding to sequential functions F: $X^* \to Y^*$ which are *finite-state*, then we get the same class of languages whether we use the functions as deciders or acceptors. We speak of languages in this class as *finite-state languages*. The reader may wish to prove, after he has read Section 3.3, that they are the same class of languages as those *generated* by finite-state (generalized) sequential functions F: $Z^* \to X^*$.

Now, we have already suggested that the Turing-computable functions F: $X^* \to X^*$ correspond to the intuitive notion of effectively computable functions. Thus the classes of sets which are decided, accepted, or generated by them should include the classes of sets decided, accepted, or generated by other finitely specified automata. (I make the proviso "finitely specified," since the mathematical automata theorist is under no compulsion to restrict his attentions to this case. Once he understands this primary focus of automata theory, he may then find it worthwhile to seek nonfinite generalizations.)

We shall see in Chapter 4 that the class of functions *decided* by Turing-computable functions—the *recursive sets*—is a *proper* subclass of the class *accepted* by Turing-computable functions—the *recursively enumerable sets*. However, the sets *generable* by Turing machines are precisely the recursively enumerable sets.

One of the centers of study in the theory of formal languages is that of *closure properties*. We may ask whether or not a class is closed under comple-

---

‡ 'iff' is the standard abbreviation for 'if and only if' and will be used throughout.

mentation—i.e., whether, for every subset R of X^* which belongs to the class, it is also true that the complement $X^* - R$ belongs to the class. It is clear that every class of *acceptable* sets is closed under complementation—we just interchange the role of a and b in the definition of the set. Similarly, one may prove that any reasonable class of generable sets is closed under the formation of finite unions—we just use the first letter of the input to switch us to the computation for generating an element of the appropriate term of the union.

We shall see in Section 3.3 not only that the finite-state languages are closed under union, set product (which replaces the sets E and F by the set $E \cdot F$ of all strings obtainable as a string of E followed by a string of F), and iteration (the operation that replaces a set E by the set E^* of all strings obtainable by concatenating a nonnegative number of strings from E)—as well as complementation and intersection—but also that these first three operations serve to characterize the finite-state languages. In fact, a set is a finite-state language iff it can be built up from finite sets, using a finite number of applications of $\cup$, $\cdot$, and $*$ operations. This will be our first taste of machine-independent characterizations of a class of languages which may also be characterised by a class of machines.

The beginnings of a hierarchy of classes of machines—with lower end defined by finite-state sequential machines, and upper end defined by the Turing machines—defines the beginning of a hierarchy of classes of languages —with lower end defined by finite-state languages, and upper end defined by the recursively enumerable sets, with the recursive sets falling properly in between. A major aim is to fill out in more and more detail the structure of these two hierarchies.

We shall see in Chapter 5 that languages can be defined in a machine-independent way by formalized "grammars," and shall then be led to study two natural classes of languages, the so-called context-sensitive and context-free languages. We shall find that the finite-state languages are a proper subclass of the context-free languages, which are similarly related to the context-sensitive languages, which in turn form a proper subclass of the recursive sets. But this is not all. We shall see that we may associate with these languages two classes of automata—each obtained by imposing natural restrictions on Turing machines—the push-down automata with the context-free languages, and the linear-bounded automata with the context-sensitive languages. And so it goes on, the literature now abounding with new classes of automata, intermediate between the finite automata (i.e., finite-state sequential machines) and the Turing machines. It is too early to provide an overview of all these variants, and to judge which are worthy of continued study and which mutations are nonviable—but the material presented in Part II of this book should more than suffice as background for the reader who wishes to approach this literature and judge for himself.

1.5 HIERARCHIES AND DIVERSITIES

A hierarchical classification of machines does not arise merely in connection with the study of formal languages.

We may impose subhierarchies on the finite automata (i.e., finite-state sequential machines) by asking how many components of a given kind are required in the construction of a given machine, as we do in Section 2.2, where the components are boolean switching elements with a fixed number of input lines, or in Section 8.6, where the components are finite automata whose inputs all serve to permute the set of states. These are studies which lay the foundations for really practical analyses of cost of realization of abstract descriptions of automata, at the same time as they give us insight into the way the *structure* of the finitely specifiable substrate *must* vary as we alter the nature of the input-output function it is to embody.

We may define subhierarchies of the Turing-computable functions in terms of inductive definitions of classes of functions, often far removed from machine definitions—in the manner of recursive function theory—and yet, as we shall see in Chapter 6, the subclasses so defined often correspond to subclasses of the Turing machines, and therein lies their interest to automata theorists.

Or we may seek to restrict our machines by limiting the time or tape space they may use in completing a computation, and then ask where in the complexity scale so induced lie the solutions of various problems. For instance, in Chapter 7 we shall give a formal proof of the old saw that "two heads are better than one" by proving that a Turing machine with two heads on one tape can recognize whether or not a string is a palindrome (i.e., reads the same backward and forward: "ABLE WAS I ERE I SAW ELBA," and the like) in a time that only increases linearly with the length of the string, while the time taken by a one-head machine will, for nearly all strings, go up with the square of the length of the string.

The reader should begin to understand why automata theory has so many different devices. Automata may be viewed in many different ways, and each way gives rise to a different set of questions. No matter how well we may evolve a unified theory of automata, these differences will remain, and the interrelations of these differing approaches will provide fertile fields for study. Just as much of the excitement of automata theory is generated by the attempt to capture diffuse aspects of reality in a convenient formalization, so there is a richness of insight to be gained in cross-formalization studies, in which we try to understand the mismatches between formalizations, and why advantages of a formalization in one context become disadvantages in another. Let us close, then, by listing some of the different ways in which we may consider automata, whether or not we have already discussed them in this chapter. We may consider automata as:

Constructs: Given a collection of components, we may ask questions of *synthesis*—can a given behavior be realized by an interconnection of these components, and if so, how?—and of *analysis*—what is the behavior of a given interconnection of the components?

Programs: Given a collection of input and output commands, data manipulation, and branch-on-test instructions, we may study the computations which can be carried out by executing a program written in terms of these commands.

Functions: We may view automata as either on-line or off-line devices for transforming input strings in X^* (not always successfully) to output strings in Y^*, thus yielding a (possibly partial) function $F: X^* \rightarrow Y^*$.

Languages: An automaton may be used for deciding whether or not input strings belong to a language, or accepting those strings which belong to a language, or generating a language as the set of its output strings. With languages, as with functions, we shall be led by our machine-theoretic investigations to study machine-independent questions, such as closure properties, which will lead us to other characterizations.

Logics: We may study devices for generating proofs of theorems from a given set of axioms, using given rules of inference; or a device for deciding whether or not a string is a theorem in a given formal system. This study may be formally like that of languages, but with the interpretation "This is a theorem" replacing the interpretation "This is grammatical."

Dynamic systems: Here the primary emphasis is on the state of the system, and the ways in which inputs may be chosen to control this state— outputs thus being relegated to a secondary role. This is the approach which links automata theory to mathematical system theory.

Algebraic systems: Here we emphasize the way in which, e.g., finite automata may be considered as a generalization of semigroups, thus enabling us to ask new questions about algebra, yet at the same time applying algebraic techniques to questions about automata. We can also study generalizations of automata suggested by generalizations of the algebraic concepts we apply.

We study the interplay between machine, language, and algebraic characterizations. We see how concepts change as we go from deterministic to possibilistic (nondeterministic yet not probabilistic) to probabilistic modes of operation. We extend our study of computation to deal with problems of construction. We impose hierarchies upon our constructs by imposing constraints of time, space, or complexity. And we ask how our formalizations compare with the complexities of real information-processors. The result is a growing, open-ended, mathematically sophisticated yet intuitively appealing abstract theory of automata.

2   ALGEBRAIC BACKGROUND

This chapter sets forth some of the basic algebraic notions required for the study of automata theory. The reader should master much of Sections 1 and 2 before going any further, so that he knows the basic terminology and procedures which aid our presentation in Part II. The generalized notion of proof by induction presented in Section 2 will play an especially important role. Some of the semigroup material of Sections 3 and 4 will be needed in Chapter 3, with a few notions of group theory being invoked in Section 3.2. Apart from this, most of the material in Sections 3 and 4 will be required only in Chapter 8.

    The exposition in this chapter is moderately full, but may be too brief for the reader to whom these ideas are completely novel, and who needs exercises to work through. For these readers I suggest MacLane and Birkhoff [1967] or Hu [1965]. For the reader whose problem is the opposite—the exposition stops just when the algebra gets interesting—Kurosh [1956] and Hall [1959] give additional group theory, while Clifford and Preston [1961, 1967] and Arbib [1968a] give a wealth of material on semigroups.

2.1   SETS, MAPS, AND DIAGRAMS

    Before starting our exposition, we list the basic notations that we shall employ throughout:

$\Rightarrow$	implies
$\Leftrightarrow$	implies and is implied by
iff	if and only if
$\square$	end of proof (or: no proof required)
$X = \{x_1, x_2, x_3, \ldots\}$	the set X has elements $x_1, x_2, x_3, \ldots$
$\emptyset$	the empty set
$x \in X$	x belongs to X or x is an element of the set X
$x \notin X$	x does not belong to X
$\{x \mid P(x)\}$	the set of all elements x such that the statement $P(x)$ is true; for example, $X = \{x \mid x \in X\}$.
$X \subset Y$	X is a subset of Y; that is, $x \in X \Rightarrow x \in Y$.
$X = Y$	$X \subset Y$ and $Y \subset X$; that is, X and Y are equal iff they have the same members
$X \cap Y$	the *intersection* of X and Y, that is, $\{x \mid x \in X$ and $x \in Y\}$
$X \cup Y$	the *union* of X and Y, that is, $\{x \mid x \in X$ or $x \in Y$ or both$\}$
$X - Y$	the *difference* of X and Y (or the *relative complement* of Y in X) = $\{x \mid x \in X$ and $x \notin Y\}$
N	the set of *nonnegative integers* $\{0, 1, 2, 3, \ldots\}$
Z	the set of *all integers* $\{\ldots, -3, -2, -1, 0, 1, 2, \ldots\}$
R	the set of all *real numbers*
$\forall$	for all
$\exists$	there exists; for example, $(\forall x \in Z)(\exists y \in Z)$ $(x + y = 0)$ means for every integer x, we may find an integer y such that the sum $x + y$ is 0.

We say two sets are *disjoint* iff $A \cap B = \emptyset$; otherwise, they are said to be *overlapping*.

Given two sets X and Y, the *cartesian product* of X and Y is

$$X \times Y = \{(x, y) \mid x \in X \text{ and } y \in Y\}$$
$$= \text{the set of all ordered pairs in which the first element belongs to}$$
$$X \text{ and the second to } Y$$

MAPS

We use the notation $f: X \to Y$ for "f is a *map* (or *function*) from the set X to the set Y"; that is, "to each $x \in X$, f assigns a unique element $f(x) \in Y$." We call $f(x)$ the *image* of x under f. We say that "f maps X into Y," and call X the *domain* of f and Y the *range* of f. We write $x \mapsto f(x)$.

Let $A \subset X$. Then the characteristic function of A in X is the function $\chi_A: X \to \{0, 1\}$ defined by

$$\chi_A(x) = \begin{cases} 0 & \text{if } x \notin A \\ 1 & \text{if } x \in A \end{cases}$$

We use Y^X to denote the set of all functions mapping X into Y.

If we label by "2" the two-element set $\{0, 1\}$, we see that we may identify 2^X with "the set of all subsets of X" by making the correspondence

$f: X \rightarrow \{0, 1\}$ corresponds to $\{x \in X \,|\, f(x) = 1\} \subset X$

$A \subset X$ corresponds to $\chi_A: X \rightarrow \{0, 1\}$

We say two functions, $f: X \rightarrow Y$ and $f': X' \rightarrow Y'$, are *equal* iff $X = X'$, $Y = Y'$, and $(\forall x \in X)f(x) = f'(x)$.

Thus if $X \subset Y$, we do *not* identify the inclusion function $i: X \rightarrow Y$. where $x \mapsto x \in Y$ with the identity function **1**: $X \rightarrow X$, where $x \mapsto x \in X$, for even though their action is equal, their ranges are not. This convention seems artificial at first sight, but turns out to be crucial in careful treatments of many parts of modern mathematics.

We say $f: X \rightarrow Y$ is *one-to-one* (1–1) or *injective* iff the images of distinct points of X are distinct, and sometimes write $f: X \hookrightarrow Y$.

Thus the inclusion function $i: X \rightarrow Y$ (which we sometimes write $i: X \subset Y$) is injective.

If $f: X \rightarrow Y$ and $A \subset X$, we write $f(A) = \{f(x) \,|\, x \in A\}$.

For $B \subset Y$ we write $f^{-1}(B) = \{x \in X \,|\, f(x) \in B\}$, the "inverse image" of B. Note that f^{-1} is *not*, in general, a map from Y to X but rather from 2^Y to 2^X. We write $f^{-1}(y)$ for $f^{-1}(\{y\})$;

$$y \in f(X) \Leftrightarrow f^{-1}(y) \neq \emptyset$$

We say $f: X \rightarrow Y$ is a function from X onto Y iff $f(X) = Y$—we then call f *surjective*, and often write $f: X \twoheadrightarrow Y$.

A function $f: X \rightarrow Y$ is called *bijective* iff it is both injective and surjec-

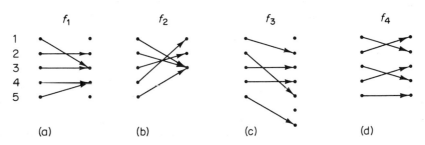

Fig. 2.1

tive, i.e., one-to-one and onto, so that $f^{-1}(y)$ contains one point for every $y \in Y$.

1 EXAMPLE: Consider the functions f_1, f_2, f_3, and f_4 which each have domain $\{1, 2, 3, 4, 5\}$ and are represented by the diagrams shown in Fig. 2.1.

If f is bijective, we *may* consider f^{-1} to be a function $f^{-1} \colon Y \to X$, and it is bijective too. The identity function $\mathbf{1} \colon X \to X$ is bijective, and has $\mathbf{1}^{-1} = \mathbf{1}.$

DIAGRAMS

If $f \colon X \to Y$, we may read this as "X is mapped by f into Y" and denote it by

$$X \xrightarrow{f} Y$$

If we should have both $X \xrightarrow{f} Y$ and $Y \xrightarrow{g} Z$, we may denote this by the diagram

$$X \xrightarrow{f} Y \xrightarrow{g} Z$$

If this case holds, i.e., the domain of g equals the range of f, we say f and g are *composable*, and define their composition $g{\cdot}f \colon X \to Z$ by the equation

$$[g \circ f](x) = g[f(x)]$$

We may also write $\qquad g{\cdot}f \quad$ or $\quad gf \quad$ for $\quad g \circ f$
Consider now the diagram

We say it is *commutative*, or *commutes*, for no matter what path we follow from one point to another, so long as we move in the directions of the arrows, and apply the stated function at each transition, we shall apply the same overall mapping. Thus, in mapping X into Z in the above diagram, it is immaterial to the overall result whether we map directly from X into Z via $g{\cdot}f$, or first map X into Y via f, and then map the result from Y into Z via g.

Frequently in the ensuing theory we will find the proof of theorems reducing to "diagram-chasing," i.e., drawing up a mapping diagram, and then checking paths to verify commutativity. Normally, when we draw such a diagram of maps, it *will* be commutative—such diagrams serve as shorthand to remind us of the equalities which hold between maps of interest.

Let us give an example of how concepts may be transferred from "evaluate-a-function-at-a-point" to "chase-a-diagram" language. The reader should verify the following characterizations:

(i) $X \xrightarrow{f} Y$ is surjective iff $X \xrightarrow{f} Y \xrightarrow{g} Z = X \xrightarrow{f} Y \xrightarrow{h} Z$

always implies $Y \xrightarrow{g} Z = Y \xrightarrow{h} Z$

(ii) $X \xrightarrow{f} Y$ is injective iff $Z \xrightarrow{g} X \xrightarrow{f} Y = Z \xrightarrow{h} X \xrightarrow{f} Y$

always implies $Z \xrightarrow{g} X = Z \xrightarrow{h} X$

Let us also note that any injective map $f = X \rightarrow Y$ has at least one "left-inverse" $\hat{f} \colon Y \rightarrow X$, that is, $\hat{f} \circ f = 1_X$—just choose $\hat{f}(y)$ arbitrarily if $y \notin f(x)$, and always set $\hat{f}(f(x)) = x$. Similarly, every surjective map has a right inverse.

With these observations we can now give an example of a "proof by diagram-chasing":

2   THE INDUCED-MAP THEOREM: *If the square*

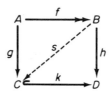

commutes (where f is onto and k is 1-1), then there is a unique $s: B \rightarrow C$ (the broken arrow indicates the map is not given, but is to be found) for which the triangles commute.

Proof. Since f is onto, it has a right inverse $\hat{f}$ such that $f\hat{f} = 1_B$. Set $s = g\hat{f}$.

The lower triangle commutes, since $ks = kg\hat{f} = hf\hat{f}$ (by commutativity of the square) $= h$.

To show that the upper triangle commutes, it suffices to show that $kg = ksf$, since k is injective, and it will then follow that $g = sf$. But $ksf = kg\hat{f}f = hff$ (by commutativity of the square) $= hf = kg$ (by commutativity of the square).

We see immediately that s is unique, since if $ks' = h = ks$, that is, the lower triangle commutes, then $s = s'$ by the injectivity of k.   □

Let $f: X \rightarrow Y$ and $A \subset X$. Then we define the *restriction* of f to A, denoted $f|A$, to be the function $g: A \rightarrow Y$ defined by $g(a) = f(a)$ for each $a \in A$.

If $g = f|A$, then the function $f: X \rightarrow Y$ is said to be an *extension* of g

over the set X. Thus, if $h\colon A \subset X$ denotes the inclusion function, it follows that the triangle

is commutative.

3 EXERCISE: Let $A = \{1\}$, $X = \{1, 2\}$, $Y = \{1, 2, 3\}$, and define $g\colon A \to Y$ by $g(1) = 3$. How many different functions $f\colon X \to Y$ exist, such that $f|A = g$?

Let A be a set of "indices," such that for each $a \in A$, there is assigned a subset X_a of X, and a function $f_a\colon X_a \to Y$. We say the family $\Phi = \{f_a | a \in A\}$ of functions is *combinable* if the functions of each pair *agree* on the overlap of their domains; i.e., for all a, $a' \in A$, we have

$$f_a|X_a \cap X_{a'} = f_{a'}|X_a \cap X_{a'}$$

This being so, we may define the *combined function* of the family Φ to be $f\colon \bigcup_{a \in A} X_a \to Y$, where

$$f(x) = f_a(x) \qquad \text{if } x \in X_a$$

N.B. If we regard a function $f_a\colon X_a \to Y$ as the set of ordered pairs $\{(x, f_a(x)) | x \in X_a\}$, then to say that a set of functions $\{f_a\}$ is *combinable* is to say that their union is a function—namely, f.

A *sequence* is just a function from the natural numbers $f\colon N \to X$. If $f(n) = x_n$, we call it the nth *term* of the sequence, and often write

$$f = (x_1, x_2, \ldots, x_n, \ldots)$$

A *finite* sequence is a map $f\colon \{1, 2, \ldots, m\} \to X$, for some $m \in N$. If $m = 0$, we denote the unique sequence of length 0 by Λ.

Let $F = \{X_\mu | \mu \in M\}$ be a family of sets indexed by the set M. Let $X = \bigcup_{\mu \in M} X_\mu$. Then the *cartesian product* of the family F of sets is the set Φ of all functions $f\colon M \to X$ such that $f(\mu) \in X_\mu$ for every $\mu \in M$. We denote Φ by $\prod_{\mu \in M} X_\mu$. Note that this reduces to the usual definition if M is finite:

$$X_1 \times X_2 \times \ldots \times X_n = \{(x_1, \ldots, x_n) | x_j \in X_j\}$$

For each $\mu \in M$, consider the function

$$p_\mu\colon \Phi \to X_u$$

defined by $p_\mu(f) = f(\mu)$ for every $f \in \Phi$; p_μ is surjective for every $\mu \in M$, and we call p_μ the *projection* of the cartesian product onto its μth *coordinate set* X_μ.

If $f: X_1 \times X_2 \to Y$, we write $f(x_1, x_2)$ rather than $f((x_1, x_2))$. $f(\circ, x_2)$ will denote the function $X_1 \to Y$ which sends x_1 to $f(x_1, x_2)$. Similarly,

$$f(x_1, \circ): X_2 \to Y: x_2 \mapsto f(x_1, x_2)$$

RELATIONS

A (binary) *relation R* on a set *S* is simply a subset of $S \times S$. We say x is *in the relation R to y* (written xRy) if and only if $(x, y) \in R$. Thus a function may sometimes be thought of as a relation R, such that for each x there is one and only one y with $(x, y) \in R$.

By a *partially ordered set* we mean a set P together with a binary relation $x \leq y$ which satisfies

P1 For all $x \in P$, we have $x \leq x$ *(reflexivity)*
P2 For all x and y in P,
    if $x \leq y$ and $y \leq x$, then $x = y$ *(antisymmetry)*
P3 For all x, y, and z in P,
    if $x \leq y$, and $y \leq z$, then $x \leq z$ *(transitivity)*

The most common example is that of the integers, where $x \leq y$ if and only if y is greater than or equal to x.

A more illuminating example, which points up that the ordering need only be *partial*, is the set of subsets of a set S, under the subset relation: if X, $Y \subset S$, then $X \leq Y$ if and only if $X \subset Y$. Here we see that, given X and Y, it may well happen that neither $X \leq Y$ nor $Y \leq X$, in contrast to the situation for the integers. We then say that X and Y are *incomparable*.

A notion of fundamental importance in mathematics is that of equivalence: A relation $\equiv$ on a set S is an *equivalence* if and only if it satisfies the three conditions:

E1 For all $x \in S$, we have $x \equiv x$ *(reflexivity)*
E2 For all x, $y \in S$, the equivalence
    $x \equiv y$ implies $y \equiv x$ *(symmetry)*
E3 For all x, y, $z \in S$, the equivalences
    $x \equiv y$ and $y \equiv z$ imply $x \equiv z$ *(transitivity)*

Familiar examples are equality in arithmetic, congruence in euclidean geometry, and similarity for nonsingular matrices.

Given a set S, and an equivalence relation $\equiv$, the *equivalence class* of $s \in S$ *modulo* $\equiv$ is $[s]_\equiv = \{t \mid t \equiv s\}$. We may define a new set $S/\equiv$ as the set of equivalence classes of S modulo $\equiv$. An equivalence relation over a set S is of *finite index* if there are only finitely many equivalence classes under the relation.

4 EXAMPLE: If Z is the set of all integers, and we set $n \equiv n'$ iff $n - n'$ is even, then we see that $\equiv$ is an equivalence relation, and that $Z/\equiv$ has two elements. Is $n \sim n'$ when $n - n'$ is *odd* an equivalence relation?

A *partition* P of S is a division of S into disjoint subsets S_k; that is,

$$S_i \cap S_j = \emptyset \qquad \text{for } i \neq j$$

and

$$S = \cup S_i$$

Each S_i is called a *block* of P.

Clearly $[s] = [t]$ as elements of $S/\equiv$ iff $t \equiv s$. We call $S/\equiv$ *the partition of S induced by the equivalence*. If, for a partition P, we define $\equiv_P$ on S by $x \equiv_P y$ if and only if x and y lie in the same block of P, then $\equiv_P$ is an equivalence and P is the partition of S induced by the equivalence $\equiv_P$.

In certain partially ordered sets, we can define "meets" and "joins." We say that m is a *meet* (or *greatest lower bound*) of a and b if $m \leq a$ and $m \leq b$ and if, for every m', $m' \leq a$ and $m' \leq b$ imply $m' \leq m$. Thus the meet of a and b is unique by antisymmetry, and we write $a \wedge b$ for m.

Dually, u is a *join* (or *least upper bound*) for a and b if $a \leq u$, $b \leq u$ and for every u' with $a \leq u'$ and $b \leq u'$ we must have $u \leq u'$. Thus the join of a and b is unique, and we write $a \vee b$ for u.

Then a *lattice* is a partially ordered set for which every pair of elements has both a meet and a join.

5 EXAMPLES

(i) N is a lattice with $a \wedge b = \min (a, b)$ and $a \vee b = \max (a, b)$.

(ii) The set of all subsets of a given set is a lattice, with $a \wedge b = a \cap b$ and $a \vee b = a \cup b$.

(iii) The partitions on a set S form a lattice under the ordering $\pi_1 \leq \pi_2$ if each block of π_1 is contained in a block of π_2. Two partitions π_1 and π_2 have meet $\pi_1 \cdot \pi_2$ with blocks the intersections of blocks of π_1 and π_2. The join $\pi_1 + \pi_2$ has s and s' in the same block just in case there are elements $s_1, \ldots, s_n$ of S with $s_1 = s$, $s_n = s'$, and s_j and s_{j+1} lying in the same block of π_1 or π_2 for each j, where $1 \leq j < n$. For instance, if $S = \{1, 2, 3, 4, 5, 6, 7\}$ and π_1 has blocks $\{1, 7\}$, $\{2, 5, 6\}$ and $\{3, 4\}$, while π_2 has blocks $\{1, 2, 7\}$, $\{3, 4\}$, $\{5, 6\}$, then

$$\pi_1 \cdot \pi_2 = \{\{1\}, \{2\}, \{3, 4\}, \{5, 6\}, \{7\}\}$$

while

$$\pi_1 + \pi_2 = \{\{1, 2, 5, 6, 7\}, \{3, 4\}\}$$

We say that 0 is a *zero element* of a partially ordered set if $0 \leq m$ for all m in the set; while 1 is a *unit element* if we always have $m \leq 1$. Note that if the set is a lattice, then $0 \wedge x = 0$, $0 \vee x = x = x \wedge 1$, and $x \vee 1 = 1$.

6 EXAMPLE

(i) N has zero 0, but no unit, under $\leq$.

(ii) The set of all subsets of S has zero $\emptyset$ and unit S, under $\subset$.

(iii) The lattice of partitions on a set S has zero 0 consisting of singleton blocks, and unit 1 comprising only one block, namely S.

DENUMERABILITY

We close this section with a short note on cardinal numbers: We remind the reader that a set is *finite* if it has finitely many members; *denumerable* if it can be put in one-to-one correspondence with the set N (in which case we say the set has cardinality aleph-null: symbolized $\aleph_0$; and *nondenumerable* if none of the previous cases holds.

Given a finite set S, with n elements, there are 2^n subsets of S since for each of the n elements we have two choices as to whether or not we include it in the subset.

By analogy, we denote by $2^{\aleph_0}$ the number of subsets of a denumerable set S—the 1-1 correspondence between S and N induces a 1-1 correspondence on their set of subsets, which thus have the same cardinality. With each subset T of S we may associate a sequence

$$t_1 t_2 t_3 \ldots t_n \ldots$$

where
$$t_n = \begin{cases} 1 & \text{if } n \in T \\ 0 & \text{if } n \notin T \end{cases}$$

We shall now give a version of the well-known Cantor diagonal argument to show that these sequences *cannot* be put in 1-1 correspondence with the integers:

Suppose we could enumerate all these sequences, so that the jth is $a_{j1} a_{j2} a_{j3} \ldots a_{jn} \ldots$. Arrange them in an array:

$$\bar{a}_1 = a_{11} a_{12} a_{13} \ldots a_{1n} \ldots$$
$$\bar{a}_2 = a_{21} a_{22} a_{23} \ldots a_{2n} \ldots$$
$$\bar{a}_3 = a_{31} a_{32} a_{33} \ldots a_{3n} \ldots$$

and so on. Now consider the sequence obtained by moving down the diagonal and changing each 1 to 0 and each 0 to 1,

$$\bar{b} = b_1 b_2 b_3 \ldots b_n \ldots$$

where each $b_n = 1 - a_{nn}$. Then $\bar{b}$ differs from $\bar{a}_n$ in the nth place, and so is not included in the enumeration. But *the choice of enumeration was arbitrary, and so the sequences are not denumerable.* Thus we have

$$2^{\aleph_0} \underset{\neq}{\geq} \aleph_0$$

We shall see analogues of this *diagonal argument* of Cantor play an important role in proofs of noncomputability in Chapter 4 and elsewhere.

2.2   GRAPHS, TREES, AND INDUCTION

We shall have occasion to use graphs not in the sense of a graph of a function, but rather in the sense of structures such as the one shown in Fig. 2.2, in which we have a set of *nodes* or *vertices* joined by *edges,* usually *directed,* and usually *labelled.*

Abstractly, a *labelled graph* may be defined as a quadruple (V, E, g, h) where V is a set, called the set of *vertices;* E is a set called the set of *edges; g*: $E \rightarrow V \times V$ assigns to each edge e a pair of

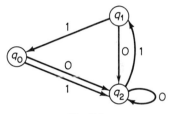

Fig. 2.2

vertices $g(e) = (v_1, v_2)$, indicating that e is an edge leading from v_1 to v_2; and h: $E \cup V \rightarrow L$, where L is some set of labels, assigns label $h(e)$ to edge e and label $h(v)$ to vertex v.

Thus we might specify the above graph by setting

$$V = \{v_1, v_2, v_3\}$$
$$E = \{e_1, e_2, e_3, e_4, e_5, e_6\}$$

with $h(v_1) = q_0$, $h(v_2) = q_1$, $h(v_3) = q_2$ and g and h given on V by the table

	e_1	e_2	e_3	e_4	e_5	e_6
h	1	1	0	0	0	1
g	(v_2, v_1)	(v_3, v_2)	(v_2, v_3)	(v_3, v_3)	(v_1, v_3)	(v_1, v_3)

It should be clear from this example that we are not interested in whether the vertex labelled q_0 is known as v_1 or v_2—the important thing is that the edge leading from the vertex labelled q_0 to that labelled q_1 is itself labelled 1.

Thus when we talk of a labelled graph, we shall mean any graph isomorphic to the given one, where:

Two labelled graphs (V, E, g, h) and (V', E', g', h') with the same label set L are *isomorphic* if there exist bijections $k_1: V \to V'$ and $k_2: E \to E'$ such that for all $v, v_1, v_2 \in V$ and $e \in E$,

$$g(e) = (v_1, v_2) \text{ implies } g'(k_2(e)) = (k_1(v_1), k_1(v_2))$$
$$h(e) = h'(k_2(e))$$
$$h(v) = h'(k_1(v))$$

In another model of a graph, we wish not only to record which vertices have edges leading to a given vertex, but also to put an order on the set of vertices leading to a given vertex:

A *directed ordered‡ graph* Γ (*DOG*) is a map $\Gamma: V \to V^*$, where V is called the set of *vertices* of Γ. (Recall that V^* is the set of all finite sequences of elements of V, and that Λ is the "empty sequence.") We often write $(v, \overset{1\to}{v}, \ldots, \overset{n(v)\to}{v})$ for $\Gamma(v)$ and call any $\overset{j\to}{v}$ an *input node for* v. v is called *initial* if $\Gamma(v) = \Lambda$. v is called *terminal* if v is not an input node for any $v' \in V$.

We say $v < v'$ if there is a sequence $v = v_1, v_2, \ldots, v_n = v'$ $(n > 1)$ with each v_i an input node for v_{i+1}.

Henceforth, all DOGs considered will be finite.

A *loop* of a DOG Γ is a sequence $v_1, \ldots, v_n, v_{n+1} = v_1$ of vertices of Γ such that v_i is an input node of v_{i+1}, where $i = 1, \ldots, n$.

A *directed order acyclic graph* (DOAG) is a DOG without any loops.

Thus a DOG is a DOAG if $v < v$ for *no* vertex v.

A *tree* is a DOAG for which a node is input to at most one other node and there is only one terminal node.

Fig. 2.3

Thus a tree can always be represented by a diagram of the form (perhaps rotated through 90° or 180°) shown in Fig. 2.3, where each vertex has a vertex leading to a unique vertex above it, but may be fed by several vertices from below.

If the vertices of a DOAG have labels from a set Σ we obtain a Σ *DOAG*: a pair (Γ, h), where $\Gamma: V \to V^*$ is a DOAG, and $h: V \to \Sigma$.

Given a DOAG Γ, we associate a *level* with each node as follows:

level $(v) = 0$ iff v is initial

level $(v) \leq k + 1$ iff level $(\overset{j\to}{v}) \leq k$ for $1 \leq j \leq n(v)$

Thus $v < v' \Rightarrow$ level $(v) <$ level (v'), but the converse is not true, even in trees.

---

‡ Here ordered refers *not* to the set of vertices (= nodes), but to each set of nodes leading to a given node.

R3
R6

QA166.G6513
. C48
. R4

P85. C47

P158. R3

This is a good place to recall the basic PRINCIPLE OF INDUCTION, which is often used in mathematical proofs:

If P(n) is a predicate which is true for n = k, and if the truth of P(n) implies the truth of P(n + 1) for each n ≥ k, then P(n) is true for all n ≥ k.
[If $P(n)$ were not true for all $n \geq k$, since $P(k)$ is true there would be some integer $n_0 > k$ such that $P(n_0)$ would be false, but $P(n)$ is true for $n < n_0$. But if $P(n_0 - 1)$ is true, then $P(n_0 - 1 + 1)$ is true—a contradiction!]

Actually, in automata theory we often do such inductions which at first sight do not appear to fit the normal mold of numerical induction, but which can be cast in this mold essentially by considering induction on a numerical parameter such as the level of a vertex in a tree.

For instance, if we wish to prove that something is true of all vertices of a tree, we prove it true for vertices of level 0, and then show that if it holds for all vertices of level k, it must also hold for vertices of level $k + 1$.

We say a set is *closed under an operation* if whenever that operation is applied to members of a set, it yields another member of the set. Thus the set N of nonnegative integers is closed under addition but not under subtraction: $1 - 2 \notin N$.

We may note that the set N is the smallest set containing zero and closed under the successor operation which replaces n by $n + 1$. By this we mean that an object is a positive integer iff it is zero, or can be obtained from zero by a finite number of applications of the successor operation. Putting it still another way, we may define

$$S_0 = \{0\}$$
$$S_{n+1} = \{m \mid m = k + 1 \text{ for some } k \text{ in } S_n\}$$

and then
$$N = \bigcup_{n \geq 0} S_n$$

This is somewhat circular as a definition, but we shall find these equivalent modes of definition useful. To exemplify this, we shall give the definition of regular set (already mentioned in Chapter 1) which will be developed in Section 3.3.

We consider subsets of X^*. We define the operations of union, which replace sets E and F by their union $E \cup F$, of product, which replace sets E and F by $E \cdot F = \{\alpha \cdot \beta \mid \alpha \in E \text{ and } \beta \in F\}$, and of closure, which replaces E by $E^* = \{\alpha_1 \cdot \alpha_2 \cdot \cdots \cdot \alpha_n \mid n \geq 0 \text{ and each } \alpha_i \in E\}$. Note that X^*, in our old notation, does equal the closure of X, and so the new notation is consistent.

We then define the class of regular sets (on X) to be the smallest class containing the sets $\emptyset$, $\{\Lambda\}$, and $\{x\}$ (for $x \in X$) and closed under the operations of union, product, and closure. By this we mean that a subset of X^* is regular iff it is one of the sets $\emptyset$, $\{\Lambda\}$, or $\{x\}$ (for $x \in X$) or can be obtained from these sets by a finite number of applications of the operation of union, product, and closure. Putting it still another way, we define

$$
\begin{aligned}
\mathcal{R}_0(x) &= \{\emptyset, \{\Lambda\}, \{x\} \text{ for } x \in X\} \\
\mathcal{R}_{n+1}(x) &= \{G | G = E \cup F \text{ for some } E, F \text{ in } \mathcal{R}_n(x)\} \\
&\quad \cup \{G | G = E^* \text{ for some } E \text{ in } \mathcal{R}_n(x)\} \\
&\quad \cup \{G | G = E \cdot F \text{ for some } E, F \text{ in } \mathcal{R}_n(x)\}
\end{aligned}
$$

and then the class of regular subsets of X equals $\bigcup\limits_{n \geq 0} \mathcal{R}_n(x)$.

Now it should be clear that we may give inductive proofs of theorems about regular sets by proving that the theorem holds for every set in $\mathcal{R}_0(x)$, and then showing that if it holds for every set in $\mathcal{R}_n(x)$, it must hold for every set in $\mathcal{R}_{n+1}(x)$. By the induction principle, it then holds for every set in every $\mathcal{R}_n(x)$, and since every regular set belongs to some $\mathcal{R}_n(x)$, it must hold for every regular set. However, to prove that if a result holds for every set in $\mathcal{R}_n(x)$, it must also hold for every set in $\mathcal{R}_{n+1}(x)$, it clearly suffices to prove that if it holds for E, it must also hold for E^*, whereas if it holds for both E and F, it must also hold for $E \cdot F$ and $E \cup F$. Thus we shall give inductive proofs which will have the structure exemplified by the proof of the following:

7   **PROPOSITION**: *For a string* $u = x_1 x_2 \ldots x_n$, *each* $x_j \in X$, *we define its reverse* u^R *to be the string* $x_n \ldots x_2 x_1$.‡ *For a subset S of X^* we define its reverse S^R to be the set* $\{u^R | u \in S\}$. *Then S^R is regular if S is regular.*

Proof. Basis: The result is true for $\emptyset$, $\{\Lambda\}$, or $\{x\}$ for $x \in X$, since $\emptyset^R = \emptyset$, $\{\Lambda\}^R = \{\Lambda\}$ and $\{x\}^R = \{x\}$.

Induction: (i) If E and F are regular with E^R and F^R regular, then $(E \cup F)^R = E^R \cup F^R$, and so is regular, being the union of regular sets.

(ii) If E and F are regular with E^R and F^R regular, then $(E \cdot F)^R = F^R \cdot E^R$, and so is regular, being the product of regular sets.

(iii) If E is regular with E^R regular, then $(E^*)^R = (E^R)^*$, and so is regular being the closure of a regular set.   □

Of course, it is easy to develop facility with such proofs, and so one might end up writing such a proof simply as: "The result is clearly true for the basis sets, and since $(E \cup F)^R = E^R \cup F^R$, $(E \cdot F)^R = F^R \cdot E^R$ and $(E^*)^R = (E^R)^*$, the result holds for all regular sets by induction." We thus leave implicit the details of the proof, as well as the underlying fact that we are giving a proof by induction on the number of operations required to define a set.

―   ―

‡ This may be *defined* inductively by $\Lambda^R = \Lambda$, and for each $u \in X^*$ and $x \in X$, $(ux)^R = x \cdot u^R$. We then obtain, for example, $(x_1 x_2 x_3 x_4)^R$ by the process $(x_1 x_2 x_3 \cdot x_4)^R = x_4 \cdot (x_1 x_2 x_3)^R = x_4 x_3 (x_1 x_2)^R = x_4 x_3 x_2 (\Lambda \cdot x_1)^R = x_4 x_3 x_2 x_1$.

2.3 SEMIGROUPS

We do not assume any knowledge of group theory in this section, but for those readers acquainted with group theory we point out that whereas a group is a set closed under a binary operation which is associative and has an identity and inverses, a semigroup is a set closed under a binary operation which is associative, the other two requirements *not* necessarily being fulfilled. Thus every group is a semigroup, but many semigroups are not groups.

By a *binary operation* on a set S we mean a map $m: S \times S \to S$. We refer to $m(a, b)$ as the *composite* of a and b (under m).

1 EXAMPLES

(i) $S = N$ or Z or R, and m is the *usual addition*

$$m(a, b) = a + b$$

(ii) $S = N$ or Z or R, and m is the *usual multiplication*

$$m(a, b) = a \times b$$

(iii) $S = Z$ or R, and m is the *usual subtraction*

$$m(a, b) = a - b$$

(iv) Let S be the set of all maps from a set X into itself, and let m be *composition*

$$m(f, g)(x) = f(g(x))$$

(v) Let $S = N$ or Z or R, and let

$$m(a, b) = 2a + 2b$$

A binary operation m on a set S will be called *abelian* or *commutative* if, for *all* a and b in S, we have

$$m(a, b) = m(b, a)$$

Thus the usual addition is commutative, but subtraction is not.

A binary operation m on a set S will be called *associative* if, for *all* a, b, and c in S, we have

$$m(a, m(b, c)) = m(m(a, b), c)$$

Thus the usual addition is associative, but the operation of example (v) is not.

2 EXERCISE: Determine which of the five examples above are commutative, and which associative, operations.

The reader will thus see that commutativity and associativity are independent properties. We shall consider many binary operations on different sets, and shall usually denote a composite, $m(a, b)$, by one of the notations: $a + b$, ab or $a \cdot b$. Even though m may be quite different from the above examples, we reserve $a + b$ for commutative operations.

In what follows, let us consider given a set S, and a binary operation ab.

Now, $u \in S$ is a *left identity* if $us = s$ for every s in S, a *right identity* if $su = s$ for every s in S, and an *identity* if it is both a left and a right identity.

In example (i) above, 0 is the only (left or right) identity; in example (ii), 1 is the only (left or right) identity; in example (iii), 0 is a right identity, but there is no left identity.

3 EXERCISE: Catalogue the (left, right) identities for examples (iv) and (v).

If a binary operation on a set S has a left identity u and a right identity v, then $v = uv = v$, and so if there is a left and a right identity, there can be only one.

An element x in S is said to be *idempotent* if $xx = x$. Thus every (left, right) identity is idempotent. In example (ii), however, 0 is idempotent but is neither a left nor a right identity.

By a *semigroup* we mean a pair $(S, \circ)$, where S is a set on which $\circ$ is an associative binary operation. The rest of this section will explore the elementary properties of semigroups.

A *monoid* is a semigroup with a (unique) identity. Example: Let $N^{\bullet} = \{1, 2, 3, \ldots\}$. Then $(N^{\bullet}, +)$ is a semigroup, but not a monoid, whereas $(N, \times)$ *is* a monoid.

We say $(S, \circ)$ is *commutative* or *abelian* if $\circ$ is commutative.

We shall often write S to denote a semigroup when we really mean $(S, \circ)$—trusting to the context to help the reader associate the correct operation with the set.

A subset W of S is *closed* (or *stable*) iff $ab \in W$ for all a and b in W. If W is stable, then the restriction $\rho = m | W \times W$ of the binary operation $m: S \times S \rightarrow S$ is an associative binary operation on W. We may thus speak of W (that is, (W, ρ)) as a *subsemigroup* of S (that is, (S, m)).

If, further, S is a monoid whose unique identity is a member of W, we call W a *submonoid* of S.

4 EXERCISE: Invent a monoid S which has a subsemigroup W which is a monoid, yet is *not* a submonoid of S (and recall an example of a semigroup which is not a monoid).

5 EXERCISE: Prove that the intersection of any family of subsemigroups (submonoids) of a semigroup (monoid) S is again a subsemigroup (submonoid) of S.

Let X be an arbitrary subset of S. Then X is contained in at least one subsemigroup of S—namely S. Let $\langle X \rangle$ denote the intersection of all subsemigroups of S which contain X. It is a subsemigroup of S containing X, and is the smallest such—we call it the *subsemigroup generated by* X. If $X = \{a\}$, we write $\langle a \rangle$ for $\langle \{a\} \rangle$. If $S = \langle a \rangle$ for some $a \in S$, we call S a *cyclic semigroup*.

If $S = \langle X \rangle$, we call X a *set of generators* for S, and say that S is *generated* by X.

Then $\{1\}$ is a set of generators for $(N, +)$, and $\{-1, 1\}$ is a set of generators for $(Z, +)$, but there is no *finite* set of generators for Z under the usual multiplication—we need -1 and all the positive prime numbers.

Given a semigroup, we have two ways of turning it into a monoid: Let

$$S^I = S \cup \{e\}$$

where $e \notin S$, with the binary operation on S extended by requiring $es = se = s$ for all $s \in S \cup \{e\}$.

$$\text{Let } S^1 = \begin{cases} S & \text{if } S \text{ is a monoid} \\ S^I & \text{if } S \text{ is not a monoid} \end{cases}$$

Note that if S is a monoid, it equals S^1 but is *not* a submonoid of S^I. Note, too, that if given $a \in S$, and B, $C \subset S$, we denote by BC the set $\{bc | b \in B, c \in C\}$, and write aC for $\{a\}\, C$, and so on, we then have

$$S^1 a = S^I a = Sa \cup \{a\} \qquad aS^1 = aS^I = aS \cup \{a\}$$

and

$$S^1 a S^1 = S^I a S^I = SaS \cup Sa \cup aS \cup \{a\}$$

6 EXERCISE: Prove that, in any given semigroup S, we have

$$(ab)(cd) = (a(bc))d = (ab)(cd)$$

and so on for any a, b, c, d in S—and so we may denote it unambiguously by $abcd$. Generalize this result to the product of any number of elements in S.

Thus, for any semigroup S, the product of n copies of an element x is uniquely defined, irrespective of the order in which we associate subproducts —call the result x^n. [We already knew that x^3 was well-defined, whether as $x(xx)$ or $(xx)\, x$.]

Prove that for any $x \in X$, and any integers $m, n > 0$, we have

$$x^m x^n = x^{m+n} \qquad (x^m)^n = x^{mn}$$

A *homomorphism* from the semigroup S_1 to the semigroup S_2 is a map $f: S_1 \to S_2$ which preserves multiplication; i.e., for all a, b in S_1, we have

$$f(ab) = f(a)f(b)$$

Consider the function $f \times f: S_1 \times S_1 \to S_2 \times S_2: (s_1, s_1') \mapsto (f(s_1), f(s_1'))$. To say that f is a homomorphism is just to say that the diagram is commuta-

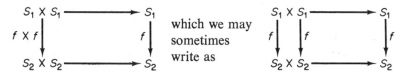

which we may sometimes write as

tive, where the horizontal arrows are the binary operations of the semigroups.

7 EXAMPLE: Multiplication by 2 is a homomorphism for $(N, +)$ but not for $(N, \times)$.

If, further, S_1 is a monoid with identity e_1, and S_2 is a monoid with identity e_2, and $f(e_1) = e_2$, we call f a *monoid homomorphism*.

8 EXAMPLE: The map $(R, +) \to (R, \times): x \mapsto e^x$ is a homomorphism, in fact, a monoid homomorphism.

9 EXERCISE: Prove that if $S_1 \xrightarrow{f_1} S_2 \xrightarrow{f_2} S_3$ with f_1 and f_2 both homomorphisms, then $f_2 \circ f_1$ is also a homomorphism.

10 EXERCISE: Let $f: S_1 \to S_2$ be a homomorphism, A_1 a subsemigroup of S_1, and A_2 a subsemigroup of S_2. Then show that $f(A_1)$ is a subsemigroup of S_2, and $f^{-1}(A_2)$ is a subsemigroup of S_1. Note that we do *not* assume that $f^{-1}: S_2 \to S_1$.

We say a homomorphism $f: S_1 \to S_2$ is a *monomorphism* iff it is injective (one-to-one), and may denote this by $f: S_1 \hookrightarrow S_2$ or $S_1 \overset{f}{\hookrightarrow} S_2$. We say it is an *epimorphism* iff it is surjective (onto), and write $f: S_1 \twoheadrightarrow S_2$. If f is both a monomorphism and an epimorphism (i.e., it is a one-to-one and onto homomorphism), we call it an *isomorphism*, and may write $f: S_1 \cong S_2$.

We say two semigroups S_1 and S_2 are *isomorphic*, denoted $S_1 \cong S_2$, iff there exists an isomorphism $f: S_1 \cong S_2$.

We say a semigroup S_2 is a *homomorphic image* of a semigroup S_1, iff there exists an epimorphism mapping S_1 onto S_2, that is, iff there exists an $f: S_1 \longrightarrow\!\!\!\!\!\rightarrow S_2$.

An *endomorphism* is a homomorphism $f: S \to S$ of a semigroup into itself.

An *automorphism* is an isomorphism $f: S \cong S$ of a semigroup onto itself.

11 EXERCISE: Let $f_1: S_1 \to S_2$ and $f_2: S_2 \to S_3$ be homomorphisms. If $f_2 \cdot f_1$ is a monomorphism, then so is f_1. If it is an epimorphism, so is f_2.

If $f: S_1 \to S_2$ is a homomorphism, we call Im $(f) = f(S_1)$ the *image* of f and denote it by Im (f). If, further, S_2 is a monoid with identity e_2, we call $f^{-1}(e_2)$ the *kernel* of f, Ker (f).

12 EXERCISE: Let $f: S_1 \to S_2$ be a homomorphism. Show that:
   (i) $a \in S_1$ idempotent $\Rightarrow f(a) \in S_2$ idempotent.
   (ii) If S_1 and S_2 are monoids, the following are equivalent:
        (a) f is a monoid homomorphism.
        (b) Im (f) is a submonoid of S_2.
        (c) Ker (f) is a submonoid of S_1.

For any set X, let X^+ denote the set of all finite sequences of elements (repetitions allowed) of the given set X. We will define a binary operation by associating with

$$\alpha = (a_1, \ldots, a_m) \qquad \text{and} \qquad \beta = (b_1, \ldots, b_n)$$

the new sequence $\alpha\beta = (a_1, \ldots, a_m, b_1, \ldots, b_n)$. This binary operation is clearly associative, and makes X^+ a semigroup.

Now, X^* is obtained by adjoining to X^+ the *empty sequence* Λ of length 0. For all α we then set $\alpha \cdot \Lambda = \Lambda \cdot \alpha = \alpha$. We denote by $l(\alpha)$ or $|\alpha|$ the *length* of α—if $\alpha = x_1, \ldots, x_n$, each $x_j \in X$, then $l(\alpha) = n$.

13 EXAMPLE: Let $X = \{0, 1\}$. Then the following is the set of all sequences of X^* of length less than 4:

$$\{\Lambda, 0, 1, 00, 01, 10, 11, 000, 001, 010, 011, 100, 101, 110, 111\}$$

and we have that

$$\Lambda \cdot 00 = 00 \qquad 11 \cdot 001 = 11001$$

and

$$|11001| = 5 = 2 + 3 = |11| + |001|$$

14 The following simple facts are all true for any set X:
   (i)   For all $\alpha \in X^*$, we have $\alpha \cdot \Lambda = \Lambda \cdot \alpha = \alpha$.
   (ii) For all $\alpha, \beta, \gamma \in X^*$, we have $(\alpha \cdot \beta) \cdot \gamma = \alpha \cdot (\beta \cdot \gamma)$.

(iii) For all α, β, $\gamma \in X^*$, we have: If $\alpha \cdot \beta = \alpha \cdot \gamma$, then $\beta = \gamma$.

(iv) For all α, β, γ, $\delta \in X^*$, we have: If $\alpha\beta = \gamma\delta$, then we can find $\theta \in X^*$ such that either

    (a) $\alpha = \gamma\theta$, $\delta = \theta\beta$; or

    (b) $\gamma = \alpha\theta$, $\beta = \theta\delta$

(v) $l(\alpha\beta) = l(\alpha) + l(\beta)$

We define $f: X \to X^+$ by defining $f(x)$ to be the finite sequence which consists of the single element x of X.

We suppose that $g: X \to S$ is an arbitrarily given function from X into a semigroup S. We may define $h: X^+ \to S$ by

$$h(a_1, \ldots, a_m) = g(a_1) \ldots g(a_m)$$

for every element $(a_1, \ldots, a_m)$ of X^+. Because of the associativity in S, it follows that h is a homomorphism. For any element $a \in X$, we have [recalling that $f(a)$ is the sequence of one element a]

$$(h \circ f)(a) = h[f(a)] = g(a)$$

and so $h \circ f = g$. This determines h uniquely, for if $k: X^+ \to S$ is another homomorphism satisfying $k \circ f = g$, then

$$
\begin{aligned}
k(a_1, \ldots, a_m) &= k[f(a_1) \ldots f(a_m)] \\
&= k[f(a_1)] \ldots k[f(a_m)] \\
&= g(a_1) \ldots g(a_m) \\
&= h(a_1, \ldots, a_m)
\end{aligned}
$$

Thus X^+ is a *free semigroup* on the set S, where

Given an arbitrary set X, we say a semigroup F, together with a function $f: X \to F$, is a *free semigroup on the set X* if for every semigroup S, and every function $g: X \to S$ from the set X into S, there exists a unique homomorphism $h: F \to S$ such that the diagram

commutes.

15 UNIQUENESS THEOREM: *If (F, f) and (F', f') are free semigroups on the same set X, then there exists a unique isomorphism*

$$j: F \to F' \quad \text{such that} \quad j \cdot f = f'$$

The proof is a nice example of diagram-chasing: The reader is asked to provide it by contemplating the four diagrams

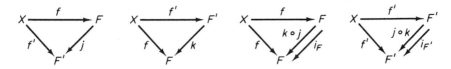

where i_F is the identity endomorphism of F, and so on.

16 If X is a set of generators for a semigroup S, then every element of S can be written as the product of a finite sequence of elements in X.

Let (X^+, f) be the free semigroup on X constructed in **14**. Let $g\colon X \subset S$ be the inclusion function (note that we do not ask S to be free). Let $h\colon X^+ \to S$ be the unique homomorphism $h\colon X^+ \to S$ such that

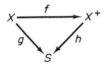

commutes. We prove that h is an epimorphism. Now, $h(X^+)$ is a subsemigroup of S. Since

$$X = g(X) = h \circ f(X) = h[f(X)] \subset h(X^+)$$

and since X generates X^+, it follows that $h(X^+) = S$. Hence h is an epimorphism.

Now let x be an arbitrary element of X. Then there exists an element $(a_1, \ldots, a_m)$ of F such that

$$h(a_1, \ldots, a_m) = x$$

where $a_1, \ldots, a_m$ are elements of X. It follows that

$$x = a_1 \ldots a_m$$

We call X^+ *the free semigroup generated by the set* X. The use of the word "free" should now be clear from **16**—any other semigroup S generated by X is "restricted" by the possible identification of "free" products $a_1 \ldots a_m$ imposed by h. That is, in general there may be unequal sequences $(a_1, \ldots, a_m)$ and $(b_1, \ldots, b_n)$ in X^+ whose images in S under h are equal—the elements of X^+ are free from any restrictions save those imposed by associativity.

An equivalence relation R over the semigroup S is *right-invariant* if whenever xRy then $xzRyz$ for all z in S. Clearly there is an analogous definition of *left-invariant* equivalence relations. A *congruence* relation is defined to be an equivalence relation over a *semigroup* S that is both right- and left-invariant.

Thus R is a congruence iff xRx' and yRy' always implies $xyRx'y'$. Define the map $N_R: S \rightarrow S/R$ by the equation

$$N_R(t) = [t]_R$$

the equivalence class of t under R.

The importance of the notion of congruence resides in the following:

If R is an equivalence relation, we may make S/R a semigroup with the multiplication

$$[x]_R \cdot [y]_R = [xy]_R$$

if and only if R is a congruence.

N_R is then a homomorphism, and we call S/R the *factor semigroup* (or quotient semigroup) of S with respect to R.

2.4 GROUPS AND SEMIGROUPS

A *group* is a monoid G with *inverse*, i.e., to each element a of G there is assigned an *inverse* element, a^{-1} say, such that

$$a^{-1} \cdot a = a \cdot a^{-1} = e$$

where e is the identity of G.

Thus $(Z, +)$ is a group with $(-a)$ as the inverse of a; $(Z, \times)$ is not a group; $(R, \times)$ is not a group, since 0 has no inverse; but $(R - \{0\}, \times)$ is a group with $1/a$ as the inverse of a. The set of endomorphisms of a semigroup into itself is not usually a group; the set of automorphisms always is.

An element can only have one inverse, for suppose

$$b \cdot a = a \cdot b = e$$

then $b = b \cdot e = b \cdot (a \cdot a^{-1}) = (b \cdot a)a^{-1} = e \cdot a^{-1} = a^{-1}$.

A *subgroup* of G is a subset which is closed under both composition and the group inverse operation.

Considering the subsemigroup of $(Z, +)$ consisting of $(N, +)$, we see that a subsemigroup of a group need not be a subgroup. However, every subsemigroup S of a *finite* group G *is* a subgroup—just take any element $a \neq e$ of G, and prove that there is an a^m, $m > 0$, with $a^m = a^{-1}$, so long as G is finite, to conclude that S, being closed under composition, is also closed under the taking of inverses.

To check that H is a subgroup of G (we write $H \leq G$), it is enough to check that ab^{-1} is in H for every a, b in G, for then $aa^{-1} = e$ is in H and so, if b is in H, so is $eb^{-1} = b^{-1}$, and thus, if a and b are in H, so is $a(b^{-1})^{-1} = ab$. That is, H is closed under inverse and composition.

Our notion of homomorphism for semigroups when applied to groups has the property that the image of the identity is the identity, and the image of an inverse is the inverse of the image.

For let G_1 and G_2 be two groups, and $h\colon G_1 \to G_2$ be a homomorphism.

Then
$$h(e_1) = h(e_1 \cdot e_1) = h(e_1) \cdot h(e_1)$$

and multiplying by $h(e_1)^{-1}$ in G_2, we have

$$e_2 = h(e_1)$$

Now, for any $a \in G_1$, we have

$$e_2 = h(e_1) = h(a \cdot a^{-1}) = h(a)h(a^{-1})$$

and so
$$h(a^{-1}) = h(a)^{-1}$$

Given a set X, the set of *all* maps $f\colon X \to X$ is a semigroup $F_R(X)$ under the composition $f * g\colon x \mapsto g(f(x))$—we call $F_R(X)$ the *full (right) transformation semigroup of X*. Similarly, this same set is a semigroup $F_L(X)$ under the composition $f \circ g\colon x \mapsto f(g(x))$, and call $F_L(X)$ the *full (left) transformation semigroup of X*.

Note that every semigroup may be *embedded in* (i.e., is isomorphic to a subsemigroup of) a full transformation semigroup:

$$L\colon S \to F_L(S^1) \qquad \text{sends } s \text{ to} \qquad L_s\colon S^1 \to S^1\colon s' \mapsto ss'$$

$$R\colon S \to F_R(S^1) \qquad \text{sends } s \text{ to} \qquad R_s\colon S^1 \to S^1\colon s' \mapsto s's$$

If we consider the subset of $F_R(X)$ containing the collection of permutations on X, that is, bijective maps $X \to X$, they constitute the largest subgroup of $F_R(X)$, called the *symmetric group* on X, and denoted by $S(X)$. If X has n elements, we may refer to $S(X)$ as S_n, the symmetric group on n letters. A_n, *the alternating group on n letters*, is the subgroup of S_n containing the even permutations, namely those which can be obtained by an even number of transpositions of elements of the set $X = \{1, 2, \ldots, n\}$.

We shall approach what are called "normal" subgroups by asking what a congruence becomes when a semigroup is a group.

Let G be a group, and let $\equiv$ be a congruence on G, with $[g]$ denoting the equivalence class of an element g of G.

Then $N = [e]$ is a subgroup of G, for if a and b are in N, so is ab^{-1}, since

$$ab^{-1} = ab^{-1} \cdot e \equiv ab^{-1} \cdot b = a \equiv e$$

Further, $[a] = aN = Na$, for all $a \in G$, since

$$\begin{aligned}
b \in [a] &\Leftrightarrow b \equiv a \\
&\Leftrightarrow a^{-1}b \equiv a^{-1} \cdot a = e \\
&\Leftrightarrow a^{-1}b \in N \\
&\Leftrightarrow b \in aN
\end{aligned}$$

and similarly $b \in [a] \Leftrightarrow b \in Na$.

Thus N is a "normal" subgroup of G (we write $N \lhd G$), where: A subgroup N of a group G is called *normal* just in case $gN = Ng$ for all $g \in G$. (This does *not* mean $gn = ng$ for each $n \in N$ and $g \in G$.)

It is well known (see, e.g., HALL, Theorem 5.4.3, p. 61) that A_n $(n \neq 4)$ has *no* proper normal subgroups. Yet if $m < n$, we may consider A_m as a subgroup of A_n, on identifying elements of A_m with permutations of $\{0, 1, \ldots, n - 1\}$ which leave $\{m, m + 1, \ldots, n - 1\}$ fixed. Thus subgroups need not be normal.

We say a group is *abelian* if multiplication is commutative: ab always equals ba. It is immediate from the definition that *every* subgroup of an abelian group is normal.

Given $H \leq G$, the sets gH form a partition of G, called the *left coset decomposition;* that is, $\forall g, g' \in G\colon gH \cap g'H \neq \emptyset \Rightarrow gH = g'H$:

If $g'' \in gH \cap g'H$, we have $g'' = gh = g'h'$ for suitable elements h, $h' \in H$. But then

$$gH = g'h'h^{-1}H = g'H$$

We have the corresponding result for right coset decomposition. The reader should verify that these two decompositions are the same. We thus have the important result:

Given $H \leq G$, the left (right) coset decomposition of G is a congruence iff $H \lhd G$. Every congruence on G is the coset decomposition of some $N \lhd G$.

If $N \lhd G$, we write G/N for the factor semigroup induced by the left (or right) coset congruence. If G is abelian, so too is G/N.

Now, G/N is a *group*—we call it the factor group of G by N—for we already know it has an associative multiplication, from our semigroup theory, with

$$aN \cdot bN = [a] \cdot [b] = [ab] = (ab)N$$

and we merely note that $N = [e]$ is the identity, and aN has inverse $a^{-1}N$.

The map $h: G \rightarrow G/N$ defined by $h(g) = gN$ is clearly an epimorphism —it is called the *canonical* epimorphism. We see that the following diagram is commutative, where $m_G: G \times G \rightarrow G$ is the group operation of G, and so on

$$
\begin{array}{ccc}
G \times G & \xrightarrow{\ h \times h\ } & G/N \times G/N \\
\downarrow {\scriptstyle m_G} & & \downarrow {\scriptstyle m_{G/N}} \\
G & \xrightarrow{\ \ h\ \ } & G/N
\end{array}
$$

emphasizing that $aN \cdot bN = (ab)N$.

1 EXAMPLES: Let Z be group of all integers under addition. Then for each integer p, the relation

$$Z_1 \equiv {}_p Z_2 \,(\mathrm{mod}\ p) \qquad \text{iff} \qquad Z_1 - Z_2 \text{ is divisible by } p$$

is a congruence relation, and so $Z/\equiv_p$, which we denote by Z_p, is an abelian group. We usually write its elements as $\{0, 1, \ldots, p-1\}$ and refer to Z_p as the group of integers under addition modulo p.

For example, $Z_2 = \{0, 1\}$ with addition given by $0 + 1 = 1 = 1 + 0$ and $0 + 0 = 0 = 1 + 1$.

2 EXERCISE: Let $f: G_1 \twoheadrightarrow G_2$ be an epimorphism of G_1 onto G_2. Consider the kernel of f, Ker $(f) = f^{-1}(e_2)$. Define $\sim_f$ on G_1 by $g \sim_f g' \Leftrightarrow f(g) = f(g')$. Then verify that $\sim_f$ is a congruence, the equivalence classes are the sets $g \cdot$Ker (f) [so Ker (f) is a normal subgroup N of G_1], and we have $G_1/N \cong G_2$. Note that $\cong$ means both one-to-one and onto.

This last result is referred to as

3 THE HOMOMORPHISM THEOREM: *If f is an epimorphism of G_1 onto G_2, then* $G_1/\mathrm{Ker}\,(f) \cong G_2$.

Every group G has at least two normal subgroups: $\{e\}$ and G, and we have $G/\{e\} \cong G$; $G/G \cong \{e\}$.

4 ISOMORPHISM THEOREMS:

(i) *Let* $H \lhd K \lhd G$. *Then* $K/H \lhd G/H$,

and
$$\frac{G/H}{K/H} \cong G/K$$

(ii) *If* $K \lhd KH$, *then* $K \cap H \lhd H$,

and $$KH/K \cong H/K \cap H$$

Proof. Part (i) follows from verifying that the map $[g]_H \to [g]_K$ is a well-defined epimorphism $G/H \twoheadrightarrow G/K$ with kernel K/H.

Part (ii) follows from verifying that the map $h \to [h]_K$ is a well-defined epimorphism $H \twoheadrightarrow KH/K$ with kernel $K \cap H$. □

We now discuss some basic results from the theory of semigroups, and tie these in with our group theory.

The great problem in dealing with semigroups is to refrain from attributing to them properties they do *not* share with groups.

We call an element r of a semigroup S a *left (right) zero* if $rs = r$ $(sr = r)$ for all $s \in S$. If r is both a left and a right zero of S, then it is the only left or right zero, and we may then denote it unambiguously by 0_S or plain 0.

Clearly zeros, as well as identities, are always idempotents. In a group G there are no zeros (unless G has only one element) and only one idempotent, namely the identity.

EXAMPLE: Consider two disjoint groups G_1 and G_2. Let S be $G_1 \cup G_2 \cup \{0\}$ with the multiplication

$$s \cdot s' = \begin{cases} ss' & \text{(group multiplication) if } s \text{ and } s' \text{ belong to the same } G_k \\ 0 & \text{otherwise} \end{cases}$$

Then 0 is a left and right zero of S, and e_1 and e_2 are idempotents of S, but S has no identities.

A subset A of a semigroup S is a *left (right) ideal* of S if $SA \subset A$ $(AS \subset A)$. We say A is *proper* if $A \neq S$, and $A \neq \emptyset$. Clearly, A is a subsemigroup of S: $AA \subset A$. We say S is *left (right) simple* if it has no proper left (right) ideals.

Any set A may be turned into a semigroup A^r, called the *right-zero semigroup* on A, by making each $a \in A$ a right zero: $a'a = a$ for all a, $a' \in A$. Now, A^l, the *left-zero semigroup* on A, is A with left-zero multiplication: $a'a = a'$ for all $a, a' \in A$.

Note that A^r is right simple, since $XA^r = A^r$ for all $X \subset A^r$, but that every subset of A^r is a left ideal.

5 PROPOSITION: *A semigroup is a group iff it has no proper left or right ideals.*

Proof. (i) If S has no proper left or right ideals, then $aS = Sa = S$ for all a in S. Pick $a \in S$. Since $Sa = S$, there is an e such that $ea = a$. For any $c \in S$, let $az = c$. Then $ec = eaz = az = c$. Thus e is a left identity. Similarly, there exists a right identity f. But then $e = ef = f$. Thus we have a two-sided identity such that $ea = ae = a$ for all a in S. Now choose a', a'' such that

$$a'a = e = aa''$$

Then $a' = a'e = a'aa'' = ea'' = a''$. Thus $a' = a''$ is an inverse for a. Thus S, having an identity and inverses, is a group.

(ii) The converse is clear—in a group G, $gG = gG = G$ for every element g of G. □

6 PROPOSITION: *Any finite semigroup S contains an idempotent. For any $a \in S$, there is an idempotent of the form a^k.*

This follows from the more careful analysis:

7 THEOREM: *Let a be an element of an arbitrary semigroup S. Let $\langle a \rangle$ be the cyclic subsemigroup of S generated by a, that is, $\{a, a^2, a^3, \ldots\}$. If $\langle a \rangle$ is infinite, then all the powers of a are distinct. If $\langle a \rangle$ is finite, there exist two positive integers, the **index** r and the **period** m of a, such that $a^r = a^{r+m}$, and*

$$\langle a \rangle = \{a, a^2, \ldots, a^{m+r-1}\}$$

the order of $\langle a \rangle$ being $m + r - 1$. The set

$$K_a = \{a^r, a^{r+1}, \ldots, a^{r+m-1}\}$$

is a cyclic subgroup of S of order m. If n is the multiple of m satisfying $r \leq n \leq m + r - 1$, then a^n is idempotent, and the identity of K_a.

Proof. If $\langle a \rangle$ is not infinite, let s be the smallest integer for which there exists a yet smaller integer r for which $a^r = a^s$. The results then follow easily from Fig. 2.4. □

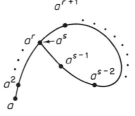

Let S be a semigroup with a proper ideal I. Then we may define a *congruence* ρ_I by setting $s\rho_I t$ iff $s = t$ or both s and t are in I. The quotient semigroup S/ρ_I is usually denoted by S/I and called the *Rees quotient* of S by I. Note that S/I is isomorphic to the set $(S - I) \cup \{0\}$ ($0 \notin S$) with multiplication defined by $s \circ 0 = 0 \circ s = 0$ and

· **Fig. 2.4**

$$s \circ t = \begin{cases} st & \text{if } st \notin I \\ 0 & \text{if } st \in I \end{cases}$$

Contrast this with the situation in group theory, in which every block of a congruence has the same number of elements. For a generalization of this notion, and much further information, see ARBIB [1968b] and VERBEEK [1968].

AN INTRODUCTION
TO AUTOMATA THEORY

3 FINITE AUTOMATA

In this chapter, we explore the implications of restricting a machine to operate sequentially with only a finite number of states. After a brief aside, relating our sequential machines to the systems of mathematical system theory, our first section analyzes the way in which we may reduce the number of states of a machine, and the experiments whereby we may determine the state of a machine. In the second section, we see that any finite automaton can be built as a network of very simple components, and then see how the complexity of a network of components varies "inversely" with the complexity of the components themselves, for networks carrying out such diverse operations as group multiplication and pattern recognition. The third section gives, and explores, the characterization of languages acceptable by finite-state sequential machines. The final section relates machine-theoretic concepts to algebraic properties of semigroups, to lay the groundwork for our analysis of machine decomposition in Chapter 8.

3.1 AUTOMATA, SYSTEMS, AND MINIMIZATION

Before we study the finite automata of Chapter 1 in detail, it is well to emphasize that automata are but special types of systems—we thus try to gain perspective by first introducing a general notion of system and then seeing how we must particularize it to obtain those systems which occupy our attention in the theory of finite automata.†

Intuitively, we view a system as a structure into which something (be it matter, energy, or information) may be put at certain times, and which itself puts out something at certain times. For instance, we may think of an electrical circuit whose input is a voltage signal and whose output is a current reading. We may think of a switching network whose input is an on-off setting of a number of input switches, and whose output is the on-off pattern of an array of lights. In the first case we may think of the time-scale as being continuous (since electrical signals usually vary continuously in time), whereas in the second case it may be more natural to think of the time-scale as discrete (the input switches are set every 5 seconds, say).

In either case, we think of the system as having an associated time set T. At each moment of time $t \in T$, our system S receives some input $x(t)$, and emits some output $y(t)$.

We assume that the input values are taken from some fixed set X; that is, at each time t an input $x(t)$ must be chosen from X. In general, the input segments‡ $\omega: [t_a, t_b) \to X$ are *not* allowed to be chosen arbitrarily, but must belong to some restricted class Ω. The choice of Ω may be inferred from physical considerations, or may be dictated by mathematical expediency, e.g., continuity. We further assume that there is some fixed set Y to which the output $y(t)$ of S at any time t must belong.

Now, we may not be able to predict $y(t)$ without knowing more than just what the present input $x(t)$ is. The past history of the system may have altered S in such a way (e.g., by hysteresis in our first example; by setting internal switches in the second example) as to modify the output. In other words, the output of S will, in general (and not surprisingly), be a function both of the present input of S, and of the history of S. We think of the *state* of S as being some (internal) attribute of the system at the present moment which, together with the input over a subsequent interval, determines the output at each moment of that interval. But to qualify as the state of S this information must have one more property, namely that the states and inputs together suffice to determine subsequent states.§

We thus demand that the set Q of internal states of S be sufficiently rich to carry *all* the information about the past history of the system needed to predict the effect of the past upon the future. We do not insist that the state be the *least* such information—this may or may not be a convenient assumption.

In a digital computer, for example, by knowing the state, we mean knowing the contents of all the registers—or at least the ones that are relevant to the output behavior of the machine.

Note that systems *do* exist in which the present output depends only on the

---

† The next few pages are based on ARBIB [1965]. ZADEH and DESOER [1963] adopt a similar viewpoint—which finds advanced expression in KALMAN, FALB, and ARBIB [1969]. Readers uninterested in this rapprochement may jump directly to Definition **13** below.

‡ The notation means that ω assigns an input $\omega(t) \in X$ for each time $t \in T$ such that $t_a \leq t < t_b$.

§ We are thus only talking here of *deterministic* systems. In Chapter 9 we shall relax this condition and study automata in which states and inputs determine only the *probability distribution* of subsequent states.

present input (though with perhaps a slight delay)—we shall usually think of such a system as having one state, which thus cannot change and which need not be specified in relating input to output. The only information carried by such a unique state is that the system still exists!

Let us now choose some set T of times at which we shall examine the behavior of our system. We shall usually assume T is the half-line $[0, \infty)$ or—as is usual in automata theory—the discrete set $\{0, 1, 2, 3, \ldots\}$. In some applications, finite time sets may be more suitable.

We give below a formal definition of what we shall mean by a system. Let us first state the three axioms informally (AS denoting Axiom for Systems):

AS_1. We specify the time set T at which we can apply inputs, and the state space Q whose elements record behaviorally different past histories of the system.

AS_2. We not only specify the sets of possible values of inputs which may be applied to the system, and outputs which might be observed from the system at given points in time, but we also specify just what types of input functions may be applied over different time intervals; i.e., for each interval $[t_0, t_1)$ we must say what input segments may be applied over the interval. Our requirements are (a) any

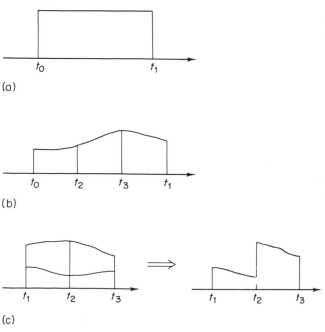

Fig. 3.1

constant function is admissible, (b) any portion of an admissible segment is admissible, and (c) splicing of admissible segments yields admissible segments, as shown in Fig. 3.1. Thus acceptable classes of input segments, with X = the real line = T would include:

(i)   step functions
(ii) piecewise continuous functions
(iii) piecewise differentiable functions

AS$_3$. We must provide explicit functions which tell us if we are given the state at time t_0, and the input to be applied from time t_0 to time t_2, how we may determine the state and output at time t_2. This is subject to a consistency condition which says that the state cannot change in time 0, and that if an input segment is decomposed into two consecutive segments, it is immaterial whether we consider the input segment as applied "all in one go" or successively in two pieces. The following

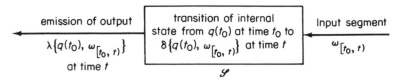

Fig. 3.2. Behavior of a system $\mathcal{S}$ from time t_0 to time t.

diagram, together with Fig. 3.2, may prove useful in following the formal statement of AS$_3$ below.

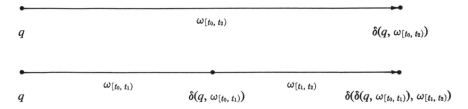

1   DEFINITION: *A system $\mathcal{S}$ is a mathematical structure*

$$\mathcal{S} = (T, X, Y, \Omega, Q, \delta, \lambda)$$

satisfying the axioms:
AS$_1$. *There is given a* **state-space** *Q and a set, T, of values of time at which the behavior of the system is defined.*
AS$_2$. *There is given an* **input set** *X, and an* **output set** *Y. An* **input segment** *$\omega_{[t_0,t)}$ is a mapping $\omega: [t_0, t) \to X$. There is given a set Ω of* **admissible input segments** *which satisfies the conditions:*
    (a) *Ω contains all constant functions.*
    (b) *(Restriction of inputs) If $\omega_{[t_0,t)}$ is in Ω and $[t_1, t_2) \subset [t_0, t)$, we require that the restriction of ω to $[t_1, t_2)$, $\omega_{[t_1,t_2)} = \omega \,|\, [t_1, t_2)$ be also in Ω.*
    (c) *(Concatenation of inputs) If $t_1 < t_2 < t_3$ and $\omega, \omega' \in \Omega$, then there is an $\omega'' \in \Omega$ such that $\omega''_{[t_1,t_2)} = \omega_{[t_1,t_2)}$ and $\omega''_{[t_2,t_3)} = \omega'_{[t_2,t_3)}$.*
AS$_3$. *There are functions δ and λ such that for any initial time t_0 in T, any initial state $q(t_0)$ in Q, and any input segment $\omega_{[t_0,t)}$, $t > t_0$ from Ω with $t, t_0 \in T$, the state $q(t)$ and the output $y(t)$ of the system $\mathcal{S}$ at time t are determined by the scheme*

$$q(t) = \delta(q(t_0), \omega_{[t_0,t)}) \in Q$$
$$y(t) = \lambda(q(t), \omega_{[t_0,t)}) \in Y$$

that is, $\delta: Q \times \Omega \to Q$ and $\lambda: Q \times \Omega \to Y$. The functions δ and λ are subject to the following conditions:

(a) (Consistency) *We may extend δ to segments of 0 length by:*

$$\delta(q, \omega_{[t_0,t_0)}) = q$$

(b) (Composition property) *For all $t_0 < t_1 \leq t$,*

$$\delta(q, \omega_{[t_0,t)}) = \delta(\delta(q, \omega_{[t_0,t_1)}), \omega_{[t_1,t)})$$
$$\lambda(q, \omega_{[t_0,t)}) = \lambda(\delta(q, \omega_{[t_0,t_1)}), \omega_{[t_1,t)})$$

It is clear from AS_3 (*b*) above that the system is *nonanticipatory*—the values of ω after time τ cannot affect the behavior of S up to time τ.

The notion of system as defined is useful for setting up terminology, for analyzing and rephrasing concepts, and for perceiving unity in a diversity of applications. Now, to get good theorems and interesting applications we must particularize and impose additional structure. One particularization which we shall use in all that follows is to assume that the response of the system to a given input segment starting from a specific state is independent of the time at which the action takes place.

DEFINITION: *A system S is **constant** (or **time-invariant**, or **stationary**) iff for all τ, with $t_0 \leq t_1$, and for all $q \in Q$ and $\omega, \omega' \in \Omega$,*

$$\omega'(t) = \omega(t + \tau) \quad for \quad t_0 \leq t < t_1 \quad implies \quad \begin{aligned} \delta(q, \omega'_{[t_0,t_1)}) &= \delta(q, \omega_{[t_0+\tau,t_1+\tau)}) \\ \lambda(q, \omega'_{[t_0,t_1)}) &= \lambda(q, \omega_{[t_0+\tau,t_1+\tau)}) \end{aligned}$$

Thus, while not denying that there are many interesting results in the study of time-varying systems, we shall henceforth concentrate on time-invariant systems. For such systems, we usually consider the input segment of the second variable as defined on a suitable interval $[0, t)$, since the result for other intervals is obtained by translation.

We now list a few basic definitions and some simple assertions whose easy proofs are left to the reader:

DEFINITION: *State q of system S is **equivalent to** state q' of system‡ S' with the same time set and input set iff for all input segments $\omega_{[t_0,t)}$ the output segment of S starting in state q is identical with the output segment of S' starting in state q'; that is,*

$$q \cong q' \quad \Leftrightarrow \quad \lambda(q, \omega_{[t_0,t)}) = \lambda'(q', \omega_{[t_0,t)})$$

for all times t_0, t (with $t_0 \leq t$) and all input segments $\omega_{[t_0,t)}$ of S and S'. Thus two states are equivalent if we cannot distinguish them by tests of input-output behavior of the systems concerned.

---

‡ Systems S and S' may or may not be identical.

4 ASSERTION: *If two states are equivalent, then so are the states into which they ar taken by a given input segment.*

5 DEFINITION: *A system* S *is in reduced form if there are no distinct states in it state space which are equivalent to each other.*

6 DEFINITION: *A state q′ is reachable from state q of* S *iff there exists an inpu segment ω in Ω which transfers* S *from state q to state q′; that is, q′ = δ(q, ω). We us r(q) to denote the set of states reachable from q.*

7 DEFINITION: *System* S *is said to be strongly connected if every state is reachabl from every other state.*

8 ASSERTION: *System* S *is strongly connected* ⟺ *r(q) = Q for all q ∈ Q.*

9 DEFINITION: *Systems* S *and* S′ *are equivalent iff for every state q of* S *there ma be found an equivalent state q′ of* S′*, and vice versa.*

10 EXERCISE: Prove that state and system equivalence are equivalence relation

Our general systems become the automata of algebraic automata theory (ofte called "sequential machines" to distinguish them from such automata as Turin machines, whose study we postpone to Chapter 4) if we quantize time and stud the behavior of our systems at successive moments $t = 0, 1, 2, 3, \ldots$, on som appropriate discrete time scale, and further require that the input and output se be finite. In some applications, we think of one unit of our time scale as bein some constant interval of "real" time, say 1 millisecond, or three days. In othe cases, n just denotes the time at which the nth happening we care to take note c took place—as in a machine which responds only when data are fed into it, wit such feedings taking place at random "real" times.

We shall *not* necessarily demand that there be only finitely many states. If, a time-quantized system, Q does have finitely many members, we shall say that ou system is a *finite automaton* or *finite-state machine*. It will be a question of intere to ask: "Given an automaton, does there exist an equivalent finite automaton?

11 EXERCISE: Prove that, for a *discrete* time-scale, the conditions of AS₂ imp that *every* finite input segment is admissible. Since we are now considering statior ary systems, we do not need to specify when n inputs are to be applied, just th sequence of inputs. Hence, in this case, we need only give X to determine Ω, whic is just X^*. [Hint: Prove by induction on the length of the segment.]

12 EXERCISE: Prove, by induction on the length of the sequence, in the discret time case, that the values of δ [resp., λ] on the set $Q \times X$ *uniquely* determine th values on $Q \times X^*$ [resp., $Q \times X^+$, where $X^+ = X^* - \{\Lambda\}$] by the relations

$$\delta(q, \Lambda) = q \qquad \left. \begin{array}{l} \delta(q, \xi x) = \delta(\delta(q, \xi), x) \\ \lambda(q, \xi x) = \lambda(\delta(q, \xi), x) \end{array} \right\} \quad \text{for all } q \in Q, \, x \in X, \text{ and } \xi \in X^*$$

Thus when we fix T to be $\{0, 1, 2, \ldots\}$, Ω is specified as soon as we give X, and δ and λ need only be specified on $Q \times X$. In this case our general notion of a *system* reduces to that of an automaton:

13 DEFINITION: *An **automaton** is a quintuple $M = (X, Y, Q, \delta, \lambda)$, where*
*X is a finite set, the set of **inputs**;*
*Y is a finite set, the set of **outputs**;*
*Q is a set, the set of **states**;*
*$\delta: Q \times X \to Q$, the **next-state function**;*
*$\lambda: Q \times X \to Y$, the **next-output function**.*
   *We say M is a **finite automaton** if Q is finite.*

We interpret this formal quintuple as being a mathematical description of a machine which, if at time t is in state q and receives input x, will at time $t + 1$ be in state $\delta(q, x)$ and will emit output $\lambda(q, x)$.

Before going into the theory of these automata, we should note two main ways of representing δ and λ: by a table and by a graph.

14 EXAMPLE (REPRESENTATIONS OF A FINITE AUTOMATON)
   (i) We may represent δ and λ by a table with rows labelled by states q_i and columns labelled by inputs j, and the ij entry being $\delta(q_i, j)/\lambda(q_i, j)$. For example,

$$\text{Input set } X = \{0, 1\}$$
$$\text{Output set } Y = \{0, 1\}$$
$$\text{State set } Q = \{q_0, q_1, q_2\}$$

$$\delta(q, x)/\lambda(q, x)$$

q \ x	0	1
q_0	$q_1/0$	$q_1/1$
q_1	$q_0/1$	$q_2/0$
q_2	$q_2/0$	$q_0/1$

   (ii) We may represent δ and λ by a directed graph with one node for each state, and so labelled, and with a directed edge labelled x/y from node q_i to node q_j iff $\delta(q_i, x) = q_j$ and $\lambda(q_i, x) = y$. Thus the above table becomes the diagram shown in Fig. 3.3.

   Now, we extend δ to $Q \times \{\Lambda\}$ by defining $\delta(q, \Lambda)$ to equal q—an input sequence of length 0 produces no change of state. However, for a general (even finite) automaton, $\lambda(q, \Lambda)$ is *not* well-defined. In the automaton for example **14**, we sce that whether we arrive at q_0 from q_1 because of an input 0, or from q_2 because of an input 1, the associated output is 1, and so we may consistently define $\lambda(q_0, \Lambda)$ as 1. However, $\lambda(q_1, \Lambda)$ cannot be defined, for the automaton puts out 0 if it was sent to q_1 from q_0 by an input 1, but puts out 1 if it was sent from q_0 to q_1 by an input 0.

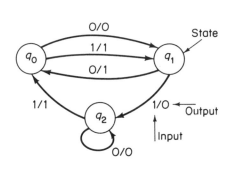

It is clear, then, that $\lambda(q, \Lambda)$ is well-defined just in case $q = \delta(q_1, x_1) = \delta(q_2, x_2) \Rightarrow \lambda(q_1, x_1) = \lambda(q_2, x_2)$.

Fig. 3.3

15   This is just in case we have a *present-output function* $\beta: Q \rightarrow Y$ such that $\lambda(q_1, x_1) = \beta[\delta(q_1, x_1)]$, or in other words, the diagram

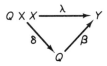

commutes. We say a machine‡ is a state-output machine if such a β exists.

16   ASSERTION: *If M is a state-output machine with* $\lambda = \beta \circ \delta$ *on* $Q \times X$, *then we may extend both δ and λ to all of $Q \times X^*$ with*

$$\delta(q, \Lambda) = q \qquad \lambda(q, \Lambda) = \beta[\delta(q, \Lambda)] = \beta(q)$$

and for all $x, x' \in X^*$:

$$\delta(q, xx') = \delta(\delta(q, x), x')$$
$$\lambda(q, xx') = \beta[\delta(q, xx')] = \lambda(\delta(q, x), x')$$

If we are given any automaton M, we may construct a new automaton

$$M = (X, Y, \hat{Q}, \hat{\delta}, \lambda)$$

in which $\hat{Q}$ is obtained by *splitting* each $q \in Q$ into several states $[q, y] \in Q \times Y$, one for each output which can be associated with a transition into state Q:

---

‡ We shall use machine interchangeably with automaton when the context allows no ambiguity.

$Q = \{[q, y] | \exists q' \in Q$ and $x \in X$ such that $\delta(q', x) = q$ and $\lambda(q', x) = y\}$.

The next-state and next-output functions are then given by

$$\hat{\delta}([q, y], x) = [\delta(q, x), \lambda(q, x)]$$
$$\hat{\lambda}([q, y], x) = \lambda(q, x)$$

Thus the present output function $\hat{\beta}: \hat{Q} \rightarrow Y: [q, y] \mapsto y$ satisfies $\hat{\lambda} = \hat{\beta} \circ \hat{\delta}$.

17   EXAMPLE: Let us note that for a state-output machine, we can label each state node q with its output $\beta(q)$, and then do not need to place output labels on the edges. With these conventions, the state graph for the state-output

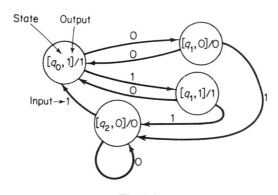

Fig. 3.4

form of the machine of example **14** is as shown in Fig. 3.4. We have thus shown the following:

18   FACT: *An arbitrary automaton may be replaced by an equivalent state-output machine.*

Automata in which outputs are associated with transitions are often called Mealy machines; those in which outputs are associated with states are often called Moore machines—recognizing the contributions of MEALY [1955] and MOORE [1956] (see also HUFFMAN [1954] for an early contribution).

We shall find it convenient to work with X^* rather than $X^* - \{\Lambda\}$, and so *we shall henceforth only consider state-output machines*, unless explicitly stated to the contrary. If $M = (X, Y, Q, \delta, \lambda)$ is a state-output machine with $\lambda = \beta \circ \delta$, we shall sometimes prefer to denote it by the quintuple (X, Y, Q, δ, β).

Thus, in defining a *finite automaton*, we need only specify δ on the *finite* set $Q \times X$ and β on the finite set Q—but in "using" the machine, we shall always feel free to use δ and $\lambda = \beta \circ \delta$ extended to $Q \times X^*$.

19 DEFINITION: *Given a machine M = $(X, Y, Q, \delta, \lambda)$, we define **the input-output behavior** of M **started in state** q to be the function*

$$M_q: X^* \to Y: x \mapsto \lambda(q, x)$$

that is, $M_q(x)$ is the output emitted by M at time $t + l(x)$ after it has read in the string x, starting in state q, at time t. We may say that M_q is the function of M when started in state q. Similarly, $N_{q'}$ would be the function of an automaton N started in state q'.

Thus if we start in state q at time 0, and feed in the string $x_0 \ldots x_{n-1}$, where each x_j is in X, the machine will emit the element of Y^* defined by

$$M_q(\Lambda) \text{ at time } 0$$
$$M_q(x_0) \text{ at time } 1$$
$$M_q(x_0x_1) \text{ at time } 2$$
$$M_q(x_0x_1 \ldots x_{n-1}) \text{ at time } n$$

We now see that our general systems definitions have the following special forms for automata (which may be read as definitions by readers who skipped our discussion of systems):

20 ASSERTION: *If M and M' have the same input set X and output set Y, then state q of M is **equivalent** to state q' of M' iff $M_q = M'_{q'}: X^* \to Y$.*

21 ASSERTION: *Machine M is in **reduced form** iff*

$$M_q = M_{q'} \quad \Rightarrow \quad q = q'$$

22 ASSERTION: *Machines M and M' are **equivalent** iff*

$$\{M_q | q \in Q\} = \{M'_{q'} | q' \in Q'\}$$

23 DEFINITION: *q' is **reachable from** q if there exists x in X^* with $\delta(q, x) = q'$. We call $r(q) = \delta(q, X^*)$ the **reachability set** of q. M is **strongly connected** if $r(q) = Q$ for every state q of M.*

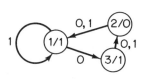

Note that if we did not choose to restrict ourselves to state-output machines, we would carry out a similar analysis with M_q restricted to X^+.

Fig. 3.5

24 EXERCISE: (a) Show that the

state output machine M with the state graph shown in Fig. 3.5 (where 0, 1 means both inputs cause the labelled transition) is in reduced form.

Compute M_1 for input sequences of length ≤ 3 (including Λ).

Write out the tabular description of the machine M' whose graph is shown in Fig. 3.6, and prove that M' is equivalent to M.

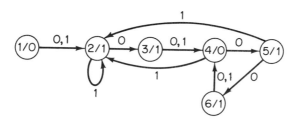

Fig. 3.6

(b) Let M be a machine with n states. The *transition matrix* of M associated with input sequence $x \in X^*$ is the matrix $M(x)$, with

$$M(x)_{ij} = \begin{cases} 1 & \text{if } \delta(q_i, x) = q_j \\ 0 & \text{otherwise} \end{cases}$$

The skeleton matrix S of M is the matrix $[s_{ij}]$, where $s_{ij} = 1$ iff there is some input $x \in X$ such that $\delta(q_i, x) = q_j$ and $s_{ij} = 0$ otherwise. In other words $s_{ij} = 1$ iff there is an arrow from q_i to q_j in the state graph of M.

(a) If we modify the method for finding the product of two matrices so that the product terms are ORed together (i.e., using $0 \vee 0 = 0$; $0 \vee 1 = 1 \vee 0 = 1 \vee 1 = 1$) rather than algebraically summed, show that S^k becomes a matrix such that $s_{ij}^k = 1$ iff there is a path of length k that takes q_i into q_j; and that $M(x)M(x') = M(xx')$ for all $x, x' \in X^*$.

(b) Express S in terms of the transition matrices for M.

(c) Find a simple test in terms of S to determine whether M is strongly connected.

25 EXERCISE: Exercise **24**(a) shows that an automaton may be equivalent to a strongly connected automaton, and yet not be strongly connected itself. Prove, however, that if an automaton M is *in reduced form*, and is equivalent to a strongly connected machine, then M must be strongly connected itself.

26 THEOREM: *Every machine M is equivalent to a machine M° in reduced form.*

Proof. We shall write this proof out in some detail, because we wish to emphasize the need to check well-definedness of a function by showing that the arbitrary choices made in its definition do not affect the end result. The idea of the proof is very simple—we merge equivalent states into a single state. (The reader should note that this is, in effect, what he did in passing from M' to M in Exercise **24**.) Formally, the process is as follows:

Let $M = (X, Y, Q, \delta, \beta)$. Write $q \sim q'$ if states q and q' are equivalent, and write $[q]$ for the block containing q in the $\sim$ partition. Let us set $M^\circ = (X, Y, Q^\circ, \delta^\circ, \beta^\circ)$, where

$$Q^\circ = Q/\sim \quad \text{(the set of blocks of the $\sim$ partition)}$$
$$\delta^\circ([q], x) = [\delta(q, x)]$$
$$\beta^\circ([q]) = \beta(q)$$

We must check three things:

(i)   that δ° and β° are well-defined;
(ii) that M° and M are equivalent;
(iii) that M° is in reduced form.

(i) We must check that if $q \sim q'$, then $[\delta(q, x)] = [\delta(q', x)]$ for all x, and that $\beta(q) = \beta(q')$—that is, our definitions of δ° and β° do not depend on our choice of representative for an element of Q°. But if $q \sim q'$, then $\lambda(q, x) = \lambda(q', x)$ by definition of equivalence, and so, taking $x = \Lambda$, we see that $\beta(q) = \beta(q')$. Further, for all x', we have

$$\lambda(\delta(q, x), x') = \lambda(q, xx')$$
$$= \lambda(q', xx') \quad \text{since } q \sim q'$$
$$= \lambda(\delta(q', x), x')$$

and thus $\delta(q, x) \sim \delta(q', x)$; that is, $[\delta(q, x)] = [\delta(q', x)]$.

(ii) Machines M° and M are surely equivalent, since state q of M is equivalent to state $[q]$ of M°.

(iii) Machine M° is in reduced form, for if states $[q]$ and $[q']$ of M° are equivalent, then states q and q' of M must be equivalent, so that $[q] = [q']$. Thus we obtain a reduced form of M simply by "merging" equivalent states.   □

Let us consider how the input-output function of the states of a machine changes under the action of inputs.

If we start in state q, and apply input sequence x, the machine goes to state $\delta(q, x)$, whose input-output function satisfies

$$M_{\delta(q,x)}(x') = \lambda(\delta(q, x), x') = \lambda(q, xx') = M_q(xx')$$

Thus if we define $L_x \colon X^* \to X^*$ to be left-multiplication by x, so that $L_x(x') = xx'$, we have

$$M_{\delta(q,x)} = M_q L_x$$

Thus we may represent the action of X^* on the input-output functions directly, without passing through the state-action.

Bearing in mind that we have a distinct function M_q for each distinct equivalence class $[q]$, the reader should have no trouble solving:

27 EXERCISE: Let $M = (X, Y, Q, \delta, \lambda)$, and set $M^1 = (X, Y, Q^1, \delta^1, \lambda^1)$, where

$$Q^1 = \{g \colon X^* \to Y | \exists q \in Q \text{ with } g = M_q\}$$
$$\delta^1(g, x) = gL_x$$
$$\lambda^1(g, x) = g(x)$$

Verify that M^1 is well-defined, in reduced form, and is equivalent to M.

Let us say that M' is a *reduced form* of M if M' is in reduced form and is equivalent to M. The reader should by now have suspected the truth of:

28 EXERCISE: There is "only one" reduced form of M, in that if M' and M'' are both reduced forms of M, they differ only in a relabelling of the states, i.e., a bijection‡ $h \colon Q' \to Q''$ such that the diagram below commutes.

$$
\begin{array}{ccc}
Q' \times X & \xrightarrow{\ \delta \times \lambda'\ } & Q' \times Y \\
h \uparrow \quad \uparrow = & & h \uparrow \quad \uparrow = \\
Q'' \times X & \xrightarrow[\ \delta'' \times \lambda''\ ]{} & Q'' \times Y
\end{array}
$$

We close this section with an algorithm for state minimization, and an "experimental" method for finding the state of a machine, due to MOORE [1956]. We first note a useful argument in general form:

29 THE NESTED-PARTITION LEMMA

If P_0, P_1, P_2, P_3, . . . is an infinite sequence of partitions on a finite set Q such that, for all k,

1. *$P_{k+1} \leq P_k$ (each block of P_{k+1} is contained in a block of P_k—we say P_{k+1} is a refinement of P_k).*
2. *$P_{k+1} = P_k \Rightarrow P_{k+2} = P_{k+1}$.*

Then there is an integer $k_0 < |Q|$ such that $P_k = P_{k_0}$ for all $k \geq k_0$.

Proof. Let $|P_k|$ be the number of blocks of P_k. Clearly, if $P_{k+1} < P_k$, then $|P_k| > |P_{k+1}|$. Since $|P_k| \leq |Q|$, this can only happen finitely many times. Let k_0 be the minimum k such that $P_{k+1} = P_k$. Then $k_0 < |Q|$, and $P_k = P_{k_0}$ for all $k \geq k_0$. □

We now present automata theory's basic application of this lemma:

---

‡ Cf. Section **2.1.**

30   We say two states of a machine M are *k-equivalent* if they yield the same output for input sequences of length $\leq k$:

$$q \equiv_k q' \qquad \text{iff } l(x) \leq k \Rightarrow M_q(x) = M_{q'}(x)$$

Let P_k be the partition corresponding to the equivalence $\equiv_k$. That $P_{k+1} \leq P_k$, for each k, is immediate from the definition. Now suppose that $P_{k+1} = P_k$—we show that $q \equiv_{k+1} q' \Rightarrow q \equiv_{k+2} q'$ to deduce that $P_{k+2} = P_{k+1}$. Let $x \in X$. Then $M_q(x) = M'_q(x)$ certainly, and since $q \equiv_{k+1} q'$, we also have $\delta(q, x) \equiv_k \delta(q', x)$. But $P_{k+1} = P_k$, so we have: $\delta(q, x) \equiv_{k+1} \delta(q, x)$. Since this is true for each x, we have $q \equiv_{k+2} q'$. Thus there is an integer $k_0 < |Q|$ such that $P_1 < P_2 < \cdots < P_{k_0} = P_{k_0+1} = \cdots$.

31   EXERCISE: Show that if M is in reduced form, then $|P_k| \geq k + 1$ for $0 \leq k < |Q|$.

32   We see that two states of M are equivalent iff they are k_0-equivalent. Since $k_0 < |Q|$, we may deduce, without knowing k_0, that to find whether or not two states are equivalent we need only check whether or not they are $(|Q| - 1)$-equivalent.

33   AN ALGORITHM FOR STATE MINIMIZATION: These results yield a simple algorithm for testing equivalence of states. We find P_0 by inspection; then, for each k, obtain P_{k+1} by noting that $q \equiv_{k+1} q'$ iff $q \cdot x \equiv_k q' \cdot x$ for each $x \in X \cup \{\lambda\}$. We then read equivalence by looking at P_{k_0}, where k_0 is the first j such that $P_j = P_{j+1}$.

34   EXAMPLE: Consider the machine M' of Exercise **15**:

q	1	2	3	4	5	6
$q \cdot 0$	2	3	4	5	6	4
$q \cdot 1$	2	2	4	2	2	4
$\beta(q)$	0	1	1	0	1	1

$P_0 = \{1, 4\}, \{2, 3, 5, 6\}$, since 1 and 4 have output 0, the rest output 1.
$P_1 = \{1, 4\}, \{2, 5\}, \{3, 6\}$, since 0 and 1 send both 1 and 4 to the second block of P_0, and similarly for 2 and 5, while 0 and 1 send 3 and 6 to the first block of P_0.
$P_2 = \{1, 4\}, \{2, 5\}, \{3, 6\}$, since 0 and 1 send both 1 and 4 to block 2 of P_1, and send both 3 and 6 to block 1 of P_1; while 0 sends both 2 and 5 to block 3 of P_1, and 1 sends both 2 and 5 to block 2 of P_1.
Since $P_1 = P_2$, our process ends here, and it follows that $q_1 \equiv q_4$, $q_2 \equiv q_5$ and $q_3 \equiv q_6$, but that no further equivalences hold.

35   Given a *reduced* machine $M = (Q, X, Y, \delta, \beta)$, we may be interested in finding its state—we do this by applying inputs and noting the resultant outputs to generate new inputs, until we can deduce, from the results of this "experiment," the present (not the original) state of M.

We may think of the experiment as carried out by a machine $E = (2^Q, Y, X, \delta', \beta')$ whose present state is the subset of states consistent with the progress of the experiment, whose input is the current output of M, and whose output is the next input we wish to administer to M. We may imagine the experimental setup as shown in Fig. 3.7. The choice for the next-state function is thus clear; for each $q \subseteq Q$, we have $\delta'(\hat{q}, y) = \{\delta(q, \beta'(\hat{q}))|q \in \hat{q}$ and $\lambda(q, \beta'(\hat{q})) = y\}$ retaining those states of $\hat{q}$ consistent with M's output of y, and updating them under the action of $\beta'(\hat{q})$.

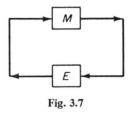

Fig. 3.7

Our problem is this: Can we choose β' in such a way that E must eventually enter a state denoting a singleton subject of Q, thus telling us the precise state of M? If so, how long will this process take?

36 LEMMA: *Given a subset $\hat{q}$ of Q, let $\bar{f}(\hat{q})$ be a shortest member of X^* such that there exist $q, q' \in \hat{q}$ with $\lambda(q, \bar{f}(\hat{q})) \neq \lambda(q', \bar{f}(\hat{q}))$. Then $l(\bar{f}(\hat{q})) \leq n - r + 1$, where $n = |Q|$, and $r = |\hat{q}| > 1$.*

Proof. Since, by **31**, there are at least $n - r + 2$ blocks of P_{n-r+1}, of which at most $n - r$ can be wholly contained in $Q - |\hat{q}|$ (which has $n - r$ elements), at least two blocks of P_{n-r+1} intersect $\hat{q}$, which thus has at least two elements distinguishable by a tape of length $\leq n - r + 1$.   □

37 Let us thus define $\beta'(\hat{q}) =$ the first member of the sequence $\bar{f}(\hat{q})$.

It is then clear that if we start with a block of k states, in time $n - k + 1$ at most it will be reduced to $k - 1$, and so on, until we obtain a block of only one state in time $\sum_{r=2}^{k} (n - r + 1) = [(k - 1)(2n - k)]/2$. In the case in which we start our experiment in complete ignorance, $\hat{q} = Q$ and has n states, and then the experiment takes at most time $[n(n - 1)]/2$.

38 EXERCISE: Why does it not matter that the definition of β' does not guarantee that E started in state $\hat{q}$ will "feed" the tape $\bar{f}(\hat{q})$ to M?

For further discussion along these lines see GILL [1962], GINSBURG [1958, 1962], HENNIE [1968], and BOOTH [1967]. See, e.g., Chapter 7 of MILLER [1965] for a careful treatment of minimization of *incomplete* machines —i.e., automata in which $\delta(q, x)$ and $\beta(q)$ are *not* specified for all q and x, and the reduced form must only be consistent with the specified values. Interestingly enough, this latitude in specification allows for *nonuniqueness* of reduced forms of a given incomplete machine.

3.2 AUTOMATA, CIRCUITS, AND COMPUTATION TIME

An acquaintance with the construction of digital computers or with the crude McCulloch-Pitts model of the brain (see McCULLOCH and PITTS [1943], and ARBIB [1964, Sections 1 and 2 of Chapter 1]) suggests the interest of considering networks made up of simple logical elements, which we shall call *modules*. We may speak of the input or output line of such a module as being *d*-state if at any moment it may carry any one element of a *d*-element set X_d as a signal.

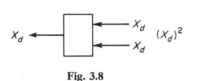

Fig. 3.8

A device whose input at any time is carried on a finite number of *d*-state input lines, and whose output is carried on a *d*-state output line will be called a *d*-module (see Fig. 3.8).

1 DEFINITION: *A **d-module** is a device with n d-state input lines and one d-state output line. It is characterized by a function f:* $(X_d)^n \rightarrow X_d$. *If the inputs of the module take values* $(x_1, \ldots, x_n)$ *at time t, then the output of the module is* $f(x_1, \ldots, x_n)$ *at time* $t + 1$.

The reader may choose to think of a *d* module as a finite automaton $(X, Y, Q, \delta, \lambda)$, where

(1) $X = (X_d)^n$, $Y = X_d$, Q has one element, q say, and

$$\delta(q, (x_1, \ldots, x_n)) = q$$
$$\lambda(q, (x_1, \ldots, x_n)) = f(x_1, \ldots, x_n)$$

or (2)

$$X = (X_d)^n \qquad Y = X_d \qquad \text{and} \qquad Q = X_d$$

with

$$\delta(q, (x_1, \ldots, x_n)) = \lambda(q, (x_1, \ldots, x_n)) = f(x_1, \ldots, x_n) \qquad \text{for all } q$$

We shall take the second viewpoint of a state-output machine.

We may now join these elements together to form a network, by splitting output lines and either leading them out of the network or else joining them to the input lines of modules of the network:

2 DEFINITION: *A **d-modular net** is a finite set of d modules and a rule of interconnections which partitions the set of input lines of the modules, and* *associates zero or one output lines with each set of the partition. The lines of each (augmented) class are then to be connected together. Each unassigned output line forms a class of its own. The classes which do not include an output line are called the* **input lines of the circuit,** *and a designated set of classes which do include an output line are called the* **output lines of the circuit.**

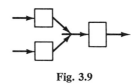

Fig. 3.9

A connection such as that shown in Fig. 3.9 is thus not allowed.

3 EXAMPLE: Suppose we have four modules with their inputs and outputs labelled as in Fig. 3.10, and we partition the set of inputs into the classes

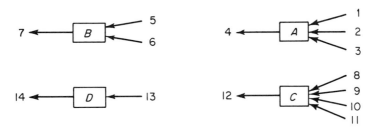

Fig. 3.10

$\{1, 8, 13\}$, $\{2, 3\}$, $\{6, 9, 10\}$, $\{6\}$, $\{11\}$; adjoin output line 4 to $\{11\}$ and output line 7 to $\{1, 8, 13\}$; and leave $\{12\}$ and $\{14\}$ as individual classes. We designate the set of classes as $\{12\}$ and $\{1, 8, 13, 7\}$.

The resultant net may be represented as shown in Fig. 3.11.

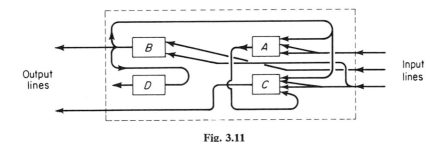

Fig. 3.11

Let a modular net N have p modules, r input lines, and s output lines. We say that we know the *input* of the net when we know the states of the r input lines—there are thus d^r inputs: X_N is $(X_d)^r$. Similarly there are d^s *outputs* in the set Y_N.

We say that we know the *state* of the net at time t if we know the state of every module of the net at time t. Thus there are d^p states of the net: Q_N is $(X_d)^p$.

The state of a module of N at time $t + 1$ is determined by the states of the module's input lines at time t. But these input lines are either fed by input lines of the net or by output lines of other modules, and so their states are determined completely by the input and the state of the net. And so, in turn, the state q and input x at time t determine the state $\delta_N(q, x)$ and output $\lambda_N(q, x)$ at time t. Thus:

4   FACT: *Any modular net is describable as a state-output finite automaton.*

5   EXERCISE: Note that our definition of a modular net did not allow through lines running from input to output without passing through a module. Modify Definition **2** and the above fact to handle this case.

Note that if we assign specific 2-module functions to the 4 modules of the above net, we have a 16-state finite automaton. It is not in reduced form, for the module D does not affect other elements or yield an output, and so may be removed to yield an 8-state machine equivalent to the original one.

What may be surprising is that even if it is not state-output, any finite automaton can, essentially, be replaced by a modular net. First we need the important concept of simulation.

We want to relax the idea of strict equivalence, by considering two machines to be equivalent if they can do the same things, *provided that their inputs and outputs are suitably coded.* The appropriate machine notion here is that of simulation—we say that M *simulates* M' if, provided that we encode and decode the input and output appropriately, M can process strings just as M' does, when started in an appropriate state. We require the encoder and decoder to be memoryless (i.e., to operate symbol by symbol) in order to

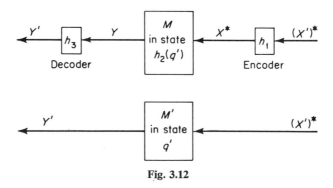

Fig. 3.12

make M do all the computational work involving memory. Machine M simulates M' if h_1, h_2, and h_3 can be so chosen that the systems of Fig. 3.12 have identical input-output behavior.

We shall say that the simulation is *weak* if $h_1(X')$ is *not* contained in X; that is, if a concatenation of several inputs to M may be required to code a single input to M'. More precisely:

6 DEFINITION: *Let $M = (X, Y, Q, \delta, \lambda)$, $M' = (X', Y', Q', \delta', \lambda')$ be two automata. We say M simulates M' if there exist (h_1, h_2, h_3), where*

(i)   *$h_1: (X')^* \to X^*$ is a monoid homomorphism with $h_1(X') \subseteq X$*
(ii) *$h_2: Q' \to Q$*
(iii) *$h_3: Y \to Y'$*

are such that the diagram

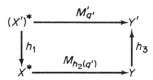

is commutative; i.e., the map from $(X')^*$ to Y' is independent of the route taken:

$$M'_{q'}(x') = h_3(M_{h_2(q')}[h_1(x')])$$

or $$\lambda'[q', x'] = h_3(\lambda[h_2(q'), h_1(x')])$$

We say that M weakly simulates M' if we remove the condition that $h_1(X') \subset X$.

Thus if we say that M simulates M' without further qualification, we shall imply that a suitable input code h_1 exists for which $h_1(X')$ is indeed contained in X.

We may now give our converse of **4**:

7 THEOREM: *For every finite automaton M, there exists a modular net N_M which simulates M.*

We shall give an inefficient construction, using binary modules (i.e. 2-modules). (See Fig. 3.13.) The main subject of switching theory is the study of how to do this efficiently when restricted to a limited set of modules (i.e., commercially available electronic components) (cf. HARRISON [1965], MCCLUSKEY [1965], and MILLER [1965]). For our present purposes it is enough to know that suitable nets may be constructed, irrespective of efficiency.

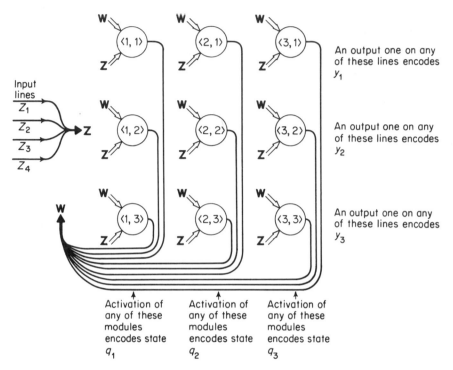

Fig. 3.13. Illustration for Theorem **7** for M with four inputs, three states, and three outputs.

Proof. Let $M = (X, Y, Q, \delta, \lambda)$ with

$$X = \{x_1, \ldots, x_n\} \qquad Y = \{y_1, \ldots, y_m\} \qquad Q = \{q_1, \ldots, q_l\}$$

Then our N_M is to have lm modules, labelled $\langle i, j \rangle$, $1 \le i \le l, 1 \le j \le m$. The idea is that *if M is in state q_i and emits output y_j at time t, then i, j is the only module of N whose output at time t takes the value* 1 (we equate X_2 with $\{0, 1\}$). Net N_M has n input lines, labelled $[1], \ldots, [n]$, and lm output lines, one from each module.

Each module has $k = lm + n$ input lines, the one labelled z_h coming from the hth input line, and the one labelled $w_{\langle i,j \rangle}$ coming from the module $\langle i, j \rangle$. Let $(\mathbf{w}, \mathbf{z})$ be the vector of inputs received by every module so that $\mathbf{z}$ is the net input, and $\mathbf{w}$ is the net state. Then let $x_{\mathbf{z}}$ be the x_j such that j is a minimum for those input lines z_j with value 1, and x_1 if none exists; and let $q_{\mathbf{w}}$ be the q_i such that $i + j$ is a minimum for those module outputs $w_{\langle i,j \rangle}$ with value 1, and q_1 if none exists.‡

‡ Under normal operating conditions only one line in the $\mathbf{z}$ bundle will be activated, and that line tells us x_i; similarly, the one active line in the $\mathbf{w}$ bundle will tell us q_i. We give more complicated definitions to handle *all* states of the network, thus covering contingencies which will not arise when we are using the net just for simulation.

The function of the module $\langle i, j \rangle$ is given by

$$f_{ij}(\underset{\text{state}}{\mathbf{w}}, \underset{\text{input}}{\mathbf{z}}) = \begin{cases} 1 & \text{if } q_i = \delta(q_w, x_z) \quad \text{and} \quad y_j = \lambda(q_w, x_z) \\ 0 & \text{otherwise} \end{cases}$$

Now we give three functions $h_1: X \rightarrow X_N$, $h_2: Q \rightarrow Q_N$, and $h_3: Y_N \rightarrow Y$ to complete the simulation:

$h_1(x_i)$ assigns 1 to the ith input line, 0 to all the others.
$h_2(q_j)$ assigns 1 to the $\langle j, 1 \rangle$ module output, 0 to all others.
$h_3(\mathbf{w})$ is the y_j such that $i + j$ is a minimum for those modules $\langle i, j /$ with output 1, and y_1 if none exists.

It should now be clear that with this coding, N_M does indeed simulate M.   □

The reader should realize the horrible inefficiency of this construction. If M is itself the modular net of our example 3 above, where we assume that all 4 of the modules are binary, we will replace it by a net with 8 input lines, 4 output lines, and 64 modules (2^4 for states $\times$ 2^2 for outputs).

8 EXERCISE: Give a construction with only one module per state for the case in which M is a state-output machine.

We may now mention another type of circuitry which may be used to build finite automata while using simple modules. Suppose we make the convenient mathematical fiction that our modules are of two kinds—pure delays (i.e., modules in the above sense with one input and one output, such that the input at time t is precisely the output at time $t + 1$), and delayless computing modules whose output at time t is some specified function of its input at time t. Wiring up a network of such modules requires some care—if we lead the output of a binary

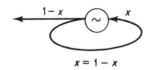

$$x = 1 - x$$

Fig. 3.14. A contradiction!

1-input delayless module for which $f(x) = 1 - x$ (in other words, a NOT-gate or inverter) back to its input, as in Fig. 3.14, we get unstable oscillations. However, such circuits are well-defined in their behavior so long as we insert one delay element in every loop (cf. COPI, ELGOT, and WRIGHT [1959]).

9 We say a network is *combinatorial* if it contains only delayless elements and is free of loops. Clearly, then, this network is such that the input pattern at time t uniquely specifies the output at time t.

Now let us introduce three special delayless binary modules, the NOT-gate (as above), the AND-gate, and the OR-gate (see Fig. 3.15). Consider the following equality, then:

$$a \vee b = 1 \text{ iff } (a = 0 \text{ and } b = 1) \text{ or } (a = 1 \text{ and } b = 0) \text{ or } (a = 1 \text{ and } b = 1)$$
$$\text{iff } (\bar{a} = 1 \text{ and } b = 1) \text{ or } (a = 1 \text{ and } \bar{b} = 1) \text{ or } (a = 1 \text{ and } b = 1)$$
$$\text{iff } (\bar{a}b = 1) \text{ or } (a\bar{b} = 1) \text{ or } (ab = 1)$$

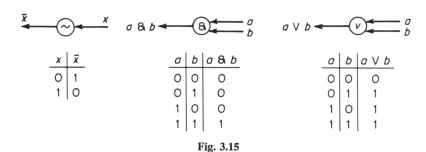

x	$\bar{x}$
0	1
1	0

a	b	$a \& b$
0	0	0
0	1	0
1	0	0
1	1	1

a	b	$a \vee b$
0	0	0
0	1	1
1	0	1
1	1	1

Fig. 3.15

where we have abbreviated $a \& b$ to ab, and so on. This allows us to write the equality

$$a \vee b = \bar{a}b \vee a\bar{b} \vee ab$$

which may be rewritten in an obvious manner as

$$a \vee b = (0 \cdot \bar{a}\bar{b}) \vee (1 \cdot \bar{a}b) \vee (1 \cdot a\bar{b}) \vee (1 \cdot ab)$$

and if we now use the notation $a^0 = \bar{a}$, $a^1 = a$, and so on, this takes on the very pleasing form

$$a \vee b = (0 \vee 0 \cdot a^0 b^0) \vee (0 \vee 1 \cdot a^0 b^1) \vee (1 \vee 0 \cdot a^1 b^0) \vee (1 \vee 1 \cdot a^1 b^1)$$
$$= \bigvee_{\substack{\alpha_1 = 0 \text{ or } 1 \\ \alpha_2 = 0 \text{ or } 1}} (\alpha_1 \vee \alpha_2) a^{\alpha_1} b^{\alpha_2}$$

Note that for each choice of a and b only one term of the conjunction is nonzero—and the coefficient of that term yields the value of $a \vee b$. The reader, if he does not know it already, should generalize the above argument to prove:

10 PROPOSITION: *Let $f: \{0, 1\}^n \rightarrow \{0, 1\}$ be an arbitrary binary function of n variables. Then we may write it in disjunctive normal form:*

$$f(x_1, x_2, \ldots, x_n) = \bigvee_{\substack{\alpha_1 = 0 \text{ or } 1 \\ \vdots \\ \alpha_n = 0 \text{ or } 1}} f(\alpha_1, \ldots, \alpha_n) x_1^{\alpha_1} \ldots x_n^{\alpha_n}$$

$$= \bigvee_{\substack{\text{those } \alpha_j = 0 \text{ or } 1 \\ \text{such that} \\ f(\alpha_1, \ldots, \alpha_n) = 1}} x_1^{\alpha_1} \ldots x_n^{\alpha_n}$$

11   COROLLARY: *For every g:* $\{0, 1\}^n \rightarrow \{0, 1\}^m$, *there exists a combinatorial binary network, consisting only of AND-, OR-, and NOT-gates, such that an input of* $(x_1, \ldots, x_n)$ *at time t yields an output of* $g(x_1, \ldots, x_n)$ *at time t.*

To make this clear we give a simple example of a two-input/two-output binary function.

12   EXAMPLE: Let $g:$ $\{0, 1\}^2 \rightarrow \{0, 1\}^2$: $(x_1, x_2) \mapsto (g_1(x_1, x_2), g_2(x_1, x_2))$ be specified by the table

x_1	x_2	g_1	g_2
0	0	1	0
0	1	0	0
1	0	0	1
1	1	1	0

Then we may write

$$g_1(x_1, x_2) = \bar{x}_1\bar{x}_2 \vee x_1x_2$$
$$g_2(x_1, x_2) = x_1\bar{x}_2$$

to obtain the combinatorial network shown in Fig. 3.16.

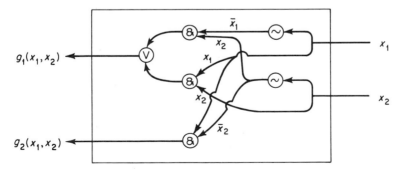

Fig. 3.16

13   Now, we may always simulate a finite automaton $M = (X, Y, Q, \delta, \lambda)$ as follows:

   (i)   Code X, Y, Q into binary vectors, using 1-1 maps:

$$X \rightarrow \{0, 1\}^m \qquad Y \rightarrow \{0, 1\}^n \qquad Q \rightarrow \{0, 1\}^r$$

   (ii)   Build a combinatorial circuit which computes the function

$$g: \{0, 1\}^{m+r} \rightarrow \{0, 1\}^{n+r}$$

for which, whenever $(z_1, \ldots, z_m)$ codes x in X and $(z_{m+1}, \ldots, z_{m+r})$ codes q in Q,

$$g(z_1, \ldots, z_{m+r}) = (y_1, \ldots, y_{n+r})$$

implies that $(y_1, \ldots, y_n)$ codes $\lambda(q, x)$, while $(y_{n+1}, \ldots, y_{n+r})$ codes $\delta(q, x)$.

   (iii) Link the new-state outputs of the g network to the old-state inputs via unit delays to obtain the network shown in Fig. 3.17 to simulate M.

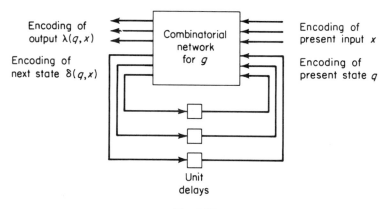

Encoding of output $\lambda(q, x)$ Combinatorial network for g Encoding of present input x

Encoding of next state $\delta(q, x)$ Encoding of present state q

Unit delays

Fig. 3.17

    Thus, even when we wish to build sequential machines, an important intermediate step may well be the construction of combinatorial networks. Now, in real life, there are no delayless elements, and so the output of such a network will often be somewhat delayed relative to the input. A crucial question then becomes—given the function g of a combinatorial network— how big must the delay be? In the circuit of example **12**, it will be three element-delays from the time we establish a new-input pattern until the correct output pattern is stabilized. If we had allowed ourselves to use arbitrary two-input binary modules, we would, of course, have used a single module for each of g_1 and g_2, and only unit delay would be required.

Clearly, then, the time required depends on the way we restrict our components. Let us study the time required for a modular net to compute a finite function if our only limitation is in the number of input lines of our modules. In what follows, a (d, r) *circuit* is a d-modular net in which each module is limited to have at most r input lines. (Notice that we are once again *assuming a unit delay* in the operation of all our modules.)

The theory that follows is based on the simple observation exemplified by Fig. 3.18. Here we see that if we consider $(d, 2)$ circuits in which an output

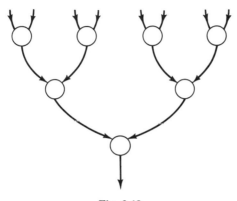

Fig. 3.18

line depends on 2^3 input lines, then it takes at least three time units for an input configuration to yield its corresponding output. Lemma **15** below formalizes this observation, and is the basis for the lower bounds we obtain on computation time for various functions.

WINOGRAD obtained such bounds especially for addition and group multiplication [1967] and numerical multiplication [1968]. SPIRA and ARBIB [1967] made explicit the methodology implicit in his work, forming a basis upon which we can erect a thoroughgoing analysis of multiplication in groups and semigroups and also can analyze computation of various finite functions. We present here part of such an analysis.

14 DEFINITION: *Let $\varphi\colon X_1 \times X_2 \times \cdots \times X_n \to Y$ be a finite function. A circuit C, with the input lines partitioned into n sets with I_j the set of possible configurations on the jth ($j = 1, \ldots, n$), and K the set of possible output configurations, is said to be capable of computing the function φ in time τ if there is a state s_0 of C, maps $g_j\colon X_j \to I_j$ ($j = 1, \ldots, n$) and a 1–1 function $h\colon Y \to K$ such that if C is started in state s_0 at time 0 and receives constant* *input* $[g_1(x_1), \ldots, g_n(x_n)]$ *from time* 0 *through time* $\tau - 1$*, the output at time* τ *will be* $h(\varphi(x_1, \ldots, x_n))$.

15 LEMMA: *In a* (d, r) *circuit the output of an element at time* τ *can depend upon preceding values on at most* r^τ *input lines.*

Proof. Just consider the fan-in with modules having r input lines each to the height of τ. ☐

Let $\lceil x \rceil$ be the smallest integer $\geq x$; let $\lfloor x \rfloor$ be the largest integer $\leq x$; let $|S|$ be the number of elements in the set S; and let $U_N = \{0, 1, \ldots, N - 1\}$.

For a (d, r) circuit let $h_j(y)$ be the value on the jth output line when the overall output configuration is $h(y)$.

16 DEFINITION: *Let* $\varphi\colon X_1 \times X_2 \times \cdots \times X_n \to Y$ *and let* $h\colon Y \to K$ *be an output function for a circuit* C *which computes* φ*. Then* $S \subset X_m$ *is called an* h_j-*separable set for* C *in the* mth *argument of* φ *if* $s_1, s_2 \in S$ *and* $s_1 \neq s_2 \Rightarrow \exists x_1, x_2, \ldots, x_{m-1}, x_{m+1}, \ldots, x_n$ *with* $x_i \in X_i$ *such that*

$$h_j(\varphi(x_1, \ldots, x_{m-1}, s_1, x_{m+1}, \ldots, x_n)) \neq h_j(\varphi(x_1, \ldots, x_{m-1}, s_2, x_{m+1}, \ldots, x_n))$$

This notion of h_j-separable set allows us to use Lemma **15** to get a completely general lower bound on computation time:

17 LEMMA (THE BASIC LEMMA): *Let* $\varphi\colon X_1 \times X_2 \times \cdots \times X_n \to Y$*. Let* C *be a* (d, r) *circuit which computes* φ *in time* τ*. Then*

$$\tau \geq \max_j \{\lceil \log_r (\lceil \log_d |S_1(j)| \rceil + \cdots + \lceil \log_d |S_n(j)| \rceil) \rceil\}$$

where $S_i(j)$ *is an* h_j-*separable set for* C *in the* ith *argument of* φ*.*

Proof. The jth output at time τ must depend upon at least $\lceil \log_d |S_i(j)| \rceil$ output lines from I_j or else there would be two elements of $S_i(j)$ which were not h_j-separable. Thus the jth output depends upon at least $\lceil \log_d |S_1(j)| \rceil + \cdots + \lceil \log_d |S_n(j)| \rceil$ input lines, from which $\tau^r \geq \lceil \log_d |S_1(j)| \rceil + \cdots + \lceil \log_d |S_n(j)| \rceil$, and the result follows, since τ is integral-valued. ☐

With Lemma **17** we have exposed the methodology implicit in Winograd's treatment of the times required for addition and multiplication.

18 COROLLARY: *Let* $\varphi\colon U_N \times U_N \to \{0, 1\}$ *be*

$$\varphi(x, y) = \begin{cases} 1 & \text{if } x \leq y \\ 0 & \text{if } x > y \end{cases}$$

Then if the (d, r) *circuit* C *computes* φ *in time* τ*, we have*

$$\tau \geq \lceil \log_r 2 \lceil \log_d N \rceil \rceil$$

Proof. If $h_j(0) \neq h_j(1)$, then U_N is an h_j-separable set for C in both the first and second arguments of φ, since if $x > y$, we have $\varphi(x, y) \neq \varphi(y, y)$ and $\varphi(x, y) \neq \varphi(x, x)$.   □

19   COROLLARY: *Let* $\varphi: U_N \times U_N \to U_N$ *be defined by* $\varphi(x_1, x_2) = \lfloor X_1 \cdot X_2 \rfloor / N$. *Then, if C computes* φ *in time* τ, *we have*

$$\tau \geq \lceil \log_r 2 \lceil \log_d \lfloor N^{1/2} \rfloor \rceil \rceil$$

Proof. Pick j such that $h_j(0) \neq h_j(1)$. Let $m = \lfloor N^{1/2} \rfloor$. Then $\{1, 2, \ldots, m\}$ is an h_j-separable set for C in both arguments of φ, since for each $x \neq y$ with $x, y \in \{1, 2, \ldots, m\}$ we may choose $z \in U_N$ to be such that $x \cdot z < N \leq y \cdot z < 2N$ to yield $\varphi(x, z) \neq \varphi(y, z)$. By symmetry, this holds for the second argument as well, and the result follows from Lemma 17.   □

The next example shows that the size of separable sets can be strongly dependent upon the output code of a circuit which computes a given φ.

20   EXAMPLE: Let $\varphi: U_N \times U_N \to U_{N^2}$ be numerical multiplication with $N = 2^8$. Consider an output code in which, if the output value is M, the ith line carries the ith value in the binary expansion for M. Then there are 16 output lines. Pick any $x \neq y$ with $x, y \in U_N$. Then their binary expansions differ in at least one place, say the kth. Choose $z = 2^{8-k}$. Then

$$h_8(\varphi(x, z)) \neq h_8(\varphi(y, z))$$

and $$h_8(\varphi(z, x)) \neq h_8(\varphi(z, y))$$

Hence there is an h_8-separable set of size 2^8 in both arguments of φ.

Now consider the same φ, but let the output code for z be binary representation of the exponents in its prime decomposition. Let the first six output lines code the exponent of 2 in the result. Pick $x, y \in U_N$ such that x and y do not have the same power of 2 in their prime decompositions, the powers differing in, say, the kth place of their binary expansions. Then, letting $z = 2^{3-k}$, we have

$$h_3(\varphi(x, z)) \neq h_3(\varphi(y, z))$$

and $$h_3(\varphi(z, x)) \neq h_3(\varphi(z, y))$$

Thus, since an element of U_N can have eight different exponents of two in its prime decomposition, there is an h_3-separable set of size 8 in both arguments of φ. One easily sees that this is the maximal size of a separable set of any output line, since 2 is the smallest prime. Note, however, that this output code requires 45 output lines.

We now show how the basic lemma may be applied to give us information about group multiplication.‡ Let G be a finite group, and let

---

‡ The reader may find it helpful to revise Section **2.4** before studying the rest of this section.

$\varphi: G \times G \to G$ be group multiplication. Let C be a (d, r) circuit which computes φ. Let $h_j(g)$ be the value on the jth output line of C when the output is $h(g)$. We follow SPIRA [1969].

21 DEFINITION: *We say x and y are K_j-equivalent if $h_j(xg) = h_j(yg)$ for all g in G; and that they are L_j-equivalent if $h_j(gx) = h_j(gy)$ for all g in G. Clearly K_j and L_j are equivalence relations, and we write $K_j(g)$ for the K_j-equivalence class of g and $L_j(g)$ for the L_j-equivalence class of g. Set $K_j = K_j(e), L_j = L_j(e)$, where e is the identity in G.*

22 LEMMA: *K_j and L_j are groups. Furthermore $K_j(g) = K_j g$ and $L_j(g) = gL_j$ for all g in G.*
   Proof. Suppose $a, b \in K_j$. Then $h_j(ab^{-1}y) = h_j(b^{-1}y) = h_j(bb^{-1}y) = h_j(y)$, for all $y \in G$. So $ab^{-1} \in K_j$, and it is a group. Now, $a \in K_j(g)$ iff $h_j(ay) = h_j(gy)$ for all $y \in G$ iff $h_j(ag^{-1}y) = h_j(y)$ for all $y \in G$ iff $ag^{-1} \in K_j$ iff $a \in K_j g$. The proof for L_j is dual.   □

23 LEMMA: *A maximal size $S \subseteq G$ which is h_j-separable in the first argument consists of a representative from each left coset of K_j in G. It thus has size $|G|/|K_j|$. A dual result holds for a maximal h_j-separable subset in the second argument.*
   Proof. The proof is direct from Lemma **22**.   □

24 THEOREM: *Let C be a (d, r) circuit which computes $\varphi: G \times G \to G$ in time τ. Then*

$$\tau \geq \max_{j} \left\{ \left\lceil \log_r \left(\left\lceil \log_d \frac{|G|}{|K_j|} \right\rceil + \left\lceil \log_d \frac{|G|}{|L_j|} \right\rceil \right) \right\rceil \right\}$$

   Proof. The proof follows from Lemma **17** and Lemma **23**.   □
   These results could be important in the design of a circuit to compute φ, since they define which are the "good" and which are the "bad" output codes, the desideratum being to make K_j and L_j as large as possible over all j.

25 DEFINITION: *Let H be a group. We say P(a, H) holds if $e \neq a \in H$ and if $\{e\} \neq K \leq H \Rightarrow a \in K$. We say P(H) holds if P(a, H) holds for some $a \in H$. If P(G) holds or $G = \{e\}$, let $\beta(G) = 1$. If not, for any $c \in G\{e\}$, let $\beta(c)$ be the maximum order of any subgroup of G not containing c and let $\beta(G) = \min_{c \in G\{e\}} \{\beta(c)\}$.*

26 EXERCISE: Prove that for any finite group G, we have $|G| \geq \alpha(G)\beta(G)$.

27 THEOREM: *Let G be a finite group. Then if C is a (d, r) circuit to multiply in G in time τ, we have*

$$\tau \geq \left\lceil \log_r 2 \left\lceil \log_d \frac{|G|}{\beta(G)} \right\rceil \right\rceil$$

(*which implies Winograd's result that* $\tau \geq \lceil \log_r 2 \lceil \log_d |\alpha(G)| \rceil \rceil$ *by Exercise* 26).

  Proof. Let $a \in G$ be such that $\beta(a) = \beta(G)$. Now $\exists j$ for which $h_j(a) \neq h_j(e)$. Thus $a \notin R_j(e)$ and $a \notin L_j(e)$. Hence

$$|R_j| \leq \beta(G) \qquad |L_j| \leq \beta(G)$$

and the result follows from Lemma **23**. (Exercise: Fill in the details for the case in which $\beta(G) = 1$.) □

  We now give, for each finite group, a construction, due to SPIRA [1969], of a circuit which computes group multiplication within one time unit of the lower bound.

28 LEMMA: *Let K be any subgroup of G. Define* $\varphi: G \times G \to \{0, 1\}$ *by*

$$\varphi(a, b) = \begin{cases} 0 & \text{if } ab \in K \\ 1 & \text{if } ab \notin K \end{cases}$$

Then there exists a (d, r) circuit to compute φ in time

$$\tau = 1 + \left\lceil \log_r \left\lceil \log_d \frac{|G|}{|K|} \right\rceil \right\rceil$$

  Proof. Let $M = |G|/|K|$. Pick a coset representative $v_i \in Kv_i$ for each right coset of K in G. Then $\{v_i^{-1}\}$ will be a set of left coset representatives, for $v_i^{-1} K = v_j^{-1} K$ iff $v_i v_j^{-1} \in K$ iff $Kv_i = Kv_j$. Define maps z_1 and z_2 from G to the space of $\lceil \log_d M \rceil$-ary vectors over z so that

$$z_1(g_1) = z_1(g_2) \qquad \text{iff} \quad Kg_1 = Kg_2$$
$$z_1(g) \oplus z_2(g^{-1}) = \bar{0}$$

where $\bar{0}$ is the all-zero vector and $\oplus$ is componentwise addition modulo d. Note that z_2 maps any two elements in the same left coset to the same vector. The first level of the circuit consists of $\lceil \log_d M \rceil$ modulo d adders. If ab is being computed, these adders sum $z_1(a)$ and $z_2(b)$ componentwise modulo d. Thus all outputs are 0 iff $\exists j$ such that $a \in Kv_j$ and $b \in v_j^{-1}K$, that is, iff $ab \in K$. The rest of the circuit is a fan-in of r input elements having output 0 iff all inputs are 0 and output 1 if at least one input is nonzero. This fan-in has depth $\lceil \log_r \lceil \log_d M \rceil \rceil$. Thus the circuit computes φ in time

$$\tau = \lceil \log_r \lceil \log_d M \rceil \rceil + 1$$ □

29 COROLLARY: *There is a (d, r) circuit to tell whether $ab \in Ku$ for any $u \in G$ in the same time.*

30 LEMMA: *If G has subgroups $K_1, \ldots, K_n$ such that $\bigcap\limits_{j=1}^{n} K_j = \{e\}$, then $\exists \, a \; (d, r)$ circuit to compute multiplication in G in time*

$$\tau = 1 + \max_{1 \leq j \leq n} \left\lceil \log_d \left\lceil \log_r \frac{|G|}{|K_j|} \right\rceil \right\rceil$$

Proof. This follows from Lemma **29**, since knowing the right cosets containing any $a \in G$ suffices to determine a. If $K_j a_1 = K_j a_2$ for all j, then $\bigcap\limits_{j=1}^{n} K_j a_1 = \bigcap\limits_{j=1}^{n} K_j a_2$, and so $a_1 = a_2$. $\square$

We now immediately obtain:

31 THEOREM: *For any $d \geq 2$ and any $r \geq 2$ there is a (d, r) circuit to multiply in a finite group G in time*

$$\tau = 1 + \left\lceil \log_d \left\lceil \log_r \frac{|G|}{\beta(G)} \right\rceil \right\rceil$$

Proof. The first part follows from Lemma **30** and the definition of $\beta(G)$; the rest follows from the fact that

$$\lceil \log_d \lceil \log_r x \rceil \rceil + 1 \geq \lceil \log_d 2 \lceil \log_r x \rceil \rceil \qquad \square$$

The above circuit is almost optimal in that its multiplication time is within one time unit of the fastest obtainable. However, the reader should estimate for himself the large number of modules required in this construction. It is still an open research problem to look for an equally good fit between upper and lower bounds for functions other than group multiplication, and to try to do so in a way which is more economical in the number of modules required.

I think it is fairly evident that results such as the above point the way to an extremely rich theory of circuit complexity. It is too early to try to delimit it, and no general theorems are available. But just to give an idea of the diversity of applications such a theory will find, we close with a few results from MINSKY and PAPERT [1967, 1969], in which we consider the input lines of our circuits arranged in a two-dimensional array, so that input configurations are to be regarded as spatial patterns. The circuits we study may then be thought of as pattern-recognition devices.

Let R be the set of input lines (to be thought of as arranged in a rectangular "Retina" in a plane on which patterns may be projected) and let us identify a binary firing pattern on those lines with the subset of R comprising those lines bearing the value 1.

We shall often think of R as a *set of squares* into which a subset of the euclidean plane is divided by constantly spaced lines parallel to the x and y axes, respectively. A subset $\tilde{X}$ of the plane is then identified with the subset

$$X = \{x \in R | x \cap \tilde{X} \neq \emptyset\} \qquad \text{of } R$$

We thus identify figures within a certain tolerance, triggering a 1 on an input line of R in case *any* point of the corresponding square belongs to the "stimulus set."

We are going to be interested in pattern predicates ψ [that is, $\psi(X)$ is true for some patterns X, and false for others]—for example, X is connected, or X is of odd parity, and so on.

With each predicate ψ we shall associate the binary function

$$\lceil \psi(X) \rceil = \begin{cases} 1 & \text{if } \psi(X) \text{ is true} \\ 0 & \text{if } \psi(X) \text{ is false} \end{cases}$$

Let us be given a set Φ of binary modules wired up to various lines of R—Minsky and Papert ask what predicates ψ can be computed by a network whose first layer consists of the modules Φ, and whose second layer consists of a single threshold module—i.e., a module whose ouput is 1 if and only if the weighted sum of its inputs exceeds its threshold. That is, we are interested in the class $L(\Phi)$, where:

32   DEFINITION: *For any collection* Φ *of functions* $2^R \to \{0, 1\}$ *we define* $L(\Phi)$, ***the class of functions linear with respect to*** Φ, *to be precisely those functions* ψ *which may be written*

$$\psi = \lceil \sum_{\Phi} \alpha_\varphi \varphi > \theta \rceil$$

[*that is,* $\psi(X) = 1$ *iff it is true that* $\sum_{\Phi} \alpha_\varphi \varphi(X) > \theta$] *for suitable choices of real numbers* α_φ (*the "weights"*) *and* θ (*the "threshold"*).

We shall say a function φ of Φ is of *degree* k if we may associate it with a module having k input lines, each a distinct line of R. We then say that the *order* of ψ is the smallest integer k for which $\psi \in L(\Phi)$ for some collection of functions for which every ψ in Φ is of degree $\leq k$. Thus a linear threshold function is of order 1, and every function is of order $\leq |R|$. In a sense, then, we may say that Winograd and Spira asked how much time is required for a function if we bound the order, whereas Minsky and Papert ask how big an order is required for a function if we bound the time (by only allowing one level to be read out by a threshold element).

33 DEFINITION: *We call φ a* **mask**, *and write it as φ_A iff there is a set A such that $\varphi(X) = \lceil A \subseteq X \rceil$. We write φ_x for $\varphi_{\{x\}} = \lceil x \in X \rceil$. Let $\mathfrak{M}_R$ be the set of all masks on R.*

Thus φ_A is of degree $|A|$, and is simply an AND-gate with one input line for each element of A.

34 PROPOSITION: *All masks are of order* 1.

Proof.
$$\varphi_A = \lceil \sum_{x \in A} \varphi_x \geq |A| \rceil \qquad \square$$

35 PROPOSITION: *If M is an integer $0 < M \leq |R|$, then the "counting function" $\psi^M(X) = \lceil |X| = M \rceil$ is of order ≤ 2.*
Proof.
$$\psi^M(X) = \lceil (|X| - M)^2 \leq 0 \rceil$$
$$= \lceil (2M - 1)|X| - |X|(|X| - 1) \geq M^2 \rceil$$
$$= \lceil (2M - 1) \sum_x \varphi_x(X) + \sum_{x \neq x'} \varphi_{\{x,x'\}}(x) \geq M^2 \rceil \qquad \square$$

36 THEOREM: *Every ψ is in $L(\mathfrak{M}_R)$—that is, every ψ is a linear threshold function with respect to the set of all masks.*
Proof. Take the disjunctive normal form **(10)** for ψ. Noting that at most one term is nonzero, we may replace $\bar{x}$ by $1 - x$ and consider it as an actual numerical expression,

$$\psi(x_1, \ldots, x_n) = \sum \psi(\alpha_1, \ldots, \alpha_n) x_1^{\alpha_1} \ldots x_n^{\alpha_n}$$

Gathering terms, we obtain

$$\psi(X) = \sum \alpha_i \varphi_i(X) \qquad (*)$$

where each $\varphi_i(X) = x_{j_1} \ldots x_{j_m}$ for some subset $(j_1, \ldots, j_m)$ of $(1, \ldots, n)$ —but this just says φ_i is a mask. Rewriting the above equation in the form

$$\psi = \lceil \sum \alpha_i \varphi_i > 0 \rceil$$

we see that ψ does indeed belong to $L(\mathfrak{M}_R)$. $\qquad \square$

37 EXERCISE: Prove the following refinements of Theorem **36**:
(i) The coefficients α_i of the masks φ_i in (*) are unique.
(ii) The function ψ is of order k iff $\psi \in L(\Phi)$, where Φ is the set of masks of degree $\leq k$.

We shall now show that if a predicate is unchanged by various permutations, then we may use this fact to simplify its coefficients with respect to the set of masks—and that this simplified form will often enable us to place a lower bound on the order of the predicate [bearing in mind **37**(ii)]. Before giving the theory, we should make this clear by a simple example:

38   EXAMPLE: Let $R = \{x_1, x_2\}$, and let $\psi(x_1, x_2) = x_1x_2 \vee \bar{x}_1\bar{x}_2$, which is unchanged by transposing x_1 and x_2. We use this fact to show that ψ cannot be expressed as a linear threshold function. For suppose

$$\psi(x_1, x_2) = \ulcorner \alpha x_1 + \beta x_2 > \theta \urcorner$$

Then by symmetry we must have $\psi(x_1, x_2) = \ulcorner \alpha x_2 + \beta x_1 > \theta \urcorner$, which yields $\psi(x_1, x_2) = \ulcorner \gamma x_1 + \gamma x_2 > \theta \urcorner$, where $\gamma = (\alpha + \beta)/2$, that is, $\psi(X) = \ulcorner \gamma |X| > \theta \urcorner$. But $\psi(0, 0) = 1$; $\psi(0, 1) = 0 = \psi(1, 0)$; $\psi(1, 1) = 1$, which would imply

$$\gamma \cdot 0 > \theta \qquad \gamma \cdot 1 \leq \theta \qquad \gamma \cdot 2 > \theta$$

which is impossible, since a linear function cannot change direction.

We shall now see how the above analysis may be generalized. Let G be a group of permutations on R, with xg the image of $x \in R$ under $g \in G$. We then write

$$Xg = \{xg | x \in X\} \qquad \text{for each} \quad X \subset R \quad \text{and} \quad g \in G$$

and use φg to denote the function with $\varphi g(X) = \varphi(Xg)$. We then say φ *is equivalent to φ' with respect to G*, and write $\varphi \underset{G}{\equiv} \varphi'$, just in case $\varphi = \varphi'g$ for *some* $g \in G$. We say ψ *is invariant under G* just in case $\psi = \psi g$ for *all* $g \in G$.

39   THE GROUP INVARIANCE THEOREM: *Let G be a group of permutations of R and let Φ be a set of functions on R closed under G (that is, $\varphi \in \Phi, g \in G$ implies $\varphi g \in \Phi$). Then if ψ in $L(\Phi)$ is invariant under G, it has a linear representation*

$$\psi = \ulcorner \sum_{\varphi \in \Phi} \beta(\varphi)\varphi > \theta \urcorner$$

in which $\beta(\varphi) = \beta(\varphi')$ whenever $\varphi \underset{G}{\equiv} \varphi'$.

Proof. Given a representation

$$\psi = \ulcorner \sum \alpha(\varphi)\varphi > \theta \urcorner$$

form

$$\beta(\varphi) = \frac{\displaystyle\sum_{g \in G} \alpha(\varphi g)}{|G|}$$

which thus depends only on the equivalence class of φ. Then

$$\psi = \lceil \sum \beta(\varphi)\varphi > \theta \rceil$$

as the reader may readily verify. □

40 COROLLARY: *Let* $\Phi = \Phi_1 \cup \ldots \cup \Phi_m$, *where each* Φ_j *is a block of* $\underset{G}{\equiv}$. *Let* $N_j(X)$ *be the **number** of* φ's *in* Φ_j *for which* $\varphi(X)$ *is true. Then if* ψ *is in* $L(\Phi)$, *with* Φ *closed, and* ψ *invariant, under* G, *then* ψ *has a representation*

$$\psi = \lceil \sum_{i=1}^{m} \alpha_i N_i > \theta \rceil$$

41 EXERCISE: Apply Corollary **40** to masks of degree 1 to prove that if G is any *transitive* group of permutations on R (that is, $xG = R$ for each $x \in R$), then the only first-order predicates invariant under G are

$$\lceil |X| > m \rceil \qquad \lceil |X| \geq m \rceil \qquad \lceil |X| < m \rceil \qquad \text{and} \qquad \lceil |X| \leq m \rceil$$

for some m.

We may now apply the group invariance theorem to show that some functions have order which increases markedly as $|R|$ increases.

42 THEOREM: *The parity function*

$$\psi_{\mathrm{PAR}}(X) = \lceil |X| \text{ is an odd number} \rceil$$

is of order $|R|$.

Proof. Since ψ_{PAR} is invariant under the group G of *all* permutations of R, Corollary **40** tells us that ψ_{PAR} has a representation

$$\psi_{\mathrm{PAR}} = \lceil \sum_j \alpha_j C_j > \theta \rceil$$

where $C_j(X)$ is the number of masks φ of degree j with $\varphi(X) = 1$ and thus equals the number of subsets of X with j elements:

$$C_j(X) = \binom{|X|}{j} = \frac{1}{j!}|X|(|X| - 1) \cdots (|X| - j + 1)$$

a polynomial of degree j in $|X|$.

If ψ_{PAR} is of order K, then $P(X) = \sum_{j=0}^{k} \alpha_j C_j(X) - \theta$ is a polynomial of degree $\leq K$ in $|X|$.

Now, let X_j have j points, $j = 0, 1, \ldots, |R|$. Then the sequence

$P(|X_0|) \leq 0$, $P(|X_1|) > 0$, $P(|X_2|) \leq 0, \ldots$, $P(|X_R|)$ changes sign $|R| - 1$ times. Thus P has degree $\geq |R|$, and so we conclude that ψ_{PAR} must have order $|R|$. □

43 EXERCISE
   (i) Prove that if $\psi_{PAR} \in L(\Phi)$ and Φ contains *only* masks, then Φ contains *every* mask. [Hint: Suppose that φ_A is not in Φ, and deduce that $\psi_{PAR}(X \cap A)$ is of order $< |A|$ to get a contradiction.]
   (ii) Prove that if $\psi_{PAR} \in L(\Phi)$, then Φ must contain at least one φ of degree $|R|$.
   (iii) Prove that $\psi_{PAR} \notin L(\Phi)$ if Φ is the set of all ψ_{PAR}^A for *proper* subsets A of R.

   MINSKY and PAPERT [1967, Section 9.1] show that, in the threshold function for realizing ψ_{PAR}, the ratio of the largest to the smallest weights must be $2^{|R|-1}$—and comment that this shows that a function which is theoretically realizable in a certain way need not be practically realizable if too fine a tolerance is required of the circuitry.

   We close our discussion of the Minsky-Papert work by proving the "One-in-a-Box" Theorem, and applying this to obtain a lower bound for the order of the connectedness predicate.

44 THE "ONE-IN-A-BOX" THEOREM: *Let $A_1, \ldots, A_m$ be disjoint subsets of R, and let*

$$\psi(X) = \lceil (\forall i)(|X \cap A_i| > 0) \rceil$$

that is, $\psi(X)$ is true only if X contains a member of each A_i.

   If $|A_i| = 4m^2$ for all i, then the order of ψ is $\geq m$ (and thus $\geq \sqrt[3]{|R|/4}$ if $R = A_1 \cup \ldots \cup A_m$).
   Proof. Let G_i be the group of all permutations which leave $R - A_i$ invariant ($i = 1, \ldots, m$). Let G be the group generated by the G_i. Then ψ is invariant *wrt* G. Let Φ^K be the set of masks of degree $\leq K$, with equivalence classes Φ_j under $\underset{G}{\equiv}$. We see that $\varphi_1 \underset{G}{\equiv} \varphi_2$ iff $|S(\varphi_1) \cap A_i| = |S(\varphi_2) \cap A_i|$ for each i, where $S(\varphi)$ is the set of lines feeding the module of φ. Then clearly

$$N_j(X) = |\{\varphi | \varphi \in \Phi_j \,\&\, \varphi(X)\}|$$

$$= \binom{|X \cap A_1|}{|S(\varphi) \cap A_1|} \cdots \binom{|X \cap A_m|}{|S(\varphi) \cap A_m|} \quad \text{(for any } \varphi \text{ in } \Phi_j)$$

So $N_j(X)$ is a polynomial $P_j(y_1, \ldots, y_n)$ of degree $\leq K$ in the numbers $y_i = |X \cap A_i|$. So if ψ can be represented in terms of Φ^K, then there is a polynomial Q of degree $\leq K$ such that

$$\psi(X) = \lceil Q(y_1, \ldots, y_m) > 0 \quad \text{with } y_i = |X \cap A_i| \rceil$$

Thus we require that for $0 \leq y_i \leq 4m^2$: $Q(y_1, \ldots, y_m) > 0 \Leftrightarrow (\forall i)(y_i > 0)$.

Set $y_i = (t - (?i - 1))^2$ so that Q becomes a polynomial of degree $\leq 2K$ in t. Now if t is odd, $y_i = 0$ for $i = (t+1)/2$, but if t is even, $y_i > 0$ for all i. Thus the degree of Q in t is $\geq 2m$. Hence $K \geq m$.   □

Let us recall our interpretation of R as a set of squares in the plane, and say that two points of R are *adjacent* if they are squares with a common edge. We then say that X is *connected* if for each p and q in X we can find a sequence $p_1, p_2, \ldots, p_n$ of points with $p = p_1$, p_j adjacent to p_{j+1} for $1 \leq j < n$ and $p_n = q$.

45   THEOREM: *The order of the predicate $\psi(X) = \ulcorner X$ is connected $\urcorner$ increases without bound as $|R| \to \infty$.*

Proof. Consider a rectangle with $(2m + 1)$ rows, each of $4m^2$ squares. A figure containing all the odd-numbered rows will be connected iff it also contains at least one point from each of the m even-numbered rows. Thus a solution to the connectedness problem for this array with $|R| = 4m^2(2m + 1)$ solves the one-in-a-box problem for the even rows, and so has order at least m. Thus the order of ψ increases at least as fast as $\frac{1}{2}\sqrt[3]{|R|}$.   □

In fact, it can be shown by a more detailed argument which, following an idea of Huffman, represents the relay states of networks by patterns in the plane, that the order of ψ increases linearly with $|R|$. For the proof of this, and an analysis of many other problems of complexity of pattern recognition, the reader is referred to MINSKY and PAPERT [1969].

3.3   FINITE-STATE LANGUAGES ARE REGULAR SETS

In Section 1.4 we called subsets of X^* *languages*. Let us see how some languages may be associated with finite automata, used as *acceptors*.

With each state q of an automaton‡ M, we have associated a function

$$M_q : X^* \to Y$$

For each $y \in Y$, consider the set $R = M_q^{-1}(y)$, that is, $\{x \in X^* | M_q(x) = y\}$. We have a simple procedure for telling whether or not an input string x belongs to R—given x, we simply feed it into M started in state q, and observe whether or not the final output is y.

1   DEFINITION: *A subset R of X^* is a **Finite-State Language (FSL)** iff there exists a finite automaton $M = (X, Y, Q, \delta, \beta)$, a state $q_i \in Q$, and an output $y \in Y$ such that*

---

‡ Recall our blanket assumption: All automata are state-output unless specified explicitly to the contrary.

$$R = M_{q_i}^{-1}(y) = \bigcup \{R_{ij}|\beta(q_j) = y\}$$

where $$R_{ij} = \{x \in X^*|\delta(q_i, x) = q_j\}$$

Thus R_{ij} is the set of strings which cause M to go from state q_i to state q_j, and thus R itself is the set of all strings sending M from state q_i to a state in which M emits output y.

2 EXAMPLE: Let R be the set of strings on $\{0, 1\}$ ending in 1. Let M be the automaton shown in Fig. 3.19. Then $R = M_{q_0}^{-1}(1)$, and so is an FSL.

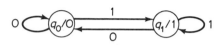

Fig. 3.19

It should be emphasized that there are finite-state languages which are *not* of the form R_{ij} for any pair of states of any finite automaton. This may be shown by an example of Bodnarchuk of the Institute of Cybernetics in Kiev (cf. GLUSHKOV [1961], Theorem 24).

3 EXAMPLE: Consider distinct letters x, x' of X, and let $E = x \cup xx'$. Then E cannot be R_{ij} for any finite automaton. For if it were, we should have $\delta(q_i, x) = q_j$ and $\delta(q_i, xx') = q_j$, whence $\delta(q_j, x') = q_j$, and thus R_{ij} must contain every string xx'^n, $n \geq 0$—a contradiction.

4 EXERCISE

(i) Show that R is an FSL iff $\exists$ a finite automaton $M = (X, Y, Q, \delta, \beta)$ with $Y = \{0, 1\}$, and a state $q \in Q$ such that

$$R = M_q^{-1}(1)$$

(ii) Deduce that if R is an FSL, then so too is $X^* - R$.

Thus when we are using an automaton as an acceptor of an FSL, and our context tells us that the input alphabet X is being considered, we need not specify Y or β—all we need specify is the set F of states which yield the desired output y. Thus:

5 DEFINITION: *If Q is a finite set, δ is a next-state function $Q \times X \rightarrow Q$, $q_0 \in Q$ is a choice of initial state, and $F \subset Q$ is a set of designated final states, we may speak of the finite **acceptor** $M = (Q, \delta, q_0, F)$ and call $T(M) = \{x|\delta(q_0, x) \in F\} \subset X^*$ the set of tapes **accepted** by M.*

6 EXAMPLE: The set of strings containing an even number of 0's and an even number of 1's is an FSL.

Proof. Consider the four-state machine with states C_{00}, C_{01}, C_{10}, C_{11}, where C_{ij} is the state corresponding to parity i for the 0's and j for the 1's.

Then $q_0 = C_{00}$, $F = \{C_{00}\}$, and the transitions are given by the graph shown in Fig. 3.20.   □

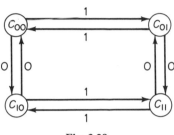

Fig. 3.20

Of course, not all subsets of X^* are FSLs. In fact (cf. **4.5**) X^* has nondenumerably many subsets, whereas there are only denumerably many finite acceptors, and hence only denumerably many FSLs. Let us exhibit an explicit example of a subset of X^* which is *not* an FSL:

7 EXAMPLE: The set $\{1^{n^2} | n \geq 1\}$ is *not* a finite-state language.

Proof. Suppose M has m states and initial state q_0, and accepts this set. Consider the states $q_0 \cdot 1^j$ [shorthand for $\delta(q_0, 1^j)$] for $0 \leq j \leq m$. Since there are $m + 1$ strings involved, and M has only m states, there must be a repetition, say $q_0 \cdot 1^{j_1} = q_0 \cdot 1^{j_2}$ with $j_2 > j_1$. Pick n so that $(n + 1)^2 - n^2 > m$. Then $q_0 \cdot 1^{n^2} = q_0 \cdot 1^{j_1} \cdot 1^{n^2 - j_1} = q_0 \cdot 1^{j_2} \cdot 1^{n^2 - j_1} = q_0 \cdot 1^{n^2 + (j_2 - j_1)}$, and so M must respond incorrectly by accepting $1^{n^2 + (j_2 - j_1)}$.   □

8 EXERCISE: For each of the following sets, either give the state graph for a finite-state acceptor, or prove that none such exists:

 (a) all strings of 0's and 1's with 3 more 0's than 1's
 (b) all strings of 0's and 1's with $3n$ more 0's than 1's
    (i) with n ranging over the integers
    (ii) with n ranging over the positive integers
 (c) $\{1^n | n$ is a prime number$\}$

In fact, there is a general result, known as "the pumping lemma," which allows us to obtain all such negative answers as simple corollaries. This lemma gives us some feel for the restriction placed on a sequential machine by having only finitely many states.

9 THEOREM (THE PUMPING LEMMA): *Let R be an FSL acceptable by an n-state finite automaton. Then every string w of R with length $\geq n$ can be written in the form xyz, where y is nonnull, where $l(yz) \leq n$, and where $xy^k z$ also belongs to R for all $k \geq 0$.*

Proof. Let $w = x_1 \ldots x_l$, $l \geq n$, each $x_i \in k$. Let $\hat{q}_k = q_0 \cdot x_1 \ldots x_k$, so $\hat{q}_0 = q_0$. Then at least two members of $\{\hat{q}_{l-n}, \hat{q}_{l-n+1}, \ldots, \hat{q}_l\}$ must be equal, say $\hat{q}_i$ and $\hat{q}_j$, with $i \neq j$. Set $x = x_1 \ldots x_i$ (so $x = \Lambda$ if $i = 0$); $y = x_{i+1} \ldots x_j$, and $z = x_{j+1} \ldots x_l$, so that $l(yz) \leq n$. Then $q_0 \cdot x = \hat{q}_i = \hat{q}_i \cdot y$. Therefore $q_0 \cdot xy^k z = q_i y^k z = \hat{q}_i \cdot z = \hat{q}_0 \cdot w$.   □

The usefulness of this is made evident by the following:

10 COROLLARY: *Let* $f: N \to N$ *be any monotonic function such that for each* $n \in N$ *there exists m such that* $f(m + 1) - f(m) > n$. *Then* **no** *finite automaton can accept* $R_f = \{1^n | n \text{ is in the range of } f\}$.

Proof. Suppose the automaton M has n states and accepts R_f. Pick m so that $f(m + 1) - f(m) > n$. Let $w = 1^{f(m)}$, and pick x, y, z so that y is nonnull, $l(yz) \leq n$, and $xy^k z \in R_f$ for all $k \geq 0$. But $xy^2 z$ is then 1^α, where $\alpha < f(m + 1)$, and so should not be in R_f: a contradiction—and so M cannot have a finite number of states.   □

Thus the set of squares and the set of primes cannot be recognized by a finite automaton when n is coded as 1^n. In fact, these sets cannot be recognized even when coded to a base ≥ 2. For proofs see [MINSKY and PAPERT, 1966], [RITCHIE, 1963b], [COBHAM, 1965], [SCHÜTZENBERGER, 1968], [HARTMANIS and SHANK, 1968] and Section 5.2 of this book. These papers have charm in that they all involve the use of theorems from number theory. Perhaps we may hope for the converse effect.

11 DEFINITION: *The* **reverse** *of a string* $\xi = x_1 x_2 \ldots x_n$, *each* $x_i \in X$, *is the string* $\xi^R = x_n \ldots x_2 x_1$. *The reverse of a subset S of* X^* *is* $S^R = \{\xi^R | \xi \in S\}$.

Rabin and Scott introduced a notion of a *dual* of an automaton to prove:

12 THEOREM: S *is an FSL iff* S^R *is an FSL*.

We prove Theorem 12 below, using a generalization of the dual due to ARBIB and ZEIGER [1968] whose properties we explore, obtaining—in particular—Theorem **14** below. Recall that Y^Q is the set of functions *from* Q *to* Y.

13 DEFINITION: *Given a machine* $M = (X, Y, Q, \delta, q_0, \beta)$ *with distinguished initial state* q_0, *its* **automaton-theoretic adjoint** *is defined to be*

$$M^\dagger = (X, Y, Y^Q, \delta^\dagger, f_0, \beta^\dagger)$$

where, denoting the dynamics of M *by* $\delta(q, v) = q \circ v$, *and those of* $M^\dagger$ *by* $\delta^\dagger(f, v) = v * f$, *we have the basic relation*

$$q(v * f) = (q \circ v)f \tag{1}$$

where, on each side, we are evaluating an element of Y^Q *at an element of* Q *to yield an element of* Y, *with the argument written on the left.*

The initial element f_0 *of* $M^\dagger$ *is precisely the output function of* M, *whereas its output function* $\beta^\dagger$ *is evaluation at* q_0, *the initial state of* M: *we set* $\beta^\dagger(f) = q_0 f$.

The Rabin and Scott definition is that of the case $Y = \{0, 1\}$, so that the state-set of $M\dagger$ may be viewed as the set of subsets of Q. β is then χ_F, the characteristic function of $F \subseteq X$. From the identity (1), it follows that the set of tapes accepted by $M\dagger$ is the reverse of the set of tapes accepted by M, thus showing the closure of the set of finite-state languages under the operation of string reversal.

We have said that an automaton M is *in reduced form* (or *observable*) if each distinct state q has a distinct input-output function M_q, that is, just in case the map $q \mapsto M_q$ is injective.

We say an automaton M is *cyclic* (or *reachable*) if each state is reachable from the initial state, i.e., just in case $\delta_{q_0}: X^* \to Q: x \mapsto \delta(q_0, x)$ is surjective.

14   THEOREM

(i) *Automaton M is cyclic iff $M^\dagger$ is in reduced form.*

(ii) *Automaton M is in reduced form if $M^\dagger$ is cyclic, but the converse is not, in general, true.*

Proof.

(i) For a state f of $M^\dagger$, the response function $M_f^\dagger$ satisfies $M_f^\dagger(v) = q_0 \circ v \circ f$. We thus have

which commutes for all $f \in Y^Q$. Thus (save in the trivial case in which Q or Y has less than two elements) δ_{q_0} is surjective iff $f \mapsto M_f^\dagger$ is surjective. That is, M is cyclic iff $M^\dagger$ is in reduced form.

(ii) The function δ_{q_0} for M corresponds to $\delta_\beta^\dagger$ for $M^\dagger$. Let ξ_q be evaluation at q. Then $M_q(v) = q \circ v \circ \lambda = \xi_q(\delta_\beta^\dagger(v))$; that is, the diagram

commutes for all q. Hence (provided that $|Y| > 1$, so that $q \mapsto \xi_q$ is injective), if $\delta_\beta^\dagger$ is surjective, then $q \mapsto M_q$ is injective. The reader may construct a counterexample to the converse, noting that most functions $X^Q \to Y$ are not of the form ξ_q.   □

We now define three operations on languages, and show that they may be used to give an alternative characterization of the FSLs (due to KLEENE [1956]).

15   DEFINITION: *If E and F are two languages on X (subsets of X^*), then we define*

$(E \cup F)$ $(E \, union \, F)$: $\{x \,|\, x \in E \text{ or } x \in F\}$

$(E \cdot F)$ $(E \, dot \, F)$: $\{ef \,|\, e \in E \text{ and } f \in F\}$

E^* $(E \, star)$: $\left\{ x \left| \begin{array}{l} \exists \text{ an integer } n, \text{ and} \\ n \text{ sequences } e_1, \ldots, e_n \text{ of } E \\ \text{such that } x = e_1 \ldots e_n \end{array} \right. \right\}$

Note that this notation is consistent with our use of X^*. If we define $E^0 = \Lambda$, $E^{n+1} = E^n \cdot E$, then we see that

$$E^* = \bigcup_{n=0}^{\infty} E^n$$

and is the smallest submonoid of X^* containing E.

16 DEFINITION: *We shall say a subset of X^* is **regular** if and only if*
    (1) *it is a finite subset of X^* (possibly empty); or*
    (2) *it can be built up from finite subsets of X^* by a finite number of applications of the union, dot, and star operations.*

The operations $\cup$ and $\cdot$ only yield finite sets when applied to finite sets. It is the * operation that yields infinite sets when applied to any set other than Λ. Since * may be applied to sets other than X, we may obtain infinite sets other than X^*, for example, $(0\ 1)^* \neq \{0, 1\}^*$. We shall often write $x_1 \ldots x_n$ for the one-string set $\{x_1 \ldots x_n\}$, EF for $(E \cdot F)$, and so on, wherever no ambiguity can arise.

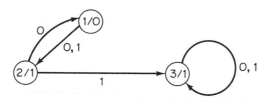

Fig. 3.21

17 EXAMPLE
    (i) Consider the three-state machine M, shown in Fig. 3.21. The set $M_1^{-1}(1)$ is the union $R_{12} \cup R_{13}$, where $R_{12} = (0 \cup 1) \cdot (0(0 \cup 1))^*$ is the set of sequences taking M from state 1 to state 2, whereas $R_{13} = R_{12} \cdot 1 \cdot (0 \cup 1)^*$ is the set of those sequences taking M from state 1 to state 3. Thus the finite-state acceptable set $M_1^{-1}(1)$ is in fact regular, and equal to

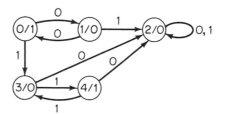

$$\{0, 1\}\ (0\{0, 1\})^* \cdot (\Lambda \cup 1\ \{0, 1\}\ ^*)$$

Fig. 3.22

Note that the set $\{0, 1\}$ is the same as the regular set $(0 \cup 1)$, and that we omit $\cdot$'s when no ambiguity should arise.

(ii) The set

$$\{0^{2n}\,1^{2m}|n \geq 0,\, m \geq 0\} = (00)^*\cdot(11)^*$$

is recognized by the automaton shown in Fig. 3.22.

18   EXERCISE: Verify the following properties which, in particular, point up the difference between the empty set $\emptyset$ and the set $\{\Lambda\}$, or Λ, as we sloppily write it, consisting of the empty string alone.

$\cdot$ is associative:	$(PQ)R = P(QR)$
distributivity:	$PQ \cup RQ = (P \cup R)Q;\; P(Q \cup R) = PQ \cup PR$
$\emptyset$ as an identity:	$R \cup \emptyset = \emptyset \cup R = R$
$\emptyset$ as a zero:	$R\emptyset = \emptyset R = \emptyset$
Λ as an identity:	$R\Lambda = \Lambda R = R$
	$\Lambda^* = \Lambda,\; \emptyset^* = \Lambda$

19   EXERCISE: Prove that the set $(0^*1 \cup 1^*0)$ is a finite-state language by constructing a finite automaton which accepts it.

20   EXERCISE: Prove whether or not the following subsets of $\{0, 1\}^*$ are regular: (i) $\{0^n1\,0^n|n \geq 0\}$; (ii) strings with the same number of 0's and 1's; (iii) strings with more 1's than 0's; $\{0^p|p \text{ prime}\}$.

We shall now show that a set *is a finite-state language iff it is regular*.

21   THEOREM: *Every regular set is a finite-state language.*

Proof. We proceed by induction, our proof being based on that of BRZOZOWSKI [1962a], which follows ARDEN [1960].

Let us fix the alphabet X. We in fact construct for each regular set E a machine M_E with two input lines, one bearing symbols from X and one bearing symbols from $\{0, 1\}$, and output set $\{0, 1\}$, such that M_E produces output 1 in response to sequence $\begin{pmatrix} x_1 \\ a_1 \end{pmatrix} \begin{pmatrix} x_2 \\ a_2 \end{pmatrix} \ldots \begin{pmatrix} x_n \\ a_n \end{pmatrix}$ iff $\exists\, i,\, 1 \leq i \leq n$, such that $a_i = 1$ and $x_{i+1} \ldots x_n \in E$. This turns out to be a form which, though it appears cumbersome, is ideally suited to inductive construction.

If we prove this, our Theorem **21** follows by our adjoining to the $\{0, 1\}$ input line a two-state machine which is in state 1 with output 1 at time 0, and resets to state and output 0 thereafter.

We start by exhibiting $M_\emptyset$, M_Λ, and $M_{x'}$ for every $x' \in X$ (see Fig. 3.23). We now proceed by induction: given that we have already constructed M_E and M_F, we construct $M_{E \cup F}$, $M_{E \cdot F}$, M_{E^*}, as in Figure 3.24 where the circle marked $\vee$ is delayless and emits a 1 iff one of its inputs is 1.

Clearly we can form M_E for $E = \{x_1 \ldots x_n\}$ by forming $M_{x_1}, \ldots, M_{x_n}$ and then using the second construction $n - 1$ times. Then for any finite set E we use the first construction to build up M_E from the machines of its constituent sequences. But any regular set can be built up from the finite sets by a finite number of applications of $\cup$, $\cdot$, and $*$, and so its machine can be built up from the machines of finite sets by the finite number of

M_ϕ has state graph

All inputs

M_Λ has state graph

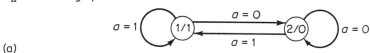

(a)

$M_{x'}$ has state graph

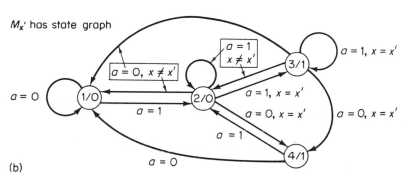

(b)

Fig. 3.23

corresponding constructions. Thus we can construct M_E for *any* regular set E, and, as outlined above, we then easily obtain a machine $\hat{M}_E$ with a state q such that $(\hat{M}_E)_q^{-1}(1) = E$. $\square$

22 THEOREM: *Every finite-state language is a regular set.*

    Proof. Our proof follows that of MCNAUGHTON and YAMADA [1960].

    Let $E = M_{q_1}^{-1}(y)$ be a finite-state language, where $M = (X, Y, Q, \delta, \beta)$, with $Q = \{q_1, \ldots, q_n\}$. Then

$$E = \cup\{R_{1j}|\beta(q_j) = y\}$$

where

$$R_{ij} = \{x \in X^*|\delta(q_i, x) = q_j\}$$

So it suffices to verify that each R_{ij} is regular.

Let us define R_{ij}^k to be the set of sequences which transfer M from q_i to q_j without passing through any state q_r for which $r > k$. In particular, R_{ij}^0 is the set of sequences which transfer M from q_i to q_j without passing through any intermediate state and so is a subset of $X \cup \{\Lambda\}$, and is thus

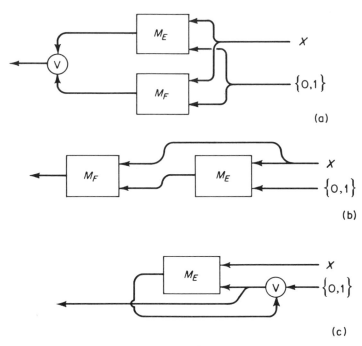

Fig. 3.24. (a) $M_{E \cup F}$ (b) $M_{E \cdot F}$ (c) M_{E*}.

regular; while $R_{ij}^n = R_{ij}$. We prove that if R_{ij}^k is regular for all i and j, and for fixed k, then R_{ij}^{k+1} is regular for all i and j. This is immediate, since

$$R_{ij}^{k+1} = R_{ij}^k \cup R_{i,k+1}^k (R_{k+1,k+1}^k)^* R_{k+1,j}^k$$

Thus R_{ij}^k is regular for every k, and, in particular, $R_{ij} = R_{ij}^n$ is regular. $\square$

If we had not chosen to discuss state-output machines, the above discussion would be changed in that we would consider subsets of X^+ rather than X^*, replace $F^* = \overset{\infty}{\underset{n=0}{\cup}} E^n$ by $E^+ = \overset{\infty}{\underset{n=1}{\cup}} E^n$, and omit all mention of Λ.

23 EXERCISE: Find regular expressions for the R_{ij} for the machine with the state graph shown in Fig. 3.25.

It is of some interest to give a different proof of the induction step of **21**, using the notion of nondeterministic automaton introduced by RABIN and SCOTT [1959]:

The idea is that if M is in state q at time t and receives input x, it emits output $\beta(q)$ at time t, and must change to any *one* state of a set $\mathfrak{M}(q, x)$ for time $t + 1$. It is *not* a probabilistic machine, for we assign no weights to the possible transitions—it should be called a *possibilistic* machine. Recall that 2^Q is the set of subsets of Q. Then we have the following:

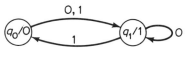

Fig. 3.25

24 DEFINITION: *A nondeterministic state-output automaton (n.d.a.) is a quintuple* $M = (X, Y, Q, \mathfrak{M}, \beta)$, *where* X, Y, *and* Q *are sets*
     $\mathfrak{M}: Q \times X \to 2^Q$ *is the nondeterministic next-state function*
     $\beta: Q \to Y$ *is the state-output function.*
     We may extend $\mathfrak{M}$ *to* $Q \times X^*$ *by setting*

$$\mathfrak{M}(q, \Lambda) = \{q\}$$
$$\mathfrak{M}(q, x'x) = \bigcup \{\mathfrak{M}(q', x)|q' \in \mathfrak{M}(q, x')\}$$

and then set

$$M_q^{-1}(y) = \{x \in X^*|\exists q' \in \mathfrak{M}(q, x) \quad \text{such that} \quad \beta(q') = y\}$$

Thus a string x is in $M_q^{-1}(y)$ iff it is *possible* for x to send M from state q to a state with output y.

25 DEFINITION: *A set* $E \subset X^*$ *is finite-state n.d.a. acceptable iff there exists an n.d.a.* M *with finite state set* Q *for which there is a state* q *and an output* y *such that*

$$E = M_q^{-1}(y)$$

Interestingly enough, for *finite-state acceptors*, this nondeterminism does *not* increase the class of acceptable sets:

26 PROPOSITION: *A set is an FSL iff it is finite-state n.d.a. acceptable.*
     Proof. Let $M = (X, Y, Q, \mathfrak{M}, \beta)$ be an n.d.a.
     Consider the finite automaton (deterministic) $M' = (X, 2^Y, 2^Q, \delta, \beta')$, where X, Y, and Q are as before with

$$\delta: 2^Q \times X \to 2^Q$$

and

$$\beta': 2^Q \to 2^Y$$

defined by

$$\delta(Q', x) = \bigcup \{\mathfrak{M}(q', x)|q' \in Q'\}$$
$$\beta'(Q') = \{\beta(q')|q' \in Q'\}$$

Then if $E = M_q^{-1}(y)$ is finite-state n.d.a. acceptable, we have that $E =$

$\cup \{[M'_{\{q\}}]^{-1}(\tilde{Y})| y \in Y \subset Y\}$ and thus finite-state acceptable, being a finite union of finite-state languages.

Conversely, any finite automaton may be viewed as a finite-state n.d.a. $\square$

We may now give an alternative proof of the induction step of Theorem **21** by proving the following:

27 PROPOSITION: *If E and F are finite-state n.d.a. acceptable, so are* $E \cup F$, $E - F$, $E \cap F$, $E \cdot F$, *and* E^*.

Proof. Let us suppose $E = M_{q_0}^{-1}(1)$ and $F = (M'_{q'_0})^{-1}(1)$.

We construct M^1, M^2, M^3 and specify states q_1, q_2, q_3 such that

$$(M_{q_1}^1)^{-1}(1) = E \cup F \qquad (M_{q_2}^2)^{-1}(1) = E \cdot F \qquad (M_{q_3}^3)^{-1}(1) = E^*$$

(a) Automaton $M^1 = (X, Y, Q \times Q', \hat{\delta}^1, \beta^1)$, where $q_1 = (q_0, q'_0)$;

$$\hat{\delta}^1((q, q'), x) = \hat{\delta}(q, x) \times \hat{\delta}'(q', x)$$
$$\beta^1((q, q')) = 1 \qquad \text{iff } \beta(q) = 1 \text{ or } \beta'(q') = 1$$

The proofs for $E - F$ and $E \cap F$ are similar.

(b) Automaton $M^2 = (X, Y, Q \cup Q', \hat{\delta}^2, \beta^2)$, where $q_2 = q_0$;

$$\hat{\delta}^2(q, x) = \begin{cases} \hat{\delta}(q, x) & \text{if } q \text{ is in } Q \text{ and } 1 \notin \beta(\hat{\delta}(q, x)) \\ \hat{\delta}(q, x) \cup \{q'_0\} & \text{if } q \text{ is in } Q \text{ and } 1 \in \beta(\hat{\delta}(q, x)) \\ \hat{\delta}(q, x) & \text{if } q \text{ is in } Q' \end{cases}$$

$$\beta^2(q) = 1 \text{ iff } q \in Q' \text{ and } \beta'(q) = 1$$

(c) Automaton $M^3 = (X, Y, Q, \hat{\delta}^3, \beta)$, where $q_3 = q_0$ and

$$\hat{\delta}^3(q, x) = \begin{cases} \hat{\delta}(q, x) & \text{if } 1 \notin \beta(\hat{\delta}(q, x)) \\ \hat{\delta}(q, x) \cup \{q_0\} & \text{if } 1 \in \beta(\hat{\delta}(q, x)) \end{cases} \qquad \square$$

28 EXERCISE [BURKS and WANG, 1957; RABIN and SCOTT, 1959]:

(i) Let M be a finite-state acceptor with n states. Prove that (recall Definition **5**) $T(M)$ is nonempty iff M accepts some string of length less than n. (This implies that there is an *effective procedure* whereby we can tell whether or not $T(M)$ is empty if we know how many states M has—we just test M on strings of length less than the number of states of M, and conclude that $T(M)$ is empty iff it accepts none of these strings.)

(ii) Let M be a finite-state acceptor with n states. Show that $T(M)$ is infinite iff it contains a string of length r, with $n \leq r < 2n$. (Thus there is an effective procedure whereby it can be decided in a finite number of steps whether or not $T(M)$ is infinite.)

(iii) Deduce an upper bound for the number of strings in $T(M)$ if M is finite, as a function of n and $|X|$.

(iv) Let M and M' be finite-state acceptors, with n and n' states, respectively. By constructing an acceptor for $[T(M) - T(M')] \cup [T(M') - T(M)]$, show that $T(M) = T(M')$ just in case any tape of length less than nn' is accepted by M iff it is accepted by M'.

29 EXERCISE: DEFINITE EVENTS [KLEENE, 1956; PERLES, RABIN, and SHAMIR, 1963]. If $x = yz$, with $x, y, z \in X^*$, we call y a *prefix* of x and z a *suffix* of x. We say a subset R of X^* is *weakly k-definite* if for any x in R which has a suffix z of length $\geq k$, we must also have z in R. Subset R is *k-definite* if k is the smallest integer j for which it is weakly j-definite, and we say R is of *degree* k. In the following questions, M will always be the finite-state acceptor (Q, δ, q_0, F).

(i) Prove that a subset of X^* is weakly k-definite iff we can build a modular net which accepts it, which has no loops, and for which no path from input line to output line passes through more than k modules. (Thus definite events correspond to loop-free automata, and their degree equals the maximum memory time required in testing strings for membership in them.)

(ii) Prove that if $T(M)$ is k-definite, then M has at least $k + 1$ states.

(iii) Prove that if M is in reduced form, and if $T(M)$ is k-definite, then for all x of length greater than or equal to k, we have $\delta(q, x) = \delta(q', x)$ for all $q, q' \in Q$.

(iv) Use results (ii) and (iii) to devise an effective procedure for telling whether or not $T(M)$ is definite (that is, k-definite for some k) for a given finite-state acceptor M.

30 EXERCISE: For a finite-state acceptor $M = (Q, \delta, q_0, F)$ let us set $R_q = \{x \mid \delta(q, x) \in F\}$, so that $T(M) = R_{q_0}$. For any subset R of X^*, set

$$\delta(R) = \begin{cases} \Lambda & \text{if } \Lambda \in R \\ \emptyset & \text{if } \Lambda \notin R \end{cases}$$

(i) Prove that the R_q satisfy the simultaneous equations

$$R_q = \delta(R_q) \cup \bigcup_{x \in X} x R_{\delta(q,x)}$$

(ii) Prove that if $\Lambda \notin A$, then the set equation $X = AX \cup B$ has the solution $X = A^*B$.

(iii) Show how, given the state graph for M, we may obtain the simultaneous equations of (i), and how we may then solve these equations by repeated applications of (ii) to obtain R_{q_0}. Apply this method to the

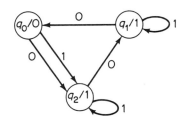

Fig. 3.26

machine with the state graph shown in Fig. 3.26.

(iv) Prove that, for all $P, Q \subset X^*$: $\delta(P \cdot Q) = \delta(P) \cdot \delta(Q)$, $\delta(P^*) = \Lambda$ and $\delta(P \cup Q) = \delta(P) \cup \delta(Q)$.

We close this section with an account, based on the work of BRZOZOWSKI [1962a, b; 1964a, b; 1965] of how we may manipulate expressions for regular sets directly to obtain the state graph of a machine which accepts the language described by that regular expression. (For related material, see McNAUGHTON and YAMADA [1960] and OTT and FEINSTEIN [1961].) To carry this out successfully we must distinguish between regular *sets*, and the regular *expressions* which describe them. Thus we make explicit the idea that a regular expression is in a *meta*language and serves to *denote* a regular set.

31   DEFINITION: *If $X = \{x_1, \ldots, x_n\}$ we introduce a new set of symbols $\bar{x}_1, \ldots,$ $\bar{x}_n$, as well as $\bar{\Lambda}$ and $\emptyset$. We then say a string on the alphabet of symbols $\{\bar{x}_1, \ldots, \bar{x}_n,$ $\bar{\Lambda}, \emptyset, +, \circ, *\}$ is a **regular expression** if it can be obtained from the expressions $\bar{x}_1, \ldots, \bar{x}_n, \bar{\Lambda}, \emptyset$, by a finite number of the combinations $\alpha, \beta \mapsto \alpha + \beta; \alpha, \beta \mapsto \alpha \circ \beta;$ $\alpha \mapsto \alpha^*$. Let L be the set of regular expressions, and let K be the set of subsets of X^*. Then we define the function $|\ \ |: L \to K$ by induction:*

$$|\bar{\emptyset}| = \emptyset \qquad |\bar{\Lambda}| = \Lambda \qquad |\bar{x}_i| = x_i, \quad i = 1, \ldots, n$$

$$|\alpha + \beta| = |\alpha| \cup |\beta| \qquad |\alpha \circ \beta| = |\alpha| \cdot |\beta| \qquad |\alpha^*| = |\alpha|^*$$

We read "$|\alpha| = E$" as "α denotes the set E" and observe that a set is regular iff it may be denoted by a regular expression. We often write $\alpha\beta$ for $\alpha \circ \beta$.

For regular expressions α, β we write $\alpha \equiv \beta$ (read: α and β are *identical*) if α and β are exactly the same strings in L; and we write $\alpha = \beta$ (read: α and β are *equal*) if α and β *denote* the same sets, that is, $|\alpha| = |\beta|$. For example, $\bar{0}^*\bar{0} + \bar{0} + \bar{1} = 1 + \bar{0}^*\bar{0}$. We observe the following identities, for all regular expressions α, β, γ:

A_1: $\alpha + (\beta + \gamma) = (\alpha + \beta) + \gamma$ A_7: $\bar{\Lambda}\, \alpha = \alpha$
A_2: $\alpha(\beta\gamma) = (\alpha\beta)\gamma$ A_8: $\bar{\emptyset}\alpha = \bar{\emptyset}$
A_3: $\alpha + \beta = \beta + \alpha$ A_9: $\alpha + \bar{\emptyset} = \alpha$
A_4: $(\alpha + \beta)\gamma = \alpha\gamma + \beta\gamma$ A_{10}: $\alpha^* = \bar{\Lambda} + \alpha^*\alpha$
A_5: $\alpha(\beta + \gamma) = \alpha\beta + \alpha\gamma$ A_{11}: $\alpha^* = (\bar{\Lambda} + \alpha)^*$
A_6: $\alpha + \alpha = \alpha$

Before describing Brzozowski's work, let us mention (without giving proofs) that some work has been done on an axiomatic theory of regular expressions.

SALOMAA [1966] has shown that *all* equalities for regular expressions may be obtained from the equalities $A_1 - A_{11}$ by repeated applications of the two rules of inference:

R1 (Substitution). Assume that γ' is the result of replacing an occurrence of α by β in γ. Then, from the equations $\alpha = \beta$ and $\gamma = \delta$, one may infer the equation $\gamma' = \delta$ and the equation $\gamma' = \gamma$.

R2 (Solution of Equations). Assume that $\Lambda \notin |\beta|$. Then, from the equation $\alpha = \alpha\beta + \gamma$, one may infer the equation $\alpha = \gamma\beta^*$.

However, REDKO [1964] has shown that if we allow only the rule of substitution, no finite collection of axioms suffices for the deduction of all regular expression inequalities. If we augment the equalities $A_1 - A_{11}$, by the denumerable set of axioms

$$\alpha^* = \bar{\Lambda} + \alpha + \alpha^2 + \cdots + \alpha^{k-1} + \alpha^k \alpha^* \qquad k = 1, 2, 3, \ldots$$

(where $\alpha^2 = \alpha \circ \alpha$, $\alpha^3 = \alpha \circ \alpha \circ \alpha$, and so on), then from this collection one may deduce all equalities of regular expressions by applications of $R1$ alone.

32 EXERCISE: Use the proof of Theorem **21** to show that if α is a regular expression with n letters (in the sense that $\bar{0}\bar{1}^* + \bar{0}^*\bar{1}\bar{0}^*$ has five letters, not two), then there is an automaton with no more than 2^n states which realizes $|\alpha|$.

Let α be a given regular expression which denotes the set $R = |\alpha| \subset X^*$. We know from Exercise 1.25 that we may obtain a minimal finite-state acceptor M for R as follows:

(i) Form the function

$$f = \chi_R \colon X^* \to \{0, 1\} \colon x \mapsto \begin{cases} 1 & \text{if } x \in R \\ 0 & \text{if } x \notin R \end{cases}$$

(ii) Find one representative for each of the distinct functions

$$fL_x \colon X^* \to \{0, 1\} \colon x' \mapsto f(xx')$$

(iii) Let M have one state for each distinct fL_x, with next-state function $(fL_x, x') \mapsto fL_{xx'}$, and output-function $fL_x \mapsto f(x)$.

Let us notice that $fL_x(x') = 1$ iff $f(xx') = 1$ iff $xx' \in R$. Thus fL_x is the characteristic function of the *left quotient of R by x*, that is, the set $\{x' | xx' \in R\}$, which we denote $x \backslash R$—the set of strings obtained by chopping off the x from strings of R with suffix x. Hence our minimal machine has one state for each left quotient of R. Brzozowski's notion is to replace the operation of finding left quotients of subsets of X^* by the *finite* operation of finding what he calls the *derivative* of a regular expression.

33 DEFINITION: *The derivative $D_x\alpha$ of a regular expression α with respect to a string x of X^* is defined inductively as follows:*

(i)   *For $x = \Lambda$, $D_\Lambda\alpha \equiv \alpha$*
(ii) *For $x \in X$ we define*
$$D_x\bar{\Lambda} \equiv \bar{\emptyset}$$
$$D_x\bar{\phi} \equiv \bar{\emptyset}$$
$$D_x\bar{x}_j \equiv \begin{cases} \bar{\emptyset} & \text{if } x \neq x_j \\ \bar{\Lambda} & \text{if } x = x_j \end{cases}$$
$$D_x(\alpha + \beta) \equiv D_x\alpha + D_x\beta$$
$$D_x(\alpha \circ \beta) \equiv D_x\alpha \circ \beta + \alpha \circ D_x\beta$$
$$D_x\alpha^* \equiv D_x\alpha \circ \alpha^*$$
(iii) *For $x = x_1 x_2 \ldots x_n$, each $x_j \in X$, we define*
$$D_x\alpha \equiv D_{x_n}(\circ \circ \circ D_{x_2}(D_{x_1}\alpha) \ldots)$$

The reader may easily check, by induction, the

34   ASSERTION. *For all* $x \in X^*$, *and all regular expressions* α *on* X, *we have*

$$|D_x \alpha| = x \backslash |\alpha|$$

35   EXAMPLE: Let $\alpha \equiv (\bar{0} + 1)^*1$. We saw in Example **2** that $|\alpha|$ is accepted by a two-state machine. Let us compute a few derivatives of α:

$$D_\Lambda \alpha \equiv (\bar{0} + 1)^* \circ 1$$
$$D_1 \alpha \equiv (\bar{\emptyset} + \bar{\Lambda}) \circ (\bar{0} + 1)^* \circ 1 + (\bar{0} + 1)^* \circ \bar{\Lambda}$$
$$D_0 \alpha \equiv (\bar{\Lambda} + \bar{\emptyset}) \circ (\bar{0} + 1)^* \circ 1 + (\bar{0} + 1)^* \circ \bar{\emptyset}$$

It should be clear that, continuing this process, we shall find that α has infinitely many derivatives, to describe only two regular sets.

It is clear that we must find some routine way of simplifying regular expressions which is powerful enough to reduce the number of dissimilar derivatives of a regular expression to within finite limits but does not require that we go to all the effort of checking equality of the sets denoted by different expressions.

36   DEFINITION: *Two regular expressions are* **similar** *if one can be transformed into another by using only the identities*

$$\alpha + \alpha = \alpha$$
$$\alpha + \beta = \beta + \alpha$$
$$(\alpha + \beta) + \gamma = \alpha + (\beta + \gamma)$$
$$\alpha + \bar{\emptyset} = \alpha \qquad \alpha\bar{\emptyset} = \bar{\emptyset}\alpha = \bar{\emptyset} \qquad \alpha\bar{\Lambda} = \bar{\Lambda}\alpha = \alpha$$

Thus, by using successive similarity reductions, we have, in the above example,

$$D_1 \alpha = \bar{\Lambda} \circ (\bar{0} + 1)^* \circ 1 + (\bar{0} + 1)^* = (\bar{0} + 1)^* \circ 1 + (\bar{0} + 1)^*$$
$$D_0 \alpha = \bar{\Lambda} \circ (\bar{0} + 1)^* \circ 1 + \bar{\emptyset} = (\bar{0} + 1)^* \circ 1 = \alpha$$

In fact, the reader may prove that there are only two similarity types among the derivatives of this α.

This renders plausible the following theorem:

37   THEOREM: *Every regular expression has only a finite number of dissimilar derivatives.*

Proof. The proof is by induction on the number $0(\alpha)$ of occurrences of letters in the expression α.

$0(\alpha) = 1$: It is certainly true for $\alpha \equiv \bar{\Lambda}$, $\bar{\emptyset}$ or $\bar{x}_i$—the only derivatives here are α, $\bar{\emptyset}$, or $\bar{\Lambda}$ (*not* respectively).

Induction step. Suppose the assertion is true for $0(\alpha) \leq n$. We show it is true for $0(\alpha) = k + 1$.

(i) Let $\alpha \equiv \beta + \gamma$. Then since $D_x(\alpha + \beta) \equiv D_x \alpha + D_x \beta$, we conclude that $\alpha + \beta$ has only finitely many derivatives.

(ii) Let $x = x_1 x_2 \ldots x_n$ with each $x_i \in X$. For each ordered subset K of $\{1, \ldots, n\}$ with $K = \{j_1, j_2, \ldots, j_k\}$ for $1 \leq j_1 < j_2 < \cdots < j_k \leq n$, let $x^K = x_{j_1} x_{j_2} \ldots x_{j_k}$ while $x_K = $ the string obtained from x by deleting $x_{j_1}, x_{j_2}, \ldots, x_{j_k}$.

Thus if $K = \{1, \ldots, n\}$, then $x^K = x$ and $x_K = \Lambda$. [We may define the *shuffle product* of two words y and z with $n = l(y) + l(z)$ to be

$$y T z = \{x \mid \text{ there exists } K \subset \{1, \ldots, n\} \text{ with } x^K = y \text{ and } x_K = z\}$$

Note that this product is commutative.] Then it is very easy to verify that using an obvious notation, made possible by the commutativity of $+$ under similarity:

$$D_{x_1 x_2, \ldots x_n}(\beta \circ \gamma) = \sum_{K \subset \{1, \ldots, n\}} D_{x^K}\beta \circ D_{x_K}\gamma$$

Thus if β and γ have only finitely many dissimilar derivatives, the same must be true for $\alpha = \beta \circ \gamma$. We leave the verification for $\alpha \equiv \beta^*$ to the reader. With this, our result follows by induction. ☐

This result assures us that the following algorithm will terminate in a finite time:

38 ALGORITHM: *To construct an automaton to accept the set denoted by a regular expression α:*
   Stage 0. Set $Q = \{\alpha\}$, $Q_0 = \{\alpha\}$. Go to stage 1.
   Stage $k + 1$ ($k \geq 0$). Form the derivatives with respect to elements of X of all the expressions in Q_k. Let Q_{k+1} be the set of all expressions so formed which are not similar to expressions in the set Q formed at stage k.
      If $Q_{k+1} = \emptyset$, exit to stage ω.
      If $Q_{k+1} \neq \emptyset$, adjoin Q_{k+1} to Q, and go to stage $k + 2$.
   Stage ω. Form the automaton $\tilde{M}_\alpha$ with state-space Q, with next-state function

$$(D_x\alpha, x') \mapsto \text{the } D_{x''}\alpha \text{ in } Q \text{ which is similar to } D_{xx'}\alpha$$

and output function

$$D_x\alpha \mapsto 1 \qquad \text{iff } \Lambda \in |D_x\alpha|$$

and initial state α. ☐

39 EXERCISE: Prove that $\tilde{M}_\alpha$ is indeed a finite-state acceptor for $|\alpha|$.

3.4 CANONICAL FORMS AND SEMIGROUPS ‡

Suppose we are given a machine $M = (X, Y, Q, \delta, \beta)$ in state q. Then the only behavior of M we could expect to see is that associated with states reachable from q—that is, states in $r(q) = \delta(q, X^*)$. Thus the machine we "see" is not M but M with its states cut down to $r(q)$:

$$M^{(q)} = (X, Y, r(q), \delta|r(q) \times X, \beta|r(q))$$

---

‡ The reader may choose to omit this section at a first reading, but will find a complete understanding of it necessary before reading Chapter 8.

where we restrict δ and β so they only act on states in $r(q)$. A machine of the form $M^{(q)}$ will be called *cyclic* (not because it contains cycles, but because the usage is analogous to that of algebra in calling a ring cyclic), and q will be called a *generator* of $M^{(q)}$, since q, together with the action of the inputs, generates all the states of $M^{(q)}$.

1   So given M started in state q_0, let us consider the reduced form of $M^{(q_0)}$ as a *canonical* form for the machine's behavior. Recalling the results of exercise **1.25**, we see that, if $f = M_{q_0}: X^* \to Y$ is the input-output function of the initial state, our canonical machine takes the form

$$M(f) = (X, Y, Q_f, \delta_f, \lambda_f)$$

where $Q_f = \{fL_x | x \in X^*\}$ contains precisely one representative of each distinct input-output function of states of M reachable from q,

$$\delta_f(g, x) = gL_x$$
$$\lambda_f(g, x) = g(x)$$

Since M is a state-output machine, so is $M(f)$, with $\beta_f(g) = g(\Lambda)$.

Note that the definition is valid for any $f: X^* \to Y$, whether or not it comes from a finite automaton M. Of course, for a general f, we cannot guarantee that Q_f will be a finite set.

2   DEFINITION: *We say that a function $f: X^* \to Y$ is finite-state computable iff there exists a finite automaton M and a state q of M such that $f = M_q$.*

We immediately have these results:

3   PROPOSITION: *$f: X^* \to Y$ is finite-state computable iff $M(f)$ is a finite automaton.*

4   PROPOSITION: *$E \subset X^*$ is a finite-state language iff its characteristic function $\chi_E: X^* \to \{0, 1\}$ is finite-state computable.*

5   A finite automaton is specified by a finite tableau. We can enumerate these tableaux in some effective manner, and so the set of finite automata [and so, a fortiori, the set of finite-state computable functions; and so (a fortiori)[2], the set of finite-state languages] is denumerable, i.e., has cardinality $\aleph_0$. But X^*, having cardinality $\aleph_0$, must have $2^{\aleph_0}$ subsets, i.e., nondenumerably many. Similarly, the collection of all functions $f: X^* \to Y$ is nondenumerable. Thus most subsets of X^* are *not* finite-state languages, and most functions $f: X^* \to Y$ are *not* finite-state computable.

It will be useful to reformulate Proposition **3**, to obtain a criterion for finite-state computability in terms of equivalence relations ([NERODE, 1959], [RABIN & SCOTT, 1959]).

6   DEFINITION: *Given a function* $f: X^* \to Y$, *let* E_f *be the equivalence relation* (*the* **Nerode equivalence**) *on* X^*:

$$xE_fx' \quad \Leftrightarrow \quad f(xz) = f(x'z) \text{ for all } z \text{ in } X^*$$

Thus $xE_fx' \Leftrightarrow fL_x = fL_{x'}$, and we see that the Nerode equivalence classes $[x]_E$ may be thought of as the elements of Q_f, the state set of $M(f)$ which is the minimal machine which computes f. Hence, recalling the terminology or equivalence relations introduced in Section **2.1**.

7   PROPOSITION
    (i) E_f is a right-equivalence relation;
    (ii) f is finite-state computable $\Leftrightarrow E_f$ is of finite index;
    (iii)   the index of E_f is the number of states of the minimal machine which computes f.

8   EXAMPLE: The set $R = \{0, 01, 01^2, \ldots\}$ is an FSL.
    Proof 1 (Nerode equivalence). Let $X = \{0, 1\}$, and write E for E_{X_R}. Then $xEy \Leftrightarrow \forall z \in X^*(xz \in R \Leftrightarrow yz \in R)$, and we have *three* equivalence classes,

$$\{\Lambda\}$$
$$R$$
$$X^* - (R \cup \{\Lambda\}) \qquad \text{that is, } E \text{ has } \textit{finite} \text{ index}$$

    Proof 2 (Direct construction of an automaton which realizes R). We may derive it as $M(\chi_R)$ (note that there will be three states, since states of the minimal machine correspond to Nerode equivalence classes), or else construct it ad hoc. Either way we get

$X = \{0, 1\}$
$Y = \{0, 1\}$
$Q = \{q_0, q_1, q_2\}$, q_0 the initial state

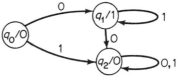

Fig. 3.27

with the state graph shown in Fig. 3.27.

9   EXERCISE: Check that if a function is finite-state computable, then so is any function that differs from it on only a finite number of elements.

    We saw in Exercise **3.28** that to tell whether two states of an n-state machine are equivalent, we need only test their equivalence on strings of length less than n. This information may be represented on a tree of depth $n - 1$, with one branch for each letter of X, emanating from any node, and with a letter of Y labelling each node. Thus if $X = \{0, 1\}$, $Y = \{0, 1\}$, the tree for f (Fig. 3.28) denotes that $f(\Lambda) = 0$, $f(0) = 0 = f(1)$, $f(00) = 0 = f(11)$, and $f(10) = 1 = f(10)$.

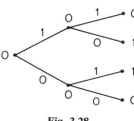

Fig. 3.28

If we know that a response function $f: X^* \to Y$ has realization with $\leq n$ states, we need only look at the trees of depth $n - 1$ depending on nodes distant at most $n - 1$ from the initial node of the tree of f to find which are the possible distinct fL_x's. We then read off a minimal representative x for each such tree, to obtain representatives for a minimal state set. By extending the tree of f to depth $2n - 1$, we may look at the trees on the nodes following each such representative to obtain the state transition function.

10   EXAMPLE: Use the tree-search method to find the minimal state machine for recognizing the set $\{0^n 1 | n \geq 0\}$, given that three states are sufficient.

Solution. Since three states suffice, we need only develop the tree of f, the characteristic function of $\{0^n 1 | n \geq 0\}$ to depth 5. To avoid cumbrous labeling, we establish the convention that the upper of two branches corre-

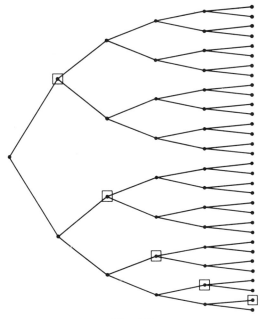

Fig. 3.29

sponds to input 1, and that a node is 0 unless marked with a square. We then have the tree shown in Fig. 3.29. Inspection quickly reveals that there are only three distinct trees of depth $(n - 1) = 2$, as shown in Fig. 3.30, and

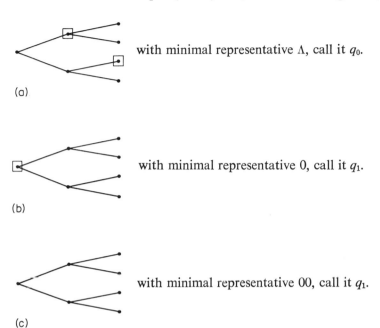

(a)   with minimal representative Λ, call it q_0.

(b)   with minimal representative 0, call it q_1.

(c)   with minimal representative 00, call it q_1.

Fig. 3.30

inspection immediately yields the state graph shown in Fig. 3.31.

11 EXERCISE: Use the tree-search method to find the minimal automaton which recognizes the set $\{0^{2n} | n \geq 0\}$.

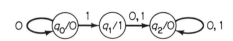

Fig. 3.31

12 EXERCISE (RANEY [1958]): Given $f: X^* \to Y$, extend it to $F: X^* \to Y^*$ by $F(\Lambda) = \Lambda$, $f(x_1x_2 \ldots x_n) = F(x_1x_2 \ldots x_{n-1})f(x_1x_2 \ldots x_n)$. Similarly, extend $g: Y^* \to X$ to $G: Y^* \to X^*$. Let I_X and I_Y be the identity functions on X^* and Y^*, respectively. We say f and g are *inverses* if $FG = I_Y$ and $GF = I_X$.

(i) Prove that if f and g are inverses, then for any $x \in X^*$, fL_x and gL_{Fx} are inverses.

(ii) Prove that if f and g are inverses, then $M(f)$ and $M(g)$ have the same number of states.

(iii) If $M(f)$ is strongly connected, then $M(fL_x)$ is strongly connected for each $x \in X^*$.

(iv) If $M(f)$ is finite, then $M(fL_x)$ is strongly connected for at least one $x \in X^*$.

(v) If f and g are inverses, then $M(f)$ is strongly connected iff $M(g)$ is strongly connected.

13   EXAMPLE: The set $R = \{0^{n^2-1}1 | n > 0\}$ is *not* an *FSL*.

Proof 1 (Nerode equivalence). $i \neq j \Rightarrow 0^i \not{E} 0^j$. So E has nonfinite index.

Proof 2. Suppose $M(\chi_R)$ has only finitely many states. Since there are infinitely many strings 0^k, we must have a pair $k > l$ such that

14
$$\chi_R \cdot L_{0^k} = \chi_R \cdot L_0 l$$

Pick any $n^2 - 1 > k > l$. Then for all positive integers t,

$$\chi_R(0^{n^2-1+t(k-l)}1) = \chi_R(0^{n^2-1}1)$$

by repeated application of (**14**), and R was not what we thought it was.

As we pointed out in Exercise **3.4**, when we use an automaton to recognize a set of inputs, we need to specify the starting state q_0, and that set F of states which yield the acceptance output, but have no other interest in the outputs, and thus may denote it by the quadruple $M = (Q, \delta, q_0, F)$ and refer to it as a *finite-state acceptor*. The quantity X is left implicit.

We may think of M as having its input sequence printed on a tape which it reads in one direction, from left to right, say. We have characterized the type of set it may recognize—the regular events—in terms of Nerode's right equivalence relation.

But what if we allow our automaton to move backward and forward on its input tapes? We are led to consider two-way automata, where:

15   DEFINITION: *A **two-way finite automaton** with input alphabet X is a quadruple:*

$$M = (Q, \delta, q_0, F)$$

where Q *is a finite set:*   *"the set of states"*
      $q_0 \in Q$:   *"the initial state"*
      $F \subset Q$:   *"the designated final states"*
and $\delta: Q \times X \to \{L, N, R\} \times Q$.

The automaton M operates as follows: It starts on the leftmost square of the given tape in state q_0. When its internal state is q and it scans the symbol x, then if $M(q, x) = (p, q')$, it goes into the new state q' and moves one square left, right, or not at all as p is L, R, or N.

The class $T(M)$ of tapes *accepted* by M is the class of tapes t such that M eventually moves off the right-hand edge of t in a state belonging to F.

RABIN and SCOTT [1959] found that any set of tapes accepted by a two-way automaton is regular. SHEPHERDSON [1959] gave the elegant proof which follows. His intuitive reason for the possibility of the reduction was that:

A machine can spare itself the necessity of coming back to refer to a piece of tape t again if, before leaving t, it thinks of all the possible questions it might later come back and ask about t, answers these questions now, and carries the table of question-answer combinations forward along the tape with it, altering the answers where necessary as it goes along.

Formally, then:

16 THEOREM: *For every two-way finite automaton M there exists a one-way finite automaton $\overline{M}$ such that $T(M) = T(\overline{M})$.*
  Proof. For each $t \in X^*$, define a function

$$\tau_t: \{\bar{q}_0\} \cup Q \to \{0\} \cup Q$$

as follows: For $q \in Q$, if M, when started in state q on the *rightmost* symbol of t, ultimately leaves t from the right in an internal state q', then $\tau_t(q) = q'$; if, on the other hand, M either leaves t from the left, or never leaves t, then $\tau_t(q) = 0$.
  The function $\tau_t(\bar{q}_0)$ similarly describes the result of the motion when M is started in the initial state q_0 on the *leftmost* symbol of t.
  Now let us define the usual Nerode equivalence relation

$$t_1 \; \mathrm{E} \; t_2 \qquad \text{iff } (\forall t \in X^*)(t_1 t \in T(M) \Leftrightarrow t_2 t \in T(M))$$

We see that if $\tau_{t_1} = \tau_{t_2}$, then $t_1 \; \mathrm{E} \; t_2$. But if n is the number of internal states of A, there are at most $(n + 1)^{n+1}$ distinct τ_t. Thus the Nerode relation has finite index, and $T(M)$ is definable by a one-way automaton $\overline{M}$. $\square$

17 EXERCISE (SHEPHERDSON). Show that $\overline{M}$ may be effectively obtained from M.

Although we have studied the case where X and Y are finite sets, we should stress that the Nerode equivalence has given us a general method whereby, given an "external" description $f: X^* \to Y$ of a system, for *arbitrary* X and Y, we can obtain a *realization*, i.e., a discrete-time system $M = (X, Y, Q, \delta, \lambda)$ with some state q_0 for which $f = M_{q_0}$:

18 *Given $f: X^* \to Y$, let us define an equivalence relation E_f by*

$$\theta_1 E_f \theta_2 \quad \Leftrightarrow \quad f(\theta_1 \theta) = f(\theta_2 \theta) \quad \text{for all} \quad \theta \quad \text{in} \quad X^*$$

and then set $[\theta_1] = \{\theta_2 | \theta_1 E_f \theta_2\}$ and $X^*/E_f = \{[\theta_1] | \theta_1 \in X^*\}$.
  Then $M(f)_{[\Lambda]} = f$ for the system $M(f)$ with internal description given by
  State-set $Q_f = X^*/E_f$
  Next-state function $\delta_f: Q_f \times X \to Q_f : ([\theta], x) \mapsto [\theta x]$
  Output function $\beta_f: Q_f \to Y : [\theta] \mapsto f(\theta)$.

We have already seen (e.g. in Example **10**) how to convert this into an algorithm if we know that the function has a realization with a number of states less than some given finite number n.

Unfortunately, the prescription **18** for determining the canonical realization of the system is not finite in the *general* case—we need an infinite test to tell whether or not $\theta_1 E_f \theta_2$, and we must find equivalence classes for infinitely many strings. We try to lay bare the true nature of the finite-state case by presenting procedures of successive approximation for these two problems, and then exhibiting two important cases in which these approximations become exact at some finite stage—one being the finite-state case, and the other that of finite-dimensional linear systems.

Let us say two sequences θ_1 and θ_2 are *k-equivalent* if they lead any realization of f to states which cannot be distinguished by experiments of length less than k—in symbols:

19
$$\theta_1 E_f^k \theta_2 \iff f(\theta_1\theta) = f(\theta_2\theta) \quad \text{for all} \quad \theta \in X^{[0,k)}$$

Then we set $Q_k = X^*/E_f^k$, the set of equivalence classes $[\theta]_k$ of strings θ under the relation E_f^k, and note that we may write $Q_f = Q_\infty$ without inconsistency. Indeed, we have for $0 < k_1 < k_2 \leq \infty$ a surjection

$$Q_{k_1} \leftarrow\!\!\!\leftarrow Q_{k_2}$$

well-defined by $[\theta]_{k_1} \leftarrow\!\!\mid [\theta]_{k_2}$ for all θ in X^*, since if θ cannot be distinguished from θ' by tests of length $< k_2$, they cannot be distinguished by shorter tests. Q_f is the "limit" of the sets Q_k as k tends to ∞.

20 LEMMA: *If in the infinite sequence*

$$Q_1 \leftarrow\!\!\!\leftarrow Q_2 \leftarrow\!\!\!\leftarrow Q_3 \leftarrow\!\!\!\leftarrow \cdots\cdots$$

we have $Q_k \cong Q_{k+1}$ for some k, then $Q_k \cong Q_{k'}$ for all $k' \geq k$, and in fact $Q_k \cong Q_f$.

Proof. We prove that $Q_k = Q_{k+1}$ implies $Q_{k+1} = Q_{k+2}$—the rest follows by induction. Since $\theta_1 E_f^{k+2}\theta_2$ implies $\theta_1 E_f^{k+1}\theta_2$ in any case, it suffices to prove the converse:

$$
\begin{aligned}
\theta_1 E_f^{k+1}\theta_2 &\Rightarrow f(\theta_1 x\theta) = f(\theta_2 x\theta) && \text{for all} && x \in X,\, \theta \in X^{[0,k)}\\
&\Rightarrow \theta_1 x \;\; E_f^k \;\; \theta_2 x && \text{for all} && x \in X\\
&\Rightarrow \theta_1 x \;\; E_f^{k+1} \;\; \theta_2 x && \text{for all} && x \in X,\text{ by assumption}\\
&&&&& \text{that } Q_k = Q_{k+1}\\
&\Rightarrow \theta_1 \;\; E_f^{k+2} \;\; \theta_2
\end{aligned}
$$
$\square$

Thus, if we can guarantee that k is such that $Q_k = Q_{k+1}$, then we may reduce the computation of Q_f to that of Q_k:

We now define a sequence of nested subsets of Q_f by simply letting S_k

be the set of states of $M(f)$ accessible with input sequences of length less than k—in symbols:

21
$$S_k = \{[\theta] | \theta \in X^{[0,k)}\}$$

Again we may equate Q_f with S_∞, and note that $S_{k_1} \subset S_{k_2}$ for all $0 < k_1 \leq k_2 \leq \infty$, since if we can reach a state in less than k_2 steps, we can reach it in less than k_1 steps. Q_f is the union of all the sets Q_k.

22 LEMMA: *If, in the infinite sequence*

$$S_1 \subset S_2 \subset S_3 \subset \cdots$$

we have $S_k = S_{k+1}$ for some k, then $S_k = S_{k'}$ for all $k' \geq k$, and in fact $S_k = Q_f$.

Proof. Again, it suffices to show that $S_k = S_{k+1}$ implies $S_{k+1} = S_{k+2}$. But if state q is in S_{k+2}, it is reachable in one step from a state q' of S_{k+1}. But if $S_k = S_{k+1}$ then q' must be reachable in $<k$ steps, and so q is reachable in $<k + 1$ steps, i.e., q is in S_{k+1}. □

Combining the two lemmas we have the following crucial result for simplifying the computation of canonical realizations.

23 THEOREM: *Let $f: X^* \to Y$ be an external description of a system for which there exist numbers M and N such that*

$$Q_M = Q_{M+1}$$
$$S_N = S_{N+1}$$

Then, in the definition of the canonical realization $M(f)$ of f, we may take

$$Q_f = U^{[0,N)}/E_f^M$$

It will now require little effort on our part to prove the following corollaries, the first of which should look familiar:

24 COROLLARY: (for finite systems) *Let $f: X^* \to Y$ be an external description for a system which has a (not necessarily minimal) realization with a finite number, at most N, of states. Then in the definition of the canonical realization $M(f)$ of f, we may take*

$$Q_f = X^{[0,N)}/E_f^N$$

25 COROLLARY: (for linear systems)† *Let $f: X^* \to Y$ be an external description, with X and Y vector spaces over some field K, which is the zero-state re-*

---

† The discussion of linear systems should be omitted by students who have not studied basic linear systems theory by the state-space approach. For more information, see Chapters 2 and 10 of [KALMAN, FALB, and ARBIB, 1969].

sponse of u (not necessarily minimal) **linear** *system whose state-space is of dimension at most N over K. Then in the definition of the canonical realization M(f) of f, we may take*

$$Q_f = U^N/E_f^N$$

To make the proofs as simple as possible we note that each comprises two applications of the following lemma, which has appeared in many guises (of which our **1.29** already constituted a generalization) in the literature, but does not seem to have been stated explicitly hitherto.

26 A TERMINATION LEMMA: *Let $A_1, A_2, A_3, \ldots$ be a sequence of objects with the jth of which is associated an integer h_j. Let it be the case that*

(i) $h_1 \leq h_2 \leq h_3 \leq \ldots$
(ii) $h_k = h_{k+1}$ *implies* $A_k \cong A_{k+1}$ *and* $h_{k+1} = h_{k+2}$

Then if $h_j \leq H$ for all j, then

$$A_{k'} \cong A_{H-h_1+1} \qquad \text{for all} \qquad k' \geq H - h_1$$

Proof. The sequence $h_1, h_2, h_3, \ldots$ must be strictly increasing until equality is first attained. Since each $h_j \leq H$, there can be at most $H - h_1$ increases before equality is obtained, and so this must occur by stage $k_1 = 1 + (H - h_1)$. The assertion follows immediately. □

27 *Proof of Corollary* **24**: We must show that $Q_N = Q_{N+1}$ and that $S_N = S_{N+1}$. But this is immediate, since the conditions of the termination lemma hold both for the sequence $Q_1, Q_2, Q_3, \ldots$ and for the sequence $S_1, S_2, S_3, \ldots$ if we take H to be N, and h_j to be the cardinality of Q_j or S_j, respectively, so that in either case $h_1 \geq 1$, and $H - h_1 \leq N$. □

28 *Proof of Corollary* **25**: To apply the termination lemma, with dimension as the parameter, some preliminary work is necessary to exhibit the X and S spaces as vector spaces.

If f is the zero-state response of the linear system

$$q(t + 1) = Fq(t) + Gx(t)$$
$$y(t) = Hq(t)$$

then $f(x_1 x_2 \ldots x_n) = \sum_{j=1}^{n} HF^{n-i}Gx_i$ and we see that f has the crucial properties

Stationarity: $f(0\theta) = f(\theta)$ for all θ in X^*
    Linearity: $f(a\theta_1 + b\theta_2) = af(\theta_1) + bf(\theta_2)$

where we have made X^* and each $X^{[0,k)}$ a vector space by decreeing that scalar multiplication is componentwise, and addition is componentwise after the shorter sequence has been made of length equal to the longer by prefixing as many 0's as necessary. Actually, it is not X^* so much as X^*/P which is a vector space, where $\theta_1 P \theta_2$ iff there exist integers k_1 and k_2 such that $0^{k_1}\theta_1 = 0^{k_2}\theta_2$. Similarly, we identify $U^{[0,k)}$ with U^{k-1} by equating θ with $0^{k-1-|\theta|}\theta$. This type of identification is possible precisely when we have a system which satisfies the stationarity condition.

29 EXERCISE: The reader should verify the following:

For any function f satisfying the conditions of linearity and stationarity, the mapping $X^* \to Q_k : \theta \mapsto [\theta]_k$ induces a linear structure on Q_k by $a[\theta_1]_k + b[\theta_2]_k = [a\theta_1 + b\theta_2]_k$, for $0 < k \leq \infty$. Further:

(a) each map $Q_k \longleftarrow Q_{k'}, 0 < k \leq k' \leq \infty$ is linear
(b) each S_k is a subspace of Q_f
(c) Let us note that $[\theta x] = [\theta 0] + [0x]$ but that $[0x] = [x]$ by stationarity. Further, $\beta_f([\theta]) = f(\theta)$ gives a linear map $Q_f \to Y$. Thus f has a linear (but not necessarily finite-dimensional) realization, which we may write

$$\delta_f([\theta], x) = F_f[\theta] + G_f x$$
$$\beta_f([\theta]) = H_f[\theta]$$

where the linear maps are defined by

$$F_f : [\theta] \mapsto [\theta 0]; \qquad G_f : u \mapsto [u]; \qquad \text{and} \qquad H_f : [\theta] \mapsto f(\theta).$$

In the case where the dimension of Q_f is known to be at most N, the termination lemma applies to both the X_j series and the S_j series, in each case with h_j equal to the dimension of the jth term, and H equal to N. The reader may readily verify that if $h_j = 0$ for the X_j series $h_1 \geq 1$; while for the S_j series, $h_1 = 0$. Since $H - h_1 + 1$ now is at most N for the X_j series, and at most $N + 1$ for the S_j series, corollary **25** follows immediately.   □

We have seen that if f has a linear realization of dimension at most N, then $X_f = U^N/E_f^N$. Let us use this to provide an algorithm for obtaining $M(f)$.

30 LEMMA: *If f is linear and stationary, then*

$$\theta_1 E_f^N \theta_2 \iff f(\theta_1 0^n) = f(\theta_2 0^n) \qquad \text{for all } n \text{ with} \qquad 0 \leq n < N$$

(where $\theta_1 0^n$ is the sequence obtained by following θ_1 with a string of n 0's).
    Proof. For any $\theta \in X^*$,

$$f(\theta_1 \theta) = f(\theta_1.0^{|\theta|} + 0^{|\theta_1|}.\theta)$$

—simply by the definition of addition in X^*—where $0^{|\theta|}$ is a string of 0's of length equal to that of θ, etc.,
$$= f(\theta_1.0^{|\theta|}) + f(0^{|\theta|}.0) \text{ by linearity of } f$$
$$= f(\theta_1.0^{|\theta|}) + f(\theta) \text{ by stationarity of } f.$$

Thus $\theta_1 E_f^N \theta_2$ $\iff$ $f(\theta_1.0^{|\theta|}) + f(\theta) = f(\theta_2.0^{|\theta|}) + f(\theta)$ for all $\theta \in X^{[0,N)}$
                    $\iff$ $f(\theta_1.0^n) = f(\theta_2.0^n)$ for all n, with $0 \leq n < N$.   □

Let us now specify that X and Y are K-vector spaces of dimension m and p, respectively, and let it henceforth be guaranteed that dim $X_f \leq N$. Let us call the pN vector

31
$$\langle\theta\rangle = \begin{bmatrix} f(\theta) \\ f(\theta 0) \\ \vdots \\ f(\theta 0^{N-1}) \end{bmatrix}$$

the *full-state vector* of the input sequence θ in X^*. We have shown that two input sequences θ_1 and θ_2 lead us from the zero-state to the same state in the minimal state-space Q_f iff they have the same full-state vector $\langle\theta\rangle$. Thus we may represent Q_f as simply the subspace (of dimension at most N) of K^{pN} spanned by the vectors $\langle\theta\rangle$. Our algorithm will consist of finding a basis for this space, and then expressing F, G and H in terms of this basis. The crucial fact given by Lemma **32** limits the domain of search for this basis:

32   LEMMA: *Let $\{e_1, \ldots, e_m\}$ be a basis for X. Then the space of all full-state vectors $\langle\theta\rangle$ for θ in X^* is spanned by the subset*

$$\langle e_j 0^n\rangle \quad for \quad 1 \leq j \leq m \quad and \quad 0 \leq n < N.$$

Proof. We already know that $\{\langle\theta\rangle | \theta \in X^*\}$ is spanned by $\{\langle\theta\rangle| \;\; |\theta| \leq N\}$ of all full-state vectors given by input sequences of length $<N$. Thus our lemma simply reduces to proving that S_N is spanned by the given vectors. But this is immediate, since by linearity of f, and the definition of $\langle\theta\rangle$, it follows that if

$$\theta = x_1 x_2 \ldots x_N = \sum_j x_{1j} e_j 0^{n-1} + \sum_j x_{2j} e_j 0^{n-2} + \ldots + \sum_j x_{Nj} e_1$$

then
$$\langle\theta\rangle = \sum_j x_{1j}\langle e_j 0^{n-1}\rangle + \sum_j x_{2j}\langle e_j 0^{n-2}\rangle + \ldots + \sum_j x_{Nj}\langle e_j\rangle$$

so that every $\langle\theta\rangle$ is a linear combination of vectors $\langle e_j 0^n\rangle$ for $1 \leq j \leq m$ and $0 \leq n < N$.   □

Thus we obtain a minimal realization as follows:

Select a basis of $n' < N$ vectors for the space spanned by

33 $[\langle e_1\rangle, \ldots, \langle e_m\rangle, \langle e_1 0\rangle, \ldots, \langle e_m 0\rangle, \ldots, \langle e_1 0^{N-1}\rangle, \ldots, \langle e_m 0^{N-1}\rangle]$

Say this basis consists of the vectors $\langle\theta_1\rangle, \ldots, \langle\theta_{n'}\rangle$. Let us write $[\theta]$ for the column vector whose entries are the coefficients of $\langle\theta\rangle$ with respect to the basis $\langle\theta_1\rangle, \ldots, \langle\theta_{n'}\rangle$. As we saw in Exercise **29**, we have

$$\delta_f([\theta], x) = [\theta 0] + [x]$$
$$\beta_f([\theta]) = f(\theta)$$

Let $[\theta] = \sum a_j[\theta_j]$; $\delta_f([\theta], x) = \sum a'_j[\theta_j]$ and $x = \sum x_j e_j$. We use the linearity of $[\theta] \mapsto [\theta 0]$, of $x \mapsto [x]$, and of $[\theta] \mapsto f(\theta)$ to deduce that

$$\sum a_i'[\theta_i] = \sum a_i[\theta_i 0] + \sum u_i[e_i]$$
$$f(\theta) = \sum a_i f(\theta_i)$$

or, in terms of components with respect to the basis

$$\begin{bmatrix} a_1' \\ \cdot \\ \cdot \\ \cdot \\ a_{n'}' \end{bmatrix} = \begin{bmatrix} [\theta_1 0], \ldots, [\theta_{n'} 0] \end{bmatrix} \begin{bmatrix} a_1 \\ \cdot \\ \cdot \\ a_{n'} \end{bmatrix} + \begin{bmatrix} [e_1], \ldots, [e_m] \end{bmatrix} \begin{bmatrix} u_1 \\ \cdot \\ \cdot \\ u_m \end{bmatrix}$$

34

$$\beta_f \left(\begin{bmatrix} a_{1'} \\ \cdot \\ \cdot \\ a_{n'} \end{bmatrix} \right) = \begin{bmatrix} [f(\theta_1), \ldots, f(\theta_{n'})] \end{bmatrix} \begin{bmatrix} a_1 \\ \cdot \\ \cdot \\ a_n \end{bmatrix}$$

Thus with respect to our basis we have the simple formulae:

35
$$G = \begin{bmatrix} [e_1], \ldots, [e_m] \end{bmatrix}$$
$$F = \begin{bmatrix} [\theta_1 0], \ldots, [\theta_{n'} 0] \end{bmatrix}$$
$$H = [f(\theta_1), \ldots, f(\theta_{n'})].$$

Any algorithm for choosing a basis yields an algorithm for finding a "canonical realization" of f—i.e., a version of $M(f)$. One such algorithm follows, but many others can be similarly constructed, and the reader may wish not to read it.

36   ALGORITHM: *Given a linear stationary input/output function* $f: X^* \to Y$*, the matrices* (F, G, H) *of a canonical realization may be computed as follows:*
Fix a basis $e_1, \ldots, e_m$ *of* X*.*
Fix a bound N *on the dimensionality of a canonical realization.*
When $\langle \theta \rangle$ *is required below for any input sequence* θ*, obtain it as the vector*

$$\begin{bmatrix} f(\theta) \\ f(\theta 0) \\ \cdot \\ \cdot \\ \cdot \\ f(\theta 0^{N-1}) \end{bmatrix}$$

e.g., by applying the sequence $\theta 0^{N-1}$ *to a system with external description* f*, started in its zero state, and recording the output vector following upon application of the last* N *elements of this input sequence.*
The algorithm proceeds by the following at most $mN + 2$ *stages:*
STAGE 0: *Set* $k(0) = 0$*.*
STAGE r: $(1 \leq r \leq mN)$*: Let* $r = j + mn$*, with* $1 \leq j \leq m$*. Compute* $\langle e^j 0^n \rangle$*. Is* $\langle e^j 0^n \rangle$

linearly dependent on $\langle\theta_1\rangle, \ldots, \langle0_{k(r-1)}\rangle$? *(If $k(r-1) = 0$, this question is to read: Does $\langle e^i0^n\rangle = \langle0\rangle$?)*

    YES: Set $k(r) = k(r-1)$. Go to Stage $r + 1$.
    NO: Set $k(r) = k(r-1) + 1$.
        Set $\theta_{k(r)} = \langle e^i0^n\rangle$.
        Does $k(r) = N$? YES: Set $k(mN) = N$ and go to Stage $mN + 1$.
                NO: Go to stage $r + 1$.

STAGE $mN + 1$: *Let $n' = k(mN)$. In what follows, for a given θ, let $[\theta]$ be the n'-vector*

$$\begin{bmatrix} a_1 \\ \cdot \\ \cdot \\ \cdot \\ a_{n'} \end{bmatrix}$$

expressing $\langle\theta\rangle$ in terms of the basis

$$\langle\theta_1\rangle, \ldots, \langle\theta_{n'}\rangle, \quad \text{i.e.,} \quad \langle\theta\rangle = \sum_{i=1}^{n'} a_i\langle\theta_i\rangle$$

Given θ, $f(\theta)$ may either be obtained directly, or read off as the first p entries of $\langle\theta\rangle$.

Compute G as $[[e_1], \ldots, [e_m]]$
Compute F as $[[\theta_10], \ldots, [\theta_{n'}0]]$
Compute H as $[f(\theta_1), \ldots, f(\theta_{n'})]$
HALT.

    The algorithm rests on two subroutines—one for telling whether or not a vector is linearly independent of a set of vectors, and another for finding the coefficients of a vector with respect to a basis.

    Presumably, we could use the algorithm to handle *noisy data* by replacing the question

        "Is $\langle e^i0^n\rangle$ linearly dependent on $\langle\theta_1\rangle, \ldots, \langle\theta_{k(r-1)}\rangle$?"

by the question

        "Can $\langle e^i0^n\rangle$ be approximated to within ϵ by linear combinations
               of $\langle\theta_1\rangle, \ldots, \langle\theta_{k(r-1)}\rangle$?"

but the choice of formalization of the phrase "approximated to within ϵ" is a difficult one determined by practical consideration of the problem at hand, and we have no suggestions to make about it.

    Note that the computation of F will fail just in case any one of the vectors $\langle\theta_j0\rangle$ cannot be expressed as a linear combination of the vectors $\langle\theta_1\rangle, \ldots, \langle\theta_{n'}\rangle$ in which case our assumption that dim $X_f < N$ is revealed as false.

    Consider the matrix $A_i = HF^{i-1}G$ corresponding to a realization of the response function f. We easily see that

$$A_i = [f(e_10^{i-1}), f(e_20^{i-1}), \ldots, f(e_m0^{i-1})]$$

It then follows that our crucial matrix **33** can be rewritten in the apparently simple but perhaps misleading form

$$\mathcal{K} = \begin{bmatrix} A_1 & A_2 & \ldots & A_N \\ A_2 & A_3 & \ldots & A_{N+1} \\ \cdot & \cdot & & \\ \cdot & \cdot & & \\ A_N & A_{N+1} & \ldots & A_{2N-1} \end{bmatrix}$$

and the reader may proceed from this observation to a comparison of our algorithm with that given by B. L. Ho (see Ho [1965], ZEIGER [1968a], and KALMAN, FALB and ARBIB [1969, Sec. 10.11]). Our novelty here is more conceptual than computational.

After this excursion into linear system theory, we return to the domain of automata in which X and Y are finite sets. For further information on the construction of minimal automata from external descriptions, see TAL [1964], and GRAY and HARRISON [1966].

37 With a machine $M(f)$, we shall now associate a *semigroup* S_f, namely the collection of transformations of the state set Q_f induced by the input strings to $M(f)$; that is,

$$S_f = \{s: Q_f \to Q_f | \exists x \in X^* \text{ such that } s(q) = \delta(q, x) \text{ for all } q \in Q\}$$

The function $\delta(\circ, x): q \mapsto \delta(q, x)$ will be called the *action* of x on Q_f, and we may speak of S_f as *the semigroup of actions of input sequences* of $M(f)$.

We write $[x]_f$ for the state transformation induced by x. If M is not in reduced form, we associate with it (and some specified starting state q) the semigroup of the reduced machine $M(f)$, where f is just M_q.

We again give a characterization in terms of an equivalence relation ([MYHILL, 1957], [RABIN & SCOTT, 1959]).

38 DEFINITION: *Given a function f:* $X^* \to Y$, *let* $\equiv_f$ *be the equivalence relation (**Myhill Equivalence**) on* X^* *defined by*

$$x \equiv_f x' \Leftrightarrow (\forall y, z \in X^*) [f(yxz) = f(yx'z)]$$

39 $$\Leftrightarrow (\forall y \in X^*) [fL_yL_x = fL_yL_{x'}]$$

40 $\Leftrightarrow$ *the input strings* x *and* x' *induce the same function on* Q_f; *that is,* $[x]_f = [x']_f: Q_f \to Q_f$,
where $([x'']_E) \circ [x]_f = [x''x]_E$.

Note that we write our semigroup as acting on the right.

41 PROPOSITION: $\equiv_f$ *is a congruence.*

Proof. $x \equiv x'$ and $y \equiv y' \Rightarrow (\forall z \in X^*)[fL_zL_{xy} = fL_{zx}L_y = fL_{zx}L_{y'}$
$$= fL_zL_xL_{y'}$$
$$= fL_zL_{x'y'}]$$
$$\Rightarrow xy \equiv x'y'$$

Thus we may define S_f equivalently by

42 DEFINITION: *The semigroup S_f of the function $f: X^* \to Y$ is the factor semigroup $X^*/\equiv_f$.*

Note that $x \equiv_f x' \Rightarrow x \mathrel{E} x'$, but the converse is not necessarily true.

43 PROPOSITION: *Let $M(f)$ have n states and S_f n' elements. Then $n \leq n' \leq n^n$.*
Proof. $n' =$ the index of $\equiv_f \geq$ the index of $E_f = n$.
Since S_f is a subsemigroup of $F_R(Q_f)$, the full transformation semigroup on Q_f,

$$n' \leq \text{the number of functions from } Q_f \text{ to } Q_f = n^n$$

$$\therefore n \leq n' \leq n^n \qquad \qquad \square$$

Analogously to Proposition **7** we thus obtain:

44 PROPOSITION (MYHILL [1957]).
　　(i)　$\equiv_f$ *is a congruence relation.*
　　(ii)　*f is finite-state computable $\Leftrightarrow \equiv_f$ is of finite index.*
　　(iii)　*The index of $\equiv_f$ is the number of state transformations in the semi-group of the minimal machine which computes f.*

45 EXERCISE: Deduce that if there exists a congruence of finite index on X^* such that $R \subset X^*$ is a union of blocks of the congruence, then R is an FSL.

We repeat that the elements of S_f correspond to input sequences regarded as state-transition functions of $M(f)$; composition is consecutive state transformation, and M_f is finite iff S_f is a finite semigroup.

For generalizations of the criterion of Exercise **45** due to O. Kulagina and S. Marcus, see MARCUS [1964, Chap. 3].

46 EXERCISE
　　(i) Show that $n' = n$ for the $M(f)$ with $X = Y$ and $n - 1$ reset inputs, $X = \{x_1, \ldots, x_{n-1}\}$ with $f(zx_k) = x_k$ for all $z \in X^*$ ($f(\Lambda) = x_1$, say).
　　(ii) Show that $n' = n^n$ when we let Y have n elements $\{y_1, \ldots, y_n\}$, X have n^n elements $\{x_1, \ldots, x_{n^n}\}$; label the n^n functions of Y into Y by elements of X, as $g_{x_1}, \ldots, g_{x_{n^n}}$; and define

$$f(\Lambda) = y_1$$
$$f(zx_i) = g_{x_i}(f(x)) \text{ for all } z \in X^*$$

[In fact (PAZ [1962]), we could choose $|X| = 3$ by taking

$c(y_n) = y_1, c(y_k) = y_{k+1} \ (1 \le k < n)$;

$e_{12}(y_j) = y_1$ if $j = 2$, y_2 if $j = 1$, y_j otherwise;

$f_1^2(y_j) = y_1$ if $j = 1$ or 2, y_j otherwise—

since it suffices that the g_x be a set of *generators* for the semigroup of maps of Y into Y.]

47 EXAMPLE: Compute S_{χ_R} for $R = \{0, 01, 01^2, \ldots\}$.

Construction. We shall use our knowledge of Q_f to compute S_f, where $f = \chi_R$, as a set of functions on Q_f.

We saw that the states of $M(\chi_R)$ are $q_0 = [\Lambda]_{E'}$, $q_1 = [0]_E$ and $q_2 = [1]_E$. We now have to further subdivide these classes into new sets such that all the strings in a given subset map Q_f identically. A little trial and error quickly yields the choice $s_0 = q_0$, $s_1 = q_1$, $s_2 = \{1^m\}$, $s_3 = q_2 - s_2$. The functions on Q_f are given by the following table:

	s_0	s_1	s_2	s_3
q_0	q_0	q_1	q_2	q_2
q_1	q_1	q_2	q_1	q_2
q_2	q_2	q_2	q_2	q_2

We thus conclude that $S_{\chi_R} = \{s_0, s_1, s_2, s_3\} = \{[\Lambda], [0], [1], [10]\}$ and has multiplication table

	s_0	s_1	s_2	s_3
s_0	s_0	s_1	s_2	s_3
s_1	s_1	s_3	s_1	s_3
s_2	s_2	s_3	s_2	s_3
s_3	s_3	s_3	s_3	s_3

48 EXAMPLE (MCNAUGHTON, cited in MYHILL [1963a]): Figure 3.32 shows

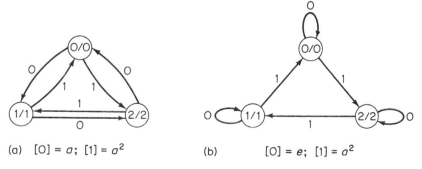

(a) $[0] = \sigma$; $[1] = \sigma^2$ (b) $[0] = e$; $[1] = \sigma^2$

Fig. 3.32

two distinct automata with the same semigroup, namely the cyclic group of order 3: $\{e, a, a^2\}$ with identity $a^3 = e$.

As an application of these ideas, we devote the next few exercises to the question "How do we design automata which are relatively insensitive to errors in their input-sequence?" For further details see WINOGRAD [1962, 1964] and HARRISON [1965]. Let E be a subset of $X^* \times X^*$. We may think of E as *a set of errors* in that if $(w, w') \in E$, and the input sequence intended for the automaton is uwv, then the actual input may be in error $uw'v$.

49   DEFINITION: *An automaton M is said to be **bounded-transient** with regard to E if and only if there exists an integer n such that for all $q \in Q$, for all $(w, w') \in E$, for all $v \in X^*$,*

$$l(v) \geq n \Rightarrow \delta(q, wv) = \delta(q, w'v)$$

The least such integer n is called the length of the transient.

50   EXERCISE: Let $\tilde{E}$ be the closure of E under reflexivity, transivity, and two-sided invariance, and symmetry. Let M be bounded-transient with regard to E, with N as the length of the transient. Then prove that M is also bounded-transient with regard to $\tilde{E}$, with N as the length of the transient.

51   EXERCISE: Show that if $(w, w') \in E$ and $M(f)$ is bounded-transient *wrt* E, with length of transient 0, then $w \equiv_f w'$.

52   EXERCISE: Define the partition E_k on X^* by

$$wE_k w' \qquad \text{iff} \quad (w, w') \in E \quad \text{and} \quad l(v) \geq k \Rightarrow \delta(q, wv) = \delta(q, w'v)$$

Use the nested-partition lemma (**1.29**) to deduce that if M has n states, and is bounded-transient with regard to E, then the length of the transient is less than n.

53   EXERCISE (MEYERS [1965]): For $E \subseteq X^* \times X^*$ and $x \in X$, define

$$E/x = \{(w_1, w_2) \in X^* \times X^* | (w_1 x, w_2 x) \in E\}$$

If $M(f)$ has n states, and for each $t \geq 0$, E_t is the maximal set of errors with respect to which $M(f)$ is bounded-transient with length of transient at most t, then show that

$$
\begin{aligned}
E_0 &= \equiv_f \\
E_t &- \bigcap_{x \in X} E_{t-1}/x \qquad \text{for } 0 < t < n \\
E_t &= E_{n-1} \qquad \text{for } t \geq n
\end{aligned}
$$

We have seen how to go from a machine to a semigroup. We now want to turn our attention to how a semigroup characterizes a machine. (We will devote Chapter 8 to exploring the structure of machines via the structure of semigroups.)

Given a machine $M(f)$, we obtained S_f, a monoid with the equivalence class of the empty string as identity.

54   Conversely, given a monoid S we may obtain a machine

$$M(S) \overset{\text{def}}{=} (S, S, S, \cdot, \cdot)$$

where $\cdot$ denotes multiplication, the *machine of the monoid S*. If $M(S)$ is in state s at time t and receives input s', then its state and output at time $t + 1$ will both be $s \cdot s' \in S$.

If we go from the monoid S_f to the machine $M(S_f)$, in what sense are this machine and the original $M(f)$ the same? *We realize they are not equal on recalling that if n is the number of states of $M(f)$, n' of $M(S_f)$, then $n \leq n' \leq n^n$, and the bounds are attainable.*

We want to find some sense in which a machine and its semigroup are equivalent. To do this we recall the notion of simulation from **2.6**:

We say M *simulates* M' if there exist (h_1, h_2, h_3), where

(i) $h_1: (X')^* \to X^*$ is a monoid homomorphism with $h_1(X') \subset X$
(ii) $h_2: Q' \to Q$
(iii) $h_3: Y \to Y'$

are such that the following diagram is commutative:

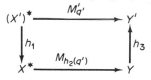

We say that M *weakly simulates* M' if we remove the condition that $h_1(X') \subseteq X$.

*We write $M'|M$ if M simulates M', and read this as M' **divides** M (note changes of order). We say that M and M' are **weakly equivalent** if each weakly simulates the other.*

This definition works whether or not the machines are state-output.

55   EXERCISE: Let M' be *in reduced form*. Then M simulates M' iff there exist (g_1, g_2, g_3), where

(i) $g_1: (X')^* \to X^*$ is a monoid homomorphism with $g_1(X') \subseteq X$;
(ii) g_2 maps a subset Q'' of Q onto Q;

$$Q \supset Q'' \xrightarrow{\ on\ } Q'$$

(iii) $g_3\colon Y \to Y'$

are such that the following diagram is commutative:

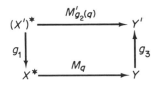

56   EXERCISE

(i)   Show that if M and M' are equivalent, then they are weakly equivalent.
(ii)   Show that if M and M' are reduced and weakly equivalent, then they are isomorphic.
(iii)   Show that $M|M'$ yields a partial order on the set of machines.

In our discussions of semigroups as representing machines, we are interested not only in the transformations from state to state, but also in what the output is. So given the semigroup S_f, we can also specify the function $i_f\colon S_f \to Y$, so that if x takes us from the initial state to the state represented by $s \in S_f$, that is, $s = [x]$, then we must have $i_f(s) = f(x)$. Note that i_f is well defined and depends only on s and *not* the choice of representative x.

If we want to look at a machine in terms of algebra, we form S_f and i_f. Now we want to look at (S_f, i_f) and recapture machine concepts.

57 $M(S_f, i_f)$ is the state-output machine $(S_f, Y, S_f, \cdot, i_f)$, that is, a state-output machine, called *the monoid machine of f*.

58   PROPOSITION: $M(S_f, i_f)$ *is weakly equivalent to* $M(f)$: *In fact*, $M(S_f, i_f)$ *simulates* $M(f)$, *whereas* $M(f)$ *weakly simulates* $M(S_f, i_f)$.

Proof. (i) That $M(S_f, i_f)$ simulates $M(f)$ is immediate from Fig. 3.33, where $j_f\colon X \to S_f\colon x \mapsto [x]_f$ (the Myhill equivalence class).

$$M(S_f, i_f)$$

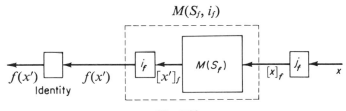

Fig. 3.33

To verify that $M(f)$ weakly simulates $M(S_f, i_f)$ we have to find maps $h_1: S_f^* \to X^*$, $h_2: S_f \to Q_f$, and $h_3: Y \to Y$ such that the diagram

$$
\begin{array}{ccc}
X^* & \xrightarrow{\ M(f)_{h_2(s)}\ } & Y \\[4pt]
{\scriptstyle h_1}\Big\uparrow & & \Big\downarrow{\scriptstyle h_3} \\[4pt]
S_f^* & \xrightarrow{\ M(S_f,\, i_f)_s\ } & Y
\end{array}
$$

commutes.‡ Note that we only required h_1 to be a homomorphism from S_f^* into X^*, not from S_f to X^*.

The obvious choices are an $x \in X^*$ such that $s = [x]_f$ for $h_1(s)$; an fL_x such that $[x]_f = s$ for $h_2(s)$ (this does *not* depend on the choice of x, since $[x]_f = [x']_f \Rightarrow fL_x = fL_{x'}$); and take $h_3(y) = y$. To verify that the diagram commutes for any of the above choices of h_1, we note that

$$
\begin{aligned}
M(S_f, i_f)_s(s') &= i_f(ss') = f(h_1(ss')) \\
&= f(h_1(s)h_1(s')) \\
&= M(f)_{[h_1(s)]_s}(h_1(s')) \\
&= M(f)_{h_2(s)}(h_1(s')) \qquad\qquad \square
\end{aligned}
$$

Now that we have established weak equivalence between $M(S_f, i_f)$ and $M(f)$, we want to see whether machine concepts can be transferred to algebraic objects. Here we shall content ourselves with exploring the algebraic counterpart of simulation.

59 DEFINITION: *We say a semigroup S' **divides** a semigroup S iff $\exists$ a subsemigroup S'' of S' and a homomorphism Z of S'' onto S':*

$$
S'|S \quad\Leftrightarrow\quad S \supset S'' \xrightarrow{Z} S'
$$

*If $i': S' \to Y'$ and $i: S \to Y$, then we say that (S', i') **divides** (S, i) iff, in addition, there is a map $H: Y \to Y'$ such that $i'(Z(s)) = H(i(s))$ for all s in S''.*

$$
(S', i')|(S, i) \quad\Leftrightarrow\quad
\begin{array}{ccc}
S \supseteq S'' & \xrightarrow{Z} & S' \\[2pt]
{\scriptstyle i|S''}\Big\downarrow & & \Big\downarrow{\scriptstyle i'} \\[2pt]
Y & \longrightarrow & H'
\end{array}
\quad commutes
$$

60 DEFINITION: *We write $f'|f$ and say that f' **divides** f if $M(f)$ weakly*

---

‡ Here is a case in which, in general, M' is not reduced, and we *cannot* find an h_2' to satisfy the criterion of exercise **55**.

simulates $M(f')$ with the state f of $M(f)$ simulating the state f' of $M(f')$. That is, iff there exist $h: (X')^* \to X^*$ and $H: Y \to Y'$ such that $f' = Hfh$.

To check that the machine concepts and the algebraic concepts mesh, we prove

61 THEOREM $f'|f \Leftrightarrow (S_{f'}, i_{f'})|(S_f, i_f)$

Proof. (i) If $f'|f$, we have a commutative diagram.

62

$$
\begin{array}{ccc}
X^* & \xrightarrow{f} & Y \\
h\uparrow & & \downarrow H \\
(X')^* & \xrightarrow{f'} & Y'
\end{array}
$$

for suitable choice of h, H, and x.

Our task is to find $S'' \subset S_f$ and a map Z such that

63

$$
\begin{array}{ccc}
X^*/\equiv_f \supset S'' & \xrightarrow{i_f|S''} & Y \\
Z\downarrow & & \downarrow H \\
(X')/\equiv_{f'} = S_{f'} & \xrightarrow{i_{f'}} & Y'
\end{array}
$$

Inspection of the diagrams suggests that Z should be in some sense the "inverse" of h. Clearly, this can only be defined on $h((X')^*)/\equiv_f$, which we take for S''. We then define

$$Z([h(x')]_f) \qquad \text{to be} \qquad [x']_{f'}$$

We must check that this is well defined, i.e., that

$$h(x_1) \equiv_f h(x_2) \Rightarrow x_1 \equiv_{f'} x_2$$

This is true, since for all y and z,

$$
\begin{aligned}
f'(yx_1z) &= Hfh(yx_1z) \\
&= Hf(h(y)h(x_1)h(z)) \\
&= Hf(h(y)h(x_2)h(z)) \qquad \text{since} \quad h(x_1) \equiv_f h(x_2) \\
&= Hfh(yx_2z) \\
&= f'(yx_2z)
\end{aligned}
$$

Clearly Z is onto and a homomorphism, and we may easily check that the above diagram **63** commutes.

(ii) Conversely, given that diagram **63** commutes, we must choose h so that diagram **62** commutes. The choice should now be clear—for each $x' \in X'$, choose $h(x')$ to be some $t \in X^*$ such that $Z([t]_f) = [x']_{f'}$. At least one such t exists, since Z is onto. Then **62** commutes, since

$$Hfh(x') = H(i_f([h(x)]_f))$$
$$= i_{f'}(Z([h(x')]_f))$$
$$= i_{f'}([x']_{f'})$$
$$= f'(x') \qquad \qquad \square$$

64 EXERCISE: Prove that $f'|f \Rightarrow M(f')|M(f)$, but that the converse is false.

65 EXERCISE: Let $f: X^* \to Y$ be such that $M(f)$ is a finite-state machine. Prove that for any $x \in X^*$, we have $S_{fL_x}|S_f$. (Note that L_x is *not* a homomorphism.)

66 EXERCISE: Consider the two statements
   (i) $M(fL_x) = M(f)$—that is, the function sets $\{fL_xL_{x'}|x' \in X^*\}$ and $\{fL_{x'}|x' \in X^*\}$ are identical.
   (ii) $S_{fL_x} = S_f$
Prove, or give counterexamples to, the claims that (i) $\Rightarrow$ (ii) and (ii) $\Rightarrow$ (i).

We close with theorems that firmly link FSLs with the monoid approach.

67 THEOREM *Let $R \subset X^*$. Then R is a regular set iff there exists a homomorphism $\varphi: X^* \twoheadrightarrow S$ of X^* onto a finite monoid S such that*

$$\varphi^{-1}\varphi R = R$$

Proof. If $\varphi^{-1}\varphi R = R$, then there is a subset R' of S such that $R = \varphi^{-1}R'$ (namely $R' = \varphi R$). Thus R is accepted by $M(S, i)$, where $i(s) = 1$ just in case $s \in R'$.

Conversely, if $R = f^{-1}(y)$ where f is finite-state computable so that S_f is finite, it is clear that we may take $S = S_f$ and φ the canonical epimorphism: $x \to [x]_f$, for then

$$\varphi R = \{[x]_f | f(x) = y\}$$

and

$$\varphi^{-1}\varphi R = f^{-1}(y) = R \qquad \qquad \square$$

Let us recall the following notions from semigroup theory (Section **2.3**):

A semigroup S is *finitely generated* if there is a finite set X which generates $S: \langle X \rangle = S$; that is, $X \subset S$ and every $s \in S$ can be written as a finite product $x_{i_1}x_{i_2} \ldots x_{i_n}$ with each $x_{i_j} \in X$.

A semigroup S is *free* if there is a (not necessarily finite) set X which not only generates S but has the property that if

$$x_{i_1}x_{i_2} \ldots x_{i_n} = x_{j_1}x_{j_2} \ldots x_{j_m} \qquad \text{each} \qquad x_{i_r}, x_{j_s} \in X$$

then $m = n$, and $x_{i_k} = x_{j_k}$ for each k, $1 \le k \le m$.

A *congruence* on a semigroup is a partition on S with the property that $x \equiv x'$

and $y \equiv y'$ implies $xy \equiv x'y'$. Equivalently, a partition is a congruence iff it is induced by a homomorphism φ of S onto a semigroup S': $x \equiv x'$ iff $\varphi(x) = \varphi(x')$. We shall say that it is a finite congruence if the congruence is of finite index.

Thus Theorem **67** simply says that a subset of X^* is an FSL iff it is a union of blocks of a finite congruence. Thus the Kleene theorems (**3.21** and **3.22**) may be rephrased as follows:

68   THEOREM: *Let S be a finitely generated free semigroup. Then:*

(i) *Every union of blocks of a finite congruence on S is a regular subset of S.*
(ii) *Let E and F be unions of blocks of finite congruences on S. Then $E \cup F$, $E \cdot F$, and $\langle E \rangle$ are all unions of blocks of finite congruences on S.*   □

The mathematician naturally asks: "Do these results extend to semigroups other than those which are both free and finitely generated?" The following partial answer is due to McKNIGHT [1964]—the reader may wish to discover further generalizations for himself.

69   THEOREM: (i) *If S is a finitely generated semigroup, then every union of blocks of a finite congruence on S is a regular subset of S.*

(ii) *If S is a free semigroup, and E and F are unions of blocks of finite congruences on S, then $E \cup F$, $E \cdot F$, and $\langle E \rangle$ are also unions of blocks of finite congruences on S.* We omit the proof, merely giving the result to indicate another way in which automata theory suggests new questions for the mathematician to study.

The semigroup approach to automata will be taken up again, in much more detail, in Chapter 8.

4

TURING MACHINES AND
EFFECTIVE COMPUTATIONS

Any effective computation, mapping strings of symbols to strings of symbols, can be carried out by a Turing machine. This is Turing's hypothesis or Church's thesis. It is our task to substantiate this claim in this chapter. Since mathematics can only prove identity between formalized notions, we cannot *prove* Turing's hypothesis—what we can do is show that the notion of computability by a Turing machine embraces so many other notions of computability that we "confirm" Turing's hypothesis by induction. It is probably fair to say that today no one really doubts that any effective computation may be carried out by a Turing machine (and we shall make use of this in the sequel by outlining effective procedures when a formal proof really demands specification of a Turing machine). The real doubts may be put the other way around—perhaps *too many* functions are Turing-computable. Can we really say a function is effectively computable when a Turing machine which computes it, even if it executes a thousand steps every microsecond, will take three times the lifetime of the universe to compute even a single answer? It is for this reason that much research is now devoted to studying not only what can be done by Turing machines, but also how long they, or other computing structures, take to produce their answers. It is to these questions of complexity of computation that we shall turn in Chapter 7, but here our task is to chart the limits of the possibly computable, to provide the general framework for any studies of the practicably computable.

125

For further reading on the classical theory of computability, see the textbooks of KLEENE [1952] and DAVIS [1958], and the lucid articles of POST [1944] and ROGERS [1959]; for a treatment of the nonmachine theory of computability, especially the study of unsolvability structures, and (to a lesser extent) logic and foundations, see the textbook of ROGERS [1967].

4.1   AN EFFECTIVE ENUMERATION OF TURING MACHINES

In Chapter 1, we captured the essential flavor of the Turing machine as a finite-state device which operates on a tape on which is printed a string of symbols, by scanning a symbol at a time, and then on the basis of this symbol and its own internal state, either halting its computation, or else carrying out the following three stages to complete a step of the computation: change the scanned symbol, move at most one square along the tape, and change the internal state. Thus, for each state-symbol pair $q_i x_j$ we must specify a triple $x_k m q_l$, where x_k is the new symbol, m is the move, and q_l is the new state. If we do not specify such a triple, then we signify that $q_i x_j$ is a halting situation.

Let us use this discussion to establish a more formal definition of a Turing machine:

1   DEFINITION: *A Turing Machine Z is a quadruple* (Q, X_b, P, q_0), *where*

> Q *is a finite set* (*the set of* **states**)
>
> X_b *is a finite set* (*the set of* **tape symbols,** *one member of which is designated the* **blank** *and denoted b—we set* $X = X_b - \{b\}$)
>
> P *is a subset of* $Q \times X \times X \times \{-, 0, +\} \times Q$, *the set of* **quintuples** *of Z, and has the properties that no two quintuples of Z have the same first two members*
>
> $q_0 \in Q$ *is the* **initial state.**

Now the configuration of a Turing Machine (henceforth TM) at any time is specified by giving the string of symbols on its tape, the position of the head, and the state of the machine. If the string is $\xi\eta$ ($\xi, \eta \in X_b^*$), and Z is in state q, scanning the leftmost symbol of η, we may succinctly summarize this information in the *instantaneous description* (ID) $\xi q\eta$. Thus the IDs are simply elements of $X_b^* Q X_b^*$. We may now introduce the relation $\vdash$ between IDs which holds when the second ID describes the configuration obtained in one step from that described by the first ID.

2   DEFINITION: *Let* $Z = (Q, X_b, P, q_0)$ *be a TM. The relation* $\vdash_{\overline{Z}}$ (*or* $\vdash$, *for short*) *is defined by the following:*

$$\xi qx\eta \vdash \xi q'x'\eta \qquad \text{if } qxx'0q' \in P$$
$$\xi q \vdash \xi q'x' \qquad \text{if } qbx'0q' \in P$$

$$\xi qx\eta \vdash \xi x'q'\eta \qquad \text{if } qxx' + q' \in P$$
$$\xi q \vdash \xi x'q' \qquad \text{if } qbx' + q' \in P$$

$$\left.\begin{array}{l} \xi \hat{x}qx\eta \vdash \xi q'\hat{x}x'\eta \\ qx\eta \vdash q'bx'\eta \end{array}\right\} \quad \text{if } qxx' - q' \in P$$

$$\left.\begin{array}{l} \xi \hat{x}q \vdash \xi q'\hat{x}x' \\ q \vdash q'bx' \end{array}\right\} \quad \text{if } qbx' - q' \in P$$

A computation of Z results when Z is started in its initial state scanning the leftmost square of a string of X_b^*—if and when it halts, the result is the string on the tape:

3 DEFINITION: *A computation of the* TM *Z is a finite sequence*

$$z_0, z_1, z_2, \ldots, z_m$$

*of IDs of z such that z_0 is an **initial** ID, that is, $z_0 \in q_0 X_b^*$; z_m is a **terminal** ID, that is, if $z_m = \xi qx\eta$ (respectively ξq), then no quintuple in P starts with qx (respectively qb); and $z_j \underset{Z}{\vdash} z_{j+1}$ for $0 \le j < m$.*

If we start Z in an initial configuration z_0, then either Z will eventually stop—in which case z_0 uniquely defines the computation of which it is the first element—or Z will never stop, in which case Z has no computation of which z_0 is the first element. Thus we may unambiguously define:

4 DEFINITION: *The function $F_Z^b \colon X_b^* \to X_b^*$ is defined by the equation*

$$F_Z^b(\theta) = \begin{cases} \xi\eta & \text{if there is a computation of } Z \text{ with initial ID} \\ & q_0\theta \text{ and terminal ID } \xi q\eta \text{ for some } q \in Q \\ \text{undefined} & \text{if there is no computation of } Z \\ & \text{with initial ID } q_0\theta \end{cases}$$

We may obtain functions on X^* by "cutting down" F_Z^b (recall that $X_b - b = X$). We present strings of X^* to Z, separated by blanks. If Z halts with a string of X^* printed on an otherwise blank tape, we let that string be the result of the computation:

5 DEFINITION: *The function $F_Z^n \colon (X^*)^n \to X^*$ is defined as follows:*

$$F_Z^n(\xi_1, \xi_2, \ldots, \xi_n) = \begin{cases} \eta & \text{if } \eta \in X^* \text{ and } F_Z^b(\xi_1 b\xi_2 b \ldots b\xi_n) = \alpha\eta\beta \\ & \text{with } \alpha \text{ and } \beta \text{ in } \{b\}^* \\ \text{undefined} & \text{if no such } \eta \text{ exists} \end{cases}$$

6 DEFINITION: *A function* $f: (X^*)^n \to X^*$ *is* (*partial*) **TM-computable** *just in case there exists a* TM Z *such that* $f = F_Z^n$. *We say* f *is* **total** *if it is defined for all elements of* $(X^*)^n$.

Thus the word *partial* reminds us that the function need not be defined for all its values. We use the word *total* if we wish to emphasize that a function is always defined—to say that a function is partial does *not* imply that it is sometimes undefined, only that it *may* sometimes be undefined. As mathematicians find it convenient to consider linear problems as a *subclass* of nonlinear problems, so do we find it convenient to consider the total functions as a subclass of the partial functions. Note, too, the result of the following:

7 EXERCISE: Construct a Turing machine Z such that F_Z^2 is a total TM-computable function, but such that F_Z^5 is *not* always defined.

8 EXAMPLE: We now give an example of programming a Turing machine to do a specific task. We construct a Z, with input alphabet $X = \{0, 1, b\}$ and states $\{q_0, q_1, q_2, q_3, q_4, q_5, q_6, q_7, q_8, q_s\}$, where b is the blank and q_s is the stop state; i.e., no quintuple starts with q_s.

Then we define the behavior of Z, just for strings which contain no blank (that is, $x \in \{0, 1\}^*$) as follows:

$$F_Z^1(x) = \begin{cases} 1 & \text{if} \quad x = 0^n 1 \quad 0^n \text{ for some } n \\ 0 & \text{if} \quad \text{not} \end{cases}$$

Z goes back and forth from one end of x to the other, deleting 0's, until there are no more pairs of 0's; thus successive snapshots taken of the tape each time Z has moved to a blank delimiting one end or the other might look (blanks being left blank!) like this:

$$0011000$$
$$011000$$
$$01100$$
$$1100$$
$$110$$

When it has completed the reduction

$$x = 0^m \tilde{x}\, 0^m \to \tilde{x} \qquad (\tilde{x} \neq 0\, x'0)$$

Z tests to see whether $\tilde{x}$ is 1. If it is, Z stops. If it isn't, Z deletes $\tilde{x}$, prints a 0, and then halts.

Having explained the operation of Z, we invite the reader to check the detailed operation of the quintuples.‡

---

‡ In this and following examples, we shall use $\{L, R, N\}$ in place of $\{-, 0, +\}$ as a mnemonic aid.

(i) If string is 0^m, $m \geq 0$, go to q_8, output is 0. In any case, delete left-most 0.

$$q_0 \ b \ b \ L \ q_8$$
$$q_0 \ 0 \ b \ R \ q_1$$
$$q_1 \ 0 \ 0 \ R \ q_1$$
$$q_1 \ 1 \ 1 \ R \ q_2$$
$$q_1 \ b \ b \ L \ q_8$$

(ii) If not, go to end of string.

$$q_2 \ 0 \ 0 \ R \ q_2$$
$$q_2 \ 1 \ 1 \ R \ q_2$$
$$q_2 \ b \ b \ L \ q_3$$

(iii) If 0 at rightmost end, delete it, return to leftmost end, and repeat process.

$$q_3 \ 0 \ b \ L \ q_4$$
$$q_4 \ 0 \ 0 \ L \ q_4$$
$$q_4 \ 1 \ 1 \ L \ q_4$$
$$q_4 \ b \ b \ R \ q_0$$

(iv) If no 0 at rightmost end, go to state q_8, and stop with 0 on tape.

$$q_3 \ 1 \ b \ L \ q_8$$
$$q_8 \ 0 \ b \ L \ q_8$$
$$q_8 \ 1 \ b \ L \ q_8$$
$$q_8 \ b \ 0 \ N \ q_s$$

(v) If 1 at leftmost end is whole string, stop; if not, go to q_6 and stop with 0 on tape.

$$q_0 \ 1 \ 1 \ R \ q_5$$
$$q_5 \ 0 \ 0 \ L \ q_6$$
$$q_5 \ 1 \ 1 \ L \ q_6$$
$$q_5 \ b \ b \ N \ q_s$$
$$q_6 \ 1 \ 0 \ R \ q_7$$
$$q_7 \ 1 \ b \ R \ q_7$$
$$q_7 \ 0 \ b \ R \ q_7$$

9 EXERCISE: One quintuple is superfluous. What is it? Why?

10 EXERCISE: Write an alternative program for a TM which computes the same function, but which will halt with output 0 if after its first scan it finds that there is not exactly one 1 on its tape.

11   EXAMPLE: (This example is to remind us that we *may* interpret the string processing of our automaton as numerical processing.) Code the number m as $\langle m \rangle$, a string of 1's and 2's, where

$$\langle m \rangle = i_1 \ldots i_n \Leftrightarrow m = \sum_{j=1}^{n} i_j 2^{n-j}$$

thus

$$111 = \langle 7 \rangle$$
$$1211 = \langle 19 \rangle$$

We do not use the usual binary coding, since it does not provide a unique string for each number—for example, $001 = 1$ in binary.

Write down the codes for 14 and 38. Use this to give an informal description of how to form $\langle 2m \rangle$ from $\langle m \rangle$. Note that numbers coded as a string of 1's alone require special treatment.

Write a program for a Turing machine with alphabet $\{b, 1, 2\}$ which if started with just $\langle m \rangle$ written on its tape and scanning the *rightmost* square, in state q_0, will eventually halt with $\langle 2m \rangle$ on its tape.

Solution.

$$\langle 7 \rangle = 111$$
$$14 = 2(4 + 2 + 1) \quad \therefore \ \langle 14 \rangle = 222$$
$$\langle 19 \rangle = 1211$$
$$38 = 16 + 8 + 8 + 4 + 2 = 1 \times 16 + 1 \times 8 + 2 \times 4 + 2 \times 2 + 2 \times 1$$
$$\therefore \ \langle 38 \rangle = 11222$$

Informal description of multiplication by 2. We must change $\sum i_j 2^{n-j}$ into $\sum i_j 2^{n-j+1}$. But $\langle m \rangle 0$ is an illegal expression, so we change the 0 to a 2 by "borrowing" one from the next column to the left. If that is a 2, we change it to 1 and stop. If it is a 1, we cannot write 0, so we put 2 and repeat the process. If the string is all 1's, we simply cancel the final 1 to get the correct answer. Thus in multiplying 7 by 2 we would get the configuration

$$111b, \ 11b2, \ 1b22, \ b222$$

and in multiplying 19 by 2 we would get the configurations

$$1211b, \ 121b2, \ 12b22, \ 11222.$$

Note that $\langle 2m \rangle = \langle m - 1 \rangle \cdot 2\ddagger$—so the above procedure, apart from placing the initial 2, is just subtraction of one. We readily see that this procedure is carried out by the Turing machine.

---

‡ Concatenation of 2, *not* multiplication.

$$q_0 \ 1 \ 1 \ R \ q_1$$
$$q_0 \ 2 \ 2 \ R \ q_1$$
$$q_1 \ b \ 2 \ L \ q_2$$
$$q_2 \ 1 \ 2 \ L \ q_2$$
$$q_2 \ 2 \ 1 \ N \ q_3$$
$$q_2 \ b \ b \ R \ q_4$$
$$q_4 \ 2 \ b \ N \ q_3$$

Note that this handles $m = 0$ (the empty string) correctly.

An alternative approach is to actually implement bit-by-bit addition. Note that in this arithmetic we may carry 0, 1, or 2. We need only observe here the rules

$$1 + 1 = 2$$
$$2 + 2 = 2, \text{ carry } 1$$
$$1 + 1 + 1 = 1, \text{ carry } 1$$
$$1 + 2 + 2 = 1, \text{ carry } 2$$
$$2 + 1 + 1 = 2, \text{ carry } 1$$
$$2 + 2 + 2 = 2, \text{ carry } 2$$

Then our multiply machine is to have three states, q_0, q_1, q_2 corresponding to the carry digit. The machine starts in state q_0 on the rightmost square, and proceeds according to the quintuples

$$q_0 \ 1 \ 2 \ L \ q_0$$
$$q_0 \ 2 \ 2 \ L \ q_1$$
$$q_1 \ b \ 1 \ L \ q_0$$
$$q_1 \ 1 \ 1 \ L \ q_1$$
$$q_1 \ 2 \ 1 \ L \ q_2$$
$$q_2 \ b \ 2 \ L \ q_0$$
$$q_2 \ 1 \ 2 \ L \ q_1$$
$$q_2 \ 2 \ 2 \ L \ q_2$$

12 EXERCISE: Using the techniques of the last part of the above solution, program a Turing machine which, if started in state q_0, scanning the leftmost symbol of the string $\langle m \rangle \ b \ \langle n \rangle$, will finally halt with the string $\langle m + n \rangle$ on the tape.

13 EXERCISE: Find a Turing machine Z with input alphabet $\{0, 1, 2, b\}$ such that

$$F_Z(x) = \begin{cases} 1 & \text{if } x \text{ is a string of } n^2 \text{ ones, for some } n \\ 0 & \text{if } x \text{ is a string of } m \text{ ones, } m \neq n^2, \text{ any } n \end{cases}$$

and we shall not worry about the value for strings not in $\{1\}*$. [Hint: If one notes the equalities $(n + 1)^2 = n^2 + 2n + 1$, $2n + 1 = (2(n - 1) + 2$, one can find a machine with 12 states which will do this task. A better trick, or slicker programming, may well lower this figure.]

Now that these examples have extended our feel for the utility of lists of quintuples for describing Turing machines, we shall show how to enumerate these lists, and in an effective way, so that given an integer n, we may effectively find our nth TM—and given a TM we may effectively find n, its position in the enumeration.

14   Let us always code the states of a TM as $q_0, q_1, \ldots, q_{m-1}$ and the inputs as $x_0, x_1, \ldots, x_{n-1}$ (with $x_0 = b$) and call the maximum of m and n the *degree* of the TM. Note that there are only finitely many TMs of a given degree.

We represent a TM of degree n by the ordered list of its quintuples—the ordering being such that $q_i x_j \ldots$ precedes $q_i x_k \ldots$ if $j < k$, and $q_i \ldots$ precedes $q_j \ldots$ if $i < j$. We may then arrange the TMs of degree n in "dictionary" order by considering the list of their quintuples as words on an appropriate alphabet.

15   Finally, by placing first the automata of degree 1, then those of degree 2, . . . we have an *effective enumeration*

$$Z_1, Z_2, Z_3, \ldots, Z_n, Z_{n+1}, \ldots$$

in which each Turing machine (represented by its list of quintuples) appears.

In **15** I have used the notion of effective enumeration only in the informal sense. However, the reader should note that if we identify a TM with its list of quintuples as printed in some finite alphabet, then it will be possible to program a TM which could go from a list of quintuples to the n (in binary notion, say) that encodes it, and, conversely, to program another TM which would convert n into the list of quintuples that it encodes.

Some readers may prefer to see a more explicit scheme for effectively enumerating the Turing machines.

Let us code x_j as the string $x\langle j\rangle_{10}$, where $\langle j\rangle_{10}$ is the number j written out in base ten with the high-order digit nonzero (but with $\langle 0\rangle_{10} = 0$). Similarly, code q_k as $q\langle k\rangle_{10}$. A typical quintuple might then be coded as $q1\ x\ 7\ x\ 13\ L\ q2$.

We then replace a list of quintuples by the string of coded-up quintuples so arranged that the $q_i x_j$ quintuple precedes the $q_k x_l$ quintuple if $i < k$, or if $i = k$, but $j < l$, successive quintuples being separated by semicolons. Thus the list

$$q_0\ x_1\ x_2\ L\ q_0$$
$$q_0\ x_2\ x_1\ R\ q_1$$
$$q_1\ x_0\ x_2\ N\ q_2$$
$$q_1\ x_2\ x_2\ R\ q_1$$

becomes $q0x1x2Lq0; q0x2x1Rq1; q1x0x2Nq2; q1x2x2Rq1$

Now notice that the only symbols we have used in our encoding are 0, 1, 2, 3, 4, 5, 6, 7, 8, 9, q, x, R, L, N, and ;. Since there are 16 symbols, we may regard this list of quintuples as a number written to the base 16.

16   Thus we have given an effective procedure for going from a Turing machine (once we have labeled the inputs and states appropriately) to a number. Given a Turing machine Z, we shall call the number so obtained its *description number*, $DN(Z)$.

Now we must verify that we can reverse the process. It is clear that most numbers cannot be obtained as description numbers of a Turing machine. Thus let us associate *every* number which is not of the form $DN(Z)$ with the trivial machine $Z_\emptyset$, which has one input and one state, and sits there—its list of quintuples is $q_0 x_0 x_0 N q_0$.

Now given a number to radix 16, we scan it from left to right. If it does not break up into a sequence of quintuples, arranged in proper order, and separated by semicolons, we stop with $Z_\emptyset$ the result of our computation. If the decoded number does break up into a sequence of quintuples, arranged in proper order, and separated by semicolons, our output is the Turing machine Z described by that list of quintuples and such that if m is the largest index j of an x_j in that list, and n is the largest index k of a q_k in that list, then Z has input alphabet $\{x_0, \ldots, x_m\}$ and set of states $\{q_0, \ldots, q_n\}$.

Thus we have an effective procedure for retrieving Z from the number $DN(Z)$.

17   We have specified two distinct ways of enumerating all the Turing machines in a list

$$Z_1, Z_2, Z_3, \ldots, Z_n, \ldots$$

such that *given Z we can effectively find that n for which $Z = Z_n$, and given n we can effectively find Z_n.*

There are many other such effective enumerations, different ones being more convenient for different purposes. However, we shall find that for general theoretical inquiries, all these enumerations are equally effective (!) and that for nearly all our studies it will suffice to know that an enumeration is effective, without bothering to specify the specific details of the encoding of TMs (lists of quintuples) as numbers.

Note that we may equally well effectively enumerate the TMs with a fixed tape alphabet $X_b = X \cup \{b\}$.

We shall now show how numerical functions may be computed by Turing machines. We shall say the string $x_1 \ldots x_n \in \{1, 2, \ldots, k\}^*$ is the k-adic encoding of $m \in N$ (recall that $N = \{0, 1, 2, 3, \ldots\}$) and write $\langle m \rangle_k = x_1 \ldots x_n$ iff $m = \sum_1^n x_j k^{j-1}$—and so $\langle 0 \rangle_k = \Lambda$. Compare this with the k-ary encoding: $\langle m \rangle_k = x_1 \ldots x_n$ with each $x_j \in \{0, 1, \ldots, k-1\}$ iff $m = \sum_1^n x_j k^{j-1}$ and $\langle 0 \rangle_k = 0 = 00 = 00 \ldots 0$.

18 DEFINITION: *A numerical function f: $N^n \to N$ is **TM-computable to radix** k iff there exists a Turing machine Z with alphabet $\{b, 1, 2, \ldots, k\}$ such that*

$$F^n(\langle m_1 \rangle_k, \ldots, \langle m_n \rangle_k) = \langle f(m_1, \ldots, m_n) \rangle_k$$

(it being understood that if either side of the equation is undefined, then both sides are).

19 EXERCISE: Prove (at least in outline) that it would not have mattered in the above definition if we had used k-ary instead of k-adic encoding.

We shall see in Chapter 6 that, in fact, a numerical function f is TM-computable to radix k ($k \geq 1$) iff it is TM-computable to radix 1. Thus we may drop the qualifying phrase "to radix k" and simply speak of a numerical function as TM-computable. In fact, the choice of coding of numbers is irrelevant so long as it is effective—for instance, it may be proved that a numerical function is (partial) TM-computable iff there exists a TM Z such that

$$f(n) = \text{the number of 1's in the string } F_Z^b(b^n 1)$$

We close this section with a result that relates our enumeration of Turing machines to our discussion of numerical functions:

20 THEOREM: *There is no total TM-computable numerical function g such that a partial TM-computable function is total iff it equals the function $F_{g(n)}^1$ computed by $Z_{g(n)}$ for some n.*

Proof outline. In this proof we shall make use of our notion that if we can outline an effective procedure for computing a function, then in fact it is TM-computable. The reader who feels this unreasonable may return and fill in the details after he has read the next two or three sections.

Let us interpret each F_n^1 (that is, $F_{Z_n}^1$) as a numerical function computed to a suitable radix. If g is a total TM-computable function, then the following is an effective procedure for computing a *total* numerical function—given n, compute $g(n)$, then find $Z_{g(n)}$ and use it to compute $F_{g(n)}^1(n)$, and then add one to this result.

Thus if $F_{g(n)}^1$ is *total* for every n, then we conclude that

$$h(n) = F_{g(n)}^1(n) + 1$$

is a total TM-computable function. But it cannot equal $F_{g(n_0)}^1$ for any n_0, for then we would have the contradiction $h(n_0) = F_{g(n_0)}^1(n_0) = F_{g(n_0)}^1(n_0) + 1$. Thus we conclude that for any total TM-computable function g, the enumeration $F_{g(0)}^1, F_{g(1)}^1, F_{g(2)}^1, \ldots$ cannot contain all and only the total functions. $\square$

4.2   GENERALIZED TURING MACHINES

The purpose of this section is to strengthen the reader's intuition that for every effective procedure for transforming input strings to output strings, there exists a Turing machine which can implement it. We shall do this by showing how computations, implementable by a host of apparently more complicated automata, can be reduced to Turing machine computations. But first we shall show that any Turing machine can be simulated by simpler devices. At this level of discussion we shall not bother to formalize the notion of simulation we have in mind—rather we shall delimit it by example.

1   THEOREM (SHANNON [1956])

(i) *Any Turing machine can be simulated by a two-state Turing machine with more symbols.*

(ii) *Any Turing machine can be simulated by a two-symbol Turing machine with more states.*

Proof of (i). Given an arbitrary Turing machine A with m tape symbols (including the blank) and n internal states, we design a machine B with two internal states and $4mn + m$ tape symbols. Machine B will act essentially like A, with identical tape configurations, save that the square under scan by A and one of those adjacent to it, will bear extra information for B, pertaining to A's current state.

Let A have symbols $x_1, \ldots, x_m$ and states $q_1, \ldots, q_n$. Then B will have two states α and β and $4nm + n$ symbols, and m of the symbols will be simply $x_1, \ldots, x_m$. In addition, $4mn$ new symbols $B_{i,j,x,y}$ correspond to state-symbol pairs of A together with two new 2-valued indices: $i(= 1, 2, \ldots, m)$ corresponds to the symbols, $j(= 1, 2, \ldots, n)$ corresponds to the states, $x = +$ or $-$ (relating to whether the square was last scanned or is to be next scanned in the operation of A which is being simulated) and $y = R$ or L (relating to whether A was to move R or L in the operation being simulated).

At the end of a cycle of the simulation in which A changes to state q_i and scans symbol x_j, the tape of B will be the same as that of A, save that the square under scan will contain either $B_{i,j,-,R}$ or $B_{i,j,-,L}$ and the state of B will be α.

To simulate a quintuple of the form $q_i x_j x_k N q_l$ is simplicity itself—we give B the quintuple

$$\alpha B_{i,j,-,y} B_{l,k,-,y} N \alpha$$

and the step is properly executed.

If A has the quintuple

$$q_i x_j x_k L q_l \qquad \text{or} \qquad q_i x_j x_k R q_l$$

we equip B with the quintuple

$$\alpha B_{i,j,-,y} B_{l,k,+,L} L\beta \qquad \text{or} \qquad \alpha B_{i,j,-,y} B_{l,k,+,R} R\alpha$$

respectively. The state β (respectively α) indicates that the state information must be transferred one square to the left (respectively right). In the symbol $B_{l,k,+,y}$, the k indicates the symbol information to be retained on the scanned square, the l indicates the state information to be transferred, the $+$ indicates that information is to be transferred *from* the square, and the y indicates the direction of transfer. We wish to reduce this symbol to x_k; and, if the square in direction y initially contains x_r, to build up there the symbol $B_{l,r,-,y'}$. This is done by bouncing the head in state β back and forth between the two squares, decreasing the state in the $+$ square by 1 at each step, and increasing the state in the $-$ by 1 at each step. The reader may easily check that the following quintuples for B ensure the successful completion of the stage of the simulation:

Moving to an x_i square in state α (respectively β), record the fact that the state information is to the right (respectively left):

$$\alpha x_i B_{1,i,-,L} L\alpha \qquad (i = 1, 2, \ldots, m)$$
$$\beta x_i B_{1,i,-,R} R\beta \qquad (i = 1, 2, \ldots, m)$$

We now bounce back and forth in state β till we remove all this information in the old square, at which stage we restore the appropriate tape symbol:

$$\beta B_{j-1,1,-,m} B_{j,2,-,m} m\beta$$
$$\beta B_{j,i,+,m} B_{(j-i),i,+,m} m\beta \qquad (i = 1, 2, \ldots, m; j = 2, \ldots, n; m = R, L)$$
$$\beta B_{1,i,+,m} x_i m\alpha \qquad (i = 1, 2, \ldots, m; x = R, L) \qquad \square$$

2 EXERCISE: Prove **1**(ii) above. (Hint: Given a Turing machine with less than 2^m symbols, we replace it by a two-symbol TM programmed to act on blocks of m symbols as the original machine would act on single symbols.)

For results related to Shannon's and for comments on other formalisms for Turing machines, see FISCHER [1965b].

The reader will note that in the above simulations the state-symbol product only changes by a small-constant multiple. Some automata theorists enjoy playing the game of minimizing the state-symbol product for a Turing machine. The present champion may be Minsky, who has a 4-symbol 7-state universal (see Section **3** of this chapter) Turing machine, thus achieving a product of 28 to nudge the 36 of the previous winner—a 6-symbol 6-state machine. I refer the reader to MINSKY [1967, Sec. 14.8] for more details of this recreational aspect of automata theory.

A W-machine (introduced by WANG [1957] and named for him by LEE [1960], who explored their relations with finite automata, and so on) is like a Turing machine with two symbols blank and mark, save that its performance at each step is guided not by a Turing quintuple $q_i x_j x_k m q_l$ but by an instruction from the following list:

e: erase the square under scan
m: mark the square under scan
+: move the read-write head one square to the right
−: move the read-write head one square to the left
t(n): conditional jump
 *: stop

The complete program for a particular machine is a finite ordered list of instructions with position in the program corresponding to the state of a TM. After execution of an instruction of the first four types, control is automatically transferred to the next instruction. The instruction *t(n)* transfers control to the *n*th instruction if the square under scan is marked, otherwise it transfers control to the next instruction. Thus *t(n)* is a program jump, *not* a move on the tape. If control is transferred to *, or to an instruction outside the program, the computation halts.

For example, here is a program which, started at the left-hand end of a string, will transform it to 1^{m+n+1} if it is of the form $1^m b 1^n$, but will leave it unchanged if it is of the form 1^m.

 1. *t*(3)
 2. *   stop if string is blank
 3. +   move right to first blank
 4. *t*(3) move right to first blank
 5. +   are there two consecutive blanks?
 6. *t*(8)
 7. *   if so, stop
 8. −   if not, fill in first blank, and stop.
 9. *m*
10. *

What will this program do to other strings?

3 EXAMPLE
 (i) Using the W-machine instructions *e*, *m*, +, −, *t(n)*, program an unconditional jump, *t(n)*: transfer control to *n*th instruction whether or not scanned square is marked.
 (ii) Simulate the Turing machine quintuples

$$q_3 \; 0 \; 1 \; N \; q_4$$
$$q_3 \; 1 \; 0 \; L \; q_4$$

with as few W-machine instructions as possible.

Solution.
We program the unconditional jump to *n* by

$$t(n)$$
$$m$$
$$t(n-1)$$

and then precede instruction n by the instructions

$$n - 2. \quad t(n)$$
$$n - 1. \quad e$$

A common mistake here is to fail to erase a mark which had been placed merely to ensure a jump.

To simulate q_3 0 1 N q_4 economically, we must combine them into one sub-
$$q_3 \ 1 \ 0 \ L \ q_4$$
program:

$$q_3 \qquad : t(q_3 + 3)$$
$$q_3 + 1: m$$
$$q_3 + 2: t(q_4)$$
$$q_3 + 3: e$$
$$q_3 + 4: -$$
$$q_4 \qquad : \text{as previously determined}$$

Note that if q_4 is not $q_3 + 5$, we will need an *unconditional* jump to q_4 at $q_3 + 5$.

4   EXERCISE: Verify the following useful equivalence:

   (i) Given a W-machine with N instructions, there is a completely equivalent two-symbol TM with not more than N states.

   (ii) Given a two-symbol TM with s states, there is a completely equivalent W-machine with not more than $10s + 1$ instructions.

Thus in questions of construction in Chapter 10, it will suffice to be able to construct W-machines rather than general Turing machines.

We now generalize Turing machines by removing the restriction that there be only one read-write head and only one tape, and then show that any multihead, multitape generalized Turing machine may be simulated by one of our ordinary one-head, one-tape machines. Up to now our tapes have been one-dimensional strings of squares—we shall now allow two-dimensional planes cut up into squares, or three-dimensional spaces cut up into equal cubes, or the like, for our tape space—without probing the problems of spatial arrangement for the resultant machine. We do not go into details, and we do not attempt to make the most economical reductions. A great deal of study has been made of economy of reductions and estimates of which are the best possible. This is studied under the heading of "Complexity of Computation" —a sample of such research is presented in Chapter 7.

The generalization of a Turing machine Z which we now consider has n tapes $\tau_1, \ldots, \tau_n$ of dimensions $l_1, \ldots, l_n$, respectively, each divided into hypercubes‡ and specified by integer coordinates if desired. $\mathfrak{M}$ has a control unit which receives inputs from heads each of which scans a "square" of tape. We assume that each head stays on a single tape, and that there are h_j heads

---

‡ Hereinafter referred to as "squares."

on tape τ_j (see Figure 4.1). We assume that each "square" is blank, b, or contains a symbol from a fixed finite alphabet X.

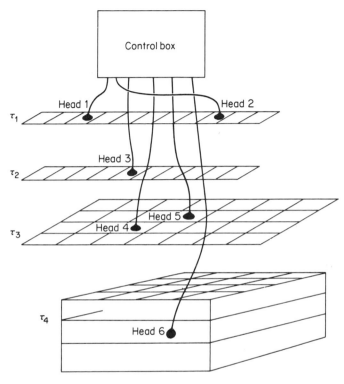

Fig. 4.1

5 EXERCISE: Show that there is no increase in generality in assigning a different alphabet to each tape.

Let $h = \sum_{1}^{n} h_j$ be the total number of heads and let us label each head with a distinct integer from 1 to h. Let $X_b = X \cup \{b\}$. The machine operates on a discrete time scale $\{0, 1, 2, 3, \ldots\}$. Then the input to the control unit is an element of $(X_b)^h$, whose jth element is the symbol scanned by the jth head.

The output of the control unit is an element of $((X_b)^h \times M) \cup \{\text{stop}\}$, where M is the set of all possible instructions to the heads to move at most distance 1 (where we use the metric $|x - x'| = \sum_{i=1}^{l} |x_i - x'_i|$ on the l-dimensional tape).

Thus the Turing machine is specified as usual by quintuples

$$q_i \; x_j \; x_k \; m \; q_l$$

with the sole difference that the x's and m's are "vectors," and that we must employ a convention for use if two heads try to print different symbols on a single "square." A computation of such a machine starts with the assignment of a state to the control unit, of nonblank symbols to a finite number of "squares," and of positions for all the heads, and proceeds in the usual fashion, stopping when and only when no $q_i\ x_j$ quintuple is applicable.

Our task is to show that any such computation can be simulated, in a suitable sense, on an "ordinary" Turing machine (that is, $n = l_1 = h_1 = 1$), and to bound the number of steps required for such a simulation. We give a number of partial reductions and then show how they may be combined to yield the overall result.

6 LEMMA: **Reduction of Heads.** *If a generalized Turing machine Z has h scanners on a single one-dimensional tape, then it may be simulated by an ordinary TM Z' in such a way that a single step of Z when its tape is n squares long may be simulated by Z' in at most $2n + 2h$ steps.*

Proof. Let our h-head machine Z have alphabet X_b. We simulate it with a one-head machine Z' with alphabet $(X_b \times S_h) \cup \{*\}$, where S_h is the set of all subsets of $\{1, 2, \ldots, h\}$ and * will mark the left-hand end of the tape. (Why don't we need a marker at both ends?) We write x for $(x\ \emptyset)$.

If Z has nonblank tape

$$x_1 x_2 \ldots x_m$$

with head j scanning x_{i_j}, we let Z have its head scan the leftmost square of

$$(x_1, \mathfrak{K}_1)(x_2, \mathfrak{K}_2) \ldots (x_m, \mathfrak{K}_m)$$

where

$$\mathfrak{K}_k = \{j | k = i_j\}$$

Thus we encode

$$\overset{3}{\downarrow} \qquad \overset{1\,2}{\downarrow\downarrow}$$

$$\boxed{3}\,\boxed{7}\,\boxed{4}\,\boxed{1}\,\boxed{2}\,\boxed{9}\,\boxed{1}\,\boxed{3}\,\boxed{4}\,\boxed{2}\,\boxed{2}$$

$$\downarrow$$

(†)

by

$$*\ 3\ 7\ 4\ (1, \{3\})\ 2\ 9\ (1, \{1, 2\})\ 3\ 4\ 2\ 2$$

Thus the head information is encoded on the tape. It is now necessary to design the logic so that this information is updated after each cycle of the simulation.

The control box of Z contains h registers which are to contain the h scanned symbols of Z.

In a simulation, Z' moves ↓ right from * until it has filled all h registers. It then "knows" the new settings required, and moves ↓ left, changing squares appropriately until it has returned to * (which may have to be displaced one square left).

If the rightmost square with second symbol non-null is n squares to the right of *, the simulation will take at most $2n + 2h$ steps—the extra $2h$ being required to simulate the worst possible repositioning of heads.   □

Another mode of simulation requires only h extra symbols $S_1, \ldots, S_h$, coding (†) by

$$3\ 7\ 4\ S_3\ 1\ 2\ 9\ S_1\ S_2\ 1\ 3\ 4\ 2\ 2$$

or with *no* extra symbols coding (†) as

$$b\ 3\ b\ 7\ b\ 4\ 3\ 1\ b\ 2\ b\ 9\ 6\ 3\ b\ 4\ b\ 2\ b\ 2$$

where we have coded $\emptyset$ $\{1\}$ $\{2\}$ $\{3\}$ $\{2, 3\}$ $\{1, 3\}$ $\{1, 2\}$ $\{1, 2, 3\}$.
$\quad\quad\quad\quad\quad\quad b\quad 1\quad\ 2\quad\ 3\quad\ \ 4\quad\ \ 5\quad\ \ 6\quad\ \ \ 7$

We chose a method which seemed easy to describe, and which can be further reduced with our knowledge of alphabet reduction [(1ii)].

7 LEMMA: *Reduction of tapes. If a generalized machine Z has n tapes, then it may be simulated by a **generalized** TM Z' with one tape, in such a way that a single step of Z may be simulated by a single step of Z'.*

Proof. This is easy. If we have n tapes of maximum dimension l, we replace them by n tapes all of dimension l, and then replace n l-dimensional tapes with alphabet X by one l-dimensional tape with alphabet X^n. Each head then works on an appropriate "track" of the new tape. The number of heads and the computation time do not change under this simulation. □

If the tapes are all one-dimensional, we may avoid the use of extra symbols by placing the n tapes end-to-end separated by punctuation marks, or letting n consecutive symbols denote the corresponding squares of n tapes. Then, of course, the simulation of a single step takes considerably longer than a single step.

We may combine **6** and **7** to conclude

8 THEOREM: *A generalized Turing machine Z with one-dimensional tapes may be simulated by an ordinary Turing machine Z' in such a way that if Z starts with initially blank tapes and computes for n steps, then Z' may simulate the action of Z in αn^2 steps, where α is a constant independent of n.*

Proof. Combine the tapes, using **7** to obtain $\tilde{Z}$ with k heads on a single tape, then reduce the number of heads of $\tilde{Z}$, using **6** to obtain Z'. At the jth step of Z', $\tilde{Z}$ will have covered at most $2j$ squares, and thus Z'' will need at most $4j + 2k$ steps to simulate this step. The total simulation time is then

$$\leq \sum_{j=1}^{n} (4j + 2k) = 2n(n + 1) + 2kn < \alpha n^2 \text{ for } \alpha = 4 + 2k. \qquad \square$$

Actually a much faster simulation of arbitrary one-dimensional tape machines is possible if we use two-tape simulators:

9 THEOREM (HENNIE and STEARNS [1966]): *A generalized Turing machine Z with one head on each of k one-dimensional tapes may be simulated by a Turing machine Z' with one head on each of two one-dimensional tapes, in such a way that if Z starts with initially blank tapes and computes for n steps, then Z' may simulate the action of Z in $\alpha n \log_2 n$ steps (for $n > 1$) where α is a constant independent of n.*

Proof abstract. The data on the k tapes of Z are stored on the second tape of Z', with the data from the jth tape of Z stored on the two levels of the jth track of this k-track tape, stored in blocks whose lengths are increasing powers of 2, cunningly arranged so that the simulation time for Z' of a step of Z increases only as the logarithm of the number of symbols stored on any tape of Z, despite the need to simulate independent movements of the k heads on the tapes of Z.

For the details, the reader is referred to HENNIE and STEARNS [1966, pp. 535–541]. $\qquad \square$

10 LEMMA: (**Reduction of dimension**) *If a generalized Turing machine Z has an l-dimensional tape τ, it may be simulated by a Turing machine Z' in which τ is replaced by one-dimensional tapes in such a way that if the "activated squares" of τ are contained in a hypercube of side n, then a single step of Z may be simulated by Z' in at most αn^l steps, where α is constant independent of n.*

Proof. We give a reduction scheme for two-dimensional tapes in a form which is immediately extendable to l-dimensional tapes for any integer $l > 2$.

We take a rectangle containing the nonblank symbols of the tape, and encode it onto one-dimensional tape by transcribing it line after line with suitable markers.

becomes

where $\cdot$ marks the ends of a line and $\cdot\cdot$ marks the ends of the encoding of a rectangle. An auxiliary tape stores the line length n_1. (Let there be n_2 lines) A second auxiliary tape is also required.

Simulating scanning and printing causes no problem, but moves may cause more trouble. Here we have to consider two main cases:

(α) *r or l (that is,* $+$ *or* $-$ *in direction* 1, $d_{\pm}^1$)

Take the case of moving *r*.

Move the head one step right.

If scanned symbol is not $\cdot$, simulation is completed.

If scanned symbol is $\cdot$, each line must be enlarged by placing a blank square at the right-hand end of each line, and increasing length of first auxiliary tape to $n_1 + 1$.

A special mark is placed whither we wish the head to return. We then move the head right counting number of $\cdot$'s encountered till we meet $\cdot\cdot$. We then transcribe a line at a time, with its appended dots, onto auxiliary tape 1, and then move it a number of steps right equal to the length of auxiliary tape 2, which we then decrease by 1. We repeat this until we return to the special mark, and carry out a similar exercise to the left. Finally we blank out the special mark. The simulation is completed.

In the worst case, the simulation time is essentially

$$\sum_{j=1}^{n_2-1} (n_1 + 1 + j) + n_2 - 1 = (n_2 - 1)(n_1 + \tfrac{1}{2}n_2 - 1)$$
$$< \tfrac{3}{2}n^2 \text{ where } n = \max(n_1, n_2).$$

(β) *u or d (that is,* $+$ *or* $-$ *in direction* 2, $d_{\pm}^2$).

Take the case of moving *u*.

We use auxiliary tape 1 to move the head $n_1 + 1$ squares right. If we do not encounter $\cdot\cdot$, the simulation is completed. If we do pass $\cdot\cdot$, we place a special mark in the square scanned, remove the old $\cdot\cdot$, place a $\cdot\cdot n_1$ squares to its right and a $\cdot$ to the left of this, and finally erase the special mark and complete the simulation with the head one square left of this position.

The simulation time is less than $3n$ steps.

In either case the simulation time $< \tfrac{3}{2}n^2$ (if $n \geq 2$). Clearly, this simulation extends to the *l*-dimensional case, where we may find a constant C_l such that if all information is contained in an *l*-dimensional cube of side *n*, we may simulate a step with a machine with one-dimensional tapes in no more than $C_l n^l$ steps.   □

11 EXERCISE (HARTMANIS and STEARNS [1965]): Show that the simulation time in **10** for simulation of *n* steps starting with a blank tape may be reduced to αn^2 by a coding which, for a two-dimensional tape, would use "$x_1 \, l \, x_2 \, d \, x_3 \, u \, x_4 \, r \, x_5 \, u$" on the tape of Z' to record that at time 1, Z printed x_1 and moved left, at time 2, Z printed x_2 and moved down, and so on.

12 EXERCISE: Prove the following:

13 THEOREM: *Given a generalized Turing machine Z with n tapes, the jth of which is of dimension l_j and is scanned by h_j heads, it may be simulated by a Turing machine Z' with a single one-dimensional tape scanned by a single head.* □

14 EXERCISE:

(i) Compute an upper bound for the time required by the Z' of Theorem **13** to simulate a single step of the computation of Z. (This will depend on the amount of nonblank tape already in use.)

(ii) Use the result of part (i) to bound the time required by Z to simulate a computation by Z in which the initial data are contained on squares distant less than N from the initial position of all the tape heads (assuming that Z starts with all heads corresponding to a single tape scanning the same square) and for which Z takes M steps.

We have now seen that anything that can be done by a generalized TM can be done by an ordinary TM—but, in general, less efficiently. We shall prove that this is so in Chapter 7—here we shall preview a result which shows that, when it comes to speed of computation, "two heads are better than one":

15 EXERCISE: Generalize the construction of example **1.8** to program an ordinary TM Z with alphabet $X_b = \{b, 0, 1\}$ which computes the symmetry predicate

$$S(x) = \begin{cases} 1 & \text{if } x = x^R \\ 0 & \text{if } x \neq x^R \end{cases}$$

that is, Z tells whether or not x is a *palindrome* such as "radar" or "amanaplanacanalpanama" and verify that Z takes less than αn^2 steps to compute the result for x of length n. Note that α can be reduced by having Z checking off more than one symbol at each pass.

16 EXAMPLE: A one-tape two-head machine can tell whether or not a string of length n is a palindrome in about $\frac{3}{2}n$ steps. Starting with both heads at the left-hand end, we move the second head to the right-hand end of the string. Then both heads move in one step at a time, erasing as they go. If, when they meet in the middle, they have always seen equal symbols they print a 1—otherwise a 0—and halt.

17 EXERCISE: Write out the quintuples for the two-head machine of example **16**.

Now a one-head machine can always check some palindromes very quickly—e.g., in one pass it can test to see whether the string is of the form

0^n or 1^n. BARZDIN [1965] has shown, however, that for any one-head one-tape TM Z, there exists a constant C such that for almost all symmetrical words x of length n, the time taken by Z to actually verify symmetry is at least Cn^2. We give the proof in Chapter 7.

The reader should appreciate how general a model of computers the generalized Turing machine is—and thus how powerful the ordinary Turing machines are in capability, though not in efficiency. For instance, any present-day computer is really a generalized Turing machine—the input system corresponds to a read-only tape, the output system to a write-only tape, the tape units (although of only finite capacity) to one-dimensional one-head TM tapes, and addressable words of core-store correspond to TM tapes only one square long (the machine can read and write but cannot move on these tapes). Thus the next time some computer scientist scoffs "Oh, Turing machines—they may be alright for automata theorists, but they have nothing to do with real computers," just reply knowingly, "Poor chap—don't tell me you're still stuck with the old one-tape one-dimension one-head model!"

4.3   UNIVERSAL TURING MACHINES AND THE
HALTING PROBLEM

We learned that for each multihead, multitape Turing machine we may effectively construct a one-head one-tape (one-dimensional) two-symbol Turing machine which simulates it on a step-by-step basis.

We now want to show that there exists a universal Turing machine, namely a Turing machine U, say, which when presented with an encoded description of a Turing machine Z and a string x to be fed to Z, will actually compute $F_Z(x)$ [and will not halt, if $F_Z(x)$ is undefined].

We shall do this in three steps. The first was accomplished in Section 2—given any TM Z we replace it by a W-machine Z_W. The second is to exhibit a three-tape machine U_3, which if given the program of the W-machine Z_W on its first tape and the data string x on its third tape, will produce the data string $F_Z(x)$, if it is defined, on its third tape. The third step is to use the methods of Section 2 to replace U_3 by a one-tape universal TM U.

We replace instructions of the form $t(n)$ by instructions of the form $t \pm (n)$—transfer control ahead ($+$) or back ($-$) n instructions if scanned square is marked, otherwise proceed to next instruction. Thus, if instruction k is $t + (n)$, then it equals $t(n + k)$. This is because relative addressing is easier to handle than absolute addressing. Given a W-machine program, we code it up as tape 1 of U_3 by coding e, m, $+$, $-$, and $*$ by a single symbol e, m, $+$, $-$ or $*$, respectively, and coding $t + (n)$ by the string of $n + 1$

symbols $\uparrow_l$ $\uparrow$ . . . $\uparrow$ $\uparrow_r$ and coding $l - (n)$ by the string of $n + 3$ symbols
$$\underbrace{\qquad}_{n-1}$$
$\downarrow_l \downarrow$ . . . $\downarrow$ $\downarrow_r$. Then the whole program is encoded by concatenating the

Tape 1 (encoded program)
symbols:
$m, e, +, -, b, \uparrow_l, \uparrow, \uparrow_r, \downarrow_l, \downarrow, \downarrow_r, *$

Tape 2
symbols: $\uparrow, \downarrow, b$

1-State
control box

Tape 3 (encoded tape)
symbols: 1, b

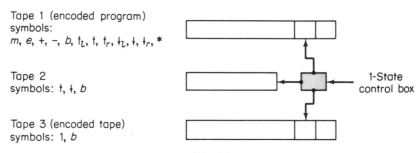

Fig. 4.2

instruction encoding in the given order. Thus we do not encode the addresses
of the instruction save implicitly by the *position* of the instruction in the
encoding.

Given a W-machine tape, we code it up as tape 3 of U, by having it
unchanged.

At the start of simulating a step in Z's computation, U_3 will have its
tape-1 head scanning the leftmost square of the encoding of the Z's present
instruction, its tape-2 head scanning a blank tape, and its tape-3 head scanning
the square representing that which Z would have under scan at that time. We
must now list the instruction which U must execute to ensure that this relation is maintained at the end of simulating the step in Z's computation.

Since we have a one-state machine,‡ rather than use quintuples we shall
use expressions such as

$$(m, r, 1) \rightarrow (R, bL, 1)$$

to mean if the symbols scanned are m on tape 1, r on tape 2, and 1 on tape 3,
move tape 1 one square right, erase the symbol on tape 2 and move it one
square left; and print a 1 on tape 3.

Simulating the $m, e, +, -$ steps in Z's computation is simplicity itself—
we carry out the order operation on tape 3, and advance tape 1 to the next
instruction,

$$(m, b, y) \rightarrow (R, N, 1)$$
$$(e, b, y) \rightarrow (R, N, b)$$
$$(+, b, y) \rightarrow (R, N, R)$$
$$(-, b, y) \rightarrow (R, N, L)$$

---

‡ This is a surprise: Prove that no one-head machine can be universal if it only has
one state.

where the y indicates that the symbol scanned on tape 3 is immaterial. Having no explicit instruction for $(*, b, y)$ yields the desired halt. The transfer instruction $t \pm (n)$ is simple if the scanned square on tape 3 is blank— we just proceed to the next instruction,

$$(A, b, b) \rightarrow (R, N, N) \qquad \text{if } A \text{ is} \quad \downarrow_l \quad \downarrow \quad \downarrow_r \quad \uparrow_l \quad \uparrow \quad \text{or} \quad \uparrow_r$$

If the scanned square on tape 3 is 1, we must transfer control n instructions back or forward, and so our first step is to store n on tape 2 as a string of $(n - 1)$ r's if the transfer is $t + (n)$, and as a string of $(n + 1)$ l's if the transfer is $t - (n)$—the extra plus or minus one being necessitated because in reading n off tape 1, we have already advanced tape 1 by $+1$ encoded instruction:

$$(\uparrow_l, b, 1) \rightarrow (R, b, 1) \qquad (\downarrow_l, b, 1) \rightarrow (R, b, 1)$$
$$(\uparrow, b, 1) \rightarrow (R, \uparrow R, 1) \qquad (\downarrow, b, 1) \rightarrow (R, \downarrow R, 1)$$
$$(\uparrow_r, b, 1) \rightarrow (R, L, 1) \qquad (\downarrow_r, b, 1) \rightarrow (R, L, 1)$$

It now only remains to advance tape 1 the requisite number of instructions. This is easily accomplished by advancing tape 1 one instruction and deleting a symbol from tape 2, and repeating the process till tape 2 is empty.

$$(x, \uparrow, 1) \rightarrow (R, N, 1) \qquad \text{if } x = \uparrow_l, \downarrow_l, \uparrow \text{ or } \downarrow$$
$$\qquad\qquad (R, bL, 1) \qquad \text{if not}$$

$$(x, \downarrow, 1) \rightarrow (L, N, 1) \qquad \text{if } x = \uparrow, \downarrow, \uparrow_r \text{ or } \downarrow_r$$
$$\qquad\qquad (L, bL, 1) \qquad \text{if not}$$

We have thus proved:

1 THEOREM: *There is a simple instruction-by-instruction coding which replaces the program of a W-machine Z by a string $\hat{e}(Z)$ of $\{m, e, +, -, \uparrow_l, \uparrow, \uparrow_r, \downarrow_l, \downarrow, \downarrow_r\}^*$; and a three-tape one-state Turing machine U which is universal in the sense that if it is started scanning the leftmost symbol of $\hat{e}(Z)$ on tape 1, with tape 2 blank, and scanning the leftmost symbol of x on tape 3, it will halt if and only if $F_Z(x)$ is defined, in which case it will halt with $F_Z(x)$ on tape 3.* $\square$

Before going further, let us recall how we used Turing machines to compute functions of several arguments. The simplest way to associate such a function $f: (X^*)^n \rightarrow X^*$ with a machine is to consider a machine Z with alphabet $X \cup \{b\}$ and then define $F_Z(x_1, \ldots, x_n)$ to be precisely $F_Z(x_1 b \ldots b x_n)$, where $'x_1'$ and $'x_2'$ and $'\ldots'$ and $'x_n'$ are strings from X^* so that $'x_1 b \ldots b x_n'$ is a string of $(X \cup \{b\})^*$.

2 Suppose, however, that $X = \{0, 1\}$ and we wish Z to have alphabet $\{0, 1\}$ as well. Then we might code the string $x = a_1 a_2 \ldots a_m (a_j = 0 \text{ or } 1)$ as the string $\tilde{x} = 1a_1 1a_2 \ldots 1a_m$ and then code $'x_1, \ldots, x_n'$ as $[x_1, \ldots, x_n]^\sim = \tilde{x}_1 00\tilde{x}_2 00 \ldots 00\tilde{x}_n$ and then define the function $F_Z(x_1, \ldots, x_n)$ of n arguments to equal our familiar one-argument function $F_Z([x_1, \ldots, x_n]^\sim)$. Combining Theorem **1** with Theorem **2.1**(ii), exercise **2.4** and the reduction steps of **2.6**(ii) (which in this case may be further simplified), and **2.7**(ii) we immediately obtain:

3 COROLLARY (TURING [1936]). *There is a quintuple-by-quintuple coding which replaces the program of a Turing machine Z with alphabet* $\{0, 1\}$ *by a binary string* $e(Z)$, *and a one-tape one-head Turing machine U with alphabet* $\{0, 1\}$ *which is **universal** in the sense that*

$$F_U(e(Z), x) = F_Z(x)$$

4 EXERCISE: Prove Corollary **3** above, making careful use of the results cited, but without rederiving them.

By a statement, we mean something which asserts a proposition that is either true or false. By a *predicate*, on the other hand, we mean an expression that contains certain symbols and becomes a statement when these symbols are replaced by any members of a specified set. If the specified set is a set of words, we may speak of a *word predicate*. Such a predicate is called *recursive* (this use of the word "recursive" for "effective" will be justified in Section **6.1**) if there is an effective procedure for telling whether the statements obtained from the predicate by replacement of the variables are true or false.

For example, "x is a noun" is a word predicate, and if we replace "x" by the word "Father" we get the true statement " 'Father' is a noun," whereas if we replace "x" by the word "runs," we get the false statement " 'runs' is a noun."

The decision problem for a predicate has a solution if there is an algorithm for determing the value of the predicate, given the values which are to replace its variables. We say the problem is unsolvable if no such solution exists.

We may rephrase this in formal terms:

5 DEFINITION: *The decision problem for a predicate* $R: (X^*)^n \rightarrow \{\text{true, false}\}$ *is called recursively solvable if there is a Turing machine Z with tape alphabet X, and two distinct strings* a_{true} *and* a_{false} *of* X^* *such that for all* $x_j \subseteq X^*$, $j = 1, \ldots, n$, *we have*

$$F_Z(x_1, \ldots, x_n) = a_{R(x_1, \ldots, x_n)}$$

*It is called **recursively unsolvable** if no such Z exists.*

One of the most important decision problems is that associated with the question "Is $F_Z(x)$ defined?" or in other words, "Will Z halt if started in state q_0, scanning the leftmost square of x?" It is called the *halting problem*.

6 DEFINITION: *Let $Z_1, Z_2, \ldots Z_n$ be an effective enumeration of the Turing machines. Then **the halting problem for Turing machines** is that associated with the predicate having variables n and x which asserts that*

$$\text{"}F_{Z_n}(x) \text{ is defined"}$$

It turns out that this problem is recursively unsolvable—we have no effective procedure which will tell us for an *arbitrary* machine Z and an arbitrary tape x whether or not Z will stop if started in state q_0, scanning the leftmost square of x. This, of course, does not preclude finding special procedures for solving the halting problem for *many* Z's and x's. A related problem for Turing machines is the *immortality problem*—to decide for a given Z whether it has *any* "immortal" tape (i.e., one for which Z never halts). For a proof that this problem, too, is recursively unsolvable, see HOOPER [1966]. Here we prove the unsolvability of the halting problem:

7 THEOREM (TURING [1936]). *The halting problem for Turing machines is recursively unsolvable.*

  Proof. We shall assume the halting problem to be recursively solvable, and derive a contradiction, thus verifying the theorem. Thus, by way of contradiction, assume that Z_k is such that

$$f_k(n, x) = \begin{cases} 1 & \text{if } f_n(x) \text{ is defined, that is, } Z_n \text{ eventually} \\ & \text{stops when started on tape } x \\ 0 & \text{if not} \end{cases}$$

when we write f_k for F_{Z_k}.

  Let $\sigma(m, n)$ be the index of the Turing machine which transforms the string x to the encoding $[n, x]$ and then transfers control to the program of Z_m:

$$f_{\sigma(m,n)}(x) = f_m(n, x)$$

The index $\sigma(m, n)$ is clearly given effectively by m and n.

  Now let r be the index of the Turing machine which, given (n, x), first computes $\sigma(n, n)$ and then computes $f_k(\sigma(n, n), x)$. If the result is 0, it prints 1 and halts. If the result is not 0, it computes $f_{\sigma(n,n)}(x)$. If this latter result is 0, it prints 1 and halts; if it is 1, it prints 0 and halts. Thus

$$f_r(n, x) = \begin{cases} 1 & \text{if } f_{\sigma(n,n)}(x) \text{ is undefined or } 0 \\ 0 & \text{if } f_{\sigma(n,n)}(x) \text{ is defined and not } 0 \end{cases}$$

Now let $s = \sigma(r, r)$ so that $f_s(x) - f_{\sigma(r,r)}(x) = f_r(r, x)$.

Then $f_s(x) = f_r(r, x) = \begin{cases} 1 & \text{if } f_s(x) \text{ is undefined or } 0 \\ 0 & \text{if } f_s(x) \text{ is defined and } \neq 0 \end{cases}$

We have our contradiction, and so the halting problem is *not* solvable. □

Thus although we are convinced that any string-manipulation problem that can be solved effectively can be solved by a Turing machine, we see that there are problems which are *well-defined* but not effectively solvable. We shall meet many more in the sequel.

8 EXERCISE: Deduce from the unsolvability of the halting problem the fact that the function

$$f(n) = \begin{cases} 1 & \text{if } Z_n \text{ eventually halts when started on a blank tape} \\ 0 & \text{if not} \end{cases}$$

is *not* TM-computable.

Another way of obtaining well-defined functions which are not computable is by defining a function which grows faster than any TM-computable function:

9 EXERCISE (RADO [1962]): Consider TMs with alphabet $\{b, 1\}$. Let E_r be the set of pairs (Z, s) such that Z is an n-state TM such that Z halts after precisely s steps if started in state q_0 on a blank tape.
  (i) Show that E_n is a finite nonempty set, and that, given a pair (Z, s), we can effectively decide whether or not $(Z, s) \in E_n$.
  (ii) If $(Z, s) \in E_n$, let $\sigma(Z, s) =$ the number of 1's in $F_Z^b(b)$. Thus $\sigma(Z, s) \leq s$. Define

$$\sum (n) = \max \{\sigma(Z, s)|(Z, s) \in E_n\}$$

Prove that if f is any numerical TM-computable function (e.g., in 1-adic), then $\sum (x) > f(x)$ for all but finitely many x. [Hint: Set $F(x) = \sum_{n=0}^{x} [f(n) + n^2]$. Let M_F be the machine for which $F_{M_F}(1^{x+1}) = 1^{x+1}01F^{(x)}+1$, and consider the function which, when started on all-zero tape, prints $1^{x+1}01F^{(x)}+101F^{(F(x))}+1$.] Thus $\sum (n)$ is well defined but not computable.

10 EXERCISE: Show that if f_n is the numerical function computed by the nth TM Z_n, then

$$g(n) = \sum_{i \leq n} f_i(n)$$

is not TM-computable.

We thus begin to appreciate the limits of the computable—these shall be made even more clear in Section **4**. In Chapter 6 we shall prove that a method of definition completely different from the Turing machine yields a class of functions—the partial recursive functions—coextensive with the partial TM-computable functions. This, together with our discussion of generalized TMs should cement our conviction in Turing's hypothesis that a function is *effectively* computable iff it is TM-computable—even though many TM-computable functions are not *practicably* computable.

4.4   RECURSIVE AND RECURSIVELY ENUMERABLE SETS

Now that we have a fairly good understanding of the partial functions $F: X^* \to X^*$ which can be computed by Turing machines, we wish to study the subsets of X^* characterized by these functions. In what follows, when we are discussing a fixed alphabet X, we shall sometimes use an integer n to refer to a string of X^*, it being understood that if $|X| = k$, then by n we really mean the string on X which serves as k-adic coding of n (under some fixed correspondence between $\{1, 2, \ldots, k\}$ and X). We shall now use the term (partial) recursive function instead of (partial) TM-computable function. The reasons for, and justification of, this identification will be given in Sections **6.1** and **6.2**.

1   DEFINITION:

(i) (*Turing machines as acceptors.*) *A subset R of X* is **recursive** just in case its characteristic function*

$$\chi_R(n) = \begin{cases} 1 & \text{if } n \in R \\ 0 & \text{if } n \notin R \end{cases}$$

is a recursive function.

(ii) (*Turing machines as generators.*) *A subset R of X* is **recursively enumerable** just in case it is the range of some total recursive function f or is the empty set, $\emptyset$.*‡

$$R = \{f(n) | n \in X^*\}$$

We now talk about sets of numbers—the reader should made a mental translation to the general case. Since set R is an actual collection of numbers we can order it (enumerate it) in many different ways. To say a set is recursively enumerable is thus to say that *for at least one enumeration*, the successive values of a recursive function f correspond to the successive (perhaps with repetitions) elements of R in the enumeration. Pick such an enumeration by

---

‡ Note that $\emptyset$ is the range of a partial recursive function, namely that undefined for all inputs. We shall prove that a set is in fact recursively enumerable iff it is the range of a partial recursive function.

some recursive function f. Now ask yourself, of some value n: Does or does not n belong to R? Now if we generate the successive values of f: $f(0), f(1),$ $f(2), \ldots$, we will eventually reach any member of R, and so effectively tell if n *does* belong to R. However, if n does *not* belong to R, we can never tell, for even if we generate a billion elements R, we cannot be sure that n is not the billion and first. So given a set R and a function f which recursively enumerates it, $R = \{f(0), f(1), f(2), \ldots\}$, one *cannot* use f directly to see if R is *recursive*, but one might be able to use it indirectly to prove that there is a total recursive function, g: $N \rightarrow \{0, 1\}$, such that

$$g(n) = 1 \quad \text{if and only if} \quad n = f(m) \quad \text{for some } m$$

If we can prove that no such recursive g exists, then we deduce that R is *not* recursive. The distinction I am trying to emphasize, then, is that the Turing machine which enumerates a set is quite distinct from the Turing machine (if there is one) which checks membership in the set.

No one denies that the design of a Turing machine may require enormous intellectual effort—the point is that a problem is recursively solvable if this intellectual effort results in a finite set of rules which can thereafter be applied *mechanically* to solve the problem, no matter what form the parameters may take. The next point is that the procedure is recursive if we can guarantee that it will terminate whenever an answer is defined—but *recursiveness* is no guarantee of practicability, for to say that a process will terminate is no guarantee that it will terminate in a reasonable span of time. (It is this difficulty that leads one to ask of a function not merely "is it recursive?" but also "how difficult is it?" and thus to the theory of difficulty in Chapter 7.)

We reiterate the hypothesis (a variant of which is often called *Church's thesis*), following Turing in his original 1936 paper: *The informal intuitive notion of an effective procedure on sequences of symbols is identical with our precise concept of one which may be executed by a Turing machine.*

Such a hypothesis can never be given a formal proof, simply because a formal proof requires definitions of the concepts involved—and such a formal definition is incompatible with the idea of an intuitive concept. All one can adduce is a "proof" by inductive inference: To date, wherever in the development of the theory of recursive functions it has been intuitively evident that an effective procedure exists, it has always been possible to devise a Turing machine to execute a rigorous analog of the process.

Let us then recouch our definitions in our intuitive language of effective procedures:

2 A *function* is called *recursive* if there exists an effective procedure for computing it (computation).

A *set* is *recursive* if there exists an effective procedure for telling whether or not an element belongs to it (decision).

A *set* is *recursively enumerable*, if there exists an effective procedure for generating its elements, one after another (generation).

The set of squares of integers is *recursively enumerable*—we take 1, 2, 3, . . . in turn and square them. It is also *recursive*—given any integer, we decompose it into its prime factors and then tell easily whether or not it is square. We shall see that every recursive set is recursively enumerable, but that the converse is not true. The latter result is deep.

We now have two sets of definitions, formal and informal. If a function is recursive in the formal sense, it is certainly recursive in the informal sense —our effective procedure is simply to compute the function with the Turing machine given to us by the formal definition. Similarly, a set which is recursive (or recursively enumerable) in the formal sense must be recursive (or recursively enumerable) in the informal sense. It is the converse statement (e.g., that if a set is recursive in the informal sense, then it is recursive in the formal sense) which constitutes, for us, Turing's hypothesis. We now prove theorems informally on recursive and recursively enumerable sets. Of course, when a formal proof doesn't involve many finicky details, we shall not hesitate to give it in full.

3   THEOREM: *If R and S are recursively enumerable sets, then so are $R \cap S$ and $R \cup S$.*

Proof. The cases in which R or S is null are trivially true. Otherwise, let $R = \{f(n)|n \in N\}$, $S = \{g(n)|n \in N\}$ for total recursive f and g. Let

$$h(n) = \begin{cases} f(m) & \text{if } n = 2m + 1 \\ g(m) & \text{if } n = 2m \end{cases}$$

Then h is clearly recursive and $R \cup S = \{h(n)|n \in N\}$ and so is recursively enumerable.

If $R \cap S = \emptyset$, it is certainly recursively enumerable. If $R \cap S \neq \emptyset$, there exists $m_0 \in R \cap S$ (though we may not have an effective means of finding it—see the following Theorem **12**). Let

$$\hat{h}(n) = \begin{cases} f(m) & \text{if } n = 2m + 1 \quad \text{and } f(m) \in \{g(0), \dots, g(m)\} \\ g(m) & \text{if } n = 2m \quad \text{and } g(m) \in \{f(0), \dots, f(m - 1)\} \\ m_0 & \text{otherwise} \end{cases}$$

Then $R \cap S = \{\hat{h}(n)|n \in N\}$ and so is recursively enumerable. $\square$

4   EXERCISE: To what extent is the above proof informal? Formalize it.

5   EXERCISE: Show that $S \subseteq X^*$ is recursive iff $\bar{S} = X^* - S$ is recursive.

6   THEOREM: *A set S is recursive iff both S and $\bar{S}$ are recursively enumerable.*
   Proof. Let S be recursive, with g a total recursive function such that

$$g(n) = \begin{cases} 1 & \text{if } n \in S \\ 0 & \text{if } n \notin S \end{cases}$$

Let n_0 be the least element of S. (We may assume such exists, since the theorem clearly holds for the empty set.) Then define the effectively computable function f as follows:

$$f(0) = n_0$$
$$f(n) = \begin{cases} f(n-1) & \text{if } g(n) = 0 \\ n & \text{if } g(n) = 1 \end{cases}$$

Then $S = \{f(n) | n \in N\}$ and so is recursively enumerable—and similarly for $\bar{S}$. Conversely, suppose S and $\bar{S}$ are recursively enumerable. Then

$$S = \{f(n) | n \in N\} \qquad \text{and} \qquad \bar{S} = \{h(n) | n \in N\}$$

for some total recursive functions f and h, and given any $m \in N$, we know m is either an $f(n)$ for some n, or an $h(n)$ for some n, but not both. So given m, simply generate the sequence $f(1), h(1), f(2), h(2), f(3), \ldots$ until we encounter m. If it is an $f(n)$, set $g(m) = 1$; if it is an $h(n)$, set $g(m) = 0$. Then

$$g(m) = \begin{cases} 0 & \text{if } m \notin S \\ 1 & \text{if } m \in S \end{cases}$$

and so S is recursive.   □

7   EXERCISE: Give a *formal* proof that if R and S are *recursive* sets, then so are $R \cap S$ and $R \cup S$.

8   EXERCISE: Prove that a subset of N is recursive iff it can be recursively enumerated in order of magnitude.

9   EXERCISE: Show that any finite set is recursive. Use this to deduce that if S is finite and R is recursive (recursively enumerable), then $R \cup S$ is recursive (recursively enumerable).

   Before turning to our next theorem, we remind the reader that there exists an effective enumeration of the ordered pairs of natural numbers, obtained by the *diagonal method* (see Fig. 4.3).

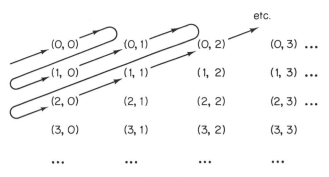

Fig. 4.3

10   The pair (x, y) appears in the xth row and yth column. We proceed by passing up successive diagonals starting from the upper left-hand corner. The first few pairs in this enumeration are $(0, 0)$, $(1, 0)$, $(0, 1)$, $(2, 0)$, $(1, 1)$, $(0, 2)$, $(3, 0)$, $(2, 1)$, ... We let $\tau(x, y)$ be the position of x, y in this enumeration. The passage from (x, y) to $\tau(x, y)$, and from $\tau(x, y)$ to x or y is total-recursive.

11   EXERCISE: Verify that the pair (x, y) falls in the $\frac{1}{2}(x^2 + 2xy + y^2 + 3y + x + 2)$th place in the sequence.

We may relax the condition that the function used to enumerate a recursively enumerable set be total:

12   THEOREM: *A set is recursively enumerable iff it is the range of a partial recursive function.*
    Proof. We have to show that $\{f(n)|n \in N\}$ is recursively enumerable, even if the partial recursive function f is *not* total. If f is completely undefined, then its range is $\emptyset$, and we are done. If not, pick some n_0 from its range. Let Z be a Turing machine which computes f. Let

$$F(n, m) = \begin{cases} 1 & \text{if } Z \text{ takes } m \text{ steps to compute } f(n) \\ 0 & \text{if not} \end{cases}$$

Now, F is total recursive—to compute it, we simply start Z with n on its tape, and run it for m steps. If it then stops, $F(n, m)$ is 1; otherwise, 0. Let us now define the function g by the equalities

$$g(n) = \begin{cases} f(x) & \text{if } n = \tau(x, y) \text{ and } F(x, y) = 1 \\ n_0 & \text{if } n = \tau(x, y) \text{ and } F(x, y) = 0 \end{cases}$$

Then g is total recursive, and $\{g(n)|n \in N\} = \{f(n)|n \in N\}$, which is thus recursively enumerable.   □

The reader should ponder the fact that *there may be an effective procedure for solving a problem—but no effective procedure for finding a solution procedure.* This is well illustrated by the above proof. If we generate a set by a partial recursive function, we run the risk that the output may be undefined —so we adopt the "run for y steps with input x" strategy to ensure that computation will halt for every input n—which we decode by solving the equation $n = \tau(x, y)$. This transition is effective, save for one catch—we must generate an element of the set even if the original computation on input x would not have taken y steps. To plug this gap, we fix on a single element n_0 of the range of the original recursive function. This we can obtain, if we are patient enough, by our "run for y steps with input x" strategy till we first obtain an output—*so long as the range of our partial function is nonempty.* But to tell whether or not it is empty is a problem akin to the halting problem and thus effectively unsolvable—as the reader should quickly convince himself. Hence, if we *know* our set is nonempty, we can find an algorithm of the desired guaranteed-to-terminate kind—but we have no general procedure which is guaranteed to terminate with the right output "the set is empty" or the "guaranteed-to-terminate" algorithm.

13 THEOREM: *The recursively enumerable sets may be effectively enumerated:* $S_1, S_2, \ldots S_n, \ldots$

Proof. Let $Z_1, Z_2, \ldots$ be an effective enumeration of Turing machines. Let f_n be the partial recursive function of one argument computed by Z_n. Let $S_n = \{f_n(m) | m \in N\}$ □

14 EXERCISE: Prove that each recursively enumerable set occurs infinitely often in the above enumeration.

The reader may find it helpful to recall Cantor's diagonal proof (see p. 30) that the set of real numbers is not denumerable when he reads the following:

15 THEOREM: *There exists a recursively enumerable set which is not recursive.*

Proof. By Theorem **6** we must exhibit a recursively enumerable set K for which $\overline{K}$ is not recursively enumerable.

Let us define the set K to be $\{n | n \in S_n\}$. Thus

$$n \in K \Leftrightarrow n \in S_n$$

where $\{S_1, S_2, \ldots\}$ is an effective enumeration of the recursively enumerable sets.

K is recursively enumerable, for, if we define f by

$$f(n) = \begin{cases} y & \text{if } n = \tau(x, y) \text{ and } y \text{ is the } x\text{th element of } S_y \\ \text{undefined} & \text{if not} \end{cases}$$

then $K = \{f(n) | n \in N\}$.

Finally, we show that $\overline{K}$ is not recursively enumerable. For were $\overline{K}$ recursively enumerable, we would have $\overline{K} = S_{n_0}$ for some n_0. But then

$$n_0 \in K \Leftrightarrow n_0 \in S_{n_0} \Leftrightarrow n_0 \in \overline{K}$$

a contradiction.   □

It is instructive to contrast the above with the following 'proof': "Since every recursive set is recursively enumerable, all recursive sets certainly occur in $S_1, S_2, \ldots$. If it were true that all sets $S_1, S_2, \ldots$ were recursive, then the set $\overline{K} = \{n | n \notin S_n\}$, which is not in the enumeration, would be recursive—for, S_n being recursive, we can effectively tell whether or not $n \in \overline{K}$ by testing whether not or whether $n \in S_n$. Contradiction—and so $S_1, S_2, \ldots$ contains nonrecursive sets—and hence there are recursively enumerable sets which are not recursive."

This proof is invalid. The reader is invited to figure out why before reading the rest of this paragraph. Why? Because, by reasoning similar to that following Theorem **12**, we cannot in general go effectively from the Turing machine Z_n which generates S_n to a decision procedure which tells whether or not a number belongs to S_n—even if we know the set is recursive. But for the above proof to work, we must show that $\overline{K}$ is recursive by *effectively* obtaining for each n a decision procedure to test its membership in S_n. What the above argument *does* prove, however, is that any effective enumeration of decision procedures for recursive sets cannot include decision procedures for all recursive sets. We shall use this argument in Section **5.2** to show that not all recursive sets are context-sensitive languages.

The reader may be interested to learn that Theorem **15** is an abstract form of *Gödel's* celebrated *incompleteness theorem*, which states that any axiomatic system whose vocabulary is *adequate* to express a sufficiently rich collection of statements about numbers, and which is *consistent* (i.e., its axioms do not imply any contradictions), must also be *incomplete* in that there are truths about numbers expressible, but not provable, in this axiomatic theory. Of course, the tough thing in studying a given axiomatic system is to show that it is consistent and adequate. We give an informal proof of Gödel's theorem—the reader may wish to fill in details after reading Section **5.1**. For a collection of many important papers related to this topic, see DAVIS [1965].

16 THEOREM (GÖDEL [1931]): *Every consistent adequate arithmetical logic is incomplete.*

Informal Proof. An axiom system is specified by a finite set of *axioms*, and a finite set of *rules of inference*—effective procedures for telling whether or not a statement may be deduced from other statements. A *proof* is a finite sequence of statements each of which is either an axiom, or deducible from earlier statements in the sequence by one of the rules of inference. A *theorem* is any statement which may occur in a proof. The proofs clearly form a recursive set of sequences—the theorems may then be obtained as a recursively enumerable set by taking the range of the function: given n, generate the nth sequence, check to see whether it is a valid proof, and if so put out its last line; otherwise, put out the first axiom.

Now, by *adequacy and consistency* we shall mean (i) that for each recursively enumerable set U and for each $n \in N$ there is a string $U(n)$ which is to represent the statement $n \in U$—and we require that given any string, we can tell if it is of the form $U(n)$, and if so, for what U and what n; and (ii) that if $U(n)$ is a theorem, then we demand that it be true that $n \in U$, and if $\sim U(n)$ [the negation of $U(n)$] is a theorem, then we demand that it be true that $n \notin U$.

Let, now, U be a recursively enumerable set which is not recursive. We show that the system is *incomplete* by showing that there exists an n for which neither $U(n)$ nor $\sim U(n)$ is a theorem. Since either $n \in U$ or $n \notin U$, one of these represents a true statement, and so must be provable if the system is to be complete.

Suppose that, in fact, for each n, one of $U(n)$ and $\sim U(n)$ is a theorem. Then, given n, we have an effective procedure for telling whether or not n belongs to U: Generate, one by one, the theorems (remember, they form a recursively enumerable set)—eventually either $U(n)$ or $\sim U(n)$ will be encountered. If it is $U(n)$, we decide that $n \in U$, if it is $\sim U(n)$, we decide that $n \notin U$. Thus if the system were complete, U would have to be recursive, which it is not. We conclude that the system is incomplete.   □

We can in fact obtain even more information by the above type of reasoning. First we explore in more detail the possible anatomy of nonrecursive sets.

17   DEFINITION: *A set R is* **creative** *if it is recursively enumerable and if there exists a total recursive function f such that*

$$S_n \subset \bar{R} \Rightarrow f(n) \in \bar{R} - S_n$$

Thus, no creative set is recursive.

18   FACT: $K = \{n | n \in S_n\}$ *is creative.*
        Proof. Since $\bar{K} = \{n | n \notin S_n\}$, $S_n \subset \bar{K}$ implies $n \in \bar{K} - S_n$, and so K is creative with $f(n) = n$.   □

19   EXERCISE: Show that if a set R is creative, then its complement contains an infinite recursively enumerable subset.
        However, not all sets have such subsets.

20   DEFINITION: *A set S is* **simple** *if it is recursively enumerable while $\bar{S}$ is infinite but contains no infinite recursively enumerable subset. Thus, no simple set is recursive.*

21   FACT: $S = \{x | \exists n$ *such that x is the first element of S_n with $x > 2n\}$ is simple.*
        Proof. If S_n is infinite, $S_n \cap S \neq \emptyset$. Thus no infinite recursively enumerable set can be contained in $\bar{S}$. However, $\bar{S}$ is infinite because the x's in $\{0, 1, \ldots, 2n + 1\}$ may only gain entry to S through the sets $S_1, \ldots, S_n$, so that at least half of any set $\{0, 1, \ldots, 2n + 1\}$ belongs to $\bar{S}$. We conclude that S is simple.   □

Now let us reassess the proof of Gödel's theorem. Implicit in it is that for any adequate consistent arithmetical logic $\mathcal{L}$, $\{n| \vdash_{\mathcal{L}} \sim U(n)\}$, the set of n for which $\sim U(n)$ is a theorem of $\mathcal{L}$, is a recursively enumerable set.

Thus if U is simple, $\{n| \vdash_{\mathcal{L}} \sim U(n)\}$ being a recursively enumerable subset of $\overline{U}$ is finite, even though $n \notin U$ for infinitely many n. Note well that this is true for *any* choice of an adequate consistent logic $\mathcal{L}$.

If K is creative, then $S_m = \{n| \vdash_{\mathcal{L}} \sim K(n)\} \subset \overline{K}$, and so $f(m) \in \overline{K}$, where $f(m) \notin S_m$. If we now construct a new logic $\mathcal{L}'$ by adjoining $\sim K(f(m))$ as an additional axiom, we have a logic in which the truth $f(m) \in \overline{K}$ is represented by a theorem.

Now, for each logic $\mathcal{L}$, we may specify a Turing machine $Z_{h(\mathcal{L})}$ which, started on a blank tape, proceeds to print out (scratchwork and) an effective enumeration of the theorems of $\mathcal{L}$. Further, the passage from $\mathcal{L}$ to $h(\mathcal{L})$ is effective, and given any n, we can tell whether it is an $h(\mathcal{L})$, and, if so, for which $\mathcal{L}$.

Given a Turing machine Z_n, let $g(n) = n$ if Z_n is not $Z_{h(\mathcal{L})}$ for some logic $\mathcal{L}$. If $n = h(\mathcal{L})$, let $Z_{k(n)}$ be Z_n modified so that it prints out only theorems of the form $\sim K(n)$ for our creative set K. But then $\sim K(k(n))$ may be consistently adjoined to the axioms of $\mathcal{L}$ to yield a new logic $\mathcal{L}'$. Let $g(n) = h(\mathcal{L}')$. Clearly, then, g is a total recursive function, and we have

22   THEOREM (MYHILL [1963b]): *There is a total recursive function g such that for the Turing machine $Z_{h(\mathcal{L})}$ which prints out theorems of the adequate consistent arithmetical logic $\mathcal{L}$, the Turing machine $Z_{g(h(\mathcal{L}))}$ is $Z_{h(\mathcal{L}')}$ for an adequate consistent arithmetical logic $\mathcal{L}'$ with more theorems than $\mathcal{L}$.*   □

Thus, while Gödel's incompleteness theorem points to an inevitable limitation of any axiomatization of arithmetic, Myhill's theorem points out the much less well known fact that this limitation can be *effectively* overcome. And, of course, the process may be iterated mechanically again and again. We shall see an amusing application of this due to MYHILL [1964] in our study of self-reproducing automata in Chapter 10.

Besides its relevance to questions of incompleteness, Theorem **15** is also of interest because it is equivalent to the unsolvability of the halting problem. Recall that the halting problem for a Turing machine Z is to determine, for each and every number n, whether or not Z will ever stop computing after being started in state q_0 scanning the leftmost square of the tape $\langle n \rangle_1$. If $\overline{R}_Z$ is the set of numbers n for which Z does not stop computing, then the question "Is the halting problem solvable for Z?" is equivalent to the question "Is $\overline{R}_Z$ recursive?"

Now, R_Z (the set of numbers n for which Z *does* stop computing) is *always* recursively enumerable: at stage n ($n = 1, 2, 3, \ldots$) we simply emit into R_Z those among the first n integers for which Z stops computing on the corresponding tapes within n steps. So, if $\overline{R}_Z$ is not recursive, then R_Z is not recursive, but is still recursively enumerable, and thus $\overline{R}_Z$ is not recursively enumerable (cf. Theorem **6**). Hence, to find a Z for which $\overline{R}_Z$ is not recursively enumerable, we have to find a Z for which $\overline{R}_Z$ is not recursive. But this is immediate (by Theorem **13**) if we can show that every recursively enumerable set is an R_Z for some Turing machine Z. This is easy, for, using Turing's hypothesis, we know that given a recursively enumerable set R, we can find a Turing machine $Z(R)$ which embodies the following effective procedure:

Given a number n, generate successive members $x_1, x_2, \ldots$ of R until an x_i is found which equals n. Emit n. Stop.

Clearly $Z(R)$ only halts if n is in R; that is, $R = R_Z(R)$.

Thus, if R is recursively enumerable but not recursive, $\bar{R}_{Z(R)} = \bar{R}$ is not recursively enumerable, and $Z(R)$ has an unsolvable halting problem.

Our next result is an amazing one, showing that any effective enumeration of the Turing machines is redundant "in any way you can specify"—more precisely:

23 THEOREM (THE RECURSION THEOREM): *For any recursive function h, there exists a string y such that*

$$f_y = f_{h(y)}$$

that is, f_y is a fixed point for the second component of the functional $(i, f_i) \mapsto (h(i), f_{h(i)})$.

Proof. Let U be a universal machine which, when presented with the string x, y, computes $f_x(y)$ if this is defined, and never stops, if not. Let U_z be the machine which, when given the string x, does the following:

(i) It computes $f_z(z)$. If this is not defined, U_z never halts, no matter what x may be.

(ii) If and when $f_z(z)$ is computed, U_z then rearranges its tape contents to obtain the string $f_z(z)$, x.

(iii) It then acts on this with U's program.

Clearly, given z we can effectively determine the program of U_z, and we then effectively find its index—$g(z)$, say. Note that g is a total recursive function—it is defined for every z—and

24
$$f_{g(z)}(x) = f_{f_z(z)}(x)$$

even though we do *not* expect $g(z)$ to equal $f_z(z)$ (since whether or not $f_z(z)$ is defined for all z is effectively unsolvable).

Now let the total recursive function $h(g(x))$ have index v, that is, $h \circ g = f_v$. Then

$$
\begin{aligned}
f_{g(v)}(x) &= f_{f_v(v)}(x) && \text{by (24)} \\
&= f_{h(g(v))}(x) && \text{by choice of } v
\end{aligned}
$$

∴ Our desired fixed point is $y = g(v)$ □

25 EXERCISE: Show that the fixed point y may be chosen effectively as a function of an index of h.

Note that the above proof did not rest on the properties of any one ordering of the Turing machines. In fact, the proof suggests there may be some interest in erecting an *axiomatic* theory of computation. We hint at such a theory by giving a generalization of the recursion theorem.

26 DEFINITION: *We say that an "enumeration" of partial functions $f_j: X_b^* \to X_b^*$, one for each $j \in X^*$,*

    (i)   *is universal if $\exists U \in X^*$ such that $\forall j \in X^*, \forall x \in X^*: f_U(j, x) = f_j(x)$*

    (ii) *is constant-rich if $\exists l$ in the enumeration which is total, and $\forall z \in X_1^*$ and all $x \in X_1^*$*

$$f_{l(z)}(x) = z$$

    (iii) *has **effective concatenation and composition** if $\exists$ functions c_n and c_m in the enumeration, each defined on all of X^*bX^* with values in X^*, such that*

$$f_{c_n(j_1, j_2)}(x) = f_{j_1}(x)bf_{j_2}(x)$$
$$f_{c_m(j_1, j_2)}(x) = f_{j_1}(f_{j_2}(x))$$

Then our proof of the recursion theorem may be formalized to prove:

27 THEOREM: *An enumeration which is universal, constant-rich, has effective concatenation and composition, and contains the identity function ($f_I(x) \equiv x$) satisfies the recursion theorem in the strong sense that there is a total function f_t such that for every total $h = f_j$ we have*

$$f_v = f_{h(v)} \qquad \text{for } v = f_t(j)$$

In fact, we may even display t explicitly.

    Proof. The proof that follows looks intricate, but this intricacy proves worthwhile, for it gives us complete control over the indices of all our functions. Clearly, $f_U(f_U(f_{l(z)}(x)bf_{l(z)}(x)), f_I(x)) = f_{l_z(z)}(x)$, and the left-hand side has index $c_m(c_n(c_m(U, c_n(l(z), l(z))), I)) = g(z)$. Let c_m have index α, c_n index β, l index γ. Then

$$g(z) = f_\alpha(f_\beta(f_\alpha(f_{l(u)}(z), f_\beta(f_\gamma(z), f_\gamma(z))), f_{l(I)}))$$

which has index,

$$c_m(\alpha, c_n(c_m(\beta, c_m(\alpha, c_n(l(U), c_m(\beta, c_n(\gamma, \gamma)))))), l(I))) = s, \text{ say.}$$

If $h = f_j$, then $h(g(x))$ has index $c_m(j, s) = f_\alpha(j, f_{l(s)}(j)) = f_t(j)$, where $t = c_m(\alpha, c_n(I, l(s)))$. Thus $f_{f_t(j)} = f_j \circ g$. Setting $v = f_{t(j)}$, we have

$$f_{g(v)}(x) = f_{f_s(v)}(x) \qquad \text{by definition of } g$$
$$\quad = f_{h(g(v))}(x) \qquad \text{by choice of } v \qquad \square$$

28 EXERCISE: What is the smallest enumeration which is universal and constant-rich, and has effective concatenation and composition?

The next two results simply say that our enumeration of TMs is a "sensible" one:

29 THEOREM (THE ENUMERATION THEOREM): *There exists a partial recursive function f of two variables n and x such that*

$$f(n, x) = \begin{cases} f_n(x) & \text{if this is defined} \\ \text{undefined} & \text{if not} \end{cases}$$

Proof. "Immediate from Turing's hypothesis." $\square$

30 THEOREM (KLEENE'S ITERATION THEOREM): *For each m, there is a recursive function $g(r, y_1, \ldots, y_m)$ such that*

$$f_r^{m+n}(y_1, \ldots, y_m, x_1, \ldots, x_n) = f_{g(r, y_1, \ldots, y_m)}^n(x_1, \ldots, x_n)$$

Proof. This just means that given an effective procedure for computing

$$f_r^{m+n}$$

and given $y_1, \ldots, y_n$, we have an effective means of producing a procedure for computing

$$g(x_1, \ldots, x_n) = f_r^{m+n}(y_1, \ldots, y_n, x_1, \ldots, x_n)$$

But the effective procedure is essentially to write down $y_1, \ldots, y_m$ on the tape in front of $x_1, \ldots, x_n$ and then proceed, using Z_r. We then let $s(r, y_1, \ldots, y_n)$ be the first index for a Turing machine embodying this procedure. Clearly s is effective. $\square$

31 EXERCISE: Show that it is clear that s is effective.

We close this section with two results of C. Y. LEE [1963], which we exhibit as corollaries of the recursion theorem.

The expression $\alpha \xrightarrow{Z} \beta$ means that the machine Z, if started with the string α (input) on its tape, will finally halt with the string β (output) on its tape. We use Λ to denote the null string.

An *admissible program encoding* is an injective function f from the set of TMs to the positive integers such that, given Z, we may effectively find $f(Z) \in N$; given $n \in N$, we may effectively tell whether or not it is of the form $f(Z)$, and if so, for which (unique) Z.

32 THEOREM: *Let f be an arbitrary admissible program encoding. Then there exists a **self-describing machine**; i.e., a machine $\hat{Z}$ such that*

$$\Lambda \xrightarrow{\hat{Z}} f(\hat{Z})$$

Proof. Define the function h by defining $h(n)$ to be so chosen that $Z_{h(n)}$ is the machine which prints $f(Z_n)$ a symbol at a time moving from left to right, then halts:

$$\Lambda \xrightarrow[Z_{h(n)}]{} f(Z_n)$$

Clearly, h is total recursive. By the recursion theorem, there is a computational fixed point $\hat{Z} = Z_{\hat{n}}$ of h,

$$x \xrightarrow[Z_{\hat{n}}]{} y \Leftrightarrow x \xrightarrow[Z_{h(\hat{n})}]{} y$$

Thus, taking $x = \Lambda$, we see $\hat{Z}$ is self-describing: $\Lambda \xrightarrow[\hat{Z}]{} f(\hat{Z})$.   □

THATCHER [1963] gives an explicit 2532-instruction program for a self-describing machine. (It takes only three pages to describe in full and verify.)

33 EXERCISE: Prove that if f is an arbitrary admissible program encoding, then there exists a self-describing and universal machine: i.e., given a decodable function $u(Z, x)$ from (machine, tape) pairs to tapes, we have a machine $\hat{U}$ such that

$$x \xrightarrow[Z]{} y \Leftrightarrow u(Z, x) \xrightarrow[\hat{U}]{} (y, f(\hat{U}))$$

5 POST SYSTEMS AND CONTEXT-FREE LANGUAGES

1. Logics and Post Systems
2. Context-Sensitive and Context-Free Languages
3. Ambiguity and Decision Problems for Context-Free Languages
4. Push-Down Automata and Linear-Bounded Automata

In this chapter, we study languages from an approach based on the axiomatic style of logic, where we "grow" the language (or set of strings or theorems) by starting from a small set of strings, and producing new strings by rewriting using various rules of inference.

In Section **1**, we relate such sets to the recursively enumerable sets defined in terms of Turing machines in Chapter **4**. In Section **2**, we restrict the rewriting rules to obtain subclasses of the recursively enumerable sets—the context-sensitive and context-free languages—and show, among other things, that such sets are recursive. In Section **3**, we apply the unsolvability of Post's Correspondence Problem, which we deduced from the unsolvability of the Turing Machine Halting Problem in Section **1**, to prove that most decision problems associated with context-free languages are unsolvable. In Section **4**, we introduce (nondeterministic) push-down automata and linear-bounded automata, and show that they are acceptors for the context-free and context-sensitive languages respectively.

5.1 LOGICS AND POST SYSTEMS

Turing originally developed his machines in order to derive theorems about what was and was not provable by finitely specified rules of inference in a formal system of deductive logic. (Compare our discussion and proof

164

of Theorem **4.4.16**.) Let us inspect this interest briefly, and compare it with the approach taken by Emil L. Post.

The Hilbert School of Formalists placed great emphasis on finitistic axiomatic systems. Many successful attempts were made to characterize these systems in such a way that they themselves were amenable to mathematical (or, more properly, metamathematical) analysis. The various characterizations proved to be equivalent, and therein lay their power. In particular, the definitions of Turing and Post proved equivalent.

A logic $\mathcal{L}$ must have a designated finite set of strings—the *axioms* of $\mathcal{L}$—together with a finite set of *rules of inference*. When $R(Y, X_1, \ldots, X_n)$ is a true inference of $\mathcal{L}$, we say that Y is a *consequence* of $X_1, \ldots, X_n$, by R, in $\mathcal{L}$.

1 A finite sequence of strings $X_1, X_2, \ldots, X_n$ is called a *proof* (of X_n) in a logic $\mathcal{L}$ if, for each i, $1 \leq i \leq n$, either

(i) X_i is an axiom, or

(ii) there exist $j, \ldots, k < i$ such that X_i is a consequence of $X_j, \ldots, X_k$ in $\mathcal{L}$ by one of the rules of inference of $\mathcal{L}$.

2 We say that W is a *theorem* of $\mathcal{L}$, or that W is *provable* in $\mathcal{L}$, if there is a proof of W in $\mathcal{L}$. We denote this by $\vdash_{\mathcal{L}} W$.

The only thing now lacking in our definition of our logic $\mathcal{L}$ is a restriction which ensures that the rules of inference operate in a strictly finitistic manner. The difference between the Turing and Post formalisms is in the way in which they effect this restriction.

The Turing form of the finistic restriction, then, is to demand that a rule of inference R be accepted for one of our logics $\mathcal{L}$ only if there exists a Turing machine $Z(R)$ such that

$$F_{Z(R)}(X_1, \ldots, X_n, Y) = \begin{cases} 1 & \text{if } R(Y, X_1, \ldots, X_n) \text{ is true} \\ 0 & \text{if not} \end{cases}$$

Let us agree to call one of our logics a *Turing system* if its rules of inference can be mediated by Turing machines, as above.

3 POST [1943] gave his finitistic restriction in terms of *productions*. A k-antecedent production is of the form

$$g_{11}u_1^{(1)}g_{12}u_2^{(1)} \ldots g_{1m_1}u_{m_1}^{(1)}g_{1(m_1+1)}$$
$$\vdots$$
$$g_{k1}u_1^{(k)}g_{k2}u_2^{(k)} \ldots g_{km_k}u_{m_k}^{(k)}g_{k(m_k+1)}$$

$$produce$$

$$g_1u_1g_2u_2 \ldots g_mu_mg_{m+1}$$

In this display, the g's represent specific strings including the null string, while the u's represent the operational variables of the production and, in the application of the production, may be identified with arbitrary strings. These variables need not be distinct—equalities among them constrain our substitutions. We then add the restriction that each operational variable in the conclusion of the production is present in at least one of the premisses of the production, it having been understood that each premiss, and the conclusion, has at least one operational variable. This production corresponds to the rule of inference R for which $R(\Theta_1, \ldots, \Theta_k, \Theta)$ is true iff there exist strings $h_j^{(i)}$ $(1 \leq i \leq k; 1 \leq j \leq m_i + 1)$ [with $h_j^{(i)} = h_{j'}^{(i')}$ if $u_j^{(i)} = u_{j'}^{(i')}$] such that $\Theta_i = g_{i1}h_1^{(i)}g_{i2}h_2^{(i)} \ldots g_{i(m_i+1)}$ $(1 \leq i \leq k)$ and $\Theta = g_1h_1g_2h_2 \ldots g_mh_mg_{m+1}$, where h_j is the $h_i^{(i)}$ such that u_j is the variable $u_i^{(i)}$.

Post called a logic in which each rule of inference is mediated by a production a *system in canonical form.*

4 EXAMPLE: Consider the one-antecedent production

$$17R3Q \rightarrow RR6Q$$

[where we replace "produce" by "$\rightarrow$"—a usage that should be familiar to readers acquainted with context-free grammars (see Section **2** below)]. We may apply this to 1735, taking $R = \Lambda$, $Q = 5$, to yield 65. We may apply this to 17634362, either taking

$$R = 6 \quad Q = 4362 \quad \text{to yield } 6664362$$

or taking

$$R = 634 \quad Q = 62 \quad \text{to yield } 634634662$$

We cannot apply this to 39617, for instance.

For a two-antecedent production, consider

$$R_13R_25 \quad \text{and} \quad 6R_14 \quad \text{produce } R_2$$

Applying this to the set of strings $\{3435, 64, 634, 33175\}$, one may combine the third and fourth elements to obtain 17, or combine the first and second to obtain 43.

5 DEFINITION: *A **Post-generation system** is a quadruple* $\mathcal{S} = (V, X, A, P)$, *where*

V is a finite set;
*$X \subseteq V$ (the **terminal** symbols);*
*A is a finite subset of V^* (the set of **axioms**); and*
*P is a set of **productions** whose fixed strings are in V^*.*

We shall say that a set is generated by $\mathcal{S}$, and call it $L(\mathcal{S})$, if it is the set of *theorems of* $\mathcal{S}$ *which lie in* X^*.

Given a set B, we write $B \vdash_S x$ if there is a proof of x using the rules of inference of S, and using B as the set of axioms. Then $L(S) = \{x \in X^* | A \vdash_S x\}$.

6 DEFINITION: *We shall say a set of strings is* **Post-generable** *if there exists a Post-generation System* S *for which the given set equals* $L(S)$.

7 DEFINITION: *A system in canonical form is said to be a* **semi-Thue‡** *system if each production is of the form*

$$u_1 g u_2 \longrightarrow u_1 g' u_2$$

for suitable strings g, g'.

8 THEOREM: *A set of strings is Post-generable, using a semi-Thue system, iff it is recursively enumerable.*

Proof outline. Certainly every semi-Thue generable set is recursively enumerable—one either believes this from Turing's hypothesis (alias Church's thesis), or else applies standard techniques for proving sets recursively enumerable. For more details, see Section **6.2**.

Conversely, one associates with a recursively enumerable set S a Turing Machine Z which produces the nth element of the set when started in state q, scanning the leftmost symbol of a string of n 1's, and halts when and only when it reaches state q_s; and then simulates Z by a semi-Thue system $\tau(Z)$ with alphabet $Q \cup X \cup \{h, k, k', k''\}$ [where we assume that Q (the state-set of Z) and X (the input set of Z) are disjoint, and that h and the k's are symbols in neither Q nor X] such that

(1) $\tau(Z)$ has the single axiom hkh

(2) There are productions to replace k by a string of $q_0 X^*$:

$$u_1 k u_2 \longrightarrow u_1 k x u_2 \qquad x \in X$$
$$u_1 k u_2 \longrightarrow u_1 q_0 u_2$$

(3) Other productions of $\tau(Z)$ mimic the quintuples of Z, for example,

$$qxx'Lq' \quad \text{yields} \quad \begin{array}{l} u_1 x_1 q x u_2 \longrightarrow u_1 q' x_1 x' u_2 \qquad \text{all} \ \ x_1 \in X \\ u_1 h q x u_2 \longrightarrow u_1 q' b x' u_2 \end{array}$$

(4) Finally, there are productions which, for a string containing q_s, remove q_s and the h's.

---

‡ Pronounced "Semi-two-way." One is tempted to say "one-way."

Thus the only strings on X^* obtainable are those which we may find on the tape of Z at the end of a computation.   □

Note that just as a Turing machine may never halt, so may a semi-Thue system produce an infinity of strings, none of which contains only "terminal" symbols—and thus generates the empty set.

9 EXERCISE: Complete steps (3) and (4) in the above proof.

This shows that any computation which can be executed by a Turing machine can be carried out by a suitable Post canonical system, though it be only a semi-Thue system. The converse result, that even a general canonical system may be simulated by a Turing machine, is harder, and we omit it. The enterprising reader may be able to supply the proof when he has finished reading Section **6.2**. We now wish to show that even simpler Post systems suffice for the simulation of Turing machines.

10 DEFINITION:

(i) *A system in canonical form is said to be in **normal form** if each of its productions is in the form $gu \rightarrow u\bar{g}$, where g and $\bar{g}$ are any two fixed strings.*

(ii) *A normal system is **monogenic** if the g's of the premises form a set $g_1, g_2, \ldots, g_k$ such that each string can be written in the form $g_i u$ for at most one i.*

(iii) *A "**tag**" **system** is a monogenic normal system in which the g's constitute all sequences of some fixed length l, while the corresponding h's are identical for all g's having the same initial symbol.*

POST [1943] proved that the normal systems are universal—i.e., any canonical system can be "simulated" by a normal system (for an elegant new proof of this result see MINSKY [1967, Chap. 13]). *He then conjectured* (POST [1943, p. 204]) *that the monogenic normal systems were universal.* MINSKY [1961; see also 1967, Chap. 14] proved the even stronger result—the "tag" systems are universal—by showing how to represent an arbitrary Turing machine as a "tag" system. Our task here is to provide the much simpler representation of a Turing machine Z as a monogenic normal system $M(Z)$; see Fig. 5.1. The reader will be invited to prove the harder result in Exercise **6.2.18**.

Our construction (ARBIB [1963]) results from a number of changes of viewpoint. First, we may remove the infinitude of blank squares of Z, agreeing to stick a new blank square on the tape whenever Z tries to move off the end of its tape. Thus we may regard the tape as finite, and can replace the linear tape by a circular tape with a square marked h (assume this is a new symbol) to mark the ends of the linear tape it replaces (see Fig. 5.1b). We can now signify our knowledge of which square is scanned and the state of

Z by inserting a new square on our circular tape immediately preceding the scanned square and writing on it the name of the internal state. We now replace Z by an arrow. (See Fig. 5.1c.) *It is this use of a circular tape, and the replacement of the Turing machine by a state-square and an arrow, that constitutes the essence of our construction.*

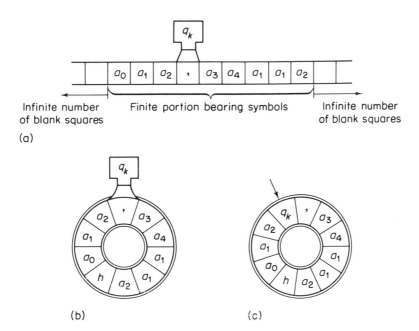

Fig. 5.1. Three portraits of a Turing machine.

We can simulate the operation of Z by rotating our circular tape until we encounter a q_j, and then operating according to the appropriate quintuple. In fact we shall apply the Turing machine state symbol changes only when the arrow points to the square *preceding* that bearing the state symbol.

To ensure monogenicity, we will have to rotate the tape more than one square at a time. In our construction, we shall cycle two squares at a time. However, if the arrow should point to a state square, and the tape has an even number of squares, such two-square cycling cannot bring the tape into "the Turing position," the position in which we can apply a production which simulates a quintuple of Z. Hence we introduce a technical device which enables the machine to extricate itself from the above impasse: we insert an additional square after the square bearing the state symbol, and on it print the symbol 1 if the number of squares on the tape is even, and 0 if the number of squares on the tape is odd. This should be enough to motivate the following construction of a monogenic normal system.

If our Turing machine is to operate on the finite string of symbols u, then we get our monogenic normal system to operate on the string

$$hq_0\xi u$$

where $\qquad \xi = \begin{cases} 0 & \text{if } u \text{ has an even number of symbols} \\ 1 & \text{if } u \text{ has an odd number of symbols} \end{cases}$

Let us agree to abbreviate productions in normal form from $gu \rightarrow u\bar{g}$ to $g \rightarrow \bar{g}$. For cycling we introduce the three productions:

$$\alpha\beta \rightarrow \alpha\beta$$
$$q_j 1\alpha \rightarrow q_j 1\alpha$$
$$q_j 0 \rightarrow q_j 0$$

(where α, β indicate nonstate symbols).

This corresponds to rotating the tape till the arrow points to the square preceding the one bearing a state symbol. This allows us to apply one of the following productions corresponding to the quintuples of the Turing machine (x_0 denotes the blank). We see that $q_i x_j x_k L q_l$ gives rise to

$$x_r q_i \xi x_j \alpha \rightarrow q_l \xi x_r x_k \alpha$$

and $\qquad\qquad hq_i \xi x_j \alpha \rightarrow hq_l (1 - \xi) x_0 x_k \alpha$

and $q_i x_j x_k N q_l$ gives rise to

$$\alpha q_i \xi x_j \beta \rightarrow \alpha q_l \xi x_k \beta$$

11   EXERCISE: To what productions does $q_i x_j x_k R q_l$ give rise?

12   THEOREM: *To each Turing machine Z there corresponds a monogenic normal system $M(Z)$, such that, if starting Z in state q_0 scanning the leftmost square of u causes Z to stop in state q_k scanning the α of the expression $Q\beta\alpha R$ printed on its tape, then starting $M(Z)$ on the string $hq_0\xi u$ will finally yield $\beta q_k\eta\alpha RhQ$ ($\eta = 0$ or 1) from which we immediately obtain the desired result $Q\beta\alpha R$.*

13   EXERCISE: Repeat the above proof without using the parity symbol ξ, but instead adding two squares each time you "extend the tape" to keep the length of the string always *odd*.

We also owe to Post an interesting problem known as:

14   POST'S CORRESPONDENCE PROBLEM: *Given elements $a_1, \ldots, a_n, b_1, \ldots, b_n$ of X^*, decide whether or not there exist integers $i_1, i_2, \ldots, i_m$ ($m \geq 1$) such that*

$$a_{i_1}a_{i_2} \ldots a_{i_m} = b_{i_1}b_{i_2} \ldots b_{i_m}$$

We shall find it most helpful in Section **4** to know that this problem is *not* recursively solvable:

15   THEOREM: *Post's correspondence problem is recursively unsolvable.*

Proof. Consider Turing machines modified to erase their tapes and go into some specified state q^* when they halt, and with no quintuple of the form $qxxNq$. Such a machine will halt after being started in state q_0 on a blank tape iff, $g_i \rightarrow h_i$ being the productions of the monogenic normal system which simulates it, there exists some sequence $i_1, \ldots, i_n$ for which

$$hq_0 0hh_{i_1}h_{i_2} \ldots h_{i_n} = g_{i_1}g_{i_2} \ldots g_{i_n}hq^*0h$$

Consider the Post correspondence problem for the pairs

$$(h_0, g_0) = (hq_0 0h, \Lambda), \qquad (h_1, g_1), \ldots, (h_m, g_m), \qquad (h_{m+1}, g_{m+1}) = (\Lambda, hq^*0h)$$

This is trivially solvable, because the pairs (h_i, g_i) corresponding to the "rotation" productions $\alpha\beta \rightarrow \alpha\beta$ have $h_i = g_i$. To avoid this trivial solvability, we recast $M(Z)$ in a new form $M'(Z)$ in which the alphabet is doubled, each symbol a in the old alphabet being matched by a new symbol a'. We replace the "rotation" productions $\alpha\beta \rightarrow \alpha\beta$, $q_j 1\alpha \rightarrow q_j 1\alpha$, $q_j 0 \rightarrow q_j 0$ by the "rotate and change alphabet" productions $\alpha\beta \rightarrow \alpha'\beta'$, $q_j 1\alpha \rightarrow q_j' 1'\alpha'$, $q_j 0 \rightarrow q_j' 0'$, and $\alpha'\beta' \rightarrow \alpha\beta$, where the last production is repeated for *all* α' and β' in the new alphabet. The quintuple productions $\alpha q_i \beta\gamma\delta \rightarrow \bar{g}$ are replaced by $\alpha q_i \beta\gamma\delta \rightarrow \bar{g}'$, where $\bar{g}'$ results from $\bar{g}$ by changing each letter to its primed counterpart. Thus we replace a single rotation in $M(Z)$ by a double rotation in $M'(Z)$, the first of which (applies a quintuple of Z and) changes all the symbols from unprimed to primed, while the second restores the symbols to the unprimed state.

Now, for the monogenic normal system $M'(Z)$, if we now use $g_1 \rightarrow h_1, \ldots, g_m \rightarrow h_m$ to label its productions, we again deduce that if Z halts when started on a blank tape, there is a solution to the Post correspondence problem for

$$(h_0, g_0) = (hq_0 0h, \Lambda), \qquad (h_1, g_1), \ldots, (h_m, g_m), \qquad (h_{m+1}, g_{m+1}) = (\Lambda, hq^*0h)$$

However, because *each h_i and g_i have no letters in common*, we can prove a sort of converse:

16   EXERCISE: Prove (recall that there is no quintuple $qxxNq$) that if

$$h_{j_1} \ldots h_{j_k} = g_{j_1} \ldots g_{j_k}$$

where no substring of $(j_1 \ldots j_k)$ is a solution of the correspondence problem, then we *must* have $j_i = 0$, $j_k = m + 1$, $\{j_2, \ldots, j_{k-1}\} \subseteq \{1, \ldots, m\}$.

It follows that if this correspondence problem were solvable, we could tell whether or not our Turing machine halted—i.e., we could solve the halting problem for Turing machines. $\square$

5.2   CONTEXT-SENSITIVE AND CONTEXT-FREE LANGUAGES

One important idea which has recurred in the previous pages is that of a relation between languages (in the formal sense of subsets of the set X^* of all strings on some vocabulary X) and automata. With finite automata we associated regular languages, whether we used the automata as generators or acceptors. Turing machines were associated with recursive sets when used as acceptors, and with recursively enumerable sets when used as generators. In Section 1 we saw how Post's symbol-manipulation systems could be used to generate languages. In particular we saw a sense in which semi-Thue systems and monogenic normal systems can be used to generate all recursively enumerable sets. In this section we study context-sensitive and context-free languages—which are the languages generated by restricted types of semi-Thue systems. In Section 4 we shall show that the context-free [context-sensitive] languages are precisely the languages accepted by what we shall call nondeterministic push-down [linear bounded] automata. CHOMSKY [1959] introduced these languages and suggested their use as a formal approximation to natural languages (Chomsky and his school have since done much to refine that approximation by augmenting it with the notion of transformational grammar). It has also been noted that the bulk of the programming language ALGOL could be treated as a context-free language (using the Backus Normal Form)—that it is not entirely so is due in a large part to the presence of so-called "semantic" rules for handling declaration statements, and so forth. As a result, there is now much interest in context-free languages as models of programming languages—part of a theory of data processing. Concepts, and unifying ideas, have come out of this, but as yet the theory has not yielded any effective measures for assessing the relative value of different computer languages.

We now present a slight modification of semi-Thue systems in a vocabulary appropriate to their interpretation as grammars. (We use Λ to denote the empty word, of length 0.)

1   DEFINITION: *A phrase-structure grammar is a quadruple*

$$G = (V, X, P, \sigma)$$

where

> V *is a finite nonempty set: the* **total vocabulary.**

> $X \subset V$: *The set of* **terminal symbols.** (*We shall be interested in languages over X, and may think of $V - X$ as grammatical symbols—elements of $V - X$ are called* (**metalinguistic**) *variables.*)

> P *is a finite set of ordered pairs (u, v) with u in $(V - X)^* - \Lambda$ and v in V^*. We usually write (u, v) as $u \to v$ and call it a* **production** *or* **rewriting rule** (*note that v may be Λ*).

> $\sigma \in V - X$: *The* **initial symbol.**

Given a grammar G, we write $y \Rightarrow z$, and say y *directly generates* z, if y and z are words on V for which we can find u, u_1, u_2, and v such that (u, v) is in P and $y = u_1 u u_2$ and $z = u_1 v u_2$.

We use $\Rightarrow^*$ to denote the transitive closure of $\Rightarrow$; that is, if y and z are in V^*, $y \Rightarrow^* z$ just in case $y = z$, or there is a sequence $z_1, z_2, \ldots, z_k$ in V^* such that $y = z_1 \Rightarrow z_2 \Rightarrow z_3 \Rightarrow \ldots \Rightarrow z_{k-1} \Rightarrow z_k = z$. We call such a sequence $z_1, \ldots, z_k$ a *derivation* or *generation* of z from y (by the rules of the grammar G).

2 DEFINITION: $L \subset X^*$ *is called a* **phrase-structure language** *if there exists a phrase structure grammar $G = (V, X, P, \sigma)$ such that*

$$L = L(G) = \{w \in X^* | \sigma \Rightarrow^* w\}$$

It turns out that the phrase-structure languages form the largest class of effectively generable subsets of X^*:

3 EXERCISE: Prove that a set of words is a phrase-structure language iff it is recursively enumerable. [Hint: This is almost a restatement of Theorem (**1.8**). How do we get around the condition that if $u \to v$, then $u \in (V - X)^* - \Lambda$?]

Since we would like a computer to be able to tell whether or not a string of symbols constitutes a valid program, the class of phrase structure languages is thus too broad for it to serve as a model for programming languages. We next present a subfamily of the recursive sets to which we can give a grammar formulation:

4 DEFINITION: *A* **context-sensitive grammar** *is a phrase-structure grammar for which each production (u, v) satisfies $l(u) \leq l(v)$. L is a* **context-sensitive language** *if $L = L(G)$ for some context-sensitive grammar G.*

5 FACT: No context-sensitive language contains Λ.

6 EXAMPLE: The set $\{a^n b^n c^n | n \geq 1\}$ is context-sensitive. (Why is $\{a^n b^n c^n | n \geq 0\}$ *not* context-sensitive?)

Proof. Let us use $V - X = \{\sigma, \sigma_1, B, B'\}$ with initial symbol σ:

$$X = \{a, b, c\}$$

and productions $\left.\begin{array}{l} \sigma \to a\sigma_1 B' \\ \sigma \to aB' \\ \sigma_1 \to a\sigma_1 B \\ \sigma_1 \to aB \end{array}\right\}$ produce strings of the form $a^n B^{n-1} B' \qquad n \geq 1$

$\left.\begin{array}{l} B' \to bc \\ Bb \to bB \\ Bc \to bcc \end{array}\right\}$ convert $a^n B^{n-1} B'$ to $a^n b^n c^n$

Sample derivations: $\sigma \Rightarrow aB' \Rightarrow abc$.

$$\sigma \Rightarrow a\,\sigma_1\,B' \Rightarrow a\,a\,\sigma_1\,B\,B' \Rightarrow a\,a\,a\,B\,B\,B' \Rightarrow a\,a\,a\,B\,B\,b\,c$$
$$\Rightarrow a\,a\,a\,B\,b\,B\,B\,c \Rightarrow a\,a\,a\,b\,B\,B\,c \Rightarrow a\,a\,a\,b\,B\,b\,c\,c$$
$$\Rightarrow a\,a\,a\,b\,b\,B\,c\,c \Rightarrow a\,a\,a\,b\,b\,b\,c\,c\,c$$

To make clear the name "context-sensitive," let us consider a grammar which is *strictly* context-sensitive in that every production is of the form $\varphi\,u\,\psi \to \varphi\,v\,\psi$, where $\varphi \in V^*, \psi \in V^*, u \in V - X$, and $v \in V^+$—that is, each production replaces a single letter by a non-null string, but the replacement may depend on the context. Let us see that *any* context-sensitive production can be replaced by a series of strictly context-sensitive productions:

Given $x_1 \ldots x_n \to x_1' \ldots x_m'$ with $m \geq n$, we introduce n new nonterminal symbols $A_n, \ldots, A_1$ and replace the above production by $2n$ strictly context-sensitive productions:

$$x_{n-1}x_n \to x_{n-1}A_n x_{n+1}' \ldots x_m'$$
$$x_{j-1}x_j A_{j+1} \to x_{j-1}A_j A_{j+1} \qquad 1 < j < n$$
$$A_{j-1}A_j \to A_{j-1}x_j' \qquad 1 < j \leq n$$
$$x_1 A_2 \to A_1 A_2$$
$$A_1 \to x_1'$$

We now relate context-sensitive languages to the families of recursive and recursively enumerable sets.

7 THEOREM: *Every context-sensitive language is a recursive set.*

Proof outline. Given v we use the length condition to see that there are only finitely many derivations which yield distinct strings of length $\leq l(v)$, and we check all of these effectively to see whether v is itself derivable. $\square$

It is of interest to contrast this with the result of the next exercise:

8 EXERCISE: Use the proof of Theorem **1.8** to show that every recursively enumerable set is the homomorphic image of a context-sensitive set.

We may use a diagonal argument, akin to that used in **4.4.15** to exhibit a nonrecursive, recursively enumerable set, to show that a recursive set need not be context-sensitive:

9 THEOREM: *There exist recursive sets which are not context-sensitive.*
    Proof. Let G_1, G_2, . . . be an effective enumeration of the context-sensitive grammars with terminal alphabet X. Enumerating the strings of X^* as $\xi_1, \xi_2, \xi_3, . . .$, we may define a set $\hat{S}$ by

$$\xi_n \in \hat{S} \Leftrightarrow \xi_n \notin L(G_n)$$

Now, $\hat{S}$ is recursive, since we may effectively test whether or not ξ_n is generable by G_n. However, $\hat{S}$ cannot be context-sensitive, for if $\hat{S}_n$ equaled $L(G_m)$, say, we should have $\xi_m \in \hat{S} \Leftrightarrow \xi_m \notin \hat{S}$, a contradiction.   □

    *The notion of context in this discussion refers to the context of a **single** letter.* This motivates the:

10 DEFINITION: *A **context-free (CF) grammar** is a phrase-structure grammar in which each production $u \to v$ has the property $l(u) = 1$; that is, each rule has the form $u \to v$ with $u \in V - X$, $v \in V^*$.*
    *L is a **context-free language (CF language; CFL)** if $L = L(G)$ for some CF grammar G.*

11 FACT: Λ may be in a CFL, but L context-free implies $L - \{\Lambda\}$ context-sensitive.

12 EXAMPLE: If $X = \{a, b\}$, $V = \{a, b, \sigma\}$, $P = \{\sigma \to a\sigma b, \sigma \to ab\}$, then $L(G) = \{a^n b^n | n \geq 1\}$, which is thus a CFL, although, as the reader may deduce from Theorem **3.3.9**, it is not regular.
    Unfortunately, it is not usually possible to obtain so explicit a description of a language defined implicitly by a CF grammar.

13 EXERCISE: Show that any context-free grammar G may be replaced by a context-free grammar G' in which every production $\xi \to x$ has $l(x) \geq 2$; and such that $L(G) - L(G')$ is a finite set, and $L(G') \subset L(G)$.

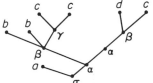

Fig. 5.2

14 EXAMPLE: Let $G = (V, X, P, \sigma)$, with $X = \{a, b, c, d\}$, $V = \{\sigma, \alpha, \beta, \gamma, a, b, c, d\}$, and $P = \{\sigma \to a\alpha, \alpha \to \beta\alpha, \alpha \to \beta, \beta \to dc, \beta \to bb\gamma, \gamma \to cc\}$. Then the derivation $\sigma \Rightarrow a\alpha \Rightarrow a\beta\alpha \Rightarrow a\beta\beta \Rightarrow a\beta dc \Rightarrow abb\gamma dc \Rightarrow abbccdc$ may be "graphed" by a tree known as the *derivation tree*, in which the word generated is given by the terminal modes, read from left to right as in Fig. 5.2, a structure reminiscent of a parsing tree.

By looking at derivations in terms of these trees, we may obtain the following result (cf. **3.3.9**) known as the *pumping lemma* for context-free languages:

15 THEOREM (BAR-HILLEL, PERLES, and SHAMIR [1961]): *Let* $G = (V, X, P, \sigma)$ *be a CF grammar. It is possible to determine two integers p and q such that every sentence z of $L(G)$ with $l(z) > p$ can be decomposed into the form $z = xuwvy$, where $u \neq \Lambda$ or $v \neq \Lambda$, $l(uwv) \leq q$, and $z_k = xu^kwv^ky \in L(G)$ for $k = 1, 2, \ldots$.*

Proof. By **13** we may assume, without loss of generality, $l(x) \geq 2$ whenever some $\xi \to x$ is in P.

Let n be the number of symbols in $V - X$, and let p be the length of the longest string that can be derived with a tree of height at most n. Then every string z of length greater than p must have some symbol W of $V - X$ occurring at least twice in a branch of its derivation tree, say $W \Rightarrow^* u'Wv' \Rightarrow^* uwv$, where $u' \Rightarrow^* u$, $W \Rightarrow^* w$, and $v' \Rightarrow^* v$. By our initial assumption, u or v is non-null. Thus $z = xuwvy$, and clearly $W \Rightarrow^* (u')^kW(v')^k \Rightarrow^* u^kwv^k$. So $z_k = xu^kwv^ky \in L(G)$. The bound q is obtained by noting that we may take $W \Rightarrow^* u'Wv' \Rightarrow^* uwv$ to have total branch length $\leq n + 1$. ☐

Actually, much more information may be obtained from the above type of argument:

16 EXERCISE (OGDEN [1968]): Let $G = (V, X, P, \sigma)$ be a CF grammar. Determine an integer k such that for every sentence z of $L(G)$ with $l(z) \geq k$, if any k or more positions in z are designated as distinguished, then there is some A in $V - X$, and words $\alpha, \beta, \gamma, \delta$, and μ in X^* such that:

(i) $\sigma \Rightarrow^* \alpha A\mu \Rightarrow^* \alpha\beta A\delta\mu \Rightarrow^* \alpha\beta\gamma\delta\mu = z$.

(ii) γ contains at least one of the distinguished positions.

(iii) Either α and β both contain distinguished positions, or δ and μ both contain distinguished positions.

(iv) $\beta\gamma\delta$ contains at most k distinguished positions.

[Hint: Call a node of a derivation tree for z a B-node if it has at least two immediate descendants with descendants occupying distinguished positions in z.]

17 EXERCISE (HARTMANIS and SHANK [1968]): Recall the number-theoretic result that $2^{p-1} \equiv 1 \pmod{p}$ for each prime $p > 2$. [This follows from the binomial expansion $(1 + 1)^p = 1 + p + \dfrac{p(p - 1)}{2} + \cdots + p + 1 \equiv 2 \pmod{p}$.] Use this to show that the set of binary strings which are the *binary* expansions of prime numbers is neither regular (use **3.3.9**) nor context-free (use **15**).

18   EXERCISE: Use **(15)** to verify that $\{a^n b^n c^n | n \geq 1\}$, which we have seen to be context-sensitive, is not a CFL. Show that $\{ww^R | w \in X^*\}$ is a CFL, whereas $\{ww | w \in X^*\}$ is context-sensitive but not a CFL.

19   FACT: *The class of CFL's is not closed under intersection.*
   Proof. $L_1 = \{a^i b^j c^j | i, j \geq 1\}$ and $L_2 = \{a^i b^i c^j | i, j \geq 1\}$ are both CFLs, but, by **(18)**, $L_1 \cap L_2$ is *not* a CFL.   □

20   THEOREM: *The class of CFL's is closed under the* $\cup$, $\cdot$, *and* * *operations.*
   Proof. Given grammars for L_1 and L_2, replace them by grammars with disjoint sets of metalinguistic variables, to obtain

$$G_1 = (X^1 \cup X, X, P_1, \sigma_1) \qquad G_2 = (X^2 \cup X, X, P_2, \sigma_2)$$

It is then easy to verify that G_3 is a grammar for $L_1 \cup L_2$, G_4 is a grammar for $L_1 \cdot L_2$, and G_5 is a grammar for L_1^*, where

$$G_3 = (X^1 \cup X^2 \cup X \cup \{\sigma\}, X, P_1 \cup P_2 \cup \{\sigma \rightarrow \sigma_1, \sigma \rightarrow \sigma_2\}, \sigma)$$
$$G_4 = (X^1 \cup X^2 \cup X \cup \{\sigma\}, X, P_1 \cup P_2 \cup \{\sigma \rightarrow \sigma_1 \sigma_2\}, \sigma)$$
$$G_5 = (X^1 \cup X, X, P \cup \{\sigma \rightarrow \Lambda, \sigma \rightarrow \sigma \sigma_1\}, \sigma)$$ □

21   COROLLARY: *The class of CFL's is not closed under complementation.*
   Proof. If it were, Theorem **20** would then imply that it was closed under intersection contrary to **19**.   □

22   THEOREM: *If L is a CFL and R is a regular set, then $L \cap R$ is also a CFL.*
   Proof. Let $M = (Q, \delta, q_0, F)$ be an acceptor for R, that is, $R = \{x \in X^* | \delta(q_0, x) \in F\}$.
   Let $G = (V, X, \sigma, P)$ be a CF grammar for L.
   Let us introduce new auxiliary symbols (q, v, q'), where each symbol is labeled by some $q \in Q$, $v \in V$, and $q' \in Q$.
   Now let $\hat{L}$ consist of all strings

$$(q_0, x_1, q_1)(q_1, x_2, q_2) \ldots (q_{n-1}, x_n, q_n)$$

such that $x_1 x_2 \ldots x_n \in L$ (with each $x_j \in X$) and $q_n \in F$. $\hat{L}$ is generated by CF grammar $\hat{G}$ with initial symbol $\hat{\sigma}$ and productions $\hat{P}$:

$$\hat{\sigma} \rightarrow (q_0, \sigma, q) \qquad \text{for each } q \in F$$

and
$$(p, \xi, q) \rightarrow (p, v_1, q_1)(q_1, v_2, q_2) \ldots (q_{n-1}, v_n, q)$$

   for each production $\xi \rightarrow v_1 v_2 \ldots v_n$ of P, each $v_j \in V$, and *any* choice of $q_1, q_2, \ldots, q_{n-1}$.

Now we adjoin to $\hat{P}$ the productions

$$(p, v, q) \rightarrow v \qquad \text{if } v \text{ is in } X \text{ and } \delta(p, v) = q$$

These productions extract the string $x_1 \ldots x_n$ of X^* from the string $(q_0, x_1, q_1) \ldots (q_{n-1}, x_n, q_n)$ of $\hat{L}$ just in case $\delta(q_0, x_1) = q_1, \ldots, \delta(q_{n-1}, x_n) = q_n$. Since $q_n \in F$, this says we obtain $x_1 \ldots x_n$ just in case it belongs not only to L but also to R. Thus $L \cap R$ is a context-free language. $\square$

23 EXAMPLE: Suppose L is CF, and let L_n be the set of all words in L whose length is divisible by n. Then $L_n = L \cap R_n^*$, where R_n is the set of words of length n. Thus L_n is a CFL.

24 DEFINITION: *For each a in X, let X_a be a finite nonempty set, and specify a subset $\tau(a)$ of X_a^*. We then extend τ to X^* by letting*

$$\tau(\Lambda) = \{\Lambda\} \qquad \tau(a_1 \ldots a_k) = \tau(a_1) \ldots \tau(a_k)$$

*Such a τ is called a **substitution mapping**.*

If L is CF, and τ is an unrestricted substitution mapping, we cannot expect $\tau(L)$ to be CF—just take $\tau(a)$ to be a non-CF language, and set $L = \{a\}$. However,

25 EXERCISE: Prove the SUBSTITUTION THEOREM: If L is CF, and τ is a substitution mapping with $\tau(a)$ CF for every a in $\sum$, then $\tau(L)$ is CF. [This is an easy exercise of the type undertaken to prove Theorem **20**.]

26 COROLLARY: *For every homomorphism $h: X^* \rightarrow Y^*$ and every CF $L \subset X^*$, we have: $h(L) \subset Y^*$ is also CF.*

Alternatively to direct substitution, we may introduce sequential dependencies:

27 DEFINITION: *A **generalized sequential machine** (gsm) is a sextuple*

$$S = (Q, X, Y, \delta, \lambda, q_0)$$

*where Q, X, and Y are finite nonempty sets (the **states**, **inputs**, and **outputs**):*

$q_0 \in Q$ *is the **start state**;*
$\delta: Q \times X \rightarrow Q$ *is the **next-state** function;*
$\lambda: Q \times X \rightarrow Y^*$ *is the **output** function.*

Note that a single input may yield no output, a single output symbol, or a whole string. If $\lambda(Q \times X) \subset Y$, we obtain our familiar finite automata (also known as complete sequential machines, and so on).

If S is a gsm, and $w \in X^*$, we set $S(w) = \lambda(q_0, w)$, on extending λ to $Q \times X^*$ in the usual way.

28 EXERCISE: If L is CF, and S is a gsm, show that $S(L)$ is also a CFL. [Hint: Mimic the proof of **22**.]

29 EXAMPLE: Let L be a CFL. Let $f(w_1 w_2 \ldots w_k) = w_2 w_4 \ldots (w_i \in X)$. Clearly f is a gsm mapping, and so $f(L)$ is also a CFL.

30 EXAMPLE: For each set of words L, let Init $(L) = \{u \neq \Lambda | \exists w \text{ with } uw \text{ in } L\}$. We show that if L is CFL, then so is Init (L). For each a in X, set $\tau(a) = \{a, ac\}$ with $c \notin X$. Then $\tau(L) \cap X^* c X^*$ is still CF. Now, let S be the gsm which acts like an identity until it reaches a c, and then just "emits" Λ. Clearly Init $(L) = S[\tau(L) \cap X^* c X^*]$ and so is a CFL.

We saw in Section **3.3** that the regular sets are those accepted by finite-state automata, whether these be deterministic or possibilistic (nondeterministic) in their operation. We may also characterize the regular sets as CFLs of a particular kind:

31 DEFINITION: *A CF grammar $G = (V, X, P, \sigma)$ is said to be* **right-linear** *if each production in P is of the form $\xi \rightarrow u$ or $\xi \rightarrow u\alpha$, where u is in X^* and α is in $V - X$.*

32 THEOREM: *A set $R \subset X^*$ is regular iff there exists some right-linear grammar G such that $R = L(G)$.*
    Proof. Let $M = (Q, X, \delta, q_0, F)$ be a finite acceptor for R (that is, $R = \{x \in X^* | \delta(q_0, x) \in F\}$), and let $G = (V, X, P, \sigma)$, where $V = X \cup Q \cup \{\sigma\}$, and let P contain

   (i)   a production $\sigma \rightarrow q_0$
   (ii)   for each $q, q' \in Q$ and $x \in X$ such that $\delta(q, x) = q$
          a production $q \rightarrow xq'$
   (iii)   for each q in F
          a production $q \rightarrow \Lambda$.

Then $L(G) = R$. A somewhat modified reversal of this construction yields the converse.   □

33 EXERCISE: Let R be a regular subset of X^* and E a symbol not in X. Construct a CF grammar G such that $L(G) = \{x E x^R | x \in R\}$, where x^R is the reversal of the string x. When is $L(G)$ regular?

34 EXERCISE: Show that if L is CFL, so too is L^R.

Thus the regular sets are all CFLs. However, as we saw in example **12**, not all CFLs are regular, an example of one which is not regular being $\{a^i b^i | i \geq 1\}$.

Recalling that $L^+ = \{x_1 \ldots x_n | n \geq 1 \text{ and } x_j \in L\}$, we may summarize the closure properties of the families of languages we have studied by the following table:

Family		Closed under					
		+	Union	Inter-section	Comple-mentation	Intersection with a regular set	Substi-tution
	Recursively enumerable	yes	yes	yes	no	yes	yes
	Recursive	yes	yes	yes	yes	yes	yes
	Context-sensitive	yes	yes	yes	?	yes	yes
	Context-free	yes	yes	no	no	yes	yes
	Regular	yes	yes	yes	yes	yes	yes
	Finite	no	yes	yes	no	yes	yes

35 EXERCISE: For each entry in the above matrix, identify where in the book its assertion is proved. If it is not proved in this book, supply the proof yourself.

5.3 AMBIGUITY AND DECISION PROBLEMS FOR CONTEXT-FREE LANGUAGES

Returning to the generation tree of (2.14), we see that it corresponds to several different derivations, but since all these derivations yield the same tree, we want to regard them as corresponding to the same "parsing" of the derived word. We may avoid this diversity of derivations for a tree, by associating with the tree the *leftmost derivation*, i.e., that in which, at each stage, a production is applied to the leftmost variable—this is always possible, since all replacements are context-free. For instance, the leftmost derivation for the tree in (2.14) is

$$\sigma \Rightarrow a\alpha \Rightarrow a\beta\alpha \Rightarrow abb\gamma\alpha \Rightarrow abbcc\alpha \Rightarrow abbcc\beta \Rightarrow abbccdc$$

We may now embody the notion of a grammar as being ambiguous if there are words of the language which can be parsed in different ways.

1 DEFINITION: *A CF grammar is* **unambiguous** *if each word in $L(G)$ has exactly one generation tree (i.e., exactly one leftmost derivation). Otherwise, G is called* **ambiguous**.

We repeat that this notion is one of *syntactic* ambiguity. In data-processing a word in the language encodes a program. A compiler must be able to break the program down uniquely into its components. Of course, a language might be ambiguous syntactically, and yet unambiguous semantically in that no matter how many different ways an ambiguous string were compiled, it would yield a program which would cause a computer to compute the same function. But such notions of semantic ambiguity are outside the scope of the present treatment.

2 EXAMPLE: Consider the language $\{a^n b^n | n \geq 1\}$. We know that it has the unambiguous grammar with the simple productions $\sigma \to a\sigma b$, $\sigma \to \Lambda$. But it also has the ambiguous grammar with productions

$$\sigma \to a\sigma_1 \qquad \sigma \to \sigma_2 b \qquad \sigma_1 \to a\sigma_1 b \qquad \sigma_2 \to a\sigma_2 b \qquad \sigma_1 \to b \qquad \sigma_2 \to a$$

In this case, the ambiguity seems somewhat forced. However, consider the language

$$\hat{L} = \{a^i b^j a^i b^k | i, j, k \geq 1\} \cup \{a^i b^j a^k b^j | i, j, k \geq 1\}$$

Here the most natural grammar, with productions

$$\sigma \to \sigma_1 \sigma_1' \qquad \sigma \to \sigma_2 \sigma_2' \qquad \sigma_1 \to a\sigma_1 a \qquad \sigma_1 \to \sigma_1' \qquad \sigma_1' \to b\sigma_1' \qquad \sigma_1' \to b$$

$$\sigma_2 \to a\sigma_2 \qquad \sigma_2 \to a \qquad \sigma_2' \to b\sigma_2' b \qquad \sigma_2' \to \sigma_2$$

is ambiguous. It is not at all clear whether or not $\hat{L}$ has an unambiguous grammar. In fact, it does not.

It is not always easy to tell, by inspection, whether or not a grammar is ambiguous. In fact we shall see that the ambiguity problem—telling whether or not a grammar is ambiguous—is *not* effectively solvable for CF grammars.

3 THEOREM (CANTOR [1962]): *The ambiguity problem for CF grammars is unsolvable.*

Proof. Let us be given an unsolvable Post correspondence problem (*cf.* **1.15**) $(a_1, \ldots, a_n)$, $(b_1, \ldots, b_n)$ over an alphabet X_1. Adjoin to X_1 the new symbols $i_1, \ldots, i_n$ to obtain the alphabet X.

Now consider the CF grammar

$$G = (V, X, \sigma, P)$$

where $V - X = \{\sigma, \sigma_1, \sigma_2\}$, and the productions in P are

$$\left.\begin{array}{ll} \sigma \rightarrow \sigma_1 & \sigma \rightarrow \sigma_2 \\ \sigma_1 \rightarrow i_j \sigma_1 a_j & \sigma_2 \rightarrow i_j \sigma_2 b_j \\ \sigma_1 \rightarrow i_j b_j & \sigma_2 \rightarrow i_j b_j \end{array}\right\} 1 \leq j \leq n$$

Then $L(G) = \{i_{j_m} \ldots i_{j_1} b_{j_1} \ldots b_{j_m}\} \cup \{i_{j_m} \ldots i_{j_1} a_{j_1} \ldots a_{j_m}\}$ and G is ambiguous if and only if the two sets displayed above are not disjoint, i.e., iff there is a solution to the Post correspondence problem for $(a_1, \ldots, a_n)$, $(b_1, \ldots, b_m)$. Hence it is undecidable whether or not G is ambiguous. $\square$

The reader may readily convince himself that every CFL has infinitely many CF grammars. Thus, given an ambiguous grammar for a language, we may seek unambiguous grammars for the language. Such a search may or may not succeed.

4 DEFINITION: *A CFL is said to be **inherently ambiguous** if every grammar generating it is ambiguous.*

That there do exist inherently ambiguous languages was first shown by PARIKH [1961], who proved that the language $\hat{L} = \{a^i b^j a^k b^l | j = l \text{ or } i = k; i, j, k, l \geq 1\}$, already mentioned in example **2**, is inherently ambiguous.

We may give a simpler proof (similar in spirit to that of Parikh) of an inherent ambiguity by using the result of Exercise **(2.16)**.

5 THEOREM (OGDEN [1968]): *Let $M = \{a^i b a^{i+1} b | i \geq 0\}$, $L_0 = abM^*$ and $L_1 = M^*\{a\}^* b$. Then the CF language $L_0 \cup L_1$ is inherently ambiguous.*

Proof. Let G be *any* grammar for $L_0 \cup L_1$, and let k be the integer presented to us by the result of Exercise **2.16**. Let $p = k!$ We shall show that $z = aba^2 ba^3 b \ldots ba^{4p} ba^{4p+1} b$, which lies both in L_0 and in L_1, has two distinct derivations.

Let z_0 be the word $aba^2 ba^3 \ldots ba^{4p-1} ba^p a^p ba^{2p+1} b$ of $L_0 - L_1$, and let us designate as distinguished the first $p(\geq k)$ symbols in the second last block of a's in z_0. Let A_0, α_0, β_0, γ_0, δ_0 and μ_0 be the strings with properties (i) through (iv) for z_0, assured by Exercise **2.16**.

Now, γ_0 contains a distinguished symbol [by (ii)], and by (iii) either α_0 and β_0 both contain distinguished positions (in which case β_0 must consist entirely of distinguished positions since the distinguished positions are consecutive) or δ_0 and μ_0 both contain distinguished positions (in which case δ_0 must consist entirely of distinguished positions). Since $p > k$, it follows that (iv) guarantees that $\beta_0 \gamma_0 \delta_0$, having at most k distinguished positions, cannot be entirely contained in the first p symbols in the second last block of a's in z_0.

Since, by (i), we must have $\alpha_0 \beta_0^n \gamma_0 \delta_0^n \mu_0$ in $L_0 \cup L_1$ for each $n \geq 0$, and since $\alpha_0 \beta_0 \gamma_0 \delta_0 \mu_0 = z_0$, the "overshoot" must be from the right-hand end. We conclude that β_0 is in the distinguished symbols of z_0, and δ_0 is in the last block of a's in z_0, and we see that $|\beta_0| = |\delta_0| = j_0$, say. Then $j_0 < k$.

Let $q_0 = 2k!/j_0 + 1$. Then $z = \alpha_0 \beta_0^{q_0} \gamma_0 \delta_0^{q_0} \mu_0$.

Similarly, considering $z_1 = aba^2 ba^3 b \ldots ba^{4p-2} ba^{2p-1} ba^p a^p ba^{4p+1} b$, and designating the last p symbols in the next to last block of a's as distinguished, we may obtain $\sigma \Rightarrow^* \alpha_1 A_1 \mu_1 \Rightarrow^* \alpha_1 \beta_1 A_1 \delta_1 \mu_1 \Rightarrow^* z_1 = \alpha_1 \beta_1 \gamma_1 \delta_1 \mu_1$ in such a way that $z = \alpha_1 \beta_1^{q_1} \gamma_1 \delta_1^{q_1} \mu_1$ for suitable $q_1 > 0$.

We thus have two derivations of z which are incompatible, and so G is ambiguous. Since G was an arbitrary grammar for $L_0 \cup L_1$, we conclude that $L_0 \cup L_1$ is inherently ambiguous. $\square$

6 EXERCISE

(i) Show that if L is an *unambiguous* CFL and R is a regular set, then $L \cap R$ is also an unambiguous CFL (compare **2.22**).

(ii) Show that the right-linear grammar for a regular set (**2.23**) may be chosen to be unambiguous.

We have already applied the fact that the following problem (Post's correspondence problem) is not effectively solvable: Let $a = (a_1, \ldots, a_n)$, $b = (b_1, \ldots, b_n)$ be two n-tuples of strings over a vocabulary V. Does there exist a sequence of indices $l_1, \ldots, l_k$, where $k \geq 1$ and $1 \leq i_j \leq n$ for $j = 1, \ldots, k$ such that $a_{i_1} \ldots a_{i_k} = b_{i_1} \ldots b_{i_k}$? We write $\mathcal{P}(a, b) = 1$ if there exists such a sequence, $\mathcal{P}(a, b) = 0$ if not.

We now lead the reader through a series of exercises to prove the following three theorems of BAR-HILLEL, PERLES, and SHAMIR, which apply this result to show that many questions related to CFLs, besides that of deciding ambiguity, are also unsolvable.

7 THEOREM: *The following decision problems are effectively unsolvable: Given two CFGs, G_1 and G_2, is $L(G_1) \cap L(G_2)$*

(a) *empty;*

(b) *finite;*

(c) *regular;*

(d) *a CFL?*

Moreover, these problems are unsolvable even in the special case in which G_1 and G_2 have a common terminal vocabulary X which contains two symbols only, and they remain unsolvable for G_1, even if G_2 is held fixed to be a certain $\bar{G}_s$ defined below.

8 THEOREM: *The following decision problems are effectively unsolvable: Given a CFG G with a terminal vocabulary X, is $X^* - L(G)$*

(a) *empty;*

(b) *finite;*

(c) *regular;*

(d) *a CFL?*

These problems are unsolvable even if X is restricted to contain two symbols only.

9 THEOREM: *The following decision problems are effectively unsolvable:*

(a) *Given two CFGs, G_1 and G_2, is $L(G_1) \subset L(G_2)$? This problem remains unsolvable for G_2 if G_1 is held fixed to be a certain G_w defined below, and remains unsolvable for G_1 if G_2 is held fixed to be a certain $\bar{G}_s$ defined below.*

(b) *Given two CFGs, G_1 and G_2, is $L(G_1) = L(G_2)$? This problem remains unsolvable for G_1 if G_2 is held fixed to be a certain G_w defined below.*

(c) *Given a CFG, G, is $L(G)$ regular?*

(d) *Given a CFG, G, and an FA, $\mathcal{Q}$, is $L(G) = T(\mathcal{Q})$? This problem remains unsolvable for G if $\mathcal{Q}$ is held fixed to a certain FA $\mathcal{Q}_w$ defined below. These four problems are unsolvable even in the special case in which the terminal vocabularies of G_1, G_2, and G and the vocabulary of $\mathcal{Q}$ each contain two symbols only.*

10   EXERCISE: Let $\hat{\imath} = 0^i$ code the natural number i. Given an n-tuple of strings $\xi = (x_1, \ldots, x_n)$, define

$$L(\xi) = \{\hat{\imath}_k \ldots \hat{\imath}_1 \text{ E } x_{i_1} \ldots x_{i_k} | k \geq 1, 1 \leq i_\nu \leq n \qquad \text{for } \nu = 1, \ldots, k\}$$

Let (a, b) be a pair of n-tuples of non-empty strings over $\{0, 1\}$. $a = (a_1, \ldots, a_n)$, $b = (b_1, \ldots, b_n)$. Define $L(a, b) = L(a) \text{ E } L(b)^R$. Exhibit grammars which show that

(i) $L(a, b)$ is a CFL.

(ii) $\{0, 1, E\}^* - L(a, b)$ is a CFL.

(iii) $L_s = \{w_1 \text{ E } w_2 \text{ E } w_2^R \text{ E } w_1^R \mid w_1, w_2 \in \{0, 1\}^*\}$ is a CFL.

(iv) $\{0, 1, E\}^* - L_s$ is a CFL.

Now, $L(a, b) \cap L_s = \{\hat{\imath}_k, \ldots, \hat{\imath}_1 \text{ E } a_{i_1} \ldots a_{i_k} \text{ E } b_{i_k}^R \ldots b_{i_1}^R \text{ E } \hat{\imath}_1 \ldots \hat{\imath}_k | k \geq 1;$ $1 \leq i_\nu \leq n$ for $\nu = 1, \ldots, k$; and $a_{i_1} \ldots a_{i_k} = b_{i_1} \ldots b_{i_k}\}$. Thus

$$\mathcal{P}(a, b) = 0 \Rightarrow L(a, b) \cap L_s = \emptyset$$

$$\mathcal{P}(a, b) = 1 \Rightarrow L(a, b) \cap L_s \text{ is infinite, since}$$

$$a_{i_1} \ldots a_{i_k} = b_{i_1} \ldots b_{i_k} \Rightarrow (a_{i_1} \ldots a_{i_k})^n = (b_{i_1} \ldots b_{i_k})^m$$

Moreover, we shall see that $\mathcal{P}(a, b) = 1 \Rightarrow L(a, b) \cap L_s$ is *not* a CFL. But in order to prove our theorems also for CFGs with *two* terminal symbols only, we shall first appropriately recode the vocabulary of $L(a, b)$ and L_s. Let

$$\varphi: \{0, 1, E\}^* \rightarrow \{0, 1\}^* \text{ be given by } \varphi(0) = 101, \varphi(1) = 1001 \text{ and}$$
$$\varphi(E) = 10001.$$

Write $\bar{x}$ for $\varphi(x)$. φ is one-to-one and so:

$$\varphi(L_1 \cap L_2) = \varphi(L_1) \cap \varphi(L_2)$$

Set $W = \{0, 1, E\}^*$ and $\overline{W} = \varphi(W)$:

$$\varphi(W - L) = \overline{W} - \varphi(L) = \{0, 1\}^* - (L' \cup \varphi(L)), \text{ where } L' = \{0, 1\}^* - \overline{W}.$$

11   EXERCISE: Exhibit a grammar which shows that L' is a CFL.

12   EXERCISE: Show that if $\mathcal{P}(a, b) = 1$ then $\overline{L}(a, b) \cap \overline{L}_s$ is not a CFL. [Hint: The proof is by a careful application of Theorem **4.1**. The proof shows that if $\mathcal{P}(a, b) = 1$, $\overline{L}(a, b) \cap \overline{L}_s$ is not only different from any CFL, but does not even *contain* an infinite CFL.]

13 *Proof of Theorem* **7.** If $\mathcal{P}(a, b) = 1$, then $\overline{L}(a, b) \cap \overline{L}_s = L(\overline{G}(a, b)) \cap L(\overline{G}_s)$ is not a CFL (and thus not an FSL, nor empty nor finite). But if $\mathcal{P}(a, b) = 1$, it is empty, and so certainly finite, an FSL and a CFL. Thus if any of (a), (b), (c), and (d) were effectively solvable, we would have an effective decision procedure for Post's correspondence problem. $\qquad \square$

14 *Proof of Theorem* **8.** Let $L(\overline{G}'_s) = \overline{W}_s - \overline{L}_s$, $L(\overline{G}'(a, b)) = \overline{W} - \overline{L}(a, b)$, $L(G') = L'$, and then construct $\overline{G}''(a, b)$ from G', $\overline{G}'_s$ and $\overline{G}'(a, b)$ so that $L(\overline{G}''(a, b)) = L(G') \cup L(\overline{G}'_s) \cup L(\overline{G}'(a, b))$. Then $\{0, 1\}^* - L(\overline{G}''(a, b)) = \overline{L}(a, b) \cap \overline{L}_s$, and so the answers to (a), (b), (c), and (d) are positive for $G = \overline{G}''(a, b)$ if $\mathcal{P}(a, b) = 0$, and negative if $\mathcal{P}(a, b) = 1$. So a decision procedure cannot exist, or else there would be one for Post's correspondence problem. $\qquad \square$

15 *Proof of Theorem* **9.**

(a) Set $L(G_W) = \{0, 1\}^*$ to reduce to **8**(a).

(b) $L(G_W) = \{0, 1\}^*$.

(c) Note that $L(G)$ is an FSL iff $X^* - L(G)$ is an FSL and use **8**(c).

(d) Let $T(\mathcal{C}_w) = \{0, 1\}^*$, and use **8**(a). $\qquad \square$

5.4   PUSH-DOWN AUTOMATA AND LINEAR-BOUNDED AUTOMATA

We have seen that the regular sets are precisely those accepted by finite automata, while the recursive sets are precisely those accepted by Turing machines. In Section **2**, we introduced two new families of languages, the context-free and the context-sensitive languages. We shall show that corresponding to these are two new classes of acceptors, the nondeterministic push-down automata and the nondeterministic linear bounded automata, respectively.

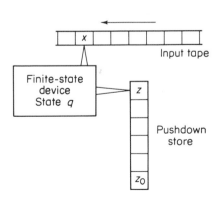

Fig. 5.3

The notion of a nondeterministic (i.e., possibilistic) push-down automaton was first introduced as a tool for mechanical translation, and as a programming concept. We may picture one as a finite-state device (see Fig. 5.3), to which is adjoined a push-down store—a finite but expandable tape, only the topmost square of which may be read by the machine at any time. Inputs come in from the right.

The triple (q, x, z) of state, input, and top push-down symbol can determine possible next states q', and possible strings γ with which to replace z, in which case the machine completes the cycle scanning the rightmost (i.e., topmost) square of γ (if $\gamma = \Lambda$, which gives an erase, the machine ends scanning the square below z). Alternatively, the machine may only use q and z to determine (q', γ), in which case the input tape is not advanced. Thus the action is nondeterministic. The push-down store is a LIFO store: Last In, First Out.

The machine halts if the push-down store is emptied, and so we introduce a special symbol z_0 to mark the end of its tape—computation always starts with just z_0 in the push-down store. Formally:

1 DEFINITION: *A **push-down automaton** (pda)‡ is a septuple*

$$M = (Q, X, \Gamma, \delta, z_0, q_0, F)$$

*where Q, X, and Γ are finite non-empty sets (the **states**, **inputs**, and **push-down symbols**, respectively),*

*$z_0 \in \Gamma$ is the **push-down start symbol***
*$q_0 \in Q$ is the **start state***
*$F \subset Q$ is the set of **designated final states***

and δ is a mapping from $Q \times (X \cup \{\Lambda\}) \times \Gamma$ into the finite subsets of $Q \times \Gamma^*$.

Given a pda, M, let $\vdash^*$ be the relation on $Q \times X^* \times \Gamma^*$ defined as follows: For z in Γ, x in $X \cup \{\Lambda\}$, write $(p, xw, \alpha z) \vdash (q, w, \alpha\gamma)$ if $\delta(q, x, z)$ contains (q, γ). Note that x may be empty.

Write $(p, w, \alpha) \vdash^* (p, w, \alpha)$. Further, for each β in Γ^* and x in $X \cup \{\Lambda\}$, $1 \leq i \leq k$, write $(p, x_1 \ldots x_k w, \alpha) \vdash^* (q, w, \beta)$ if there exists $p = p_1, p_2, \ldots, p_{k+1} = q$ in Q, and $\alpha = \alpha_1, \alpha_2, \ldots, \alpha_{k+1} = \beta$ in Γ^* such that $(p_i, x_i \ldots x_k w, \alpha_i) \vdash (p_{i+1}, x_{i+1} \ldots x_k w, \alpha_{i+1})$ for $1 \leq i \leq k$.

2 DEFINITION: *A word $w \in X^*$ is **accepted** by a pda M if*

$$(q_0, w, z_0) \vdash^* (q, \Lambda, \alpha)$$

for some $q \in F$ and some α in Γ^*. The set of all tapes accepted by M is denoted by $T(M)$.

In other words a word is accepted by M if it is possible to start M in state q_0, with the single symbol z_0 on its stack (push-down store), and have it read in the word to finish in a state of F, with an empty stack.

We shall in fact prove the

---

‡ The nondeterministic pda is so important that we omit the label—and only make special comment if a pda is deterministic.

3 CHARACTERIZATION THEOREM: *A set L of words is a CFL iff L = T(M) for some pda M.*

This theorem is an important tool in showing that we may prove a language CF by exhibiting a pda which accepts it. Unfortunately, this task may be a hard one—it is usually easy to prove that all strings of a language are accepted by a suitable pda, but hard to show that the pda accepts no other strings.

4 EXAMPLE: Let $X = \{a, b\}$, and let L be the set of words with exactly as many occurrences of a as occurrences of b. Consider the pda M which reads an input symbol at a time and deletes the top letter from the push-down store if it is the "opposite" of the input letter, whereas we add the input letter to the store if it is equal to that atop the store. At the first step, of course, we must add whatever input is scanned. Let the device be in its final state if the symbol z_0 is atop the push-down store. Then it may be proved that $L = T(M)$. Thus L is CF.

5 EXERCISE: Show that without loss of generality we assume $L(G) \subset X^* - \{\Lambda\}$ and that each production $\xi \to x$ has $x \in X \cup (V - X)^2$.

We shall approach the characterization theorem via an algebraic characterization which I believe gives the most insight into the real meaning of the theorem. For a combinatorial proof see GINSBURG [1966, Sec. 2.5].

How might we proceed to test whether or not a string belongs to $L(G)$ for a given context-free grammar G? The natural way seems to be to erect all possible trees (there are only finitely many when we restrict the grammar in the way validated by Exercise **5**) which have the given word spelled out on their terminal nodes. We then test each of these trees to see whether it is a valid derivation tree. As soon as we find a valid derivation tree, we accept the word—if none of the trees is valid, we reject the word.

6 EXAMPLE: Consider the grammar (V, X, σ, P), where $X = \{a, b\}$, $V - X = \{\sigma\}$, and $P = \{\sigma \to a\sigma b, \sigma \to \Lambda\}$, which generates the set $L = \{a^n b^n | n \geq 0\}$. We may put this grammar in standard form (while losing Λ) as (V', X, σ', P'), where $V' - X' = \{\sigma', \sigma_1, \alpha, \beta\}$ and productions

    1. $\sigma' \to \alpha\sigma_1$
    2. $\sigma_1 \to \sigma'\beta$
    3. $\sigma' \to \alpha\beta$
    4. $\alpha \to a$
    5. $\beta \to b$

Figure 5.4 shows sample trees on the string $a^3 b^2$, neither of which is valid—

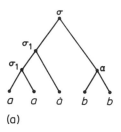
(a)

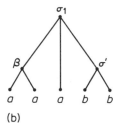
(b)

Fig. 5.4

an exhaustive search shows that none is. However, the trees on a^2b^2 include Fig. 5.5a, which is not valid, and Fig. 5.5b, which is valid.

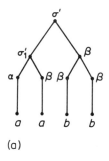
(a)

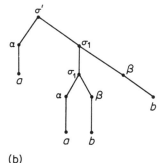
(b)

Fig. 5.5

We now want to replace this procedure of generating trees and checking them by one of generating strings and checking them.

Given a grammar, let us number the productions $1, 2, \ldots, n$ and then, if the jth production is of the form $\xi \to \alpha\beta$, let us modify it to read $\xi \to [_j\alpha_j]\beta$, where $[_j$ and $_j]$ are two new terminal symbols. If the jth production is of the form $\xi \to a$, modify it to read $\xi \to aa'$, where we introduce a new terminal a' for each terminal a. Now the valid derivation tree of the above example becomes the tree shown in Fig. 5.6.

Now consider the terminal string of this tree:

$$[_1aa_1'][_2[_3aa_3']bb_2']bb'$$

It has three important properties:

1. The homomorphism f generated by $f(a) = a$, $f(b) = b$, $f(a') = f(b') = f([_j) = f(_j]) = \Lambda$, recaptures the original string.
2. The string tells us its derivation.
3. If we consider a as a left bracket whose matching bracket is a', we see that the string is a well-bracketed expression.

Thus we replace the process of constructing a tree on a string by a process of inserting brackets $[_j$ and $_j]$ and then transforming each a to aa' in such a way as to obtain a well-bracketed formula.

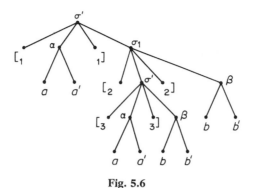

Fig. 5.6

But a nondeterministic push-down store is, par excellence, the device for doing such a job. Let us start with the given string. We may do one of three things—print a symbol j on top of the stack, in which case we print $[_j$ on our output string; read a symbol a from our input string, in which case we print aa' on our output string; or pull the top symbol j off the stack, in which case we print $_j]$ on our output string. The reader should convince himself that any pass on such a device which starts and ends with an empty stack will lead to a well-bracketed version of the input string; and conversely any such well-bracketed string can be obtained in this way. This explains the role of nondeterminism (many trees have to be tested—one on each possible pass) and of the push-down stack (making sure the brackets are placed properly). The role of the finite automaton will be made clear when we show below that there is a regular set R such that a well-bracketed string belongs to R iff it encodes a valid derivation tree. R will contain many strings which do not encode valid derivations, but they will not be well bracketed, and the job of the push-down store is to ensure that we shall not be bothered with them.

With all this motivation, the reader should now have no trouble in following our proof of the characterization theorem, and filling in the details. First, we formalize the above discussion to obtain an algebraic characterization of the context-free languages:

7   THEOREM: *Given X, we may find a set X', a language $D \subset X'^*$, and a homomorphism $h: X'^* \twoheadrightarrow X^*$ such that for any CF $L \subset X^*$ there exists a regular set $R \subset X'^*$ such that*

$$L = h(D \cap R)$$

Proof. Let us be given the set $X = \{a_1, \ldots, a_m\}$. Introduce the set $X' = \{a_1, a_1', \ldots, a_m, a_m', c, c', d, d'\}$. Regarding unprimed symbols as left brackets and primed symbols as right brackets, let D be the set of all words on X' consisting of properly bracketed expressions; that is, D is the CFL generated by the productions $\sigma \rightarrow \Lambda$ and $\sigma \rightarrow \sigma a \sigma a' \sigma$ for $a \in X \cup \{c, d\}$.

Define $h: X'^* \twoheadrightarrow X^*$ by

$$h(a) = \begin{cases} a & \text{if } a \in X \\ \Lambda & \text{if } a \in X' - X \end{cases}$$

We must now show how to go from a grammar G to a regular set R such that $h(D \cap R) = L = L(G)$.

Now let $G = (V, X, P, \sigma)$ with $P = \{\pi_1, \ldots, \pi_m\}$.

Let us define a new language L'' with productions P''

$$\xi \rightarrow aa' \qquad \text{if } \xi \rightarrow a \text{ is in } P$$
$$\eta \rightarrow [_i \alpha_i] \beta \qquad \text{if } \eta \rightarrow \alpha\beta \text{ is } \pi_i \text{ in } P$$

Now code $[_i$ as $dc^i d$ and $_i]$ as $d'c'^i d'$. Then clearly $L'' \subset D$ and $h(L'') = L$.

We now construct a regular event R such that $L'' = D \cap R$, and the result follows.

Given a derivation using P'' for a string of L,'' we give productions which chase down the leftmost branch remaining. For example, given the tree shown in Fig. 5.7, we apply the sequence of productions

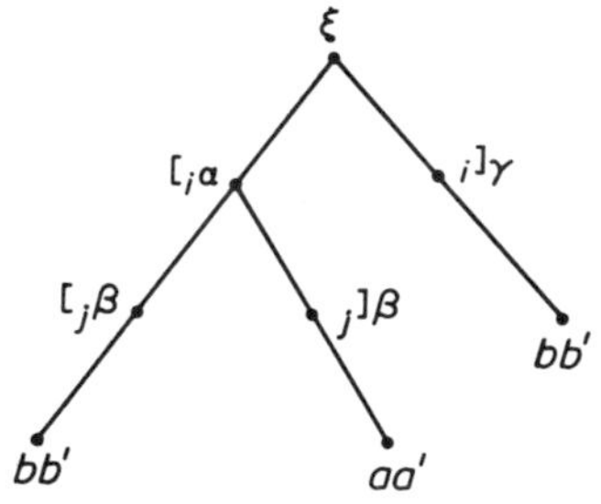

Fig. 5.7

$$\xi \rightarrow [_i \alpha$$
$$\alpha \rightarrow [_j \beta$$
$$\beta \rightarrow bb_j'] \beta \qquad (1)$$
$$\beta \rightarrow aa_i'] \gamma \qquad (2)$$
$$\gamma \rightarrow bb'$$

Note that we could have interchanged the application of (1) and (2) in our derivation, but then the resulting string would not be a member of D. It is D that provides the "control" which ensures that the brackets match up properly.

With this example in mind we may define explicitly:

$$P' = \{\xi \rightarrow aa' | a \text{ in } X, \xi \rightarrow a \text{ in } P\}$$
$$\cup \{\xi \rightarrow aa_i'] \beta | \xi \rightarrow a \text{ in } P, \pi_i = \eta \rightarrow \alpha\beta\}$$
$$\cup \{\eta \rightarrow [_i \alpha | \pi_i = \eta \rightarrow \alpha\beta\}$$

Then $R = L(G')$ is regular, since the productions are all right-linear. The reader may convince himself that $L = h(D \cap R)$, as desired, by formalizing the discussion of the above example.   □

We now use this algebraic result to prove the characterization theorem. Our idea is that *nondeterminism* allows us to "try out" arbitrary bracketings on an input string to find possible derivation trees, with the push-down store keeping track of the brackets, and the control box testing for membership in R.

8 *Proof of the Characterization Theorem for Context-Free Languages:*
    (i) Let A be the finite acceptor for R, where $L = h(D \cap R)$.

The idea is that the pda feeds A a $[_i$ every time it prints i on the stack, and feeds A an $_i]$ every time it takes i off the stack, and feeds aa' to A every time it reads a off the input tape. The nondeterminacy is given by the fact that an $_i]$ or $[_i$ may be added to or removed from the stack at any time while reading Λ off the input tape. Then if F is the set of designated final states for A, then a string is in L iff it leaves the stack empty (the string fed to A is in D) and A is in a state of F (the string fed to A is in R), it being clear that the input tape equalled h of the string fed to A.

    (ii) Let the pda have the productions $(p, xw, \alpha z) \vdash (q, w, \alpha \gamma)$.

Then if the string read in so far comprising inputs and bracketings from the stack is θ, and $\gamma = z_1, \ldots, z_n$ the string "seen" by the control box becomes $\theta x x'_z] [_{z_1} [_{z_2} \ldots [_{z_n}$ (where $\Lambda' = \Lambda$, of course) and the box of the pda acts as a nondeterministic automaton which is such that $q \in p \cdot (x x'_z] [_{z_1} [_{z_2} \ldots [_{z_n})$. Let R be the regular set accepted by this finite automaton. If we empty the stack, we have a word of D_z (augmented) produced by the productions $p \to x x'_z] [_{z_1} [_{z_2} \ldots [_{z_n} q$. So $L = h(D \cap R)$. By (2.22) and (2.26) we conclude that L is CF.   □

We now turn to the characterization of the context-sensitive languages. The appropriate acceptor turns out to be the linear-bounded automaton (introduced in its deterministic form by MYHILL [1960]) which is essentially a Turing machine which cannot use any tape except that on which the initial data are presented. (Since augmenting the alphabet is equivalent to using an amount of tape increased by a constant multiple, this condition is equivalent to requiring that the length of tape used be a linear function $an + b$ of the length n of tape on which the input string is presented—thus the name linear-bounded automaton). Formally:

9 DEFINITION: *A nondeterministic linear-bounded automaton (lba) is a quintuple*

$$M = (Q, X, \delta, q_0, F)$$

*where Q and X are finite nonempty sets (the **states** and **inputs**, respectively),*

$q_0 \in Q$ is the **start state**

$F \subset Q$ is the set of **designated final states**

and δ is a mapping from $Q \times X$ into the finite subsets of $Q \times X \times \{-1, 0, 1\}$. For p and q in Q, u and v in X^*, and a, b, c in X, we write

$$ucpav \vdash uqcbv \qquad \text{if } (q, b, -1) \in \delta(p, a)$$
$$upav \vdash uqbv \qquad \text{if } (q, b, 0) \quad \in \delta(p, a)$$
$$upav \vdash ubqv \qquad \text{if } (q, b, 1) \quad \in \delta(p, a)$$

that is, if $(q, b, m) \in \delta(p, a)$, an admissible next configuration is obtained by changing the scanned symbol a to b and the state p to q, and moving m squares along the tape. Note that this is just like a Turing machine (**4.1.1–3**) save that no provision is made for moving off the end of the string.

As usual, we use $\vdash^*$ to denote the ancestral relation of $\vdash$. Then the *set of strings accepted by M* is that which can lead to Ms leaving the right-hand end of its tape in a designated final state; that is,

$$T(M) = \{w \text{ in } X^* | q_0 w \vdash^* \beta \text{ for some } \beta \in X^* F\}$$

10   THEOREM (LANDWEBER [1963]). *$T(M)$ is context-sensitive for each lba $M = (Q, X, \delta, q_0, F)$.*

Proof. We exhibit a context-sensitive grammar G, for which $L(G) = T(M)$.

For each x in X, introduce new symbols x' and x''. Let $X' = \{x' | x \in X\}$ and $X'' = \{x'' | x \in X\}$ and set $\overline{X} = X' \cup X''$. Now let $G = (V, X, \sigma, P)$, where the auxiliary alphabet

$$V - X = \{\sigma\} \cup F \cup [\{\#\} \times (\overline{X} \cup [Q \times X''])] \cup (Q \times X'') \cup \overline{X}$$

where σ and $\#$ are new symbols. Then for arbitrary members a, b, c of X and p, q of Q, we introduce in P three sets of productions. The idea of G is that it simulates the action of M *working backward*. Thus the first set of productions lead to strings of the form $(\#, x_1')x_2'' \ldots x_n'' q$ just in case q is in F, representing a possible successful completion $x_1 \ldots x_n q$ of a computation by M:

$$\sigma \rightarrow (\#, a')q \qquad \text{if } q \text{ is in } F$$
$$(\#, a') \rightarrow (\#, a'')$$
$$(\#, a') \rightarrow (\#, a')b'$$
$$(\#, a'')b' \rightarrow (\#, a'')b''$$
$$b''c' \rightarrow b''c''$$

The second set of productions simulates the reversal of the actions of M:

$$b''q \rightarrow (p, a'')$$
$$(\#, b'')q \rightarrow (\#, p, a'')$$
$$b''(q, c'') \rightarrow (p, a'')c''$$
$$(\#, b'')(q, c'') \rightarrow (\#, p, a'')c'' \quad \Bigg\} \quad \text{if } (b, q, 1) \in \delta(p, a)$$

$$(q, b'') \rightarrow (p, a'')$$
$$(\#, q, b'') \rightarrow (\#, p, a'') \quad \Bigg\} \quad \text{if } (b, q, 0) \in \delta(p, a)$$

$$(q, c'')b'' \rightarrow c''(p, a'')$$
$$(\#, q, c'')b'' \rightarrow (\#, c'')(p, a'') \quad \Bigg\} \quad \text{if } (b, q, -1) \in \delta(p, a)$$

The final set of productions lets us get rid of the state symbol and recapture the terminal symbols just in case we have successfully retraced a computation to a stage at which the state symbol is q_0, and at the left-hand end,

$$(\#, q_0, a'') \rightarrow a''$$
$$a'' \rightarrow a$$

It should now be clear that $L(G) = T(M)$.   □

In fact we may show, following KURODA [1964], that every context-sensitive language is accepted by some nondeterministic linear-bounded automaton. The proof proceeds by reducing grammars for CS languages to a standard form, and then exhibiting an lba for each CS grammar in standard form.

11 DEFINITION: *A CS grammar is of order n if n is the length of the longest string appearing in any production. It is **length-preserving** if for each production $\varphi \rightarrow \psi$, either φ is the initial symbol, or ψ does not contain the initial symbol and $|\varphi| = |\psi|$. A CS grammar is **linear-bounded** if it is of order 2 and length-preserving, and if, σ being the initial symbol, $\sigma \rightarrow EF$ implies $E = \sigma$.*

12 LEMMA: *To every CS grammar G there corresponds a linear-bounded CS grammar G' equivalent in that $L(G) = L(G')$.*

  Proof. (i) we show that G of order $n > 2$ is equivalent to a CS grammar G' of order $n - 1$, whence it is equivalent to one of order 2 by induction:

  We may assume that no production has a nonterminal on either side unless it is of the form $A \rightarrow a$.

  Let $\varphi \rightarrow \psi$ be a production of G. If $|\psi| < 3$, we let $\varphi \rightarrow \psi$ be a rule of G'. Otherwise, we write $\varphi = A\varphi'$, $\psi = BCD'$, where A, B, C, D are nonterminal symbols.

  If $\varphi' = \Lambda$, we introduce two new nonterminals A_1 and A_2, and let $A \rightarrow A_1A_2$, $A_1 \rightarrow BC$, $A_2 \rightarrow D\psi'$ be rules of G'.

If $\varphi' \not\prec \Lambda$, write $\varphi' = E\varphi''$, with E a nonterminal symbol, introduce two new nonterminals A' and E', and let $AE \to A'E'$, $A' \to B$, and $E'\varphi'' \to CD\psi'$ be rules of G'.

Giving G' all the productions obtained from those of G in this fashion, we see that G' is of order $n - 1$ and equivalent to G.

(ii) We show that any CS grammar G of order 2 is equivalent to a linear-bounded grammar G':

Let $G = (V, X, \sigma, P)$ and let $V' = V \cup \{\sigma', q'\}$, where q' and σ' are new auxiliaries. Let $G' = (V', X, \sigma', P')$ with the productions

$$\sigma' \to \sigma'q \quad \sigma' \to \sigma$$
$$qA \to Aq \quad Aq \to qA \qquad \text{for all } A \text{ in } V$$

$$
\begin{aligned}
A &\to B & &\text{if } A \to B \text{ is a rule of } G \\
AB &\to CD & &\text{if } AB \to CD \text{ is a rule of } G \\
Aq &\to BC & &\text{if } A \to BC \text{ is a rule of } G
\end{aligned}
$$

G' is clearly linear-bounded. We show that it is equivalent to G'. Define a homomorphism $f: (V')^* \to V^*$ by requiring $\sigma' \mapsto \sigma$, $q \mapsto \Lambda$, and $A \mapsto A$ for $A \in V$. Then $x \to y$ in G' implies $f(x) \overset{*}{\Rightarrow} f(y)$ in G, and so $L(G') \subseteq L(G)$. Conversely, $x \to y$ in G implies $x \to y$ in G or $xq \to y$ in G'. So if $x \overset{*}{\Rightarrow} y$ in G then, for some n, $xq'' \overset{*}{\Rightarrow} y$ in G' and so, by the first two productions of G', if $\sigma \overset{*}{\Rightarrow} y$ in G, then $\sigma' \overset{*}{\Rightarrow} y$ in G' and so $L(G) \subset L(G')$. Thus G and G' are equivalent.

(i) and (ii) combine to yield the theorem. $\square$

13 LEMMA: *For any linear-bounded grammar G, there exists an lba which accepts $L(G)$.*

Proof. Let $G = (V, X, \sigma, P)$. We construct an lba M with alphabet V and states Q as follows. $Q = \{t_0, t_1, s_0, s_1, r_0, r_1, s_A$ for each A such that there is a rule $AB \to CD$ in $G\}$. t_0 is the initial and only final state. M has the following instructions.

$$
\begin{aligned}
(\#, t_0) &\to (\#, t_1, 1) \\
(a, t_1) &\to (a, t_1, 1) & &\text{for all } a \text{ in } X \\
(\#, t_1) &\to (\#, s_0, -1) \\
(A, s_0) &\to (A, s_0, 1) & &\left.\right\} \\
(A, s_0) &\to (A, s_0, -1) & &\left.\right\} \quad \text{for all } a \text{ in } V \\
(B, s_0) &\to (A, s_0, 0) & &\text{for all rules } A \to B \text{ of } G \\
(C, s_0) &\to (A, s_A, 1) & &\left.\right\} \\
(D, s_A) &\to (B, s_0, 0) & &\left.\right\} \quad \text{for all rules } AB \to CD \text{ of } G \\
(\sigma, s_0) &\to (\sigma, r_0, -1) \\
(\#, r_0) &\to (\#, r_1, 1)
\end{aligned}
$$

$$(\sigma, r_1) \rightarrow (\#, s_1, 1) \Big\}$$
$$(A, s_1) \rightarrow (\sigma, s_0, 0) \Big\}$$
for all rules $\sigma \rightarrow \sigma A$ of G

$$(\#, s_1) \rightarrow (\#, t_0, 1)$$

$$(X, x) \rightarrow (X, x, 0) \qquad \text{for all other pairs } (X, x)$$

The reader may easily check that M accepts $L(G)$. □

We thus have the characterization theorem for context-sensitive languages:

14 THEOREM: *A set of strings is a context-sensitive language iff it is accepted by an lba.*

15 EXERCISE: Use the theory to prove that the intersection of context-sensitive languages is context-sensitive.

16 OPEN QUESTIONS: (i) Is every context-sensitive language acceptable by a *deterministic* lba?

(ii) Are the context-sensitive languages closed under complementation?

17 EXERCISE: Prove that if the answer to (i) is "yes," then so is the answer to (ii).

This open question is of some interest, since deterministic push-down automata do *not* accept all context-free languages—for if they did, the CFLs would be closed under intersection. For a discussion of the languages they do accept see GINSBURG [1966].

We close this section with a result which relates context-free languages and *deterministic* lba's:

18 THEOREM (KURODA [1964]): *Context-free languages are accepted by deterministic lba's.*

Proof. Take a CF grammar in "normal" form: productions of the forms $A \rightarrow BC$ or $A \rightarrow a$. A derivation of a string of length n then takes $2n - 1$ steps. Let $D(x) = [\varphi_1, \varphi_2, \ldots, \varphi_{2n}]$ be the leftmost derivation of x, and let R_i be a rule of G which derives φ_{i+1} from φ_i. Thus $D(x)$ is fully characterized by an N-ary number of $2n - 1$ digits, each N-ary digit labeling one of the N productions of G.

Then the tape of M has three tracks—the top one holds the string x to be accepted and is not changed, the second one contains an N-ary number, two digits to a square, and the third tape is used to generate the string of L whose derivation is encoded on tape 2. If this string equals x, we accept x; if it doesn't, we add 1 to the number of tape 2, repeating the process again and again until it is accepted or we have worked through all numbers up to N^{2n-1} on tape 2, whereupon we reject x. □

19 COROLLARY: *The Boolean closure of the CFL's (that is, the smallest class of languages containing the CFLs and closed under intersection and complementation) is contained in the class of languages accepted by deterministic lba's.*

With this we end our discussion of Post systems, context-sensitive languages, and context-free languages. For more information on Post systems, see Part III of MINSKY [1967] and the collection of Post's original papers in DAVIS [1965]; for a monograph on context-free languages and a wealth of further reading see GINSBURG [1966]. For a treatment of automata theory which takes the notion of semi-Thue system as its starting point, see NELSON [1968].

SELECTED TOPICS

6 PARTIAL RECURSIVE FUNCTIONS

1. Partial Recursive Functions: Strings and Numbers
2. Equivalence with Turing-Computable Functions
3. Hierarchies

Partial recursive functions are usually presented as numerical functions. However, we wish to emphasize that they may also be presented as functions on strings of symbols. The definition we give follows that of SHEPHERDSON and STURGIS [1963], but much of the theory of these symbol-string functions that we present here seems to be new, though hardly surprising.

In Section 1, we introduce partial recursive functions as a subclass of the Turing-computable function and show that if numerical functions are partial recursive with respect to one radix, they are partial recursive with respect to all radishes. In Section 2, we demonstrate the equivalence of partial recursive functions to Turing-computable functions. In Section 3, we concentrate on numerical functions, and consider some important subclasses and hierarchies.

The theory of partial recursive functions is a branch of mathematics in its own right, and the reader is referred to the texts of KLEENE [1952], DAVIS [1958], and ROGERS [1967] for a full treatment of the topic—or to MINSKY [1967] for a useful introduction. Our aim here is simply to go into enough detail for the automata theorist to understand why the classes of partial recursive functions and TM-computable functions are co-extensive, and how this theory may lend itself to studies of complexity of computation.

6.1   PARTIAL RECURSIVE FUNCTIONS: STRINGS AND NUMBERS

In Section **4.2**, we saw that if a partial function $f\colon (X^*)^n \to X^*$ can be computed by a generalized Turing machine, then it can be computed by an ordinary Turing machine. We shall use this fact to give simple proofs of certain closure properties of the TM-computable functions, and then give what in Section 2 will prove to be an equivalent characterization—as what are called the (partial) recursive functions.

We first introduce some simple functions which are all TM-computable.

1   DEFINITION:

(i)   *For each* $x \in X$, *let* $S_x\colon X^* \to X^*$ *be the* **post-fixing** *function* $\xi \mapsto \xi x$.

(ii)   *For each* $n \in N$, *let* $\Lambda^n\colon (X^*)^n \to X^*\colon (x_1, \ldots, x_n) \mapsto \Lambda$ *be the function which replaces n arguments by the* **empty** *string.*

(iii)   *For each* $n \in N$, *and* $1 \le j \le n$, *let* $U_j^n\colon (X^*)^n \to X^*\colon (x_1, \ldots, x_n) \to x_j$ *be the function which* **selects** *the jth of n arguments.*

2   EXERCISE: Verify that S_x, Λ^n, and U_j^n are all TM-computable.

We now introduce three operations on functions, and check that, when applied to computable functions, they yield computable functions.

3   DEFINITION:

(i)   **Composition** *is the operation which, when applied to the functions* $h\colon (X^*)^m \to X^*$ *and* $g_j\colon (X^*)^n \to X^*$, *for* $1 \le j \le m$, *yields the function* $f\colon (X^*)^n \to X^*$ *defined by*

$$f(x_1, \ldots, x_n) = h(g_1(x_1, \ldots, x_n), \ldots, g_m(x_1, \ldots, x_n)).‡$$

(ii)   **Recursion** *is the operation which, when applied to the functions* $g\colon (X^*)^{n-1} \to X^*$ *and* $h_x\colon (X^*)^n \to X^*$, *one for each* $x \in X$, *yields the function* $f\colon (X^*)^n \to X^*$ *defined* **recursively** *by*

$$f(\Lambda, x_2, \ldots, x_n) = g(x_2, \ldots, x_n)$$
$$f(zx, x_2, \ldots, x_n) = h_x(f(z, x_2, \ldots, x_n), z, x_2, \ldots, x_n) \quad (x \in X)$$

(iii)   **Minimization in** $\{x\}^*$, *where x is a given element of X, is the operation which, when applied to* $g\colon (X^*)^n \to X^*$, *yields the function* $f\colon (X^*)^{n-1} \to X^*$ *defined by*

---

‡ Since we are dealing with functions which may be only partially defined, every such equation must be understood as having an implicit qualifying clause such as, in this case, "so that f is only defined for $x_1, \ldots, x_n$ if each of $g_1(x_1, \ldots, x_n), \ldots, g_m(x_1, \ldots, x_n)$ is defined, and further, that h is defined for the argument vector $g_1(x_1, \ldots, x_n), \ldots, g_m(x_1, \ldots, x_n)$."

$$f(x_1, \ldots, x_{n-1}) = \mu_x y[g(x_1, \ldots, x_n, y) = \Lambda]$$

*which is the word x^k for which k is the smallest integer such that $g(x_1, \ldots,$
$x_{n+1}, x^k) = \Lambda$, while $g(x_1, \ldots, x_{n-1}, x^l)$ is defined, but non-null, for $0 \le l < k$.*

Our task is now to prove that these operations yield TM-computable functions when applied to TM-computable functions.

4   THEOREM

(i) *If h and $g_1, \ldots, g_m$ are TM-computable, and f is obtained from them by composition,*

$$f(x_1, \ldots, x_m) = h(g_1(x_1, \ldots, x_m), \ldots, g_m(x_1, \ldots, x_n))$$

then f too is TM-computable.

(ii) *If g and h_x, for $x \in X$, are TM-computable, and f is obtained from them by recursion,*

$$f(\Lambda, x_2, \ldots, x_n) = g(x_2, \ldots, x_n)$$
$$f(zx, x_2, \ldots, x_n) = h_x(f(z, x_2, \ldots, x_n), z, x_2, \ldots, x_n)$$

then f too is TM-computable.

(iii) *If g is TM-computable, and f is obtained from g by minimization,*

$$f(x_1, \ldots, x_{n-1}) = \mu_x y[g(x_1, \ldots, x_n, y) = \Lambda]$$

then f too is TM-computable.

Proof outline. By the results of section **4.2**, it suffices to show that if we have an ordinary Turing machine program for each of the g's and h's, then we may construct a generalized Turing machine program for f.

We now outline the proof for cases (ii) and (iii).

(ii) We use three tapes. In computing $f(x_1, \ldots, x_n)$, the computation will proceed in $|x_1|$ stages, at the $(i + 1)$st of which tape 1 will contain $_i|x_1, x_1|_i$ (where $x_1|_i$ is the string of the first i letters of x_1, and $x_1 = x_1|_i \cdot {_i|x_1}$); tape 2 will contain $f(x_1|_i, x_2, \ldots, x_n)$; tape 3 will contain $x_1, \ldots, x_n$. Then the program for f may be outlined as follows:

Stage 1. Start with tapes 1 and 2 blank, and with $x_1, \ldots, x_n$ on tape 3. Read $x_2, \ldots, x_n$ onto tape 2; and z, Λ onto tape 1. Execute the program for g on tape 2. Go to stage 2.

Stage $i + 1$. Let the contents of tape 1 be y_1, y_2. If y_1 is empty, erase tapes 1 and 3 and halt with the answer on tape 2. Otherwise transfer $x_1, \ldots, x_n, y_2$ (from tapes 1 and 3) to the left of the string on tape 2. Transfer the first symbol of y_1 to the end of y_2 on tape 1. If this symbol is x, execute the program for h_x on tape 2. Go to stage $i + 2$.

(iii) We use two tapes. In computing $f(x_1, \ldots, x_{n-1})$, we shall proceed in stages, at the $(i + 1)$st of which tape 1 will contain $x_1, \ldots, x_{n-1}, x^i$ and tape 2 will contain $g(x_1, \ldots, x_{n-1}, x^i)$. Then the program for f may be outlined as follows:

Stage 1. Start with $x_1, \ldots, x_{n-1}$ on tape 1, and tape 2 blank. Print the symbol "," to the right of the expression on tape 1. Go to stage 2.

Stage $i + 1$. Replace the contents of tape 2 with the present contents of tape 1. Execute the program for g on tape 2. If tape 2 is empty, delete $x_1, \ldots, x_{n-1}$ from tape 1, and halt with answer on tape 1. If tape 2 is not empty, print an x at the right end of the string on tape 1, and go to stage $i + 2$. □

5 EXERCISE: Prove (i), closure under composition.

6 DEFINITION: *The class of* **partial recursive functions** *on X is the smallest collection of functions of the form $f: (X^*)^n \to X^*$ with $n \in N$ which contains the functions S_x, Λ^n and U_j^n on X and is closed under the operations of composition, recursion, and minimization. f is called* **total** *if it is defined for all arguments.*

It is now immediate from Exercise **2** and Theorem **4** that we have proved

7 THEOREM: *Every partial recursive function is TM-computable.*

In Section **2**, we shall prove the converse. In the remainder of this section, let us gain some more facility with recursive definitions, and see what *numerical* functions are partial recursive.

Let $X_k = \{a_1, \ldots, a_k\}$. In what follows let the variables $x_1, x_2, \ldots, x_n, \ldots, y, z$ take values in X_k^*. The number n of arguments in the functions considered may be 0, 1, 2, 3, . . .—a 0-argument function is a constant.

Our next lemma shows that we may re-order and relabel the variables in a partial recursive function with impunity.

8 LEMMA: *If $f(x_1, \ldots, x_n)$ is partial recursive, and $\rho = (\rho_1, \ldots, \rho_n)$ is any subset (perhaps with repetitions) of $(1, \ldots, m)$, then*

$$f_\rho(x_1, \ldots, x_m) \underset{\text{def}}{=} f(x_{\rho_1}, \ldots, x_{\rho_n})$$

is also partial recursive.

Proof. $f_\rho(x_1, \ldots, x_m) = f(U_{\rho_1}^m(x_1, \ldots, x_m), \ldots, U_{\rho_n}^m(x_1, \ldots, x_m))$ □

9 LEMMA: *Any constant function is total recursive.*

Proof. $a_{i_1} \ldots a_{i_n} = S_{a_{i_1}}(\ldots S_{a_{i_n}}(\Lambda(x_1)) \ldots)$ □

10 LEMMA: *The concatenation function* $\mathrm{con}^n (x_1, x_2, \ldots, x_n) = x_1 x_2 \ldots x_n$ *is total recursive for each n.*

Proof. Let $h^2(\Lambda, x_2) = U_1^1(x_2)$; $h^2(za_i, x_2) = S_{a_i}(h^2(z, x_2))$

Let $h^{j+1}(x_1, \ldots, x_j, x_{j+1}) = h^2(x_1, h^j(x_2, \ldots, x_{j+1}))$

Then $\text{con}^n(x_1, \ldots, x_n) = h^n(x_n, \ldots, x_1)$ is total recursive.   □

11   LEMMA: $h^{(n)}(x_1) = \underbrace{x_1 \ldots x_1}_{n \text{ times}}$ *(the n-folding of a string) is total recursive.*

Proof. $x_1^n = \text{con}^n(x_1, \ldots, x_1)$ □

Often, but by no means most often, our interest in string manipulation is in actual numerical computation. We would then want to interpret a string on the alphabet $\{a_1, \ldots, a_k\}$ to be a number in radix k.

Given a positive integer m, let $\langle m \rangle_k$ be its coding as a number to base k using the alphabet $\{a_1, \ldots, a_k\}$; that is,

$$\langle m \rangle_k = a_{i_1} \ldots a_{i_n} \Leftrightarrow m = \sum_1^n i_j k^{n-j} \qquad (0 < i_j \leq k)$$

for example,

$$\langle 4 \rangle_2 = a_1 a_2 \qquad \langle 13 \rangle_3 = a_1 a_1 a_1 \qquad \langle 0 \rangle_k = \Lambda$$

We are thus emphasizing the difference between strings and the numerals they denote. Given a string α on $\{a_1, \ldots, a_k\}$ let $_k\langle \alpha \rangle$ be the number it denotes when read as a number in radix k; that is,

$$_k\langle \alpha \rangle = m \Leftrightarrow \alpha = a_{i_1} \ldots a_{i_n} \qquad \text{and} \qquad m = \sum_1^n i_j k^{n-j}$$

12   EXERCISE: What are $_6\langle a_3 a_5 a_2 \rangle$ and $_5\langle a_3 a_5 a_2 \rangle$?

In particular, we shall deem the representation of m by a string of m a_1's to be in the "base" or "radix" 1. Thus $_1\langle a_1 a_1 a_1 a_1 \rangle = 4$, and so on.

13   DEFINITION: *We say a function $f: N^m \to N$ on the natural numbers is* **partial recursive when computed to base k** *if the function $\hat{f}_k: (X_k^*)^m \to X_k^*$, defined by*

$$\hat{f}_k(\langle n_1 \rangle_k, \ldots, \langle n_m \rangle_k) = \langle n \rangle_k \Leftrightarrow f(n_1, \ldots, n_m) = n$$

is partial recursive wrt X_k. We say f is **partial recursive** *if it is partial recursive when computed to base 1.*

We shall reassure ourselves that this collection of functions *does not depend on the choice of radix*—i.e., for any $k, l \geq 1$, a function is partial recursive when computed to base k iff it is partial recursive when computed to base l, thus justifying our definition of numerical functions which are partial recursive (without further qualification). To this end we shall eventually prove:

14 THEOREM: *Given any positive integer k: a function $f: N^m \rightarrow N$ is partial recursive when computed to base k iff it is partial recursive when computed to base 1.*

Reinterpreting Definition **6** for alphabet X_1 as a definition of partial recursive functions of numbers (using radix 1), we immediately have

15 PROPERTY: *A function $f: N \times N \times \cdots \times N \rightarrow N$ is **partial recursive** iff it can be obtained from the functions of the list*

I $S(n) = n + 1$

II $0^n(x_1, \ldots, x_n) = 0$

III $U_j^n(x_1, \ldots, x_n) = x_j$

by zero or more applications of the following schemata:

IV **Composition:** *If $h, g_1, \ldots, g_m$ are partial recursive, then so is the function f defined by*

$$f(x_1, \ldots, x_n) = h(g(x_1, \ldots, x_n), \ldots, g_m(x_1, \ldots, x_n))$$

V **Recursion:** *If g, h are partial recursive, so is the function f defined recursively by*

$$f(0, x_2, \ldots, x_n) = g(x_2, \ldots, x_n)$$
$$f(z + 1, x_2, \ldots, x_n) = h(z, f(z, x_2, \ldots, x_n), x_2, \ldots, x_n)$$

VI **Minimization:** *If g is partial recursive, then so is the function f defined by*

$$f(x_1, \ldots, x_n) = \mu y[g(x_1, \ldots, x_n, y) = 0]$$

which is the smallest number y such that $g(x_1, \ldots, x_n, y) = 0$ and $g(x_1, \ldots, x_n, z)$ is defined for $z < y$ (f may thus be undefined).

16 EXAMPLE: We want to illustrate the fact that the phrase "and $g(x_1, \ldots, x_n, z)$ is defined for $z < y$" is *not* redundant in the definition of minimization. To show this we shall use the fact (whose proof in this and the next section does not depend on this example) that a function is partial recursive if and only if it is computable by a Turing machine. Now, let W be a recursively enumerable set which is not recursive, so that we may define a partial recursive function by

$$\varphi(x, 1) = 0$$
$$\varphi(x, 0) = \begin{cases} 0 & \text{if } x \in W \\ undefined & \text{otherwise} \end{cases}$$

Then clearly $f(x) =$ "the least y such that $\varphi(x, y) = 0$" is *not* partial recursive since it is the characteristic function of a non-recursive set.

To indicate how we may use our schemata to build up functions, we shall now give examples of numerical partial recursive functions.

17   EXAMPLE: The following numerical functions are partial recursive:

(i)   Addition $x + y$

(ii)   Multiplication $x \cdot y$

(iii)   Exponentiation x^y

(iv) $x \doteq y = \begin{cases} x - y & \text{if } x \geq y \\ 0 & \text{if } x < y \end{cases}$

(v) $|x - y|$

(vi) $n!$

(vii)   The nth prime $\Pr(n)$: $\Pr(1) = 2$, $\Pr(2) = 3$, $\Pr(3) = 5, \ldots$,

Solutions.

(i) We know $S(n) = n + 1$ and $U^1(n) = n$ are partial recursive; By composition, $g(z, w, y) = S(U^2(z, w, y)) = w + 1$ is partial recursive. So, if we define $f(x, y)$ by recursion with

$$f(0, y) = U^1(y)$$
$$f(z + 1, y) = g(z, f(z, y), y) = f(z, y) + 1$$

then f is partial recursive, and clearly $f(x, y) = x + y$. We have written this example out in tedious detail—we shall in the future abbreviate such an application of the recursion schema to

$$f(0, y) = y$$
$$f(z + 1, y) = f(z, y) + 1$$

(ii) $0 \cdot y = 0$; $(x + 1) \cdot y = x \cdot y + y$.

(iv) We first define $1 \doteq x$ as a partial recursive function of one variable by the recursion

$$1 \doteq 0 = 1$$
$$1 \doteq (z + 1) = 0$$

and then set up $x \doteq y$ by

$$x \doteq 0 = x$$
$$x \doteq (y + 1) = (x \doteq y) \doteq 1$$

(vii) $\Pr(n + 1)$ is the least m such that $m > \Pr(n)$ which is not divided by any number between 1 and m. We thus have to express the predicates of comparison and divisibility as partial recursive functions.

Let us first define the function

$$\text{equ}(x, y) = \begin{cases} 1 \text{ if } x = y \\ 0 \text{ if } x \neq y \end{cases}$$

Then clearly

$$\text{equ } (x, y) = 1 \doteq ((x \doteq y) + (y \doteq x))$$

and so is partial recursive.

The predicate "x exceeds y" is given by

$$\text{exc } (x, y) = \begin{cases} 1 \text{ if } x > y \\ 0 \text{ if } x \leq y \end{cases}$$

and is partial recursive, since

$$\text{exc } (x, y) = (1 \doteq (y \doteq x)) \doteq \text{equ } (x, y)$$

Let's check this.

If $x > y$, the right-hand side is $(1 \doteq 0) \doteq 0 = 1$
If $x = y$, the right-hand side is $(1 \doteq 0) \doteq 1 = 0$
If $x < y$, the right-hand side is $\leq (1 \doteq 1) \doteq 0 = 0$

Now for divisibility. y divides x if the remainder is 0 when y is divided into x. We define

$$[x/y] = \text{if } y = 0 \text{ then } 0 \text{ else the greatest integer } \leq x/y.\ddagger$$

Thus $z = [x/y]$ and $y \neq 0$ implies $y \cdot z \leq x < y \cdot (z + 1)$. Then

$$[x/y] = \mu z[\{y \cdot (1 \doteq \text{exc } (y \cdot z + 1, x))\} = 0]$$

and so is partial recursive. We then define the partial recursive function

$$R(x, y) = x \doteq y[x/y]$$

which is the remainder after dividing y into x.

If we now define

$$P(m) = \begin{cases} 1 \text{ if } m \text{ is a prime number} \\ 0 \text{ if } m \text{ is composite} \end{cases}$$

then $$P(m) = \text{equ } (m, \mu z[(1 \doteq \text{exc } (m, 1)) + R(m, z) = 0])$$

that is, m is the smallest number greater than 1 which divides m. This is only defined for $m > 1$. Now we may exhibit the nth prime as a partial recursive function. Setting $\text{Pr } (0) = 1$ for convenience, we then use the simple recursion

---

‡ This conditional expression, familiar to users of modern computer languages, is shorthand for

$$[x/y] = \begin{cases} 0 & \text{if } y = 0 \\ \text{the greatest integer } \leq x/y & \text{if } y \neq 0 \end{cases}$$

$$\text{Pr} (n + 1) = \mu z[(1 \div \text{exc} (z, \text{Pr} (n))) + (1 \div P(z)) = 0]$$

18 EXERCISE: Verify **17** (iii), (v), and (vi).

We may now turn to the "if" part of Theorem **14**, by first proving some very useful lemmas. We return to the general alphabet X_k.

19 EXERCISE: Let g_k be the encoding of strings on X_k,

$$g_k(a_{i_1} \ldots a_{i_n}) = \text{a string of} \left(\sum_1^n i_j k^{n-j} \right) a_1\text{'s}$$

Show that g_k is total recursive on X_k, and that X_1 is total recursive on X_1. [Hint: Lemma **11** may or may not be useful.]

20 LEMMA:

$$\text{equ} (x_1, x_2) = \begin{cases} \Lambda \text{ if } x_1 = x_2 \\ a_1 \text{ if not} \end{cases}$$

is total recursive, wrt X_k.

Proof. As in example **17**, we may show that

$$\text{equ}^1 (x_1, x_2) = \begin{cases} \Lambda \text{ if } x_1 = x_2 \text{ and both are in } X_1^* \\ a_1 \text{ if not} \end{cases}$$

is recursive on X_k, and then define equ in general by

$$\text{equ} (x_1, x_2) = \text{equ}^1 (g_k(x_1), g_k(x_2)) \qquad\qquad \square$$

21 LEMMA: *Let f be a total recursive function which maps X_1^* one-to-one onto X_k^*. Then f^{-1} is also total recursive.*

Proof. $f^{-1}(x) = \mu_1 y[\text{equ} (f(y), x) = \Lambda]$. $\qquad\qquad \square$

22 *Proof of the "if" part of Theorem* **14**.

Let the function $f: N^m \to N$ be represented as f_k in radix k, and as f_1 in radix 1. Then $f_k = g_k^{-1} f_1(g_k \times \ldots \times g_k)$ and so is partial recursive wrt X_k if f_1 is partial recursive wrt X_1, and so, *a fortiori*, wrt X_k. $\qquad\qquad \square$

To prove the "only if" part of Theorem **14** we must show that the schemata whereby we built up f_k over X_k can be simulated by schemata for building up f_1, the radix 1 encoding of f, over X_1.

23 PROBLEM: State and verify the simulations of the base functions S_{a_i}, Λ^n, and U_i^n, and verify that the composition schemata **IV** goes over unchanged.

24 EXERCISE: Let $d(x)$ be x with its last letter deleted (or Λ, if $x = \Lambda$). Let e_Λ be Λ if x is Λ, a_1 if not. Let e_j be Λ if x ends in a_j, a_1 if not. Then d, e_Λ, and the e_j are partial recursive, wrt X_k.

25 NOTE: The computer scientist acquainted with LISP and ALGOL may find the above material easier to assimilate if he ponders the translations of some of the above material:

$$e_\Lambda(x) = \textit{if } x = \Lambda \textit{ then } \Lambda \textit{ else } a_1$$
$$e_j(x) = \textit{if } x \textit{ ends in } a_j \textit{ then } \Lambda \textit{ else } a_1$$

Let us recall our coding function $g_k \colon X_k^* \to X_1^*$, where

$$g_k(a_{i_1} \ldots a_{i_n}) = \sum_1^n i_j k^{n-i}$$

identifying the number n with a string of n a_1's.

If we have a string x on X_1 coding the string za_i on X_k, then, recalling the notation introduced in the solution to **17** (vii)

$$a_i \text{ is coded by } R(x, k) + k \cdot (1 \mathbin{\dot-} R(x, k))$$

which we shall call $\alpha(x)$. (Why is the second term necessary?)

$$z \text{ is coded by } [x \mathbin{\dot-} \alpha(x)/k]$$

which we shall call $\beta(x)$.

We now show how to simulate base k schema V in base 1. Suppose g' and h_i' are the X_1-simulands of the X_k-functions g, h_i and that

$$f(\Lambda, x_2, \ldots, x_n) = g(x_2, \ldots, x_n)$$
$$f(za_i, x_2, \ldots, x_n) = h_i(z, f(z, x_2, \ldots, x_n), x_2, \ldots, x_n) \qquad (1 \le i \le k)$$

We have to find a function f', partial recursive over X_1, which simulates f. Clearly, we set

$$f'(\Lambda, x_2, \ldots, x_n) = g'(x_2, \ldots, x_n)$$

The induction step is harder. Since

$$f(za_i, x_2, \ldots, x_n) = h_i(z, f(z, x_2, \ldots, x_n), x_2, \ldots, x_n)$$

we must have

(1) $f'(y, x_2, \ldots, x_n) = h_i'(\beta(y), f'(\beta(y), x_2, \ldots, x_n), x_2, \ldots, x_n)$ if $\alpha(y) = i$

We use this to find a single function h', primitive recursive over X_1, such that

(2) $f'(za_1, x_2, \ldots, x_n) = h'(z, f(z, x_2, \ldots, x_n), x_2, \ldots, x_n)$

Comparing (1) and (2), we are cursed with the fact that the f' on the right-hand side of (1) depends on $\beta(za_1)$, whereas the f' on the right-hand side of (2) depends on z. There is a clear case for a theorem:

26 THEOREM: *If g, h, ρ', and ρ are partial recursive over X_1, and ρ' and ρ are total recursive with the property that $\begin{cases} \rho'(x) \leq x \\ \rho(x) \leq x \end{cases}$, then the function f defined by*

$$f(\Lambda, x_2, \ldots, x_n) = g(x_2, \ldots, x_n)$$
$$f(za_1, x_2, \ldots, x_n) = h_1(\rho'(z), f(\rho(z), x_2, \ldots, x_n), x_2, \ldots, x_n)$$

is also partial recursive.

Proof. Here we shall only outline the proof, using a suggestion by Paul Young that rather than work with $f(z, x_2, \ldots, x_n)$ we work with

$$F(z, x_2, \ldots, x_n) = \prod_{k=1}^{z} \Pr(k)^{f(k, x_2, \ldots, x_n)}$$

where $\Pr(1) = 2, \Pr(2) = 3, \ldots, \Pr(k) = $ the kth prime and we are now interpreting functions on X_1 as numerical functions.

One then shows that the function

$$\mathrm{et}(x, y) = \text{the exponent of } \Pr(x) \text{ in } y$$

is total recursive in the integers x and y. Then F is defined by the recursion relations

$$F(\Lambda, x_2, \ldots, x_n) = g(x_2, \ldots, x_n)$$
$$F(z + 1, x_2, \ldots, x_n) = F(z, x_2, \ldots, x_n) \Pr(z)^{h(\rho'(z), \mathrm{et}(\rho(z), F(z, x_2, \ldots, x_n)), x_2, \ldots, x_n)}$$
$$= H(z, F(z, x_2, \ldots, x_n), x_2, \ldots, x_n)$$

where $H(z, y, x_2, \ldots, x_n) = y \Pr(z)^{h(\rho'(z), \mathrm{et}(\rho(z), y), x_2, \ldots, x_n)}$ is clearly partial recursive when h is. Thus F is partial recursive. Finally,

$$f(z, x_2, \ldots, x_n) = \mathrm{et}(z, F(z, x_2, \ldots, x_n))$$

is also partial recursive. □

27 EXERCISE: Fill in the details of the above proof.

28 LEMMA: *If $h'_1(z, y, x_2, \ldots, x_n), \ldots, h'_k(z, y, x_2, \ldots, x_n)$ are partial recursive, then so is*

$$h'(z, y, x_2, \ldots, x_n) = h'_i(z, y, x_2, \ldots, x_n) \qquad \text{when } \alpha(za_1) = i$$

Proof. Define $C(x_1, x_2, x_3) = \begin{cases} x_1 \text{ if } x_2 = x_3 \\ \Lambda \text{ if not} \end{cases}$

Set $\gamma(\Lambda, x_2) = x_2$, $\gamma(za_1, x_2) = \Lambda$, which is thus partial recursive. Then $C(x_1, x_2, x_3) = \gamma(\mathrm{equ}(x_2, x_3), x_1)$ is also partial recursive. Then

$h'(z, y, x_2, \ldots, x_n)$
$\quad = \mathrm{con}(C(h'_1(z, y_1, x_2, \ldots, x_n), a_1^1, \alpha(za_1)), \ldots, C(h'_k(z, y, x_2, \ldots, x_n), a_1^k, \alpha(za_1)))$

and is thus partial recursive. □

Applying Theorem **26** and Lemma **28**, we use the equation

$$f'(za_1, x_2, \ldots, x_n) = h'(\beta(za_1), f(\beta(za_1)), x_2, \ldots, x_n), x_2, \ldots, x_n)$$

to assure ourselves that f' is partial recursive computed in X_1. It remains to show that if h' is partial recursive over X_1 and simulates h, which is partial recursive over X_k, and if

$$f(x_1, \ldots, x_n) = \mu_1 y[h(x_1, \ldots, x_n, y) = \Lambda]$$

then the function f', which simulates f, is partial recursive on X_1. Notice that μ_1, wrt X_k is *not* the same as μ_1, wrt X_1. Let g_k be the encoding function of Lemma **10**. Let

$$m_j(x_1) = \begin{cases} \Lambda \text{ if } x_1 = g(a_j^s) \text{ for some } s \\ a_1 \text{ if not} \end{cases}.$$

29   EXERCISE: Prove that m_j is partial recursive, wrt X_1. Then $f'(x_1, \ldots, x_n) = \mu y[\text{Con}(g(x_1, \ldots, x_n, y), m_j(y)) = \Lambda]$ and so is partial recursive, wrt X_1.
With this, the verification of Theorem **14** is complete, and we may change base with impunity in describing a function as partial recursive.

6.2   EQUIVALENCE WITH TURING-COMPUTABLE FUNCTIONS

The main aim of this section is to prove the converse to Theorem **1.7**—namely that every TM-computable function is partial recursive. We shall approach the proof in so general a fashion that we will add even further credence to our claim that the TM-computable functions (and thus, ipso facto, the partial recursive functions) are an appropriate formalization of our intuitive notion of effectively computable functions.

We first give a horrendously general definition of a class of computers, which we shall call the recursive computers, and indicate that Turing machines form a very special case. We shall then show that every function computable by a recursive computer is partial recursive, from which the partial recursiveness of TM-computable functions follows immediately.

Let us recall the way in which a function $f: (X^*)^n \rightarrow X^*$ is computed by a Turing machine Z.

First, recalling that $X_b - X = \{b\}$, where b denotes the blank, we apply a function $\alpha: (X^*)^n \rightarrow X_b^* Q X_b^*$, which takes the argument $(x_1, \ldots, x_n)$ into the initial ID $q_0 x_1 b x_2 \ldots b x_n$.

Secondly, we operate upon the ID with a function λ, such that $\xi = \lambda(\eta)$ just in case $\eta \vdash_{\overline{Z}} \xi$, and we do this successively until such time (if one exists) as we obtain an ID which is terminal.

Thirdly, we recapture the result $f(x_1, \ldots, x_n)$ by applying a function $\beta: X_b^* Q X_b^* \to X^*$, which takes the ID $\xi q \eta$ into the string $\xi \eta$ on X.

The reader may already be prepared to believe that the functions α, β, and λ, as well as the test for whether or not an ID is terminal, are all partial recursive functions. We invite the reader to prove this for himself as an exercise in the techniques of Section 1—if the effort fails, see MINSKY [1967] or DAVIS [1958]. In any case, the above discussion applied to a (universal) Turing machine motivates the following very general definition:

1   DEFINITION: *A **recursive computer** $\mathcal{C}$ on the alphabet Y is a partial recursive function $f_{\mathcal{C}}: Y_b^* \to Y_b^*$. We call $\hat{Q} = Y_b^*$ the set of **complete states** for $\mathcal{C}$.*

The idea is that if at some time a computer has n registers, the jth of which contains the word Y_j, we may say that its *complete state* is the word $Y_1 b \ldots b Y_n$ of $\hat{Q}$, and then, if the state of the computer $\mathcal{C}$ is $\xi \in \hat{Q}$ at time t, the state $\mathcal{C}$ will be $f_{\mathcal{C}}(\xi)$ at time $t + 1$ (and may thus be undefined). We view $\mathcal{C}$ as *halting* in state $\xi \in \hat{Q}$ just in case $f_{\mathcal{C}}(\xi) = \xi$.

2   A computation *of $\mathcal{C}$ is then any finite sequence*

$$\xi_0, \xi_1, \xi_2, \xi_3, \ldots, \xi_n$$

of elements of $\hat{Q}$ such that $\xi_{j+1} = f_{\mathcal{C}}(\xi_j)$ for $0 \leq j < n$, whereas $\xi_n = f_{\mathcal{C}}(\xi_n)$.

Given a state ξ of $\hat{Q}$, we define $f_{\mathcal{C}}^*(\xi)$ to be the end result of a computation of $\mathcal{C}$ which starts with ξ (which is thus unique, if it is defined).

3   A program Π *for $\mathcal{C}$ is then a pair of maps $\alpha: (X^*)^m \to \hat{Q}$ and $\beta: \hat{Q} \to (X^*)^n$ partial recursive on $(X \cup Y)_b$. The (partial) **function computed by** $\mathcal{C}$ **with program** Π is the function $\mathcal{C}_\Pi: (X^*)^m \to (X^*)^n$ defined by commutativity of the diagram*

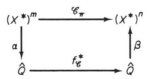

In other words, $\mathcal{C}_\Pi$ is the computation obtained (i) by using α to read in the data and appropriate instructions into memory, then (ii) computing with $\mathcal{C}$ until the computation halts, whereupon (iii) β is used to read the result from the registers.

4   THEOREM: *If $\mathcal{C}$ is a recursive computer and Π is a program for $\mathcal{C}$, then the function $\mathcal{C}_\Pi$ is partial recursive.*

Proof. Define the function

$$p(\xi) = \begin{cases} \Lambda & \text{if } f_e(\xi) = \xi \\ x, & \text{some element of } X, \text{ if not} \end{cases}$$

It is a simple exercise of the techniques of recursive function theory to show that p is partial recursive. Let $f_e(\xi, x)$ be the $|x|$ step consequent of ξ. We see that it is partial recursive from the recursion scheme

$$f_e(\xi, \Lambda) = \xi$$
$$f_e(\xi, zx) = f_e(f_e(\xi, z)) \qquad \text{for all } x \in X$$

Then
$$\eta(\xi) = \mu_x y[p(f_e(\xi, y)) = \Lambda]$$

is partial recursive, and is x^n if n is the number of steps in a computation starting with ξ, if such exists, and is otherwise undefined. But then, clearly,

$$f_e^*(\xi) = f_e(\xi, \eta(\xi))$$

and so is partial recursive. Thus $\mathcal{C}_{\Pi}(x) = \beta(f_e(\alpha(x)))$ is also partial recursive. $\square$

It is a straightforward application of Theorem **1.14** to prove that the use of an augmented alphabet does not enlarge the class of functions partial recursive over a given alphabet. We may thus conclude:

5   THEOREM: *A function is* TM-*computable iff it is partial recursive.* $\square$

We showed in Section **1** that every partial recursive function is TM-computable by appealing to our discussion of generalized Turing machines. Another approach due to SHEPHERDSON and STURGIS [1962] (but see also MINSKY [1967, Chap. 11]) uses various formalized versions of a programmed computer. They introduce a limited-register machine LRM (X_k) with alphabet $X_k = \{a_1, a_2, \ldots, a_k\}$ and show that any partial recursive function on X_k can be computed by LRM(X_k) when supplied with a suitable program. They then make the reduction to a single-register machine, SRM(X_k). Finally, they make the reduction to Turing machines, and note other possible reductions. In this way, they show that every partial recursive function is computable by a Turing machine.

The limited-register machine, LRM(X_k), has at any moment of time only a finite number, N, of registers, but also has the facility of adding and deleting registers. Each register can store any string from X_k^*. Henceforth $\langle n \rangle$, $\langle n' \rangle$ denote the contents of register n before and after carrying out the instruction. In the instructions listed below, the subscript N means that the instruction is to be applied when the number of registers is N, and is to leave all registers unchanged, save where the instruction specifies to the contrary. The possible instructions for LRM(X_k) are (for $N = 1, 2, 3, \ldots$; $n = 1, 2, \ldots, N$)

$P_N^{(i)}(n)$: Place a_i on the end of $\langle n \rangle$ $(i = 1, \ldots, k)$.

$D_N^{(n)}$: Delete the first letter of $\langle n \rangle$.

$J_N^{(i)}(n)[E1]$: Jump to 1 if $\langle n \rangle$ begins with a_i.

$N \to N + 1$: Bring in a new register, numbered $N + 1$.

$N \to N - 1$: Remove register N.

We define a *program* as a finite sequence of instructions from the above list, numbered serially.

A *computation* of the LRM starts with the specification of a program, of the number of registers, and of their contents. The machine starts by executing instruction 1. When it has executed instruction k, it always proceeds to instruction $k + 1$, unless instruction k was of the form $J_N^{(i)}(n)[l]$ and $\langle n \rangle$ began with a_i, in which case the machine next executes instruction l. The computation *halts* if the machine is sent to an instruction number which is outside the domain of the program. We only consider "legal" programs, i.e., those in which N-register instructions are to be executed when and only when there actually are N registers.

We shall present the Shepherdson-Sturgis results in a series of exercises:

6   EXERCISE: Program auxiliary subroutines for the following useful operations:

  (a) $\bar{J}_N(n)[E1]$: Jump to exit 1 if $\langle n \rangle \neq \Lambda$.

  (b) $J_N[E1]$: Jump to exit 1.

  (c) $J_N(n)[E1]$: Jump to exit 1 if $\langle n \rangle = \Lambda$.

  (d) $\Lambda_N(n)$: Clear register n (that is, place Λ in it).

7   EXERCISE: Suppose we have subroutines $F_N^{(i)}$ $(i = 1, \ldots, k)$ for performing certain operations. It is convenient to have a subroutine which will perform subroutine $F_N^{(i)}$ if $\langle n \rangle$ begins with a_i $(i = 1, \ldots, k)$ and will do nothing if $\langle n \rangle = \Lambda$.

Denote this by $\sum_{i=1}^{k} (n) F_N^{(i)}$. Program this subroutine.

Now we define $\{F_N^{(1)}\} \langle n \rangle$ to have the following effect: If $\langle n \rangle = a_{i_1} \ldots a_{i_l}$, then it performs the sequence of operations $F_N^{(i_1)}, \ldots, F_N^{(i_l)}$ (if $\langle n \rangle = \Lambda$, it does nothing) and reduces $\langle n \rangle$ to Λ. Here we assume that $n \leq N$, and that the $F_N^{(i)}$ do not disturb register n. It is executed as follows:

  1. $\sum_{i=1}^{k} (n) \{F_N^{(i)}, D_N(n), \bar{J}_N^{(n)}[1]\}$

Use this device to write a subroutine for

$$C_N(m, n): \text{Copy } \langle m \rangle \text{ into register } n$$

8   EXERCISE: Write the following subroutines:

  I.   Subroutine $R_N(\langle y \rangle = S_{a_i}(\langle x \rangle))$

  II.   Subroutine $R_N(\langle y \rangle = \Lambda^n(\langle x_1 \rangle, \ldots, \langle x_n \rangle))$

III. Subroutine $R_N(\langle y \rangle = U_i^n(\langle x_1 \rangle, \ldots, \langle x_n \rangle))$

IV. Subroutine $R_N(\langle y \rangle = f(\langle x_1 \rangle, \ldots, \langle x_n \rangle))$, using subroutines for $g_1, \ldots, g_m$, and h, where

$$f(x_1, \ldots, x_n) = h(g_1(x_1, \ldots, x_n), \ldots, g_m(x_1, \ldots, x_n))$$

V. Subroutine $R_N(\langle y \rangle = f(\langle x_1 \rangle, \ldots, \langle x_n \rangle))$, using subroutines for g and the h_i, where

$$f(\Lambda, x_2, \ldots, x_n) = g(x_2, \ldots, x_n)$$
$$f(za_i, x_2, \ldots, x_n) = h_i(z, f(z, x_1, \ldots, x_n), x_2, \ldots, x_n)(i = 1, \ldots, k)$$

VI$_i$. Subroutine $R_N(\langle y \rangle = f(\langle x_1 \rangle, \ldots, \langle x_n \rangle))$, using subroutine for g, where $f(x_1, \ldots, x_n) = \mu_1 y g(x_1, \ldots, x_n, y) = \Lambda]$

From Exercise **8** we may immediately deduce the

9 THEOREM: *For each function f on n arguments, partial recursive on X_k, and each set of natural numbers (to be considered as addresses of registers) $x_1, \ldots, x_n, y, N$ (where the x_i and y are $n + 1$ distinct numbers $\leq N$) there exists a program $R_N(\langle y \rangle = f(\langle x_1 \rangle, \ldots, \langle x_n \rangle))$ for LRM(X_k) such that if $\langle x_1 \rangle, \ldots, \langle x_n \rangle$ are the initial contents of registers $x_1, \ldots, x_n$, then*

(i) *if $f(\langle x_1 \rangle, \ldots, \langle x_n \rangle)$ is undefined, the machine will not stop; whereas*

(ii) *if $f(\langle x_1 \rangle, \ldots, \langle x_n \rangle) = m$, say, the machine will stop with the final contents of register y, $\langle y \rangle$, equal to m, and with the final contents of all registers $1, 2, \ldots, N$ except register y the same as their initial contents.*

At the start and end of computation, LRM will have exactly N registers.

Note that if we take $R_{n+1}(\langle n + 1 \rangle = f(\langle 1 \rangle, \ldots, \langle n \rangle))$ and precede it by $n \rightarrow n + 1$, we get a routine which when started with n registers containing $x_1, \ldots, x_n$ finishes with $n + 1$ registers containing $x_1, \ldots, x_n, f(x_1, \ldots, x_n)$. If we add a routine for copying the contents of register $n + 1$ into register 1, and deleting all registers except 1, we finish with a single register containing $(x_1, \ldots, x_n)$.

Consider the machine SRM(X_k) which has a single register in which may be stored words on the enlarged alphabet $X_k \cup \{,\}$, where the symbol "," does not belong to X_k. Then the information stored in the N registers of LRM(X_k) may be stored as one word $A = \langle 1 \rangle, \langle 2 \rangle, \ldots, \langle N \rangle$ in the single register of SRM. Setting $a_0 = $, we let i run from 0 to k in the SRM instruction list:

$P^{(i)}$: Place a_i at the rightmost end of A.
D: Delete the first letter of A.
$J^{(i)}[E1]$: Jump to exit 1 if A begins with a_i.

Unfortunately, we can now operate only on the ends of the word A, rather than on the constituents $\langle n \rangle$.

10 EXERCISE: Show how to recapture the instructions of LRM(X_k) by writing the following subroutines for SRM(X_k):

(a) Subroutine for $\bar{J}[E1]$: Jump if $A \neq \Lambda$

Note that if we are simulating the case $N > 1$, then A is always non-null—it contains at least one comma—and so $\bar{J}$ is then an unconditional jump.

(b) Subroutine T for cycling $A_1, A_2, \ldots, A_N$ into $A_2, \ldots, A_N, A_1$:

Now write out the subroutines for simulating *legal* programs of LRM(X_k)—bringing A_n to the appropriate position by repeated application of T, operating on it, then restoring the position of the substrings.

We may thus deduce the truth of the:

11 THEOREM: *All partial recursive functions over X_k are computable by a single-register machine with alphabet $X_k \cup \{,\}$ and instructions*

$$P^{(i)}: A \to Aa_i$$
$$D: a_iA \to A$$
$$J^{(i)}[E1]: \text{Jump to exit 1 if } A \text{ begins with } a_i.$$

12 EXERCISE: Prove that Theorem **11** is valid even if we replace the last two operations by the single scan-and-delete operation

Scd $[E1, \ldots, E(k + 1)]$: scan the first letter of A. If $A = \Lambda$, take the normal exit. If A starts with a_i, delete it, and take exit $i + 1$ ($i = 0, \ldots, k$).

If we take X_1 as the single-letter alphabet $\{1\}$ and use 0 as a comma, this shows that all numerical partial recursive functions are computable by the machine shown in Fig. 6.1, which has a single one-way tape, two tape symbols 0, 1, and two heads —a reading head at the left-hand end and a writing head at the right-hand end, each capable of moving to the right only, and connected to a suitable control center and program store.

For the reader who recalls the material of Section **5.1**, we note that Theorem **11** as modified by Exercise **12** shows that any partial recursive function can be computed by a Post normal system as follows:

Given a program of m lines on alphabet $\{a_0, \ldots, a_k\}$, we consider a Post normal system on alphabet $\mathcal{C} = \{a_0, \ldots, a_k, g_1, \ldots, g_m\}$ obtained by the replace-

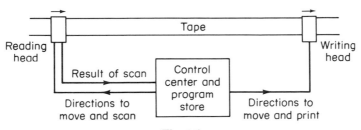

Fig. 6.1

ments

$$\text{Scd } [i_1, \ldots, i_{k+1}] \quad \text{is replaced by} \quad g_i a_j P \to P g_{i_{j+1}} \,(j = 0, \ldots, k)$$
$$P^{(j)} \quad \text{is replaced by} \quad g_i P \to P a_j g_{j+1}$$

to which are added the productions $a_j P \to P a_j$. Thus we may go from $g_1 W$ to $g_m W_1$ iff the program started on W would end with W_1.

To prove that any $\text{SRM}(X_k)$ machine can be simulated by a Turing machine, it suffices to prove that we can do the job with a Turing-like machine with alphabet $\{0, a_1, \ldots, a_k\}$ (where 0 serves as a blank) and programmed with a finite sequence of instructions from the list:

> L: Move the head one square left.
> R: Move the head one square right.
> $P^{(i)}$: Print a_i $(i = 0, 1, \ldots, k)$ on the scanned square.
> $J^{(i)}[E1]$: If the symbol on the scanned square is a_i, take exit 1.
> We denote $P^{(0)}$ by E (for erase).

We represent a word $A_1, \ldots, A_N$ of the $\text{SRM}(X_k)$ by the tape expression

$$- 0 \downarrow A_1\, 0\, A_2\, 0\, A_3 \ldots 0\, A_N\, 0^\infty$$

where $\downarrow$ indicates the standard position of the reading head on the first square to the right of the arrow, and the horizontal line on the left indicates that we do not care what is printed on the tape there. (Thus we could use a one-way infinite tape— but we do not refer to a fixed origin.) Ambiguity between $A_1, A_2, \ldots, A_N$ and $A_1, A_2, \ldots, A_N, \Lambda$, and so on is no problem, since we always keep track of N. Subroutine R_0: "Proceed to next blank to the right" may be given as

> 1. $R, J^{(1)}[1], \ldots, J^{(k)}[1]$

Similarly for L_0. We may now give the subroutines for simulating the operations of $\text{SRM}(X_k)$:

$$P_N^{(i)} = 1.L, R_0^N, P^{(i)}, L_0^N, R$$
$$D_N = 1.E, R$$
$$J_N^{(i)}[E1] = J_N^{(i)}[E1]$$

Using Theorem **11**, we may immediately deduce

13 THEOREM: *Every partial recursive function f of n arguments over the alphabet X_k is computable by a Turing machine over the alphabet $X_k \cup \{0\}$ in the sense that if the initial tape configuration is*

$$- 0 \downarrow x_1\, 0\, x_2\, 0 \ldots x_{n-1}\, 0\, x_n\, 0^\infty$$

then if $f(x_1, \ldots, x_n)$ is undefined, the machine will not stop; whereas if $f(x_1, \ldots, x_n)$ is defined it will stop with tape configuration

$$— 0 \downarrow x_1\, 0\, x_2\, 0 \ldots 0\, x_n\, 0\, f(x_1, \ldots, x_n)\, 0^\infty$$

(*or, if desired,* $0 \downarrow f(x_1, \ldots, x_n)\, 0^\infty$).

Suppose we have a weak Turing machine whose alphabet $\mathfrak{B}$ has $X_k \cup \{0\}$ as a proper subset, and whose operations are

L: Move the head one square left.
R: Move the head one square right.
E: Replace the symbol on the scanned square by a symbol in $\overline{X}_k = \mathfrak{B} - (X_k \cup \{0\})$. (It doesn't matter which symbol.)
$P^{(i)}$: Print a_i on the scanned square, provided that this is blank ($i = 1, \ldots, k$).
$J^{(i)}[E1]$: Jump to exit 1 if the scanned symbol is a_i ($i = 1, \ldots, k$).

Let us choose some symbol $\bar{a}$ of $\overline{X}_k$ and represent the sequence of words $A_1, \ldots, A_N$ over X_k by the tape configuration

$$— \bar{a} \downarrow A_1\, \bar{a}\, A_2\, \bar{a} \ldots \bar{a}\, A_N\, 0^\infty$$

We immediately have

14 THEOREM: *Every partial recursive function f over X_k is computable by a weak Turing machine over any alphabet $\mathfrak{B}$ properly containing $X_k \cup \{0\}$ in the following sense: If the initial tape configuration is* $— \bar{a} \downarrow x_1\, \bar{a}\, x_2\, \bar{a} \ldots \bar{a}\, x_n\, 0^\infty$, *then the final tape configuration, when $f(x_1, \ldots, x_n)$ is defined, is*

$$— \bar{a} \downarrow x_1\, \bar{a}\, x_2\, \bar{a} \ldots \bar{a}\, x_n\, \bar{a}\, f(x_1, \ldots, x_n)\, 0^\infty$$

or
$$— \bar{a} \downarrow f(x_1, \ldots, x_n)\, 0^\infty$$

(*if desired*).

15 EXERCISE: Prove the result (WANG [1957]) that any partial recursive function can be computed by a non-erasing W-machine, i.e., with alphabet $\{b, *\}$ (b = blank) and operations

←: Move head one square left.
→: Move head one square right.
*: Mark the scanned square.
C: Jump to exit 1 if scanned square is marked.

[Hint: Code 0 as bb, 1 as $*b$, 2 as $**$, and then apply Theorem **14** with $X_1 = \{1\}$, $\mathfrak{B} = \{0, 1, 2\}$, and use E to replace the scanned symbol by 2. Show that C may be replaced by C': jump to exit 1 if scanned square is blank.]

We now present a number of related results due to MINSKY [1961]. The proofs may be found in Section 10 of SHEPHERDSON and STURGIS [1962] and in Chapter 14 of MINSKY [1967]:

16   EXERCISE: Prove the following: A single-register machine working on non-negative integers, and with operations

(α) x_k: Multiply the number in the register by k.
(β) $\div k$: Divide the number in the register by k.
(γ) Div ? $k[E1]$: Test whether the number in the register is divisible by k; if
         so, take exit 1. If not, proceed with next instruction.

can compute all partial recursive functions f in the following sense: if the number in the register is initially $p_1^{x_1} p_2^{x_2} \ldots p_n^{x_n}$ (where p_j is the jth prime), then it will finally be $p_1^{f(x_1, \ldots, x_n)}$.

17   EXERCISE: Prove the following: With the same representation of arguments and values as in **16** but with the operations

a. $P(n)$: Add one to $\langle n \rangle$.
b. $D(n)$: Subtract one from $\langle n \rangle$.
f̄. $J(n)[E1]$: Jump to exit 1 if $\langle n \rangle \neq 0$.

two registers are adequate for the computation of all partial recursive functions.

The reader acquainted with Section **5.1** may wish to emulate MINSKY [1961] by showing that "tag" systems are universal:

18   EXERCISE: Use **17** to prove that "tag" systems are universal in that they can compute all partial recursive functions.

We shall conclude this section by showing how the limited-register machine fits into our general notion of a recursive computer. We shall, in fact, generalize the LRM to obtain our own *stored-program version* of the limited-register machine, SPM(X_k), which has at any moment of time only a finite number, N, of registers but also has the facility of adding and deleting registers. Each register can store any string from X_k^*. These strings may be interpreted either as instructions or as data.

The possible instructions for SPM(X_k) are

$P^{(i)}(n)$: $\langle n' \rangle = \langle n \rangle a_i$ ($i = 1, \ldots, k$).
$D(n)$: Delete the first letter of $\langle n \rangle$.
$J^{(i)}(n)[E1]$: Jump to exit 1 if $\langle n \rangle$ begins with a_i.
    Reg $+$: Bring in a new register (i.e., increase N to $N + 1$).
    Reg $-$: Remove the last register (i.e., decrease N to $N \doteq 1$).

Each of these instructions has a standard, uniquely decipherable encoding as a string in X_k^*. We do not bother to specify an encoding, and simply use the above notations both for an instruction and as shorthand for the encoding of an instruction.

A *state* of the SPM consists of the specification of the number of its registers, their contents, and of at most one register which contains the next string to be decoded for possible instruction execution. Denote the address of this register by I.

If there are N registers, the nth having contents $\langle n \rangle$, and $I = i$, then we may represent the state of SPM by the string

$$q = \langle 1 \rangle, \langle 2 \rangle, \ldots, \downarrow \langle i \rangle, \langle i + 1 \rangle, \ldots, \langle N \rangle$$

where we assume that "," and " $\downarrow$ " are distinct symbols not in X_k.

If no register is singled out for the next possible instruction, we say "SPM has halted," set $I = \emptyset$, and represent its state as

$$q = \langle 1 \rangle, \langle 2 \rangle, \ldots, \langle n \rangle, \ldots, \langle N \rangle$$

and we call q a *passive* state. Otherwise, q is *active*. Let Q be the set of all such state-representatives.

We define a next-state function λ as follows:

(i) If q is passive, $\lambda(q) = q$.

(ii) If q is active, but $\langle I \rangle$ is not a valid instruction (i.e., it is not decodable as an instruction; or, if it is, the n of the instruction is larger than the N of q), then, again, we set

$$\lambda(q) = q$$

(iii) If $q = \langle 1 \rangle, \langle 2 \rangle, \ldots, \downarrow \langle I \rangle, \ldots, \langle N \rangle$ is active, with $\langle I \rangle$ a valid instruction, we have‡

   (a) $\langle I \rangle = P^{(i)}(n)$ with $n \leq N$, then

$$\lambda(q) = \langle 1 \rangle, \ldots, \langle n - 1 \rangle, \langle n \rangle a_i, \ldots, \langle I \rangle, \downarrow \langle I + 1 \rangle, \ldots, \langle N \rangle$$

   and is the corresponding passive state if $I = N$.

   (b) $\langle I \rangle = D(n)$ with $n \leq N$, then

$$\lambda(q) = \langle 1 \rangle, \ldots, \langle n - 1 \rangle, d(\langle n \rangle), \ldots, \langle I \rangle, \downarrow \langle I + 1 \rangle, \ldots, \langle N \rangle$$

   and is the corresponding passive state if $I = N$.

   (c) $J^{(i)}(n)[k]$ with $n \leq N$.

   (α) $\langle n \rangle$ begins with a_i

$$\lambda(q) = \langle 1 \rangle, \ldots, \langle I \rangle, \ldots, \downarrow \langle k \rangle, \ldots, \langle N \rangle$$

   and is the corresponding passive state if $k > N$.

---

‡ We do not rule out $n \geq I$, and so on, but show $I > n > 2$ for ease of diagramming.

(β) $\langle n \rangle$ does not begin with a_i

$$\lambda(q) = \langle 1 \rangle, \ldots, \downarrow \langle I + 1 \rangle, \ldots, \langle N \rangle$$

(d) $\langle I \rangle = \text{Reg} +$

$$\lambda(q) = \langle 1 \rangle, \ldots, \langle I \rangle, \downarrow \langle I + 1 \rangle, \ldots, \langle N \rangle, \Lambda$$

where Λ is the empty string.
(e) $\langle I \rangle = \text{Reg} -$

$$\lambda(q) = \langle 1 \rangle, \ldots, \langle I \rangle, \downarrow \langle I + 1 \rangle, \ldots, \langle N - 1 \rangle$$

and is the corresponding passive state if $I = N - 1$ or N.
If $N = 0$ or 1, then $\lambda(q) = \Lambda$.

The crucial point to observe (the details of the proof are quite straightforward once we have chosen any "reasonable" encoding of the instructions as strings and may be supplied by the reader after studying Section 1) is that:
λ *is a total recursive function from* $\hat{Q}$ *into* $\hat{Q}$.
A *computation* of the SPM starts with the specification of a state q_1, and is then simply the sequence

$$q_1, q_2, q_3, \ldots, q_j, q_{j+1}, \ldots,$$

where $q_{j+1} = \lambda(q_j)$.
We say the computation *halts* if q_j is passive for some j, and call q_j the *result* of the computation. If no q_j is passive, we call the computation *non-terminating*.
We shall say that a partial function $f: (X_k^*)^n \to X_k^*$ is *SPṀ-computable* if there exists
(a) a sequence $W_1, \ldots, W_s$ of words of X^* (the "program for f") and
(b) an integer $\mathfrak{M}$ (the "result address")
such that the computation with initial state

$$\downarrow W_1, W_2, \ldots, W_s, x_1, \ldots, x_n$$

halts with at least $\mathfrak{M}$ registers if and only if $f(x_1, \ldots, x_n)$ is well-defined, in which case $f(x_1, \ldots, x_n)$ will be the contents of the $\mathfrak{M}$th register.

19   THEOREM: *Every partial recursive function on* X_k *is SPM-computable.*
   Proof. Let f be a partial recursive function, and let $R_{n+1}(\langle n + 1 \rangle = f(\langle 1 \rangle, \ldots, \langle n \rangle))$ be the LRM-program guaranteed by Theorem **9**. Suppose it contains s instructions, and let $W_1, \ldots, W_s$ be the sequence of instructions

obtained from these by adding s to all the register indices (i.e., the n's, but not the El's), dropping subscript N's, and changing each $N \rightarrow N + 1$ to Reg $+$, each $N \rightarrow N - 1$ to Reg $-$.

Then it is obvious that f is SPM-computable, in that if we start SPM in state

$$\downarrow W_1, \ldots, W_s, x_1, \ldots, x_n$$

and $f(x_1, \ldots, x_n)$ is well-defined, the computation will terminate with $f(x_1, \ldots, x_n)$ in its $(s + n + 1)$st register. $\qquad \square$

20   THEOREM: *Every SPM-computable function is partial recursive.*
   Proof. Just check that Theorem **4** is applicable. $\qquad \square$

Intermediate between the SPM and the general recursive computer is a whole family of mathematical models of computation. For instance, if we enlarge the Q of the SPM by allowing any number of registers to be preceded by arrows, and then restrict λ to be a total function which in some sense executes the instructions stored in those registers, we get a model of a parallel computer—but are still assured that it only computes partial recursive functions.

6.3   HIERARCHIES

In this section, we wish to study an important subclass of the partial recursive functions—namely the primitive recursive functions—and embed them in various hierarchies, indicating the recursive function theory approach to complexity as a foil for our more extensive study of complexity of computation in Chapter 7. However, the material in this section is *not* a prerequisite for Chapter 7, and many readers may choose to omit it on a first reading.

We restrict our study in this section to numerical functions—in any case, the primitive recursive functions are those partial recursive functions which may be obtained without the use of minimization:

1   DEFINITION: *The **primitive recursive** functions are the smallest class of numerical functions containing* S: $n \mapsto n + 1$, 0^n: $(x_1, \ldots, x_n) \mapsto 0$ *and* $U_j^n(x_1, \ldots, x_n) \mapsto x_j$ *and closed under composition and recursion.*

Note that this definition implies that every primitive recursive function is *total*. Primitive recursive functions are, in a sense, more computable than partial recursive functions in that their computation does not involve the a priori unbounded searches which may arise in applying the minimization operator.

The reader should by now be able to prove that the primitive recursive functions *can* be effectively enumerated and thus form a *proper* subclass of the total recursive functions—if g_n is the nth primitive recursive function in such an enumeration, then $g_n(n) + 1$ is a total recursive function which is not in the enumeration, and is thus not primitive recursive.

2 DEFINITION: *The operation of **explicit transformation** is one that replaces a function $f: N^n \rightarrow N$ by a function $g: N^m \rightarrow N$, where $g(x_1, \ldots, x_m) = f(\xi_1, \ldots, \xi_n)$, where for each j it is decreed that ξ_j must always be a certain constant or a certain x_k.*

3 EXERCISE: Prove that if a class of functions contains S, 0^n, and U_j^n and is closed under composition, then it is closed under explicit transformation.

Thus the classes of partial recursive functions, total recursive functions, and primitive recursive functions are all closed under explicit transformation.

4 EXERCISE: Prove that the following functions are primitive recursive: $x + y$; $x \cdot y$; $x \div 1$; $n!$; x^y; $1 \div x$ and $|x - y|$.

Let us now use $\mathbf{x}$ to denote a vector $(x_1, \ldots, x_m)$ of integers, and so on.

5 PROPOSITION: *If $f(k, \mathbf{x})$ is primitive recursive, then so too are*

$$g(n, \mathbf{x}) = \sum_{k=0}^{n} f(k, \mathbf{x})$$

and
$$h(n, \mathbf{x}) = \prod_{k=0}^{n} f(k, \mathbf{x})$$

*We say that g is obtained from f by **limited addition**, and that h is obtained from f by **limited multiplication**.*

Proof. For g, we have $g(0, \mathbf{x}) = f(0, \mathbf{x})$
$$g(n + 1, \mathbf{x}) = g(n, \mathbf{x}) + f(n + 1, \mathbf{x})$$
For h, we have $h(0, \mathbf{x}) = f(0, \mathbf{x})$
$$h(n + 1, \mathbf{x}) = h(n, \mathbf{x}) \cdot f(n + 1, \mathbf{x}) \qquad \square$$

We now examine the primitive recursive functions in more detail, following the treatment of GRZEGORCZYK [1953]:

6 DEFINITION: *If $\mathcal{X}$ is a class of functions on N, let $\mathcal{X}_n$ denote the class of n-argument functions in $\mathcal{X}$. We say that $F(x_1, \ldots, x_n, t)$ is a **universal function for $\mathcal{X}_n$** if*

$$f \in \mathcal{X}_n \quad \Leftrightarrow \quad (\exists t \in N)(f(\mathbf{x}) = F(\mathbf{x}, t))$$

We say that $P: N^2 \to N,\ddagger\ Q: N \to N,\ R: N \to N$ *form a* **triple of pairing functions** *if*

$$P(Qz, Rz) = z$$
$$Q(P(x, y)) = x$$
$$R(P(x, y)) = y$$

7 PROPOSITION:

(i) *If* $\mathfrak{X}$ *is closed under composition and explicit transformation and contains a triple of pairing functions, then* F_n, *a universal function for* $\mathfrak{X}_n$, *can be expressed in terms of* F_1.

(ii) *If* $\mathfrak{X}$ *is closed under composition and explicit transformation and contains S, then the universal function for* $\mathfrak{X}_n$ *cannot belong to* $\mathfrak{X}$.

Proof. (i) Let P, Q, R be a triple of pairing functions belonging to $\mathfrak{X}$.

Then
$$f(x_1, x_2, \mathbf{x}) \in \mathfrak{X}_{n+1} \Rightarrow f(Qz, Rz, \mathbf{x}) \in \mathfrak{X}_n$$
$$f(z, \mathbf{x}) \in \mathfrak{X}_n \quad \Rightarrow f(P(x_1, x_2), \mathbf{x}) \in \mathfrak{X}_{n+1}$$

It follows that if $F_n(x_1, x_2, \ldots, x_n, t)$ is a universal function for $\mathfrak{X}_n$, then $F_n(P(x_1, x_2), x_3, \ldots, x_{n+1}, t)$ is a universal function for $\mathfrak{X}_{n+1}$, and the result follows by induction.

(ii) Consider $f(x_1, \ldots, x_n) = F_n(x_1, x_1, \ldots, x_n) + 1$.   □

8 DEFINITION: *The class $\mathcal{E}$ of functions* **elementary** (*in the sense of* KALMAR [1943]) *is the smallest class of functions containing* $S(x)$, $x + y$, *and* $x \doteq y$, *and closed under composition, explicit transformation, limited addition, and limited multiplication.*

It is clear, then, that every elementary function is primitive recursive.

9 EXERCISE:

(i) Verify that $x \cdot y$, x^y, and $x!$ are elementary functions.

(ii) Verify that $\mathcal{E}$ is closed under the operation of *limited minimum* which transforms $F(h, \mathbf{x})$ to

$$f(y, \mathbf{x}) = \mu t \le y[F(n, \mathbf{x}) = 0]$$
$$= \begin{cases} \text{the smallest } t \le y \text{ such that } F(\mathbf{x}, t) = 0; \\ 0 \text{ if no such } t \text{ exists} \end{cases}$$

The reader may consult KALMAR [1943] if he reads Hungarian and GRZEGORCZYK [1953] if he reads English to see equivalent definitions of the class of elementary functions, and proofs that the following functions

---

‡ Compare the function τ of 4.4.10.

are elementary (recalling that for a predicate $P(\mathbf{x})$, $\ulcorner P(\mathbf{x})\urcorner = 0$ if $P(\mathbf{x})$ is false, and 1 if $P(\mathbf{x})$ is true): $\ulcorner x \leq y\urcorner$, $\ulcorner x = y\urcorner$, $\ulcorner x$ is divisible by $y\urcorner$, $\ulcorner x$ is a prime$\urcorner$, $[x/y]$, $r(x, y)$, $x^+ = x^z$, $x^{++} = x^{z+}$, $[\overset{y}{\sqrt{}}x]$, and so on.

10   DEFINITION: *We say f is obtained from g, h, and j by the operation of* **limited recursion** *if*

$$f(0, \mathbf{x}) = g(\mathbf{x})$$
$$f(n + 1, \mathbf{x}) = h(n, f(n, \mathbf{x}), \mathbf{x})$$

and $$f(n, \mathbf{x}) \leq j(n, \mathbf{x})$$

that is, f is obtained from g and h by recursion, but is only "accepted" if its size is limited by that of the already available function j.

11   EXERCISE: Prove, starting from $S(x)$ and x^y, that $x \cdot y$ and $x + y$ can be obtained by limited recursion.

We then have the following characterizations:

12   THEOREM: *The following classes are identical:*

(i)   *The class $\mathcal{E}$ of elementary functions;*

(ii)   *The class $\mathcal{E}'$, being the smallest class including $x + 1$, $x \div y$, and x^y and closed under composition, explicit transformation, and limited* **minimum**.

(iii)   *The class $\mathcal{E}''$, being the smallest class including $x + 1$ and x^y and closed under composition, explicit transformation, and limited* **recursion**.

(iv)   *The class $\mathcal{E}'''$, being the smallest class including $x + 1$, $x \div y$, $x \cdot y$, and x^y and closed under composition, explicit transformation, and limited* **summation**.

Proof. This should not be beyond the reach of many readers. The details may be found in GRZEGORCZYK [1953, pp. 15–20].   □

We now introduce a class of functions by the definition:

$$f_0(x, y) = y + 1$$
$$f_1(x, y) = x + y$$
$$f_2(x, y) = (x + 1) \cdot (y + 1)$$

and, for $n \geq 2$, $$f_{n+1}(0, y) = f_n(y + 1, y + 1)$$
$$f_{n+1}(x + 1, y) = f_{n+1}(x, f_{n+1}(x, y))$$

The monotonicity of these functions is indicated by the following results:

13   EXERCISE: Prove that

(i) $$f_n(x, y) > y \qquad\qquad \text{for } n > 1 \; (f_0(0, y) = y)$$

(ii) $f_n(x + 1, y) > f_n(x, y)$ for $n \geq 1$

(iii) $f_n(x, y + 1) > f_n(x, y)$ for $n \geq 0$

We may now introduce a denumerable collection of classes of functions:

14 DEFINITION: *Let $\mathcal{E}^n$ be the smallest class of numerical functions including $S(x)$, U_1^2, U_2^2, and $f_n(x, y)$, and closed under the operations of composition, explicit transformation, and limited recursion.*

The smallest of these classes is amazingly powerful in that GRZEGORCZYK [1953, Theorem 5.3] proves that every recursively enumerable set can be enumerated by a function of $\mathcal{E}^0$. We shall not go into proofs here, referring the reader to GRZEGORCZYK [1953] for further details, but simply list other properties of these sets $\mathcal{E}^n$ that attract our interest:

15 EXERCISE: Prove that $\mathcal{E}^3$ is the class of elementary functions. [Hint: Use $x^y < f_3(x, y)$ to prove $\mathcal{E} \subset \mathcal{E}^3$; and $f_3(x, y) = g(2^x, y)$ where

$$g(0, y) = y$$
$$g(x + 1, y) = (g(x, y) + 2)^2$$
$$g(x, y) < (y + 2)^{2^{2^{2^x}}}$$

to prove $\mathcal{E}^3 \subset \mathcal{E}$.]

16 *Each $f_i \in \mathcal{E}^n$ for $i \leq n$, and so $\mathcal{E}^n \subset \mathcal{E}^{n+1}$ for each n.*

17 *The function $f_{n+1}(x, x)$ increases faster than any function of the class $\mathcal{E}^n$, and so $\mathcal{E}^n$ is a **proper** subclass of $\mathcal{E}^{n+1}$.*

18 *For $n > 2$, the class $\mathcal{E}^{n+1}$ includes the universal function for the class $\mathcal{E}_1^n$.*

It is clear that each function in some $\mathcal{E}^n$ is primitive recursive. In fact, the converse is also true:

19 *If a primitive recursive function f is obtained from the basis functions by applying at most n of the operations, then $f \in \mathcal{E}^{n+3}$. Thus the union of the classes $\mathcal{E}^n$ is the class of all primitive recursive functions.*

Thus the classes $\mathcal{E}^n$ form a hierarchy, now known as the *Grzegorczyk hierarchy*, which stratifies the primitive recursive function, with $\mathcal{E}^0$ being totipotent for purposes of enumerating sets of integers, and with $\mathcal{E}^3$ comprising the elementary functions.

RITCHIE [1963] imposed a subhierarchy on $\mathcal{E}^3$ in a study based on the amount of tape required by a Turing machine for its computation—we let $a_f(x)$ denote an‡ amount of tape for computing $f(x)$ and write $l(x) =$

---

‡ Since many Turing machines can compute f, a statement like "$a_f(x) = g(x)$" is shorthand for "at least one Turing machine which computes f is such that its computation time for input x is at most $g(x)$).

$\sum_{i=1}^{n} |x_i| + (n - 1)$ for the amount of tape required to write out the vector $\mathbf{x} = (x_1, \ldots, x_n)$. We assume that all numbers are encoded in binary form.

20   EXERCISE: Verify the following relations:
(a) $f(\mathbf{x}, y) = h(\mathbf{x}, g(y)) \Rightarrow a_f(\mathbf{x}, y) = l(\mathbf{x}, y) + \max\,[l(\mathbf{x}) + a_g(y), a_h(\mathbf{x}, g(y))]$
(b) $f(\mathbf{x}, 0) = g(\mathbf{x}), f(\mathbf{x}, s(y)) = h(\mathbf{x}, y, f(\mathbf{x}, y)) \Rightarrow$
$$a_f(\mathbf{x}, y) = 2[l(\mathbf{x}, y) + \max_{z < y}\,[\max\,(a_h(\mathbf{x}, z, f(\mathbf{x}, z))), a_g(\mathbf{x})]]$$
(c) $f(x_1, \ldots, x_n) = g(\xi_1, \ldots, \xi_k) \Rightarrow a_f(x_1, \ldots, x_n) = a_g(\xi_1, \ldots, \xi_k) + l(\mathbf{x}).$

21   DEFINITION: *Let F_0 be the class of functions computable by finite automata (that is, TMs which only move right)—so $a_f(\mathbf{x}) = l(\mathbf{x}) + Q$—where Q is the number of states of the TM. For $i > 0$, a numerical function f is said to be in the class F_i iff*
   (i) *it is computable by a TM;*
   (ii) *there is a function $g \in F_{i-1}$ such that $a_f(\mathbf{x}) \le g(\mathbf{x})$ for all n-tuples $\mathbf{x}$ of nonnegative integers (that is, f can be computed by a TM, using an amount of tape bounded above by a function of F_{i-1}). The class of **predictably computable functions**, $\mathfrak{F}$, is then the union of the F_i.*
   Clearly $F_i \subset F_{i+1}$ for all i—we shall see that the containment is proper.

22   EXERCISE: Prove that each class F is closed under explicit transformations. [Hint: Verify that this is true for F_0, and proceed by induction.]

23   LEMMA: *$\mathfrak{F}$ is closed under composition. More precisely,*

$$h \in F_i \text{ and } g \in F_j \Rightarrow f \in F_{i+j}, \text{ where } f(\mathbf{x}, y) = h(\mathbf{x}, g(y))$$

Proof. $f'(\mathbf{x}, y) = g(\mathbf{x}) + g'(y) \Rightarrow a_{f'}(\mathbf{x}, y) = a_g(\mathbf{x}) + a_{g'}(y)$, so F_0 closed under addition yields, by induction, each F_i closed under addition.

$g \in F_j$ and $h \in F_0$ certainly implies $h(\mathbf{x}, g(y)) \in F_j$.

Now use induction on i, recalling **20**(a).   □

24   DEFINITION: *Set $f_0(x) = x, f_{i+1}(x) = 2^{f_i(x)}$ for all $i \ge 1$. ($f_i(x) = 2^{2^{\cdot^{\cdot^{\cdot^2}}}} i$ times).*

25   LEMMA: *For each $i > 1$ and each $f \in F_i$, there is an integer K such that $f(\mathbf{x}) < f_i\,(K \max\,(\mathbf{x}, 1))$ and $a_f(\mathbf{x}) < f_{i-1}\,(K \max\,(\mathbf{x}, 1))$.*
   Proof. For $f \in F_1$, we may check that $a_f(\mathbf{x}) < K \max\,(\mathbf{x}, 1)$. Thus $f(\mathbf{x}) < 2^{l[f(\mathbf{x})]} < 2^{a_f(\mathbf{x})} < 2^{k \max(\mathbf{x}, 1)} = f_1(K \max\,(\mathbf{x}, 1))$. Then, by induction, assuming that for $f \in F_{i+1}$, we have $a_f(\mathbf{x}) < f_i(K \max\,(\mathbf{x}, 1))$, then we also have

$f(\mathbf{x}) < f_1(l[f(\mathbf{x})]) < f_1(a_f(\mathbf{x})) < f_1(f_i(K \max (\mathbf{x}, 1))) = f_{i+1}(K \max (\mathbf{x}, 1))$. $\square$

For any constant a, the function $x \mapsto a^x$ is in F_1, and so $f_i(x) \in F_i$ for each i. However, $f_i \notin F_{i-1}$, since $a_{f_i}(x) \geq l(f_i(x)) = f_{i-1}(x) + 1$, and so $a_{f_i} \notin F_{i-1}$, by induction. Thus:

26 THEOREM: $F_0 \subset F_1 \subset F_2 \subset \ldots \subset F_n \subset \ldots$ *each containment being proper, with* f_i *lying in* F_i *but not* F_{i-1}. $\square$

27 EXERCISE: Prove that $\mathfrak{F}$ is closed under limited recursion. More precisely, let

$$f(\mathbf{x}, 0) = g(\mathbf{x})$$
$$f(\mathbf{x}, y + 1) = h(\mathbf{x}, f(\mathbf{x}, y), y)$$
$$f(\mathbf{x}, y) \leq j(\mathbf{x}, y)$$

Then $h \in F_i, j \in F_k, g \in F_{i+k} \Rightarrow f \in F_{i+k}$. [Hint: Use **20**(b), Lemma **25**, and Lemma **23** twice.]

28 THEOREM: *The class* $\mathcal{E}$ *of elementary functions is contained in* $\mathfrak{F}$.

Proof. From Theorem **12**(iii), we know that $\mathcal{E}$ is the smallest class containing the successor function and the exponential function x^y which is closed under explicit transformations, composition, and limited recursion. Noting that $x^y \in F_2$, we find that the result follows from the lemmas. $\square$

RITCHIE [1963, Appendix 1] gives an encoding of TMs and their IDs in terms of which he constructs elementary U and T_n such that an n-argument function f is computable (in binary) iff there is a number z_0 such that, for all $\mathbf{x}$,

$$f(\mathbf{x}) = U(\mu y[T_n(z_0, \mathbf{x}, y)])$$

where $T_n(z_0, \mathbf{x}, y)$ is the predicate "y encodes the terminal ID of a computation of the z_0th TM with initial data $\mathbf{x}$" and $U(y)$ is "the number encoded by ID y." f is then elementary if there is a $g(\mathbf{x}) \in \mathcal{E}$ such that

$$f(\mathbf{x}) = U(\min y \leq g(x)[T_n(z_0, \mathbf{x}, y)])$$

We find such a g for $f \in F_i$:

$$a_f(\mathbf{x}) \leq h(\mathbf{x}) = f_{i-1}(K \max (\mathbf{x})), \text{ which is elementary.}$$

We may then take $g(\mathbf{x}) = [\text{Pr}(h(\mathbf{x}) + 1)^M]^{h(\mathbf{x})+1}$ where M is the maximum number encoding a tape symbol internal state of the z_0th TM. We thus obtain Ritchie's main result:

29 THEOREM: *The class* $\mathfrak{F}$ *of predictably computable functions is precisely the class* $\mathcal{E}$ *of elementary functions.*

In Section 4 of his work, Ritchie shows that if F' is the class of all computable functions f for which the amount of tape used in computing $f(\mathbf{x})$ is $\leq$ a constant K_f times $l(\mathbf{x})$, then F' is precisely Grzegorczyk's $\mathcal{E}^2$. In his Section 5, he gives a similar characterization of each of the F_i's.

CLEAVE [1963] extended Ritchie's hierarchy to a refinement of the whole Grzegorczyk hierarchy, using a variant of the Shepherdson-Sturgis machines, involving an analog of limited recursion. Given a denumerable set Σ of functions taking N into N, a J-limited machine over Σ is like a Shepherdson-Sturgis machine save that the program contains functions from Σ instead of the usual print and delete instructions, and there is also specified a function h, called a J-limiter, such that, given initial data $(x_1, \ldots, x_n)$, the computation will be terminated without answer if it does not terminate in less than $h(x_1, \ldots, x_n)$ steps. Let $\mathcal{C}(\Sigma)$ be the set of programs on Σ. We write $f = [P, h]$ for the function computed on a J-limited machine with program P, and J-limiter h. We then define the hierarchy, analogous to Ritchie's, of

$$E(\Sigma)_0 = \{f \mid f = [P, h], P \in \mathcal{C}(\Sigma), h \in C\}$$

where C is the set of constant functions

$$E(\Sigma)_{r+1} = \{f \mid f = [P, h], P \in \mathcal{C}(\Sigma), h \in E(\Sigma)_r\}$$

If we now set $E_\omega = \bigcup_{r \geq 0} E(\Sigma)_r$, we may extend this chain by setting

$$\left.\begin{aligned} E_{\omega r+s} &= E(E_{\omega r})_s \\ E_{\omega r} &= \bigcup_{i < \omega r} E_i \\ E_{\omega^2} &= \bigcup_{i < \omega^2} E_i \end{aligned}\right\} r, s < \omega$$

Let $\delta(x, y)$ be the Kronecker delta:

$$\delta(x, y) = \begin{cases} 1 & \text{if } x = y \\ 0 & \text{if not} \end{cases}$$

Cleave ties this hierarchy in with Grzegorczyk's by showing that if $\Sigma = \{+, x, \delta\}$, then, for $s \geq 1$, $E_{\omega s} = \mathcal{E}^{2+s}$.

Much other work has been done on complexity of partial recursive functions in the manner of this section (see, e.g., FISCHER [1965c] for a partial review). However, we now turn to studies of complexity in which techniques automata theory predominate over those of recursive function theory.

7

COMPLEXITY OF COMPUTATION

We know that any computation which can be carried out effectively can be carried out by a Turing machine. The classical theory of recursive functions is concerned with characterizing what can and cannot be done effectively. This has proved a fertile new field of mathematical investigation, and one of great attractiveness to people in the computer sciences. However, the theory of Turing machines is a far cry from a theory of programming, and we mention two reasons. The first is that the operation of a Turing machine is so doggedly serial that few of the tricks of the programmer for improving computer performance can find a place in the theory. Our study of polycephalic machines has already indicated how this may be overcome. The second is that the theory tells what can be done *effectively*, but gives us no clue to what can be done *practically*—it is no good knowing that something can be computed if we cannot be sure that Earth is large enough to hold the requisite tape units, or that life is long enough to see the end of the computation. Our preoccupation in this chapter will be mainly in augmenting the theory of computable functions in the light of the second of these complaints. The resulting theory is still mathematical rather than practical, but as a new chapter in the theory of recursive functions, we hope that it is an apt prolegomenon to the theory of programming.

7.1 CROSSING SEQUENCES FOR ONE-TAPE MACHINES

Our emphasis in our study of Turing machines was on delimiting the possible effective computations. In particular, we saw that anything that could be done by a multihead, multitape machine could be done by a one-head one-tape machine. However, we must suspect that there are many tasks for which a multihead, multitape machine is far more efficient in some sense —e.g., takes less time. That this is so can be made precise, and constitutes a fast-growing but as yet unsystematized area of automata theory. We now present a small sampling of results from this area.

In this section we shall only consider TMs with one-dimensional tapes. A TM will have one head and one tape unless specified explicitly to the contrary.

We may use a TM either as an on-line machine or as an off-line machine (see Section 1.3). In the first case, by an n-tape machine we mean one which actually has $n + 1$ tapes, it being stipulated that one of these tapes is a one-way read-only tape on which the input is written, the other n tapes then being referred to as work tapes. An n-tape off-line machine, however, does indeed have n tapes, with the input actually placed on one of these tapes, it now being the case that there is no necessary restriction that the machine may not write and move both ways on the tape on which the input is presented. We may use such a Turing machine as a function computer, or as an acceptor. We judge acceptance by the state of the machine when computation halts in the off-line case, and by the state of the machine when it moves off the given segment of input tape in the on-line case. Thus a 0-tape on-line acceptor is a finite-state acceptor, and a 1-tape off-line acceptor is an ordinary Turing machine.

We may associate with any machine which computes a total function a number $T(n)$ which bounds the number of steps (i.e., the time) required by the machine to process any input sequence of length n. If we now turn to 1-tape (on-line or off-line) machines, we may introduce $L(n)$ to bound the number of tape squares (i.e., the length) of work tape, while $C(n)$ bounds the number of times a Turing machine crosses the line dividing two adjacent squares of its work tape in processing strings of length n.

If $F_i^Z(x)$ is the number of steps taken by a machine Z in processing the string x, we shall say that Z *defines* $T(n)$ if $T(n) = \max\{F_t(x)|\ |x| = n\}$. Similarly, we may speak of Z as defining a certain $L(n)$ and $C(n)$.

We have already seen in Section 6.3 results due to RITCHIE [1963a] which classify functions on the basis of the minimal $L(n)$ for ordinary Turing machines which compute them. In this section, our emphasis will be on the acceptance of sets, using an analysis of $C(n)$ as our basic tool.

The notion of *trace* of an ordinary Turing machine computation was introduced in Russia by TRAKHTENBROT [1964], in the U.S.A. by HENNIE [1965] (under the name of "crossing sequence"), and in Israel by RABIN [1964] (under the name of "scheme"). Let us denote the successive letters of a string x by $x(1), x(2), \ldots, x(|x|)$. Let Z be any one-head, one-tape TM. By a point of the tape we shall mean the line dividing two successive squares. We number these points sequentially so that at the start of the computation of Z, point i, for $1 \leq i < |x|$, lies between the symbols $x(i)$ and $x(i + 1)$.

Let Z, in the process of its calculating, be in state $q(j)$ on the jth time it

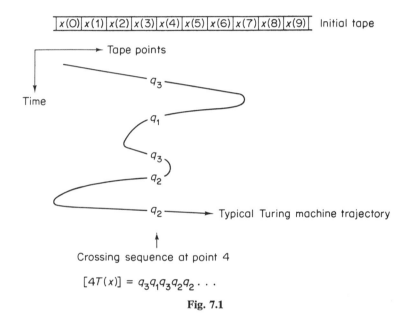

Crossing sequence at point 4

$$[4T(x)] = q_3 q_1 q_3 q_2 q_2 \ldots$$

Fig. 7.1

passes through point i—we then say that the word x has at the point i the *trace* or *crossing sequence* (compare Fig. 7.1)

$$[iT(x)] = q(1)q(2) \ldots$$

We call $x|_i = x(1) \, x(2) \ldots x(i)$ the i-left end of the word x
$$_i|x = x(i + 1) \, x(i + 2) \ldots x(|x|)$$ the i-right end of the word x.
We set $[x, i, y] = x|_{i \cdot i}|y$. If $x|_i = w_1$ and $_i|x = w_2$, we may also write $C(w_1; w_2)$ for $[iT(x)]$.

The crucial point to notice from Fig. 7.1 is that the way in which Z processes $x|_i$ depends on $_i|x$ only insofar as $_i|x$ determines the crossing sequence of Z at i—if we replace $_i|x$ by any $_i|y$ for which $[iT(x)] = [iT(x|_{i \cdot i}|y)]$, then $x|_i$ will be processed the same way whether Z acts on x or $x|_{i \cdot i}|y$. Thus the crossing sequence is a spatial analogue of the temporal

notion of state of a finite automaton, but is two-sided in that the crossing
sequence supplies information about the patterns that appear on both sides
of its occurrence. We obtain lower bounds on computation time by seeing
how long a crossing sequence is required at various points to carry the
requisite information from one part of the tape to the other—a method
reminiscent of the argument used in the Nerode test for finiteness of a sequential machine, in which we study which input sequences must lead the machine
to distinct states so as to obtain a lower bound on the number of states
required.

Note that the total computation time of an ordinary Turing machine
equals the sum of the lengths of all the crossing sequences, if, as we may do
without loss of generality, we insist that every quintuple is of the form
$qxx'Lq'$ or $qxx'Rq'$.

In the analysis that follows, it will be convenient to consider Turing
machines which act on a tape which is only one-way infinite. By looking at
Fig. 7.2, we see that this involves no change in computation time if we are

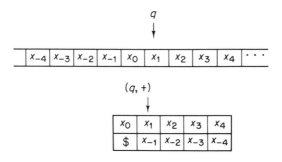

Fig. 7.2

prepared to enlarge the tape alphabet. In any case, we know from **4.3.2** that
if we do not enlarge the alphabet, simulating an increase in the alphabet only
results in an increase by a constant factor in the computation time (but *does*
increase the number of tape reversals immensely).

Suppose we are given a Turing machine Z (which we are using as an off-
line acceptor), with a tape bounded on the left with initial tape segment t and
a crossing sequence ξ. Then we can effectively tell whether t *supports* ξ at its
right-hand end, i.e., we can tell if

$$\xi = q(1), q(2), q(3), \ldots, q(n)$$

is such that Z would first leave t in state $q(1)$ (t changed to t_1), and that, for
$k > 0$, Z, if it enters t_k from the right in state $q(2k)$ would leave it in state
$q(2k + 1)$ (t_k changed to t_{k+1}) and whether the sequence is transient (that is,

n is odd, so Z leaves t), *accepting* (that is, n is even and Z halts on t in an accepting state) or *nonaccepting* (that is, n is even and Z halts on t in a nonaccepting state). With this notion, we can obtain:

1 THEOREM (HENNIE [1965]): *If every crossing sequence in every computation performed by a given ordinary TM (off-line acceptor) Z contains at most K members, then the set it accepts is regular.*

Proof. We use an argument of the Nerode type. We say that two tape segments t and t' are equivalent iff they support the same crossing sequences, each with the same classification of transient, accepting, or nonaccepting. We easily see that this is a right-equivalence relation such that for all t'', tt'' is accepted iff $t't''$ is accepted. Since it has finite index, the set accepted by Z is regular.   □

2 COROLLARY: *If there is a constant K such that every computation by the one-tape off-line acceptor Z involves less than K tape reversals, then the set accepted by T is regular.*   □

The conditions of Theorem **1** imply that the time bound $T(n) \leq Kn$. However, the condition that $T(n) \leq Kn$ is weaker, and does not bound the crossing sequences by a constant. It does, however, suffice to ensure regularity:

3 EXERCISE (HENNIE [1965]): If a one-tape, off-line Turing machine performs all of its computations within the time bound $T(n) \leq Kn$, where K is a constant, then the set it accepts is regular. [Hint: Since K is fixed, replace Z by a new Z' (Fig. 7.3) with K-track tape which never leaves the input

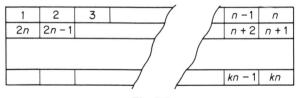

Fig. 7.3

portion of its tape, yet takes the same time as Z. Each time Z enters a new block of n squares, Z' merely zigs or zags onto a fresh track of tape. The bound of K assures us that we can get away with a finite alphabet. Show that if Z' has m states, then no crossing sequence is longer than $2Km^K + K$, to deduce the result.]

Actually, the above result is a corollary to an even stronger result due to TRAKHTENBROT [1964] and to HARTMANIS [1968] which states that for the set accepted by Z to be regular, it is sufficient that

$$\lim_{n \to \infty} \frac{T(n)}{n \log n} = 0$$

As before, we study the length $C(n)$ of crossing sequences of Z's computation of length n, and then use the result on C to obtain the time-bound result.

4   LEMMA: *Let $C(w_1; w_2)$ be the crossing sequence generated by a one-tape off-line TM Z on the boundary between the initial tape segments w_1 and w_2. Then*

(i) $C(w_1w_2; w_3w_4w_5) = C(w_1w_2w_3; w_4w_5)$

$\Rightarrow C(w_1; w_2w_4w_5) = C(w_1; w_2w_3w_4w_5)$

and $C(w_1w_2w_4; w_5) = C(w_1w_2w_3w_4; w_5)$

$\Rightarrow Z$ *accepts (rejects) $w_1w_2w_3w_4w_5$ iff Z accepts (rejects) $w_1w_2w_4w_5$.*

(ii) *If any crossing sequence of Z on a tape is generated three times or more, then for **every** crossing sequence on that tape there exists a shorter tape on which it occurs.*

Proof. (i)   is   immediate.   As   for   (ii),   suppose $C(w_1; w_2w_3w_4) = C(w_1w_2; w_3w_4) = C(w_1w_2w_3; w_4)$. Then every crossing sequence occuring in $w_1w_2w_3w_4$ on w_1, w_2, or w_4 will occur on the tape $w_1w_2w_4$, on w_1, w_2, or w_4, respectively, whereas every crossing sequence occurring on w_3 in $w_1w_2w_3w_4$ will occur on w_3 in $w_1w_3w_4$.   □

5   THEOREM: *If A is $C(n)$-recognizable, by a one-tape off-line TM, then*

$$\lim_{n \to \infty} \frac{C(n)}{\log n} = 0 \quad \Rightarrow \quad A \text{ regular}$$

Proof. Let Z recognize A and define $C(n)$. We show that $C(n)$ is bounded to deduce that A is regular by Theorem **1**.

To obtain a contradiction, assume that $C(n)$ is unbounded, so there exists an infinite sequence $0 < n_1 < n_2 < n_3 < \ldots$ of integers such that $C(n) < C(n_i)$ for $n < n_i$.

Let t_i be a segment of length n_i on which a $C(n_i)$-long crossing sequence is generated. By **4**(ii), no crossing sequence of *any* length is generated more than twice, otherwise we would have a sequence of length $n < n_i$ with a crossing sequence of length $C(n_i)$, contradicting the minimality of n_i.

If Z has $Q (\geq 2)$ states, then the number of different crossing sequences of length $\leq r$ is $\sum_{i=0}^{r} Q^i \leq Q^{r+1}$.

Now if on a segment of length n_i no crossing sequence can be generated more than twice, then we must have

$$2Q^{C(n_i)+1} \geq n_i$$

that is, $C(n_i) + 1 + \log 2 \geq \log n_i$

and thus
$$\lim_{n \to \infty} \frac{C(n)}{\log n} \neq 0$$

a contradiction.   □

6 COROLLARY: *If a one-tape off-line* TM *recognizes a nonregular set and defines* $C(n)$, *then*

$$\sup_{n \to \infty} \frac{C(n)}{\log n} > 0$$

To realize how tight the bound is, we note that there is a set with $\lim_{n \to \infty} [C(n)/\log n] = $ constant which is *not* regular:

7 EXERCISE: Show that there exists a one-tape TM which started on 1^n computes the binary representation of n with $C(n) = 2 \lceil \log_2 n \rceil$, to deduce that the nonregular set $\{1^{2^k} | k = 1, 2, \ldots\}$ is $C(n) = 2 \lceil \log n \rceil$-recognizable. [Hint: Just sweep back and forth, marking off every second unmarked square each time.]

8 THEOREM: *If A is* $T(n)$-*recognizable and* $\lim_{n \to \infty} [T(n)/n \log n] = 0$, *then A is regular*.

9 EXERCISE: Prove Theorem **8** by reworking the proof of **5**, relating time to number of crossings. If $T(n_i)$ is the computation time for t_i with a non-regular sequence, then

$$T(n_i) \geq 2 \sum_{j=0}^{r} jQ^j$$

where $r = \lceil \log_Q n_i \rceil - 3$

N.B. $\{1^{2^k} | k \geq 1\}$ is $T(n) = 2n\lceil \log n \rceil$-recognizable—so $\exists$ nonregular sets which are $T(n) = 2n\lceil \log n \rceil$-recognizable.

The reader may wish to consult HARTMANIS [1968] for further results, especially those on $L(n)$; for example, one may prove, using techniques similar to the above, that if A is $L(n)$-recognizable and $\lim_{n \to \infty} [L(n)/\log \log n] = 0$, then A must be regular.

We now return to the work of HENNIE [1965] and show that for each p with $1 < p \leq 2$, there exist nonregular sets which can be recognized by a one-tape off-line TM in a time proportional to n^p, but not in a time proportional to n^q for $q < p$.

Let $S = \{w_1 w_2 w_3 | w_1 \in \{0, 1\}^*, w_2 = 2^{|w_1|}$ and $w_1 = w_3\}$. For an ordinary TM, just by removing the last symbol of w_1 and checking the last symbol of w_3, we can check an acceptable tape in $n/3$ passes of length $\frac{2}{3}n$—in a total time of about $\frac{2}{9}n^2$. In fact, an 8-state machine exists to process tapes in time

$T(n) = \frac{4}{9}n^2 + n$. We can speed this up by using a $(k + 1)2^{k+1}$-state machine to compare k symbols at a pass. The corresponding computation time is at most

$$\frac{2n^2}{\log_2 Q} + 4n \qquad \text{for } Q \geq 8$$

where Q is the number of states of the machine.

Consider *acceptable* sequences of length n. There are clearly $2^{n/3}$ of these, and n must be divisible by 3. It is also clear that all the crossing sequences in the middle third of the tape must be distinct.

Let s denote the number of distinct crossing sequences which are "short" in that their length does not exceed $\lambda = [n/(3 \log Q)] - 1$, where Q is the number of states of the machine.

$$s = \sum_{i=1}^{\lambda} Q^i < Q^{\lambda+1} = Q^{n/(3 \log Q)} = 2^{n/3}$$

Since no one crossing sequence can appear in the center portion of two different computations, we see that there are not enough of the "short" crossing sequences to have one in the center of each computation. Thus some computation must have every crossing sequence in the center portion of length $> \lambda$, so its computation time is greater than

$$\frac{n}{3}(\lambda + 1) = \frac{n^2}{9 \log Q}$$

A more delicate argument involving the *whole* tape yields $2n^2/(9 \log Q)$. But we know the time need not exceed $(2n^2/\log Q) + 4n$. For $Q = 8$, this is $2n^2/27$ versus $12/27n^2 + n$—bracketing in a factor of 6 for large multiples of 3.

S is recognizable in real time on a two-tape machine. We know that going from a two-tape TM to a one-tape TM can be accomplished by squaring the computation time—here then is an example in which the squaring is necessary.

S is a set with a "recognition growth rate" of n^2. We now exhibit sets with "recognition growth rate" n^p, for $1 < p \leq 2$. The reader may generalize the argument to solve the following exercise:

10   EXERCISE: Let $p = 1 + q/r$ be a rational number, with $q \leq r$ integers. Let S_p be the set of strings $w_1w_2w_3$ such that $w_1 \in \{0, 1\}^*$ with $|w|$ a power of 2^q, $w_2 = 2^{|w_1|^{r/q}}$ and $w_3 = w_1$. Then prove that there exist constants α_4, α_5, α_6 such that S_p can be recognized in time at most $\alpha_4 n \log n + \alpha_5 n(n^{q/r}) \leq \alpha_6 n^p$. Show then that a growth rate of n^p is necessary. [Hint: A machine can compute the integer part of the base-k logarithm of the length of a block of tape

by making a series of passes across that block. On the first pass it marks the
1st previously unmarked square, then the $(k + 1)$st, then the $(2k + 1)$st, and
so on. The number of passes required to mark all the squares will then be
1 greater than the integer part of the logarithm of the length of that block.
Furthermore, the length of that block will be a power of k iff the rightmost
square of the block is the last square marked, as in Fig. 7.4.]

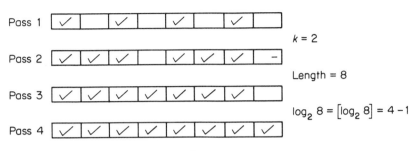

Fig. 7.4

⋅ Summarizing the above discussion and exercise:

11   THEOREM (HENNIE [1965]): *For any rational number p in the range
$1 < p \leq 2$, there exists a set S_p such that*
    (a) *S_p can be recognized by a one-tape off-line TM within a computation
        time that is less than $C_1(p, Q)n^p$, and*
    (b) *S_p cannot be recognized by a one-tape off-line TM within a computation
        time that is less than $C_2(p, Q)n^p$*
*where C_1 and C_2 are functions only of p and the number of internal states Q
available for the computation.* □

12   COROLLARY: *If p and q are real numbers with $1 \leq q < p \leq 2$, then
there exists a set that can be recognized by a one-tape off-line TM within
a computation time that is proportional to n^p but cannot be recognized within a
computation time proportional to n^q.* □

We now present exercises designed to guide the reader through other applications of the crossing-sequence argument. Exercises **13–16** are based on the work
of BARZDIN [1965], whereas Exercises **17–19** present results of RABIN [1964].

13   EXERCISE: We say that *almost all* words which have the property S also have
the property E if $E_S(n)/S(n) \to 1$ as $n \to \infty$, where $S(n)$ is the number of words of
length n which have the property S, and $E_S(n)$ is the number of words of length n
which have both properties E and S. Solve the following subproblems to deduce
the truth of the theorem: *For any one-head, one-tape machine Z which accepts the
set S of palindromes $\{x | x \in \{0, 1\}^* \text{ and } x = x^R\}$, a constant C exists such that for
almost all symmetrical words x we have that*

$$F_i^z(x) \geq C|x|^2$$

(i) Show that if x and y are symmetrical words and $[x, i, y]$ is nonsymmetrical, then the crossing sequence $[iT(x)] \neq [iT(y)]$.

(ii) Let A be some set, with $|A|$ elements. Let ζ be a word of Q^*, where Q is the set of internal states of the machine Z. Let us designate as $A^n(i, \zeta)$ the set of all symmetrical words of length n for which the crossing sequence $[iT(x)] = \zeta$. Show that for $i = 1, 2, \ldots, [n/2]$, we have $|A^n(i, \zeta)| \leq 2^{[(n+1)/2]-i}$. [Hint: Use the fact that for $i \leq [n/2]$, if symmetrical words $x, y \in A^n(i, \zeta)$ have $x|_i \neq y|_i$, the word $z = [x, i, y]$ must be asymmetrical. (Note: This is not true if $i = [(n + 1)/2]$, for if $n = 3$, $i = 2$, $x = aba$, $y = aca$, then $x|_i \neq y|_i$, but $[x, i, y]$ *is* symmetrical.)]

(iii) Given a positive constant C, let $A_C^n(i)$ be the set of symmetrical words of length n for which $|[iT(x)]| < Cn$. Show that, for $i = 1, 2, \ldots, [n/2]$, we have

$$|A_C^n(i)| < 2^{[(n+1)/2]-i+Cn\, \log_2 r}$$

where r is the number of internal states of the machine Z.

(iv) Let us designate as B_C^n the set of all symmetrical words of length n for which at least at one of the points

$$i \in \left[\left[\frac{n}{4}\right], \left[\frac{n}{2}\right]\right]$$

the length of the trace $|[iT(x)]| < Cn$. Then prove that

$$|B_C^n| < \left(\left[\frac{n}{2}\right] - \left[\frac{n}{4}\right]\right) \cdot 2^{[n+1/2]-[n/4]+Cn\, \log_2 r}$$

(v) Let us designate by S^n the set of all symmetrical words of length n, and by D_C^n, the set $S^n - B_C^n$. Note that

$$|S^n| = 2^{[(n+1)/2]}$$

and prove that there exists a constant C such that

$$\frac{|D_C^n|}{|S^n|} \to 1 \qquad \text{for } n \to \infty$$

(vi) Use the above results to obtain a constant C_Z such that for all $x \in D_{C_0}^n$, for appropriate C_0, the time required by Z to verify that x is a palindrome exceeds $C_Z|x|^2$. Deduce that for almost all x, the time required to recognize symmetry increases with $|x|^2$.

(vii) Verify that (vi) still goes through if we replace $[[n/4], [n/2]]$ in the definition of B_C^n by any interval of the form $[[an], [bn]]$ with $0 < a < b \leq \frac{1}{2}$ and find the choice of a and b which maximizes C_Z in (vi).

It is also possible to obtain lower estimates of the complexity for certain other predicates and functions by the *method* developed in **13**:

14 EXERCISE: Let the ordinary TM Z realize inversion of *all* words. Let us designate as $t_Z(x)$ the number of steps which the machine requires for inversion of the word x. For any machine Z which realizes inversion of *all* words a constant C_Z exists such that for almost all words x, we have $t_Z(x) \geq C_Z|x|^2$.

15 EXERCISE: Let f be some function such that if $x \neq y$, then $f(x) \neq f(y)$. The word z will be called an f component if it has the form $x \cdot f(x)$, where either $\cdot$ is an auxiliary symbol or, for $|x| = |y| = n$ and $i < n$, $x \neq y \Rightarrow [x, i, y] \notin \{z \cdot f(z)\}$. Let us designate as P_f the predicate which is true for those words and only those words which are f components. Prove the following theorem: *For any machine Z which realizes the predicate P_f, there exists a constant C_Z such that for almost all words x*

$$t_{P_f, Z}(x \cdot f(x)) \geq C_Z|x|^2$$

16 EXERCISE: Let x be a word on the alphabet $\{0, 1\}$. This word is a binary notation of some number, say $d(x)$. Let us say that the machine Z realizes the multiplication of words if for each two words x and y in the alphabet $\{0, 1\}$ it processes the word $x * y$, where $*$ is an auxiliary symbol, into the word z so that $d(z) = d(x)d(y)$. Let us designate as $t_Z(x, y)$ the number of steps which the machine Z requires for processing the word $x * y$. For any machine Z which realizes multiplication of words, a constant C_Z exists such that for almost all pairs of words x, y

$$t_Z(x, y) \geq C_Z|x|\,|y|$$

where we say that almost all pairs of words x, y have the property E if

$$\frac{E(n, m)}{S(n, m)} \to 1 \qquad (n \to \infty, m \to \infty)$$

where $S(n, m)$ is the number of all pairs of the words x, y such that $|x| = n$ and $|y| = m$, and $E(n, m)$ is the number of all pairs of words x, y such that (a) the pair x, y has the property E, and (b) $|x| = n$ and $|y| = m$.

We now turn to the results of RABIN [1964]:

17 EXERCISE: Let $\sum' = \{a, b, 0, 1, \alpha, \beta\}$. Words on $\{a, b\}$ will be called *ab words* and the set of *ab* words will be denoted by A. Words on $\{0, 1\}$ will be called *01 words* and the set of 01 words will be denoted by A'. Let

$$T_2 = \{uvau^R | u \in A, v \in A'\} \cup \{uv\beta v^R | u \in A, v \in A'\}$$

Show that the set T_2 is acceptable in $T(n) = n$ by a two-tape on-line TM.

18 EXERCISE: Solve the following subproblems to deduce the truth of this theorem: *The set T_2 is not acceptable in $T(n) = n$ by a one-tape on-line TM.* (Consequently, two-tape "real-time" computation can do more than one-tape "real-time" computation.)

To prove that T_2 is not real-time definable by a one-tape machine assume by way of contradiction that the one-tape machine Z does define T_2 in real time. Let the number of states of Z be m and the number of letters in its working alphabet be n.

If Z has input w, then the work space $t(w)$ of Z on w is the segment of work tape visited by Z while reading the input sequence w. (Thus $|t(w)| \leq |w|$.)

(i) Prove that $c = [2 \log_2 n]^{-1}$ is such that for every $u \in A$ and every integer $i > 0$ there exists a $v \in A'$ such that $|v| = i$ and $ci \leq |t(uv)|$.

(ii) Prove that $d = [10/c + 1]$ is such that for every $u \in A$ and every integer $i \geq |u|$ there exists a sequence $v \in A'$, $|v| = i$, such that

(a) $ci \leq |t(uv)|$,

(b) fewer than $\frac{1}{5}$ of the squares of $t(uv)$ are covered by Z more than d times.

(iii) The proof of the theorem rests on the idea that in working on certain input sequences, the machine Z develops "bottleneck squares" on its work tape through which information cannot flow in sufficient quantity.

Let $u \in A$, $v \in A'$. A square B on $t(uv)$ is called a bottleneck square of $t(uv)$ if (1) under input uv the machine passes through B no more than d times [where d is as in (ii)]; (2) B lies outside the work space $t(u)$; (3) the length of the section of $t(uv)$ determined by B which does not contain $t(u)$ exceeds $|u| + 1$. Then prove that for every $u \in A$ there exists a $v \in M'$ such that the tape $t(uv)$ has a bottleneck square (cf. Fig. 7.5).

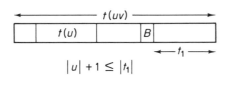

$$|u| + 1 \leq |t_1|$$

Fig. 7.5

(iv) Now use a crossing-sequence type of argument to use the above results to prove the theorem. A careful analysis of the quantities introduced in the proof should enable you to deduce that if Z has m states and n letters in its working alphabet, and we set

$$c = (2 \log_2 n)^{-1} \quad d = \left[\frac{10}{c} + 1\right] \quad \text{and} \quad N = 2m + 2m^2 + \cdots + 2m^d$$

and let g be the smallest integer such that $N < 2^g$ and let i be the smallest number such that $5g < ci$, then there exists a sequence $x \in \Sigma^*$ such that $|x| \leq 2g + i + 1$ and Z accepts x even though $x \notin T_2$ or Z rejects x even though $x \in T_2$.

19 EXERCISE: Rabin concluded his paper with a blow to what intuition one may have built up in seeing the above Theorem. He shows that if

$$T_1 = \{a^n 0^m \alpha \, a^n | n, m = 1, 2, 3, \ldots\} \cup \{a^n \, 0^m \beta \, 0^m \, n, m = 1, 2, \ldots\}$$

then T_1 is recognizable in $T(n) = n$ by a one-tape, on-line machine. Verify this.

The above results show how we may trade-off time against the number of tapes employed. The reader may wish to turn to HENNIE [1966] for an analysis of how time bounds may be decreased by increasing the *dimensionality* of a single tape.

It should be noted that a lower bound obtained from a crossing sequence will only be close if a machine makes optimal use of the crossing sequences to carry information from one half of a tape to the other. The reader should convince himself from a study of the above proofs that a crossing sequence argument cannot show necessity for a lower bound $> n^2$.

It is thus appropriate to close this section by showing how diagonal arguments may be used to give us insight into the complexity of computations with $T(n) \geq n^2$. The following result was obtained by HARTMANIS [1968] in collaboration with John Hopcroft.

20   THEOREM: *Let the time-bound $T(n) \geq n^2$ be defined by a one-tape off-line TM and computed with length-bound $L(n) \leq \lceil \log T(n) \rceil$. Then there exists a set which is $T(n) \lceil \log T(n) \rceil$ acceptable, but not $T_1(n)$ acceptable for any $T_1(n)$ such that $\lim_{n \to \infty} [T_1(n)/T(n)] = 0$.*

Proof outline. Consider a TM Z which carries out two different computational processes (on different tracks of the tape):

(a) Z attempts to interpret some initial part of the input tape w as a description of a TM Z_i and then proceeds to simulate what this machine Z_i would have done when presented with the input tape w. If Z completes the simulation and Z_i accepts w, then Z rejects it, and vice versa. If w does not describe a TM, and the simulation cannot be carried out, then the computation is stopped and w is rejected. It can be shown that for every w whose prefix describes a machine Z_i, there is a constant k_i such that every operation of Z_i can be simulated in k_i operations by Z.

(b) Z counts the number of operations which Z has performed in (a) and stops and rejects the first input if the first computation exceeds $T(n)$ operations for an input w of length n.

It can be shown that no more than $3T(n) \lceil \log T(n) \rceil$ operations are required. One then gets rid of the factor of 3 by replacing Z by a similar machine with three symbols on each tape square. The other result follows, since Z can catch up somewhere with, and disagree with, a $T_1(n)$ computation for which $\lim_{n \to \infty} [T_1(n)/T(n)] = 0$.   □

In the next two sections we shall make much use of such diagonalization arguments.

7.2   COMPUTATION OF SEQUENCES

In this section, we analyze the time required by generalized Turing machines to compute sequences. More specifically, consider an n-tape machine to have n work tapes, no input tape, and a write-only, one-way output tape. We assume that there is a fixed integer k such that the symbols printed on squares of the output tape correspond to strings of 0's and 1's of length $\leq k$. The output tape may then be read as a sequence of 0's and 1's, and we shall say that a binary sequence α is *T-computable* iff there exists a multitape Turing machine which prints $\alpha(n)$, the nth term of α, within $T(n)$ steps of the start of its operation.

We say a sequence is *computable* if it is T-computable for some T. If we restricted ourselves to one-tape machines, the class of computable sequences would remain the same, but in general, the class of T-computable sequences would decrease for each T. (We may say that a real number between 0 and 1 is computable if its binary expansion is a computable sequence—essentially this notion was introduced by TURING [1936], although he used alternate squares of a single tape for work-space and output, rather than a separate tape. See MINSKY [1967, Chap. 6] for an exposition of computable numbers.)

Perhaps the first to consider computable sequences in relation to limitations on the time required to produce their elements was YAMADA [1960: 1962] who introduced essentially the following definition:

1   DEFINITION: *A function $f: N \to N$ is real-time countable if the function f is strictly increasing, and the sequence α^f with $\alpha^f_n = 1$ iff $n = f(m)$ for some m is T-computable for $T(n) = n$.*

Before turning to a more general study of differing choices of T, we present a number of theorems and exercises which indicate some of the properties of the class e of real-time countable functions presented in YAMADA [1960]. The reader is invited to fill in the details of the proofs.

We call a machine which enumerates the computable sequence α_f an *f-counter* if it has the additional property of possessing an input line such that the machine only functions on those times at which a 1 is applied on the input line. Clearly, an f-counter exists for each α_f in e.

2   THEOREM: *If f and g are in e, then so is $f + g$.*

Sketch of proof. Take an f-counter and a g-counter. A control box feeds 1's into the f-counter till it gets an output, then feeds 1's into the g-counter till it gets an output, and so on; it emits an output 1 only when g emits a 1. □

3 LEMMA: *Given a counter M, we may define an automaton M^e behaviorally equivalent to M save that it has an extra input line e such that the firing of e causes M^e to return to its initial configuration, provided that between erasures we require "increasing amounts of work done."*

Proof. Replace each tape of M by two push-down stores, to get M'. M^e is then two copies M_1 and M_0 of M' so controlled that at any time one, say M_i, acts like M. An input e switches the M-simulation from M_i, causing M_{1-i} to act like an initially blank M, and starts to empty the stacks of M_i. The time condition ensures that M_i will have returned to its initial state by the time it is again required to stand in for M. □

Note that there certainly is a counter M_s for $1 + 2 + \cdots + x$—it just goes back and forth along a single work tape, one more each time. With the aid of this counter, and the construction of Lemma **3**, we may discover new properties of $\mathcal{C}$.

4 THEOREM: *If $f \in \mathcal{C}$, then $g(x) = \sum\limits_{i=1}^{x} f(i) \in \mathcal{C}$; that is, $\mathcal{C}$ is closed under limited addition.*

Proof.

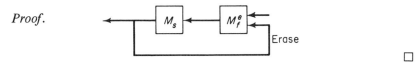

□

5 THEOREM: *$f, g \in \mathcal{C}$ implies $f \circ g \in \mathcal{C}$; that is, $\mathcal{C}$ is closed under composition.*

Proof.

□

6 THEOREM: *$f, g \in \mathcal{C}$ implies $f(x) \cdot g(x) \in \mathcal{C}$; that is, $\mathcal{C}$ is closed under multiplication.*

Proof.

$$f(x + 1)g(x + 1) - f(x)g(x) = $$
$$f(x + 1)[g(x + 1) - g(x)] + g(x)[f(x + 1) - f(x)].$$

So keep a tape $\hat{T}$ with x 1's stored on it. Use this to run M_g^e to transfer a 1 to M_f each time $g(x)$ is obtained. When M_f emits a 1, add a 1 to the tape $\hat{T}$ to record $x + 1$. Use this to run M_f^e to transfer a 1 to M_g each time $f(x + 1)$ is obtained. When M_g emits a 1, then $M_{f(x) \cdot g(x)}$ emits a 1, and the cycle restarts. □

7 EXERCISE

(i) Prove that $\mathcal{C}$ is closed under limited multiplication. [Hint: Note that if $g(x) = \prod_{i=1}^{x} f(i)$, then $g(x + 1) - g(x) = (f(x + 1) - 1) \prod_{i=1}^{x} f(i)$.]

(ii) Note that any constant function is countable, to deduce that any polynomial is countable.

(iii) Prove that for any integer, a, a^x is in $\mathcal{C}$. [Hint: Just use two tapes—at each iteration, we chase along one tape $a - 1$ times to fill up the other in such a way that the first pass fills up the one tape while making the first entry on the other.] Deduce that $a^{f(x)}$ is in $\mathcal{C}$ if $f \in \mathcal{C}$. One can also prove that $x^{f(x)}$ is in $\mathcal{C}$ if f is in $\mathcal{C}$, but this is hard. Deduce from this that $f(x)^{g(x)}$ is in $\mathcal{C}$ if $g = u \circ f$ with f, g, u in $\mathcal{C}$.

8 EXAMPLE: Using a machine which may print several symbols per tape per input symbol, prove the following:

(i) $f, g \in \mathcal{C}$ and $f(x + k) - f(x) \geq c/(c - 1) [g(x + k) - g(x)]$ for some $c > 1$ implies $f - g \in \mathcal{C}$. [Hint: Use k copies of M_f and k copies of M_g.]

(ii) If $\sum_{i=1}^{x} f(i) \in \mathcal{C}$ and $f(x + k) - f(x) \geq 1/(m - 1) \sum_{i=x}^{x+k-1} f(i)$ some m and k, then $f \in \mathcal{C}$. Deduce that if $f(1) = a$ and $f(x + 1) = a^{f(x)}$, then $f \in \mathcal{C}$. [Hint: Use (i) and $f(x) = \sum_{i=1}^{x} f(i) - \sum_{i=1}^{x-1} f(i)$.]

(iii) If $f, g \in \mathcal{C}$, then $f(x)^{g(x)} \in \mathcal{C}$. [Hint: Show $\sum f^g \in \mathcal{C}$, then apply (ii).]

Let us now, for a given T, denote by S_T the set of all T-computable sequences. We shall only consider T for which $T(n) \geq kn$ for some rational number k, otherwise T-computable sequences would be unprintable. We call such a T a *time-function*. Then following HARTMANIS and STEARNS [1965], we may obtain the following results about such sets of sequences. First, simply by changing from one machine to another with more symbols per tape square, we may note the following:

9 FACT: *For any integer k, $S_T = S_{\lceil kT \rceil}$.* □

10 THEOREM: *For any $T: N \to N$, the set S_T is recursively enumerable.*

Proof. Take any effective enumeration of the multitape TMs, and let Z_m be the mth member of the enumeration. Modify Z_m so that it checks for $n = 1, 2, 3, \ldots$ whether the computation time for α_n of the sequence α that it computes exceeds $T(n)$. If such an n is found, the modified machine $\hat{Z}_m$ henceforth puts out 0's, if not $\hat{Z}_m$ computes the sequence α.

The interesting point to note is that the enumeration $\{\hat{\alpha}^m\}$ of the sequences computed by the $\hat{Z}_m$ is in fact an effective enumeration of the T-computable sequences, since if a sequence is only nonzero for finitely many terms, it can be T-computed for $T'(n) = n$ by a finite automaton, but in general, the machine $\hat{Z}_m$ does *not* compute $\hat{\alpha}^m$ in time T. □

As we shall see below in Theorem **14**, however, S_T will not be recursive.

11   COROLLARY
    (i)   *For no T is S_T the set of all computable binary sequences.*
    (ii)   *For any time function T, there exists a time function U such that S_T is strictly contained in S_U. Thus there are infinitely long chains $S_{T_1} \subset S_{T_2} \subset \ldots$ of distinct complexity classes.*
    (iii)   *The set of all complexity classes is denumerable.*
    Proof.
    (i)   This follows from a diagonal argument—if $\{\hat{\alpha}^m\}$ is an effective enumeration of the T-computable sequences, then α with $\alpha_n = 1 - \hat{\alpha}_n^n$ is a computable sequence not in S_T.
    (ii)   Pick $\alpha \notin S_T$. If it takes $V(n)$ steps to compute α_n, then the assertion is clearly true for $U(n) = \max [T(n), V(n)]$.
    (iii)   This is immediate, since there are only denumerably many recursively enumerable sets of sequences. □

12   THEOREM
    (i)   *If U and T are time-functions such that* $\inf\limits_{n \to \infty} T(n)/U(n) > 0$ *[or,*

equivalently, $\sup\limits_{n \to \infty} U(n)/T(n) < \infty$*], then $S_U \subset S_T$*
    (ii)   *If* $0 < \lim\limits_{n \to \infty} T(n)/U(n) < \infty$, *then $S_U = S_T$.*
    (iii)   *$S_n \subset S_T$ for all time functions T.*
    (iv)   *$S_T = S_U$, where $U(n) = \max [T(n), n]$.*
    Proof. If $\inf\limits_{n \to \infty} T(n)/U(n) > 0$, then there exists an integer k such that $kU(n) \le T(n)$ for all n, and (i) follows from Fact **9**. The proofs of (ii), (iii), and (iv) are immediate. □

13   EXERCISE
    (i)   Prove that if $T(n) = \min [T_1(n), T_2(n)]$, then $S_T = S_{T_1} \cap S_{T_2}$.
    (ii)   Show that if α and β only differ for finitely many n, then $\alpha \in S_T$ iff $\beta \in S_T$.

14   THEOREM: *For each time function T, S_T is not recursive.*
    Proof. Pick $\alpha \notin S_T$ and *any* Turing machine Z. We show that if S_T were recursive, we could solve the halting problem for Z—to deduce that S_T is *not* recursive.
    Define the sequence β by

$$\beta_n = \begin{cases} \alpha_n \text{ if } Z \text{ halts for input } \Lambda \text{ in more than } n \text{ steps} \\ 0 \text{ if not} \end{cases}$$

Then $\beta = \alpha$ if Z never halts, but is eventually all zero if Z does halt—thus β is in S_T iff Z halts, and so S_T would be recursive only if we could solve any halting problem.   □

15 EXERCISE: Try to transcribe results **9–14** to computation of functions— where we say a function f is T-computable if there is a multitape TM which, when presented with the binary coding of n on its tape, can halt with the binary coding of $f(n)$ on that tape in at most $T(n)$ operations.

To tie in the classes S_T with Yamada's work, let us observe that if a sequence α is computable, then it is T-countable for some function T which itself is real-time countable—for if a machine M computes α, we may modify it to print a 1 whenever it would print a digit of α, and a 0 at every other time, to obtain a real-time-countable function with respect to which α is computable. This observation lessens the apparent harshness of the restriction on U and T in the following theorem:

16 THEOREM: *If U and T are real-time-countable monotone-increasing functions and*

$$\inf_{n \to \infty} \frac{T(n)\lceil \log T(n) \rceil}{U(n)} = 0$$

then there is a sequence that is in $S_U - S_T$.

Proof summary. We outline the proof, which uses a careful diagonalization argument, resting on the result of Hennie and Stearns cited in Section **4.3** that every multitape machine can be simulated by a two-tape machine at the cost of replacing a time-bound $T(n)$ by $kT(n)\lceil \log T(n) \rceil$.

Since T is real-time countable, there is an enumeration $\{Z_i\}$ of binary-output multitape Turing machines operating in time $2T$, and such that each $\alpha \in S_T$ is the α^i printed by some Z_i.

A device Z can be constructed which, when supplied (on a tape) with the instructions for Z_i, gives out the nth digit of α_i within $C_i T(n)\lceil \log T(n) \rceil$ operations—C_i is a constant to take care of the time required to retrieve an instruction from the tape, and the factor of $\lceil \log T(n) \rceil$ comes from the Hennie-Stearns result, since the number of tapes is fixed.

A device Z' can now be specified to run a diagonal process on the Z_i and print in time U. Because the inf is zero, the simulation of Z_i will eventually catch up to U regardless of how much initial delay D_i exists before the simulation begins; that is, $D_i + C_i T(N_i)\lceil \log T(N_i) \rceil < U(N_i)$ for some large N_i. Thus if we put out an output only at times $U(n)$ [and this is possible, since $U(n)$ is real-time], there is enough time to simulate all the Z_i, one after another, and print out the complement of $Z_i(N_i)$ at time $U(N_i)$, $N_1 < N_2 < \ldots < N_i \ldots$.

More explicitly, suppose at stage n we simulate $Z_{i(n)}$. If

$$D_{i(n)} + C_{i(n)}T(n)\lceil \log T(n) \rceil < U(n),$$

print out the complement of $\alpha_n^{i(n)}$, since simulating $Z_{i(n)}$ for n steps takes less than $U(n)$ steps, and set $i(n + 1) = i(n) + 1$. Otherwise, print out 1, and set $i(n + 1) = i(n)$. Go to stage $n + 1$.

Thus we are able to print out a U-computable sequence different from all T-computable sequences.   □

For a full proof (of the weaker result with $\inf\limits_{n \to \infty} T(n)^2/U(n) = 0$, using the simulation of a multitape TM on a single tape at the cost of replacing a time-bound $T(n)$ by $kT(n)^2$, rather than the Hennie-Stearns two-tape simulation), see HARTMANIS and STEARNS [1965, pp. 299–301].

17   COROLLARY: *Let $(\sigma T)(n) = T(n + 1)$. Then there exists a time function T such that S_T is a proper subset of $S_{\sigma T}$.*

Proof. From Exercise **7**(i) and (iii) it follows that $2^{n!}$ is real-time computable, and so, setting $T(n) = 2^{n!}$ and noting that

$$\inf_{n \to \infty} \frac{2^{n!} \log 2^{n!}}{2^{(n+1)!}} = 0$$

we see that the result follows from Theorem **16**.   □

Results analogous to the above may be obtained if we use multitape TMs as on-line recognition devices. The reader may wish to verify the following by imitating the above proofs.

18   EXERCISE: (HARTMANIS and STEARNS [1965]; HENNIE and STEARNS [1966]). Prove the following:

(i)   The collection of T-recognizable sets is recursively enumerable, and thus there are arbitrarily complex recognition problems.

(ii)   If R is T-recognizable and $T(n) = n + E(n)$, for $E(n) \geq 0$, then R is U-recognizable, where $U(n) = n + [kE(n)]$, for $k > 0$.

(iii) $\inf\limits_{n \to \infty} [T(n) + n]/U(n) > 0$ and R U-recognizable implies that R is T-recognizable.

(iv) R T-recognizable by a multitape, multihead TM implies that R is $T(n)\lceil \log T(n) \rceil$-recognizable by a two-tape TM with one head per tape.

(v)   If U and T are real-time-countable monotone-increasing functions, and $\inf\limits_{n \to \infty} [T(n) \log T(n)]/U(n) = 0$, then $\exists$ an R which is U-recognizable but not T-recognizable.

We close with an explicit example, from HARTMANIS and STEARNS [1965], of a context-free language which is not recognizable in real time.

19 EXAMPLE: Let $R \subset \{0, 1, s\}^*$ be the context-free language

$$\{yxs\{(0, 1)^*s\}^*x^R \quad | \quad x \in \{0, 1\}^* \text{ and } y \in \Lambda \cup \{0, 1, s\}^*s\}$$

We shall show that R is *not* n-recognizable: Suppose Z is a device with d states, m tapes, and at most k symbols per tape square with which we try to recognize R in time n.

Assume that Z has already performed some unspecified number of operations. We wish to put an upper bound on the number of past histories Z can distinguish in i additional operations. At most $d \cdot k^{(2i+1)m}$ can be distinguished. There are (2^{2i-1}) subsets of $\{0, 1\}^{i-1}$ which are possible x's.

But $2^{(2^{i-1})} > dk^{(2_{i+1})m}$ for large i, and so Z must eventually fail. □

The reader may wish to contrast this with the results of Barzdin (**1.15**) and Rabin (**1.18**), which tell us that there are recognition problems which require $T(n) = n^2$ on a single tape, but can be accomplished in "real time" ($T(n) = n$) with two tapes.

For extensions of this work, see, e.g., FISCHER [1968], in which it is shown that if $\alpha \in S_T$ for a real-time-countable T, then there exists a multitape TM which so generates α that each α_n appears *exactly* at time $T(n)$ (this is easy if we allow two heads on one of the work tapes, but seems to be rather hard if we only allow one head per tape), thus strengthening various results. RUBY and FISCHER [1965] show that if R and V are real-time-countable functions, and U is any function for which $S_{V(R(n))} - S_{U(R(n))}$ is nonempty, it follows that $S_V - S_U$ is nonempty. This allows one to deduce that $S_{n!} \neq S_{(n+1)!}$ and $S_n \neq S_{n2^n}$. YOUNG [1968] obtained some of the Hartmanis-Stearns results in an axiomatic framework—we shall indicate his methods, though not these results, in the latter part of the next section.

7.3 THE AXIOMATIC APPROACH

Let us view a Turing machine as a programmed computer as follows:

It is a device equipped with a container for cards, a tape scanner-printer-mover, and a tape that is infinite in both directions. The tape is divided into squares along its length and the scanner can look at one square at a time. The device can print the blank, or one of *a finite set X of symbols*, on the square it is examining and shift the tape one square to right or left. The container can hold an arbitrarily large but finite number of cards, together called the program. On each card is printed a single 5-tuple $q_i x_j x_k m q_l$. The q_i denotes internal states of the device; the x_j are tape symbols, and m is a move L (left), R (right), or N (none). When the device is in state q_i and scans the symbol x_j, it prints the symbol x_k, moves the tape m, and changes its internal state to q_l. If there is no card starting with $q_i x_j$ in the container when the machine is in state q_i and scanning the symbol x_j, then the machine stops. Any program is allowed, subject to the condition that any two cards must differ in the initial pair $q_i x_j$.

We can associate with each program a partial recursive function ϕ as follows:

The program is placed in the container, an input integer x is written in some *suitably encoded* form as a finite string of symbols on the tape, the scanner is placed over the rightmost digit of this string, and the device is put in state q_0. The device then operates in accordance with the instructions printed in the program. If it never stops, we say $\phi(x)$ is undefined. If it does stop, we let $\phi(x)$ be the integer obtained from the string of symbols on the tape by some *standard decoding*.

Note that we thus obtain many different such machines, one for each choice of X and of the encoding and decoding functions.

A Turing machine as we usually know it is any such machine equipped with a suitable program.

Let us pick some particular X and some simple encoding and decoding functions, e.g., binary notation, and let M be the machine so specified.

Just as we usually enumerate the Turing machines $Z_1, Z_2, \ldots$, so may we now effectively enumerate the programs $P_1, P_2, P_3, \ldots$ of our machine M. Let ϕ_i be the partial-recursive function computed by M when supplied with program P_i. We recall from Section **4.4**.

1   THE RECURSION THEOREM: *For any recursive function h, there exists an integer y such that*

$$\phi_y = \phi_{h(y)}$$

2   THE ITERATION THEOREM: *For each partial-recursive function f of $m + n$ variables, there is a total recursive function $s(y_1, \ldots, y_m)$ such that*

$$f(y_1, \ldots, y_m, x_1, \ldots, x_n) = \phi_{s(y_1, \ldots, y_m)}(x_1, \ldots, x_n)$$

The Iteration Theorem is also called the *s-m-n* theorem.

Let now $\Phi_i(x) = \begin{cases} \text{number of steps } M \text{ takes to compute } \phi_i(x) \text{ when supplied} \\ \quad \text{with program } P_i, \text{ if } \phi_i(x) \text{ is defined}; \\ \text{undefined if } \phi_i(x) \text{ is undefined.} \end{cases}$

We call $\Phi_i(x)$ a *measure function*. Immediately we obtain:

3   THE MEASURE-FUNCTION THEOREM: *The functions $\Phi_i(x)$ are partial recursive and satisfy*
  (i) *For all i and x, $\phi_i(x)$ is defined if and only if $\Phi_i(x)$ is defined.*
  (ii) *There exists a total recursive function α such that for all i and x*

$$\alpha(i, x, y) = \begin{cases} 1 \text{ if } \Phi_i(x) = y \\ 0 \text{ otherwise} \end{cases}$$

To sec (ii) informally, note that we may find $\alpha(i, x, y)$ effectively by supplying M with program P_i and input x, and letting it run for y steps.

The above discussion leads us to the following very abstract formulation of a computer:

4 DEFINITION: *An M-computer C is an effective enumeration of pairs of partial-recursive functions*

$$(\phi_1, \Phi_1), (\phi_2, \Phi_2), (\phi_3, \Phi_3), \ldots$$

such that every partial-recursive function f is a ϕ_i for some i, and such that the ϕ_i satisfy the recursion theorem and the iteration theorem; and the measure-function theorem is satisfied by the Φ_i and ϕ_i.

We say that C *computes* ϕ_i (*with measure function* Φ_i) *when supplied with program* P_i. The idea of a program is purely an intuitive device here.

We owe to MANUEL BLUM [1964; 1967] the understanding that much deep insight into complexity of computation can be gained by taking an axiomatic approach, studying questions of complexity in such frameworks as that provided by M-computers.

Given a partial-recursive function f, there may well be many ϕ_i which equal f (in our intuitive version: many programs P_i which compute f): for such an i, we may well find it convenient to write f_i for ϕ_i, F_i for Φ_i, and to refer to i as an *index* for f.

Suppose P_i and P_j are two programs. What shall we mean by "P_j is no faster than P_i"?
It will be

(a) $d(\phi_j) \subset d(\phi_i)$ (where $d(\phi_j) = \{x \mid \phi_j(x) $ is defined$\}$, the domain of definition of ϕ_j)

(b) $\Phi_i(x) \leq \Phi_j(x)$ for almost all $x \in d(\phi_j)$

(In this section "almost all x" means "for all but finitely many x.") The "almost all" phrase in (b) merely ensures that our comparison is not vitiated by any purely transient advantage that P_j may have—e.g., in ordinary computer terminology, because of a table look-up which allows the machine to obtain the $\phi_j(x)$ very quickly for the finitely many x in the table.

One question that immediately arises is this: Does every partial-recursive function f have a fastest program—i.e., is there an index i for f such that if j is any other index for f, then P_j is no faster than P_i? The answer to this question is negative—there are very many functions with no fastest program. In fact, the speed-up theorem below says much more:

5 DEFINITION: *Let i and j be two indexes for f; and let $r(x, y)$ be any total-recursive function. We shall say that program P_i is an **r-speed-up** of program P_j if*

$$r(x, F_i(x)) < F_j(x) \qquad \textit{for almost all } x$$

Thus P_i is faster than P_j if it is in e-speed-up of P_j, where $e(x, y) = y$. Since we may choose $r(x, y)$ to grow very quickly indeed, for example,

$$r(x, y) = 2^{2^{2^{2^{2^{x+y}}}}}$$

we see that an r-speed-up of P_j may be very much faster than P_j indeed.

The speed-up theorem (BLUM [1964, 1967]—for a generalization, see MEYER and FISCHER [1968]) tells us that no matter how large we choose r to be, we may then find a 0–1 valued characteristic function f such that *any* program P_j for f has an r-speed-up P_i which computes f—and this means that P_i, in turn, has an r-speed-up P_k which computes f, and so ad infinitum! This is a most surprising result, and the proof is a long one. Perhaps we should discourage the reader who wishes to treat this as a theorem about real computers, rather than partial-recursive functions—the r-speed-up fails for finitely many x, and this finitude may well contain all those integers (for example, $0 \le x \le 2^{32} - 1$) that we consider in a real computer. And yet the theorem is not without interest.

The reader should note, of course, that many computations cannot be sped up—e.g., consider multiplication by 2 in radix 2—save at best by a constant factor, as attested to by many of the results in Section **1**.

Before proving Blum's speed-up theorem, we note (ARBIB [1966c]) that even weaker structures than M-computers can give us insight into complexity of computation:

6   DEFINITION: *A **weak M-computer** $\{(\phi_n, \Phi_n)\}$ is a recursive enumeration $(\phi_n, \Phi_n)(n = 1, 2, 3, \ldots)$ of partial-recursive functions such that:*

     1. *Every partial-recursive function is a ϕ_n for at least one n.*
     2. *$\{\Phi_n\}$ is a **measure sequence** for $\{\phi_n\}$; that is,*
        (a) *$\Phi_n(x)$ is defined $\Leftrightarrow \phi_n(x)$ is defined.*
        (b) *There is a total-recursive function $\alpha(i, x, y)$ such that*

$$\alpha(i, x, y) = \begin{cases} 1 \textit{ if } \Phi_i(x) = y \\ 0 \textit{ otherwise} \end{cases}$$

that is, we do not require that the sequence $\{\phi_n\}$ satisfy the recursion or the iteration theorem. We now generalize a theorem of RABIN [1960]:

7   THEOREM: *Let $C = \{(\phi_n, \Phi_n)\}$ be a weak M-computer. Let h be a partial-recursive function. There exists a partial-recursive function f with $d(f) = d(h)$ and assuming only the values 0 or 1, and such that for any index m for f we have*

$$h(n) < \bar{F}_m(n) \text{ for almost all } n \in d(h)$$

Proof. We define by induction both the function $f(n)$ and an auxiliary sequence of finite sets. Set $I = H = H_0 = \emptyset$. The set I may increase, at each stage of the induction. Pick an index $\#$ for h, and leave it fixed throughout.

Stage n. For each $k \notin H_{n-1}$, $k \leq n - 1$, compute $\alpha(\#, k, n)$. If it is 1, we adjoin k to H and compute $h(k)$. Then check $\alpha(\#, n, i)$ for $1 \leq i \leq n$. If any of these is 1, adjoin n to H and compute $h(n)$. Let H_n be the elements in H at this stage. If $H_n - H_{n-1}$ is empty, go to stage $n + 1$. If $k_1, \ldots, k_r (r \geq 1)$ are elements of $H_n - H_{n-1}$ in ascending order, carry out stages $n(k_1), \ldots, n(k_r)$ and then go to stage $n + 1$.

Stage n(k). Let $m = m(k)$ be the smallest $m \leq k$, with $m \notin I$ for which $F_m(k) \leq h(k)$. If there is no such m, set $f(k) = 1$, and do not change I. Otherwise, set $f(k) = \max (1 - f_{m(k)}(k), 0)$ and adjoin $m(k)$ to I.

Clearly f is partial-recursive, $d(f) = d(h)$, and takes only the values 0, 1.

Assume now that m is an index for f. We prove that there are only finitely many integers k such that

8 $$F_m(k) \leq h(k) \qquad \text{and } h(k) \text{ is defined}$$

Clearly, since $f = f_m$, we have $m \notin I$. Let I_k comprise those integers which are in I at the end of stage k. Since $I_k \subset I_{k+1}$ for each k, there is an integer s (which we may assume $\geq m$) such that if $j < m$ ever enters I, it must be in I_s.

We now show that no $p > s$ satisfies **8**: Assume that $p > s$ does satisfy **8**, and that $q = \max (p, F_\#(p))$. We note that $m \notin I_{q-1}$ and that $F_m(p) \leq h(p)$. Now consider stage $q(p)$. No $j < m$ can qualify for addition to I_q at this stage, since $q > s$. But this means that m must be placed in I_q at stage $q(p)$—a contradiction. Thus p cannot satisfy (*) if $p > s$.   □

If we examine the construction of f, we see that we have even proved

9   COROLLARY: *There is a partial-recursive function g of two variables such that if $\#$ is an index for h, then $f(x)$ in the above theorem may be taken as $g(\#, x)$.*

This immediately yields the further

10   COROLLARY: *If the $\{f_k\}$ satisfy the iteration theorem for $n = 1$ [that is, for each partial-recursive function $g(\#, x)$ there is a total recursive function γ such that $f_{\gamma(\#)}(x) = g(\#, x)$], then if $\#$ is an index for h, the f in the above theorem may be taken as $\phi_{\gamma(\#)}$.*

The γ function thus exists if C is an M-computer, rather than just a weak M-computer. This form of the result first appeared in BLUM [1967].

Note that for an M-computer, Theorem **7** is an immediate corollary of the next theorem on setting $r(x, y) = h(x)$, for then $F_i(x) > r[x, F_j(x)]$

reduces to $F_i(x) > h(x)$—but this proof does not yield the γ function of the corollary.

11 THE SPEED-UP THEOREM: *Let r be a total-recursive function of two variables. Then there exists a total recursive function f, taking values 0 or 1, such that for every index i for f, there corresponds another index j for f such that*

12 $F_i(x) > r(x, F_j(x))$ *for almost all x*

A great deal of work for this theorem can be done simply by appealing to the recursion and iteration theorems to prove the next lemma:

13 LEMMA: *Let $t(u, v, i)$ be a total recursive function with the property that*

14 $\phi_{t(u,v,i)}(z + u)$ *is defined whenever $u \leq z$, $v \leq z$ and $\phi_i(x)$ is defined for $x \leq z$.*

Then there exists a total recursive function ϕ_{i_0} such that given any u and v we have

15 $r[x, \Phi_{t(u,v,i_0)}(x)] \leq \phi_{i_0}(x - u + 1)$

for almost all x.

Proof:

Define the partial recursive function h by the recursion scheme:

16 $\begin{cases} h(i, 0) = 0 \\ h(i, z + 1) = \max_{\substack{0 \leq v \leq z \\ 0 \leq u \leq z}} r[z + u, \Phi_{t(u,v,i)}(z + u)] \end{cases}$

By the Iteration Theorem, there exists a total recursive function s such that

$$h(i, z) = \phi_{s(i)}(z)$$

By the Recursion Theorem, there exists an index i_0 such that

$$\phi_{s(i_0)}(z) = \phi_{i_0}(z) \text{ all } z,$$

whence

$$\phi_{i_0}(z) = h(i_0, z)$$

Thus $\phi_{i_0}(0) = h(i_0, 0) = 0$. Now assume $\phi_{i_0}(x)$ converges for $x \leq z$. On inspecting **16** we see that $\varphi_{i_0}(z + 1)$ converges, since r is total recursive, and convergence of $\phi_{i_0}(x)$ for $x \leq z$ implies convergence of $\phi_{t(u,v,i_0)}(z + u)$ and thus of $\Phi_{t(u,v,i_0)}(z + u)$ for $u, v \leq z$ by **14**. Hence ϕ_{i_0} is total recursive.

Fix u and v. Then for $x > \max[2u, u + v]$, we have $u, v \le x - u$ and so, putting $z = x - u$ and $i = i_0$ in **16** we obtain **15**. $\qquad\square$

Now let us assess our progress. Given any t satisfying **13** there exists an index i_0 such that

15 $$r[x, \Phi_{t(u,v,i_0)}(x)] \le \phi_{i_0}(x - u + 1)$$

But our task is to find a function f such that for each index i for f there exists an index j for f such that

12 $$r[x, F_j(x)] < F_i(x)$$

Now this would certainly follow if we could prove the following lemma; which, interestingly enough, is independent of our choice of speed-up function r:

17 LEMMA: *There is a total recursive function $t(u, v, i)$ with the following properties:*

18 $\phi_{t(u,v,i)}(x)$ *takes only the values* 0 *and* 1, *and, further,* $\phi_{t(u,v,i)}(z + u)$ *is defined whenever* $v \le z$, $u \le z$ *and* $\phi_i(x)$ *is defined for* $x \le z$ *(and so* $\phi_{t(u,v,i)}$ *is total recursive for each u and v if ϕ_i is total).*

19 *If ϕ_{i_0} is total recursive and f is defined to be* $\phi_{t(o,o,i_0)}$, *then for each index i for f,*

$$\phi_{i_0}(x - i) < F_i(x) \quad \text{for almost all } x$$

20 *If ϕ_{i_0} is total recursive, then for each u there exists a v such that*

$$\phi_{t(u,v,i_0)} = \phi_{t(o,o,i_0)}$$

For, given this t we choose an index i_0 for which ϕ_{i_0} is total recursive, and **15** holds. Taking $u = i + 1$, **15** and **19** together yield

$$r[x, \Phi_{t(i+1,v,i_0)}(x)] < F_i(x)$$

for each index i for $f = \phi_{t(o,o,i_0)}$, and then we choose $v(i)$ by **20** so that $\phi_{t(i+1,v(i),i_0)} = \phi_{(o,o,i_0)}$, so that **12** follows with $j = t(i + 1, v(i), i_0)$.

Construction of t: We actually construct a partial recursive function $e(x, u, v, i)$, and then use the iteration theorem to deduce the existence of a total recursive function t such that

$$\phi_{t(u,v,i)}(x) = e(x, u, v, i) \text{ for all } x, u, v, \text{ and } i.$$

Let us fix u, v and i. We compute $e(x, u, v, i)$ as follows:

(i) If $v \leq u$, set $e(x, u, v, i) = e(x, u, u + 1, i)$ and then use (ii).

(ii) If $v > u$, we compute $e(x, u, v, i)$ as follows (reference to the figure may be helpful):

Consider those pairs (k, y) for which $k \leq y \leq x$ and we either have $y < v$ or $u \leq k$.

1. Compute $\phi_i(y - k)$ for each of these pairs. $e(x, u, v, i)$ is thus undefined if any of these is undefined.

2. Let A_x be the subset comprising those pairs (k, y) for which

$$\Phi_k(y) \leq \phi_i(y - k)$$

3. Let B_x be the subset of A_x obtained by including $(0, 0)$ if it belongs to A_x and from each "column" y, including the first entry such that no entry in the same row has already been placed in B_x. There is thus at most one entry per row.

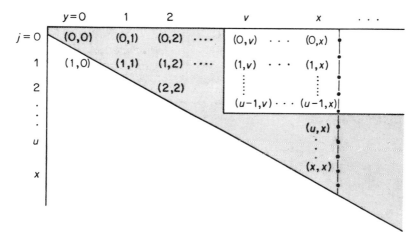

Fig. 7.6. Visualization for the computation of $e(x, u, v, i)$.

4. If B_x has no entry in column x, set $e(x, u, v, i) = 0$.
   If (k, x) is the entry in column x, set

$$e(x, u, v, i) = \begin{cases} 0 & \text{if } \phi_k(x) \neq 0 \\ 1 & \text{if } \phi_k(x) = 0 \end{cases}$$

21 VERIFICATION OF 18: We see that $e(x, u, v, i)$ is defined unless we encounter an undefined $\phi_i(y - k)$ in step 1. But if $y < v$, then certainly $y - k < v$, whereas if $u \leq k$ and $y \leq x$ we must have $y - k \leq x - u$. Thus, if $x = z + u$, $u \leq z$ and $v \leq z$, the largest $y - k$ we shall encounter is z. Hence it does follow that if $\phi_i(x)$ is defined for $x \leq z$, it is true that $\phi_{t(u,v,i)}(z + u)$ is defined for all $u, v \leq z$.

That ϕ, when defined, only takes values 0 or 1 is immediate from the construction.

22   VERIFICATION OF **20**: In the computation of $\phi_{t(o,o,i)}$, the number of rows above row u which can have an entry in any B_x is clearly finite, since a row contains at most one entry in any B_x (and note that if that entry is in B_x, it is also in $B_{x'}$ for all $x' \geq x$). Let column v be immediately to the right of all the B_x entries above row u. Then it is clear that $\phi_{t(o,o,i_0)}(x) = \phi_{t(u,v,i_0)}(x)$ for all x.

23   VERIFICATION OF **19**: Suppose i is an index for $f = \phi_{t(o,o,i_0)}$. If $F_i(x) \leq \phi_i(x - i)$ for infinitely many $x = x_1, x_2, x_3, \ldots$ then row i must have infinitely many entries in the A_x's, and hence at least one entry, say (i, x_k) in the B_x's. But then we must have

$$\phi_i(x_k) \neq e(x_k, 0, 0, i_0)$$

but the latter term is $f(x_k)$ and so we have a contradiction. This completes the proof of Lemma **17**, and thus of the speed-up theorem.   □

We note that we could obtain **19** and **20** simply by setting

$$e(x, 0, 0, i_0) = \min\{z \,|\, [i < x \;\&\; F_i(x) \leq \phi_{i_0}(x - i)] \Rightarrow z \neq \phi_i(x)\}$$

and $e(x, u, v, i_0) = e(x + (u \mathbin{\dot-} v), 0, 0, i_0)$—the reader is invited to use this to prove a suitable lemma for the speed-up theorem, but success may not be achievable.

We have already stressed how important it is that much insight can be gained into complexity of computation by adopting an axiomatic approach in which we use results of recursive-function theory rather than delicate surgery on actual abstract automata. This theme has recently been taken up with vigor by PAUL YOUNG [1968], and we devote the rest of this section to sampling a few of the results in his paper. We might mention that PAGER [1968] has also successfully explored computational techniques with subtle techniques of recursion theory (for much detail on which, see ROGERS [1968]). We now provide the axiomatic framework in which Young establishes his results.

Let $\{D_i\}$ be a fixed canonical enumeration of all the finite subsets of N. We also fix a total recursive bijection $N \times N \to N$: $(x, y) \to \langle x, y \rangle$ which indexes ordered pairs of integers.

Corresponding to the idea of elements of a recursively enumerable set being produced in stages, say over time by a Turing machine, or for various lengths of proof by a Post system, we introduce the following notion:

24   DEFINITION: *An **enumeration technique** is a total-recursive function*
$E: N \times N \to N$ *such that for every r.e. set (i.e., recursively enumerable
subset of N) W there is some integer e such that* $W = \bigcup_n D_{E(e,n)}$. *We then
write* $W_e = W$ *and call e an **index** for W given by the enumeration technique E
(e may be regarded as an encoding of the **structure** of a **device** for enumerating
W).*

   If E is any enumeration technique, we denote by E' *the enumeration
technique given by* $D_{E'(e,n)} = \bigcup_{j \leq n} D_{E(e,j)}$.

   We now specify conditions on an enumeration, the second of which
requires that we can effectively find the index $G(x, i, y, z)$ of the set $\hat{W}$ defined
by the following prescription: "Simultaneously enumerate both W_x and W_y,
putting the members of W_x into $\hat{W}$ until i turns up in W_y. If and when i turns
up in W_y, stop enumerating W_x and W_y, and instead begin enumerating W_z,
adding the members of W_z to those already put into $\hat{W}$."

25   DEFINITION: *An enumeration technique E is said to satisfy **Condition
1′** if*

   (a) *The enumeration* $\{W_e\}$ *satisfies:*
   (i) *the* S^1_1 *theorem; i.e., there exists a total-recursive function such that*

$$W_{S^1_1(e,x)} = \{y | \langle y, x \rangle \in W_e\}$$

   (ii) *the recursion theorem: from an index j for a recursive function h we
can effectively find an* i_0 *such that*

$$W_{h(i_0)} = W_{i_0}$$

   (b) *If we set* $L(i, y) = (\mu n)[i \in D_{E(y,n)}]$, *then there is a total-recursive
function G satisfying:*

   (i) $W_{G(x,i,y,z)} = \begin{cases} W_x & \text{if } i \notin W_y \\ D_{E'(x,L(i,y))} \cup W_z & \text{if } i \in W_y \end{cases}$

   (ii) *if* $i \in W_y$, *then there exists n such that*

$$D_{E'(G(x,i,y,z),n)} = D_{E'(x,L(i,y))}$$

and for all z, z′, and $m \leq n$

$$D_{E(G(x,i,y,z),m)} = D_{E(G(x,i,y,z'),m)}$$

   It is easily seen that Post systems, semi-Thue systems, and Turing
machines all satisfy this condition. YOUNG [1968] does construct an example
of an enumeration technique which fails to satisfy condition 1′, but suggests

that all such examples should be considered pathological. In all that follows, we shall only consider enumeration techniques satisfying condition 1′. By a time function we shall mean any nondecreasing total function.

Being able to generate elements slowly enough to match some other ongoing process turns out to be useful. We thus prove the following lemma, akin to one of BLUM [1967]:

26   LEMMA: *Let h be any unbounded time function, and W_e any infinite r.e. set. From e and h we can effectively find an index i_0 such that the device i_0 enumerates W_e in roughly the same order as does device c, but at a much slower rate— more precisely:*
   (i) $W_{i_0} = W_e$
   (ii) $D_{E'(i_0,n)} \subset D_{E'(e,n)}$ *for all n; and*
   (iii) $|D_{E'(i_0,n)}| \le h(n)$ *for all n.*

Proof. Given i, we define a set $W_{\sigma(i)}$ as follows: Enumerate $D_{E(i,0)}$, $D_{E(i,1)}$, $D_{E(i,2)}$, ... If

27 $$|D_{E'(i,n)}| \le h(n) \quad \text{and} \quad D_{E'(i,n)} \subset D_{E'(e,n)}$$

we put the first $z = \min \{h(n), |D_{E'(e,n)}|\}$ elements of W_e into $W_{\sigma(i)}$. We stop if either of the conditions of **27** fails to hold.

By the recursion theorem, there is an index i_0, which can effectively be found from e, such that

28 $$W_{\sigma(i_0)} = W_{i_0}$$

Now, if the enumeration of $W_{\sigma(i_0)}$ were to stop, say after the computation of $D_{E(i_0,n)}$, we would have either

$$|W_{i_0}| \ge |D_{E'(i_0,n)}| > h(n) \ge h(n-1) \ge |W_{\sigma(i_0)}|$$

or $\qquad W_{\sigma(i_0)} \subset D_{E'(e,n)} \quad \text{but} \quad D_{E'(i_0,n)} \not\subset D_{E'(e,n)}$

either of which contradicts **28**. Thus the enumeration of $W_{\sigma(i_0)}$ does not stop, and we have $W_{i_0} = W_e$, while for all n, $D_{E'(i_0,n)} \subset D_{E(e,n)}$ and $|D_{E'(i_0,n)}| \le h(n)$.   □

The result from Young which we wish to present has as corollary the result that there exist disjoint sets W and W' such that W can only be enumerated slowly, but that the union of W with portions of W' can be enumerated rapidly—as if the difficulty in enumerating W were in deciding how to avoid generating those things which are members of W'. The proof uses a technique similar to that used by FRIEDBERG [1958] to show that *every non-recursive r.e. set is the union of disjoint nonrecursive r.e. sets.*

29 DEFINITION: *Let h be a time function. The r.e. set W_i is an h **barrier** to the infinite r.e. set W_j (with respect to the enumeration technique E) if*
   (i) $W_i \subset \overline{W}_j$ *(that is, W_i and W_j are disjoint)*
   (ii) *If z is such that for infinitely many n $D_{E'(z,n)} \cap W_i$ contains at least $h(n)$ elements, then $W_z \cap W_i$ is infinite [and thus, by* (i), *if $W_z = W_j$, then $|D_{E'(z,n)}| < h(n)$ for all but finitely many n]; and*
   (iii) *W_j is contained in some W_y for which $|D_{E'(y,n)} \cap W_j| \geq h(n)$ for all n.*

Thus by (iii) we can generate more than $h(n)$ elements of W_j in the first n stages of computation (using device y), but by (ii) if we insist that *only* elements of W_j be generated, then, for all but finitely many n, we cannot hope to generate even as many as $h(n)$ elements of W_j in the first n stages of computation, no matter what device we use.

30 THEOREM: (YOUNG [1968]) *Let i be any device for enumerating an infinite set. Let h be an unbounded time function, and let*

$$h'(n) = \min\left\{ h(n), \left\lceil \frac{1}{4} |D_{E'(i,n)}| \right\rceil \right\}.$$

Then one can effectively find disjoint infinite r.e. sets P and Q whose union is W_i such that each of P and Q is an h' barrier to the other.
   Proof. Let $m_1, m_2, m_3, \ldots$ be the elements of W_i in the order in which they occur in the enumeration $D_{E(i,0)}, D_{E(i,1)}, \ldots$, using the natural ordering of the numbers within $D_E(i, n)$. By Lemma **26**, there is a device i_0 which enumerates W_i with

$$|D_{E'(i_0,n)}| \leq h'(n) \mathbin{\dot-} 1$$

We indicate how to form the sets P and Q by stages, with P^n (respectively, Q^n) being the set of elements put into P (respectively, Q) by the start of stage n. We shall make use of "priority markers," a sequence $\{\Lambda_j\}$ of symbols, each indexed by an integer j. We set $P^1 = Q^1 = \emptyset$.
Stage n ($n \geq 1$): Calculate m_n, and then find the first y such that

$$m_n \in D_{E'(i_0,y)} - D_{E'(i_0,y-1)} \qquad (\text{setting } D_{E'(i_0,-1)} = \emptyset)$$

To all devices $z \leq y$ which have not yet been assigned priority markers, we assign priority markers by arranging the devices in numerical order and successively assigning priority markers which have not previously been used but which have the lowest index among those not yet used. We shall see that markers can be changed during a process called *attacking* but that once a device has sampled the virtues of owning a marker, it will never be without one.

Next, examine all $j \leq y$ such that

$$m_n \in D_{E'(j,y)}$$

If there is no such j, put m_n into P if $|P^n| < |Q^n|$, into Q otherwise.

If there is such a j, choose that device $j_0 \leq y$ which has $m_n \in D_{E'(j,y)}$ and such that j_0 has beside it a marker Λ_q of lowest possible index q. If Λ_q has not previously been attacked, we attack it and the device i_0 by putting m_n into P if $|P^n| < |Q^n|$, into Q otherwise. If Λ_q has previously been attacked, we add m_n to Q [respectively, P] if the prior attack on Λ_q contributed to P [respectively, Q], and by replacing the marker Λ_q on the device j_0 by a new marker with the lowest index among all those markers never used before. Note that only in this last case can we ever augment the *larger* of P or Q. Thus no marker is ever attacked more than twice.

Go to stage $n + 1$.

Clearly, the above construction yields P and Q as disjoint r.e. sets whose union is W_i, and we can effectively find P and Q from i and h. Further, P and Q are disjoint, and thus (i) of Definition **29** holds.

We now show that P and Q are infinite, and that each can be computed relatively fast modulo their intersection with W_i [thus satisfying (iii) of Definition **29**] by showing that

31   For each n, at least $\lceil n/4 \rceil$ of the set $\{m_1, m_2, \ldots, m_n\}$ are in each of P and Q; and

32   For each n', $|D_{E'(i,n')} \cap Q| \geq h'(n')$, and similarly for P.

Certainly, $m_1 \in P$ and $m_2 \in Q$. Thus if $|P^n|$ or $|Q^n|$ is ever less than $\lceil n/4 \rceil$, then $n > 4$ and there must be some largest integer p, $0 < p < n$, such that $|P^p| = |Q^p|$, and we have, say, $|Q^{p+q}| < \lceil (p+q)/4 \rceil$ where $p + q = n$, and thus, certainly, $|P^x| > |Q^x|$ for $P < x \leq p + q$.

Thus, for $p < x \leq p + q$, since P^x is always larger than Q^x, elements can be added to P during stage x only if they are forced into P during an attack on a marker Λ_j which contributed to Q during an earlier attack on Λ_j. Thus if a is the number of elements added to Q during stages $p + 1, \ldots, p + q$, we must have

$$\frac{|P^{p+q}|}{|Q^{p+q}|} \leq \frac{|P^p| + |Q^p| + a}{|Q^p| + a} = \frac{2|Q^p| + a}{|Q^p| + a}$$

Recall that $|Q^p| \geq 1$. Hence $|P^{p+q}|/|Q^{p+q}|$ is at most $3|Q^p|/|Q^p|$ if $a \leq |Q^p|$, and at most $3a/a$ if $a \geq |Q^p|$, hence in any case we have $|P^{p+q}| \leq 3|Q^{p+q}|$, and thus

$$p + q = |P^{p+q}| + |Q^{p+q}| \leq 4|Q^{p+q}|$$

contradicting the assumption that $|Q^{p+q}| < \lceil p + q/4 \rceil$.

We have thus proved **31**. The proof of **32** follows when we note that if, given n', we let n be such that $D_{E'(i,n')} = \{m_1, m_2, \ldots, m_n\}$, then

$$|D_{E'(i,n')} \cap Q| = |Q^{p+q}| \geq \frac{n}{4} = \frac{1}{4}|D_{E'(i,n')}| \geq h'(n')$$

the latter inequality following from the definition of h'.

It only remains to show that (iii) of Definition **29** holds. Suppose, e.g., that we had

$$|D_{E'(x,n)} \cap P| \geq h'(n) \qquad \text{for infinitely many } n$$

Then $\qquad |D_{E'(x,n)} \cap P| \geq h'(n)|D_{E'(i_0,n)}| \qquad$ for infinitely many n

by our choice of i_0. For each such n there is an m and a $y > n$ such that

33 $\qquad m \in D_{E'(x,y)} \qquad$ and $\qquad m \in D_{E'(i_0,y)} - D_{E'(i_0,y-1)}$

Now for $n \geq x$, we will have this $y > x$, and thus at the stage where **33** occurs, x will have beside it a marker Λ_q. Now this marker Λ_q must be attacked unless some marker of smaller index is attacked. But after two attacks, a marker is retired. Thus any such marker Λ_q will be attacked twice, forcing W_x to contribute to both P and Q, and introducing a new marker beside x. Thus if $|D_{E'(x,n)} \cap P| \geq h'(n)$ for infinitely many n, then W_x contributes infinitely often to both P and Q. A similar analysis for Q yields (iii) of Definition **29** both ways, and we conclude that each of P and Q is an h' barrier to the other. $\qquad\square$

The reader may wish to recapture Friedberg's proof from the above analysis. On this high note, we close this section, urging the reader to study the wealth of further material in YOUNG [1968] and BLUM [1967], and to ponder whether Blum's proof of his speed-up theorem can be couched in Friedberg's priority-attack form.

7.4 SPEED-UP AND INCOMPLETENESS THEOREMS

The speed-up theorem for M-computers bears a resemblance to GÖDEL's [1936] speed-up theorem for proofs in recursive logics, and is proved by MOSTOWSKI [1957] in his exposition of Gödel's theory of incompleteness.

Let us briefly recall the setup in Mostowski's monograph. The basic notions of addition, equality, and ordering of the natural numbers are formalized in first-order logic to yield a system S. It is shown that S is undecidable, and in fact an actual statement, call it φ, is exhibited which is such that neither φ nor its negation is provable within S if S is consistent. A new system

S_1 is then formed, essentially by adjoining to S the axioms of second-order quantification, in which φ is provable. However, more turns out to be true.

If $\vdash_S \varphi$ (that is, φ is provable in S), let $p(\varphi)$ denote the length of the shortest proof of φ in S. Define $p_1(\varphi)$ similarly for φ provable in S_1.

Since S_1 is an extension of S, any S proof of φ is an S_1 proof of φ, and so we immediately conclude that $p_1(\varphi) \leq p(\varphi)$ for every φ provable in S. But we even have (see MOSTOWSKI [1957, pp. 112–115]):

1   THE GÖDEL SPEED-UP THEOREM: *For every recursive function F there exists a sentence φ of S such that $\vdash_S \varphi$ and $\vdash_{S_1} \varphi$ and such that the minimal S and S_1 proofs of φ satisfy the inequality $p(\varphi) \geq F(p_1(\varphi))$.*   □

The proof is based on a study of specific properties of the two systems (all the axioms of which are known), and uses results obtained in proving the incompleteness of S. It is of interest to study the incompleteness of logics and speed-up theorems for logics in a framework as close as possible to the M-computer formulation of the Blum speed-up theorem—following ARBIB [1966c], we now study the most abstract properties of a recursive logic for which we have some measure on the difficulty of proofs.

2   DEFINITION: *A PM system (proof-measure system) on the alphabet X is a quadruple $L = (G, \varphi, p, t)$, where*

1. *G is a recursive set of words on the alphabet X, the members of which are called well-formed formulas (wff).*
2. *A recursive enumeration $(\varphi_1, p_1), (\varphi_2, p_2), (\varphi_3, p_3), \ldots p_n \in N$ is called the measure of the nth proof.*

$$T_L = \{\varphi_n | n = 1, 2, 3, \ldots\}$$

*We say φ is a theorem of L, $\vdash_L \varphi$, if and only if $\varphi \in T_L$. By definition, $p(\varphi) = \min \{p_n | \varphi = \varphi_n\}$, and this is defined only on T_L. $p(\varphi)$ is the minimal proof measure of φ, and is called the **difficulty** of φ in L).*

3. *t is an increasing total recursive function t such that*

$$n > t(m) \Rightarrow p_n > m$$

N.B. Item 3 above implies that if $m = p(\varphi)$, then $\varphi = \varphi_n$ for some $n \leq t(m)$. In particular, $\min \{n | \varphi = \varphi_n\} \leq t(p(\varphi))$ if $\varphi \in T_L$.

We then define the relation between PM systems of major interest to us.

3   DEFINITION: *Let L and L_1 be two PM systems, with sets of wff's G and G_1 and difficulties p and p_1, respectively. We say that L_1 is a **speed-up** of L if*
    (a) *$T_L \subseteq T_{L_1}$*
    (b) *For every total recursive function r, L_1 is an r speed-up of L; that is, there exists $\varphi^r \in T_L$ such that $p(\varphi^r) \geq r(p_1(\varphi))$.*

4 LEMMA: *Let L be a PM system, and let H be any infinite recursive subset of X*. Then $L|H \underset{\mathrm{def}}{=} (G \cap H, \psi, q, t)$ is a PM system, where*

   (a) $\psi_n = \varphi_{\alpha(n)}$, *where* $\alpha(0) = 0$, $\alpha(m + 1) = min \; \{n > \alpha(m)|\varphi_n \in H\}$
   (b) $q_n = p_{\alpha(n)}$

Proof. We have only to verify item 3 of the definition. But

$$n > t(m) \Rightarrow \alpha(n) > t(m) \Rightarrow p_{\alpha(n)} > m \Rightarrow q_n > m \qquad \square$$

We now easily obtain a theorem which, roughly speaking, says that if a system L_1 can do some things arbitrarily quicker than L can, then L_1 can do some things that L cannot do at all.

5 THEOREM: *Let L_1 be a speed-up of L. Then there is a $\theta \in G \cap G_1$ such that*

$$\theta \in T_{L_1} - T_L$$

Proof. Let $\hat{L}_1 = L_1|G = (G \cap G_1, \psi^1, q^1, t^1)$:

$$\hat{L} = L|G_1 = (G \cap G_1, \psi, q, t)$$

Clearly, $\hat{L}_1$ is a speed-up of $\hat{L}$.

Let us assume, by way of contradiction, that $T_{L_1} \subseteq T_L$. Then we may define the total-recursive function g by $g(n) = q_{s(n)}$, where

$$s(n) = min \; \{m|\psi^1_n = \psi_m\}$$

Now set $\bar{g}(m) = max \; \{g(n)|n \leq t^1(m)\}$. Since $\hat{L}_1$ is a speed-up of $\hat{L}$, we may pick $\varphi \in T_L$ such that

$$\bar{g}(q^1(\varphi)) < q(\varphi)$$

Let $m_0 = min \; \{m|\varphi = \psi_m\}$, $n_0 = min \; \{n|\varphi = \psi^1_n\}$, so that $q_{m_0} = g(n_0)$. But

$$\begin{aligned} q_{m_0} &\geq q(\varphi) \\ &> \bar{g}(q^1(\varphi)) && \text{by choice of } \varphi \\ &> g(n_0) && \text{by definition of } \bar{g} \end{aligned}$$

A contradiction! Thus there exists $\theta \in T_{\hat{L}_1} - T_{\hat{L}}$, whence $\theta \in T_{L_1} - T_L$. $\square$

The remainder of this section is devoted to extremely weak forms of consistency, completeness, and adequacy, and the proof of correspondingly abstract (and insanely general) incompleteness theorems. For much of this work we do not need the proof measures, and we consider *weak systems*.

6 DEFINITION: *A **weak system** on the alphabet X is a pair $L = (G, T_L)$, where*

1. *G is a recursive subset of X^*.*
2. *T_L is a recursively enumerable subset of G. We say φ is a **theorem** of L, $\vdash_L \varphi$, if and only if $\varphi \in T_L$.*
    N.B. Each PM system "is" a weak system.

7 DEFINITION: *A **bi-recursive function** f: $A \to B$ is a total-recursive function f: $A \to B$ such that*
    1. *$f(A)$ is a recursive subset of B.*
    2. *There is a total recursive function f^{-1}: $f(A) \to A$ such that $f^{-1}(f(a)) = a$ for all $a \in A$.*

8 DEFINITION: *Let $L = (G, T_L)$ be a weak system and $\sim: G \to G$ a bi-recursive function. We say that L is **consistent** w.r.t. $\sim$ if for no $\theta \in G$ are both θ and $\sim\theta$ in T_L.*

9 DEFINITION: *Let $L = (G, T_L)$ be a weak system consistent w.r.t. $\sim$, and let C be a recursive subset of G for which $\sim(C) \subset C$. We say L is **complete** (w.r.t. $\sim$ and C) if, for every $\theta \in C$, **either** θ **or** $\sim\theta$ is in T_L.*
    N.B. If L were formalized in first-order logic, we would take $\sim$ as negation and C as the collection of closed wff's, that is, wff's with no free variables.

Our next theorem may be regarded as a generalized converse of the Gödel speed-up theorem.

10 THEOREM: *Let S be a PM system consistent w.r.t. $\sim$, and let S possess a speed-up S_1, also consistent w.r.t. $\sim$. Then S is a complete w.r.t. to **no** nonempty recursive subset C of G, for which $\hat{S}_1 = S_1|C$ is a speed-up of $\hat{S} = S|C$.*
    Proof. By the last theorem, there exists $\theta \in C$ such that

$$\theta \in T_{\hat{S}_1} - T_{\hat{S}}$$

S_1 consistent $\Rightarrow \sim\theta \notin T_{S_1} \Rightarrow \sim\theta \notin T_S$. Thus neither θ nor $\sim\theta$ is in T_S, and so S is incomplete w.r.t. C. $\qquad\square$

To represent a set of integers in a weak system L, we want to generate a sequence of words $W_1, W_2, W_3, \ldots$ such that W_n may be interpreted "$n \in U$," and with the property that if n actually belongs to U, then W_n is provable in L.

11 DEFINITION: *Let $L = (G, T_L)$ be a weak system, with C a recursive subset of G. We say L **represents a set** U in C if there exists a bi-recursive function W: $N \to C$ [we write W_n for $W(n)$] such that*

$$U = \{n | \vdash_L W_n\}$$

N.B. We can take $C = G$ if desired.

12 THEOREM: *If L represents U in C, then U is recursively enumerable.*
Proof. Since T_L is recursive enumerable,

$$U = \{n \mid W_n \in [\{W_1, W_2, \ldots\} \cap T_L]\}$$

is recursively enumerable.   □

Thus, given L and C, the most we can expect is that L represents all recursively enumerable sets in C. This motivates

13 DEFINITION: *Let $L = (G, T_L)$ be a weak system, with C a recursive subset of G. We say L is **adequate** through C if L represents every recursively enumerable subset of N in C. [If L is consistent, we also demand $\sim(C) \subseteq C$.]*
We now have our abstract Gödel-type incompleteness theorem:

14 THEOREM: *If a system L is consistent and adequate through C, then L is incomplete w.r.t C.*
Proof. Let L be consistent w.r.t. $\sim$.
Let U be a recursively enumerable subset of N which is *not* recursive, so that $\bar{U} = N - U$ is not recursively enumerable. By adequacy, there is a bi-recursive function $W: N \to C$ such that

$$U = \{n \mid \vdash_L W_n\}$$

Since $\sim$ is recursive, and $\sim(C) \subseteq C$,

$$\check{U} = \{n \mid \vdash_L \sim W_n\}$$

is represented by L in C, and is thus recursively enumerable. Since L is consistent w.r.t. $\sim$,

$$\vdash_L \sim W_n \Rightarrow W_n \text{ is } not \text{ a theorem of } L \Rightarrow n \notin U$$

Thus $\check{U} \subseteq \bar{U}$, but $\check{U} \neq \bar{U}$, since $\check{U}$ is recursively enumerable, while $\bar{U}$ is not.
Pick any $m \in \bar{U} - \check{U}$. Then neither W_m nor $\sim W_m$ is a theorem of L, even though both are in C. Thus L is incomplete w.r.t. C.   □

N.B. If L is a recursive logic whose axioms include the usual ones of propositional logic, then L is consistent $\Leftrightarrow G \neq T_L$. Thus every such system is consistent if it is adequate. For if $G = T_L$, then only N and φ are representable in L.

15 DEFINITION: *A weak system (G, T_L) is said to be **decidable** if T_L is recursive.*

16 THEOREM: *If L is adequate through C, then L is undecidable.*

Proof. Suppose L is decidable. Let $W: N \to C$ be a bi-recursive function with $U = \{n | \vdash_L W_n\}$. Given n, we generate W_n. Since T_L is recursive, we can tell effectively whether or not $W_n \in T_L$, and thus whether or not $n \in U$. Hence U is recursive, and so L is not adequate. □

17 THEOREM: *Let S and S_1 be two PM systems for which $T_S \subset T_{S_1}$, and there exists a recursively enumerable subset $V_1, V_2, V_3, \ldots$ of $G \cap G_1$ such that*

$$V = \{x| _{S_1}V_x\} - \{x| _SV_x\}$$

is not recursively enumerable. Then S_1 is a speed-up of S.

Proof. Suppose there is a recursive g such that, for all $\varphi \in T_S$,

$$g(p_1(\varphi)) \geq p(\varphi)$$

Given x, generate V_x, and then generate T_{S_1} until first finding φ_n^1 with $\varphi_n^1 = V_x$. Then generate the φ_m with $m \leq t(g(p_n))$. Emit x if no such $\varphi_m = V_x$. This yields a recursive enumeration of V. A contradiction—and no such g exists. □

To gain more insight into this matter, we must add more structure to our logics. Following A. EHRENFEUCHT [personal communication], consider axiomatic systems with negation and implication satisfying the usual axioms of propositional logic.‡ For a theory (i.e., set of theorems) T, we denote by $T\{\theta\}$ the set of all theorems deducible from the theorems of T and the additional axiom θ, using propositional logic.

18 THEOREM (EHRENFEUCHT): *Let T be a theory and φ a sentence, such that the set $T\{\sim\varphi\}$ is undecidable (i.e., not recursive). Then $T\{\varphi\}$ is a speed-up of T.*

Proof.

1. By propositional logic,

$$\vdash_{T\{\sim\varphi\}} \theta \iff \vdash_T \sim\varphi \supset \theta \iff \vdash_T \sim\theta \supset \varphi$$

Further,

$$\vdash_{T\{\varphi\}} \sim\theta \supset \varphi$$

2. Assume, then, that $T\{\varphi\}$ is not a speed-up of T, and thus there is a total recursive function g such that if $\vdash_T\psi$, then $p_T(\psi) \leq g(p_{T\{\varphi\}}(\psi))$.

Then we may effectively decide whether or not $\vdash_{T\{\sim\varphi\}}\theta$ by searching the theorems of T with the proof measure $\leq g(p_{T\{\varphi\}}(\sim\theta\cdot\varphi))$ for $\theta \supset \varphi$. This contradicts the undecidability of $T\{\sim\varphi\}$. □

‡ The reader unacquainted with propositional logic may have to omit the next two results.

19   EXERCISE. As a corollary to Ehrenfeucht's proof, obtain:

Let T be a theory, and φ a sentence, such that $T\{\sim\varphi\}$ is undecidable. Then the difference set

$$T\{\varphi\} - T$$

is *not* recursively enumerable.

We started with a discussion of difficulty of computation and then found ourselves, via the Gödel speed-up theorem, discussing the difficulty of proofs in PM systems. It is thus interesting to recall that RABIN [1960] defined a difficulty of computation in terms of a measure on proofs in Post logics. For a summary of some of his work, and its generalization to our framework of PM systems and M-computers, we refer the reader to ARBIB [1966c].

7.5   PARTIAL ORDERINGS OF DIFFICULTY

We have tried to isolate the relative computational efficiency of different machines for different tasks—it is clear that a machine working in radix 2 multiplies by 2 faster than a machine working in radix 10, whereas the reverse is true for multiplication by 10. However, moving away from the details of a particular machine, we might seek an ordering of complexity of functions in which multiplications by 2 or by 10 are considered equally difficult, but less difficult than, say, exponentiation. Following ARBIB and BLUM [1965], then, we introduce a partial ordering on complexity of functions with respect to computation by a given machine, and then show how to "smear" this ordering so that it is relatively machine-independent. The exposition has been improved by comments of P. FAURRE and D. PAGER [personal communications]. The resultant ordering with its relatively gross distinctions has much in common (though this has not been formally explored) with the hierarchical approach of Section **6.3**, though the subdivision is finer than, e.g., Ritchie's hierarchy.

Blum's speed-up theorem motivates the definition of a degree of difficulty ordering induced by the M-computer C.

1   DEFINITION: *Let f and g be two partial recursive functions. We say that f is no more difficult to compute than $g(f \leq g)$ if for each index i for g, there exists an index j for f such that*

(a) $d(f) \subset d(g)$

(b) $F_j(x) \leq G_i(x)$ *for almost all $x \in d(g)$*

This is in distinction to the relation on recursive functions introduced by RABIN [1960], which in the present terminology takes the form:

(i) $f < g$ if there is an index j for f such that if i is *any* index for g,

$$F'_j(x) < G_i(x) \qquad \text{for almost all } x$$

(ii) $f \leq g \Leftrightarrow f < g \qquad$ or $\qquad f = g$

We introduce the new definition, since Rabin's definition contains a flavor of the assumption that the index j for f is that of the fastest program for f—and the speed-up theorem vitiates any such assumption in the present framework. Secondly, we would hope that many functions would have the same degree of difficulty.

In order to generalize the partial ordering (F greater than G) between partial recursive functions which is defined by $F \geq G$ iff

(i) $F(x)$ defined $\Rightarrow G(x)$ defined
(ii) $F(x) \geq G(x) \qquad$ for almost all x

we introduce the S-bound relation, where:

2 DEFINITION: *If S is a class of functions of two variables $S = \{p \mid p = p(x, y), x, y \in N\}$, we say F S-bounds G iff*

(i) $d(F) \subset d(G)$
(ii) $\exists p \in S$ such that $p(x, F(x)) \geq G(x) \qquad$ *for almost all x*

Note that $\geq$ is an S-bound relation with S consisting of the single function $e(x, y) = y$.

In order to get a meaningful relation, we want S-bounding to be reflexive and transitive.

If $e(x, y) \in S$, then the S-bound relation is reflexive because $e(x, F(x)) = F(x) \geq F(x)$, so then F S-bounds F.

Now, suppose F S-bounds G and G S-bounds H; that is, $\exists p \in S$ such that $p(x, F(x)) \geq G(x)$ for almost all x, and $\exists p' \in S$ such that $p'(x, G(x)) \geq H(x)$ for almost all x.

Suppose now that $p'(x, y)$ is an increasing function of y, and that $p'(x, p(x, y)) = p''(x, y) \in S$, then $p''(x, F(x)) \geq H(x)$ for almost all x, and F S-bounds H.

So we have proved

3 THEOREM: *In order for the S-bound relation to be reflexive and transitive, it is sufficient that S be a monoid of functions of two variables $x, y \in N$ increasing with respect to y, with composition*

$$p * p'(x, y) = p(x, p'(x, y))$$

and identity $e(x, y) = y$.

4 EXERCISE. Show that for $S = S_{\max} = \{$all the functions $p(x, y)$ increasing with respect to $y\}$, F S-bounds G and G S-bounds F for any total recursive functions F and G and that even for the smaller $S = S^* = \{$all total recursive functions $p(x, y)$ increasing with respect to y} the same result holds. This result is no longer true if we require S to be a monoid of increasing functions with respect to x and y. On the other hand, if we take $S = S_{\min} = \{e(x, y)\}$, the S-bound relation becomes the $\geq$ relation.

5 DEFINITION: $f \geq_M g$ (f is at least as difficult as g, using M) if and only if, to each program P_i for computing f, there corresponds a program P_j for computing g such that Φ_i S-bounds Φ_j.

We chose S to be a monoid with a monotony condition simply so that we might deduce:

6 THEOREM: $\geq_M$ is reflexive and transitive.

In describing the machine dependence of the ordering $\geq_M$, we want to know, for each machine M, which are those machines N that give rise to the same ordering:

7 DEFINITION: Two machines M and N are S-equivalent, $M \equiv_S N$ iff, for all partial recursive functions f and g,

$$f \geq_M g \Leftrightarrow f \geq_N g$$

This equivalence relation is related to partial ordering $\geq_S$ on machines. We say that M is at least as complex as N (modulo S), and write $N \geq_S M$, iff each program $^N P_i$ for machine N can be replaced by a corresponding program $^M P_j$ for machine M so that $^N \Phi_i$ S-bounds $^M \Phi_j$ ($^N P_i$ and $^M P_j$ are programs for the same function). In other words, M is at least as complex as N if, up to elements of S, M can compute any function as quickly as N can. It is now immediate that:

8 THEOREM:
  (i) $\geq_S$ is reflexive and transitive.
  (ii) $M \equiv_S N$ if $M \geq_S N$ and $N \geq_S M$

9 EXERCISE: Prove that the converse of **8** (ii) is false.

Now think of a Turing machine as being *programmed* with its list of quintuples. It is just specified by its tape alphabet X and the choice of coding and decoding functions for numbers on its tape.

In the following discussion we let $^k T$ be the machine with the constraint that $X = \{0, 1, \ldots, k - 1\}$ (with each of these k numbers considered as a single symbol) and that the coding of input and output is to be in radix k $(k \geq 1)$. In particular, we shall be interested in machines equivalent to $^{10} T$.

Then the reader is invited to apply the results of Section **4.3** to prove the assertion of the:

10   EXERCISE: Let $\tilde{S}$ be the monoid $\tilde{S} = \{q | q(x, y) = P(\log x, y)$, where $P(z, y)$ is a positive polynomial increasing with respect to y for positive integers z and $y\}$.

Then prove that:

(i) ^{10}T is $\tilde{S}$-equivalent to any generalized Turing machine with a radix k input and radix l output ($k > 1, l > 1$) with a finite number of input tapes, each of finite dimension, and with a finite number of scanners on each tape.

(ii)   With respect to $\tilde{S}$, 2^x is more difficult to compute than x on ^2T.

(iii) ^1T is not equivalent to ^{10}T. [Hint: Consider 2^x.]

8

ALGEBRAIC
DECOMPOSITION THEORY

We saw in Section **3.2** that any finite automaton may be simulated by a network of AND- and NOT-modules, provided that we allow loops of arbitrary complexity in the network. In other words, a very simple set of components can be used to build up arbitrary finite automata *if we allow loops*. We shall see, in the next few sections, that we cannot realize arbitrary automata from a finite set of component types if we only allow loop-free synthesis, just as there is no finite set of integers from which all other integers can be built by multiplication, but all integers can be built from 1 and -1 by addition.

8.1 COMPOSITION AND PAIR ALGEBRAS

1 DEFINITION: *A machine* $M = (X', Y', Q', \delta', \beta')$ *is a **submachine** of the machine* $M = (X, Y, Q, \delta, \beta)$ *if and only if*

$Q' \subset Q, X' \subset X, Y' \subset Y$
$\delta' = \delta$ *restricted to* $Q' \times X'$
$\beta' = \beta$ *restricted to* Q'

Two machines are *isomorphic* if they only differ in the labelling of their states.

2   DEFINITION: *M_1 realizes the state behavior of M_2 if and only if a submachine M_1' of M_1 is isomorphic to M_2.*

Thus, if M_1 realizes the state behavior of M_2, it certainly *simulates M_2*. However, a machine M_1 may well simulate M_2 *without* realizing the state behavior of M_2. Let us ponder this distinction awhile, and realize that the state-behavior realization of M can be restrictive and that the most economical realizations of a machine need not be state-behavior realizations. If we build M from binary modules, for instance, its state set must have cardinality a power of 2. Suppose we have a complicated machine presented to us in reduced form. To simplify our design task in realizing it as a network of components, we may well want to split it into a series connection of two machines for each of which the network design problem is far simpler. But such a useful series decomposition may yield a machine which certainly *realizes* our initial machine, but is *not in reduced form* and so *does not realize its state behavior*. In other words, there are many practical reasons for preferring to realize a machine from other machines rather than restricting ourselves to the realization of its state behavior.

We shall start by summarizing lattice-theoretic‡ criteria for the possibility of constructing state realizations for parallel and series synthesis. This will motivate the introduction of the notion of a *pair algebra*, in terms of which HARTMANIS and STEARNS [1964] develop criteria for more general realizations.

3   DEFINITION: *An ordered pair of partitions (π, τ) defined on the set of states of $M = (X, Y, Q, \delta, \beta)$ is a partition pair on M if and only if $q \equiv q'(\pi)$ implies that for all x in X, $\delta(q, x) \equiv \delta(q', x)(\tau)$; that is, each function $\delta(\cdot, x): Q \to Q$ carries blocks of π into blocks of τ.*

A partition π on Q of M is said to have the substitution property (SP) only in the case in which (π, π) is a partition pair.

4   EXERCISE: Let L be the lattice of all partitions on the set Q, and let $\cdot$ denote the meet and $+$ the join in the lattice. Then

1. If (x_1, y_1) and (x_2, y_2) are partition pairs, then so are $(x_1 \cdot x_2, y_1 \cdot y_2)$ and $(x_1 + x_2, y_1 + y_2)$.
2. For any x and y in L, both $(x, 1)$ and $(0, y)$ are partition pairs.

Let us state the definitions of serial and parallel connection of machines in a (slightly restricted) form suitable to the present theory.

---

‡ The reader uninterested in lattice theory may omit this material and just read **5** to **7** and **10** through **21** in this section. The reader interested in lattice theory will find HARTMANIS AND STEARNS [1966] a lucid detailed presentation of its use in automata theory, with a wealth of examples.

5   DEFINITION: *The series connection of two machines*

$$M_1 = (X_1, Y_1, Q_1, \delta_1, \beta_1) \quad and \quad M_2 = (X_2, Y_2, Q_2, \delta_2, \beta_2)$$

for which $Y_1 = X_2$ *is the machine*

$$M = (X_1, Y_2, Q_1 \times Q_2, \delta, \beta)$$

where $\delta((q, q'), x) = (\delta_1(q, x), \delta_2(q', \beta_1(q)))$

and $\beta(q, q') = \beta_2(q')$

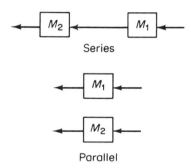

Series

M₁

M₂

Parallel

Fig. 8.1

6   DEFINITION: *The parallel connection of two machines*

$$M_1 = (X_1, Y_1, Q_1, \delta_1, \beta_1) \quad and \quad M_2 = (X_2, Y_2, Q_2, \delta_2, \beta_2)$$

is the machine $M = (X_1 \times X_2, Y_1 \times Y_2, Q_1 \times Q_2, \delta, \beta)$

where $\delta((q, q'), (x, x')) = (\delta_1(q, x), \delta_2(q', x'))$

and $\beta(q, q') = (\beta_1(q), \beta_2(q'))$

7   EXAMPLE. Let the Z_2-machine have $X = Y = Q = \{0, 1\}$, its state equal to its output, and its next-state function being addition of the state and input modulo 2.

(i) If we relabel 00 as 0, 01 as 1, 10 as 2, and 11 as 3, then the parallel combination of two copies of Z_2 (see Fig. 8.1a) has state equal to output, and next-state table

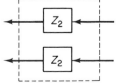

Fig. 8.1a

q \ x	0	1	2	3
0	0	1	2	3
1	1	0	3	2
2	2	3	0	1
3	3	2	1	0

The reader should notice that every input permutes the states, with the result that the semigroup is a group—in fact isomorphic to $Z_2 \times Z_2$.

Notice that the states 0 and 1 of the first machine correspond to the blocks $\{0, 1\}$ and $\{2, 3\}$ of a partition, π_1 say, on the state set, whereas the blocks $\{0, 2\}$, $\{1, 3\}$ of a partition, π_2 say, correspond to the states of the second machine. These partitions have the property that $\pi_1 \cdot \pi_2 = 0$. π_1 and π_2 each have SP:

$$\{0, 1\} \cdot 0 = \{0, 1\} \qquad \{0, 2\} \cdot 3 = \{3, 1\} \qquad \text{and so on}$$

(ii) If we now consider the two Z_2 machines in series,

the output is the output of the second machine, and the next-state table is

q \ x	0	1
0	0	2
1	1	3
2	3	1
3	2	0

Notice that π_1 still has the substitution property but that this is no longer true for π_2.

The semigroup is again a group, but it has *eight* distinct elements corresponding to whether $\{0, 1\}$ maps into $\{0, 1\}$ or $\{2, 3\}$, and then corresponding to the order in which the blocks are mapped. This example emphasizes that the series composition can have a larger semigroup than the parallel composition because the action of an input now depends on the state of the first machine.

We now state the two main results of HARTMANIS [1962] on realizability of *state* behavior, exemplified in the above example. The proofs are similar to the proofs of Theorems **32** and **33** below, and are thus left as exercises.

8 EXERCISE: The state behavior of M can be realized by a series connection of two smaller machines M_1 and M_2 if and only if there exists a nontrivial SP partition π on S of M. (By nontrivial, we mean $0 \neq \pi \neq 1$.)

9 EXERCISE: The state behavior of M can be realized by a parallel connection of two smaller machines M_1 and M_2 if and only if there exist two nontrivial SP partitions, π_1 and π_2 on S of M such that

$$\pi_1 \cdot \pi_2 = 0$$

The composition of machines in series and parallel may be subsumed in the following portmanteau way of combining machines, which explicitly includes encoding and decoding maps:

10 DEFINITION: *Given (state-output) machines* $M' = (X', Y', Q', \delta', \beta')$ *and* $M = (X, Y, Q, \delta, \beta)$, *and a triple K comprising maps*

$$\eta: \tilde{X} \to X \qquad Z: \tilde{X} \times Y \to X' \qquad \text{and} \qquad \gamma: Y \times Y' \to \tilde{Y}$$

we define **the cascade of M' and M with connection K to be the machine**

$$M' \ominus_K M = (\tilde{X}, \tilde{Y}, Q' \times Q, \delta_K, \beta_K)$$

where we may read δ_K and β_K from Fig. 8.2:

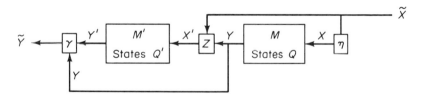

$$M' \ominus_K M$$

Fig. 8.2

$$\delta_K[(q', q), \tilde{x}] = [\delta'\{q', Z(\tilde{x}, \beta(q))\}, \delta\{q, \eta(x)\}]$$
$$\beta_K(q', q) = \gamma(\beta'(q'), \beta(q))$$

We usually omit η and γ from explicit mention, and speak of $M' \ominus_Z M$. To get *series* composition (albeit preserving the input of M) we make Z independent of $\tilde{X}$ and $\gamma(q', q) = q'$ (see Fig. 8.3(a)); to get *parallel* composition, take $\tilde{X} = X \times X'$ and set $Z((x, x'), y) = x'$, $\eta(x, x') = x$ and $\gamma(y', y) = (y', y)$ (see Fig. 8.3(b)).

The precise notion of loop-free composition we shall employ is then that of repeated formation of cascades (which thus includes symbol-by-symbol encodings and decodings).

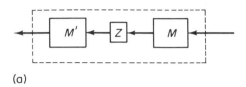

(a)

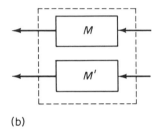

(b)

Fig. 8.3. (a) M and M' connected in series via a memoryless encoder Z. (b) M and M' "connected" in parallel.

As an example of the use of cascades, let us briefly study a class of machines which will be important for us in the sequel— machines for which an input resets the machine to a state determined by that input, or else the input leaves all states unchanged:

11 DEFINITION: M is an *identity-reset machine* if, for each $x \in X$ the map $\delta(\circ, x): Q \to Q$: $q \mapsto \delta(q, x)$ is either the identity map on Q, or else is a constant (= reset) map; and if the output of the machine is its state.

Now let us consider the two-state identity-reset machine:

12 The "*flip-flop*" F: has states $\{q_0, q_1\}$, and inputs $\{e, x_0, x_1\}$ with the actions:

$$\delta(q, e) = q \qquad e \text{ is the identity input}$$
$$\delta(q, x_i) = q_i \qquad x_i \text{ is the "reset to } q_i\text{" input}$$

13 PROPOSITION: *Any identity-reset machine may be simulated by a repeated cascade of copies of the "flip-flop" F.*

Construction. In fact, we use only coding, decoding, and parallel composition. If M is an n-state identity-reset machine, choose m so that $n \leq 2^m$; place m copies of F in parallel to obtain F^m. We select n of the 2^m states of

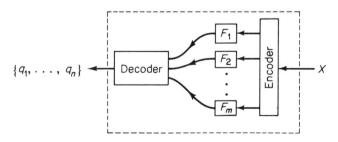

Fig. 8.4. Identity-reset machine stimulated by a parallel combination of flip-flops.

F^m at our whim and decode these as the outputs (= states) $(q_1, \ldots, q_n)$ of M. If an input x to M acts as an identity, we code it as the identity input to all m copies of F. If x acts as a reset to state q_i, we code it as that configuration of resets which will cause F^m to go into the state which will be decoded as q_i.   □

14   EXERCISE: Prove that F has semigroup $U_3 = \{1, r_0, r_1\}$ whose elements are the Myhill equivalence classes $1 = [e]$, $r_0 = [x_0]$ and $r_1 = [x_1]$ and with multiplication $u \cdot 1 = u$, $u \cdot r_i = r_i$ (1 is the identity, r_0 and r_1 are called "right zeros").

15   DEFINITION: *UNITS is the set of semigroups which divide U_3.*

Now U_3 has subsemigroups U_3; $U_2 = \{r_0, r_1\}$; $U_1 = \{1, r_0\}$ and its isomorph $\{1, r_1\}$; and $U_0 = \{1\}$.

If $S|U_3$, we must have a diagram $U_3 \supset S' \twoheadrightarrow S$, and so it follows that if $S|U_3$, it must be isomorphic to a member of the set

$$\text{UNITS} = \{U_0, U_1, U_2, U_3\}$$

We owe to KROHN-RHODES [1965] the following important structure theorem:

16   PROPOSITION: *Given a machine $M(f)$, we can simulate it by a cascade of flip-flops and the machines of (not necessarily all) the simple groups which divide the semigroup S_f.*

We shall prove this theorem in Section **8.3**. It is clear that to understand it we must first understand such notions of group theory as that of a simple group. These are presented in Section **8.2**. In the next portion of this section we shall explore those basic properties of the cascade which can be studied without reference to the semigroup.

Consider the reduced state-space $\hat{Q}$ of a cascade $M' \ominus_K M$ with state set $Q' \times Q$. We may introduce a relation on Q by saying that $\hat{q}_1$ is related to $\hat{q}_2$ only in the case in which there is a state $q \in Q$ such that both $\hat{q}_1$ and $\hat{q}_2$ correspond to states of $Q' \times Q$ with Q component equal to q. Since state reduction merges states, we cannot expect the collection of blocks corresponding to the elements of Q to be a partition. However, each input to the machine carries such a block into another—this follows from the motion of states of M under the input action. These considerations lead us to the notion of *cover*, due in various forms to HARTMANIS and STEARNS [1964], GINZBURG and YOELI [1964, 1965], and ZEIGER [1964].

For a machine M, and $x \in X_M$, let us introduce the notation

$$qx_M = \delta_M(q, x)$$

$$x_M: Q \rightarrow Q: q \mapsto \delta_M(q, x)$$

We use $\beta_M: Q_M \rightarrow Y_M$ to denote the state-output function of M.

For a machine M, S_M is the semigroup of functions $x_M: Q_M \rightarrow Q_M$ with $x \in X_M^*$.

17   DEFINITION: *A **cover** C for a machine M is a nonempty collection of nonempty sets whose union is Q_M, such that for each $w \in S_M$ and $R \in C$ there exists $R' \in C$ such that $Rw \subset R'$.*

The condition says that given $R \in C$ and $x \in X^*$ we can find $R' \in C$ (depending on x and R) such that $q \in R \Rightarrow qx_M \in R'$, *independent* of the choice of q within R.

18   DEFINITION: *If C is a cover for M, and N is a machine, then N **tells where M is in** C if*

(1) *$X_N = X_M$ and β_N maps Q_N onto C*

(2) *for each $x \in X_M$ and each $q \in Q_N$, $\beta_N(q) \cdot x_M \subset \beta_N(q \cdot x_M)$*

that is, N is a machine whose outputs are names of blocks of C, and N keeps track of how inputs to M move around the blocks of C considered as subsets of Q_M, but N need not tell us anything about how individual states move within the blocks of C. Note that a block of C may have an image lying in the intersection of two blocks of C, with the result that M and C need not determine N even up to isomorphism.

Given a machine M and a cover C, we may define a machine N which tells us where M is in C simply by taking

$$X_M = X_N \qquad C = Q_N = Y_N \qquad \beta_N(R) = R$$

and, for each $R \in C$ and $x \in X_N = X_M$, taking $R \cdot x_N$ to be some element of C which contains $R \cdot x_M = \{q \cdot x_M | q \in R\}$. Such a choice is always possible by the condition in the definition of a cover.

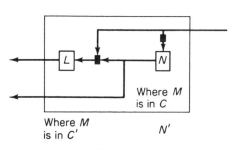

19   DEFINITION: *A cover C' is a **refinement** of the cover C if each set of C' is a subset of a set of C. It is **proper** if C is not a refinement of C'.*

Conversely to the discussion which led us to introduce the notion of a cover, we have:

Fig. 8.5

20   THEOREM: *Suppose the cover C' is a refinement of the cover C, and that N tells where M is in C, then we may find a machine N' which tells us where M is in C', that can be realized as a cascade of N with a new machine L.*

Proof. The job of L is to supply the additional information which speci-fies, given which set of C we are in, say R, the additional information as to which C' subset of R we are in.

Given an element R of C, we number its C' subsets in some arbitrary order as $R_1, R_2, \ldots, R_{j(R)}$, say, each $R_i \in C'$.

Let $l = \max \{j(R) | R \in C\} \geq 1$

Let $X_L = X_M \times Y_N$
$\quad Q_L = Y_L = \{1, \ldots, l\}$
$\quad \beta_L(i) = i$

The cascade of N and L is to tell us where M is in C', and so if the output of N is R, and the output of L is i, this should mean that the current state of M is an element R_i in C'. It should now be clear that we can always define $(\circ)x_L = \delta_L(\circ, x)$ to meet this requirement.   □

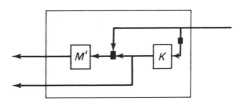

Fig. 8.6. Simulator of M.

21 If C' is the cover of Q_M by singletons (one-element sets), we conclude from **20** that given any cover C of M, and a machine K which tells where M is in C, we may cascade K with a machine M' to obtain a new ma-chine (see Fig. 8.6) which simu-lates M, that is, which tells where M is in C'. If we now refine C to obtain C'', we may break M' into two boxes L and M'' such that K cascades with L to tell us where M is in C', and M'' con-tains the remaining information for a complete simulation of M (see Fig. 8.7).

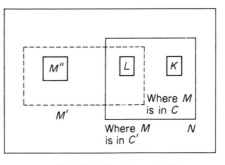

Fig. 8.7. Simulator of M.

Let us see how this notion of cover lends itself to lattice-theoretic treatment in the hands of HARTMANIS and STEARNS [1964].

22 DEFINITION: *A collection of distinct subsets* $\varphi = \{Q_\alpha\}$ *of the set* Q *is a set system if*
(i) $\cup Q_\alpha = Q$
(ii) $Q_\alpha \subset Q_\beta$ *implies* $Q_\alpha = Q_\beta$
Thus a set system φ subdivides Q into subsets so that every element of Q is contained in at least one subset (or block) of φ and no proper containment exists between the blocks of φ. Hence $\varphi = \max \varphi$, where for any collection φ', $\max \varphi' = \{R' \in \varphi' | R' \subset R \in \varphi'$ implies $R = R'\}$ is the collection of *maximal* subsets of Q'.

For a set system φ we shall write, for q, q' in Q,

$$q \equiv q'(\varphi)$$

if and only if there is a block in φ which contains both q and q'.

23 DEFINITION: *If φ_1 and φ_2 are set systems on Q, then $\varphi_1 \leq \varphi_2$ if and only if every block of φ_1 is contained in a block of φ_2.*

24 LEMMA: *The set of all set systems, L_Q, forms a lattice under the ordering of the above definition.*
   Proof. Let $\varphi_1 = \{Q_\alpha^1\}$ and $\varphi_2 = \{Q_\beta^2\}$ in L_Q. Then it can easily be verified that

$$\varphi_1 \cdot \varphi_2 = \text{g.l.b.} \ (\varphi_1, \varphi_2) = \max \{Q_\alpha^1 \cap Q_\beta^2\}$$
$$\varphi_1 + \varphi_2 = \text{l.u.b.} \ (\varphi_1, \varphi_2) = \max [\{Q_\alpha^1\} \cup \{Q_\beta^2\}] \qquad \square$$

We see from **4** that the partition pairs of a machine M form a pair algebra on $L \times L$ as soon as we make the:

25 DEFINITION: *Let L_1 and L_2 be finite lattices. Then a subset Δ of $L_1 \times L_2$ is a pair algebra on $L_1 \times L_2$ if and only if the two following postulates hold:*

   P_1 *(x_1, y_1) and (x_2, y_2) in Δ implies that $(x_1 \cdot x_2, y_1 \cdot y_2)$ and $(x_1 + x_2, y_1 + y_2)$ are in Δ.*
   P_2 *For any x in L_1 and y in L_2, $(x, 1)$ and $(0, y)$ are in Δ.*

Thus a pair algebra is a binary relation on $L_1 \times L_2$ which is closed under componentwise operations (P_1) and contains all the elements specified by P_2.

26 LEMMA: *If Δ is a pair algebra on $L_1 \times L_2$ and (x, y) is in Δ, then $x' \leq x$ and $y \leq y'$ implies that (x', y), (x, y') and (x', y') in Δ.*
   Proof. By P_2, (x', I) in Δ.
      By P_1, $(x' \cdot x, I \cdot y) = (x', y)$ is in Δ.
   The other two cases are similar. $\square$

Thus, if a pair is in the pair algebra Δ on $L_1 \times L_2$, we can obtain another pair by replacing the first component by a smaller element, or the second component by a larger element. The next definition characterizes the largest possible first component of a pair in Δ, and the smallest possible second component.

27 DEFINITION: *Let Δ be a pair algebra on $L_1 \times L_2$. For x in L_1 we define*

$$m(x) = \Pi \ \{y_i | (x, y_i) \ in \ \Delta\}$$

For y in L_2 we define

$$M(y) = \Sigma \ \{x_i | (x_i, y) \ in \ \Delta\}$$

28 Returning to the pair algebra of partition pairs, we see that π has the substitution property if and only if $m(\pi) \leq \pi$.

We now state some properties of pair algebras, culled from the 16 listed in Theorem 1 of HARTMANIS and STEARNS [1964]. The proofs are all left as simple exercises for the reader.

29 EXERCISE: If Δ is a pair algebra, then
    (i) $(M(y), y)$ and $(x, m(x))$ are in Δ.
    (ii) $y \geq m(x)$ if and only if (x, y) is in Δ.
    (iii) $x \leq M(y)$ if and only if (x, y) is in Δ.
    (iv) $M(m(x)) \geq x$.
    (v) $m(M(y)) \leq y$.
    (vi) $m^k(x) = 0$ if and only if $x \leq M^k(0)$.

We shall now define a pair algebra on the lattice of set systems associated with a machine M.

30 DEFINITION: *The pair (φ, φ') of set systems on the set of states of $M = (X, Y, Q, \delta, \beta)$ is a* **system pair** *on M if and only if for each block A of φ and each x in X, there exists at least one block B of φ' (depending both on A and on x) such that*

$$q \in A \qquad implies \qquad \delta(q, x) \in B$$

Clearly:

31 THEOREM: *The set Δ of all system pairs on Q of M is a pair algebra on $L_Q \times L_Q$.* $\square$

If φ is a set system on Q of M, then let $|\varphi|$ denote the number of blocks in φ and let $\#(\varphi)$ denote the number of elements in the largest block of φ.

32 THEOREM: *Let M be a machine and φ a set system on Q of M such that*

$$m(\varphi) \leq \varphi$$

Then M can be realized as a serial connection of two machines M_1 and M_2, where M_1 has $|\varphi|$ states and M_2 has $\#(\varphi)$ states.
Proof. The condition $m(\varphi) \leq \varphi$ just says that φ is a cover, and the result is immediate from the proof of Theorem **20**. $\square$

33 THEOREM: *Let φ_1 and φ_2 be set systems on M such that*

$$m(\varphi_1) \leq \varphi_1 \qquad m(\varphi_2) \leq \varphi_2 \qquad and \qquad \varphi_1 \cdot \varphi_2 = 0$$

Then M can be realized by a parallel connection of two machines M_1 and M_2 having $|\varphi_1|$ and $|\varphi_2|$ states, respectively.
Proof. Since $m(\varphi_i) \leq \varphi_i$, states contained in the same block of φ_i are mapped into a common block of φ_i. Thus each set system can be used to define a machine M_i whose states are the blocks of φ_i and whose transitions are defined by the state transitions of M. $\varphi_1 \cdot \varphi_2 = 0$ ensures that the state of M is completely specified by the state of the parallel composition of M_1 and M_2. $\square$

Explicit decomposition of some simple machines, after the style of the above theorems, are given in HARTMANIS and STEARNS [1964, 1966].

We close this section with a brief study of feedback in machines.

34 DEFINITION: *The state behavior of M has a feedback-free realization if and only if the present state of M is only a function of the last k inputs for some $k \leq n$, where $n = |Q|$.*

Recall from Exercise **3.3.24** that an FSL is *definite* if it can be realized by a finite automaton which possesses a feedback-free realization.

We now apply the previously developed concepts to the study of feedback in machines (HARTMANIS and STEARNS [1963, 1964]). We first introduce a new pair algebra Δ_f, which is important for this end:

35 DEFINITION: *Given $M = (Q, X, Y, \delta, \beta)$ and a function $f: Q \times X \to U$ (U any finite set); then (φ, φ') is in Δ_f if and only if for any set $C \subset B$, where B is a block of φ such that $f(q, x) = f(q', x)$ for all q, q', in C, we must have $\delta(C, x) \subset B'$ for some block B' of φ'.*

Again, we immediately have:

36 LEMMA: *The set Δ_f is a pair algebra.* $\square$

The m and M operators in Δ_f of M have a simple intuitive interpretation. For a given set system φ, the operator $m(\varphi)$ yields the smallest system (largest amount of information) which can be computed about the state of M after one operation if we know only some block of φ which contained the previous state of M, the input, and the f value. Similarly, the M operator gives for a given φ, the largest system $M(\varphi)$ (least amount of information) from which the block of φ containing the present state of M can be computed if we know the block of $M(\varphi)$ which contained the state of M, the input, and the f value.

37 THEOREM: *Let M be a reduced machine. Then the state of M is only a function of the last n inputs and the last n values of f if and only if (where $m^{i+1}(1) = m(m^i(1))$, and so on):*

    (i) $m^n(1) = 0$ *in* Δ_f
    (ii) $M^n(0) = 1$ *in* Δ_f

Proof. Conditions (i) and (ii) are equivalent by (vi) of Exercise **29** and thus we only have to show that (i) holds. From the definition we know that, if $m^n(k) = 0$, then from any input sequence of length n, and the corresponding n values of f, we can compute the state of M. If

$$m^n(1) = \varphi > 0$$

then there exist two states, q and p, and an input sequence $x_1 x_2 \ldots x_n$ such that this input sequence transfers q into q' and p into p', $q' \neq p'$, and the corresponding f sequences are identical for both transitions. Thus the state of M is not a function of only the last n inputs and f values. $\square$

The reader may prove the easy generalization:

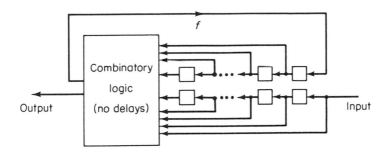

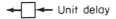 Unit delay

Fig. 8.8. A canonical form for the realization of M, using f for feedback.

38 EXERCISE: Let M be a reduced machine. Prove that $m^n(1) = \varphi$ in Δ_f if and only if there exists a function of the last n inputs and last n f values which selects a set of φ which contains the state of M.

39 DEFINITION: *The reduced machine M has a realization using $f: Q \times X \to U$ as feedback if and only if for some value n, the state of M is a function of the last n inputs and f values.*

A realization of M using f for feedback was given in Fig. 8.8. A schematic representation is given in Fig. 8.9.

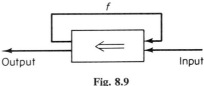

Fig. 8.9

40 *Note that this says that f is sufficient as feedback, not that it is necessary.* Observe that $m^k(1) = 0$ implies $m^{k+1}(1) = 0$, and that if r is the number of states in S, $m^r(Q)$ cannot be refined by further applications of the operator m. Then Theorem **37** immediately yields the

41 COROLLARY: *A reduced sequential machine M with r states can be realized using f for feedback if and only if the following (equivalent) conditions hold:*
    1. $m^r(1) = 0$ *in* Δ_f.
    2. $M^r(0) = 1$ *in* Δ_f.
HARTMANIS and STEARNS [1964] also derive, within their pair-algebra formalism, several results on feedback realizations originally due to LIU [1963], but we shall not discuss them here.

8.2   GROUPS AND DIVISIBILITY

It is our purpose in this section to present a number of results about finite groups and semigroups which play a crucial role in the theory of decomposition of finite automata. The first notion is that of a simple group, and the way such groups may be associated with arbitrary groups:

1 DEFINITION: *We say a group G with identity e is **simple** if it has only {e} and itself as normal subgroups.*

Given a group G, we call a series

2
$$G = G_0 \triangleright G_1 \triangleright \cdots \triangleright G_k = \{e\}$$

a *normal series* for G.

(Note that if $G \triangleright H \triangleright K$, it need not follow that $G \triangleright K$.) Since $G \triangleright H$ implies $G \triangleright H \triangleright \{e\}$, we see that any normal subgroup of G is contained in a normal series of G.

The *factors* of **2** are the factor groups G_i/G_{i+1}.

3 EXAMPLE: Consider $Z_K = \{0, 1, \ldots, K-1\}$ as a group under addition modulo K. Then Z_2 and Z_3 are simple. Since they are abelian, it is clear that

$$Z_6 \triangleright Z_3 \triangleright \{0\}$$

and
$$Z_6 \triangleright Z_2 \triangleright \{0\}$$

are two normal series for Z_6, and since

$$Z_6/Z_3 \cong Z_2 \cong Z_2/\{0\}$$

$$Z_6/Z_2 \cong Z_3 \cong Z_3/\{0\}$$

we see that they have the same factors but in different orders, i.e., they are "isomorphic," where:

4 We say that two normal series are *isomorphic* if their factors may be put into one-one correspondence such that corresponding factors are isomorphic.

We call the normal series

$$G = H_0 \triangleright H_1 \triangleright H_2 \triangleright \cdots \triangleright H_n = \{e\}$$

a *refinement* of **2** if every G_i is an H_j.

A *composition series* of a group is a normal series which has no proper refinements (i.e., the only refinements are those obtained by repeating groups already present).

The crucial result on groups we need for automata theory is

5 THE JORDAN-HÖLDER THEOREM: *Any two composition series of a group are isomorphic.*

Of course, any *finite* group *must* have a composition series.

If we consider a group as being built up, in some sense, from the factors of its composition series, the Jordan-Hölder theorem says that G uniquely determines its building blocks—but as Example **3** shows, G may be built up from these blocks in different ways.

For a proof of the Jordan-Hölder theorem see KUROSH [1956, pp. 77–78; 110–112] or any other good textbook on group theory.

One proof of the Jordan-Hölder theorem rests on:

6 ZASSENHAUS' LEMMA: *If A, A', B and B' are subgroups of a group G, with $A' \triangleleft A$, $B' \triangleleft B$.*

Then $A'(A \cap B') \triangleleft A'(A \cap B)$
$B'(B \cap A') \triangleleft B'(B \cap A)$
and the corresponding factor groups are isomorphic:

$$A'(A \cap B)/A'(A \cap B') \cong B'(B \cap A)/B'(B \cap A')$$

which is used to prove

7 SCHREIER'S THEOREM: *Any two normal series of an arbitrary group have isomorphic refinements.*

This immediately yields the Jordan-Hölder Theorem, since the only refinements of two composition series are themselves.

8 EXERCISE: Show that a normal series is a composition series iff each factor is simple. [Hint: First prove $A \rhd B \rhd C$ and $A \rhd C \Rightarrow A/C \rhd B/C$.]

9 EXERCISE: Show that if P is a factor of a composition series of G, then P is simple and $P|G$.

The converse of **9** is *not* true, since a *simple* group may have nontrivial (though not normal) subgroups. For example, if A_n (see below) is the alternating group on n letters, both A_3 and A_5 are simple, but we still have $A_3|A_5$.

Now that we know how to uniquely associate a collection of simple groups with a finite group, we should learn what these simple groups are.

10 THEOREM: *A cyclic group is simple iff it is of prime order.*
Proof. Let $G = \langle a \rangle$ have order m, that is, $a^m = e$, but $a^n \neq e$ for $0 < n < m$. If m is prime, every element a^i except e generates the whole group, which is thus simple having no proper subgroups, normal or otherwise. If m has a proper prime factor p, $m = jp$, $j \neq 1$, then $\langle a^j \rangle$ is a cyclic subgroup of order p, and is thus a simple subgroup of G, being a normal subgroup since every subgroup of an abelian group is normal. $\square$

11 THEOREM: *Every abelian group G is isomorphic to the direct product of* *cyclic groups whose order is a power of a prime. Thus the composition factors of G are isomorphic to Z_p, for those primes p that divide $|G|$.*

Proof. For the first part, we must refer the reader to a text on group theory. But the reader may then deduce the second part, using Theorem **10**. □

Note that Z_4 is not isomorphic to $Z_2 \times Z_2$—in adding numbers expressed in binary notation, componentwise addition is modified by carry digits.

Since we shall show that any group machine with group G can be simulated by a cascade of group machines, one for each factor in G's composition series, it follows that every machine with abelian group G for its semigroup may be simulated by a composition of mod p counters for primes p dividing $|G|$.

In fact, an even wider class of groups have only "counters" (i.e., cyclic groups) for their composition factors. We may sum these up in a

12   DEFINITION: *A group is **solvable** iff it has a normal series in which every quotient is abelian (so that its composition factors are all "counters").*

We owe to FEIT and THOMPSON [1963] the knowledge that

13   THEOREM: *Every group of odd order is solvable.*

This statement is deceptive in its simplicity—the paper of which this is the central result is 244 pages long. (The proof is omitted here.) Anyway, the theorem tells us that no matter how we form a group, if it has an odd number of elements, then all its composition factors are cyclic groups of prime order.

It is *not* true that all groups of even order are solvable. It is well known (see any good group theory textbook) that A_n (the alternating group, comprising all permutations of n letters which may be obtained by an even number of transpositions of pairs of letters) is simple unless $n = 4$. $A_2 \cong Z_1$, $A_3 \cong Z_3$, but A_n is not abelian for $n > 5$ and so A_n is not solvable for $n > 5$.

It is a dismaying fact that simple groups can be extremely complex. It is not our task to classify these groups here, but let us at least give a quick survey (compiled by Fred S. Roberts, to whom I also owe Exercise **5.23**) of some of the SNAGs (simple nonabelian groups).

The following results from the textbook by BURNSIDE [1897, see especially pages 365, 367, 370] give some indication of the progress made in finding simple groups by the end of the 19th century:

(1) If the order of a group G contains less than four prime factors, then G is simple if and only if it is cyclic of prime order. [The proof rests on the demonstration (given at some length in Burnside) that all groups of orders p_1, p_1^2, $p_1 p_2$, p_1^3, $p_1^2 p_2$, or $p_1 p_2 p_3$ (for p_i prime, $i = 1, 2, 3$) are solvable.]

(2) The only simple groups whose orders are products of four or five primes are groups of orders 60, 168, 660, and 1092. For each of these orders, the simple group of that order is unique. [For example, the unique simple group of order 60 is A_5, the alternating group on 5 letters.]

(3) As we have already observed, for every $n > 4$, the group A_n (alternating group on n letters) is a simple nonabelian group of order $n!/2$. Thus there are infinitely many simple groups.

(4) A group of even order cannot be simple unless 12, 16, or 56 is a factor of the order (with the exception of the trivial group of order 2).

(5) The only simple groups of order up to 1092 have either prime order or order 60, 168, 360, 504, 660, or 1092. In each case, there is only one simple group of the given order.

Starting formally with the work of L. E. DICKSON [1901], the emphasis has shifted from the search for a complete determination of all simple groups of any higher order to the orderly classification of all *known* simple groups. We shall turn to a discussion of this approach shortly. First, however, it is of interest to ask: Is it true that whenever a simple group of a given order exists, it is unique (up to isomorphism)? (An affirmative answer would be of some interest machine-theoretically. Namely, then we would need at most one type of "building block" of each fixed size.)

The answer to the question is unfortunately negative (DICKSON [1901, p. 259, p. 309]; ARTIN [1955b, p. 458]): There are two distinct simple groups of order 20,160. The coincidences in order for nonisomorphic simple groups are summarized for all known simple groups in Artin's classic paper. The only coincidences for orders different from 20,160 involve the groups he calls $S_{2n}(q)$ and $0_{2n+1}(q)$, for $2n \geq 6$. These groups have orders at least $2^9.3^4.5.7$, which is 1,461,520. (See ARTIN [1955b, pp. 458, 460]).

For every classification suggested so far, there have been new simple groups found which do not belong to any of the classes involved. It is of interest to survey the history of classification attempts, emphasizing in very general terms the techniques used to describe or build up different classes of simple groups. The following discussion is based in part on Wilhelm Magnus' introduction to the 1958 reprint of DICKSON [1901] and in part on ARTIN's [1955b] paper.

The first formal classification of all known simple groups was published in 1901 by Dickson in his classic book *Linear Groups*. His work is based heavily on that of such predecessors as Jordan, Burnside, Netto, and Weber. Dickson divided all known simple groups into 10 infinite classes and used this classification to list all then known finite simple groups of order less than one billion. Mostly, his work is a summary of known results, using vastly improved proof techniques, especially the theory of Galois fields. In subsequent papers, Dickson discovered two more infinite classes of finite simple groups.

Among other things, Dickson listed as many isomorphisms among groups of different classes as he could discover. (We have already seen above the interest of the question of whether or not two simple groups of the same order are isomorphic.) It was left to DIEUDONNÉ [1951] to prove that these, indeed, were the only isomorphisms among the groups known to Dickson.

DIEUDONNÉ [1948] also incorporated all new proof techniques which had been invented after Dickson and brought Dickson's classification up to date. It is remarkable, however, that there was no basic difference between Dieudonné's classification and Dickson's. In particular, no new finite simple groups had been discovered.

It was CHEVALLEY [1955] who finally discovered a class of simple groups not known to Dickson. His technique was to represent a simple group as a group of automorphisms of a simple Lie algebra (cf. CARTER [1965]).

ARTIN [1955] was able to incorporate these groups in a new classification scheme which involved fewer basic types of groups. Moreover, Artin's schema made proofs of simplicity and isomorphism considerably shorter. Artin's classification, unfortunately, met the same fate as that of Dickson. In 1960, Suzuki proved the following theorem: *For every $n \geq 1$, there is a group $G(q)$ with $q = 2^{2n+1}$ such that $G(q)$ is simple and has order $q^2(q - 1)(q^2 + 1)$.*

Since each such order is relatively prime to 3, and each known simple group (except the trivial group of order 2) has order divisible by 3, it followed that each $G(q)$ was a new simple group. Thus in particular, taking $n = 1$ and hence $q = 8$, there is a simple group of order $2^6.7.(2^6 + 1) = 29,120$ which was unknown to both Dickson and Artin.

Suzuki's examples were just one of a whole rash of new infinite families of simple groups, discovered by Suzuki, Steinberg, Tits, and Ree. Most of these examples are based on the technique Chevalley first used in getting a new type of simple group, namely that simple groups can be obtained as groups of automorphisms of simple Lie algebras. CARTER [1965] wrote a survey article describing the construction of these new simple groups, and we refer the reader to this article for further information on simple groups.

In what follows, we shall assume that all groups and semigroups are *finite.* We now show that our concept of divisibility has rather special implications for groups:

14   LEMMA: *If G' is a group dividing the finite semigroup S:*

$$S \supset S'' \xrightarrow{z} G'$$

then there is a group $G \subset S$ such that $Z(G) = G'$ (that is, G' is isomorphic to a factor group of G).

Proof. Since S is finite, we may find a subsemigroup S_1 of S'' such that $Z(S_1) = G'$, and such that for any proper subsemigroup S_2 of S_1, $Z(S_2) \neq G'$.

We show that S_1 has no proper left or right ideals, and is thus the desired group G.

Suppose there were a right ideal $S_2 \subset S_1$. Then S_2 contains an idempotent e. Since $Z(e^2) = Z(e)$, we must have $Z(e) = e_{G'}$.

Take any $g \in G'$ and an $s \in S_1$ with $Z(s) = g$. Then $es \in S_2$, since e is in the right ideal S_2. Thus $Z(es) = Z(e)Z(s) = e_{G'}g = g$, and so $Z(S_2) = G'$, whence $S_1 = S_2$.

Similarly, S_1 contains no proper left ideals.   □

15   DEFINITION: *S is **simple (left simple, right simple)** iff S contains no proper two-sided (left, right) ideal.*

*If S has a zero element 0, then S is called **0-simple** (**left 0-simple, right 0-simple**) if 0 is the only proper two-sided (left, right) ideal of S.*
*S is called **left** (**right**) **cancellative** if, for all a, x, y in S, ax = ay (xa = ya) implies x = y.*

16 EXERCISE: Show that if S has a zero element 0, then if 0 is the only proper (left, right) ideal of S, it follows that $S^2 \neq 0$.

17 DEFINITION: *S is a **right group** if S is right simple and left cancellative, i.e., if for any a, b in S, there is one and only one x in S such that ax = b.*
*S is a **right-zero semigroup** if all its elements are right zeros, i.e., if for all x, y in S, we have xy = y.*
Such an S is thus a right group.
Given two semigroups S_1, S_2, we define their direct product to be $S_1 \times S_2$ with term-by-term multiplication; that is, $(s_1, s_2)(s_1', s_2') = (s_1 s_1', s_2 s_2')$.

18 EXERCISE: Show that $S_1 \times S_2$ is a semigroup, and is a monoid iff both S_1 and S_2 are monoids. Show also that the direct product of two right groups is a right group.

19 PROPOSITION: *Every idempotent element of a right-simple semigroup S is a left-identity element of S.*
   Proof. Let e be an idempotent. Since eS is a right ideal, we must have $eS = S$, so that given $a \in S$, we find x such that $ex = a$.

Then
$$ea = e^2 x = ex = a \qquad \qquad \square$$

20 THEOREM: *The following are equivalent for finite semigroups:*
   (i)   *S is a right group.*
   (ii) *S is right simple.*
   (iii) *S is the direct product $G \times E$ of a group G and right-zero semigroup E.*
   Proof. (iii) $\Rightarrow$ (i) : Trivial.
           (i) $\Rightarrow$ (ii) : Trivial.
           (ii) $\Rightarrow$ (iii): Let E be the set of idempotents of S. Since S is finite, $E \neq \emptyset$. Every element of E is a left-identity element of S. In particular, $ef = f$ for every e, f in E, and so E is a right-zero subsemigroup of S.
   Clearly S is *left-cancellative* (so that (ii) $\Rightarrow$ (i)), for were we to have $sx = sy$ for some s and $x \neq y$, the sS would be a proper right ideal of S.
   We next prove that if $e \in E$, then Se is a *subgroup* of S with two-sided identity element e. If $a \in Se$, we can solve $ax = e$ for x in S. But then $a(xe) = e^2 = e$, and so a has the right inverse xe in Se.
   Let g be a fixed element of E, and let G be the group Sg. Form the direct product $G \times E$, and define the map

$$\varphi \times \varphi: \; G \times E \rightarrow S \quad \text{by} \quad (a, e)\varphi = ae \; (a \text{ in } G, \, e \text{ in } E)$$

φ is a homomorphism since

$$[(a, e)\varphi] \cdot [(b, f)\varphi] = (ae)(bf) = a(eb)f = abf$$
$$[(a, e) \cdot (b, f)]\varphi = (ab, ef)\varphi = (ab)(ef) = abf$$

To see that φ is one-one, suppose $(a, e)\varphi = (b, f)\varphi$, that is, $ae = bf$. $(a, b \in G;$ $e, f \in E)$. Since g is the identity element of G,

$$a = ag = aeg = bfg = bg = b$$

Hence $ae = af$. Since S is left-cancellative, $e = f$.

Finally, to show that φ maps $G \times E$ onto S, let $a \in S$. Solve $ae = a$ for e in S. Then $ae^2 = ae$, and $e^2 = e$ by left-cancellation, hence $e \in E$. Then $ag \in Sg = G$, and $(ag, e)\varphi = age = ae = a$. Hence φ is an isomorphism: $G \times E \cong S$. □

21 COROLLARY: *If S is a left-simple finite semigroup, then $S \cong G \times L_A$, where G is a group, and L_A is a set A with left-zero multiplication.* □

The remainder of this section is designed to appraise the reader of some of the richness of theorems available in the algebraic theory of semigroups. However, none of this material is required in later sections, and so it may be omitted without detriment to their understanding.

We shall find that Corollary **21** is most useful in Section **3**. It is thus of some interest to see that there is a very powerful structure theorem—the Rees theorem—of which it is a special case. We shall thus state the Rees theorem for finite semigroups and deduce Corollary **21** from it. For a proof of the Rees theorem, and other useful structure theorems, see CLIFFORD and PRESTON [1961], and KROHN, RHODES, and TILSON [1968b].

Let G be a group. Then G^0 is the semigroup $G \cup \{0\}$ with $g0 = 0g = 0$ for all g in G^0.

Let X and Y be any sets. By an $X \times Y$ *matrix over* G^0 we mean a mapping A of $X \times Y$ into G^0.

By a *Rees $X \times Y$ matrix over* G^0 we mean an $X \times Y$ matrix over G^0 having at most one nonzero element. If $a \in G$, $x \in X$, $y \in Y$, then $(a)_{xy}$ will denote the Rees $X \times Y$ matrix over G^0 having a in the (x, y) position and 0 elsewhere.

Now we cannot hope to multiply two $X \times Y$ matrices together directly if $X \neq Y$. We then introduce a "sandwich" matrix $P = (p_{yx})$, which is an arbitrary but fixed $Y \times X$ matrix over G^0. We define a binary operation by

$$A \circ A' = APA'$$

that is,

$$(a)_{xy} \circ (a')_{x'y'} = (ap_{yx'}a')_{xy'}$$

This operation is clearly associative. Thus the set of all Rees $X \times Y$ matrices over G^0 is a semigroup with respect to the binary operation $(\circ)$; we call it the *Rees $X \times Y$ matrix semigroup over the group with zero G^0 with sandwich matrix P* and denote it by

$$\mathfrak{M}^0(G; X, Y; P)$$

We call G the *structure group* of $\mathfrak{M}^0$. We say $\mathfrak{M}^0$ is *regular* if P is nonzero at least once in each row and column.

Alternatively, we may start with $G \times X \times Y$ and define $(\circ)$ by

$$(a; x, y) \circ (a'; x', y') = (a p_{yx'} a'; x, y')$$

$\mathfrak{M}^0(G; X, Y; P)$ is then this semigroup with a 0 adjoined, where we may identify 0 with $(0; x, y)$ for all x and y.

The Rees theorem may then be stated with beautiful simplicity:

22   THEOREM: *A semigroup is 0-simple iff it is isomorphic with a regular Rees matrix semigroup over a group with zero.*

We may deduce Corollary **21** as follows:

If S is right simple, it is certainly simple, and so $S \cup \{0\}$ is isomorphic to some $\mathfrak{M}^0(G; X, Y; P)$. But the right ideal generated by $(a; x, y)$ can only contain elements of the form $(a'; x, y')$ for the same x, and so we conclude that $|X| = 1$.

Thus each element in S can be written (a, y) with $a \in G$, and $y \in Y$, and multiplication $(a; y)(a'; y') = (a p_y a'; y')$.

We thus conclude that $S \to G \times A: (a; y) \mapsto (a p_y, y)$ is an isomorphism (using regularity to tell us that each p_y is nonzero), and we have Corollary **21**.

We close this section by drawing to the reader's attention the fact that semigroup theory has a notion of building semigroups out of smaller semigroups other than that associated with cascading of machines, which is also called "decomposition." By a *decomposition* of a semigroup S we mean a partition of S into the union of disjoint subsemigroups $S_\alpha (\alpha \in \Omega)$. Such a decomposition is not complete, of course, until we specify how we multiply elements lying in distinct subsemigroups.

To give some of the flavor of this approach, we recall some elementary terminology. A (lower) *semilattice* Y is a partially ordered set such that every pair of elements $\{a, b\}$ has a *meet* in Y, that is, an element $a \wedge b$ such that if $y \leq a$ and $y \leq b$, then $y \leq a \wedge b$, while $a \wedge b \leq a$ and $a \wedge b \leq b$. Note that $a \leq b$ iff $a \wedge b = a$.

Let $S = \cup \{S_\alpha | \alpha \in \Omega\}$. If for each $\alpha, \beta \in \Omega$ there is a γ such that $S_\alpha S_\beta \subset S_\gamma$, we may define a multiplication on Ω by $\alpha \beta = \gamma$.

If this turns Ω into a semilattice under the relation $\alpha \leq \beta$ iff $\alpha \beta = \alpha$, we say that S is *the union of the semilattice Ω of semigroups $S_\alpha (\alpha \in \Omega)$*.

The smallest [left, right] two-sided ideal containing a is just $[S^1 a, a S^1] S^1 a S^1$. We call each ideal of the form $S^1 a S^1$ a *principal ideal* of S.

The *Green's relations* on a semigroup are obtained by considering elements to be equivalent when they generate the same ideals, in some sense. Precisely,

$$a\mathcal{L}b \text{ iff } S^1a = S^1b$$
$$a\mathcal{R}b \text{ iff } aS^1 = bS^1$$
$$a\mathcal{H}b \text{ iff } a\mathcal{L}b \text{ and } a\mathcal{R}b$$
$$a\mathcal{D}b \text{ iff there exists } c \text{ such that } a\mathcal{L}c \text{ and } c\mathcal{R}b$$
$$a\mathcal{J}b \text{ iff } S^1aS^1 = S^1bS^1$$

These are all equivalence relations. We have $\mathcal{D} \subset \mathcal{J}$ ($\mathcal{D} = \mathcal{J}$ if S is finite); $\mathcal{H} \subset \mathcal{L}, \mathcal{R}; \mathcal{L}, \mathcal{R} \subset \mathcal{D}$. Thus S may be decomposed into a union of $\mathcal{J}$ classes, each $\mathcal{J}$ class into a union of $\mathcal{D}$ classes, and so on. These decompositions have many beautiful properties, treated at length in Chapter 2 of CLIFFORD and PRESTON [1961]. In fact, these relations are intimately related with the Rees theorem.

We say S is *simple* if it has no proper ideals (that is, $A \subset S$ and $S^1AS^1 \subset A$ implies $A = S$); and *completely simple* if it is simple and contains a primitive idempotent e (that is, $e^2 = e$, and, for any other idempotent f, we must have $ef = fe = e$).

We may now quote a striking decomposition theorem due to Clifford:

23   THEOREM: *The following assertions concerning a semigroup S are equivalent:*

(1) *S is a union of groups.*

(2) *S is a union of completely simple semigroups.*

(3) *S is a semilattice Y of completely simple semigroups $S_\alpha (\alpha \in y)$, where Y is the semilattice of principal ideals, and each S_α is a $\mathcal{J}$ class of S.*

With extra conditions on S, one may completely characterize the multiplication in S of elements lying in different subgroups (see CLIFFORD and PRESTON [1961, Sec. 4.2]).

For commutative semigroups, we may get an even more striking decomposition result. If S is commutative, and a and b are in S, we say a *divides* b, $a|b$, iff there is an x in S^1 such that $ax = b$. We say S is *archimedean* if for every a and b in S there exists a positive integer n such that $a|b^n$. (For instance, if we consider R^+, the positive reals under addition, $a|b$ iff $a \leq b$ and R^+ is clearly archimedean.)

TAMURA and KIMURA (see CLIFFORD and PRESTON [1961, Sec. 4.3]) proved the:

24   THEOREM: *Every commutative semigroup S is uniquely expressible as a semi-lattice Y of archimedean semigroups $S_\alpha(\alpha \in Y)$.*

8.3   A PROOF OF THE DECOMPOSITION THEOREM

We now give a proof of the theorem (KROHN and RHODES [1965]) that tells us what simple groups we need to build arbitrary machines by repeated cascading with flip-flops:

1   THEOREM: *Any machine with semigroup S can be simulated by a cascade of flip-flops and machines of simple groups which divide S.*

We shall first prove this for machines whose inputs either permute the states or reset them.

2 DEFINITION: *A **PR-machine** is one for which every input produces either a permutation or a reset, and the output of the machine is its state, i.e., given* $x \in X$,

either $\delta(\circ, x): Q \to Q$ is 1-1 (a permutation)

or $\cdot\delta(\circ, x): Q \to Q$ is a constant map (a reset)

The permutations generate a group, called the **group** of the *PR*-machine, which is not quite the semigroup of the machine, but is obtained from it by deleting resets.

3 LEMMA: *If M is a PR-machine with permutation group G, then M can be simulated by a cascade of M(G) and an identity-reset machine with the same state space as M.*

Proof. In the diagrams below, we label each machine with its state at time t. s on a line means that the line carries signal s at time t; s/ss' on a line means that the line carries signal s at time t and signal ss' at time $t + 1$. IR is an identity-reset machine with state set Q, the same as that of M. The identity input of IR is 1, while input $q \neq 1$ resets it to state q. $M(G)$ is the machine of group G. h_1 codes "reset to state q" as $(q, 1)$; and "permute by g" as $(1, g)$. h_2 codes $(1, g)$ as $(1, g)$, but for $q \neq 1$ codes (q, g) as $(g^{-1}(q), g)$. h_3 codes (q, g) as $g(q)$, and it is the output of h_3 that serves to indicate the state of M in our simulation. To reset to q', with $M(G)$ initially in state g, and IR initially in state q (thus simulating M in state $g(q)$) we have the action shown in Fig. 8.10. This rather complicated action is required because we cannot reset $M(G)$ back to 1 without using a loop.

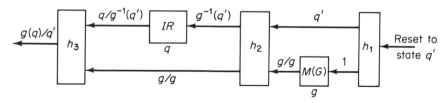

Fig. 8.10

To permute the state by g', we have the action shown in Fig. 8.11. This completes our construction.   □

4 LEMMA: *If G is a group, then M(G) can be simulated by a cascade of the machines of the composition factors of G, and so a fortiori of simple groups which divide G.*

Proof. It will be enough to verify that, given a group G and a normal

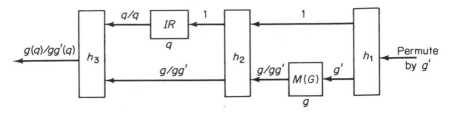

Fig. 8.11

subgroup H, we can simulate $M(G)$ by a cascade of $M(H)$ and $M(G/H)$. This is because repeated application of the lemma yields the full result by induction: Suppose $G = G_0 \rhd G_1 \rhd \cdots \rhd G_{k-1} \rhd G_k \rhd \{1\}$. Then construct $M(G_{k-1})$ by cascading $M(G_{k-1}/G_k)$ with $M(G_k)$; $M(G_{k-2})$ from $M(G_{k-2}/G_{k-1})$ and $M(G_{k-1})$, and so on; until finally we construct $M(G)$ as a cascade of the machines of its composition factors.

Let $H \lhd G$ and $K \cong G/H$ (see Fig. 8.12). For every coset $[g]$ of H in

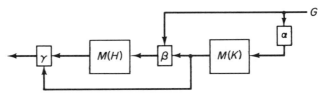

Fig. 8.12

G we choose a fixed coset leader denoted by g'. Suppose $M(K)$ is in state $[a]$ corresponding to coset leader a' and $M(H)$ is in state h, and we interpret, via γ, the pair $(h, [a])$ as coding the element $\hat{g} = ha'$ of G. If, as seems natural, we use α to code an input g in G as an input $[g]$ to $M(K)$, so that $M(K)$ changes state to $[a][g] = [a'g]$, then the input $\beta(g, [a])$ to $M(H)$ will change its state to $h\beta(g, [a])$. Thus, if the new state is to correspond to $\hat{g}g'$, we must have $h\beta(g, [a])(a'g)' = \hat{g}g' = ha'g$ so that $\beta(g, [a]) = (a'g)[(a'g)']^{-1}$, which clearly lies in H. The mappings α, β, γ are thus defined as follows:

$$\alpha\colon G \to K\colon g \to [g]$$
$$\beta\colon G \times K \to H\colon (g, [a]) \to (a'g)[(a'g)']^{-1}$$
$$\gamma\colon H \times K \to G\colon (h, [a]) \to ha'$$

Then the above cascade indeed simulates $M(G)$—more precisely, if at time t the input is g' and the output is g, then at time $t + 1$ the output will be gg'. $\square$

Thus **1** is true for permutation-reset machines. To prove it true for all machines, it suffices to prove it true for all semigroup machines, since every machine is simulatable by the machine of its semigroup. Our proof rests on a critical lemma, slightly improving one of KROHN and RHODES [1965]:

5 LEMMA: *Let S be a finite semigroup. Then either*

(i)   *S is a cyclic semigroup;*

(ii) *S is right-simple (that is, S has no proper right ideals); or*

(iii) *∃ a proper right ideal T and a proper subsemigroup V of S for which $S = T \cup V$, and either:*

(a) *there is an element s in S such that $V = sT$; or*

(b) *T is a two-sided ideal.*

Proof. Either case (ii) holds, or we can find a maximal proper right ideal T of S.

Suppose there exists $s \in S$ such that $sT \not\subseteq T$. Then $sT \cup T$ is a right ideal properly containing T, and so must equal S. But then $V = sT$ is a *proper* subsemigroup, since finiteness implies $\#(sT) \leq \#(T) < \#(S)$.

In the remaining case, $sT \subset T$ for all $s \in S$, and so T is a two-sided ideal of S. Then either $S - T$ is a subsemigroup, and we are done, or we can find $a, b \in S - T$ with $ab \in T$. Then $T' = aS \cup T$ is a right ideal. Using finiteness, and recalling that $aT \subset T$ by assumption, we see that it is proper, since $\#(T') \leq \#[a(S - T - b)] + \#(T) \leq \#(S) - 1$, and so must equal T. Thus $aS \subset T$, and so $\{a\} \cup T$ is a right ideal, hence $\{a\} \cup T = S$ so that $\{a\} = S - T$. Then either $\langle a \rangle = S$ and case (i) holds, or we may take $V = \langle a \rangle$, and case (iii) holds.   □

This lemma provides the basis for the proof of **1**. Before so applying it, we may note a connection with the regular languages studied in Section **3.3**.

6 EXERCISE: For a regular set $R \subseteq X^*$ let $S(R)$ be the finite semigroup of the minimal finite state acceptor, $M(\chi_R)$, of R. We say the set R is *group-free* if $S(R)$ is *combinatorial*, i.e., has no subgroup with more than one element. We say that R is *star-free* if it can be obtained from finite sets by a finite number of applications of the $\cup$ (union), · (set product), and $^-$ (complement with respect to X^*) operations.

(i) Prove that if S is a finite combinatorial semigroup, then either S is cyclic with period 1, or is a right-zero semigroup, or is the union of two proper combinatorial subsemigroups.

(ii) Consider a finite transformation semigroup (Q, S) and any map $X \to S$ which extends to a homomorphism $\varphi \colon X^* \to S$. For each a and b in Q let $S_{ab} = \{x \in X^* | a \cdot \varphi(x) = b\}$. Use (i) to prove, by induction, that if S is combinatorial, each S_{ab} is star-free.

(iii) Deduce from (ii) that if R is group-free, then it is star-free.

The result (iii) and its converse are due to PAPERT and MCNAUGHTON [1966], but the proof of (iii) above is new. For another proof, see SCHÜTZENBERGER [1966] and MEYER [1968, and see Exercise **5.22** below]. We now sketch the proof of the converse. Say that a regular set $R \subset X^*$ is *noncounting* iff there is an integer $k_R \geq 0$ such that for all $x, y, z \in X^*$

$$xy^{k_R}z \in R \quad \Leftrightarrow \quad xy^{k_R+1}z \in R$$

(iv) Prove that every star-free set is a noncounting regular set by considering the numbers max $\{k_u, k_v\}$, k_u, and 2 max $\{k_u, k_v\}$ in connection with $U \cup V$, $\bar{U}$, and $U \cdot V$.

(v) Prove that the semigroup S is combinatorial if there is an integer k such that $s^{k+1} = s^k$ for all s in S. Deduce that every noncounting regular set (and thus every star-free set) is a group-free regular set.

Returning to the proof of Theorem **1**, let us first settle cases (i) and (ii) of Lemma **5**.

7 LEMMA: *If S is a cyclic semigroup, then* **1** *holds for S.*

Proof. Suppose S is a cyclic semigroup with index r and period m. Let A be a cyclic semigroup with index r and period 1, and let B be a cyclic group with period m.

The reader may easily check that $M(S)$ may be simulated by a cascade of $M(A)$ and $M(B)$. Thanks to Lemma **4**, to complete the proof we need only show that $M(A)$ can be simulated by a cascade of flip-flops. To do this we cascade r flip-flops, decode the state of the cascade as s if only the first s flip-flops are in state 1; and, when the system input is t, box s flips to state 1 if $s \leq t$ or box $t - s$ is in state 1. $\square$

8 LEMMA: *If S is right simple, then* **1** *holds for S.*

Proof. By Corollary **2.17**, S is the direct product of a group G and a right-zero semigroup B. But $M(B)$ is then a reset machine and so can be built of flip-flops. Since $M(S)$ can be obtained as a parallel composition of $M(G)$ and $M(B)$, and $G|S$, the result clearly follows, if we use Lemma **4**. $\square$

To tackle case (iii) we need the following lemmas, inspired by [ZEIGER, 1967]:

9 LEMMA: *Let the semigroup $S = T \cup V$, where T is a proper right ideal and V is a proper subsemigroup. Then $M(S)$ can be simulated by a cascade of machines whose semigroups only involve T, V, resets, identities, and flip-flops.*

Proof. Case 1. $ST = S$. (Note that this case holds if T is a maximal right ideal which is not two-sided.) Consider Fig. 8.13; M_1 has state-set T,

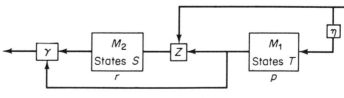

Fig. 8.13

M_2 has state-set S. If the cascade is in state $(p, r) \in T \times S$, the output $\gamma(p, r) = r \cdot p$. The input set is S. If the input u is in T

$$\eta(u) = \text{reset to } u; \quad Z_p(u) = p$$

If u is not in T,

$$\eta(u) = u \qquad Z_p(u) = 1$$

In either case $p \cdot \eta(u)$ is in T and the next state encodes $(r \cdot p) \cdot u$: For u not in T we have $\gamma(p \cdot u, r) = r \cdot (p \cdot u)$. For u in T, we have $\gamma(u, r \cdot p) = (r \cdot p) \cdot u$. Clearly, $S_1 | V \cup \{\text{resets}\}$ and $S_2 | T^1$.

Case 2. Let us now tackle the case of $ST \neq S$. If we start $M(S)$ in a state belonging to ST, we can never leave ST, and so we can use the construction of Lemma **9**. The problem is to handle the fact that we may start in a state not contained in ST. Our idea then is this—if we start in a state $v \in V$ and receive input sequence $v_1, \ldots, v_n, t, s_1, \ldots, s_m$, where each v_j is in V, t is in T, and the s_i are arbitrary, we use an $M(V^1)$ machine to compute $v \cdot v_1 \cdot \ldots \cdot v_n$. On receiving T we switch to the ST-machine—built as a cascade of $M(T^1)$ and $M(V \cup \text{resets})$—to compute $ts_1 \ldots s_m$, which certainly lies in ST since T is a right ideal. Our output decoder then reads off the result $vv_1 \ldots v_n ts_1 \ldots s_n$, while a flip-flop controls the switching.

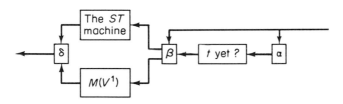

Fig. 8.14

The [t yet ?] box is just a flip-flop with states 0 and 1. α codes an element of $V - T$ as the identity, and an element of T as a reset to 1. If the box is initially in state 1, it will change to state 1 only if an element of T has occurred in the input sequence.

$$\beta_x(t) = \begin{pmatrix} t \\ 1 \end{pmatrix} \qquad \text{for } x = 0 \text{ or } 1 \text{ and } t \in T$$

$$\beta_x(v) = \begin{cases} \begin{pmatrix} 1 \\ v \end{pmatrix} & \text{for } x = 0 \text{ and } v \in V - T \\[2ex] \begin{pmatrix} v \\ 1 \end{pmatrix} & \text{for } x = 1 \text{ and } v \in V - T \end{cases}$$

Thus β always sends inputs to the ST-machine, unless the input is an element of $V - T$ arriving before any element of T has occurred in the input sequence. Finally, $\delta(v, t) = v \cdot t$.

Then the reader may check that if we start this cascade in state $\frac{1}{s} 0$ if s is in V, or state $\frac{s}{1} 1$ if s is in T, its response to subsequent inputs will always simulate the behavior of $M(S)$ started in state s. $\square$

The reader may wish to try replacing the above two-part proof by a more straightforward one. In doing so, he should bear in mind that cutting down a semigroup S to its actions on a proper right ideal T of S need not reduce the size of S; that is, it may be that for all $s \neq s'$, we have $t \mapsto ts \neq t \mapsto ts'$ as maps from T to T. For example, given any set T, consider $F_R(T)$, the semigroup of all maps $T \rightarrow T$, and identify T with the constant maps in $F_R(T)$.

Unfortunately, Lemma **9** does not immediately tell us that **1** is true for all semigroups S. This is because, although we know from Lemma **3** that resets can be peeled off a group machine in the form of flip-flops, it is an open problem whether or not $M(T^1 \cup \text{resets})$ can be obtained from $M(T)$ by cascading with flip-flops. However, this lacuna can be filled by the following:

10   EXERCISE: Show that if $M(T)$ can be simulated by a cascade of group machines and flip-flops, then $M(T^1 \cup \text{resets})$ can be simulated by a cascade of the same group machines and perhaps additional flip-flops. [Hint: Use **3** and Induction.]

11   OPEN QUESTION: Can, in general, $M(T^1 \cup \text{resets})$ be simulated by a cascade of $M(T)$ and flip-flops?

Using **3** and **10,** you will be able, with a simple modification of the proofs of **7** and **8,** to solve the next two exercises.

12   EXERCISE: If S is a cyclic semigroup, show that $M(S^1 \cup \text{resets})$ can be simulated by a cascade of flip-flops and of simple groups which divide S.

13   EXERCISE: If S is right simple, show that $M(S^1 \cup \text{resets})$ can be simulated by a cascade of flip-flops and of simple groups which divide S.

With this machinery at our disposal it is now a simple task to prove our main theorem:

14   PROOF OF **1.** The proof is by induction. Let $X(S)$ be true if and only if not only $M(S)$ but also $M(S^1 \cup \text{resets})$ can be simulated by a cascade of flip-flops and of machines of simple groups dividing S. Certainly $X(S)$ is true if $\#(S) = 1$. Now suppose $X(S)$ is true for all semigroups S with $\#(S) \leq n$. We will prove it true for semigroups S with $\#(S) = n + 1$. If S is cyclic or right simple, we are done by **12** and **13**. In the remaining case, we know by **9** that $M(S)$ can be simulated by a cascade of $M(V \cup \text{resets})$ and $M(T^1)$, where T is a proper right ideal and V is a proper subsemigroup of S. Thus $\#(T) \leq n$ and $\#(V) \leq n$, and so $X(T)$ and $X(V)$ hold. Thus $M(S)$ can be simulated by a cascade of flip-flops and of the machines of simple groups which divide T or V and so, a fortiori, S. But then, by **10**, it is immediate that $X(S)$ is true. Thus the induction goes through, and the decomposition theorem is proved. □

Above we have given a strongly machine-theoretic proof of the Krohn-Rhodes theorem. The essential logic of the proof is, however, similar to that of the original proof in KROHN and RHODES [1965]. For an alternative exposition, see KROHN, RHODES, and TILSON [1968a].

8.4   COVERS AND THE DECOMPOSITION THEOREM

It is important to notice that Theorem **3.1** does not simply tell us that every (finite-state) machine with semigroup S can be simulated by a cascade of flip-flops and machines of simple groups, but adds that we do not need any groups which do not divide S. In fact, the weaker result is much easier to prove, as we see from the next lemma, which is an application of Theorem **1.20**.

1   LEMMA [ZEIGER, 1964]: *Consider a machine M with n states in Q, and let $C_n, C_{n-1}, C_{n-2}, \ldots, C_1$ be the nested sequence of covers with C_j the collection of j-element subsets of Q, so that each C_j is a refinement of each C_i with $j \leq i$. Then we may choose a PR-machine which tells where M is in C_n (trivial!); and, given a machine M_j which tells where M is in C_j, we may cascade it with a PR-machine L, to obtain a machine M_{j-1} which tells where M is in C_{j-1}.*

Proof. Let M_j have states which we may regard as elements of C_j, and let its state equal its output at any time. Let L_j have states $\{1, \ldots, j\}$. We can order the elements of Q so that for each block of C_j we may talk of the 1st, 2nd, $\ldots$, jth elements. We then decode the output of the cascade so that if M_j tells that M is in block R of C_j, and L_j is in state i, $1 \leq i \leq j$, then M_j is to have output encoding that block of C_{j-1} obtained by deleting the ith element of R.

Now suppose that we apply input x to the cascade in state (i, R). By assumption, M_j will change to some state corresponding to a block R' of C_j with $R \circ x \subset R'$.

If the inclusion is proper, there is some element, say the i'th of R' which is not contained in R'. Setting $Z(R, x)$ equal to "reset to i'," we will then ensure that M_{j-1} continues to tell where M is in C_{j-1}.

However, if in fact $R \circ x = R'$, then the ith element of R is mapped by x to the $i \circ x_R$th element, say, of R', in such a way that $i_1 \neq i_2$ implies $i_1 \cdot x_R \neq i_2 \cdot x_R$—in other words $Z(R, x)$ is uniquely defined as a *permutation* if $R \cdot x = R'$.

Thus in any case L_j is a PR-machine. □

Thus *every finite-state machine may be obtained as a cascade of PR-machines*, and hence, by Lemmas **3.3** and **3.4**, as a cascade of machines of simple groups, and flip-flops.

The trouble with this construction is that, although it allows us to reduce a machine to a cascade of PR-machines, it gives us no control over the size of the cascade. One PR-machine is required for each state of M—and the method will yield this large cascade even if M itself is a PR-machine! Worse still, the method can yield PR-machines whose groups are even larger than the largest subgroup of the semigroup of the original machine—an example follows:

Let M be the group machine of $Z_2 \times Z_2$ with states 1, 2, 3 and 4 coding $(0, 0)$, $(1, 0)$, $(1, 1)$ and $(0, 1)$ respectively. Then states 1, 2, 3 of L_3 code states 2, 3, 4 of M if M_3 is in state 1, and code states 1, 3, 4 of M if M_3 is in state 2, etc. The reader may then check that input $(a_1, 2)$ to L_3 induces the permutation $\begin{pmatrix} 123 \\ 132 \end{pmatrix}$ and input $(a_2, 3)$ to L_3 induces the permutation $\begin{pmatrix} 123 \\ 312 \end{pmatrix}$. However, these permutations suffice to generate the group S_3 of *all* permutations of $\{1, 2, 3\}$—and this group has two more elements than $Z_2 \times Z_2$, the semigroup of the machine with which we started.

Hartmanis and Stearns were the first people to give us an algebraic feel for the loop-free decomposition of a machine. They used lattice theory—we gave many of their key results in Section **8.1**. However, they failed to ask the crucial question: "How do we obtain loop-free decompositions *in which we keep control of the size of the component machines?*" This is the question that informs our present approach, couched more technically as "How do we replace a machine M by a cascade of machines, where each component has semigroup dividing that of M?"

PAUL ZEIGER [1964] showed‡ that we could always break M down into a cascade of PR-machines, where the group of each PR-machine divides the semigroup of M. The clue to Zeiger's proof is provided by our proof of Lemma **1**, but rather than decompose all blocks of the cover, we shall choose only a certain subset D, in such a way that we may impose a common set of coordinates on the fragments into which each block in D is decomposed. We must choose these fragments so that if $R \circ x = R'$ for blocks R, R' of D and

---

‡ The proof given here follows KALMAN, FALB, and ARBIB [1969]. For alternative expositions of Zeiger's method see ZEIGER [1968] and A. GINZBURG [1968].

x in R, then we may represent this as a permutation of the coordinates representing fragments of R to give us fragments of R'. Extra care will be required to ensure that the resulting permutations belong to a group dividing the original semigroup. Of course, if $R \circ x$ is a proper subset of R', then there must be a fragment of R' which contains the result, and which is contained in the cover so that the appropriate input to the tail machine is simply a reset. Zeiger's crucial inductive step is the

2   THEOREM: *Let M be a machine, C a cover for M not consisting entirely of singletons, and K a machine which tells where M is in C. Then there exist machines N and L, and a cover C' for M for which*

    (1) *C' is a proper refinement of C.*
    (2) *N tells where M is in C'.*
    (3) *N is a cascade of K and L.*
    (4) *L is a PR-machine.*
    (5) *There is an $R_1 \subset Q_M$ such that the permutation group in S_L is a homomorphic image of $\{w \mid w \in S_M$ and $w \mid R_1$ is a permutation of $R_1\}$.*

3   EXERCISE: Verify that condition (5) really does tell us that the group in S_L divides S_M.

Before proving **2**, we note its consequences. Consider the case in which C consists of Q_M alone. Then we may take K to be a one-state machine. But this means that we may disregard K and, in particular, consider N and L identical in this case. Hence we have the immediate

4   COROLLARY: *There exists a nontrivial cover C' for M and a PR-machine L which tells where M is in C', such that there is an $R \subset Q_M$ for which the permutation group in S_L is a homomorphic image of*

$$\{w \mid w \in S_M \text{ and } w \mid R \text{ is a permutation}\}$$

Thus, applying the corollary once, and then repeatedly applying the theorem, we get a sequence of covers $C', C'', \ldots, C^{(k)} \ldots$, and a corresponding sequence of PR-machines $L^{(k)}$ such that the group part of the semigroup of $L^{(k)}$ always divides the semigroup of M, and such that we may obtain $M^{(k)}$, a machine which tells us where M is in $C^{(k)}$ by cascading $L', L'', \ldots, L^{(k)}$. Now the process of refinement of covers can only terminate when we reach an n with $C^{(n)} = \{$singletons$\}$. But this must happen for some finite n. The corresponding $M^{(n)}$ tells us where M is in $C^{(n)}$, but since $C^{(n)}$ is made up of singletons, $M^{(n)}$ actually simulates M. We have thus proved (modulo the proof of **2**):

5   THEOREM: *Any machine M can be simulated by a cascade of PR-machines whose groups divide the semigroup of M.*

For a semigroup S of transformations on a set Q, let $\tilde{S}$ be the *augmented* semigroup got from S by adjoining both the identity, E_Q say, and the reset maps W_q with $W_q(Q) = q$—one for each $q \in Q$.

We say elements R_1 and R_2 of a cover C of M are *similar*, $R_1 \sim R_2$, if $\exists w_1, w_2 \in \tilde{S}_M$ such that $R_1 = R_2 \cdot w_1$ and $R_2 = R_1 \cdot w_2$. Similarity is clearly an equivalence relation, and so we may split C up into similarity classes.

We call $R \in C$ *initial*, if $R = R' \cdot w$ for some $R' \in C$ and $w \in \tilde{S}_M$ implies $R \sim R'$, and further, no block of C has more elements than R does.

We easily deduce that if $R \sim R'$ and R is initial, then R' is initial, too. An *initial class* is any similarity class composed of initial elements. Since C is finite, at least one similarity class is initial (if we assumed this false, we would end up with an infinite regression of "ancestors," and a contradiction!).

6 EXERCISE: Prove that if an initial element R of C contains only one element, then C consists only of singletons.

If C is a collection of subsets of a set Q, then we have already said that

$$\max C = \{x \in C | x \subseteq x' \text{ with } x' \in C \text{ implies } x = x'\}$$

is the set of all elements of C *maximal* with respect to set inclusion.

Given a cover C not composed entirely of singletons, we may choose an initial class D of C, that is, a collection of equivalent initial elements all of whose members have (by **6**) at least two elements. We then form

$$
7 \quad C' = C - D \cup \left\{ \bigcup_{R \in D} \max \left[\{Hw | H \in C, w \in \tilde{S}_M, Hw \subset R\} - R \right] \right\}
$$
$$
= C_1 \cup C_2
$$

where $C_1 = C - D$ and $C_2 = \{\ldots\}$.

Thus we obtain C' from C by decomposing the blocks in the initial class D into smaller fragments. Note immediately that we put the max operation *inside* the union sign. If we had put it outside, we would have ended up with a less redundant cover, but it is precisely the redundancy which will allow us to put common coordinates on the fragments of each block of D. We can see that C' is a cover for M, since, for every block H of C' and every $w \in \tilde{S}_M$, Hw either is included in a block of $C - D$, or is some subset of a block in D, which will be included in a block of C_2. Note that $R \in D$ can be an image (onto) of a block $R' \in D$ only, but *all* these blocks are deleted. This discussion shows why, in defining C', we did not take D to be an arbitrary subset of C', but asked that it comprise initial elements. C' is a proper refinement of C because the blocks in D of C are "replaced" in C' by smaller ones.

We now have our refinement C' of C. It remains to be seen that we can choose the "correction-term" machine L so that it has the properties advertised in conditions (4) and (5) of **2**. Before proving this, we present two examples to increase the reader's feel for what the construction **7** tells us to do.

8 EXAMPLE: Let us apply **7** to the machine with the next-state table

x	0	1
q		
0	0	2
1	1	3
2	3	1
3	2	0

Start with the trivial cover $C = \{\{0, 1, 2, 3\}\}$ with initial class $D = C$. Then

$$C' = \{\{1\} \quad \{2\} \quad \{3\} \quad \{4\}\}$$

and we recapture the machine itself. This is to be expected, since the machine is already a PR-machine.

9 EXAMPLE: Consider the series connection

Let us apply Zeiger's method to this machine M, which has the next-state table

x	0	1
q		
0	0	4
1	1	5
2	1	5
3	0	4
4	6	2
5	7	3
6	6	3
7	7	2

on identifying a binary triple with the digit it encodes. Start with the trivial cover $C = \{\{0, 1, 2, 3, 4, 5, 6, 7\}\}$ with initial class $D = C$. Then

$$C' = \{\{0, 1, 6, 7\} \quad \{2, 3, 4, 5\}\}$$
$$= \{C'_0, C'_1\} \quad \text{say}$$

Then we have the next-state table

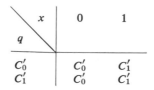

x	0	1
q		
C_0'	C_0'	C_1'
C_1'	C_0'	C_1'

that is, we find where M is in C' with a two-state reset machine K. Now apply the method to C' with $D = C'$ to obtain

$$C'' = \{\{0\} \quad \{1\} \quad \{2\} \quad \{3\} \quad \{4\} \quad \{5\} \quad \{6\} \quad \{7\}\}$$

which recaptures the original machine M, and we do indeed find that M is a cascade of K and a PR-machine L with states $0'$, $1'$, $2'$, $3'$ (see Fig. 8.15).

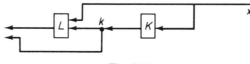

Fig. 8.15

The machine L gets input k from K as well as M's input x. Let us code the states of M by (K, L)-state pairs as follows:

$$
\begin{array}{cccccccc}
0 & 1 & 2 & 3 & 4 & 5 & 6 & 7 \\
(0, 0') & (0, 1') & (1, 0') & (1, 1') & (1, 2') & (1, 3') & (0, 2') & (0, 3')
\end{array}
$$

Applying this coding to the next state table for M we see that the machine L has the next-state table

(k, x)	00	01	10	11
q				
$0'$	$0'$	$2'$	$1'$	$2'$
$1'$	$1'$	$3'$	$0'$	$3'$
$2'$	$2'$	$1'$	$2'$	$0'$
$3'$	$3'$	$0'$	$3'$	$1'$

and we recognize from example 1.7(ii) that L has the same semigroup as the series composition of two copies of Z_2.

A point well worth noting from this example is that a machine may be obtained as a cascade in several different ways, even when we use the same semigroups—in this case U_2 and two copies of Z_2. Note further that L cannot be strictly simulated by the series composition of two copies of Z_2, but can be strictly simulated by the machine of the semigroup of that composition— this corresponds to weak divisibility rather than strong (i.e., length-preserving codes) divisibility.

Let us now recall the statement of Theorem 2 and verify that it is indeed true.

Remember that K is the machine which tells where M is in C. Hence if M is in a block R' of C' which is also a block of C, then the state of L is irrelevant—we need no extra information. However, if R' is not in C (that is, it is a subset of an element of D), K will tell us the element R of D of which R' is a subset, and the job of L is to specify which subset R' actually is. The trick is to show that the states of L need correspond to the C' subsets of just *one* element of D, and that we may use the output of K to interpret these coordinates appropriately, *without blowing up the size of the semigroup of L.* It was the desire to make this possible that motivated the construction of C' from C given above. To check that this is so, we first need a technical lemma:

10 LEMMA: *If P, $R \in D$ then $\exists$ maps v_P^R and $v_R^P \in S_M$ (not augmented) for which $v_P^R | P$ and $v_R^P | R$ are inverses:*

$$P \xrightarrow{v_P^R} R \xrightarrow{v_R^P} P$$

Proof. Since P and R are similar, we can find w and $y \in S_M$ for which $w(P) = R$ and $y(R) = P$. Hence $yw(P) = P$ and $wy(R) = R$. Thus yw and wy are permutations, but we have no reason to expect them to be inverses. However, we can find integers n, m for which $(yw)^n E_P = E_P$ and $(wy)^{nm} E_R = E_R$, since every permutation has a power which is the identity. Let $v_P^R = w$ and $v_R^P = (yw)^{nm-1}y$, and observe that they are inverses. $\square$

We have now reached the home stretch, where we construct N and L. Let $D = \{R_1, \ldots, R_k\}$. For each $R_j \in D$, we select maps $v_1^j = v_{R_1}^{R_j}$ and $v_j^1 = v_{R_j}^{R_1}$ as in Lemma **10**, and stick to this selection henceforth. Let $B_j = \{H \in C' | H \subset R_j\}$. Our choice for the state space of L is now $Q_L = B_1$, which is just the set of "fragments" of elements of D comprising R_1. We now show that our choice of v_1^j and v_j^1 allows us to assign these fragments to other elements R_j of D as well; i.e., our choice of v_1^j and v_j^1 imposes within each element of D a common coordinate system, the state space of L. We use a lemma due to GINZBURG [1968]:

11 LEMMA: *Each B_j has the same cardinality, say α. Further, the blocks of B_j may be so labelled as $H_{j1}, \ldots, H_{j\alpha}$ that*

$$H_{1p}v_1^j = H_{jp} \quad and \quad H_{jp}v_j^1 = H_{1p} \quad for \ 1 \le p \le \alpha \quad 1 \le j \le k$$

Proof. Let H_{1p} be in B_1. Then $H_{1p}v_j^1$ lies in R_j, and so must be contained in some block, H_{jq} say, of B_j. Now

$$H_{1p} = H_{1p}v_j^1 \bar{v}_j^1 \subset H_{jq}\bar{v}_j^1$$

Since v_j^1 maps R_j onto R_1, there is a block, H_{1r} say, of B_1 such that $H_{jq}\bar{v}_j^1 \subset H_{1r}$. The maximality of the blocks of B_1 implies that $H_{1p} = H_{1r} = H_{jq}\bar{v}_j^1$. V_j^1 is a one-to-one mapping, hence $|H_{1p}| = |H_{jq}|$, and since v_j^1 is also one-to-one, $H_{1p}v_j^1 = H_{jq}$.

For $H_{1p_1} \neq H_{1p}$ the same reasoning gives $H_{1p_1}v_j^1 = H_{jq_1}$ with $H_{jq_1} \neq H_{jq}$ because otherwise v_j^1 would take $H_{1p} \cup H_{1p_1}$ onto H_{jq}, while $|H_{1p} \cup H_{1p_1}| > |H_{1p}| = |H_{jq}|$.

Thus v_j^1 maps distinct blocks of B_1 onto distinct blocks of B_j. The roles of B_1 and B_j can be reversed—hence the conclusion that each B_j has the same cardinality.

Enumerate the blocks of B_1 arbitrarily as $H_{11}, \ldots, H_{1\alpha}$, and then label $H_{1p}v_j^1$ as H_{jp} to obtain the complete result, since it then follows that $H_{jp}v_j^1 = H_{1p}$. □

N is the cascade of K and L which is to tell where M is in C', so we set

$$X_N = X_K = X_M$$
$$X_L = X_K \times Q_K \qquad \text{(we identify the state and output of } K\text{)}$$
$$Q_N = Q_K \times Q_L$$

We have to define $\beta_N: Q_N \overset{\text{onto}}{\longrightarrow} C'$ so that N does indeed tell us where M is in C'. So, given $(P, r) \in Q_N$, we proceed as follows:

(i) If $P \notin D$, then P is an element of C which is also an element of C', and K already tells where M is in C', without any extra help from L. We take $\beta_N(P, r) = P$.

(ii) If $P \in D$, then we need to use the information in L to go from the element P of C to the fragment in C'. In line with our choice of "coordinate system" above, we take $\beta_N(P, r)$ to be some element of C' including $r \cdot v_{R_1}^P$. It only remains to specify our state transitions consistently with our choice of the output map:

We have to specify, for each r in $B_1 = Q_L$, each P in $X_K = C$, and each x in X, just which element of Q_L is to be the value of $r \circ (x, P)_L$.

If, in fact, $P \cdot x_K$ is an element of $C - D$, then the tail machine L need supply no further information, and so we may define $(x, P)_L$ as a reset map to satisfy condition (4).

If, however, $P \cdot x_K$ is an element of D, then there are two cases to consider. If $P \cdot x_M$ is a proper subset of an element of D, then in fact it is contained in some fragment and we may choose $(x, P)_L$ to be the reset to the coordinate which fixes such a fragment in $P \cdot x_K$. Should $P \cdot x_M$ actually equal an element R' of D, then the reader may apply Lemma **11** to verify the

12 EXERCISE: $(x, P)_L$ may then be defined as a permutation on L, which is the restriction of an element of S_M to its action on R_1.

Thus L can in fact be defined as a PR-machine whose permutation group is a homomorphic image of

$$\{w | w \in S_M \text{ and } w | R_1 \text{ is a permutation of } R_1\} \qquad \square$$

This completes the proof of **2,** and thus again assures us that "Any machine M can be obtained by cascade synthesis from PR-machines whose groups divide the semigroup of M," from which Theorem **3.1** follows immediately.

8.5   IRREDUCIBILITY RESULTS FOR CASCADE DECOMPOSITION

We have seen that any machine divides a cascade of flip-flops and the machines of simple groups. This naturally raises the question: To what extent can these components themselves be decomposed?

At this stage, we may make the natural definition

1 DEFINITION:
    (i) *A machine M is **irreducible** if for each cascade $M_1 \ominus_K M_2$ which is divided by M we must have*

$$M | M_1 \qquad or \qquad M | M_2$$

that is, M cannot be broken down into a cascade of "smaller" parts.

    (ii) *A machine M is **s-irreducible** if whenever M divides a cascade $M_1 \ominus_K M_2$, where M_j has semigroup S_j, we must have $M|M(S_1)$ or $M|M(S_2)$.*

Unfortunately, it turns out that (i) gives a very weak notion, and that *most* machines are indeed reducible, as is shown in Exercise **4**. One reason for this is simply that the output maps of M_1 and M_2 may make their output sets so small that neither M_1 nor M_2 alone can simulate M, though one of $M(S_1)$ and $M(S_2)$ is big enough to simulate M. We shall see that (ii) is more useful, and that flip-flops and the machines of simple groups are s-irreducible, with the result that every finite-state machine can be simulated by a cascade of s-irreducible machines.

2 EXAMPLE. Consider the machine M which does addition mod 3—its output always equals its state, and the state transitions are given by the table

	1	2	3
1	2	3	1
2	3	1	2
3	1	2	3

Now let M_1 (respectively, M_2) be the machine M with an output coder adjoined, whose function h_1 (respectively, h_2) is given by

$$h_1(1) = 1 \qquad h_1(2) = s \qquad h_1(3) = s$$
$$h_2(1) = s \qquad h_2(s) = 1 \qquad h_2(3) = s$$

Let us simulate M, started in state 1, by a cascade of M_1 started in state 1 and M_2 started in state 1, as shown in Fig. 8.16. The reader may verify that if we define k by

$$k \binom{1}{s} = 1 \qquad k \binom{s}{1} = 2 \qquad k \binom{s}{s} = 3$$

then this cascade behaves exactly as M. In short, $M | M_2 \times M_1$, and

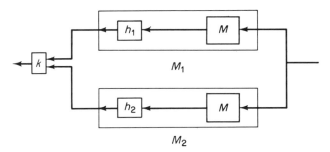

Fig. 8.16

$S = S_1 = S_2$, but it is not possible that $M | M_2$ or $M | M_1$, since the output set of M_1 alone is too small to encode all the outputs of M.

3   EXAMPLE (MYHILL [1963a]): There exist automata A and B (even ones with groups for their semigroups) such that the group of B is isomorphic to a subgroup of that of A, while A cannot simulate B (even though B is reduced).

Proof. Define A and B by the state graphs shown in Fig. 8.17. Pick one state of B to be both final and initial—so B is reduced. B's semigroup is the cyclic group of order 6, with generator [1], and this is isomorphic to subgroup of A's semigroup generated by [1]. If, however, A could simulate B, there would have to be a string σ such that A rejected σ, σ^2, σ^3, σ^4, and σ^5 and accepted σ^6. But this is impossible, no matter how outputs are assigned to A, since A has only five states. $\square$

While on the topic of clarification, note that we can only be sure of simulating a machine M by the machine $M(S)$ of its semigroup if M is *cyclic*,

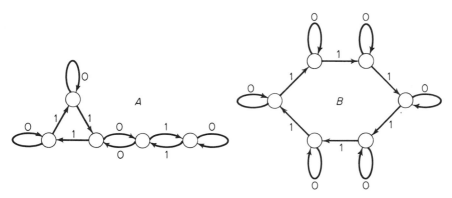

Fig. 8.17

in the algebraic (*not* graph-theoretic) sense that all states are reachable from some initial state q, so that if state $q' = \delta(q, x)$, we may encode it as $[x]$, and several choices may be available. If M is not cyclic, then it has superfluous states which can never be encountered in a "run" on the machine, and S has several orbits (i.e., maximal sets $q' \cdot S$) on the state space of M, so we may only be able to code up the states of one orbit—in general we need one copy of $M(S)$ for each orbit, and a selector switch which keys in the machine which encodes the appropriate initial state.

4   EXERCISE

   (i) Show that any machine M with n (≥ 3) outputs can be simulated by a cascade of two $(n - 1)$-output machines dividing M.

   (ii) (WEGBREIT [1967]): Show that any two-output machine M with at least three states can be simulated by a parallel composition of machines M_1 and M_2 such that M divides neither M_1 nor M_2. [Hint: Obtain M_1 and M_2 by simply changing the output function of M in two "complementary" ways. It is the proof of nondivision that is harder.]

5   COROLLARY: *Any machine M can be simulated by a cascade of two-output machines which divide M.*

6   COROLLARY: *Let P be a simple group with more than two elements. Then $M(P)$ is **not** irreducible.*

   Thus the machine of a simple group P may be made up as a cascade of machines with *less states*, although we shall show that one of the components must have a semigroup at least as big as P. To find such decompositions, we may use the decomposition techniques of Hartmanis and Stearns, as presented in Section **8.1**, but I know of no elegant techniques for ensuring the economy of such further decompositions.

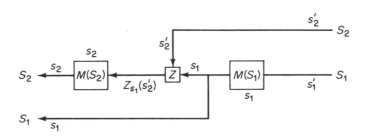

Fig. 8.18

Now, suppose that in the definition of the cascade of two machines, we take $\hat{X} = S_2 \times S_1$, $\eta(s_2, s_1) = s_1$ and have Z independent of the s_1 of $\hat{x}$, so that we may write $Z_{s_1}(s_2')$ for $Z((s_1', s_2'), s_1)$.

Further, let machine M be replaced by the semigroup machine $M(S_1)$ while M' is replaced by $M(S_2)$. We then have

$$\delta_Z[(s_2, s_1), (s_2', s_1)] = [s_2 Z_{s_1}(s_2'), s_1 s_1']$$

Comparing the expressions

$$[s_2 Z_{s_1}(s_2') Z_{s_1 s_1'}(s_2''), s_1 s_1' s_1'']$$

and
$$[s_2 Z_{s_1}(s_2' Z_{s_1'}(s_2'')), s_1 s_1' s_1'']$$

we see that the operation δ_Z becomes *associative* if we require that Z enjoy the properties

7
$$\left. \begin{array}{l} Z_{s_1 s_1'}(s_2) = Z_{s_1}(Z_{s_1'}(s_2)) \\ Z_{s_1}(s_2 s_2') = Z_{s_1}(s_2) Z_{s_1}(s_2') \end{array} \right\} \quad (s_1, s_1' \in S_1, s_2, s_2' \in S_2)$$

This leads us naturally to consider the semidirect product of S_1 and S_2, where we have the following:

8   DEFINITION: *Let S_1 and S_2 be semigroups, and Z a homomorphism of S_1 into* End (S_2) *(that is, the monoid of endomorphisms of S_2 under composition):* $s_1 \rightarrow Z_{s_1}(\cdot)$

*Then **the semidirect product of S_1 and S_2 with connecting***

homomorphism Z *is the semigroup* $S_2 \times_Z S_1$ *with elements the cartesian product set* $S_2 \times S_1$ *and multiplication*

$$(s_2, s_1)(s_2', s_1') = (s_2 Z_{s_1}(s_2'), s_1 s_1')$$

and the corresponding

9 DEFINITION: *A semigroup S is **irreducible** if for all semidirect products* $S_2 \times_Z S_1$ *such that* $S | S_2 \times_Z S_1$, *we must have*

$$S | S_2 \quad or \quad S | S_1$$

Our definitions have been so worded as to render highly plausible the result that a machine is s-irreducible if and only if its semigroup is irreducible, and we shall see that this is indeed true.

10 EXERCISE: Verify that the direct product is a semidirect product.

Given a cascade machine $M' \ominus_K M$ with semigroup $\tilde{S}$, it is tempting to believe that we can always find a suitable homomorphism $\check{Z}$ such that

$$\tilde{S} | S' \times_{\check{z}} S$$

where S' is the semigroup of M', and S that of M.

However, this is usually impossible, since the original map Z may so completely "cut across" the multiplicative structure of the semigroups that no $\check{Z}$ can be found with the desired homomorphism properties **7**. For example, we see in Example **1.7** (ii) that the series connection of two Z_2 machines has an eight-element semigroup, whereas any semidirect product $Z_2 \times_{\varphi} Z_2$ only has four elements.

Simulating M with $M(S)$, and M' with $M(S')$, we may represent $M' \ominus_K M$ by the diagram shown in Fig. 8.19.

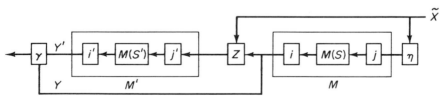

Fig. 8.19

11 EXERCISE: Given that $\tilde{M} | M' \xleftarrow[Z]{\eta} M$, find η' and Z' such that

$$\tilde{M} | M(S') \xleftarrow[Z']{\eta'} M(S)$$

The (not necessarily reduced) state space of this cascade is $S' \times S$. We consider $\hat{S}$, the semigroup of transformations of $S' \times S$ induced by input sequences.

Let t be an input sequence, i.e., an element of $\bar{X}^*$. The action of t on the $M(S)$ machine is simply multiplication by an appropriate element, $I_S(t)$, of S. However, the action of t on the *second* machine, $M(S')$, will depend on the state of $M(S)$ at the beginning of the operation—if the latter is s, then let us denote the former by $I_{S'}(t)(s)$. Thus $I_{S'}(t)$ is an element of $F(S, S')$, the semigroup of *maps* (not just homomorphisms) of S into S', with composition defined by $(f_1 \circ f_2)(s) = f_1(s) \cdot f_2(s)$.

Thus S is obtained by replacing the element t of the free input semigroup by the element $(I_{S'}(t), I_S(t))$ of the *set* $F(S, S') \times S$. What is the semigroup multiplication induced on this set by the input action? The action of t_1 followed by t_2 yields

$$(I_{S'}(t_1), I_S(t_1)) \cdot (I_{S'}(t_2), I_S(t_2)) = (I_{S'}(t_1 t_2), I_S(t_1 t_2))$$

But the action of $t_1 t_2$ on $M(S)$ is simply that of t_1 multiplied by that of t_2:

$$I_S(t_1 t_2) = I_S(t_1) I_S(t_2)$$

while the action of $t_1 t_2$ on $M(S')$ when $M(S)$ is started in state s is that of t_1 on $M(S')$ when $M(S)$ is started in state s, multiplied by that of t_2 on $M(S')$ when $M(S)$ is started in state $s \cdot I_S(t_1)$:

$$I_{S'}(t_1 t_2)(s) = [I_{S'}(t_1)(s)] \cdot [I_{S'}(t_2)(s \cdot I_S(t_1))]$$

12   If the reader will refer back to the definition of the semidirect product, and consider the map

$$W : S \to \text{End}\,(F(S, S'))$$

defined by

$$W_{s_1}(l)(s) = l(ss_1)$$

he will see that the multiplication defined on $F(S, S') \times S$ is that of the semidirect product $F(S, S') \times_W S$. This suggests that the latter semigroup deserves our special attention—we call it the **wreath product** of S and S', and denote it S' wr S.

Note that W is completely defined when we give S and S', and so need not be mentioned explicitly.

Now, $\hat{S}$ is a subsemigroup of the wreath product of S and S'. But the semigroup of $M' \ominus_K M$ is a homomorphic image of $\hat{S}$, being simply the action of $\bar{X}^*$ on the reduced state space. We thus have this crucial result:

13 THEOREM: *Let M have semigroup S, and M' have semigroup S'. Then, for any connection K, the semigroup $\hat{S}$ of M' $\ominus_K$ M divides the wreath product S' wr S.*

Note that the Z of K does *not* have to satisfy the associativity conditions **7**.

Thus, although in general there is no semidirect product of S' and S which is divisible by $\hat{S}$, it is always true that S divides that semidirect product of $F(S, S')$ with S known as the wreath product.

14 EXERCISE: Prove that the machine of the wreath product S wr S' may be obtained as a cascade of $M(S)$ and $M(S')$. (Thus the wreath product is a "universal" semigroup for cascades of cyclic machines with semigroups S and S'.)

We can now prove

15 THEOREM: *If M is s-irreducible as a machine, its semigroup S is irreducible as a semigroup.*

Proof. Suppose M is s-irreducible. To say that S divides the semidirect proof $S_2 \times_z S_1$ is just another way of saying that $M(S)$ divides the cascade of machines $M(S_2) \times_z M(S_1)$. Since $M|M(S)$ we have $M|M(S_2) \times_z M(S_1)$, and by s-irreducibility $M|M(S_1)$ or $M|M(S_2)$. But divisibility of machines implies divisibility of their semigroups, and so $S|S_1$ or $S|S_2$. Thus S is irreducible. □

16 THEOREM: *If M is a machine whose semigroup S is irreducible as a semi-group, then M is s-irreducible.*

Proof. Let S be irreducible. Now, if $M|M_2 \times_z M_1$, then S must divide S_2 wr S_1, and so divides S_1 or $F(S_2, S_1)$. If S divides S_1, then $M(S)$ divides $M(S_1)$. But $F(S_2, S_1) \cong S_2 \times \ldots \times S_2(\#(S_1)$ times). So if S divides $F(S_2, S_1)$, then S must divide S_2, by irreducibility, in which case $M(S)$ divides $M(S_2)$. Thus $M|M(S_1)$ or $M|M(S_2)$. □

Thus the proof of **15**, together with **16**, implies

17 THEOREM: *A machine is s-irreducible if and only if its semigroup is irreducible.*

The treatment so far in this section follows ARBIB [1968b], to which the reader is referred for further details. We now apply these notions to prove simply (ARBIB [1968c]) the theorem of TREVOR EVANS [1952] that every countable, i.e., finite or denumerably infinite, semigroup can be embedded in (is isomorphic to a subsemigroup of) a two-generator semigroup. For this discussion we may regard our automata as without outputs, i.e., as triples (Q, X, δ) where Q is the set of states, X is the input set, and $\delta: Q \times X \to Q$. M is called countable [finite] if Q is countable [finite]—so we are relaxing our usual finiteness condition. We reduce Evans' theorem to the obvious statement that every countable automaton can be embedded in one with binary inputs. Further, our techniques yield a proof of the Evans theorem, using wreath products, as in NEUMANN [1960].

Given a countable semigroup S with generators $G(S)$, we may represent it as the semigroup of the machine $M_S = (S^1, G(S), \delta_S)$, where δ_S is multiplication in the semigroup S, and S^1 is S with a unit adjoined only if S is not a monoid. We then replace M_S by a machine which has input set $\{0, 1\}$ and which reads in strings until a code for an element of $G(S)$ has been read, and then acts accordingly.

We now give two examples of codes and the corresponding constructions. One which works whether or not $G(S) = \{s_1, s_2, \ldots\}$ is finite is to code s_j as 1^j0, that is, a string of j ones followed by a zero. Then $M_1 = (N \times S^1, \{0, 1\}, \delta_1)$ (taking $N = \{1, 2, 3, \ldots\}$) with

$$\delta_1((n, s), 0) = (0, s \cdot s_n)$$
$$\delta_1((n, s), 1) = (n + 1, s)$$

and the map $s_j \to 1^j0$ yields an embedding of S in the two-generator semigroup $S(M_1)$. If $G(S) = \{s_1, \ldots, s_d\}$ is finite, we can replace N by $\{1, \ldots, d\}$, addition then being modulo d to handle sequences not coding words of S, so that $S(M_1)$ is finite if S is finite.

If $G(S) = \{s_1, \ldots, s_d\}$ is finite and $2^{m-1} < d \leq 2^m$, we may give a "faster" construction, encoding each s_j as a distinct string t_j of m zeros and ones. Then if A is the set of strings of at most $m - 1$ zeros and ones (including the empty string Λ) we may set

$$M_2 = (A \times S^1, \{0, 1\}, \delta_2)$$

with $\delta_2([u_1 \ldots u_k, s], u) = \begin{cases} [u_1 \ldots u_k u, s] & \text{if } 0 \leq k < n - 1 \\ [\Lambda, s \cdot s_j] & \text{if } k = n - 1 \text{ and } t_j = u_1 \ldots u_k u \\ [\Lambda, s] & \text{otherwise} \end{cases}$

and the map $s_j \mapsto t_j$ yields an embedding of S in the two-generator semigroup $S(M_2)$.

It should be clear how this construction can be extended to arbitrary codes.

The reader should verify that when the output equals the state of a cascade $A_2 \ominus_K A_1$, the semigroup of $A_2 \ominus_K A_1$ can be *embedded* in the wreath product of $S(A_2)$ and $S(A_1)$.

Now it is clear from the definitions of δ_1 and δ_2 that both M_1 and M_2 are cascades of some machine A_1 with M_{S^1}. In the case of the first construction, the semigroup T_0 of A_1 is $N^0[\{1, \ldots, d\}^0$ if $G(S)$ is finite]—i.e., the integers under addition [modulo d] with a *multiplicative* zero adjoined. In either case, we see that S can be embedded in a two-generator semigroup which can in turn be embedded in the wreath product of $S(A_1)$ and S^1.

We must now answer the crucial question: What machines are *s*-irreducible? The following answer will be our main target of proof in the rest of the section.

18   THEOREM (KROHN and RHODES [1965]): *A machine M is s-irreducible iff M has either an element of* UNITS *or a simple group for its semigroup.*

We already know that M is s-reducible if its semigroup is *not* a UNIT (compare **1.15**) or a simple group. It thus remains simply to verify that UNITS and simple groups are irreducible.

19 THEOREM: *Simple Groups are Irreducible.*
    Proof. Let G' be simple. Given that $G' | S_2 \times_Z S_1$, we are to prove:

$$G' | S_2 \quad \text{or} \quad G' | S_1$$

By **7.25** we can choose a subgroup G of $S_2 \times_Z S_1$ mapping onto G'

$$S_2 \times_Z S_1 \geq G \xrightarrow{\varphi} G'$$

G has elements (s_2, s_1) for $s_i \in S_i$. The projection map $\pi\colon G \to S_1$ with $\pi(s_2, s_1) = s_1$ is a homomorphism, and so $\pi(G)$, call it G_1, must be a subgroup of S_1.

    Let $e'' = (e', e)$ be the identity of G. Then $G_2' = \{(s_2, e) | s_2 \in S_2 \quad (s_2, e) \in G\}$ is the kernel of π, and thus a normal subgroup of G.
Define $\psi\colon G_2' \to S_2$ by

$$\psi(s_2, e) = Z_e(s_2)$$

We shall show that ψ is a monomorphism.

$$
\begin{aligned}
\psi((s_2, e)(s_2', e)) &= \psi(s_2 Z_e(s_2'), e) \\
&= Z_e(s_2 Z_e(s_2')) \\
&= Z_e(s_2) Z_e(Z_e(s_2')) \\
&= Z_e(s_2) \cdot Z_e(s_2')
\end{aligned}
$$

so ψ is a homomorphism.
    If $\psi(s_2, e) = \psi(s_2', e)$

then
$$
\begin{aligned}
(s_2, e) &= (e', e)(s_2, e) \\
&= (e' Z_e(s_2), e) \\
&= (e' \psi(s_2, e), e) \\
&= (s_2', e)
\end{aligned}
$$

and so ψ is also one-to-one. Thus $\psi(G_2')$, call it G_2, is a subgroup of S_2.
    Now, G' is exactly the homomorphic image of G under φ:

$$G' \cong G/\ker(\varphi)$$

But G' is simple, so $K = \ker(\varphi)$ is a maximal normal subgroup of G. Recall that if A, B, C are groups, and $A \triangleleft B$, $C \triangleleft B$, then $A \cdot C \triangleleft B$. Hence we have $K \triangleleft K \cdot G_2' \triangleleft G$, with K maximal in G. Therefore either $K = K \cdot G_2'$ or $K \cdot G_2' = G$.

Case 1 $(K = K \cdot G_2')$:

$$G' = \frac{G}{K} = \frac{G/G_2'}{K/G_2'}$$

by the isomorphism theorem. But $G/G_2' \cong G_1$, and so $G' = G_1/K/G_2$; that is, $G'|G_1$. Since G_1 is a subgroup of S_1, we conclude that $G'|S_1$.

Case 2 $(G = K \cdot G_2')$:

$$G' = \frac{K \cdot G_2'}{K} = \frac{G_2'}{G_2' \cap K}$$

by the isomorphism theorem. Since $G_2' \cong G_2$, we conclude that $G'|G_2 \subset S_2$, and so $G'|S_2$. $\qquad\square$

20 THEOREM: *Each member of UNITS is irreducible.*

Proof. We prove U_3 is irreducible—the proofs for the remaining units are analogous and easier.

(i) We first prove that if $\{e, r_0, r_1\} = U_3|S$, then $U_3 \subset S$ (that is, U_3 is isomorphic to a subsemigroup of S).

Suppose $S \supset S' \xrightarrow{\varphi} U_3$. Let $x = \varphi^{-1}(e)$. Then, since S is finite, there is an idempotent e' which is a power of x, and so $\varphi(e') = e$ and $\varphi(e'S'e') = U_3$, and e' is an identity for $e'S'e'$.

Let S_1 be a subsemigroup of $e'S'e'$ of smallest order for which $\varphi(S_1) = U_1 = \{r_0\}$. Then for each $s_1 \in S_1$ we have $\varphi(s_1 \cdot S_1) = \varphi(s_1)U_1 = U_1$. Thus $s_1 \cdot S_1 = S_1$, and so S_1 is right simple.

Thus by **2.20** $S_1 \cong G \times B^r$, where G is a group and B^r is a set B under right-zero multiplication. B must contain at least two members, b_1 and b_2, since U_1 is not a group. Then, if 1 is the identity of G,

$$U_3 \cong \{e', (1, b_1), (1, b_2)\} \subset \{e'\} \cup S_1 \subset S$$

(ii) We show that if $U_3|S_2 \times_Z S_1$, then U_3 divides S_2 or S_1. By the above,

$$U_3 \cong \{(b, a), (b_0, a_0), (b_1, a_1)\} \subset S_2 \times_Z S_1$$

Let $\pi_1(s_2, s_1) = s_1$. We have

$$\pi_1(U_3) = \{a, a_0, a_1\} \subset S_1$$

and a is an identity of $\pi_1(U_3)$.

If a, a_0, and a_1 are distinct, then $\pi_1(U_3) \subset S_1$ is isomorphic to U_3, whence $U_3|S_1$.

If $a_0 \neq a_1$ and $a = a_i (i = 0$ or $1)$, then for any $\hat{a} \in \{a, a_0, a_1\} \hat{a}a = \hat{a}a_i$ and so $\hat{a} = a_i$, and $U_3 \cong \{b, b_0, b_1\}$ and divides S_1.

If $a_0 = a_1$, then $b_0 \neq b_1$. Let $p_2 \colon U_3 \to S_2$, with $p_2(b', a') = Z_{a_0}(b')$.

21 EXERCISE: Show that p_2 is a homomorphism and (e.g., by enumeration of possibilities) that it is $1 - 1$. Thus in this case $p_2(U_3) \cong U_3$, and $p_2(U_3) \subset S_2$, so that $U_3 | S_2$. ☐

Thus if a machine M with a simple group or a UNIT for its semigroup divides a cascade, then its semigroup divides that of one of the component machines. Thus flip-flops and the machines of simple groups are s-irreducible.

These results, together with those of Section **3**, tell us the following:

(1) Any machine may be simulated by a (repeated) cascade using only flip-flops and the machines of the simple groups which divide them.

(2) If a machine is simulated by a (repeated) cascade of components, then each simple group dividing the semigroup of the machine must divide the semigroup of at least one component.

We noted that the alternating group A_n of any order other than 4 is simple, yet divides any other A_m, for $m > n$. Thus (1) and (2) do *not* imply that, e.g., every simple group G appearing in the composition series of a subgroup of S must occur as the semigroup of a component in a simulation of $M(S)$ by a cascade using only flip-flops or machines of simple groups—only that G must divide one of the simple groups associated with a component.

We see from the discussion which started this section that the semigroup is the right measure of irreducibility for a machine because any machine M with at least three states or outputs can be simulated by a cascade of smaller machines, but if M has a UNIT or a simple group for a semigroup, then at least one of the components must have the same semigroup so that, while the decomposition may be practically useful, it is not theoretically significant. In particular, we note that the only machines which can be built from machines irreducible in the strict sense of definition **1** have semigroups that are either combinatorial, or are divided by no nontrivial groups other than Z_2 (consider the only transformation groups on a set of two elements)—whereas any finite-state machine can be built from s-irreducible machines.

22 EXERCISE

(i) Prove that S is combinatorial, i.e., has no proper subgroups, iff $M(S)$ can be simulated by a cascade of flip-flops.

(ii) (MEYER [1968]) Let $M = M' \ominus M''$ be a cascade of flip-flop M' with another machine M''. Let $M_{a,b}$ denote the set of input strings which send M from state a to state b. Prove that if each $M''_{p,q}$ is star-free, then so too is each $M_{a,b}$. (Hint: Prove that $M_{(0,p),(1,q)} = M''_{p,q} \cap [\bigcup M''_{p,r}x \overline{(\bigcup M''_{r\sigma,s}x'X^*)}]$ for suitable finite ranges of r, s, x, and x'.) Deduce that every group-free regular set is star-free (*cf.* Exercise **3.6**).

(iii) (CUTLIP [1968]) Recall that a set R is k-definite if $l(x) \geq k$, and $y \in X^*$ implies that $x \in R$ iff $yx \in R$. Prove directly that if R is k-definite, then $S(R)$ has no proper subgroups. (You may also deduce it be proving that R is star-free if it is k-definite. Can you prove that the converse is false?) Deduce that R can be accepted by a cascade of flip-flops. In addition, give a direct proof using **3.3.29** instead of Krohn-Rhodes theory.

23 EXERCISE: Let us call a PRIME machine one of the form $M(P)$ for a simple nontrivial group P. Use the discussion of simple groups in Section **2** to prove the following:

(i) Say a machine is *solvable* if every subgroup of its semigroup is solvable. Then a machine is solvable iff it can be simulated by a cascade of flip-flops and counters (i.e., machines of cyclic groups of prime order). What happens if the semigroup is abelian?

(ii) The only PRIME machines with an even number of states greater than 2 must have the number of states divisible by 12, 16, or 56.

(iii) The only PRIME machines with an odd number of states are counters.

(iv) The only PRIME machines with at most 1092 states have p (a prime), 60, 168, 360, 504, 660, or 1092 states and for each such there is only one. [Open question: How big must N be for the version of this result, with 1092 replaced by N, to tell us, for all *practical purposes*, what building block is required?]

(v) The statement "for each $n \leq N$, there is at most one PRIME machine with n states" is true for $N = 1092$ but false for $N = 20{,}160$.

8.6 GROUP COMPLEXITY FOR CASCADE DECOMPOSITION ‡

We say that a machine M is a *group* or *permutation* machine if each input to M permutes its states—in this case the semigroup M^S of M is a group. We say that a machine M is a *basic combinatorial* or *identity-reset* machine if each input to M is a reset (i.e., constant map) or the identity map. We say that a machine is *combinatorial* or *group-free* if it can be simulated by a cascade of identity-reset machines—in this case M^S is combinatorial, i.e., has no subgroups of order greater than 1.

Then the decomposition theorem says that any reduced finite-state sequential machine has a GC-decomposition X; that is, it can be simulated by a cascade X of machines $M_1, \ldots, M_n$, where each M_j is a finite-state reduced sequential machine which is a group machine or else combinatorial, where as usual the input to M_j at time t is determined by the input to the system at time t and the outputs at time t of each of $M_1, \ldots, M_{j-1}$, and no feedback occurs.

---

‡ This section is based on KROHN, MATEOSIAN, and RHODES [1967] and ARBIB, RHODES, and TILSON [1968], the theory in which is greatly extended in KROHN, RHODES, and TILSON [1968c].

A natural question that arises is then "What is the smallest number of groups required for decomposing a semigroup machine $M(S)$ in the above fashion into group and combinatorial machines?" We call this number the group complexity of S, $\#_G(S)$, and devote this section to exploring some of its basic properties.

1   DEFINITION: *Let X be a GC-decomposition of a semigroup machine $M(S)$ into a cascade of group and combinatorial machines $M_1, \ldots, M_n$.*

Let $\#_G(X)$ denote the number of group machines among $M_1, \ldots, M_n$. Then the **group complexity** *of S is*

$$\#_G(S) = \min \{\#_G(X) : X \text{ is a GC-decomposition of } M(S)\}.$$

2   EXERCISE

(i) We write $S_n \times_{Y_{n-1}} S_{n-1} \times_{Y_{n-2}} \ldots \times_{Y_1} S_1$ for the iterated semidirect product of $S_n, \ldots, S_1$:

$$(((\ldots S_n \times_{Y_{n-1}} S_{n-1}) \times_{Y_{n-2}}) \ldots \times_{Y_1} S_1)$$

Define the group complexity of S [definition (b)], $\#_G^b(S)$ to be the smallest nonnegative integer n for which

$$S | C_n \times_{Y_{2n}} G_n \times_{Y_{2n-1}} \ldots \times_{Y_2} G_1 \times_{Y_1} C_0$$

where the G_j are groups $\neq \{1\}$ and the C_j are combinatorial semigroups. Prove that $\#_G(S) = \#_G^b(S)$.

(ii) Prove that if semidirect product is replaced by wreath product in definition (b), the measure of complexity obtained does not change.

It is hoped that the above exercise attests to the naturalness and importance of $\#_G(S)$, either in the cascade decomposition of finite state machines or in the structure theory of finite semigroups. It represents a step in going from the mere description of necessary components to a discussion of the possible order in which they may occur in the composition of a machine or semigroup. In exploring the properties of this measure, we first note the obvious

3   LEMMA

(a) *If $T | S$, then $\#_G(T) \leq \#_G(S)$*

(b) *If $T | S$ wr S_1 (or, equivalently $M(T)$ is simulatable by a cascade of M_1 and M_2 with $M_1^S = S_1$ and $M_2^S = S_2$), then $\#_G(T) \leq \#_G(S_2) + \#_G(S_1)$.*

(c) *Cascading a machine with combinatorial machines cannot increase its complexity.*

4   EXERCISE: We say a semigroup N is *null* if $n_1 \cdot n_2 = 0$ for all $n_1, n_2 \in N$. We know from **2.18** that a semigroup is 0-simple iff it is isomorphic to a Rees matrix semigroup $\mathfrak{M}^0(G; A, B; P)$. Prove the following:
(a) If S is a null semigroup and $T|S$, then $\#_G(T) = 0$.
(b) If S is a 0-simple semigroup and $T|S$, then $\#_G(T) \leq 1$. [Hint: Construct a cascade, using one group machine and two identity-reset machines, to simulate $S = \mathfrak{M}^0(G; A, B; P)$ in which $(g; a, b)(g'; a', b') = (g''; a, b')$ with $g'' = gP(b, a')g'$.]

5   EXERCISE: If S is a semigroup with a subsemigroup T and an ideal V such that $T \cup V = S$, then $T \cap V$ is an ideal of T, and we may introduce the Rees quotient $T_V = T/T \cap V$. Retrace the argument leading to **3.9** to prove that $M(S)$ may be simulated by a cascade of $M(T_V^1)$ and $M(V^1)$.

6   DEFINITION: *We say of ideals I_1 and I_2 of a semigroup S that I_1 is **nearly maximal** in I_2 if $I_1 \subset I_2$ and the Rees quotient I_2/I_1 divides a null or 0-simple semigroup.*

7   LEMMA: *Let I_1 and I_2 be ideals of a semigroup, with I_1 nearly maximal in I_2. Then*

$$\#_G(I_1) \leq \#_G(I_2) \leq \#_G(I_1) + 1$$

Proof. By Exercise **5** it follows that

$$\#_G(I_2) \leq \#_G(I_1) + \#_G(I_2/I_1)$$

and the result is then immediate from Exercise **4**.   □

The reader may verify that if I_1 is *maximal* in I_2, then I_1 is *nearly maximal* in I_2. Thus we may immediately deduce

8   THEOREM:
(a) *Let I_1 and I_2 be ideals of a semigroup S with I_1 maximal in I_2. Then*

$$\#_G(I_1) \leq \#_G(I_2) \leq \#_G(I_1) + 1$$

(b) *Let V be an ideal of S with $\#_G(S) = n \geq k = \#_G(V)$. Then there are ideals $V_n, \ldots, V_k$ of S with*

$$V = V_k \subset V_{k+1} \subset \ldots \subset V_n \subset S$$

and $\#_G(V_j) = j$, $k \leq j \leq n$.
(c) *Let T be a subideal of S, that is, there exist subgroups $S_0, \ldots, S_k$ such that*

$$T = S_k \subset S_{k-1} \subset \ldots \subset S_0 = S$$

with S_j an ideal of S_{j-1} for $j = 1, \ldots, k$. Assume that $\#_G(S) = n \geq k = \#_G(T)$.
Then there exist subideals $V_n, \ldots, V_k$ with

$$T = V_k \subset V_{k+1} \subset \ldots \subset V_n = S$$

and V_i a subideal of V_{i+1} for $i = k, \ldots, n - 1$, and $\#_G(V_i) = i, i = k, \ldots, n$. $\square$

The fact that each ideal I of S is contained in a chain of ideals

$$I \subset I_1 \subset I_2 \subset \ldots \subset S$$

through which $\#_G$ increases in steps of 1 is called "*continuity of G-complexity.*"

9   THEOREM: *Let M be a reduced finite-state sequential machine with semi-groups S and state space Q.*
   (a) *Let $r_k = \{f \in S \colon |f(Q)| \leq k\}$.*
Then r_k is an ideal of S, and $\#_G(r_k) \leq \#_G(r_{k+1}) \leq \#_G(r_k) + 1$ for $1 \leq k \leq |Q|$.
   (b) *Let spec $(M) = \{k > 1 \colon r_k \neq \emptyset\}$ (**the spectrum** of M).*
Then $\#_G(M) \leq |{\rm spec}\,(M)|$.
   (c) *When $S = F_R(Q)$, then $\#_G(M) = |{\rm spec}\,(M)| = |Q| - 1$.*
   Proof. To prove (a) and (b) we need only show that if k and $k + j$ are in
spec (M), but $r_{k+i} \not\subseteq$ spec (M) for $i = 1, \ldots, j - 1$, then r_k is nearly maximal
in r_{k+j}, for we may then apply Lemma **7**. This is left as an exercise for the
reader.

Part (b) implies half of (c), namely that $\#_G(F_R(Q)) \leq |Q| - 1$. The con-
verse result, that $\#_G(F_R(Q)) \geq |Q| - 1$ is much harder, and for it we refer the
reader to Section 5 of RHODES [1966]. $\square$

(b) may also be proved by applying Zeiger's cover construction (Sec-
tion **4** above) to the nested sequence of covers $\{C_j \colon j \in$ spec $(M)\}$, on taking
C_j to be the cover composed of j-element subsets of Q.

We claimed, but did not prove, in Theorem **9**(c) that $\#_G(F_R(Q)) = |Q| -$
1, thus implying that there are semigroups of every complexity. In this section
we shall sketch the verification of this implication, and reveal some subtler
properties of complexities as well. But first, let us introduce a more subtle
measure of complexity.

10   DEFINITION: *Let S be a semigroup. Then $\#(S)$, the complexity number‡*
of S, is the smallest positive integer n such that

$$S | T_n \text{ wr} \ldots \text{wr } T_1$$

where either

---

‡ It is *not* the same as the group complexity $\#_G(S)$.

(a) $T_1, T_3, T_5, \ldots$ *are groups and* $T_2, T_4, T_6, \ldots$ *are combinatorial semigroups;*
or
(b) $T_1, T_3, T_5, \ldots$ *are combinatorial semigroups and* $T_2, T_4, T_6, \ldots$ *are groups.*
The complexity of S**,** $C(S)$**,** *equals*
$(n, \mathbf{G})$ *iff* (a) *above holds with* $n = \#(S)$, *but* (b) *never holds with* $n = \#(S)$
$(n, \mathbf{C})$ *iff* (b) *above holds with* $n = \#(S)$, *but* (a) *never holds with* $n = \#(S)$
$(n, \mathbf{C} \vee \mathbf{G})$ *iff both* (a) *and* (b) *can hold with* $n = \#(S)$.

11 FACT: *The set of complexities is a lattice under the ordering* $\leq$, *where* $(n, \alpha) \leq (m, \beta)$ *iff* $(n, \alpha) = (m, \beta)$ *or* $n < m$ *or* $n = m$ *and* $\alpha = \mathbf{C} \vee \mathbf{G}$.

12 LEMMA: $C(S_1 \times \ldots \times S_n) = \text{LUB } \{C(S_k): k = 1, \ldots, n\}$.

Proof. $\geq$: Obvious, since $S_j | S_1 \times \ldots \times S_n$.
$\leq$: If we have $m = \max \#(S_k)$ and some $C(S_1) = (n, \mathbf{C})$ *and* another $C(S_C) = (n, \mathbf{G})$, then

$$\text{LUB } \{C(S_k)\} = (n + 1, \mathbf{C} v \mathbf{G})$$

Thus in any case we can line up the cascades for the n semigroups S_k, with groups lined up with groups, and so on, to obtain a cascade for $S_1 \times \ldots \times S_n$ with complexity LUB $\{C(S_k)\}$. The reader is invited to supply the details. $\square$

The crucial result is the following:

13 THEOREM.
(a) $C(S) = (n, \mathbf{G}) \Rightarrow C(S \text{ wr } U_3) = (n + 1, \mathbf{C})$
(b) $C(S) = (n, \mathbf{C}) \Rightarrow C(S \text{ wr } G) = (n + 1, \mathbf{G})$ *for any group* $\mathbf{G} \neq \{1\}$.

14 COROLLARY: *Semigroups of every complexity exist.*

Theorem **13** is proved on the basis of three lemmas, which we now proceed to state. For the missing proof, the reader is referred to ARBIB, RHODES, and TILSON [1968c, Sec. 2]. For a semigroup S we set $IG(S) = \langle E(S) \rangle$, the subsemigroup of S generated by its idempotents.

15 LEMMA: *Let* $S | M \text{ wr } H$, *where* H *is a finite group. Then* $IG(S) | F(H, M^1)$.
Proof. Note that if $\varphi \colon S_1 \twoheadrightarrow S_2$, then $\varphi(IG(S_1)) = IG(S_2)$. Now let $M \text{ wr } H \supset T \twoheadrightarrow S$, and let P_1 be the projection $M \text{ wr } H \twoheadrightarrow H$. Then $P_1(IG(T)) = IG(H) = \{1\}$. Thus $IG(T)$ is a subsemigroup of

$$\{(f, 1) \in M \text{ wr } H\} \cong F(H, M^1). \qquad \square$$

16 LEMMA: *Let* S_1 *be a monoid, with* $S_2 = S_1 \text{ wr } U_3$. *Then* $S_1 | IG(S_2)$.
Proof. For $1 \neq x \in U_3 = \{1, a, b\}$ let

$$I_x = \{(f, x) \in S_2 | f(x) = 1\}$$
$$P_x = \{(f, x) S_2\}$$

Set $Q_x(f, x) = f(x)$. Then Q_x: $P_x \rightarrowtail S_1$ is an epimorphism. Given $g \in S_1$, we may clearly choose $f \in F(U_3, S_1)$ such that $f(a) = g$, while $f(b) = 1$; that is, $(f, b) \in I_b$, while $Q_a(f) = 1$. (*)

Let C be the constant function in $F(U_3, S_1)$ with value 1. Then $(C, a) \in I_a$ and $(f, b) \cdot (C, a) = (f, a)$. Let T be the subsemigroup of S_2 generated by I_b and (C, a). Then T is a subsemigroup of $IG(S_2)$, and it follows from (*) that

$$Q_a(T \cap P_a) = S_1$$

and thus $S_1 | IG(S_2)$. $\square$

We omit the proof of the next lemma.

17 LEMMA: *Let $S_1 = S_2 \, \mathrm{wr} \, G_1$ with G_1 a nontrivial group. $C(S_2) = (n-1, C)$. Then if $T_1 | S \times_Y C$ with C a combinatorial semigroup, it follows that $T_2 | S$.*

18 PROOF OF THEOREM **13**

(a) Clearly $(n, \mathbf{G}) = C(S) \leq C(S \, \mathrm{wr} \, U_3) \leq (n+1, \mathbf{C})$. If $C(S \, \mathrm{wr} \, U_3) \neq (n+1, \mathbf{C})$, then $C(S \, \mathrm{wr} \, U_3) = (n, \mathbf{G})$ or $C(S \, \mathrm{wr} \, U_3) = (n+1, \mathbf{C} \vee \mathbf{G})$. In either case $S \, \mathrm{wr} \, U_3 | T \, \mathrm{wr} \, G$ for some T with $C(T) \leq (n, \mathbf{C})$ and some nontrivial group G. Then by lemma **15**, $C(IG(S \, \mathrm{wr} \, U_3)) \leq (n, \mathbf{C})$. By lemma **16**, $S | IG(S \, \mathrm{wr} \, U_3)$, and so $C(S) \leq (n, \mathbf{C})$, a contradiction. Thus $C(S \, \mathrm{wr} \, U_3)$ does equal $(n+1, \mathbf{C})$.

(b) Similarly, if (b) is false, then $S \, \mathrm{wr} \, G | T \, \mathrm{wr} \, C$ for some T with $C(T) \leq (n, \mathbf{G})$ and some combinatorial C. Then, by lemma **17**, $C(S) \leq (n, \mathbf{G})$, a contradiction. $\square$

Since we know that any nontrivial combinatorial semigroup C has complexity $(1, \mathbf{C})$ and any nontrivial group has complexity $(1, \mathbf{G})$, it follows immediately that semigroups of every complexity exist. In other words, given an arbitrary cascade of group machines and combinatorial machines, it is not in general possible to rearrange them so that all the group machines are grouped together.

With this, we close our discussion of the semigroup approach to automata theory, referring to the collection edited by ARBIB [1968a] for a wealth of further material, especially that in the chapters by Krohn, Rhodes, and Tilson.

9 STOCHASTIC AUTOMATA

1. Markov Chains
2. Stochastic Automata and Minimization
3. Realization of Stochastic Systems
4. Stochastic Acceptors

9.1 MARKOV CHAINS

In this section we give an informal treatment of Markov chains as background for our study of stochastic automata.

1 We consider a set X of possible occurrences. An *event* is merely a subset of X.

If we toss three coins, the set X consists of the vectors

$$
\begin{array}{ll}
\text{HHH} & \text{THH} \\
\text{HHT} & \text{THT} \\
\text{HTH} & \text{TTH} \\
\text{HTT} & \text{TTT}
\end{array}
$$

where, for example, HHT is the occurrence of the first two coins coming up heads, while the third coin is tails. An example of an event is "there are two heads" and is the subset {HHT, HTH, THH}.

Let X then be an occurrence space, and let $x_1, x_2, x_3, \ldots$ be events, i.e., subsets of X.

2 We associate with X a probability measure which assigns to each event x_i a number $p(x_i)$ called the *probability* of the event. We may then talk of the *probability space* (X, p). Generally, as in our treatment of state sequences below (from **11** on), we only define p on a *restricted* family of subsets of X—the "*measurable*" sets—accepting that the probabilities of certain events may not be theoretically relevant.

Let a *trial* be the selection of a point in X, and assume that we make successive trials in which no selection is influenced in any way by the outcome of previous selections. The intuitive idea of $p(x_i)$ is that if we make n trials, and obtain an occurrence of the event x_i (that is, a point of x_i) some m_i times, then for large n, (m_i/n) will be a good approximation to $p(x_i)$. Since $0 \leq m_i/n \leq 1$, this implies $0 \leq p(x_i) \leq 1$ for each x_i.

3 We say that two events x_1 and x_2 are *mutually exclusive* if they are *disjoint* when considered as subsets of X. Our frequency interpretation implies that if

$x_1 \cup x_2 =$ the event of either x_1 *or* x_2 occurring

and if x_1 and x_2 are mutually exclusive, then

$$p(x_1 \cup x_2) = p(x_1) + p(x_2)$$

Let $x_1 \cap x_2 =$ the event of both x_1 *and* x_2 occurring. Then we see from Fig. 9.1 that, for *all* x_1 and x_2,

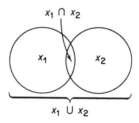

Fig. 9.1

4
$$p(x_1 \cup x_2) = p(x_1) + p(x_2) - p(x_1 \cap x_2)$$

5 We say x_1 and x_2 are *independent* just in the case

$$p(x_1 \cap x_2) = p(x_1) \cdot p(x_2)$$

Note that if we consider X itself as an event x_0, then in n trials obviously $m_0 = n$, and so we infer

$$p(X) = 1$$

6 We say that events $x_1, \ldots, x_n$ are *exhaustive* if $\cup x_i = X$. If the events $x_1, \ldots, x_n$ are exhaustive and mutually exclusive, it is clear that

$$p(x_1) + p(x_2) + \ldots + p(x_n) = 1$$

We sometimes say $x_1, \ldots, x_n$ form a *complete set of alternatives*.

7 Let us now turn to the idea of *conditional probabilities*. Suppose that we make a series of trials in which the occurrences are always constrained to be in x_2, and we want to estimate how often we obtain an occurrence of the event x_1. We may express this another way. Let us make a sequence of n unconstrained trials, and then discard those in which we do not get an occurrence of x_2. This means that approximately $p(x_2) \cdot n$ trials remain. In which of these remaining trials do we get an occurrence of x_1? Precisely when we have an occurrence of $x_1 \cap x_2$, that is, in approximately $p(x_1 \cap x_2) \cdot n$ cases. Thus the frequency with which x_1 occurs, when we know that x_2 occurs (assuming $p(x_2) \neq 0$), is approximated by

$$\frac{p(x_1 \cap x_2) \cdot n}{p(x_2) \cdot n} = \frac{p(x_1 \cap x_2)}{p(x_2)}$$

This leads us to define the *probability of x_1 conditional upon x_2* as

8
$$p(x_1 | x_2) = \frac{p(x_1 \cap x_2)}{p(x_2)}$$

and this is the probability that x_1 occurs if we already know that x_2 must occur. We set $p(x_1 | x_2) = 0$ if $p(x_2) = 0$.

Let us return to our example of three coin tosses. The events {two heads} and {two tails} are mutually exclusive. The events {at least one head} and {at least one tail} are exhaustive. Let us define our probability measure on X by assigning probability $1/8$ to each point. Then

$$p(H_i) = p(i\text{th coin comes up heads}) = 1/2$$

We see that if $i \neq j$, then H_i and H_j (or H_i and T_j) are independent, since

$$p(H_i \cap T_j) = 1/4 = p(H_i) \cdot p(T_j)$$

But if $i = j$, then $p(H_i \cap T_j) = 0 \neq p(H_i) \cdot p(T_j)$, and these results accord well with our intuitive notions of independence. Again, the probability that we get two heads if the first coin comes up heads is

$$p(2H | H_1) = \frac{p(2H \cap H_1)}{p(H_1)} = \frac{1/4}{1/2} = 1/2$$

and as we might expect is greater than the probability that we get two heads if the first coin comes up tails, which is

$$p(2H | T_1) = \frac{p(2H \cap T_1)}{p(H_1)} = \frac{1/8}{1/2} = 1/4$$

Note the following:

9 $$p(x_1 \cap x_2) = p(x_2) \cdot p(x_1 | x_2)$$

If $x_1, \ldots, x_n$ are mutually exclusive events, and $\cup x_i = x$, then

10 $$p(x) = p(x_1) + \cdots + p(x_n)$$

Consider a device M which has a set Q of internal states, and which operates on a time scale $T = \{0, 1, 2, 3, \ldots\}$. We may associate with this device the occurrence space Q^T of all T sequences of elements of Q. The sequence $q: T \to Q$ corresponds to the device being in state $q(t)$ at time t.

Of special interest are the events corresponding to fixing the values of $q(t)$ on some initial finite interval. Setting

11 $$(q_{i_1}, \ldots, q_{i_m}) = \{q \in Q^T | q(t) = q_{i_t} \text{ for } 1 \leq t \leq m\}$$

we may identify this space of events with Q^*, where $(q_{i_1}, \ldots, q_{i_m}) \in Q^*$ corresponds to the device M being in state q_{i_j} at time j, for $1 \leq j \leq m$. Let p be a probability measure on Q^T (p would usually be a probability defined only on certain subsets of the given space—we assume that it includes all the subsets of Q^T corresponding to elements of Q^*). Consistency with **11** demands that the probability of obtaining a finite sequence not depend on future behavior, i.e., that $p(q_{i_1}, \ldots, q_{i_m})$ should equal the sum of the $p(q_{i_1}, \ldots, q_{i_m}, q)$'s for all q in Q. This, and related considerations, suggest the importance of the notion of a *stochastic process:*

12   DEFINITION: *A stochastic process is a map* $p: Q^* \to [0, 1]$ *such that*
   (i) $\sum\limits_{q \in Q} p(q) = 1$

   (ii) $\sum\limits_{q \in Q} p(q_{i_1}, \ldots, q_{i_m}, q) = p(q_{i_1}, \ldots, q_{i_m})$

Let $q_k(t) = \{q \in Q^T | q(t) = q_k\}$, the event that M is in state q_k at time t. Then

$$p(q_j(t+1) | q_k(t)) = \frac{\sum\limits_{q_{i_r} \in Q, 1 \leq r < t} p(q_{i_1}, \ldots, q_{i_{t-1}}, q_k, q_j)}{\sum\limits_{q_{i_r} \in Q, 1 \leq r < t} p(q_{i_1}, \ldots, q_{i_{t-1}}, q_k)}$$

(which we take as 0 if the denominator is 0) is the probability that M should be in state q_j at time $t + 1$, given that it was in state q_k at time $t + 1$.

Consider the functions $p: \{0, 1\}^* \to [0, 1]$ defined for sequences of length ≤ 3 as follows:

$$p(\Lambda) = 1$$

$$p(0) = \tfrac{1}{3} \quad p(1) = \tfrac{2}{3}$$

$$p(00) = \tfrac{1}{6} \quad p(01) = \tfrac{1}{6} \quad p(10) = \tfrac{1}{2} \quad p(11) = \tfrac{1}{6}$$

$$p(000) = \tfrac{1}{12} \quad p(001) = \tfrac{1}{12} \quad p(010) = 0 \quad p(011) = \tfrac{1}{4} \quad p(100) = \tfrac{1}{4} \quad p(101) = \tfrac{1}{6}$$
$$p(110) = \tfrac{1}{6} \quad p(111) = 0$$

Note that this definition can be continued indefinitely, where at each stage we may choose $p(x\ 0)$ to take *any* value between 0 and $p(x)$, but must then take $p(x\ 1) = p(x) - p(x\ 0)$.

We now compute some transition probabilities:

$$p(q_0(3)|q_0(2)) = \tfrac{1}{2} = p(q_0(2)|q_0(1))$$
$$p(q_0(3)|q_1(2)) = \tfrac{1}{2} \neq p(q_0(2)|q_1(1))$$
$$p(q_0(3)|q_1(2) \cap q_0(1)) = 0$$
$$p(q_0(3)|q_1(2) \cap q_1(1)) = 1$$

Thus we see that the probability of a transition from state i to state j at time t for a general stochastic process may or may not depend on the time t, and may or may not depend on the states of the process prior to time t.

p is a *Markov process* if it is a stochastic process with the additional property that the probability of the next state being q_j when the present state is q_k is independent of any further information about the past. Formally, we have the following:

13   DEFINITION: *p is a **Markov process** if and only if for all t, for all q_j, q_k in Q, for all choices of m, $q_j \in Q$ distinct $s_i < t$ and $q_{r_i} \in Q$ for $1 \leq 1 \leq m$, we have*

$$p(q_j(t+1)|q_k(t)) = p(q_j(t+1)|\underset{1 \leq 1 \leq m}{\cap}\ q_{r_i}(s_i) \cap q_k(t))$$

We call this the *Markov property*. It has the pleasant paraphrase "A process is Markov if, given the present, the past and future are independent." In other words, "All relevant information about the past is contained in the present state," which means that a state of a Markov process shares the basic property of a state of a deterministic automaton.

14   DEFINITION: *We say the Markov process p is **stationary** (temporally homogeneous) if for all j and k, $p(q_j(t+1)|q_k(t))$ is independent of t. For a stationary p, we denote this constant value by p_{kj}.*

15   EXERCISE: Show how the function $p: Q^* \rightarrow [0, 1]$ for a stationary Markov process p may be reconstructed from a knowledge of the transition probabilities p_{ij} and the initial values $p_j = p(q_j(0))$, $q_j \in Q$.

Henceforth, we assume stationarity. Now we may immediately deduce

16 $$0 \leq p_{ij} \leq 1$$

17 $$\sum_{j=1}^{|Q|} p_{ij} = 1$$

In other words, if we are in state q_i at time t, we *must* (that is, with probability one) land up in some state at time $t + 1$.

18 A matrix P whose elements p_{ij} satisfy **16** and **17** is called a *Markov matrix*, or *stochastic matrix*.

19 EXAMPLE: Given a stationary Markov process with n states $\{q_1, \ldots, q_n\}$ and stochastic matrix P, compute the probability p_{ij}^2 that if in state q_i at time t, we will be in state q_j at time $t + 2$.

This event is the union of n mutually exclusive events x_k, where x_k is the event that the device is in state q_i at time t, q_k at time $t + 1$, and q_j at time $t + 2$.

$$
\begin{aligned}
p(x_k) &= p[q_i(t) \cap q_k(t + 1) \cap q_j(t + 2)] \\
&= p(q_i(t)) \cdot p[q_k(t + 1) \cap q_j(t + 2)|q_i(t)] \\
&= p(q_i(t)) \cdot p[q_k(t + 1)|q_i(t)] \cdot p[q_j(t + 2)|q_i(t) \cap q_k(t + 1)] \\
&= p(q_i(t)) \cdot p_{ik} p_{kj}
\end{aligned}
$$

where we have used the Markov property and stationarity. Then

$$
p_{ij}^2 = \frac{p(q_i(t) \cap q_i(t + 2))}{p(q_i(t))}
$$

$$
= \frac{\sum\limits_{k=1}^{n} p(x_k)}{p(q_i(t))} = \sum\limits_{k=1}^{n} p_{ik} p_{kj}
$$

Thus p_{ij}^2 is the generic element of the square of the matrix P, and we may thus write without ambiguity $P^2 = (p_{ij}^2)$.

20 It is now immediate by an easy induction that the kth power of P, P^k, equals (p_{ij}^k), where p_{ij}^k is the probability that if our device is in state q_i at time t, it will be in state q_j at time $t + k$.

This we may think of a Markov chain as being a stochastic process taking place on a discrete time scale, characterized by n states $q_1, \ldots, q_n$ and a Markov matrix P. P is called the transition matrix of the chain. The process has the Markov property.

For thoroughgoing introductory treatments of the material in this section, and its ramifications, see the textbooks by KEMENY and SNELL [1960] and by FELLER [1957].

9.2 STOCHASTIC AUTOMATA AND MINIMIZATION

In previous sections, we have considered deterministic automata in which the present state q and input x uniquely determine the next state and output.

We now turn to probabilistic automata in which q and x determine only the *probability* that the next output will be y and the next state will be q'. Such an automaton arises, e.g., from a network in which we have a certain amount of random malfunctioning of components.

It is worthwhile to note that stochastic sequential machines were introduced by SHANNON [1948] as models for communication channels. He also used deterministic automata as models for encoders and decoders. This seems a good point, therefore, at which to assert the belief that the theory of probabilistic automata will gain much from a rapprochement with information theory. Many results obtained for probabilistic automata may be interpreted (but not here, unfortunately) either in relation to facts about deterministic automata, or as properties of finite-state communication channels.

1 DEFINITION: *A stochastic sequential machine (SSM) is a quadruple* $M = (X, Y, Q, P)$, *where*
   X *is a finite set: the set of* **inputs**
   Y *is a finite set: the set of* **outputs**
   Q *is a finite set: the set of* **states**, *and*
   P *is a conditional probability function* $P(q', y|q, x)$; *that is,* $P(q', y|q, x) \geq 0$
      and $\displaystyle\sum_{y \in Y} \sum_{q' \in Q} P(q', y|q, x) = 1$

We interpret $P(q', y|q, x)$ as the probability that if the machine is started in state $q \in Q$ and input $x \in X$ is applied, then the output should be $y \in Y$ and the next state should be $q' \in Q$.

2 Rather than concentrating on the finite set Q, it is more natural to consider Π, the set of probability distributions on Q, as an extended state space. If $Q = \{q_1, q_2, \ldots, q_n\}$, a typical element of Π will be $\pi = (\pi_1, \pi_2, \ldots, \pi_n)$ with each $\pi_i \geq 0$ being the probability that M is in state q_i, and with $\sum \pi_i = 1$. We may embed Q in Π by identifying q_j with the probability vector with 1 in the jth place, 0 elsewhere.

We define a next-state function by

$$\tau_P[\pi, (y|x)]_j = \begin{cases} 0 & \text{if } \sum_j P(q_j, y|q_i, x) = 0 \\[2mm] \dfrac{\sum_i \pi_i \cdot P(q_j, y|q_i, x)}{\sum_j P(q_j, y|q_i, x)} & \text{if not} \end{cases}$$

It is the probability distribution obtained subsequent to π if an input x yielded an output y. The 0 is a "sink state" for the case in which an output y is impossible in these circumstances.

The *input-output function* of a state π is defined to be the function

$$P_\pi^M(y_1, \ldots, y_n | x_1, \ldots, x_n) = \sum_{\substack{q_k \in Q \\ 1 \leq k \leq n}} \pi_{q_i} \prod_{k=1}^{n} P(q_{k+1}, y_k | q_k, x_k)$$

and is the probability, given initial distribution state π and input sequence $x_1, \ldots, x_n$, that the output sequence will be $y_1, \ldots, y_n$.

We say distribution states π and π' are equivalent if they have the same input-output functions, that is, if $P_\pi^M(\cdot | \cdot) \equiv P_{\pi'}^M(\cdot | \cdot)$.

3 DEFINITION: *Two SSM's are equivalent if they have the same set of input functions.*

4 DEFINITION: *A state output SSM is one in which the output y is a function f of the state q', that is,*

$$P(q', y | q, x) = 0 \qquad unless \ y = f(q')$$

5 THEOREM: *Every SSM is equivalent to a state-output SSM.*

Proof. Just take new finite-state set $Q \times Y$, and use the transition function

$$\tilde{P}((q, y'), y'' | (q, y), x) = \begin{cases} 0 & \text{if } y' \neq y'' \\ P(q, y' | q, x) & \text{if } y' = y'' \end{cases} \qquad \square$$

Note that we should not expect the state-output SSM to be minimal-state.

Let us now reexamine Definition **1**. A stochastic sequential machine has its behavior determined by the conditional probability function P, where $P(q', y | q, x)$ is the probability that the next state will be q' and the next output will be y conditional upon the knowledge that the present state is q and the present input is x. Thus a stochastic sequential machine is not only a generalization of an automaton but also a generalization of a Markov chain. In fact a stochastic machine may be thought of as a controlled Markov chain, in that the transition matrix depends upon a parameter which may be chosen at each step by the experimenter. The fact that we have outputs as well as states need cause no difficulty, since by **5** we may regard the state-output pairs as elements of an enlarged state set.

The techniques of **1.18** are immediately applicable to this more general situation, and we obtain the following results:

6 Let M have n states, and let $M(y|x)$ be the $n \times n$ matrix with ij element $m_{ij}(y|x) = P(q_j, y | q_i, x)$. Then $M(x) = \sum_{y \in Y} M(y|x)$ is a Markov matrix, called the *state-transition matrix*. $m_{ij}(x)$ is the probability that M will go into state q_j if it receives input x when in state q_i. If $u = x_1 \ldots x_n \in X^*$, and $v = y_1 \ldots y_n \in Y^*$, then

$$M(v|u) = M(y_1|x_1)M(y_2|x_2) \ldots M(y_n|x_n)$$

has for ij element the probability that if we start M in state q_i and apply. input sequence u, we shall receive output sequence v and end up in state q_j.

Similarly, $M(u) = M(x_1) \ldots M(x_n)$ has for ij element the probability that if we start M in state q_i and apply input sequence u, we shall end up in state q_j.

7 EXERCISE: Show that deterministic automata may be identified with stochastic automata every entry of whose $M(x|y)$ and $M(x)$ matrices are either 0 or 1.

As in the deterministic case, we may draw state graphs to describe a machine. However, an arrow leading from one state to another must now be labelled not only with the output accompanying the transition, but also with the probability of that transition.

Consider the automaton with $X = Y = Q = \{0, 1\}$ and with matrices

$$M(0|0) = \begin{bmatrix} 0 & \frac{1}{2} \\ \frac{3}{4} & 0 \end{bmatrix} \qquad M(1|0) = \begin{bmatrix} \frac{1}{4} & \frac{1}{4} \\ 0 & \frac{1}{4} \end{bmatrix}$$

$$M(0|1) = \begin{bmatrix} \frac{1}{3} & 0 \\ 0 & 0 \end{bmatrix} \qquad M(1|1) = \begin{bmatrix} \frac{2}{3} & 0 \\ 0 & 1 \end{bmatrix}$$

We *omit* arrows for 0-probability transitions, to obtain the state graph shown in Fig. 9.2. We can say q_i is *reachable* from q_j if there is some sequence

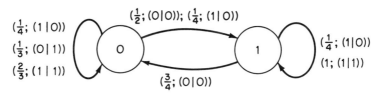

$(\frac{1}{4}; (1\,|\,0))$

$(\frac{1}{3}; (0\,|\,1))$

$(\frac{2}{3}; (1\,|\,1))$

$(\frac{1}{2}; (0\,|\,0)); (\frac{1}{4}; (1\,|\,0))$

$(\frac{3}{4}; (0\,|\,0))$

$(\frac{1}{4}; (1\,|\,0))$

$(1; (1\,|\,1))$

Fig. 9.2

in X^* which takes us from q_i to q_j with positive probability—i.e., just in the case in which there is a directed path from q_i to q_j in the graph.

q_i is *accessible* from a distribution state π if there is a sequence x such that $\pi \cdot M(x)_j > 0$, that is, the jth entry of $\pi \cdot M(x)$ is nonzero—just in the case in which there is a state q_k from which q_i is reachable, and with $\pi_k > 0$. Let now M have n states.

8 EXERCISE: Show that if q_i is accessible from π, then there is a string x of length $\leq n - 1$ such that $\pi \cdot M(x)_j > 0$.

Let $h(v|u)$ be the n-component column vector whose ith component is $\sum_{j=1}^{n} p(j, v|i, u)$, which we now label as $p_i(v|u)$. Let e have all components 1. Then clearly

$$h(v|u) = M(v|u)e$$

since
$$p_i(v|u) = \sum_{j=1}^{n} M_{ij}(v|u) \cdot 1$$
$$= \{M(v|u)e\}_i$$

We then have

9
$$h(vv'|uu') = M(vv'|uu')e$$
$$= M(v|u)M(v'|u')e$$
$$= M(v|u)h(v'|u')$$

Let $\pi = (\pi_1, \ldots, \pi_n)$ be any initial distribution for M; that is, π_i is the probability that M is in state q_i at the initial moment. Then

10
$$p_\pi(v|u) = \pi \cdot h(v|u)$$

is the probability $\sum \pi_i p_i(v|u)$ that v is the response of M when u is applied starting with initial distribution π.

We now give an analysis of equivalence of distribution states due to CARLYLE [1963], which generalizes MOORE's results [1956] for the deterministic case (cf. Sec. **3.1**).

11 DEFINITION: *Let k be a nonnegative integer. We say that the initial distribution π for the stochastic machine M is **k-equivalent** to the initial distribution λ for the stochastic machine N; or that (M, π) and (N, λ) are **k-equivalent systems**, if*

$$P_\pi^M(v|u) = P_\lambda^N(v|u)$$

*for all u and v of length k. If k-equivalence holds for all k, then (M, π) and (N, λ) are **equivalent**; otherwise, they are **distinguishable**.*

12 THEOREM: *If M is a stochastic machine with n states, and if π and λ are any two initial distributions for M, then $(n - 1)$-equivalence for π and λ is a necessary and sufficient condition for their equivalence.*

Proof. Recalling **10**, we see that π and λ are k-equivalent if

$$(\pi - \lambda)h(v|u)$$

vanishes for all v and u of length k, that is, if and only if the linear functional $\varphi(z) = (\pi - \lambda)z$ vanishes on the linear subspace of n-dimensional space spanned by the vectors $h(v|u)$ for all v and u of length k—call it $L_k(M)$. Equation **9** immediately implies:

(i) $L_k \subset L_{k+1}$

(ii) $L_k = L_{k+1} \Rightarrow L_g = L_k$ for all $g \geq k$

Thus L_k must eventually become constant—let J be the first k such that $L_g^k = L_k$ for all $g \geq k$. Since our space only has n dimensions and since L_0 is spanned by e and thus has dimension 1, we conclude that $J \leq n - 1$. Thus $L_J(M)$ is the union of the $L_k(M)$'s.

Hence π and λ are equivalent if and only if they are $(n - 1)$-equivalent. $\square$

13   THEOREM: *If M has n states, N has m states, and π and λ are initial distributions for M and N, respectively, then $(n + m - 1)$-equivalence of (M, π) and (N, λ) is a necessary and sufficient condition for their equivalence.*

Proof. Let $M + N$ be the *sum machine*, with state set the union of those of M and N, defined by

$$(M + N)(y|x) = \begin{bmatrix} M(y|x) & 0 \\ 0 & N(y|x) \end{bmatrix}$$

(M, π) and (N, λ) are equivalent if $(\pi, 0)$ and $(0, \lambda)$ are equivalent with regard to $M + N$. The result follows. $\square$

14   DEFINITION: *M and N are said to be state-equivalent if to each pure-state of M there corresponds an equivalent pure state of N, and vice versa. A* **reduced form** *of M is a machine state-equivalent to M and having the minimal number of pure states for such equivalents. A machine is in* **reduced form** *if any two pure states are distinguishable.*

The next two theorems (CARLYLE [1963]) tell us that N is a reduced form of M if and only if N is in reduced form (and hence justifies our terminology), but that, unlike reduced forms for deterministic machines, those for stochastic machines may *not* be unique.

15   THEOREM: *Let M be an n-state machine with at least one pair of equivalent states. Then there exist $(n - 1)$-state machines which are state equivalent to M. In particular, if s and t are equivalent states of M, let $N(y|x)$ be the matrix obtained from $M(y|x)$ by deleting row t and column t and replacing column s with the sums of column s and t; then $N = N(y|x)$ is a $(n - 1)$-state machine which is equivalent to M.*

16   EXERCISE: Prove Theorem **15**.

17   THEOREM: *Let M be a machine having n states; let $L = L_J(M)$ be the associated linear space (introduced in the proof of Theorem* **12***), and let H* be an $n \times (\dim L)$ *matrix whose columns form a basis for* L. *Let* $N(y|x)$ *be any set of* $n \times n$ *matrices with nonnegative elements satisfying*

18 $$N(y|x)H = M(y|x)H$$

Then $N = \{N(y|x)\}$ *is an n-state machine which is state-equivalent to* M; *in fact,*

19 (N, q_i) *is equivalent to* (M, q_i) *for* $n = 1, \ldots, n$

Conversely, if an n-state machine satisfies **19**, *then it must also satisfy* **18**.
   Proof. The converse follows immediately from **9**,

$$h(vv'|uu') = M(v|u)h(v'|u')$$

and the fact that **19** can be rewritten in the form

$$h^N(v|u) = h^M(v|u) \qquad \text{for all } u, v$$

For the direct assertion: first observe that if $N(y|x)$ is a set of matrices satisfying **18**, then in particular (since $e \in L$),

$$N(y|x)e = M(y|x)e$$

Summing over y for fixed x, we obtain

$$N(x)e = M(x)e$$

and so $N(x)$ is Markov, and thus $N(y|x)$ specifies a machine. The rest follows from **9** and **18**.   □

9.3   REALIZATION OF STOCHASTIC SYSTEMS

1   Let X and Y be finite sets, R the real line, and $\mathcal{P}(X, Y)$ the space of all functions $p: (X \times Y)^* \to R$. For $p \in \mathcal{P}(X, Y)$ we write $p(y_1, \ldots, y_n | x_1, \ldots, x_n)$ for $p((x_1, y_1), \ldots, (x_n, y_n))$.

2   DEFINITION: *A function* $p \in \mathcal{P}(X, Y)$ *is called a **stochastic system** if it satisfies the three conditions*
   (S1) $p((X \times Y)^*) \subset [0, 1]$
   (S2) $\sum\limits_{y \in Y} p(y|x) = 1$
   (S3) $\sum\limits_{y \in Y} p(y_1, \ldots, y_n, y | x_1, \ldots, x_n, x) = p(y_1, \ldots, y_n | x_1, \ldots, x_n)$
for all $x \in X$.

We denote by $\mathcal{P}_s(X, Y)$ *the convex subset of* $\mathcal{V}(X, Y)$ *comprising the stochastic systems.*

Clearly any input-output function for a state of an SSM is a stochastic system. Our central aim in this section is to characterize such stochastic systems.

Henceforth we shall restrict our attention to $\mathcal{P}_s(X, Y)$, but the reader should note that many of our notions and proofs carry over almost unchanged to the general case of $\mathcal{P}(X, Y)$.

Let $\mathcal{P}^1(X, Y)$ be the set of restrictions of functions p in $\mathcal{P}_s(X, Y)$ to the domain $X \times Y$.

3   DEFINITION: *A restricted stochastic system (RSS) is a quintuple* $\mathcal{R} = (X, Y, \Pi, \tau, \delta)$, *where, setting* $Z = Y \times Y$, *we have:*

Π *is a convex set and* 0 *is a point not in* Π.

$\tau: \Pi \times Z \to \Pi$ *is such that if* π_1 *and* π_2 *are in* Π, *then for all convex combinations* $\alpha_1\pi_1 + \alpha_2\pi_2$, *it follows that* $\tau(\alpha_1\pi_1 + \alpha_2\pi_2, z)$ *is a convex combination of the nonzero images among* $\tau(\pi_1, z)$ *and* $\tau(\pi_2, z)$—*and is* 0 *if there are no nonzero images.*

$$\delta: \Pi \cup \{0\} \to \mathcal{P}^1(X, Y) \cup \{0\} \qquad with \qquad \delta(0) = 0.$$

We call any π *such that* $\delta(\pi)$ *is the* 0-function *a* ***zero*** *of* Π *and denote it by* 0.

Given an RSS, $\mathcal{R}$, we may associate with each "state" $\pi \in \Pi$ an "input-output" function $\hat{p}_\pi$ by the equation

$$\hat{p}_\pi(y_1 \ldots y_n | x_1 \ldots x_n) = \prod_{k=0}^{n-1} \delta(\pi_k)[y_{k+1} | x_{k+1}]$$

where $\pi_0 = \pi$,

$$\pi_{k+1} = \tau[\pi_k, (y_{k+1} | x_{k+1})] \qquad (0 \le k < n)$$

4   DEFINITION: *An RSS* $\mathcal{R}$ *is a* ***realization*** *of the function* $p \in \mathcal{P}_s(X, Y)$ *iff there is a state* π *of* $\mathcal{R}$ *whose input-output function* $\hat{p}_\pi$ *is equal to* p.

An RSS is said to be in *reduced form* if $\hat{p}_{\pi_1} = \hat{p}_{\pi_2} \Rightarrow \pi_1 = \pi_2$, and all states are *reachable* from some state; that is, $\exists \pi \in \Pi$ such that $\Pi = \tau(\pi, Z^*)$.

The reader should note that any state π of an SSM M induces a realization (X, Y, Π, π, δ) with $\delta(\pi')(y|x) = p_{\pi'}(y|x)$.

Given any SSM M, we may map its distribution states π into elements p_π of $\mathcal{P}_s(X, Y)$.

5   DEFINITION: *An SSM is in* ***minimal-state form*** *iff no pure state* q_j *is equivalent to a distribution state* π *with* $\pi_j = 0$.

Surprisingly, distinct *distribution* states of a minimal-state machine may map to the same stochastic system (A. Paz). Consider the four-state deterministic machine for which all inputs cause a transition to the fourth state, but the respective outputs for inputs 0 and 1 are 1 and 1 for state q_1, 0 and 0 for state q_2, 1 and 0 for state q_3, and 0 and 1 for state q_4. If we consider this a stochastic machine, it is clearly in minimal-state form. However, $\pi_1 = (\frac{1}{2}, \frac{1}{2}, 0, 0)$ and $\pi_2 = (0, 0, \frac{1}{2}, \frac{1}{2})$ have $p_{\pi_1} = p_{\pi_2}$.

6   LEMMA: *Let $p \in \mathcal{P}_s(X, Y)$ be induced by a state π of an SSM M. Let M' be the subautomaton of M comprising the pure states reachable from π with positive probability. Then any reduced realization of p may be obtained from M', by mapping its distribution states into the corresponding elements of $\mathcal{P}_s(X, Y)$.*

7   THEOREM: *Every function in $\mathcal{P}_s(X, Y)$ has a realization.*
     Proof. We define an action of Z^* on $\mathcal{P}_s(X, Y)$ as follows:
     For $z = (y|x) \in Z^*$ and $p \in \mathcal{P}_s(X, Y)$, we define the function $p \cdot z$ by the equation

$$[p \cdot z](y_1|x_1) = \begin{cases} \dfrac{p(yy_1|xx_1)}{p(y|x)} & \text{if } p(y|x) > 0 \\ 0 & \text{if not} \end{cases}$$

The reader may readily verify that
     (i) $p \cdot z$ is in $\mathcal{P}_s(X, Y) \cup \{0\}$
     (ii) for all $\tilde{z}$ and $\bar{z}$ in Z^*, $[p \cdot \tilde{z}] \cdot \bar{z} = p \cdot (\tilde{z}\,\bar{z})$
     (iii) z carries convex combinations of points into (usually different) convex combinations of their *nonzero* images—and into 0 if there are none.

$$\sum_j \alpha_j p_j \cdot z = \sum_j (\alpha_j p_j(z) / \sum_k \alpha_k p_k(z)) p_j \cdot z$$

unless all $p_j \cdot z$ are 0.
It then follows that $(X, Y, \mathcal{P}_s(X, Y), \hat{\tau}, \hat{\delta})$ is a realization of $p \in \mathcal{P}_s(X, Y)$ as soon as we take

$$\hat{\tau}(p', z) = p' \cdot z$$
$$\hat{\delta}(p') = p'|Z \qquad\qquad \square$$

8   THEOREM: *Every $p \in \mathcal{P}_s(X, Y)$ has a reduced realization. Furthermore, this realization is unique up to isomorphism, i.e., if $(X, Y, \Pi_1, \tau_1, \delta_1)$ and $(X, Y, \Pi_2, \tau_2, \delta_2)$ are both reduced realizations of p, then there is a one-to-one correspondence $\theta: \Pi_1 \to \Pi_2$ such that*

$$\tau(\theta\pi, z) = \theta\tau(\pi, z)$$
$$\delta(\pi) = \delta(\theta\pi)$$

Proof. To get a reduced realization, we merely replace $\mathcal{P}_s(X, Y)$ in the realization of Theorem **1** by $p \cdot Z^*$. Uniqueness follows from the observation that any realization $(X, Y, \Pi, \tau, \delta)$ enjoys the property that for all $z \in Z^*$,

$$\delta(\tau(\pi, z)) = (p \cdot z)|Z$$

(extending τ to a function $\Pi \times Z^* \to \Pi$ in the natural fashion).   □

9   THEOREM [ARBIB, 1967b]: *The stochastic system p is induced by a state of an SSM iff the function p is contained in a polyhedral convex set whose union with 0 is closed under the action of Z^* in $\mathcal{P}_s(X, Y)$, that is, iff $\exists$ a finite set $\{q_1, \ldots, q_n\} \subset \mathcal{P}_s(X, Y)$ of nonzero q_i such that p and each nonzero $q_i \cdot z$ may be expressed as a convex combination $\sum \lambda_i q_i$ for suitable constants $\lambda_i (0 \le \lambda_i \le 1, \sum \lambda_i = 1)$.*

Proof. The "if" part is obvious. For the "only if" part, suppose that $q_1, \ldots, q_n$ have the stated properties. We exhibit an SSM M with finite state set $q_1, \ldots, q_n$ and for which $\pi = (\pi_1, \ldots, \pi_n)$ implies that the corresponding p_π for M is just $\sum \pi \hat{p}_{q_i}$. Our task is to find matrices

$$P(q_j, y|q_i, x) = m_{ij}(y|x)$$

which describe the transition and output probabilities. To do this we must simply solve the equations

(1) $$\delta(q_1)[y|x] = \sum_j m_{ij}(y|x)$$

(2) $$q_i \cdot (y|x) = \begin{cases} \dfrac{\sum_j m_{ij}(y|x)q_j}{\sum_j m_{ij}(y|x)} & \text{if } \sum_j m_{ij}(y|x) > 0 \\ 0 & \text{if not} \end{cases}$$

Multiplying the coefficient of q_i in (2) by the $\sum_j m_{ij}(y|x)$ of (1), we determine an $m_{ij}(y|x)$ for the given set $\{q_1, \ldots, q_n\}$. Note that, by Paz's example, the m_{ij} are not unique.   □

A stochastic process may be thought of as a stochastic system in which we have no control over the input. Thus X has but one element, and we identify $X \times Y$ with Y. Replacing Y by S, our conditions $(S\ 1\text{–}3)$ yield:

(a) $p(S^*) \subset [0, 1]$

(b) $\sum_{s \in S} p(s) = 1$

(c) $\sum_{s \in S} p(s_1, \ldots, s_n, s) = p(s_1, \ldots, s_n)$

which agrees with our definition of *stochastic process* in **1.11**. Note that a stochastic system is *not* a stochastic process in which $X \times Y$ replaces S.

A stochastic process which is, in our terminology, a state-output stochastic system is usually called "a stochastic process induced by a Markov chain."

HELLER (1965) gave a necessary and sufficient condition that a stochastic process be induced from a Markov chain. ARBIB [1967b] showed that Heller's result is a special case of our Theorem **9.**

Heller worked in terms of modules (in the algebraic, rather than network, sense) which are essentially the dual of our $\mathcal{P}(X, Y)$ setup. Independently, HELLER [1967] generalized his result to the input-output case, although still using his module formulation, which I believe to be cumbersome. However, Heller obtained some other results, to which, translated into our terminology, we devote the rest of this section. There are some questions of interest specifically related to the module framework—but, for these we must refer the reader to Heller's paper.

10   DEFINITION: $\sim_t$ is the equivalence relation on $\mathcal{P}(S)$ of *"agreement up to time t":*

$$p, p' \in \mathcal{P}(S): p \sim_t p' \Leftrightarrow p|S^t = p'|S^t$$

Thus $t' < t$ and $p \sim_t p' \Rightarrow p \sim_{t'} p'$.

11   *A Stochastic Transformation is a map* $\varphi: \mathcal{P}(X) \to \mathcal{P}(Y)$ *such that for all* $p, p' \in \mathcal{P}(X)$:
  (i) $\varphi(\lambda p + (1 - \lambda)p') = \lambda\varphi p + (1 - \lambda)\varphi p' \ 0 \leq \lambda \leq 1$
  (ii) $p \sim_t p' \Rightarrow \varphi p \sim_t \varphi p'$

12   PROPOSITION: *Each stochastic system* $f \in \mathcal{P}_s(X, Y)$ *defines a stochastic transformation* $\varphi_f: \mathcal{P}(X) \to \mathcal{P}(Y)$ *by the formula*

$$(\varphi_f p)(y_1, \ldots, y_r) = \sum_{x_1, \ldots, x_r} f(y_1, \ldots, y_r | x_1, \ldots, x_r)p(x_1, \ldots, x_r)$$

Moreover, the map $f \to \varphi_f$ *is one-to-one and onto.*

13   EXERCISE: Verify that φ_f is a stochastic transformation.

14   EXERCISE: Show how to obtain the inverse of $f \to \varphi_f$, by "driving" φ_f with stochastic processes p that have $p(x_1, \ldots, x_r) = 1$ for some sequence $x_1, \ldots, x_r$.

Under this correspondence, our finite automaton stochastic systems are just Heller's automatic stochastic transformations. Let us henceforth use $\mathcal{P}_{\text{aut}}(X, Y)$ to denote this subset of $\mathcal{P}_s(X, Y)$.

There are two natural items of structure on the stochastic transformations, namely composition and convex combination, and it is natural to see how they affect stochastic systems.

15   PROPOSITION: *Let* $f \in \mathcal{P}_s(X, Y)$ *and* $g \in \mathcal{P}_s(Y, Z)$. *Then, if we set*

$$f \,\square_Y\, g(z_1, \ldots, z_n | x_1, \ldots, x_n)$$
$$= \sum_{1 \ldots y_n} f(y_1, \ldots, y_n | x_1, \ldots, x_n) \cdot g(z_1, \ldots, z_n | y_1, \ldots, y_n)$$

we have:

$$f \square_Y g \in \mathcal{P}_s(X, Z) \qquad and \qquad \varphi_{f \square_Y g} = \varphi_g \cdot \varphi_f$$

16 EXERCISE: Prove this.

Also, it is obvious that:

17 PROPOSITION: *Let f and g both be in $\mathcal{P}_s(X, Y)$, and $0 \le \lambda \le 1$. Then $\lambda f + (1 - \lambda)g$ is in $\mathcal{P}_s(X, Y)$, and $\varphi_{\lambda f + (1-\lambda)g} = \lambda \varphi_f + (1 - \lambda)\varphi_g$.*

We now observe that $\mathcal{P}_{\text{aut}}$ is also closed under these transformations, as the following constructions show.

Let $M = (X, Y, Q, P)$ have a distribution-state π such that $p_\pi^M = f \in \mathcal{P}_{\text{aut}}(X, Y)$. Let $N = (Y, Z, Q_1, P_1)$ have a distribution state ρ such that $p_\rho^N = g \in \mathcal{P}_{\text{aut}}(X, Y)$.

18 EXERCISE: Show that the state (π, ρ) of the series composition $M \to N$ of M and N (see Fig. 9.3) has input-output function $p_{(\pi, \rho)}^{M \to N} = f \square_Y g \in \mathcal{P}_{\text{aut}}(X, Z)$.

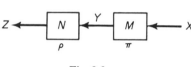

Fig. 9.3

Let, further, $M' = (X, Y, Q', P')$ have a distribution-state π' such that $p_{\pi'}^{M'} = f' \in \mathcal{P}_{\text{aut}}(X, Y)$. Let $M + M'$ be the *sum machine*

$$M + M' = (X, Y, Q \cup Q', \hat{P})$$

where

$$\hat{P}(q', y|q, x) = \begin{cases} 0 & \text{if } q \in Q \text{ and } q' \in Q' \\ 0 & \text{if } q \in Q' \text{ and } q' \in Q \\ P(q', y|q, x) & \text{if } q, q' \in Q \\ P'(q', y|q, x) & \text{if } q, q' \in Q' \end{cases}$$

Note that $M + M'$ has $|Q| + |Q'|$ states, and is *not* to be confused with $M \times M'$, consisting of M and M' in parallel, which has $|Q| \times |Q'|$ states.

The state graph of $M + M'$ contains two components completely disconnected from each other—one for Q, and one for Q'. (These components, in turn, may be further disconnected.)

19 EXERCISE: Show that the state $\lambda\pi + (1 - \lambda)\pi'$ $(0 \le \lambda \le 1)$ of $M + M'$ has input-output function

$$P_{\lambda\pi + (1-\lambda)\pi'}^{M+M'} = \lambda f + (1 - \lambda)f' \in \mathcal{P}_{\text{aut}}(X, Y)$$

20 COROLLARY: *$\mathcal{P}_{\text{aut}}(X, Y)$ is a convex subset of $\mathcal{P}_s(X, Y)$.*

21 DEFINITION: *Let $p \in \mathcal{P}_s(X, Y)$. We set **order** $(p) = \infty$ if $p \notin \mathcal{P}_{\text{aut}}(X, Y)$. If $p \in \mathcal{P}_{\text{aut}}(X, Y)$, then **order** (p) is the smallest number of states of an SSM which realizes p.*

Equivalently, order (p) is the smallest n for which **9** works—i.e., the smallest number of vertices of a simplex S such that $S \cup \{0\}$ contains p and is closed under the action of X^*.

22   COROLLARY: *Let* $f, f' \in \mathcal{P}_s(X, Y)$, $g \in \mathcal{P}_s(Y, Z)$, $0 \le \lambda \le 1$. *Then*

$$\text{order } (f \square_Y g) \le \text{order } (f) \cdot \text{order } (g)$$
$$\text{order } (\lambda f + (1 - \lambda)f') \le \text{order } (f) + \text{order } (f')$$

It is clear from the preceding comments that *any finite-state realization of a stochastic system may be uniquely expressed as a sum of submachines corresponding to connected components of its state graph.*

9.4   STOCHASTIC ACCEPTORS

If we wish to use a stochastic machine as a recognition device, we may use the following version akin to that of RABIN [1963].

1   DEFINITION: *A **probabilistic acceptor** with input set* X *is a pair* (A, λ), *where* A *is a quadruple* $\{Q, M, \pi, F\}$ *with*
     Q *a set with n elements: the set of **states**,*
     For each $x \in X$, $M(x)$ *is a Markov matrix: the **state-transition matrix**.*
     $\pi \in \Pi$, *where* Π *is the set of probability distributions on* Q, *and* π *is the **initial** distribution*
     $F \subseteq Q$: *the set of designated final states.*
and λ *is a real number* $0 \le \lambda \le 1$ *called a **cut-point**.*

Then
$$p(x) = \sum_{q_i \in Q} \sum_{q_j \in F} \pi_i m_{ij}(x) \qquad (x \in X^*)$$

is the probability that if we start A in state q_i with probability π_i and apply input sequence x, we shall end up in a designated final state. We identify q_i with the element of Π having 1 in the ith place.

2   DEFINITION: *Let* (A, λ) *be a probabilistic acceptor. The set of tapes (i.e., subset of* X^**)* $T(A, \lambda)$ *is defined to be*

$$\{x \mid x \in X^* \text{ and } p(x) > \lambda\}$$

If $x \in T(A, \lambda)$, we shall say that x is **accepted** by A with **cut-point** λ. We now want to put a restriction, due to Rabin, on the cut point λ of A. If we have the situation in which $|p(x) - \lambda|$ is relatively large, then it doesn't take many trials to assure ourselves that $p(x) > \lambda$ or $p(x) < \lambda$, and thus x is or is not in $T(A, \lambda)$, with a reasonable level of confidence. However, if the gap between $p(x)$ and λ is very small, we need many more trials to determine whether $x \in T(A, \lambda)$. But this raises the question: How many trials $N(x, \lambda)$ do we need to decide whether $x \in T(A, \lambda)$? The answer is most unfortunate —The number of trials is determined by $p(x)$, and this is precisely what we are trying to determine by making the trials. To avoid this vicious circle, Rabin emphasized the case in which a δ neighborhood around λ contains no $p(x)$'s. Then we can determine a sufficient number of trials $N(\delta, \lambda)$, independently of x.

3 DEFINITION: λ *is called an* **isolated** *cut-point for A if* $\exists \delta > 0$ *such that* $|p(x) - \lambda| > \delta$.

Note: The question of how to determine whether such a δ exists for given λ and A has not been answered yet.

RABIN [1963] proves

(a) There exists a probabilistic acceptor (A, λ) such that $T(A, \lambda)$ is *not* acceptable by a finite automaton.

(b) If A has an isolated cut-point λ, then $T(A, \lambda)$ *is* finite-state acceptable. [Rabin's ingenious proof of (b) is closely akin to the sphere-packing method of proof used so often in communication theory for coding theorems.]

4 LEMMA: *Let* $P_0 = \begin{bmatrix} 1 & 0 \\ \frac{1}{2} & \frac{1}{2} \end{bmatrix}$, $P_1 = \begin{bmatrix} \frac{1}{2} & \frac{1}{2} \\ 0 & 1 \end{bmatrix}$

If $\qquad P_{\delta_1} P_{\delta_2} \ldots P_{\delta_n} = \begin{bmatrix} 1 - p & p \\ 1 - r & r \end{bmatrix}, \qquad \delta_i \in \{0, 1\}$

then $p = .\delta_n \delta_{n-1} \ldots \delta_1$, *where p is written in binary expansion.*

Proof. (By induction.) This is clearly okay for $n = 1$. For $n > 1$, let:

$$P_{\delta_1} P_{\delta_2} \ldots P_{\delta_n} = \begin{bmatrix} 1 - p & p \\ 1 - r & r \end{bmatrix}$$

where $p = .\delta_{n-1} \delta_{n-1} \ldots \delta_1$. Then

$$P_{\delta_1} \ldots P_{\delta_{n-1}} P_0 = \begin{bmatrix} 1 - p & p \\ 1 - r & r \end{bmatrix} \begin{bmatrix} 1 & 0 \\ \frac{1}{2} & \frac{1}{2} \end{bmatrix}$$

$$= \begin{bmatrix} 1 - p' & p' \\ 1 - r' & r' \end{bmatrix}$$

where $p' = \frac{1}{2}p$;

$$P_{\delta_1} \ldots P_{\delta_{n-1}} P_1 = \begin{bmatrix} 1 - p & p \\ 1 - r & r \end{bmatrix} \begin{bmatrix} \frac{1}{2} & \frac{1}{2} \\ 0 & 1 \end{bmatrix}$$

$$= \begin{bmatrix} 1 - p'' & p'' \\ 1 - r'' & r'' \end{bmatrix}$$

where $p'' = \frac{1}{2} + \frac{1}{2}p$. $\qquad\qquad \square$

5   THEOREM: *Let $A = \{Q, M, q_0, F\}$ be an automaton over $X = \{0, 1\}$ such that $Q = \{q_0, q_1\}$, $M(0) = P_0$, $M(1) = P_1$, $F = \{q_1\}$. There exists a $0 \le \lambda < 1$ such that $T(A, \lambda)$ is not a regular event.*

Proof. If $x = \delta_1 \ldots \delta_n$, then $p(x) = \cdot \delta_n \delta_{n-1} \ldots \delta_1$. The values $p(x)$ are dense in the whole interval 0, 1. This implies that if $0 \le \lambda < \lambda_1 < 1$, then $T(A, \lambda_1) \subset T(A, \lambda)$, where the inclusion is proper. The sets $T(A, \lambda), 0 \le \lambda < 1$, therefore form a nondenumerable pairwise different collection of sets. But there is only a denumerable collection of regular events (since finite automata are denumerable). Therefore there exists a λ such that $T(A, \lambda)$ is not regular.   □

PAZ [1966, Theorem 5], making ingenious use of the eigenvalues of Markov matrices, actually defines an automaton with only *one* input and three states which, for some cut-point, does not define a regular event, but also shows (Corollary 9) that an automaton with one input and two states can only define regular events. SALOMAA [1965] gives an even more thorough analysis of the limitations of probabilistic automata with one input letter.

Paz also gives a generalization of the automaton A of Theorem **5,** which he calls "*m*-adic two state p.a.'s," M_m. The above A is then M_2.

Let $X = \{0, 1, \ldots, m - 1\}$ be the alphabet of M_m. The matrix corresponding to the symbol i is

$$M(i) = \begin{bmatrix} 1 - \dfrac{i}{m} & \dfrac{i}{m} \\[2ex] 1 - \dfrac{i+1}{m} & \dfrac{i+1}{m} \end{bmatrix}$$

Just as in the proof of Lemma **4,** we see that if $x = \sigma_1 \ldots \sigma_k$, then $p(x) = m_{12}(x) = 0.\sigma_k \sigma_{k-1} \ldots \sigma_1$, this being a usual *m*-adic fraction. Clearly, Rabin's Theorem **5** generalizes to any *m*-adic two-state automaton.

It is useful at this point to recall Nerode's regularity criterion: An event U is finite-state acceptable iff the explicit right-invariant equivalence relation $E(xEy$ iff $(\forall z)(xz \in U \Leftrightarrow yz \in U))$ is an equivalence relation of finite index.

The index of E is the minimum number of states of any machine which accepts U.

Paz gives (with a longer proof):

6   THEOREM: *The set of tapes defined by any m-adic two-state automaton with cut-point λ is a regular set if and only if λ is a rational number.*

Proof. We shall show that Nerode's equivalence relation E, when applied to the event defined by the *m*-adic two-state p.a. with cut-point λ, is of finite index if and only if λ is a rational number. If x is the tape $\sigma_1 \ldots \sigma_k$, we write $0.x^R$ for the *m*-adic fraction $0.\sigma_k \ldots \sigma_1$.

Tapes x and y belong to different classes of E iff there is a tape W s.t.

$$p(xW) \leq \lambda < p(yW)$$

or

$$p(yW) \leq \lambda < p(xW)$$

that is, if

$$.W^R x^R \leq \lambda < .W^R y^R$$

or

$$.W^R y^R \leq \lambda < .W^R x^R$$

Restricting ourselves to the former case, we have

$$\lambda = .W_n \ldots W_1 U_{n+1} U_{n+2} \ldots$$

with $.x^R \leq \lambda_n < .y^R$
where $\lambda_n = .U_{n+1} U_{n+2} \ldots$
Thus every set of tapes $\{x | \lambda_n < .x^R \leq \lambda_m\}$ for $\lambda_n < \lambda_m$ is a union of E classes. Further, if $\lambda_n < \lambda_m$ is such that $\lambda_n < \lambda_k < \lambda_m$ for *no* k, then $\{x | \lambda_n < .x^R \leq \lambda_m\}$ is actually an E class. There are only finitely many distinct λ_m's if and only if λ is rational. Hence, E is of finite index if and only if λ is rational.   □

7 EXERCISE: Use the above proof to show that there exists an automaton A with just two states and a sequence λ_n ($1 \leq n < \infty$) of cut-points such that for each n the deterministic automaton B_n with the least number of states which satisfies $T(A, \lambda_n) = T(B_n)$ has at least n states.

This shows that we can indeed save states when we use a p.a. for a tape recognition job—the price we pay is the increased number of trials required.

RABIN [1963] shows that this result may also be obtained with *isolated* cut-points.

8 THEOREM: *If A has n states, and F (the set of terminal states) contains r states, and $\exists \delta$ such that $|p(x) - \lambda| > \delta$ $\forall x \in X^*$ (that is, λ is an isolated cut-point of A), then E_λ, the Nerode equivalence relation of $T(A, \lambda)$ has index $\leq (1 + r/\delta)^{n-1}$.*

Proof. Suppose $xE_\lambda y$ is not true. Then, without loss of generality, we may pick a z such that

$$p(xz) < \lambda < p(yz)$$

Since λ is an isolated cut-point (by hypothesis), we have

9 $$p(yz) - p(xz) > 2\delta$$

Assume for the moment that F has only one state, q_n. Then

$$p(yz) = m_{1n}(yz) = [M(y)M(z)]_{1n}$$
$$p(xz) = m_{1n}(xz) = [M(x)M(z)]_{1n}$$

We adopt the following notation:

$$\text{1st row of } M(x) \text{ is } \xi_1, \ldots, \xi_n$$
$$\text{1st row of } M(y) \text{ is } \eta_1, \ldots, \eta_n$$
$$n\text{th column of } M(z) \text{ is } \zeta_1, \ldots, \zeta_n$$

Then **9** becomes

$$2\delta < \sum_{j=1}^{n} (\eta_j - \xi_j)\zeta_j$$

But ζ_j is a probability, so $|\zeta_j| \leq 1$, and thus we have

10 $$2\delta < \sum_{j=1}^{n} |\eta_j - \xi_j|$$

(If F has r states instead of 1, then δ is replaced by δ/r in **10**)
Now let the m tapes $x_1, \ldots, x_m$ be pairwise nonequivalent w.r.t. E_λ (where $m = $ index of E_λ), and let $M(x_k)$ have the 1st row $(\xi_1^k, \ldots, \xi_n^k)$. Then define

$$\sigma_k = \{(\xi_1, \ldots, \xi_n) | \xi_j \geq \xi_j^k \ (1 \leq j \leq n) \quad \text{and} \quad \sum_{j=1}^{n} (\xi_j - \xi_j^k) = \delta\}$$

(all the components in this vector σ_k maximize the corresponding elements in the 1st row of $M(x_k)$). Each σ_k is just a recentering about x_k of the basic set

$$\sigma = \{(\xi_1, \ldots, \xi_n) | \xi_j \geq 0 \ (1 \leq j \leq n) \quad \text{and} \quad \sum_{j=1}^{n} \xi_j = \delta\}$$

From **10** we see that the sets σ_i, σ_j are disjoint (for $i \neq j$), but each σ_k is contained in the set $\mathfrak{J}$:

$$\mathfrak{J} = \{(\xi_1, \ldots, \xi_n) \ | \ \sum_{j=1}^{n} \xi_j = 1 + \delta, 0 \leq \xi_i\}$$

so that if V_{n-1} means the $n - 1$ dimensional volume, then

11 $$V_{n-1}(\sigma_1) + \cdots + V_{n-1}(\sigma_m) \leq V_{n-1}(\mathfrak{J})$$

Since there is a volume constant e such that for $i = 1, 2, \ldots, m$

$$V_{n-1}(\sigma_i) = e\delta^{n-1} \quad \text{and} \quad V_{n-1}(\mathfrak{J}) = e(1 + \delta)^{n-1}$$

we see from **11** that $me\delta^{n-1} \leq e(1 + \delta)^{n-1}$; that is, $m \leq (1 + 1/\delta)^{n-1}$. And if F has r states, we may replace δ by δ/r to obtain the general result:

$$\text{Index } E_\lambda \leq (1 + r/\delta)^{n-1} \qquad \square$$

12   EXERCISE (Paz). Sharpen the bound from $(1 + r/\delta)$ to $(1 + 1/2\delta)^{n-1}$. [Hint: To get rid of r, consider a sum of columns instead of a single column. To get 2δ instead of δ, one proves that $\sum (y_j - \xi_j)\xi_j > 2\delta \Rightarrow \sum |y_j - \xi_j| > 4\delta$ by summing over positive and negative summands separately.]

In certain actual situations it is natural to assume about an automaton A that all transitions between states have strictly positive (though sometimes very small) probabilities. This led Rabin to define actual automata as follows:

13   DEFINITION: *A is called an **actual automaton** if for all $q_i, q_j \in Q$, and $x \in X$ the transition probability $m_{ij}(x) > 0$.*

14   DEFINITION: *The **spread** of a column vector* $\alpha = \begin{pmatrix} a_1 \\ \cdot \\ \cdot \\ \cdot \\ a_n \end{pmatrix}$ *is*

$$s(\alpha) = \max_i a_i - \min_i a_i.$$

*The **spread** of a matrix A with columns $\alpha_1, \ldots, \alpha_n$ is $s(A) = \max_j s(\alpha_j)$.*

15   LEMMA: *Let P be a stochastic matrix with $P_{ij} \geq \Delta > 0$ for all i and j. Then $s(P) \leq 1 - 2\Delta$.*
    Proof. $s(P) \leq \max_{i,j} P_{ij} - \min_{i,j} P_{ij} \leq (1 - \Delta) - \Delta.$ $\square$

16   COROLLARY: *Let $P_1, \ldots, P_m$ be stochastic matrices with lower bound $\Delta > 0$ for all their elements. Then $s(P_1 P_2 \ldots P_m) \leq (1 - 2\Delta)^m$.*
    Proof. Induction on m. $\square$

17   DEFINITION: *Given a matrix A, write $|A| = \max_{i,j} |a_{ij}|$.*

18   LEMMA: *If P is a stochastic matrix and A an arbitrary matrix, then $|PA - A| \leq s(A)$.*
    Proof. The absolute value of a typical element of $PA - A$ is

$$\left| \sum_k P_{ik} a_{kj} - a_{ij} \right| \leq \max_k a_{kj} - \min_k a_{kj} \leq s(\alpha_j) \leq s(A).$$ $\square$

We recall the

19   DEFINITION: *A set $T \subset X^*$ is called **definite** if for some integer k the following holds: If $k \leq l(x)$, then $x \in T$ iff $y = yz$, where $k = l(z)$ and $z \in T$.*

For the theory of such events, see PERLES, RABIN, and SHAMIR [1963], and our Exercise **3.3.29**.

20 THEOREM: *Let A be an actual machine with isolated cut-point λ. Then $T(A, \lambda)$ is definite.*

Proof. By definition of isolated cut-point, $\exists \delta > 0$ such that for all $x \in X^*$ we have $|p(x) - \lambda| > \delta$, and by definition of actual machine, $\exists \Delta > 0$ such that for all $x \in X$ and all i, j, $m_{ij}(x) > \Delta$.

Let F, the set of designated final states, have r elements. Choose a positive integer k so large that $(1 - 2\Delta)^k < 2\delta/r$ by applying corollary **16**. Hence, for any $y \in X^*$,

$$|p(yz) - p(z)| = |\sum_{q_i \in F} m_{1j}(yz) - \sum_{q_i \in F} m_{1j}(z)|$$

$$\leq \sum_{q_i \in F} |m_{1j}(yz) - m_{1j}(z)|$$

$$\leq r|M(y)M(z) - M(z)|$$

$$\leq rs(M(z)) < 2\delta$$

if we use Lemma **18**. Hence $yz \in T(A, \lambda) \Leftrightarrow z \in T(A, \lambda)$, so by definition $T(A, \lambda)$ is a definite event. □

We conclude with stability results, which deal with the behavior of $T(A, \lambda)$ under slight changes in the transition probabilities.

21 THEOREM (*Stability Theorem for Actual Automata*): *Given an actual automaton A with isolated cut-point λ, there exists $\epsilon > 0$ such that if A' is a machine with the same states, initial state, final states, and input set as A, and A' satisfies $|m_{ij}(x) - m'_{ij}(x)| < \epsilon$ for all states q_i, q_j and each $x \in X$, then we have $T(A, \lambda) = T(A', \lambda)$.*

Proof. Let F contain r states, and let $\delta > 0$ be such that $\forall x \in X^*$, $|p(x) - \lambda| > \delta$. Let $\eta = \delta/2r$. The proof proceeds in two stages:

(i) If A' satisfies $|m_{ij}(x) - m'_{ij}(x)| < \eta$ for all i, j and each $x \in X^*$, then $T(A, \lambda) = T(A', \lambda)$.

(ii) We can find $\epsilon > 0$ such that $|m_{ij}(x) - m'_{ij}(x)| < \epsilon$ for all i, j and each $x \in X \Rightarrow |m_{ij}(x) - m'_{ij}(x)| < \eta$ for all i, j and each $x \in X^*$.

Note that (i) depends on the isolated cut-point, (ii) on the fact that A is actual.

Proof of (i). $|p(x) - p'(x)| \leq \sum_{q_i \in F} |m_{ij}(x) - m'_{ij}(x)| < r\eta = \delta/2$. Therefore

$$p(x) > \lambda \Rightarrow p(x) - p'(x) > \lambda - p'(x)$$

$$\Rightarrow p'(x) > \lambda + \frac{\delta}{2}$$

Similarly,

$$p(x) < \lambda \Rightarrow p'(x) < \lambda - \frac{\delta}{2}$$

Therefore $p(x) > \lambda \Leftrightarrow p'(x) > \lambda$ for each $x \in X^*$. We also see that λ is an isolated cut-point for A'.

Proof of (ii). Let $\Delta > 0$ be such that for all i, j and $x \in X$, we have $m_{ij}(x) > \Delta$. Choose k to be a positive integer so large that $(1 - \Delta)^k < \eta/3$. Now we can find $\epsilon > 0$ so small that if $A_1, \ldots, A_k$ and $B_1, \ldots, B_k$ are $n \times n$ matrices (where n is the number of states in Q) satisfying $|A_j - B_j| < \epsilon$ for $j = 1, \ldots, k$, .then $|A_1 A_2 \ldots A_l - B_1 B_2 \ldots B_l| < \eta/3$ for each $l \le k$. We may also choose $\epsilon < \Delta/2$. Fix this choice of ϵ. Let A' be such that $|M(\sigma) - M'(\sigma)| < \epsilon$ for each $\sigma \in X$. For any $x \in X^*$ of length $l \le k$, we have $x = \sigma_1 \ldots \sigma_l$ with $\sigma_i \in X$, $|M(x) - M'(x)| = |M(\sigma_1) \ldots M(\sigma_l) - M'(\sigma_1) \ldots M'(\sigma_l)| < \eta/3$ by choice of ϵ. Also for each $\sigma \in X$, we have $m'_{ij}(\sigma) = M'_{ij}(\sigma) - m_{ij}(\sigma) + m_{ij}(\sigma) > -\epsilon + \Delta > \Delta/2$, again by choice of ϵ. So for $z \in X^*$ of length k, we have $S(M(z)) \le (1 - 2\Delta)^k < (1 - \Delta)^k < \eta/3$ and $S(M'(z)) \le (1 - 2\Delta/2)^k = (1 - \Delta)^k < \eta/3$. Now let $x \in X^*$. If length $(x) \le k$, we have already $|M(x) - M'(x)| < \eta/3 < \eta$. If length $(x) > k$, write $x = yz$ with length $(z) = k$.

$$
\begin{aligned}
|M(x) - M'(x)| &= |M(yz) - M(z) + M(z) - M'(z) + M'(z) - M'(yz)| \\
&\le |M(y)M(z) - M(z)| + |M(z) - M'(z)| + |M'(y)M'(z) - M'(z)| \\
&\le S(M(z)) + |M(z) - M'(z)| + S(M'(z)) < \eta
\end{aligned}
$$

So $|M(\sigma) - M'(\sigma)| < \epsilon$ for each $\sigma \in X \Rightarrow$
$|M(x) - M'(x)| < \eta$ for each $x \in X^*$ and this is equivalent to (ii). ☐

Theorem **21** above need not hold true if the automaton A is not actual.

22 EXERCISE (Kesten, mentioned but not given, in RABIN [1963]). Let $\rightarrow$ indicate a transition under input σ_1, $\dashrightarrow$ under input σ_2, and consider the four-state p.f.a. shown in Fig. 9.4. Let q_1 be the initial state, and let q_2 be the only designated final state. Show that

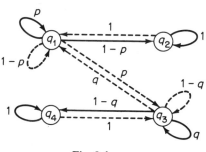

Fig. 9.4

(i) If $p = q = p_0 < \frac{1}{2}$, then any point in $[0, \frac{1}{2}(1 - p_0)]$ is an isolated cut-point.

(ii) If $q < p = p_0$, then there are points in $[0, \frac{1}{2}(1 - p_0)]$ which are *not* isolated cut-points.

[Hint: The key idea is that when $p = q$, transition from q_1 to q_2 *cannot* be improbable, but as soon as $p > q$, mass tends to shift from q_1 and q_2 down to q_3 and q_4. If P is $M(\sigma_1)$ and Q is $M(\sigma_2)$, compute P^n, and $P^n Q$ and then consider products of the form $P^{n_1} Q P^{n_2} Q \ldots P^{n_m} Q P^{n_{m+1}}$, and note that the transition from q_1 to q_2 has nonzero probability only if $n_{m+1} > 0$.]

10 MACHINES WHICH COMPUTE AND CONSTRUCT

10.1 INTRODUCTION

von Neumann in his 1948 Hixon symposium lecture (VON NEUMANN [1951]) suggested that automata theory should include a study of the way in which initial information serves to regulate the growth and change in structure of an automaton. He noted that we associate with machines used for construction a certain degenerating tendency—we expect an automaton to build an automaton of less complexity. However, when organisms reproduce, we expect their offspring to be of complexity at least equal to that of the parent. In fact, because of long-term processes of evolution, we even expect to see increases in complexity during reproduction. In view of this apparent conflict, von Neumann felt it worthwhile to see what could be formulated rigorously in the way of construction theorems for automata.

Apart from a brief account of networks in Section **2.2**, we have considered only the logical specifications of our computers, but not the implementation of these specifications in terms of a restricted set of components. Since our computations are, in general, executed by automata with no a priori bound on their size, the implementation problem contains dimen-

349

sions essentially distinct from those of conventional switching theory. Just as the tape of a Turing machine may grow without bound, so we must consider networks which grow without bound. And once we consider the growth of networks under their own control, it is but a short step to consider networks being constructed by other networks. If such a network, N, should construct a replica of itself, we say that N is self-reproducing.

Turing's result that there exists a universal computing machine suggested to von Neumann that there might be a *universal construction machine A*, that is, an automaton which when furnished with the description I_N of any other automaton N in terms of appropriate functions, will construct a copy of N. In what follows, all automata for whose construction the facility A will be used are going to share with A the property that their description will include the specification of a place where an instruction I can be inserted. We may thus talk of "inserting a given instruction I into a given automaton." The reader may at this stage think of the automaton A with the description I_A inserted into it. This entity will proceed to construct a copy of A. But note that this does not make A self-reproducing, for A with appended description produces A without an appended description—it is as if a cell had split in two with only one of the daughter cells containing the genetic message. Such a consideration suggested to von Neumann that the correct strategy might involve "duplication of the genetic material." He thus introduced an automaton B which can make a copy of any instruction I that is furnished to it—I being an aggregate of elementary parts, and B just being a "copier."

von Neumann then combined the automata A and B with a control mechanism C which does the following. Let A be furnished with an instruction I. Then C will first cause A to construct the automaton which is described by this instruction I. Next C will cause B to copy the instruction I referred to above, and insert the copy into the automaton referred to above, which has been constructed by A. Finally, C will separate this construction from the system $A + B + C$ and "turn it loose" as an independent entity.

Let us then denote the total aggregate $A + B + C$ by D. In order to function, the aggregate D must have an instruction I inserted into A. Let I_D be the description of D, and let E be D with I_D inserted into A.

E *is* self-reproductive. Note that no vicious circle is involved. The decisive step occurs in E when the instruction I_D, describing D, is constructed and attached to D. When the copying of I_D is called for, D exists already, and it is in no wise modified by the construction of I_D; I_D is simply added to form E.

We thus see that once we can prove the existence of a universal constructor for automata constructed of a given set of components, the logic required to proceed to a self-reproducing automaton is very simple. (There is, of course, something whimsical in the idea of a universal constructor, as if a mother could have offspring of any species, depending only on the father. While this may be appropriate to Greek mythology, it does not seem appropriate to biological modelling.) Our concern now is to examine the difficulties involved in actually providing a universal constructor. von Neumann did not do this in his original paper, and the task involves hundreds of pages of his book on *The Theory of Self-Reproducing Automata* which was published in 1966 after A. W. Burks had edited and extensively annotated the manuscript left at von Neumann's death in 1956. The problem is essentially this: A Turing machine is only required to carry out logical manipulations on its tape, sensing symbols, moving the tape, printing symbols, and carrying out elementary logical operations. A universal computer only has to carry out these same operations. But a universal constructor must also be able to recognize components, move them around, manipulate them, join them together. Thus, presumably, constructors of Turing machines require more components than do Turing machines themselves. We are immediately confronted with the possibility of an infinite regress. Given a set of components C_1 to construct machines which build all the automata made of components from C_1, you may need a bigger set of components C_2. To build all machines constructed of components C_2, you may need machines put together from a bigger set of components C_3. The question is: "Is there a fixed point?" Can we find a set of components C such that a sufficiently rich collection of automata built from components of C can be constructed by automata built from the same collection? This *fixed-point problem for components* is the fundamental problem in the theory of self-reproducing automata.

Once we have found a set of components C in which, for each automaton A, there can be found an automaton $c(A)$ which constructs A, it turns out to be a fairly routine matter to prove the existence of a universal constructor. We then know from von Neumann that it is a simple matter to prove *the construction fixed-point theorem*, namely that there exists a self-reproducing machine U which can construct a copy of U. There have been several procedures following on von Neumann's to exhibit a set of components which satisfy the component fixed-point theorem. VON NEUMANN [1966] used 29-state components and gave an elaborate construction taking about 200 pages. JAMES THATCHER [1965] used the same components but gave a much more elegant construction taking less than 100 pages. E. F. CODD [1965] with remarkable ingenuity and considerable use of a real computer, showed that a construction similar to von Neumann's could be done, using components with only 8 states. In the next few sections I shall show that the construction can be done with great simplicity, in a matter of a few pages, if one allows the use of much more complicated components. My rationalization for this use of complex components is that if one wishes to understand complex organisms, one should adopt a hierarchical approach, seeing how the organism is built up from cells, rather than from macromolecules.

We shall also present MYHILL's [1964] axiomatic theory of self-reproduction. Unfortunately, the axioms are formulated in a way which does not allow them to be directly applied to different sets of components but only allows one to generate theorems about self-reproduction when one already has theorems about universal constructors. However, Myhill's paper shows that results in recursive function theory can lead to rather startling conclusions about finite programs containing the possibility of infinite improvements in successive generations of offspring without requiring any randomness in the mutations.

10.2 MODULES AND CO-MOVING SETS

Our basic module is shown in Fig. 10.1 We are to think of copies of this module as placed at the lattice points of a cartesian plane. The resultant array is called a tessellation. Using coordinates (m, n), we label directions in the tessellation as follows:

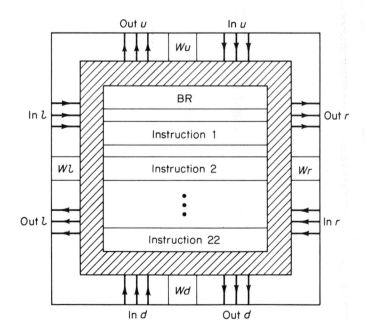

Fig. 10.1. The basic module.

u (= up):	increasing n
d (= down):	decreasing n
l (= left):	decreasing m
r (= right):	increasing m

Given the cell at (m, n), we say it has four neighbors, the cells with coordinates $(m + 1, n)$, $(m - 1, n)$, $(m, n + 1)$, and $(m, n - 1)$.

Each cell has input and output channels for communicating with its neighbors, and weld positions by which it may be joined to them. In addition there is a bit register, BR, plus the 22 registers which can hold an internal program.

The hatching denotes the combinatorial circuitry which combines the inputs and the setting of the registers and welds at time t to determine the move between t and $t + 1$, and new register settings and output of the module at time $t + 1$.

The state in which all 27 registers (including the 4 weld registers) are set to 0, is called quiescent.

Each weld may be on (state 1) or off (state 0); and two neighboring cells are said to be welded if either of the welds on their common boundary is in state 1.

Let W be the ancestral relation of welding on cells, i.e.,

$$W(\alpha, \beta) \Leftrightarrow \alpha \text{ and } \beta \text{ are welded neighbors}$$
$$\text{or } \exists \, \gamma \text{ such that } W(\alpha, \gamma) \text{ and } W(\gamma, \beta).$$

A collection C of cells is called *co-moving* if

$$\alpha \in C \quad \Rightarrow \quad : \beta \in C \Leftrightarrow W(\alpha, \beta)$$

We denote by $\bar{\alpha}$ the co-moving set of $\alpha = \{\beta | W(\alpha, \beta)\}$. By a co-moving set we mean $\bar{\alpha}$ for any nonquiescent cell α. Thus a single cell forms a co-moving set iff α is *not* quiescent and α is welded to none of its neighbors.

Our idea is this—that if any cell in a co-moving set, C, is instructed to move left, say, then all the cells in C move left.‡ To accommodate this notion, however, requires the elaboration of a rather complex set of conventions. As a first approximation, we might decree: If *any* cell in a co-moving set C receives at time t an instruction to move in direction x (u, d, l, or r), and *no* cell in the set receives at time t an instruction to move in the direction opposite x, then every cell of C will move one square in the direction x.

---

‡ I have rather loosely talked of a cell moving in direction x when in fact it is the contents of the registers that are moved. This should cause no confusion. Thus a co-moving set really comprises a *pattern*, rather than actual cells of the tessellation.

This is all right if no cell into which C is to move is nonquiescent. But what if these cells are already activated and thus presumably contain information we do not wish to lose? Thinking of the various co-moving sets as rigid bodies, we shall thus require that if a co-moving set C_1 is to the right, say, of a co-moving set C_2, and C_1 is instructed to move left, then it will push C_2 left as it moves left—unless C_2 is simultaneously instructed to move right. This prescription is enough for the models described in this section and the next. In more general situations, a more careful analysis is required—we present one later in this section.

We now present a specific instruction code for the internal program of our modules. For intelligibility, we write these instructions in semi-English. In what follows, A may take on any of the directions values, $u, l, d,$ or r; $b \in \{0, 1\}$ denotes the contents of BR or a weld register; $k, k' \in \{BR, 1, 2, \ldots, 22\}$ denote registers. An instruction of the form "$\langle A \rangle x$" tells the module to emit on its output in direction A the order x.

"weld Ab"
tells the module to change the state of its A weld to b. Here we allow A the extra value lr (20 possible instructions).

"emit Ak"
tells the module to emit in direction A the contents of its k register (88 possible instructions).

"move A"
tells the module to move in direction A (4 possible instructions).

"$A = 0$; YES(k), NO(k')"
if the input *from* direction A equals 0, execute instruction k next; if not, execute instruction k' next (1936 possible instructions).

"go to k"
tells the module to execute instruction k next (it may be regarded as an abbreviation for $'A = 0$: YES(k) NO(k')$'$).

"$(A)k; k'$"
executed by a module α causes the contents of α's register k to be stored in the register k' of the A neighbor of α (1936 possible instructions).

"A place b"
tells the module in direction A to place b in its BR (8 possible instructions).

"stop"
This is overridden by an input instruction but will be executed when control of inputs lapses, unless inputs transfer control to some other instruction of the internal program (1 possible instruction).

For each instruction, x say, of the above list, there are 4 instructions $\langle A \rangle x$, which, when executed by a module, order its neighbor in direction A

to execute instruction x. We do *not* allow such forms as $\langle A \rangle \langle A \rangle x$ obtained by repeated application. The number of possible instructions is thus

$$5(20 + 88 + 4 + 1936 + 1936 + 8 + 1) \sim 20,000 < 2^{15}$$

and so 15 bits serve to specify the state of each instruction register, while 335 bits serve to specify the state of the module.

Several of the above instructions could be avoided by reprogramming. Other instructions could be added to make our cell aggregates more useful and economical for executing tasks other than that which occupies it here.

To complete our specification, we should say what happens if a module receives contradictory instructions from its neighbors. However, we leave this open, since we shall not need to invoke such a convention in the programming that follows.

We devote the rest of this section to a discussion of co-moving conventions—this should be omitted on a first reading unless the reader wishes to acquire a new party game.

For a direction x, let x_n denote the rotation of x through n right angles (see Fig. 10.2); that is,

$$u_1 = r$$
$$r_3 = u$$
$$l_2 = r$$
$$x_{4n} = x$$

Fig. 10.2

and so on.

Let us say that a set moves in direction $x + y$ if it moves both in direction x and in direction y; and in direction 0 if it moves not at all. The addition of directions is commutative with $l + r = 0 = u + d$, and idempotent, that is, $x + x = x$.

Our convention of Sec. **1** becomes: If a cell of one co-moving set S_1 tries to move in direction x into a cell of a co-moving set S_2 which is instructed to move in direction y, then S_2 will move in direction $x + y$. S_1 moves in direction x if $y \neq x_2$, and 0 if $y = x_2$.

The prescription is not yet complete, however, as we see by considering Fig. 10.3a. Our convention applied to S_1 and S_2 tells us that S_2 should move $r + u$, while applied to S_2 and S_3 it tells us that S_2 should move $l + u$. Sticking to our rigid-body analogy, we expect the r of S_1 to cancel the l of S_3 by interacting through S_2, while S_2 still moves up, pushing S_3 with it. The result is shown in Fig. 10.3b.

Figure 10.3c shows that (on replacing 7 by $2n + 1$) the final move of a co-moving set can depend on interactions through arbitrarily many intermediaries. S_4 and S_5 do not impede each other's motion, and S_4 would push S_3 and S_2 ahead of it—were it not that this would cause S_1 to move left, in turn pushing S_7 and S_6, and thus coming up against S_5, which was moving right. Result: No motion.

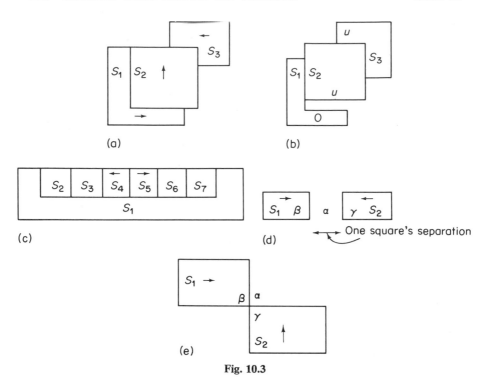

Fig. 10.3

The next problem is that raised by Fig. 10.3d. If S_1 moves right while S_2 moves left, then should cell β or cell γ occupy position α? We may make a convention that the contents of both α and γ are lost, that a specified one is kept, or—that to be used below—that neither S_1 nor S_2 moves. Similarly for Fig. 10.3e.

With this prolegomenon, we may lay down formal conventions for how cells are to move.

We let each cell contain in its combinational circuitry four registers, u, r, d, l. The x-register of cell α is denoted by α_x.

In Fig. 10.4, we introduce the extended set of directions $\{0, u, u + r, r, d + r, d, l + d, l, l + u, 0\}$ and the corresponding neighborhood of a cell. In what follows, a direction x is to be thought of as being any one of these values. If, for example, $x = l + d$, we shall use "set $\alpha_x = 1$" as shorthand for "set $\alpha_l = \alpha_d = 1$." $x(\beta)$ denotes the neighbor of β in direction x. $(x + y)_n = x_n + y_n$—for example, $(l + u)_3 = l_3 + u_3 = d + l = l + d$.

We say x is simple if $x \in \{u, l, r, d\}$, compound if $x \in \{u + r, d + r, l + d, d + l\}$.

At time t certain cells will be instructed to move in some direction. The move registers are set in stages. We henceforth assume that there are only finitely many nonquiescent cells—and thus only finitely many co-moving sets—at any finite time t. We then apply the following procedure to activated cells. (Use extended directions.)

Stage 0: We set $\alpha^x = 1$ if $\exists \beta \in \bar{\alpha}$ which is instructed to move x.

Stage k + 1: We increase α_x to 1 if $\exists \beta \in \bar{\alpha}$ such that (i) $x_2(\beta)_x = 1$ (for

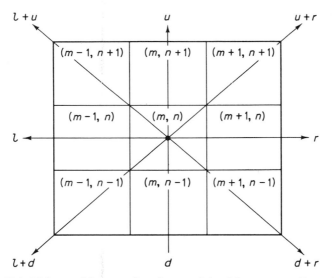

Fig. 10.4. Eight possible move directions, and the eight corresponding neighbors of the cell (m, n).

example, if $x = l$, we set α_l to 1 if any $\beta \in \bar{\alpha}$ has a cell to its right which is pushing left), and (ii) x is simple or $x = a + b$, $a \in \{b, b_2\}$ with neither $a_2(\beta)$ nor $b_2(\beta)$ in $\bar{\beta}$.

If there are n co-moving sets, the contents of the registers will stabilize in at most n stages. Let $\bar{\alpha}_x$ be the resulting value in α_x.

Figure 10.5 illustrates the distinctions of stage $k + 1$; and Fig. 10.6 gives a complete example where we need not take quiescent cells into account—we place in $\bar{\alpha}$ the symbol $\uparrow$ to indicate $\alpha_u = 1$, the symbol $\top$ to indicate $\alpha_u = 0$, $\alpha_l = \alpha_d = \alpha_r = 1$, and so on. We now have to take quiescent squares into account.

Formulation 1: Treat any quiescent square adjoining a co-moving set as a one-element co-moving set, and then carry out the above stages (the extra elements mean that more stages will, in general, be required). Then $\bar{\alpha}$, α nonquiescent, moves in direction x between time t and time $t + 1$ just in the case $\alpha_x^\sim = 1$ and $\alpha_{x_2}^\sim = 0$.

Stage 0:

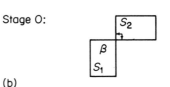

(a)

Stage 0:

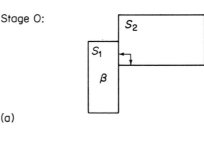

(b)

Fig. 10.5. (a) β has $\alpha = (l + d)_2(\beta)$ with $\alpha_{l+d} = 1$. But $d_2(\beta) \in \bar{\beta}$, so we do not set $\beta_{l+d} = 1$. However, $\gamma = d_2(\beta)$ has $\alpha = l_2(\gamma)$ with $\alpha_l = 1$, and so we do set $\gamma_l = 1$. Thus: Stage 1: S_1: $\leftrightarrow$ S_2: $\dashv$. (b) β has $\alpha = (l + d)_2(\beta)$ with $\alpha_{l+d} = 1$. Neither $d_2(\beta)$ nor $l_2(\beta)$ is in $\bar{\beta}$, so we do set $\beta_{l+d} = 1$. Thus: Stage 1: S_1: $\dashv$ S_2: $\dashv$.

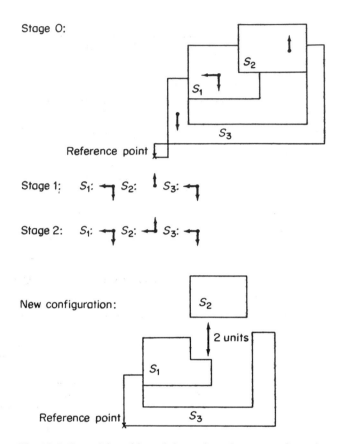

Fig. 10.6. Stage 2 is stable and determines the new configuration.

However, consider Fig. 10.7, and we see that the formulation is inadequate. So now only consider the quiescent squares after we have computed the $\alpha_x^{\sim}$.

Formulation 2: Compute $\alpha_x^{\sim}$, using only activated squares. Let x be the sum of those directions such that $\alpha_x^{\sim} = 1$ and $\alpha_{x_2}^{\sim} = 0$. Say x is the p move for $\bar{\alpha}$. We decree that $\bar{\alpha}$ will move in direction x between time t and time $t + 1$ iff there is no quiescent cell which is not only an x neighbor of some cell of $\bar{\alpha}$ but also a y neighbor of a cell β for which $\bar{\beta} \neq \bar{\alpha}$ and y is a p move for $\bar{\beta}$. If $x = 0$, or if a move of $\bar{\alpha}$ in direction x would cause a collision with some set $\bar{\beta}$ moving in direction y, then $\bar{\alpha}$ will not move.

But Fig. 10.8 shows that even this formulation is inadequate.

The remedy is to introduce a second set of registers—the "prohibition" registers—which accumulate data on the availability of jump space. The registers in cell α will be called $\alpha_x'(x = u, d, r, l)$.

Stage 0: Compute the p moves for each $\bar{\alpha}$ as before. Let x be the p move of $\bar{\alpha}$. If any cell of $\bar{\alpha}$ has as x neighbor a cell γ which is also the y neighbor of a cell β

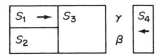

Stage 1: S_1:   ▬▶ S_2:   • S_3:   ▬▶ S_4: ◀▬▶ γ: ◀▬▶ β: ▬▶

Stage 2: S_1:   ▬▶ S_2:   • S_3: ◀▬▬▶ S_4: ◀▬▶ γ: ◀▬▬▶ β: ◀▬▬▶

Stage 3: S_1: ◀▬▬▶ S_2: ◀▬▶ S_3: ◀▬▬▶ S_4: ◀▬▬▶ γ: ◀▬▬▶ β: ◀▬▬▶

Fig. 10.7. Treat the quiescent cells γ, β as one-element co-moving sets. The only object that moves is S_2, "pushed" by S_4. This is a flaw in the formulation—we do not want a push transmitted across quiescent squares.

Stage O:

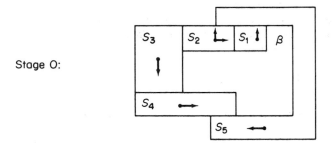

Stage 1: S_1: ⌐▶ S_2: ⌐▶ S_3: ▮ S_4: ▶ S_5: ◀⌐

Stage 2: S_1: ⌐▶ S_2: ⌐▶ S_3: ▮ S_4: ⊢▶ S_5: ◀⌐

Stage 3: S_1: ⊢▶ S_2: ⊢▶ S_3: ▮ S_4: ⊢▶ S_5: ◀⌐

New configuration:

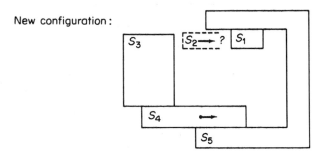

Fig. 10.8. In Stage 0, β is the only quiescent square we need consider. Stage 3 is stable and determines the new configuration. Since only one square β separates them, Formulation 2 stops S_1 moving right, and stops S_5 moving left. But S_2 tries to move into S_1. So—how do we stop S_2 from moving?

for which $\bar{\beta} \neq \bar{\alpha}$ and y is the p move for $\bar{\beta}$, then set the register $\delta'_x = 1$ for all $\delta \in \bar{\alpha}$ (that is, if $x = u + l$, we set $\delta'_u = \delta'_l = 1$).

Stage $k + 1$: We set $\alpha'_x = 1$ if $\exists \beta \in \bar{\alpha}$, which has a neighbor γ in direction x with $\gamma'_x = 1$.

If there are n co-moving sets, the contents of the registers will stabilize in at most n stages. Let $\alpha^{\#}_x$ be the resulting value.

Finally, we decree that $\bar{\alpha}$ will move in direction x iff both $\alpha^{\sim}_x = 1$, $\alpha^{\sim}_{x2} = 0$ and $\alpha^{\#}_x = 0$.

Figure 10.9 shows the appropriate solution for the problem of Fig. 10.8. A final example is shown in Fig. 10.10.

Note that we have assumed the "setting-down" time can always fall within one time step. This is akin to the assumption of rigid-body mechanics which allows the motion of one rigid body to be instantaneously transmitted along any chain of bodies against which it presses.

I hope this formulation is contradiction-free. Other conventions are permissible, as long as they are adhered to, and it is an amusing parlor-game to "de-bug" any new set of conventions.

Setting of the α'_x registers:

Stage 0: S_1: → S_2: • S_3: • S_4: • S_5: ←

Stage 1: S_1: → S_2: → S_3: • S_4: • S_5: ←

Stage 2: S_1: → S_2: → S_3: → S_4: • S_5: ←

This is stable, and determines, with the $\alpha^{\sim}_x$'s of Fig. 10.8, the new configuration. Of all the p moves, only the leftward motion of S_4 is not prohibited by the α settings.

New configuration:

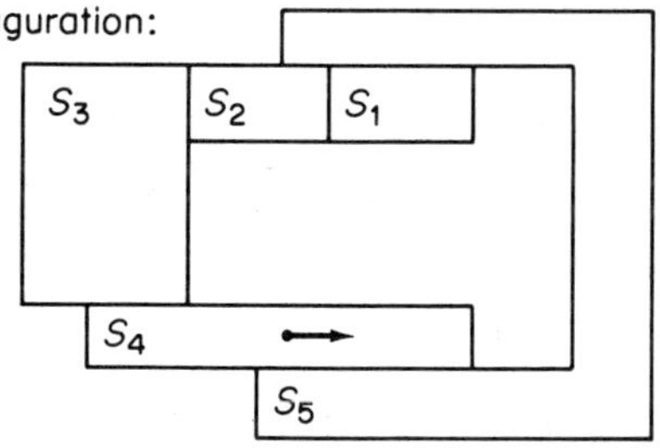

Fig. 10.9

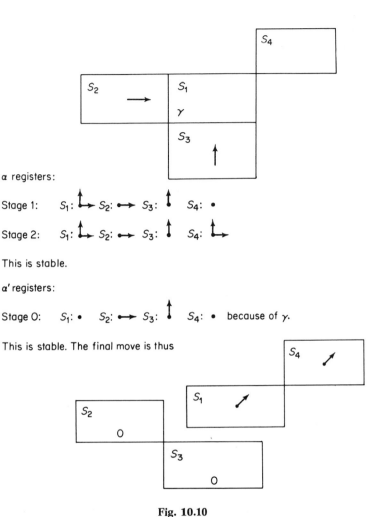

Fig. 10.10

10.3 EMBEDDING TURING MACHINES

Our task is to show how [ARBIB, 1966a] any Turing machine may be simulated by an array of active modules in the tessellation we introduced in Section 2. We shall represent the W-machine version (compare Section **4.2**) in which tape squares are either marked or blank, and the computation proceeds by executing a program comprising instructions from this list:

+   move tape left one square
−   move tape right one square

e	erase scanned square (print 0)
m	mark scanned square (print 1)
$t + (n), t - (n)$	If instruction k is $t \pm (n)$, and the scanned tape square is marked, proceed to instruction $k \pm n$; if not, go to instruction $k + 1$.
*	stop

The overall plan of the machine is very simple, as shown in Fig. 10.11. It is the same basic organization as that of the universal TM of Chapter 4. In

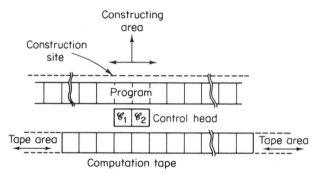

Fig. 10.11. Overall plan of embedded machine.

fact *that* construction was based on the present one. The program is represented as a linear string of co-moving cells, partitioned into substrings of ≥ 1 adjacent cells the leftmost of which has $\langle BR \rangle = 0$. The mth such substring from the left represents the mth instruction of the CT program, and contains one cell unless the mth instruction is $t \pm (n)$, in which case it contains $1 + n \mp 1$ cells.

The tape head, comprising two cells, serves to read T instructions from the program; to execute them; and to move the program. The tape consists of a linear string of co-moving cells, one for each square of the tape of the simuland—with $\langle BR \rangle$ of a cell being 1 or 0 as the corresponding square of the simuland is marked or not.

The "constructing area" shown in Fig. 10.11 will not concern us here, where we are only simulating computations.

We now show how each of the instructions listed above may be coded into the cells which represent our program in such a way as to enable the control head to appropriately manipulate the string of cells representing the data string on which our machine is computing.

To avoid confusion, we use i instruction to denote an instruction stored in a register of one of our modules, CT instruction to refer to an instruction of the CT program of the Turing machine we are simulating, and so on.

CT *instructions* $m, e, +, -$. These instructions are coded by a four i instruction program in the first four registers in the program square $\mathcal{P}$ (which, of course, has BR set to 1): $\mathcal{P}$ is the square above $\mathcal{C}_1$ at the start of the simulation of a CT instruction.

> $\mathcal{P}$: 1. (d) 4, 5
>   2. $\langle d \rangle$ go to 4
>   3. stop

The contents of register 4 depend on the CT instruction:

> m: $\langle d \rangle$ place 1
> e: $\langle d \rangle$ place 0
> $+$: $\langle d \rangle$ move l
> $-$: $\langle d \rangle$ move r

$\mathcal{P}$ will be above the first square of the control head $\mathcal{C}_1$ which will act by activating the $\mathcal{P}$, which loads the appropriate i instruction in register 5 of $\mathcal{C}_1$, which then proceeds to make sure that the tape square below it is welded into the tape, execute the CT instruction, and then advance the program tape and activate the new program square $\mathcal{P}$, thus completing the cycle:

> $\mathcal{C}_1$: 1. $\langle u \rangle$ move l
>   2. $\langle u \rangle$ go to 1
>   3. stop
>   4. $\langle d \rangle$ weld lr 1
>   5. (to be loaded by $\mathcal{P}$)
>   6. go to 1

CT *instructions* $t \pm (n)$. Most of the logic is contained in the second square C_2 of the control head. A small routine in $\mathcal{P}_1$ loads i instruction 20 of $\mathcal{C}_2$, telling whether the transfer is left or right:

> $\mathcal{P}$: 1. $\langle d \rangle$ l
>   2. (d) 5, 20
>   3. $\langle d \rangle$ go to 1
>   4. stop

The contents of register 5 depend on the CT instruction.

> $t+$: $\langle u \rangle$ move l
> $t-$: $\langle u \rangle$ move r

Now, for a transfer instruction $t \pm (n)$, $\mathcal{P}_1$ is followed by $k = n \mp 1$ squares with their BR set to 0. The first job of $\mathcal{C}_2$ is to test whether the scanned tape square is 1—if not, it simply advances the program to the next instruction, and returns control to $\mathcal{C}_1$:

$\mathcal{C}_2$:   1. $\langle d \rangle$ emit u BR
 2. $d = 0$: YES(3), NO(9)
 3. $\langle u \rangle$ move l
 4. $\langle u \rangle$ emit d BR
 5. $u = 0$: YES(3), NO(6)
 6. move r
 7. $\langle l \rangle$ go to 2
 8. stop

If the tape square is marked, $\mathcal{C}_2$ has now to generate on its right a string of k squares with Wr set to one, so that it may remember k while moving the program tape:

$\mathcal{C}_2$:   9. $\langle u \rangle$ move l
 10. $\langle u \rangle$ emit d BR
 11. $u = 0$: YES(12), NO(15)
 12. $\langle r \rangle$ move l
 13. $\langle r \rangle$ weld r 1
 14. go to 9

Having done this, $\mathcal{C}_2$ has advanced the program tape by one instruction string. So for $t + (n)$ it must move the program tape a further $k = n - 1$ instruction strings left; for $t - (n)$ it must move the program tape $k = n + 1$ instruction strings right:

$\mathcal{C}_2$:   15. $\langle r \rangle$ emit l Wr
 16. $r = 0$: YES(6), NO(17)
 17. $\langle r \rangle$ move l
 18. $\langle r \rangle$ weld r 0
 19. move r
 20. (to be loaded by $\mathcal{P}_1$: $\langle u \rangle$ move l/r)
 21. $\langle u \rangle$ emit d BR
 22. $u = 0$: YES(20), NO(15)

We are at a loss to use the "simpler" switching methods of digital computers, since we have no *a priori* bound on the number of *CT* instructions, and thus (because of transfers) none on the length of these instructions.

Note that it is the number 22 of i instructions in the program of $\mathcal{C}_2$ that determined our choice of 22 as the number of instruction registers in each module. If we had allowed more registers, we could have used a one-module control head. Using more squares in the control head, and some ingenious reprogramming, we can reduce the number of registers per module.

We have now shown that any Turing machine may be embedded in our tessellation. Thus any partial recursive function can be computed in the tessellation.

Also, any finite automaton may be simulated in our tessellation, since any finite automaton may be represented by a Turing machine with no move-right instructions (*cf.* Fig. 10.12).

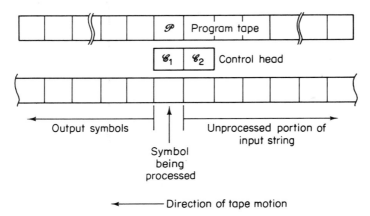

Fig. 10.12. Embedded finite automaton.

Note that the simulation of the *CT* instructions $m, e, +, -$ takes seven time steps. On the other hand, the transfer instruction $t \pm (n)$ takes $10 + 3(n \mp 1)$, if the tape square scanned has $BR = 0$, and considerably more if it has $BR = 1$. This means that *there is no constant k such that all finite automata can be simulated with at most k steps of the simulation for each time-step of the original automaton.* (This is in fact a general theorem true for any choice of a finite set of components embodying unit delays, with which to construct finite automata, and depends not at all either on our particular choice of components, or the mode of simulation we have employed —*cf.* the theorem on p. 226 of HOLLAND [1966].)

10.4 SPECIAL AND UNIVERSAL CONSTRUCTORS

Reconsider Fig. 10.11, where we now pay attention to the construction area. We shall see that we may construct automata by acting only on the square up two from e_1, and then moving constructed cells about in the construction area by appropriate programming.

"Construction" then occurs in the square above the program square above $\mathcal{C}_1$. If we want to load BR, all 22 instructions, set all four welds of the construction square, and then move the constructed cell one square in some direction, we may do it with three program cells, $\mathcal{P}_1$, $\mathcal{P}_2$, $\mathcal{P}_3$, activated in that order by the control cell $\mathcal{C}_1$.

$\mathcal{P}_1$:
1. $\langle u \rangle$ 13, 1
⋮   ⋮
10. $\langle u \rangle$ 22, 10
11. $\langle d \rangle$ go to 1
12. stop

13.⎤
⋮ | instructions
22.⎦ to be loaded

$\mathcal{P}_2$:
1. $\langle u \rangle$ 13, 11
⋮   ⋮
10. $\langle u \rangle$ 22, 20
11. $\langle d \rangle$ go to 1
12. stop

13.⎤
⋮ | instructions
22.⎦ to be loaded

$\mathcal{P}_3$:
1. $\langle u \rangle$ 11, 21
2. $\langle u \rangle$ 12, 22
3. $\langle u \rangle$ place b
4.⎤
⋮ | up to four
   | instructions
7.⎦ $\langle u \rangle$ weld Ab
8. $\langle u \rangle$ move A
9. $\langle d \rangle$ go to 1
10. stop
11.⎤
   | instructions
12.⎦ to be loaded

Let us call a machine a *CT* machine if it is programmed with the e, m, $+$, $-$, $t \pm (n)$ instructions of a W-machine, as well as register-setting and cell-moving (u, l, or r) instructions. The above paragraph, together with Section **10.3**, shows that any *CT* machine may be embedded in our tessellation, in the manner shown in Fig. 10.11. We now show:

1 THEOREM: *For each embedded CT machine $\mathcal{A}$, we may effectively find an embedded CT machine $c(\mathcal{A})$ (read "constructor of $\mathcal{A}$") which when started (by telling its $\mathcal{C}_1$ square "go to 2") will proceed to construct $\mathcal{A}$ in the three rows of its construction area immediately above it, and activate $\mathcal{A}$ by telling $\mathcal{A}$'s $\mathcal{C}_1$ square to "go to 2".*

Proof. $c(\mathcal{A})$ merely needs a control head, a program of instruction, and a blank tape. If $\mathcal{A}$ has a program comprising n squares then at most the first $3n$ squares of the program of $c(\mathcal{A})$ suffice to construct this program, in the first row of the construction area, as a co-moving set. This is then moved left or right the appropriate number of squares, and then up one square.

The control head of $\mathcal{A}$ is then built and moved up one (thus pushing the program of $\mathcal{A}$ up a further row), after which the tape of $\mathcal{A}$ is constructed as a co-moving set and moved left or right to position it appropriately.

The final square of the program of $c(\mathcal{A})$ (or, at least, of that part used in the construction of $\mathcal{A}$) then serves to activate the control head:‡

---

‡ The instructions loaded in the square below the $\mathcal{C}_1$ of $\mathcal{A}$ do not affect its functioning as a tape square.

1. $\langle u \rangle$ 5, 1
2. $\langle u \rangle$ 6, 2
3. $\langle u \rangle$ go to 1
4. appropriate transfer of control instruction: for example, $\langle d \rangle$ go to 1, or stop
5. $\langle u \rangle$ go to 2
6. stop   □

We now wish to show there is a universal *CT* machine, analogously to Turing's result that there is a universal Turing machine. We outline below the program for such a machine—that it can be embedded follows from our general considerations.

Every *CT* program is made up of the instructions $t \pm (n)$ for manipulating its tape; and instructions to load *BR*, a weld register, or one of the 22 instruction registers of the square 2 above $\mathcal{C}_1$ appropriately; and telling the co-moving set in the constructing area to move one square u, l, or r. Viewing $t \pm (n)$ as merely two instructions, $t+$ and $t-$, for the moment (we shall soon see why), we see that there are only finitely many instructions which our universal *CT* machine need simulate (*Exercise:* How many?)—let m be the least integer such that there are $< 2^m$ of them. Choose, and *fix*, an ordering of the instructions as $g_1, g_2, \ldots, g_\alpha (\alpha < 2^m)$. Let $\langle j \rangle_2^r$ denote the binary encoding of the integer j, $0 < j < 2^r$, as a string of r 0's and 1's. For example,

$$\langle 2 \rangle_2^4 = 0010$$
$$\langle 13 \rangle_2^5 = 01101$$

We then encode instruction g_j by the string of 0's and 1's:

$$e(g_j) = \langle j \rangle_2^m$$

Finally, if $t+ = g_{j+}$, $t- = g_{j-}$, we encode

$$e(t + (n)) = \langle j+ \rangle_2^m \, 1 \, 0^{n+m}$$
$$e(t - (n)) = \langle j- \rangle_2^m \, 1 \, 0^{n+m}$$

For instance, if we have $m = 6$ (it's actually larger), and $t+ = g_{17}$ (that is, $j+ = 17$), we would code $t + (2)$ as 0100011100000000.

Since n is always ≥ 1 (or can be so decreed), we are assured by our choice of $n + m$ zeros above that we have no trouble telling where an instruction starts and ends, whether we enter it from left or right in a string of such instructions. We reserve 0^m for punctuation, in a way to be explained below.

If now the program $\mathcal{P}$ of a *CT* machine consists of the sequence of instructions‡

---

‡ Where each g_j may be an g_f with $0 \leq f < 2^m$ and $j \neq t +$ or $t -$; or a $t \pm (n)$.

$$\mathcal{P} = \mathcal{g}_{j1}\ \mathcal{g}_{j2}\ \mathcal{g}_{j3}\ldots \mathcal{g}_{jL(p)}$$

we encode $\mathcal{P}$ by the string of 0's and 1's:

$$e(\mathcal{P}) = 1e(\mathcal{g}_{j1})1e(\mathcal{g}_{j2})1\ldots 1e(\mathcal{g}_{jL(p)})$$

We set $e(k, \mathcal{P}) = 1e(\mathcal{g}_{j1})1\ldots 0e(\mathcal{g}_{jk})1\ldots 1e(\mathcal{g}_{jL(p)})$.

Suppose the CT machine to be simulated has at a moment of time the tape configuration

$$T = x_1 x_2 \ldots \downarrow x_j \ldots x_s$$

that is, we specify s bits $x_1, \ldots, x_s$ and also specify that the bit under scan is the jth.

We encode T by the string

$$e(T) = 1x_1\ 1x_2 \ldots 0x_j 1 \ldots 1x_s$$

Suppose that at time t the machine we wish to simulate is about to execute the kth instruction of its program $\mathcal{P}$, that its tape-configuration is T, and some pattern $\mathfrak{M}$ has been constructed in the construction area. Then we require that at the end of its tth simulation cycle, our universal CT machine will be about to execute the *first* instruction of its program $\mathfrak{U}$, it will have

$$e(k, \mathcal{P})10^m\ 1e(T)$$

on its tape, with its control square scanning the 0 preceding $e(\mathcal{g}_{jk})$, and will have the pattern $\mathfrak{M}$ in its construction area.

We now outline the program $\mathfrak{U}$ which will enable the proper relation to hold at the end of the $(t + 1)$st simulation cycle.

1. Replace the 0 under scan by a 1.‡

2. Move right m squares along the tape, branching on each bit, so that the instruction γ_k reached in the program $\mathfrak{U}$ will be a result of decoding $\mathcal{g}_{jk}$, and will enable $\mathfrak{U}$ to simulate these instructions.

A. If $\mathcal{g}_{jk}$ is an instruction for modifying $\mathfrak{M}$, then γ_k and its successors will carry out this modification, move the tape left and replace the 1 there by a 0, and finally return control to the first instruction of $\mathfrak{U}$, to complete the $(t + 1)$st simulation cycle.

B. If $\mathcal{g}_{jk}$ is $+$, $-$, m, or e, γ_k and its successors will move the tape left and replace the 1 there by a 0, then continue moving the tape left until passing the string 10^m1, which means it has reached $e(T)$, then continue

---

‡ This is, of course, shorthand for "set BR to 1 in the cell down 1 from c_1." We use similar language in what follows.

moving it left until finding the first odd-numbered square thereafter which bears a 0 instead of a 1. The next move depends on g_{jk}:

+ : Replace the 0 by a 1. Move the tape left two squares‡ and replace the 1 by a 0.

− : Replace the 0 by a 1. Move the tape right two squares and replace the 1 by a 0.

m: Move the tape left one square and print a 1.

e: Move the tape left one square and print a 0.

The machine then moves its tape right until it passes the string 10^m1, and as soon as it has passed a 1 and a nonzero string of length m which is preceded by a 0, it scans the 0 and transfers control to the first instruction of $\mathfrak{U}$.

C. If g_{jk} is $t\pm$, γ_k and its successors will

(i) move the tape left until it has passed 10^m, and then use the 0^n preceding the next 1 to excrete a string of $n \mp 1$ cells to the right of $\mathfrak{C}_2$. The 1 is replaced by a 0.

(ii) Move the tape left until passing the string 10^m1, then continue until scanning the square to the right of the first odd-numbered square thereafter which bears a 0 instead of a 1.

(a) If the square bears a 0, reel in the string to the right of $\mathfrak{C}_2$, and move the tape right until it passes the string 10^m1, and then, as soon as it has passed a 1 and a nonzero string of length m which is preceded by a 0, it scans the 0 and transfers control to the first instruction of $\mathfrak{U}$.

(b) If the square bears a 1, move the tape right until it passes the string 10^m1, and then as soon as it has passed a 1 and a nonzero string of length m which is preceded by a 0, it changes that 0 to a 1. Then:

α. If the string to the right of $\mathfrak{C}_2$ is exhausted, print a 1 and transfer control to the first instruction of $\mathfrak{U}$.

β. If not, shorten it by one square, and move the machine tape $m + 1$ squares left. Say this is square X. The machine moves the tape left until it encounters a 1. If this takes less than m squares, it moves the tape back till it scans X, and transfers control to α. If at least m squares, it transfers control to α immediately.

With this, our outline description of $\mathfrak{U}$ is complete, as soon as we stipulate that it will decode 0^m as the stop instruction.

2 EXERCISES (Many): Fill in the details of part of the above program. Thus we have proved:

---

‡ *Exercise.* Analyze the case in which this breaks down.

3   THEOREM: *Let the CT machine with program $\mathcal{P}$ produce array $\mathfrak{M}_{\mathcal{P},T}$ in its construction area and configuration $T'_{\mathcal{P},T}$ on its tape when it stops after having been started in configuration T. Then $\exists$ a program $\mathcal{U}$, such that for all $\mathcal{P}$ and T, if we start the CT machine with program $\mathcal{U}$, scanning the leftmost square of the tape*

$$e(1, \mathcal{P})10^m1e(T)$$

it will eventually stop with $\mathfrak{M}_{\mathcal{P},T}$ in its construction area, and

$$e(\mathcal{P})0^{m+1}1e(T')$$

on its tape.   □

4   COROLLARY: *There is an encoding $f(\mathcal{A})$ of CT machines $\mathcal{A}$ as strings of 0's and 1's such that if $\mathcal{U}$ is started scanning the leftmost square of $f(\mathcal{A})$ on its tape, it will move off the rightmost square of $f(\mathcal{A})$, having constructed $\mathcal{A}$ in its construction area.*

   Proof. Let $c(\mathcal{A})$ be the constructor of $\mathcal{A}$. Then simply set

$$f(\mathcal{A}) = e(c(\mathcal{A}))$$ □

With this apparatus, it is now possible to give explicit program outlines for a host of machines with interesting properties. We give just one sample and invite the reader to supply his own:

5   THEOREM: *There exists a CT machine which is self-reproducing; that is, $\exists$ a program $\tilde{\mathcal{P}}$ and tape configuration $\tilde{\mathfrak{z}}$ such that $\mathfrak{M}_{\tilde{\mathcal{P}},\tilde{\mathfrak{z}}}$ is precisely the machine with program $\tilde{\mathcal{P}}$ and tape configuration $\tilde{\mathfrak{z}}$.*

   Proof. Let $\mathcal{V}$ be the program which causes a *CT* machine to produce a replica of its tape in the construction area, such that its rightmost square is to the left of the square 2 up from $\mathcal{C}_1$, and then repositions the tape. Let $\mathcal{W}$ be a program which takes a co-moving tape with its rightmost square to the left of the square 2 up from $\mathcal{C}_1$, and moves it right until its rightmost square is 2 up from $\mathcal{C}_1$.

   Note that $c(\mathcal{A})$ always adjoins new cells to the *left* of $\mathcal{A}$'s partially constructed program, which thus needs no repositioning before being moved up if $\mathcal{A}$ starts with the first instruction.

   Now let $\hat{\mathcal{A}}$ be the machine with program $\mathcal{V}\mathcal{U}\mathcal{W}$ (that is, the instructions of $\mathcal{V}$ followed by the instructions of $\mathcal{U}$, followed by those of $\mathcal{W}$), and no tape.
   Let $\tilde{\mathcal{P}} = \mathcal{V}\mathcal{U}\mathcal{W}$
   Let $\tilde{\mathfrak{z}} = f(\hat{\mathcal{A}})$.
Then $\tilde{\mathcal{P}}$ and $\tilde{\mathfrak{z}}$ are as advertised (*cf.* Fig. 10.13).   □

6   EXERCISE: Reprogram the above proof so that a modified version of $\mathcal{V}$ is executed *after* $\mathcal{U}$ is executed.

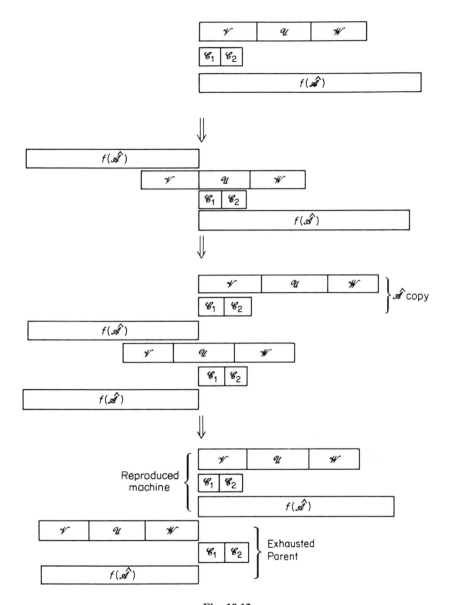

Fig. 10.13

10.5 ABSTRACT THEORY OF CONSTRUCTORS

MYHILL [1964] has given an axiomatic development of constructing machines. This seems the appropriate place to present his axioms, show that they are indeed theorems for the scheme we have just presented, and follow the deductions Myhill makes.

Pick any effective enumeration of machines (in our case, each one is a *CT* machine defined by its program and tape configuration) as

$$\mathfrak{M}_i^{(n)} \ (n = 0, 1, 2; i = 1, 2, 3, \ldots)$$

where $\mathfrak{M}_i^{(n)}$ is to be interpreted as an *n*-input machine (in our case, one to whose tape may be prefixed *n* coded programs of instructions). Let $\{I_j\}$ be an enumeration of the coded programs of instructions. $I_i: \mathfrak{M}_a^{(1)}$ denotes the 0-input machine which results from affixing the instruction I_i to the 1-input machine $\mathfrak{M}_a^{(1)}$, and $\mathfrak{M}_x^{(0)} \to \mathfrak{M}_y^{(0)}$ means that the machine $\mathfrak{M}_x^{(0)}$ builds the machine $\mathfrak{M}_y^{(0)}$. Similarly $[I_i/I_j]: \mathfrak{M}_a^{(2)}$ is the 0-input machine produced by affixing the instructions I_i, I_j to the first and second inputs of the 2-input machine $\mathfrak{M}_a$; $[\phi/I_j]: \mathfrak{M}_a^{(2)}$ is the 1-input machine formed by affixing the instruction I_j to the second input of $\mathfrak{M}_a^{(2)}$ and leaving the first input open. Thus

$$I_i: [\phi/I_j]: \mathfrak{M}_a^{(2)} = [I_i/I_j]: \mathfrak{M}_a^{(2)}$$

We now state four of Myhill's axioms, and prove their *CT* machine interpretations.

1   AXIOM *A*1: *Let h be a total recursive function; then there is a machine* $\mathfrak{M}_a^{(1)}$ *such that for all n*

$$I_n: \mathfrak{M}_a^{(1)} \to \mathfrak{M}_{h(n)}^{(0)}$$

Proof. Let *f* be the encoding of Corollary **3.3**, and let *h′* be the function which extracts *n* from I_n and proceeds to compute $f(\mathfrak{M}_{h(n)}^{(0)})$. Then $\mathfrak{M}_a^{(1)}$ is the *CT* machine whose program computes *h′* of the tape presented to it (say I_n, to produce $f(\mathfrak{M}_{h(n)}^{(0)})$) and then repositions the tape and acts on it with $\mathfrak{U}$, so that it finally constructs $\mathfrak{M}_{h(n)}^{(0)}$ □

2   AXIOM *A*2: *For every recursive function h of two arguments, there is a machine* $\mathfrak{M}_a^{(2)}$ *such that*

$$[I_m/I_n]: \mathfrak{M}_a^{(2)} \to \mathfrak{M}_{f(m,n)}^{(0)}$$

Proof. Exercise.   □

The next two axioms are trivial, and say only that we have chosen our encodings sensibly:

3   AXIOM *B*1: *There is a total recursive function t_1 such that*

$$\mathfrak{M}_{t_1(a,b)}^{(0)} = I_a: \mathfrak{M}_b^{(1)}$$ □

4   AXIOM $B2$: *There is a total recursive function t_2 such that*

$$\mathfrak{M}^{(1)}_{t_2(a,b)} = [\phi: I_a]: \mathfrak{M}^{(1)}_b \qquad \square$$

5   THEOREM: *For any computable function g, there exists a machine $\mathfrak{M}^{(0)}_a$ such that*

$$\mathfrak{M}^{(0)}_a \longrightarrow \mathfrak{M}^{(0)}_{g(a)}$$

Proof. Let $\mathfrak{M}^{(0)}_{s(x)} = I_x: \mathfrak{M}^{(1)}_x$.

Then s is a recursive function, and so is $g \circ s$. Thus, taking $h = g \circ s$ in $A1$, we have

$$I_n: \mathfrak{M}^{(1)}_c \longrightarrow \mathfrak{M}^{(0)}_{h(n)} = \mathfrak{M}^{(0)}_{g(s(n))}$$

Setting $n = c$, we obtain

$$\mathfrak{M}^{(0)}_{s(c)} = I_c: \mathfrak{M}^{(0)}_c \longrightarrow \mathfrak{M}^{(0)}_{g(s(c))}$$

and thus $a = s(c)$ satisfies the theorem. $\square$

For instance, g could be the function taking $\mathfrak{M}$ into its mirror image, and so on. Taking $g(x) = x$, we have

6   COROLLARY: *There exists a self-reproducing machine.* $\square$

7   THEOREM: *Let $h(x, y)$ be a total recursive function of two arguments. There is then a machine $\mathfrak{M}^{(1)}_d$ for which always*

$$I_a: \mathfrak{M}^{(1)}_d \longrightarrow \mathfrak{M}^{(0)}_{h(a,d)}$$

Proof. By reasoning similar to the above, we may find r so that

$$[I_a/I_n]: \mathfrak{M}^{(2)}_r \longrightarrow \mathfrak{M}^{(0)}_{h(a,t_2(n,n))}$$

Now set $d = t_2(r, r)$ and we have

$$I_a: \mathfrak{M}^{(0)}_d = [I_a/I_r]: \mathfrak{M}^{(2)}_r \longrightarrow \mathfrak{M}^{(0)}_{h(a,d)} \qquad \square$$

To present Myhill's final theorem, we recall from Section **4.4** that there is a total recursive function g such that if $\mathfrak{M}^{(0)}_{a_0}$ is a Turing machine which enumerates the theorems of arithmetic provable in some recursive axiomatization, then $\mathfrak{M}^{(0)}_{g(a_0)}$ is a Turing machine which enumerates the larger set of theorems of arithmetic provable in some expanded recursive axiomatization. If we let $\mathfrak{M}^{(0)}_a < \mathfrak{M}^{(0)}_b$ mean that $\mathfrak{M}^{(0)}_b$ prints out all the strings that $\mathfrak{M}^{(0)}_a$ prints and more, and all the strings that $\mathfrak{M}^{(0)}_b$ prints out are true statements of arithmetic; we immediately deduce

8 $$\mathfrak{M}_{a_0}^{(0)} < \mathfrak{M}_{g(a_0)}^{(0)} < \mathfrak{M}_{gg(a_0)}^{(0)} < \ldots$$

9 THEOREM: *There exists an infinite sequence of machines* $\{\mathfrak{M}_{z_i}^{(0)}\}$ *such that we have simultaneously*

$$\mathfrak{M}_{z_i}^{(0)} < \mathfrak{M}_{z_{i+1}}^{(0)}$$

and $$\mathfrak{M}_{z_i}^{(0)} \rightarrow \mathfrak{M}_{z_{i+1}}^{(0)}$$

We may call each $\mathfrak{M}_{z_i}$ a machine each of whose descendants "outsmarts" its predecessor. Myhill observes that the theorem is a brutal parody of the growth, in any usable sense, of intelligence, but is of methodological significance in that it suggests the possibility of encoding a potentially infinite number of "directions to posterity" on a finitely long "chromosomal" tape.

Since Myhill's axiomatization at this point does not accord well with our notion of *CT* machines, we leave as an

10 EXERCISE: Use **8** and the methods of Section **4** to prove Theorem **9** for *CT* machines directly.

Note that *implicit in the last discussion is an extra axiom* in Myhill's scheme—namely, that given any Turing machine Z, one may effectively find a machine $\mathfrak{M}_a^{(0)}$ which represents it.

Myhill's axioms are not very satisfactory because we know, from Section **4**, that it is hard work to verify that a tessellation satisfies these axioms. What is wanted is a set of axioms which apply directly to the modules and their scheme of interconnections.

11 RESEARCH PROJECT: Find a set of axioms satisfied by the von Neumann, Codd, and Arbib modules which guarantee self-reproduction, but which are not as cumbrous to apply as the Myhill axioms.

10.6 TESSELLATIONS AND MODULAR COMPUTERS

We devote this section to recalling the general language for describing tessellation automata as given by THATCHER [1965] and CODD [1965], with such modifications as are necessary to accommodate the co-moving sets of ARBIB [1966a], and the path-forming abilities of the iterative circuit computers of HOLLAND [1965, 1966] and the modular computers of WAGNER [1964, 1965].

G is a finitely generated abelian group [the underlying lattice: it is thus an n-dimensional array, cylinder or toroid. We have studied the case $Z \times Z$, which has two generators $(0, 1)$ and $(1, 0)$].

$G^0 = \{g^{(0)} = 0, g^{(1)}, \ldots, g^{(s)}\}$—a finite nonempty subset of G which contains a set of generators for G and which is closed under inversion. We call G^0 the basic neighborhood. (A cell at a point g of the lattice is connected to the cells at $g + g^{(i)}$. We have studied the case $s = 4$, with $G^0 = \{0, (0, 1), (0, -1), (1, 0), (-1, 0)\}$.)

At any time t, the cell at g will have a total neighborhood $N(g; t)$ which will always contain the set $g + G^0$. The cells of $N(g; t)$ are those which can affect the behavior of g from time t to $t + 1$ and will depend on past laying down of cables and forming of welds.

The basic cycle of operation comprises three phases:

(i) Pooling of relevant information from $N(g, t)$ in suitable registers of g.

(ii) Execution of computations on the basis of register contents of g.

(iii) Moves, welds, path-formation prior to next cycle.

Phase (i) includes all checks to avoid contradictions.

The finite automata in all cells are identical. Each cell has

n_1 instruction registers
n_2 data registers
s weld registers
n_3 path-formation registers

The set of states Q comprises the settings of the $n_1 + n_2 + n_3 + s$ registers, as well as the specification of which (if any) of the n_1 instructions is currently being executed.

In phase (i), certain of the n_2 data registers are set.

In phase (ii), a function $Q \rightarrow Q$ is executed.

In phase (iii), certain moves, welds, and the like are executed.

The quiescent state $q_0 \in Q$ is that in which all registers have their null setting, and no instruction is being executed. If a cell g and its basic neighborhood are all in state q_0 at time t, then g will be in state q_0 at time $t + 1$, too.

The state of all the cells at time t constitute a configuration, i.e., a map $c: G \rightarrow Q$ assigning a state to each cell of the tessellation, $c(g)$ being the state of the cell at g.

We require that the *support* of c, sup $(c) = \{g | c(g) \neq q_0\}$ be finite Interesting questions arise on relaxing this condition—but we shall not discuss them here.

We have a global transition function F such that $F(c)(g)$ is the state of the cell at g at time $t + 1$, given that the configuration was c at time t. F has the property that if sup (c) is finite, then so is sup $(F(c))$.

A configuration c' is a *subconfiguration* of c if

$$c|\sup(c') = c'|\sup(c')$$

that is,

$$c'(g) \neq q_0 \Rightarrow c'(g) = c(g)$$

c is called *passive* if $F(c) = c$, that is, it does not change with time; and *completely passive* if every subconfiguration of c is passive.

If W is the set of states which occur in the configuration c, we say that W is the *alphabet* of c, and c is called a *configuration over W*.

A subset W of Q is called *passive* or *completely passive* if all configurations over W are such.

We say that configurations c and c' are *disjoint* if their supports are. If c and c' are disjoint, we define their *union* by

$$(c \cup c')(g) = \begin{cases} c(g) & \text{if } g \in \sup(c) \\ c'(g) & \text{if } g \in \sup(c') \\ q_0 & \text{otherwise} \end{cases}$$

1   EXERCISE: The union of two completely passive configurations is *not necessarily* completely passive.

If c and c' are disjoint, Codd says that c *passes information* to c' if $\exists$ a time t such that

$$F^t(c \cup c')|S \neq F^t(c')|S, \text{ where } S = \sup(F^t(c'))$$

This is unsatisfactory, since c may push c', in view of our co-moving conventions, without modifying c' computations. So perhaps, using T_g to denote translation by g, it would be better to say that c does *not* pass information to c' if for all t there exists g_t such that

$$F^t(c \cup c')|T_{g_t}S = T_{g_t}(F^t(c')|S)$$

which says, essentially, that c has no effect on c', save to push it a distance g_t. One usually studies computation in cellular arrays by "embedding" Turing machines in the tessellation—a similar approach is Wagner's, embedding spider automata,‡ to gain some measure of parallel processing. We have followed this procedure here *but* we want to emphasize that this is highly unsatisfactory, and does not take into account the full parallel processing power of the array. Papers published so far which do try to take account of this power strike me as being rather preliminary. To move away from this into an exploration of the real subtleties and possibilities of parallel com-

---

‡ A spider automaton is a Turing machine with tape G, and $2n$ heads for some integer n, with such restrictions as that the distance between heads $2j$ and $2j + 1$ ($j = 1, \ldots, n$) is bounded.

putation on a modular computer (i.e., tessellation-embedded computer) seems a real challenge at the interface of automata theory with the design of real computers. We shall not leave the domain of Turing-computable (i.e., recursive) functions, but we shall compute them far more efficiently than with a Turing machine, and even a collection of multihead Turing machines (e.g., Wagner's spider automata).

Given a tape of a Turing machine, it will be represented square by square.

Let W be a completely passive alphabet.
Let X be the alphabet of a Turing machine.
Let $h: W \rightarrow X$ be a map.

Then a tape t_1 of the tessellation represents a tape t_2 of the Turing machine if

$$t_2(g) = h(t_1(g))$$

For instance, h could be the mapping which extracts the content of certain data registers, or it could be just a relabeling.

Let $\mathfrak{I}$ be the set of tapes, and ψ a function mapping tapes into tapes. ψ is *computable* if there exists a configuration c such that, for any configuration $d \in \mathfrak{I}$, $\psi(h(d))$ is defined iff there exists a time t such that

$$h[F^t(c \cup d)|\sup (\mathfrak{I})] = \psi(h(d))$$

where
$$\sup (\mathfrak{I}) = \bigcup_{d \in \mathfrak{I}} \sup (d)$$

and $F^t(c \cup d)\overline{|\sup (\mathfrak{I})}$ does not pass information to $F^t(c \cup d)|\sup (\mathfrak{I})$.

We say that c *computes* ψ. This definition does *not* require the computer c ultimately to become passive.

A *Turing domain* is a set of tapes $\mathfrak{I}$ such that $h(\mathfrak{I})$ is in effective one-to-one correspondence with the set of nonnegative integers. A tessellation (cellular space) is *computation-universal* if there exists a Turing domain $\mathfrak{I}$ such that for any Turing-computable partial function ψ from $\mathfrak{I}$ into $\mathfrak{I}$, $\exists$ a configuration c disjoint from $\mathfrak{I}$ such that c computes ψ.

Let $\tilde{Z}$ be a cellular space which has Turing domain $\mathfrak{I}$. Suppose $\exists$ a configuration c disjoint from $\mathfrak{I}$ such that for any Turing computable partial function ψ from $\mathfrak{I}$ into $\mathfrak{I}$, $\exists d \in \mathfrak{I}$ and a translation δ such that d_δ is disjoint from $\mathfrak{I}$ and from c, and furthermore $c \cup d_\delta$ computes ψ. Then c is called a *universal computer* with domain $\mathfrak{I}$.

This is really rather unsatisfactory, since in our earlier formulation we could interpret the above as saying that the control head $\mathcal{C}_1\mathcal{C}_2$ is a universal computer. Under certain assumptions to be explicated below, we may prove the

2   THEOREM: *There exists a universal computer in cellular space $\tilde{Z}$ iff $\tilde{Z}$ is computation universal.*

   Proof. $\Leftarrow$ Obvious.

   $\Rightarrow$ Let us desire to compute $f_n(x)$, and let $t_x \in \mathfrak{Z}$ be the tape which encodes x. Let t_n encode n.

   Assume: That we may choose δ so that $T_\delta t_n \cup t_x \in \mathfrak{Z}$ may be uniquely decomposed to obtain t_n and t_x. That is, $\exists$ an invertible recursive function k such that $T_\delta t_n \cup t_x = t_{k(n,x)}$. Then let c be the configuration which simulates the recursive function $(m) = f_n(x)$ if $m = k(n, x)$, undefined otherwise. $\square$

   Codd says that c *constructs* c' if there exists a time t such that
   (1) c' is a subconfiguration of $F^t(c)$ disjoint from c; and
   (2) $F^t(c) - c'$ does not pass information to c'.

   However, this does not exclude a simple translation. We have to know more about our representation of automata, e.g., if we are to distinguish between a configuration of an automaton and what the automaton has constructed. A tentative formulation follows:

   Let $A(t)$ = the configuration of automaton A at time t.

   Let c_t^A = the embedding of $A(t)$.

For instance, in our CT machine setup an automaton might be defined by its program, with different position and tape contents being interpreted as configurations of the one machine.

   Then c *constructs* c' if there exists an automaton A and time t such that
   (1) $c = c_0^A$
   (2) c' and c_t^A are disjoint subconfigurations of c_t^A
   (3) $F^t(c') - c$ does not pass information to c'.

Let $\mathfrak{Z}$ be a Turing domain wrt $\tilde{Z}$ which is a computation-universal cellular space. **C** is called a *complete set of computers* with domain $\mathfrak{Z}$ if each $c \in$ **C** computes a Turing-computable partial function on $\mathfrak{Z}$, and any such function is computed by at least one $c \in$ **C**.

   $\tilde{Z}$ is *construction-universal* if there is a complete set **C** of computers such that every member of **C** is constructable by some configuration disjoint from **C**. A *universal constructor* is a configuration which, when augmented by a suitable tape (disjoint from **C**) constructs an arbitrary member of **C** (*cf.* our comment on universal computers). A single configuration which is both a universal computer and universal constructor is called a *universal computer-constructor.*

   We have seen that by suitable choice of modules it is fairly too easy to show that there is a cellular space with a universal computer-constructor.

   von Neumann and Thatcher earlier proved the harder result that one may get away with only 29 states for the basic module; while Codd's thesis shows, by ingenious and arduous programming, that 8 states suffice.

3 EXERCISE: Write a critical discussion of the notions of "passing information," "self-reproduction," and "universal computer."

We next present the novel results of E. F. MOORE's [1962] "Machine Models of Self-Reproduction."

A configuration c^* *contains* n *copies* of a configuration c, if $\exists$ n *disjoint* subsets of the array of c^*, and each of these subsets is a copy of c.

A configuration will be said to be *capable of reproducing* n *offspring* by time T if starting with a copy of c, remaining cells quiescent, at time 0, there is a time $T' > T$ such that at time T' the set of all nonquiescent cells will be an array whose configuration contains at least n copies of c.

A configuration is *self-reproducing* in the sense of Moore if for each positive integer n, $\exists$ T such that c is capable of reproducing n offspring by time T. We now restrict ourselves to the case of a plane lattice. The generalizations are clear.

4 THEOREM: *If a self-reproducing configuration is capable of reproducing* $f(T)$ *offspring by time* T, *then there exists a positive real number* k *such that* $f(T) \le kT^2$.

Proof. Let c be the self-reproducing configuration. Let the smallest square array large enough for a configuration containing a copy of c be of size $D \times D$. Then at each time T, the total number of nonquiescent cells is at most $(2T + D)^2$. If r is the number of cells in the array of c, then $f(T) \le (2(T-1) + D)^2/r$. $\square$

By an *environment* is meant a specification of states for all cells of the tessellation except those of a square piece. By the insertion $E(c)$ of a configuration c (some cells of which may be quiescent) of appropriate size into an environment E is meant simply the result of specifying the states of the unspecified cells of E to be the states of the corresponding cells of c.

Two configurations c_1, c_2 of the same size are said to be *distinguished* by the environment E if $F(E(c_1)) \ne F(E(c_2))$.

5 LEMMA: *Let* E_0 *be the environment consisting entirely of passive cells. If every pair of distinct configurations can be distinguished by some environment (possibly depending on the choice of configurations), then for any two distinct configurations)* c_1, c_2, *we have* $E_0(c_1) \ne E_0(c_2)$.

Proof. If $E_0(c_1) = E_0(c_2)$, and c_1^* and c_2^* are obtained by adjoining to c_1 and c_2 a border of passive cells of width 2, then c_1^* and c_2^* would have identical sequents in *every* environment. $\square$

c is called a *Garden-of-Eden* configuration if there is no c' such that c is a subconfiguration of $F(c')$; that is, c can only be set up in the tessellation by an external agency.

6 LEMMA: *Given $A > 1$ and $n > 1$, there exists a positive integer k such that*

$$(A^{n^2} - 1)^{k^2} < A^{(kn-2)^2}$$

Proof. Since $A^{n^2}/(A^{n^2} - 1) > 1$, we may choose k so large that

$$\log_A \left(\frac{A^{n^2}}{A^{n^2} - 1} \right) > \frac{4n}{k} - \frac{4}{k^2} > 0$$

Then
$$\frac{A^{n^2}}{A^{n^2} - 1} > A^{\left(\frac{4n}{k} - \frac{4}{k^2} \right)}$$

$$A^{n^2 - (4n/k) + (4/k^2)} > A^{n^2} - 1$$

$$A^{n^2} - 1 < A^{[n - (2/k)]^2}$$

that is,
$$(A^{n^2} - 1)^{k^2} < A^{(kn-2)^2} \qquad\qquad \square$$

7 THEOREM: *A tessellation has a Garden-of-Eden configuration iff there are two distinct but indistinguishable configurations.*

Proof. Fix n, and choose k as in Lemma **6**.

Suppose there is an $n \times n$ Garden-of-Eden configuration G. A $kn \times kn$ square is made up of k^2 $n \times n$ squares. There are A^{n^2} configurations for an $n \times n$ array, but at least one of these, G, is Garden-of-Eden. Thus the number of non-Garden-of-Eden $kn \times kn$ arrays is $\leq (A^{n^2} - 1)^{k^2}$.

Suppose every distinct pair of configurations is distinguishable. Choosing k as in Lemma **6**, we see, in particular, that distinct $(kn - 2) \times (kn - 2)$ configurations, embedding in the blank configuration, must have distinct sequents. But the nonblank portion of such a sequent is contained in a $kn \times kn$ square. Thus the number of distinct non-Garden-of-Eden $kn \times kn$ configurations is at least equal to the total number of distinct $(kn - 2) \times (kn - 2)$ configurations. But this implies that $A(kn - 2)^2 \leq (A^{n^2} - 1)^{k^2}$, contradicting Lemma **6**. Thus either at least two distinct $(kn - 2) \times (kn - 2)$ configurations are indistinguishable, or there is no Garden-of-Eden configuration. $\qquad \square$

8 EXERCISE: Relate this result to the tessellation studied in Sections **10.2** through **10.4**.

SMITH [1968] has shown that Lee's results on self-description of Turing machines (cf. **4.4**) may be used to construct self-reproducing configurations in a manner far simpler than that of Sections **2** to **4**—by moving in the opposite direction, so to speak, of the biological trend outlined in the next section.

The basic observation is a simple one, refinement of which may be found in Smith's paper.

9 EXERCISE: Show that for any Turing machine Z we can define a one-dimensional cellular space $\tilde{Z}$ which simulates M in real time. [Hint: Let the state of each cell encode a state-symbol pair of Z, having introduced a new "null-state." Then let all cells but one in the space at any time have their state-symbol null, and define the next-state function on the basis of immediate neighbors in the obvious way.]

For such a space, we say that Z is *wired-in* $\tilde{Z}$, or that $\tilde{Z}$ has Z wired in. As in Section **4.4**, the notation $x \underset{P}{\rightarrow} y$ will mean that Turing machine program P acting on initial tape x halts with y on the tape as its final result.

Let the wired-in computer U be a universal Turing machine, i.e., one for which

$$f(P',x') \underset{U}{\rightarrow} y'$$

where f is the encoding function required by U and $x' \underset{P'}{\rightarrow} y'$. We require a prógram P such that

$$x \underset{\uparrow\ P}{\rightarrow} (f(P, x), y, \underset{\uparrow}{f(P, x)}) \underset{P}{\rightarrow} \cdots$$

where y is the result of some computation on x.

10 LEMMA [SMITH, 1968; cf. LEE, 1963]: *For an arbitrary one-to-one recursive function f from (program, tape) pairs to tapes and for an arbitrary total recursive function g such that $g(x) = y$, there exists a self-describing machine with program P such that*

$$x \underset{\uparrow\ P}{\rightarrow} (f(P, x), y, \underset{\uparrow}{f(P, x)}).$$

Proof. Define the functior h from programs to programs such that $h(Q)$ is the first program which reads arbitrary input tape x, encodes program Q and tape x by given function f to get $f(Q, x)$, prints $f(Q, x)$, computes $g(x)$ to get y, prints y, prints $f(Q, x)$ again (either by re-encoding $f(Q, x)$ or by copying the result of the first encoding), and finally moves the head to the leftmost symbol in the rightmost encoding $f(Q, x)$. That is,

$$x \underset{\uparrow\ h(Q)}{\longrightarrow} (f(Q, x), y, \underset{\uparrow}{f(Q, x)}).$$

Clearly h can be chosen total recursive. Thus, by the recursion theorem, there exists P which is a computational fixed point of h such that

$$x \underset{\uparrow}{\underset{P}{\rightarrow}} (f(P, x), y, \underset{\uparrow}{f}(P, x)). \qquad \square$$

Thus in cellular space $\tilde{U}$ with U wired in, the following situation can hold:

$$f(P, x) \underset{\tilde{U}}{\rightarrow} (f(P, x), y, f(P, x))$$

at some time $T > 0$. If we decree that $U_{(,)}$ is U so modified that on completing such a computation it will backtrack to the rightmost comma, and start anew without reading or writing to the left of that comma, we will obtain

$$f(P, x) \underset{U_{(,)}}{\longrightarrow} (f(P, x), y, f(P, x), y, f(P, x))$$

at some later time $T' > T$ and so forth. Hence we have shown the following:

11 THEOREM: *Let $\tilde{U}_{(,)}$ be a computation-universal cellular space with a modified universal Turing machine $U_{(,)}$ wired in. Then there exists a configuration c in Z_U which is self-reproducing and computes any given total recursive function g.* $\qquad \square$

We close this small sample of Smith's results with the vexing question, emphasized by our discussion in the next section: Has he actually *constructed* machines, or merely given copying routines somehow distinct from construction?

10.7 TOWARD BIOLOGICAL MODELS‡

We wish to show how to modify the model of Sections 2 through 4 so that it may provide a logical framework for understanding embryological processes. The great excitement over DNA-RNA prompted many people to claim that at last we had found the "secret of life." However, the simple DNA $\rightarrow$ RNA and RNA $\rightarrow$ enzyme transductions, while important biologically, are of little interest to the experienced automata theorist. It seems to me that the notion of DNA $\rightarrow$ RNA $\rightarrow$ enzyme transduction is of as vital importance to understanding life as the conversion of decimal numbers to binary notation is to understanding digital computers. However, just as computers may be built to operate in nonbinary mode, so may there be life without DNA; and we are no more entitled to say we understand embryology when we understand DNA than we are entitled to say we understand computation when we understand radix two.

The challenging question seems to be "How can a complex multicellular

---

‡ This section is based on Sections 4 and 5 of ARBIB [1967a].

automaton grow from a single cell, given that a finite program can be executed within each cell?" Such a question as this is nontrivial, and becomes a fit topic for automata theory, though it must be confessed that, at present, the emphasis is on ingenious programming of cellular arrays rather than on weaving a rich texture of theorems. We saw how a multicellular organism could construct a copy of itself, but we did not answer the question "How can a complex multicellular automaton grow from a *single* cell." In this final section, I want to sketch how our model can be modified to yield an answer, and wherein that model differs from the embryological situation.

Let us first note that the self-reproduction we have studied is a far narrower concept than the embryological one—a human zygote grows into a human, not into a replica of one of the parents. The zygote contains only an outline, a program which, in interaction with the environment, produces an organism of a certain species (we are now discarding questions of mutation and evolution). This leads to a whole series of questions—which here I can merely raise—of the "identity" of an automaton. What does it mean to say two automata belong to the same "species"? Embryological reproduction gives rise to offspring with similar structure, and this implies similarity of function. What are measures of structural similarity and functional similarity, such that the first implies the second? Are there interesting classes of automata for which we may carry out decompositions into a species-dependent automaton, and an individuality-expressing automaton? Can we study reliability of reproduction for such systems, where the genetic information determines the species-dependent automaton with high probability, random influences making their appearance chiefly in modifying the individuality-expressing automaton? Incidentally, I envisage such decompositions as being at the functional, rather than structural, level.

We have used modules far more complex than von Neumann's 29-state elements. This seems admirable, rather than sad, now that we are turning to biological questions (in fact, we shall shortly introduce a model with far larger modules). The living cell, with its synthetic machinery involving hundreds of metabolic pathways can rival any operation of our module, as well as being under the control of DNA molecules, we believe, with far more bits of information than our cell can store. So, perhaps we lose biological significance by unduly limiting the information content of the module.

Our construction rests on the assumption that we can produce new cells at will, our only problem being to ensure that they contain the proper instructions. Given cell reproduction, how do we replicate an organism? This is the topic we treat—and it makes sense to ignore a lot of hard work by using complicated cells. In fact, we might hypothesize that "sophisticated" organisms can evolve (by whatever mechanism) only when there are complicated reproducing cells available. Contrasting our model with organism reproduction, we note that

(1) Our program was embedded in a string of cells, whereas the biological program is a string stored in *each* cell.

(2) We use a complete specification, whereas "Nature" uses an incomplete specification.

(3) We didn't use anything like the full power of our model (i.e., the operation was sequential instead of parallel).

(4) We constructed a passive configuration—we set up all the cells with their internal program, and only then did we activate the machine by telling the control head to execute its first instruction. Contrast the living, growing embryo. Our construction *relied* on the passivity of the components, and demanded that any subassembly would stay fixed and inactive until the whole structure was complete. The biological development depends on active interaction and induction between subassemblies.

The logic of taking factors (2)–(4) into account is hard, and we do not treat it here. To modify our model to take account of factor (1), we still think of a cell of the tessellation as corresponding to a cell of the organism—with the active cells in the construction area corresponding to the embryo—but now each cell contains the whole program. So in a sense activation of different subroutines in a cell of our modified model would correspond to differentiation of cells of the embryo. Each module stores a whole program, but with only a substring loaded into the 22 instruction registers. Biologically, we put all the available information in one cell and let it grow. In our new model, we can think of the machine as starting as a single cell with two strings (one corresponding to our Mark I program, one to the tape). It secretes new cells and manipulates tape to produce a discrete aggregate of cells. Starting with one cell containing this information in our model, we would program it to secrete extra cells for tape as well as for the growing organism. The tape cells are discarded "at birth." (We still haven't used parallel processing—for we put a large but bounded amount of information in the individual cell, and then used extra cells for tape—this captures nothing of the embryological organization. "A germ cell doth not a living embryo make.")

We have not said anything about where cells came from: this corresponds to the question of the evolution of life. There are two distinct problems of evolution. One is, starting from a relatively unstructured universe, how do you get cells? The next evolutionary problem is how do cells start aggregating? I think at the present moment it is relatively easy, at least qualitatively, to get the idea of cells competing for various nutrients in the environment, cooperating to form aggregates, and these aggregates then evolving in a classical domineering fashion. The question of where the cells came from is a very different and very difficult one.

The question of how reproducing cells evolved in the first place is somewhat outside the scope of the present paper, but should be borne in mind. CODD (1965) considers tessellations with even simpler components than von

Neumann's. A pure automata problem is to embed our module in Codd's model, where one of our cells is simulated as an aggregate of Codd's cells with appropriate change of time scale (HOLLAND, personal communication). Perhaps we can approach the cellular-evolution problem by imagining a subtessellation with components comparable to the macromolecules of biology, and consider reproduction of our modules as aggregates of these pseudo macromolecules. Our constructions would then treat arrays of arrays.

The Mark II module is shown in Fig. 10.14. We have kept the tessellation structure, side-stepping the morphogenesis of individual cells. The control string is segmented in words which correspond to the possible i-instructions of the original module. The whole control string corresponds to the whole CT program in our original model. Only a small portion of the control string can be read by an individual cell. *Every cell in an organism has the same control string.* Individual cells differ only in the portion of the control string which can currently be read out.

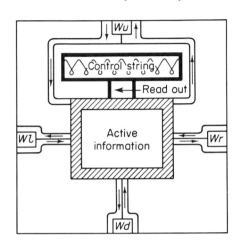

Fig. 10.14. Mark II module.

The change in activation of portions of the control string is our analog of differentiation. The increase in the number of cells in a co-moving set is our analog of growth.

A cell computes under the control of its activated control-string portion and of its inputs. Thus a cell which functions one way as part of a co-moving set may well behave in a completely different way when removed from the aggregate—a phenomenon familiar in embryological experiments.

Besides computation on inputs to produce outputs, a cell can divide (this corresponds to the activity in the construction site in the original model) or die (this corresponds to returning a cell to the quiescent state).‡ Thus we are really considering the quiescent cell of Mark I as a noncell in the Mark II model, and thus our tessellation is to be thought of as empty save where there are co-moving sets. These masses grow only when individual cells divide.

The "active information" region corresponds to the bit register and 22 instruction registers of the Mark I module. It has access to the activated portion of the control string.

---

‡ To obtain sexuality one simply requires a means for two cells to redistribute the instruction of their control strings.

When a cell divides, the original cell may be considered as preserved at its original site, while a replica has been produced at a neighboring site. This replica will have the same control string as the original cell, but may have "differentiated" in that the activated region of the control string may be adjacent to, rather than identical with, that of the original cell.

Given an automaton α in the Mark I model, we may replace it by a Mark II automaton simply by replacing each cell by a Mark II cell. We then grow α from a single cell by encapsulating the program of the constructor within a single cell $\hat{c}(\alpha)$. This single cell grows into the Mark II version of $c(\alpha)$ simply by "reading out" the control string into a linear string of cells, the last two (leftmost) of which then produce a control head. This proceeds to build a copy of α.

This procedure has several fascinating concomitants.

The first is that the problem of self-reproduction becomes very simple in this model. We simply require that $\hat{c}(\alpha)$ initially produces a copy of itself (a single cell!) which is rendered dormant. $\hat{c}(\alpha)$ then produces $c(\alpha)$. $c(\alpha)$ in turn builds α, but before turning α loose, attaches to it the "germ cell," i.e., the copy of $\hat{c}(\alpha)$. α then reproduces by releasing this copy of $\hat{c}(\alpha)$ into the tessellation at "maturity."

The second is that, in this model, the control string is not that of the reproducing automaton α itself, but rather that of the constructor of α.

At this stage, I would not push the latter observation as a clue to the operation of real biological systems. Rather, its purpose is to shock the biologist, and the theoretician, into a reappraisal of how devious genetic coding may be. Our progress in decoding the fashion in which DNA directs the production of enzymes has been so impressive of late that we tend to forget how little we know about the way this relates to overall cell function, let alone the morphogenesis of the multicellular organism. I should also emphasize that we have considered the basic units of our control string as explicit instructions with respect to cellular computation or reproduction. This must be contrasted with the exceedingly indirect commands in the control string (DNA) of a real cell, which serve to bias overall metabolic activity rather than explicitly modify specific bits of data storage.

Let me reiterate that this model shares with the Mark I model an essentially serial mode of operation. We shall have a far greater feel for the demands we must make on a genetic coding system when we have programmed the Mark II system in a parallel growth mode, in which *every cell of an organism may be considered a growth point.*

In "designing" an organism, we must use subroutines to build "components," i.e., tissues with a basically repetitive structure. Higher-level routines then serve to arrange these components in appropriate topographical relations. This is one way in which we reduce the length of the program required to specify the growth of an organism. Another factor which helps economize the growth program is that *an organism will only grow normally in an appropriate highly structured environment.* Thus the growth program may rely on "self-organizing mechanisms" to select information out of the environment, thus economizing on the information required in the zygote. That is why both nature and nurture are important.

BIBLIOGRAPHY

ARBIB, M. A. See also KALMAN, FALB, and ARBIB; SPIRA and ARBIB.

ARBIB, M. A. [1963], "Monogenic Normal Systems are Universal," *J. Austral. Math. Soc.*, III, Part 3, 301–6. *168*.

ARBIB, M. A. [1964], *Brains, Machines, and Mathematics*. New York: McGraw-Hill Book Company. *13, 66*.

ARBIB, M. A. [1965], "A Common Framework for Automata Theory and Control Theory," *J. SIAM Control, Ser. A*, III, No. 2, 206–22. *52*.

ARBIB, M. A. [1966a], "A Simple Self-Reproducing Universal Automaton," *Inform. Control*, IX, 177–89. *361, 374*.

ARBIB, M. A. [1966b], "Automata Theory and Control Theory—A Rapprochement," *Automatica*, III, 161–89. *52*.

ARBIB, M. A. [1966c], "Speed-up Theorems and Incompleteness Theorems," in *Automata Theory*, ed. E. R. Caianiello. New York: Academic Press, Inc., 6–24. *251, 262, 267*.

ARBIB, M. A. [1967a], "Automata Theory and Development: Part I," *J. Theoret. Biol.*, XIV, 131–56. *382*.

ARBIB, M. A. [1967b], "Realization of Stochastic Systems," *Ann. Math. Stat.*, XXXVIII, 927–33. *338, 339*.

ARBIB, M. A., ed. [1968a], *The Algebraic Theory of Machines, Languages, and Semigroups*. New York: Academic Press Inc. *22, 323*.

ARBIB, M. A. [1968b], "Automaton Decompositions and Semigroup Extensions," in *The Algebraic Theory of Machines, Languages, and Semigroups*, ed. M. A. Arbib. New York: Academic Press Inc., 37–54. *47, 313*.

ARBIB, M. A. [1968c], "The Automata Theory of Semigroup Embedding," *J. Austral. Math. Soc.*, VIII, 568–70. *313*.

ARBIB, M. A., and M. BLUM [1965], "Machine Dependence of Degrees of Difficulty," *Proc. Amer. Math. Soc.*, XVI, 442–47. *267*.

ARBIB, M. A., J. L. RHODES, and B. R. TILSON [1968], "Complexity and Group Complexity of Finite-State Machines and Finite Semigroups," in *The Algebraic*

Theory of Machines, Languages, and Semigroups, ed. M. A. Arbib. New York: Academic Press Inc., 127–45. *318, 322.*

ARBIB, M. A., and H. P. ZEIGER [1968], "An Automata-Theoretic Approach to Linear Systems," presented at the Theory Session of the IFAC/IE Aust. Conference, University of New South Wales, August 1968. *89.*

ARDEN, D. N. [1960], "Delayed Logic and Finite-State Machines," in *Theory of Computing Machine Design*, Ann Arbor: University of Michigan Press, 1–35. *92.*

ARTIN, E. [1955a], "The Orders of the Linear Groups," *Comm. Pure Appl. Math.*, VIII, 355–66. *288.*

ARTIN, E. [1955b], "The Orders of the Classical Linear Groups," *Comm. Pure Appl. Math.*, VIII, 455–72. *287, 288.*

BAR-HILLEL, Y., M. PERLES, and E. SHAMIR [1961], "On Formal Properties of Simple Phrase Structure Grammars," *Z. f. Phonetik Sprachwissenschaft und Communikationsforschung*, XIV, 143–72. *176, 183.*

BARZDIN, Y. M. [1965], "Complexity of Recognition of Symmetry in Turing Machines," *Problemy Kibernetiki*, XV. *144, 237, 248.*

BIRKHOFF, G. See MACLANE and BIRKHOFF.

BLUM, M. See also ARBIB and BLUM.

BLUM, M. [1964], "Measures on the Computation Speed of Partial Recursive Functions," *Quarterly Progress Report 72*, Res. Lab. Electronics, M.I.T., 237–53. *251.*

BLUM, M. [1967], "A Machine-Independent Theory of the Complexity of Recursive Functions," *J.A.C.M.*, XIV, 322–36. *251, 252, 258, 261, 262, 267.*

BODNARCHUK, See *87.*

BOOTH, T. L. [1967], *Sequential Machines and Automata Theory*. New York: John Wiley & Sons Inc. *65.*

BRZOZOWSKI, J. A. [1962a], "A Survey of Regular Expressions and Their Applications," *IRE Trans. Elec. Comp.*, EC-11, 324–35. *92, 98.*

BRZOZOWSKI, J. A. [1962b], "Canonical Regular Expressions and Minimal State Graphs for Definite Events," *Proc. Symp. Math. Theory of Automata*, Brooklyn, N.Y., 529–61. *98.*

BRZOZOWSKI, J. A. [1964a], "Derivatives of Regular Expressions," *J.A.C.M.*, XI, 481–94. *98, 99.*

BRZOZOWSKI, J. A. [1964b], "Regular Expressions from Sequential Circuits," *IEEE Trans. Elec. Comp.*, EC-13, 741–44. *98.*

BRZOZOWSKI, J. A. [1965], "Regular Expressions for Linear Sequential Circuits," *IEEE Trans. Elec. Comp.*, EC-14, 148–56. *98.*

BURKS, A. W., and H. WANG [1957], "The Logic of Automata," *J.A.C.M.*, IV, 193–218, and 279–97. *96.*

BURNSIDE, W. [1897], *Theory of Groups of Finite Order*. New York: Dover Publications, Inc., 1965. *286.*

CANTOR, D. G. [1962], "On the Ambiguity Problem of Backus Systems," *J.A.C.M.*, IX, 477–79. *181.*

CARLYLE, J. W. [1963], "Reduced Forms for Stochastic Sequential Machines," *J. Math. Analysis Appl.*, VII, 167–75. *333, 334.*

CARLYLE, J. W. [1964], "On the External Probability Structure of Finite-State Channels," *Inform. Control*, VII, 385–97. *333.*

CARTER, R. W. [1965], "Simple Groups and Simple Lie Algebras," *J. Math. Soc. London*, XL, 193–240. *288.*

CHEVALLEY, C. [1955], "Sur Certains Groups Simples," *Tohoku Math. J.* (2), VII, 14–66. *288.*

CHOMSKY, N. [1959], "On Certain Formal Properties of Grammars," *Inform. Control*, II, 137–67. *172.*

CLEAVE, J. P. [1963], "A Hierarchy of Primitive Recursive Functions," *Z. f. Math. Logik und Grundlagen d. Math.*, IX, 331–45. *227.*

CLIFFORD, A. H., and G. B. PRESTON [1961 and 1967], *The Algebraic Theory of Semigroups* (2 vols.). Providence, R.I.: American Mathematical Society. *22, 290, 292.*

COBHAM, A. [1964], "The Intrinsic Computational Difficulty of Functions," in *Proceedings of the 1964 International Congress for Logic, Methodology, and Philosophy of Science.* Amsterdam: North-Holland Publishing Company, pp. 24–30. *228.*

CODD, E. F. [1965], "Propagation, Computation and Construction in 2-Dimensional Cellular Spaces," Technical Publication of the University of Michigan. Reprinted in 1968 as *Cellular Automata.* New York: Academic Press Inc. *351, 374, 376, 378, 384.*

COPI, I., C. ELGOT, and J. WRIGHT [1958], "Realization of Events by Logical Nets," *J.A.C.M.*, V, 181–96. *71.*

CUTLIP, W. F. [1968], "On the Cascade Decomposition of Prefix Automata," *IEEE Trans. Elec. Comp.*, EC-17, 94–95. *318.*

DAVIS, M. [1958], *Computability and Unsolvability.* New York: McGraw-Hill Book Company. *199, 211.*

DAVIS, M., ed. [1965], *The Undecidable.* Hewlett, N.Y.: Raven Press. *157, 196.*

DESOER, C. A. See ZADEH and DESOER.

DICKSON, L. E. [1901], *Linear Groups.* Reprinted by Dover Publications Inc., New York, 1958. *287.*

DIEUDONNÉ, J. [1948], "Sur Les Groups Classiques," *Actualités Sci. Ind.*, No. 1040. Paris: Hermann. *287.*

DIEUDONNÉ, J. [1951], "On the Automorphisms of the Classical Groups," *Mem. Amer. Math. Soc.*, II. *287.*

EHRENFEUCHT, A. See *266, 267.*

ELGOT, C. See COPI, ELGOT, and WRIGHT.

EVANS, T. [1952], "Embedding Theorems for Multiplicative Systems and Projective Geometries," *Proc. Amer. Math. Soc.*, III, 614–20. *313.*

FALB, P. L. See KALMAN, FALB, and ARBIB.

FAURRE, P. See *266*.

FEINSTEIN, N. See OTT and FEINSTEIN.

FEIT, W., and J. G. THOMPSON [1963], "Solvability of Groups of Odd Order," *Pac. J. Math.*, XIII, 775–1029. *286*.

FELLER, W. [1957], *An Introduction to Probability Theory and Its Applications*, 2nd ed., I. New York: John Wiley & Sons, Inc. *329*.

FISCHER, P. C. See also MEYER and FISCHER; RUBY and FISCHER.

FISCHER, P. C. [1965a], "Generation of Primes by a One-Dimensional Real-Time Iterative Array," *J.A.C.M.*, XII, 388–94.

FISCHER, P. C. [1965b], "On Formalisms for Turing Machines," *J.A.C.M.*, XII, 570–80. *136*.

FISCHER, P. C. [1965c], "Multi-Tape and Infinite-State Automata—A Survey," *Comm. A.C.M.*, VIII, 799–805. *228*.

FISCHER, P. C. [1967], "Turing Machines with a Schedule to Keep," *Inform. Control*, XI, 138–46. *248*.

FRIEDBERG, R. [1958], "Three Theorems on Recursive Enumeration," *J. Symbolic Logic*, XXIII, 309–16. *258, 261*.

GILL, A. [1962], *Introduction to the Theory of Finite-State Machines*. New York: McGraw-Hill Book Company. *65*.

GINSBURG, S. [1958], "On the Length of the Smallest Uniform Experiment Which Distinguishes the Terminal States of a Machine," *J.A.C.M.*, V, 266–80. *65*.

GINSBURG, S. [1962], *An Introduction to Mathematical Machine Theory*. Reading, Mass.: Addison-Wesley Publishing Company, Inc. *65*.

GINSBURG, S. [1966], *The Mathematical Theory of Context-Free Languages*. New York: McGraw-Hill Book Company. *195, 196*.

GINZBURG, A. [1968], *Algebraic Theory of Automata*. New York: Academic Press Inc. *300, 305*.

GINZBURG, A., and M. YOELI [1964], "On Homomorphic Images of Transition Graphs," *J. Franklin Institute*, CCLXXVIII, 291–96. *277*.

GINZBURG, A., and M. YOELI [1965], "Products of Automata and the Problem of Covering," *Trans. Amer. Math. Soc.*, CXVI, 253–66. *277*.

GLUSHKOV, V. M. [1961], "Abstract Theory of Automata," *Russian Math Surveys*, XVI, 1–53 (translated from *Uspekhi. Mat. Nauk*, Tom XVI, Sept.–Oct. 1961). *87*.

GÖDEL, K. [1931], "Über formal unentscheidbare Sätze der Principia Mathematica und verwandter Systeme I," *Monatshefte fur Mathematik und Physik*, XXXVIII, 173–98 (translation in DAVIS [1965]). *157*.

GÖDEL, K. [1936], "Uber die Länge der Beweise," *Ergeb. eines math. Kolloquiums*, VII, 23–24 (translation in DAVIS [1965]). *261*.

GRAY, J. N., and M. A. HARRISON [1966], "The Theory of Sequential Relations," *Inform. Control*, IX, 435–68. *115*.

GRZEGROCZYK, A. [1953], "Some Classes of Recursive Functions," *Rozprawy Matematczyne*, IV, Warsaw, 1–45. *222, 223, 224.*

HALL, M., JR. [1959], *The Theory of Groups*. New York: The Macmillan Company. *22, 44.*

HARRISON, M. A. See also GRAY and HARRISON.

HARRISON, M. A. [1965], "On the Error Correcting Capacity of Finite Automata," *Inform. Control*, VIII, 430–50. *69, 118.*

HARTMANIS, J. [1962]. *274.*

HARTMANIS, J. [1968], "Computational Complexity of One-Tape Turing Machine Computations," *J.A.C.M.*, XV, 325–39. *233, 235, 241.*

HARTMANIS, J., and H. SHANK [1968], "On the Recognition of Primes by Automata," *J.A.C.M.*, XV, 382–89. *89, 176.*

HARTMANIS, J., and R. E. STEARNS [1963], "A Study of Feedback and Errors in Sequential Machines," *IEEE Trans. Elec. Comp.*, EC-12, 223–32. *282.*

HARTMANIS, J., and R. E. STEARNS [1964], "Pair Algebras and Their Application to Automata Theory," *Inform. Control*, VII, 485–507. *272, 277, 279, 281, 282, 283.*

HARTMANIS, J., and R. E. STEARNS [1965], "On the Computational Complexity of Algorithms," *Trans. Amer. Math. Soc.*, CXVII, 285–306. *143, 244, 247, 248.*

HARTMANIS, J., and R. E. STEARNS [1966], *Algebraic Theory of Sequential Machines*. Englewood Cliffs, N.J.: Prentice-Hall, Inc. *272, 282, 300, 310.*

HELLER, A. [1965], "On Stochastic Processes Derived from Markov Chains," *Ann. Math. Stat.*, XXXVI, 1286–91. *339.*

HELLER, A. [1967], "Probabilistic Automata and Stochastic Transformations," *Math. Systems Theory*, I, 197–208. *339.*

HENNIE, F. C. [1965], "Crossing Sequences and Off-Line Turing Machine Computations," *Proc. 6th Ann. Symp. Switching Theory*, 168–72. *231, 233, 235, 237.*

HENNIE, F. C. [1966], "On-Line Turing Machine Computations," *IEEE Trans. Elect. Comp.*, EC-15, 35–44. *241.*

HENNIE, F. C. [1968], *Finite-State Models for Logical Machines*. New York: John Wiley & Sons, Inc. *65.*

HENNIE, F. C., and R. E. STEARNS [1966], "Two-Tape Simulation of Multi-Tape Turing Machines," *J.A.C.M.*, XIII, 533–46. *142, 247.*

HO, B. L. [1966], "An Effective Construction of Realizations from Input/Output Descriptions," Ph.D. Thesis, Stanford Univ. *115.*

HOLLAND, J. H. See also *385.*

HOLLAND, J. H. [1965], "Iterative Circuit Computers: Characterization and Resume of Advantages and Disadvantages," *Proc. Symp. Microelectronics and Large Systems*. Washington, D.C.: Spartan Press, Inc. *374.*

HOLLAND, J. H. [1966], "Universal Spaces: A Basis for Studies of Adaptation," in E. R. Caianiello, ed., *Automata Theory*. New York: Academic Press Inc., 218–30. *365, 374.*

HOOPER, P. K. [1966], "The Undecidability of the Turing Machine Immortality Problem," *J. Symbolic Logic*, XXXI, 219–34. *149.*

HOPCROFT, J. See *241*.

HU, S. T. [1965], *Elements of Modern Algebra*. San Francisco: Holden-Day, Inc. *22*.

HUFFMAN, D. A. [1954], "The Synthesis of Sequential Switching Circuits," *J. Franklin Inst.*, CCLVII, 161–90, 275–303. Also in MOORE [1964]. *59*.

KALMAN, R. E., P. L. FALB, and M. A. ARBIB [1969], *Topics in Mathematical System Theory*. New York: McGraw-Hill Book Company. *52, 109, 115, 300*.

KÁLMÁR, L. [1943], Egyszerü példa eldönthetetlen aritmetikai problémára (Ein einfaches Beispiel fürein unentscheidbares arithmetisches Problem), *Matematika és fizikai lapok*, L, 1–23 (in Hungarian with German abstract). *223*.

KEMENY, J. G., and J. L. SNELL [1960], *Finite Markov Chains*. Princeton, N.J.: D. Van Nostrand Company, Inc. *329*.

KLEENE, S. C. [1952], *Introduction to Metamathematics*. Princeton, N.J.: D. Van Nostrand Company, Inc. *126, 199*.

KLEENE, S. C. [1956], "Representation of Events in Nerve Nets and Finite Automata," in C. E. Shannon and M. McCarthy, eds., *Automata Studies*, Annals of Math Studies No. 34, Princeton, N.J., 3–41. *90, 97*.

KROHN, K., R. MATEOSIAN, and J. RHODES [1967], "Complexity of Ideals in Finite Semigroups and Finite-State Machines," *Mathematical System Theory*, I, 59–66. *318*.

KROHN, K., and J. L. RHODES [1965], "Algebraic Theory of Machines, I: The Decomposition Results," *Trans. Amer. Math. Soc.*, CXVI, 450–64. *277, 292, 295, 299, 314*.

KROHN, K., J. L. RHODES, and B. R. TILSON [1968a], "The Prime Decomposition Theorem of the Algebraic Theory of Machines," in *The Algebraic Theory of Machines, Languages, and Semigroups*, ed. M. A. Arbib. New York: Academic Press Inc., 81–125. *299*.

KROHN, K., J. L. RHODES, and B. R. TILSON [1968b], "Local Structure Theorems for Finite Semigroups," in *The Algebraic Theory of Machines, Languages, and Semigroups*, ed. M. A. Arbib. New York: Academic Press Inc., 147–89. *290*.

KROHN, K., J. L. RHODES, and B. R. TILSON [1968c], "Axioms for Complexity of Finite Semigroups," in *The Algebraic Theory of Machines, Languages, and Semigroups*, ed. M. A. Arbib. New York: Academic Press Inc., 233–66. *318*.

KULAGINO, O. See MARCUS.

KURODA, S-Y. [1964], "Classes of Languages and Linear-Bounded Automata," *Inform. Control*, VII, 207–23. *193, 195*.

KUROSH, H. G. [1956], *The Theory of Groups* (2 vols.). New York: Chelsea Publishing Company. *22, 285*.

LANDWEBER, P. S. [1963], "Three Theorems on Phrase Structure Grammars of Type 1," *Inform. Control*, VI, 131–37. *192*.

LEE, C. H. [1963], "A Turing Machine which Prints Its Own Code Script," in *Proc. Symp. Math. Theory of Automata*. Brooklyn, N.Y.: Polytechnic Press, 155–64 (Vol. XII of the Microwave Research Institute Symposia Series). *162, 380, 381*.

LEE, C. Y. [1960], "Automata and Finite Automata," *Bell System Tech. J.*, XXXIX, 1267–95. *136*.

LIU, C. L. [1963], *Some Memory Aspects of Finite Automata*, M.I.T. Research Laboratory of Electronics, Report 411. *283.*

MACLANE, S., and G. BIRKHOFF [1967], *Algebra.* New York: The Macmillan Company. *22.*

MARCUS, S. [1964], "Gramatici si Automate Finite" (Grammars and Finite Automata), Editurá Academieí Republicii Populare Romîne. *116.*

MATEOSIAN, R. See KROHN, MATEOSIAN, and RHODES.

MCCARTHY, J. See SHANNON and MCCARTHY.

MCCLUSKEY, E. J. [1965], *Introduction to the Theory of Switching Circuits.* New York: McGraw-Hill Book Company. *69.*

MCCULLOCH, W., and W. PITTS [1943], "A Logical Calculus of the Ideas Immanent in Nervous Activity," *Bull. Math. Biophys.*, V, 115–33. *13, 66.*

MCKNIGHT, J. [1964], "Kleene Quotient Theorems," *Pac. J. Math*, XIV, 1343–52. *124.*

MCNAUGHTON, R. See also PAPERT and MCNAUGHTON. *417.*

MCNAUGHTON, R., and H. YAMADA [1960], "Regular Expressions and State Graphs for Automata," *IRE Trans. Elec. Comp.*, EC-9, 39–47. *92, 96.*

MEALY, G. H. [1955], "A Method for Synthesising Sequential Circuits," *Bell System Tech. J.*, XXXIV, 1045–79. *59.*

MEYER, A. R. [1969], "A Note on Star-Free Events," *J.A.C.M.*, XVI, 220–25. *295, 317.*

MEYER, A. R., and P. C. FISCHER [1968], "On Computational Speed-Up," IEEE Conference Record of 1968 Ninth Annual Symposium on Switching and Automata Theory, 351–55. *251.*

MEYERS, W. J. [1965], Term Paper for EM 270a, Stanford University. *118.*

MILLER, R. E. [1965], *Switching Theory, Vol. 2—Sequential Circuits and Machines.* New York: John Wiley & Sons, Inc. *65, 69.*

MINSKY, M. L. [1961], "Recursive Unsolvability of Post's Problem of 'Tag' and Other Topics in Theory of Turing Machines," *Ann. Math.*, LXXIV, 437–54. *168, 217, 218.*

MINSKY, M. [1967], *Computation: Finite and Infinite Machines.* Englewood Cliffs, N.J.: Prentice-Hall, Inc. *136, 168, 196, 199, 211, 212, 217, 242.*

MINSKY, M., and S. PAPERT [1966], "Unrecognizable Sets of Numbers," *J.A.C.M.*, XXXI, 281–86. *89.*

MINSKY, M. L., and S. PAPERT [1967], "Linearly Unrecognizable Patterns," in *Mathematical Aspects of Computer Science, Proc. Symp. Appl. Math.*, XIX. Providence, R.I.: Amer. Math. Soc., 176–217. *80, 85.*

MINSKY, M. L., and S. PAPERT [1969], *Perceptions.* Cambridge, Mass.: M.I.T. Press. *86.*

MOORE, E. F. [1956], "Gedanken-Experiments on Sequential Machines," *Automata Studies.* Princeton, N.J.: Princeton University Press, 129–53. *59, 63, 333.*

MOORE, E. F. [1962], "Machine Models of Self-Reproduction," *Math. Prob. Biol. Sci., Proc. Symp. Appl. Math.*, XIV, 17–33. *379.*

MOSTOWSKI, A. [1957], *Sentences Undecidable in Formalized Arithmetic.* Amsterdam: North-Holland Publishing Company. *261, 262.*

MYHILL, J. [1957], "Finite Automata and the Representation of Events," WADC Tech. Rept. 57–624, Wright-Patterson AFB, Ohio. *113, 116.*

MYHILL, J. [1960], "Linear-Bounded Automata," WADD Technical Note 60-165, Wright-Patterson AFB, Ohio. *191.*

MYHILL, J. [1963a], "Finite Automata, Semigroups and Simulation," in lecture notes for a summer conference on Automata Theory, University of Michigan. *117, 308.*

MYHILL, J. [1963b], "Notes for a Series of Lectures on Recursive Functions," in lecture notes for a summer conference on Automata Theory, University of Michigan. *159.*

MYHILL, J. [1964], "The Abstract Theory of Self-Reproduction," in *Views on General Systems Theory*, ed. M. D. Mesarovic. New York: John Wiley & Sons, Inc., pp. 106–18. *159, 352, 371, 372, 373, 374.*

NELSON, R. J. [1968], *Introduction to Automata.* New York: John Wiley & Sons, Inc. *196.*

NERODE, A. [1958], "Linear Automaton Transformations," *Proc. Amer. Math. Soc.,* IX, 541–44. *103.*

NEUMANN, B. H. [1960], "Embedding Theorems for Semigroups," *J. London Math. Soc.,* XXXV, 184–92. *314.*

OGDEN, W. [1968], "A Helpful Result for Proving Inherent Ambiguity," *Math. Syst. Theory*, II, 191–94, in press. *176, 182.*

OTT, G., and N. FEINSTEIN [1961], "Design of Sequential Machines from their Regular Expressions," *J.A.C.M.,* VIII, 585–600. *98.*

PAGER, D. See also *267.*

PAGER, D. [1968], On the Problem of Finding Minimal Programs for Tables. Mimeographed Paper, Dept. of Information Sciences, Univ. of Hawaii. *256.*

PAPERT, S. See also MINSKY and PAPERT.

PAPERT, S., and R. MCNAUGHTON [1966], "On Topological Events," *Theory of Automata*, University of Michigan Engineering Summer Conferences. *295.*

PARIKH, R. J. [1961], "Language Generating Devices," *MIT Res. Lab. Electron. Quart. Progr. Rept. 60*, 199–212. (Reprinted as "On Context-Free Languages," *J.A.C.M.,* XIII [1966], 570–81.) *182.*

PAZ, A. See also *337, 346.*

PAZ, A. [1962], "Homomorphisms between Finite Automata," *Bull. Res. Council Israel*, 10F, 93–100. *117.*

PAZ, A. [1966], "Some Aspects of Probabilistic Automata," *Inform. Control*, IX, 26–60. *343.*

PERLES, M. See also BAR-HILLEL, PERLES, and SHAMIR.

PERLES, M., M. O. RABIN, and E. SHAMIR [1963], "Theory of Definite Automata," *IEEE Trans. Elec. Comp.,* EC-12, 233–43. *97, 347.*

PITTS, W. See MCCULLOCH and PITTS.

POST, E. L. [1936], "Finite Combinatory Processes—Formulation I," *J. Symbolic Logic*, I, 103–5. *11.*

POST, E. L. [1943], "Formal Reductions of the General Combinatorial Decision Problem," *Am. J. Math.*, LXV, 197–268. *164, 168.*

POST, E. L. [1944], "Recursively Enumerable Sets of Positive Integers," *Bull. Amer. Math. Soc.*, L, 284–316. *126.*

PRESTON, G. B. See CLIFFORD and PRESTON.

RABIN, M. O. See also PERLES, RABIN, and SHAMIR.

RABIN, M. O. [1960], *Degree of Difficulty of Computing a Function and a Partial Ordering of Recursive Sets*, Hebrew University, Jerusalem, Israel. (For an abstract see his "Speed of Computation of Functions and Classification of Recursive Sets," *Bull. Res. Counc. of Israel*, 8F [1959], 69–70.) *251, 267.*

RABIN, M. O. [1963], "Probabilistic Automata," *Inform. Control*, VI, 230–45. *341, 342, 344, 346, 348.*

RABIN, M. O. [1964], "Real Time Computation," *Israel Journal of Mathematics*, I, 203–11. *231, 237, 239, 248.*

RABIN, M. O., and D. SCOTT [1959], "Finite Automata and their Decision Problems," *IBM J. Res. Dev.*, III, 114–25. *89, 94, 96, 103, 106, 115.*

RADO, T. [1962], "On Non-Computable Functions," *Bell System Tech. J.*, XLI, 877–84. *150.*

RANEY, G. [1958], "Sequential Functions," *J.A.C.M.*, V, 177–80. *105.*

REDKO, V. N. [1964], "On Defining Relations for the Algebra of Regular Events," *Ukrain. Mat. Ž.*, XVI, 120–26 (in Russian). *98.*

RHODES, J. See also ARBIB, RHODES, and TILSON; KROHN, MATEOSIAN, and RHODES; KROHN and RHODES; KROHN, RHODES, and TILSON.

RHODES, J. [1966], "Some Results on Finite Semigroups," *J. Algebra*, IV, 471–504. *321.*

RITCHIE, R. W. [1963a], "Classes of Predictably Computable Functions," *Trans. Amer. Math. Soc.*, CVI, 139–73. *224, 226, 230, 267.*

RITCHIE, R. W. [1963b], "Finite Automata and the Set of Squares," *J.A.C.M.*, X, 528–31. *89.*

ROBERTS, F. S. See *286, 318.*

ROGERS, H., JR. [1959], "The Present Theory of Turing Machine Computability," *J. SIAM*, VII, 114–30. *126.*

ROGERS, H., JR. [1967], *Theory of Recursive Functions and Effective Computability*. New York: McGraw-Hill Book Company. *126, 199, 256.*

RUBY, S., and P. C. FISCHER [1965], "Translational Methods and Computational Complexity," *Proc. 6th Ann. Symp. Switching Theory*, 173–78. *248.*

SALOMAA, A. [1965], "On Probabilistic Automata with One Input Letter," *Annales Universitatis Turkuensis, Series A*, I, 85, Turku. *343.*

SALOMAA, A. [1966], "Two Complete Axiom Systems for the Algebra of Regular Events," *J.A.C.M.*, XIII, 158–69. *98.*

SCHÜTZENBERGER, M. P. [1968]. *89, 295.*

SCHÜTZENBERGER, M. P. [1966a], "Sur Certaines Varieties de monoides finis," in *Automata Theory*, ed. E. R. Caianiello. New York: Academic Press Inc., 314–19. *295, 317.*

SCHÜTZENBERGER, M. P. [1966b], "On a Family of Sets Related to McNaughton's L-Language," *Automata Theory*, ed. E. R. Caianiello. New York: Academic Press Inc., 320–24. *295, 317.*

SCOTT, D. See also RABIN and SCOTT.

SCOTT, D. [1967], "Some Definitional Suggestions for Automata Theory," *J. Comp. Syst. Sciences*, I, 187–212. *16.*

SHAMIR, E. See BAR-HILLEL, PERLES, and SHAMIR; PERLES, RABIN, and SHAMIR.

SHANK, H. See HARTMANIS and SHANK.

SHANNON, C. E. [1956], "A Universal Turing Machine with Two Internal States," *Automata Studies* (*Annals of Math. Studies*, XXXIV), Princeton. *135.*

SHANNON, C. E. [1948], "A Mathematical Theory of Communication," *Bell System Tech. J.*, XXVII, 379–423 and 623–56. *330.*

SHANNON, C. E., and J. MCCARTHY, eds. [1956], *Automata Studies*. Princeton, N.J.: Princeton University Press. *13.*

SHEPHERDSON, J. C. [1959], "The Reduction of Two-Way Automata to One-Way Automata," *IBM J. Res. Dev.*, III, 198–200. *106, 107.*

SHEPHERDSON, J. C., and H. E. STURGIS [1963], "Computability of Recursive Functions," *J.A.C.M.*, X, 217–55. *199, 212, 217.*

SMITH, A. R., III [1968], "Simple Computation-Universal Cellular Spaces and Self-Reproduction," Conf. Record, IEEE 9th Ann. Symp. Switching and Automata Theory, 269–77. *380, 381.*

SNELL, J. L. See KEMENY and SNELL.

SPIRA, P. M. [1969], "The Time Required for Group Multiplication," *J.A.C.M.*, XVI, 235–43. *78, 81.*

SPIRA, P. M., and M. A. ARBIB [1967], "Computation Times for Finite Groups, Semi-groups and Automata," *Proc. IEEE 8th Ann. Symp. Switching and Automata Theory*, 291–95. *75, 81.*

STEARNS, R. E. See HARTMANIS and STEARNS; HENNIE and STEARNS.

STURGIS, H. E. See SHEPHERDSON and STURGIS.

SUZUKI, M. [1960], "A New Type of Simple Groups of Finite Order," *Proc. National Academy of Sciences*, XLVI, 868–70. *288.*

TAL, A. A. [1964], "Questionnaire Language and Abstract Synthesis of Minimal Sequential Machines," *Automat. i. Telemekh.*, XXV, 946–62. *115.*

THATCHER, J. W. [1963], "The Construction of a Self-Describing Turing Machine,' in *Proc. Symp. Math. Theory of Automata*. Brooklyn, N.Y.: Polytechnic Press (Vol. XII of the Microwave Research Institute Symposia Series), 165–71. *162.*

THATCHER, J. W. [1965], "Universality in the von Neumann Cellular Model," University of Michigan Technical Report. *351, 374, 378.*

THOMPSON, J. G. See FEIT and THOMPSON.

TILSON, B. R. See ARBIB, RHODES, and TILSON; KROHN, RHODES, and TILSON.

TRAKHTENBROT, B. A. [1964], "Turing Computations with Logarithmic Delay," *Algebra i Logika*, III, 4, 33–48 (in Russian). *231, 233*.

TURING, A. M. [1936], "On Computable Numbers, with an Application to the Entscheidungs-Problem," *Proc. London Math. Soc.*, *Ser.* 2–42, 230–65, with a correction, *Ibid.*, Ser. 2–43 (1936–7), 544 46. *11, 13, 148, 149, 164, 242*.

VERBEEK, L. A. M. [1968], "Semigroup Extensions," Doctoral Thesis in Mathematics for the Technische Hogeschool, Delft, Uitgeverij Waltman-Delft; 77 pages. *47*.

VON NEUMANN, J. [1951], "The General and Logical Theory of Automata," in *Cerebral Mechanisms in Behavior: The Hixon Symposium*. New York: John Wiley & Sons, Inc. *13, 348*.

VON NEUMANN, J. [1966], *Theory of Self-Reproducing Automata* (edited and completed by A. W. Burks). Urbana: University of Illinois Press. *351, 374, 378*.

WAGNER, E. G. [1964], "An Approach to Modular Computers, I: Spider Automata and Embedded Automata," *IBM Res. Rept.* RC-1107. *374, 376*.

WANG, H. See also BURKS and WANG.

WANG, H. [1957], "A Variant to Turing's Theory of Computing Machines," *J.A.C.M.*, IV, 63–92. *136*.

WEGBREIT, B. [1967], "SD-irreducible Machines," unpublished term paper, Harvard University. *309*.

WINOGRAD, S. [1962], "Bounded Transient Automata," *Proc. AIEE 3rd Ann. Switching Theory Logical Design Symp.*, 138–41. *118*.

WINOGRAD, S. [1964], "Input Error Limiting Automata," *J.A.C.M.*, XI, 338–51. *118*.

WINOGRAD, S. [1967], "On the Time Required to Perform Multiplication," *J.A.C.M.*, XIV, 793–802. *75, 79, 81*.

WINOGRAD, S. [1968]. *75*.

WRIGHT, J. See COPI, ELGOT, and WRIGHT.

YAMADA, H. See also MCNAUGHTON and YAMADA.

YAMADA, H. [1960], "Counting by a Class of Growing Automata," Doctoral Thesis, University of Pennsylvania. *242*.

YAMADA, H. [1962], "Real-Time Computation and Recursive Functions Not Real-Time Computable," *IRE Trans. Elec. Comp.*, EC-11, 753–60. *242, 246*.

YOELI, M. See GINZBURG and YOELI.

YOUNG, P. R. [1968], "Toward a Theory of Enumerations," IEEE Conference Record of 1968 Ninth Annual Symposium on Switching and Automata Theory, 334–50 (see also *J.A.C.M.*, XVI [1969], 328–48). *248, 256, 257, 258, 259, 261*.

ZADEH, L. A., and C. A. DESOER [1963], *Linear System Theory*. New York: McGraw-Hill Book Company. *52*.

ZEIGER, H. P. See also ARBIB and ZEIGER.

ZEIGER, H. P. [1964], "Loop-Free Synthesis of Finite-State Machines," Ph.D. Thesis, Dept. of Electrical Engineering, M.I.T. *277, 299, 300, 303, 321*.

ZEIGER, H. P. [1967a], "Yet Another Proof of the Cascade Decomposition Theorem for Finite Automata," *Math. Systems Theory,* I, 225–28. *296.*

ZEIGER, H. P. [1967b], "Ho's Algorithm," *Inf. Control,* XI, 71–79. *115.*

ZEIGER, H. P. [1968], "Cascade Decomposition of Automata Using Covers," in *The Algebraic Theory of Machines, Languages, and Semigroups,* ed. M. A. Arbib. New York: Academic Press Inc., 55–80. *300.*

INDEX

A

A^* (set of finite sequences), 6
A-machine, 13
Abelian binary operation, 35
Abelian group, 44, 285
Abelian semigroup, 36
abstract description of machines, 15
acceptable set, 16
acceptor, 86, 151, 341
access memory, 11
action of an input, 115
actual automaton, 346
   stability theorem for, 347
actual machine with isolated cut-point, 347
addition, 35, 205
adequate axiomatic system, 157
adequate weak system, 265
admissible input segment, 54
admissible program encoding, 162
aleph-null ($\aleph_0$), 30
algebraic characterization of context-free language, 189
algebraic system, 20
ALGOL, 172, 208
algorithm, 11
all ($\forall$), 23
"almost all," 250
alphabet, 6
alternating group, 285
   on n letters (A_n), 43, 44
alternatives, complete set of, 325

ambiguity problem for context-free grammar, 181
analysis, 20
and-gate, 72
antisymmetry, 28
archimedean semigroup, 292
associative binary operation, 35
attacking, 259
automata theory, 4
automaton, 3–5, 51, 57, 90
   actual, 346
automaton-theoretic adjoint, 89
automorphism, 39
axiom, 157, 165, 166
   for systems, 53
axiomatic approach to complexity, 248
axiomatic system, 157
axiomatic theory:
   of computation, 161
   of regular expressions, 98

B

Backus normal form, 172
barrier to enumeration, 259
basic combinatorial machine, 318
basic lemma for bounding computation time, 76
bijective function, 24
binary multiplication, 10
binary operation, 35
biological models of automata, 382